MILTON

Modern Essays in Criticism

MILTON

Modern Essays in Criticism

Edited by ARTHUR E. BARKER

OXFORD UNIVERSITY PRESS
LONDON   OXFORD   NEW YORK

OXFORD UNIVERSITY PRESS

London   Oxford   New York
Glasgow   Toronto   Melbourne   Wellington
Cape Town   Ibadan   Nairobi   Dar es Salaam   Lusaka   Addis Ababa
Delhi   Bombay   Calcutta   Madras   Karachi   Lahore   Dacca
Kuala Lumpur   Singapore   Hong Kong   Tokyo

PREFACE

The essays reprinted in this volume have been selected from the very large body of commentary on Milton for their excellence and usefulness, and principally to serve two purposes. They review Milton's poetic career by providing authoritative and stimulating introductions to some of his more notable early poems, to *Paradise Lost* and its main themes and centers of interest, and to *Paradise Regained* and *Samson Agonistes*. They also illustrate, each with distinction in its kind, current varieties of approach to and interpretation of Milton, and therewith a number of significant preoccupations and problems.

It was observed by Mr. F. R. Leavis in a moment of irritation that Miltonists "command" the academic world (*The Times Literary Supplement*, 19 September 1958). As Miltonists are well aware, that is hardly a more accurate appraisal of the situation than the appraisal of his situation achieved by the commanding and bad-tempered figure of the opening books of Milton's epic. But this volume of selections certainly illustrates—what Miltonists are aware of and may happily rejoice in—the exemplary scholarship, vigor and variety of interest, sensitivity of critical perception, and humanity, just now generally characteristic of work on Milton—and perhaps more so, and with more vital learning and humane purpose, than in most other areas of comparable activity.

The selection of a limited number of items from so very large a body of notable material must cause the editor much unavoidable distress and others justifiable disappointment. In its vigor and variety, interpretation of Milton reflects many decided differences of scholarly and critical opinion—sometimes even approaching a Miltonic acerbity —which much enliven Miltonic activity, though sometimes inclining to eccentricity to save appearances. An editor of selections—a harmless drudge—is required to do what he can, within the limits allowed, to illustrate the spectrum of such differences (saving the certifiable eccentricities) while at the same time endeavoring to keep main matters, so far as he can see them, in some degree of focus. The selection of an item for this volume does not of course imply unreserved editorial agreement with all its arguments and conclusions, but only the considered opinion that the item is notably useful for the volume's purposes in being perceptive and well supported and in expressing a point of view meriting close attention. In some cases, any one of several other articles on the poem or topic in hand might have been selected in these terms; and the choice has depended, not on mere editorial whim—though, as to what little whim has been involved, the editor, with Emerson, cannot spend the day in explanation—but on considerations of coverage and the representation of points of view.

In order to provide some lead for readers who may need it, an editorial note has been added to each of the essays, giving, in addition to such citations as are provided by the author in his notes, some other discussions of the poem or topic in hand, including in some cases earlier studies whose findings are in general now taken for granted by later authorities and in most cases studies more recent than the essay reprinted here. An editor can certainly hope to do no more for a reader in these circumstances than the Archangel Raphael was able to do for unfallen Adam. But these editorial notes will be found to provide guidance for the further consideration of the poem or topic and for further contemplation of the differences of opinion and method it has evoked. In most cases, the selected list, with the author's citations, represents the course of commentary from at least the early twentieth century on. This may help the reader to realize that he is not alone in his responses to Milton, his perplexities, or his perceptions; and it should confirm for him what has been abundantly confirmed for the editor by the process of review whence these notes issue—the sense of the vigorously continuous, developing, and, of a certainty, increasingly knowledgeable and perceptive character of commentary on Milton, not least in the thirty-odd years past during which the editor has been striving to keep abreast of it or at least to keep from falling so far behind as to be unqualified even to bring up the rear.

In brief editorial lists it is of course quite impossible to include everything that is worth some attention. The notes of the additional studies thus listed will themselves carry the self-reliant reader further. And for yet more lists to 1957, he should consult the bibliographical guides prepared by D. H. Stevens, H. F. Fletcher, and C. Huckabay. For studies after 1957, for items in 1964 that have as yet escaped the editorial net, and for those yet to come, he should consult the sections on Milton in the annual bibliographies published in *PMLA* (whose standard abbreviations for the titles of periodicals are used throughout this volume) and in *Studies in Philology*. Much of the current work is reviewed annually in "Recent Studies in the English Renaissance" in *Studies in English Literature,* and most current single items are summarized in *Seventeenth-Century News*. Selected lists are attached to the authoritative account of Milton in the fifth volume of *The Oxford History of English Literature: The Earlier Seventeenth Century,* by D. Bush, to such general studies or introductions as those by M. H. Nicolson, K. Muir, J. H. Hanford, and A. E. Barker, and to such editions of Milton as those edited by J. T. Shawcross, M. H. Nicolson, and M. Y. Hughes.

I am of course greatly obliged to the authors represented in this volume, not only for permission to reprint (and for this to the original publishers indicated in each case) but for their ready response, often with corrected copy, and further to them and the other authorities consulted for (without exception) their uniform good will and immediate interest and support. I must also record my happy debt to my research assistant, Mr. John Via, of the Graduate College, University of Illinois, for comment, advice, criticism, and firm supervision, well beyond the call of duties otherwise required of him and most efficiently, expeditiously, and cheerfully performed.

Urbana, Illinois   ARTHUR E. BARKER
April 1965

CONTENTS

B. Rajan.   "Simple, Sensuous, and Passionate"   3

Hugh N. Maclean.   Milton's *Fair Infant*   21

Laurence Stapleton.   Milton and the New Music   31

John Hollander.   Milton's Renewed Song   43

Rosemond Tuve.   Structural Figures of *L'Allegro* and *Il Penseroso*   58

John M. Wallace.   Milton's *Arcades*   77

Sears Jayne.   The Subject of Milton's Ludlow *Mask*   88 ⁊ 4

Jon S. Lawry.   "Eager Thought": Dialectic in *Lycidas*   112

Macon Cheek.   Of Two Sonnets of Milton   125

Thomas Wheeler.   Milton's Twenty-third Sonnet   136

Arthur E. Barker.   Structural Pattern in *Paradise Lost*   142

Douglas Bush.   *Paradise Lost* in Our Time: Religious and Ethical Principles   156

D. C. Allen.   Milton and the Descent to Light   177

C. S. Lewis.   Satan   196

Helen Gardner.   Milton's "Satan" and the Theme of Damnation in Elizabethan Tragedy   205

A. B. CHAMBERS. Wisdom at One Entrance Quite Shut Out: *Paradise Lost*, III, 1-55   218

MAURICE KELLEY. The Theological Dogma of *Paradise Lost,* III, 173-202   226

IRENE SAMUEL. The Dialogue in Heaven: A Reconsideration of *Paradise Lost*, III, 1-417   233

WILLIAM G. MADSEN. Earth the Shadow of Heaven: Typological Symbolism in *Paradise Lost*   246

ARNOLD STEIN. Milton's War in Heaven—An Extended Metaphor   264

GEORGE WILLIAMSON. The Education of Adam   284

H. V. S. OGDEN. The Crisis of *Paradise Lost* Reconsidered   308

KESTER SVENDSEN. Adam's Soliloquy in Book X of *Paradise Lost*   328

WILLIAM H. MARSHALL. *Paradise Lost: Felix Culpa* and the Problem of Structure   336

LAWRENCE A. SASEK. The Drama of *Paradise Lost*, Books XI and XII   342

MERRITT Y. HUGHES. Some Illustrators of Milton: The Expulsion from Paradise   357

DONALD R. PEARCE. The Style of Milton's Epic   368

GEOFFREY HARTMAN. Milton's Counterplot   386

ALBERT COOK. Milton's Abstract Music   398

WARNER G. RICE. *Paradise Regained*   416

NORTHROP FRYE. The Typology of *Paradise Regained*   429

A. S. P. WOODHOUSE. Tragic Effect in *Samson Agonistes*   447

JOHN M. STEADMAN. "Faithful Champion": The Theological Basis of Milton's Hero of Faith   467

B. RAJAN

"Simple, Sensuous and Passionate"

Most accounts of Milton's opinions on poetry lay their emphasis on certain parenthetical passages in the *Apology for Smectymnuus* and the *Reason of Church Government*. This autobiographical game (complete with conjectures about the Arthuriad) is no doubt fascinating to play, but it is apt to ignore the possibility that a great poet may have said something important, and even systematic, about the nature and limits of his profession. As a result, Saintsbury's three-volume *History of Criticism* contains only passing references to Milton. Spingarn[1] limits himself to an occasional sentence. Miss Langdon[2] conscientiously presents Milton as a classicist, and Professor Haller,[3] with fine eloquence, presents him as a Puritan. Such simplifications may be necessary, but it is also arguable that the discovery of what Milton said is hindered by interpreting it according to settled systems to which we suppose his thought to be reducible. It is difficult, on any other grounds, to explain the extraordinary neglect of the part played by the Tractate on Education in the formulation of Milton's theory of poetry. We may, of course, discount the retrospective pleading of the "Second Defence."[4] But we cannot do away with the reference in *Areopagitica* to "those unwritt'n, or at least unconstraining laws of vertuous education, religious and civill nurture, which *Plato*

From *The Review of English Studies*, XXI (1945), 289-301. Reprinted by permission of the author and the Clarendon Press, Oxford.

3

there mentions, as the bonds and ligaments of the Commonwealth, the pillars and the sustainers of every writt'n Statute."[5] And the importance of Education in this scheme is emphasized by the almost supernatural powers with which Milton endows the man of learning. This is brought out clearly in the "Seventh Prolusion." Having argued that happiness is inaccessible except to a mind "saturated and perfected by knowledge and training," Milton goes on to describe the compass of learning in terms very similar to his statement of poetic aims in the "Vacation Exercise." The resemblance may mean nothing (the descriptive pattern is a Renaissance commonplace)[6] but Milton's next reference to the powers conferred by learning puts the matter beyond serious doubt.

> He will seem to be one whose power and authority the stars will obey, the land and the sea will follow implicitly, the winds and the storms will strive to please; one to whom Mother Nature even will hand over herself in surrender quite as if some god, having abdicated power on earth, had delegated to him, his court, his laws, his executive power, as though to some prefect.[7]

The end is not Macaulay's schoolboy but the prophet,[8] and when due allowance has been made for the kind of over-statement inevitable in a Prolusion, Milton's conception of the sage corresponds quite adequately to his conception of the poet. Consequently we should not be surprised to find the educational process in the "Tractate" terminating in the study of poetics. This is of a piece with Milton's thinking and even the exaltation of poetry above rhetoric (in opposition to Cicero and Bacon) can be found in its beginnings in the "Third Prolusion."[9]

Yet, if not surprising, the matter is important. To possess and understand the Mistress knowledge, we must follow the steps which, for Milton, lead towards it. The terms of the argument are very largely commonplace, but it ends, I think, in a far from conventional dénouement. Thus the beginning is quite conventional:

> The end then of Learning is to repair the ruines of our first Parents by regaining to know God aright, and out of that knowledge to love him, to imitate him, to be like him as we may the neerest by possessing our souls of true vertue, which being united to the heavenly grace of faith makes up the highest perfection.[10]

To which we may compare a quotation from Baxter:

> The great means of promoting love to God is duly to be-
> hold Him in his appearances to man in the ways of Nature,
> Grace and Glory. First therefore learn to understand and im-
> prove His appearances in Nature, and to see the Creator in all
> His works, and by the knowledge and love of them, to be
> raised to the knowledge and love of Him.[11]

And Milton, too, draws the moral:

> But because our understanding cannot in this body found it
> self but on sensible things, nor arrive so clearly to the knowl-
> edge of God and things invisible, as by orderly conning over
> the visible and inferior creature, the same method is necessarily
> to be follow'd in all discreet teaching.[12]

Wisdom, the power to vivify details with the unity of purpose in
which those details participate, is grounded on the study and regis-
tration of particulars. The unseen is arrived at through a progressive
apprenticeship to the visible. Milton begins the ascent with the preliminary study of grammar. This is followed by agriculture and the
arts of subsistence. Side by side with this goes the study of mathematics, geography, and physics. This equips one for the mechanical
arts of fortification, architecture, and engineering, and while the in-
vestigation is under way, the study of physics is simultaneously pursued through the various refinements of natural philosophy.[13] The
sequence is obviously based on prevalent interpretations of the Great
Chain.[14] One therefore progresses from the study of matter to that of
plants, and from plants to living creatures. Next come anatomy and
physics, and Milton at this stage also allows the study of bucolic poetry.[15] By this time the faculty of reason has been sufficiently strengthened to permit the contemplation and judgment of good and evil.
Plato, Xenophon, Cicero, and Plutarch follow. This completes the
study of man the individual, which is preparatory to that of man in
Society. Ethics, which is concerned with the individual's duty to himself, is therefore followed by Economics, which deals with his duties
towards his neighbours. By now the details comprehended under
comedy have been mastered, and Milton also admits the cautious
sampling of domestic tragedies such as the *Trachiniæ* and the *Alcestis*.

The student can now investigate the limits and grounds of political
organization. Such a study, initially factual, permits him to proceed

to the abstract principles of law and legal justice. This is the highest attainable point in the analysis of temporal order and it therefore leads to the consideration of the eternal problems of church history and theology. It is only after the acquisition of such knowledge that history, heroic poetry, and tragedy can be understood. Thus Milton's introduction to the various literary *genres* is very far from haphazard. The implication is that each type covers a perfectly definite sector of reality, and this in turn suggests that no type can be understood without an understanding of the details it embraces. One proceeds, as always, from the visible to the invisible, from the particular to the abstract, from the dusty catalogue of facts to the creative principle which enriches and controls them. The organization behind art can only be revealed to a mind not distracted with the appraisal of components. Familiarity does not breed contempt. On the contrary it liberates a response to entelechies which transform and sustain the facts of the familiar.

The definitions which emerge from this "placing" are, in other words, deliberate, and they correspond to a similar division by Hobbes.

As Philosophers have divided the Universe, their subject, into three Regions, *Celestiall, Aëriall,* and *Terrestriall,* so the Poets . . . have lodg'd themselves in the three Regions of mankinde, *Court, City,* and *Country,* correspondent in some proportion to those three Regions of the World. For there is in Princes and men of conspicuous power, anciently called *Heroes,* a lustre and influence upon the rest of men resembling that of the Heavens; and an insincereness, inconstancy, and troublesome humour of those that dwell in populous Cities, like the mobility, blustring, and impurity of the Aire; and a plainness, and though dull, yet a nutritive faculty in rurall people, that endures a comparison with the Earth they labour. From hence have proceeded three sorts of Poesy, *Heroique, Scommatique,* and *Pastorall* . . . the Heroique Poem narrative . . . is called an *Epique Poem.* The Heroique Poem Dramatique is *Tragedy.* The Scommatique Narrative is *Satyre,* Dramatique is *Comedy.* The Pastorall narrative is called simply *Pastorall,* anciently *Bucolique;* the same Dramatique, *Pastorall Comedy.*[16]

Hobbes, you may say, is merely being ornamental. But Milton is deadly serious in his contention that only walking encyclopædias should be permitted to read tragedies. His curriculum, fantastic as it is, is merely the result of a thorough-going empiricism. The organic arts include all reality. Therefore one must study reality in its hierarchic details before proceeding to its patterning in art. Always the ascent is from the sensible to the intelligible, from things to words, from facts to poems, and from poems to poetics. And Milton, with a magnificent disregard to the practical, makes no attempt to glide over these necessities. His end is after all the poet of Ben Jonson:

> I could never thinke the study of *Wisdome* confined only to the Philosopher, or of *Piety* to the *Divine,* or of *State* to the *Politicke:* But that he which can faine a *Common Wealth* (which is the *Poet*) can govern it with *Counsels,* strengthen it with *Lawes,* correct it with *Judgements,* inform it with *Religion* and *Morals,* is all these.[17]

The claim recalls that of Comenius:

> Can any man be a good Naturalist, that is not seene in the Metaphysicks? Or a good Moralist, who is not a Naturalist? Or a Logician who is ignorant of real Sciences? Or a Divine, a Lawyer, or a Physician, that is no Philosopher? Or an Oratour or Poet, who is not accomplished with them all?[18]

So when Downame (referring to the pulpit beside which poetry is a power) remarks that "Grammar, Rhetoric, Logicke, Physics, Mathematicks, Metaphysicks, Ethics, Politicks, Oeconomicks, History and Military Discipline"[19] are all useful, he is saying nothing that Milton would not have endorsed.

There is, then, something both traditional and consistent in this remorseless advancement of learning to the appreciation and practice of the arts. But consistency applied to a traditional apparatus (one has in mind Bruno's manipulation of a Platonic paradox)[20] can lead sometimes to astonishing results. This is precisely what happens in the Tractate.

> And now lastly will be the time to read with them those organic arts which inable men to discourse and write perspicuously, elegantly, and according to the fitted stile of lofty, mean,

> or lowly. Logic therefore so much as is useful, is to be referr'd
> to this due place withall her well coucht Heads and Topics,
> untill it be time to open her contracted palm into a gracefull
> and ornate Rhetorick taught out of the rule of *Plato, Aristotle,*
> *Phalereus, Cicero, Hermogenes, Longinus.* To which Poetry
> would be made subsequent, or indeed rather precedent, as
> being less suttle and fine, but more simple, sensuous and pas-
> sionate.[21]

The first fact we must establish concerning this difficult but important passage is the meaning of the equivocation "subsequent, or indeed
rather precedent." Is Milton not sure what he has to say—and if so,
which of these alternatives is valid? My feeling is that he is sure and
that both terms in the equivocation are intended. Poetry is subsequent to rhetoric in the educational scheme. It is precedent in its
value, its intrinsic dignity. Now this, in itself, is not unconventional.
If Milton has Bacon and Cicero against him, he can quote Ben Jonson, Puttenham and Sidney in his defence.[22] It is not what he says
that is surprising, but the reasons he gives for saying it. Poetry is superior to rhetoric and logic because it is less subtle and fine, but more
"simple, sensuous and passionate." In saying this, is Milton denying
his Tractate—the movement of the understanding from the senses,
the orderly ascent from the visible to the invisible? Is he denying the
fibre of his future epic—the treatment of the Fall as a surrender to
the passions? Is he denying the sun-clad power of chastity which the
Lady in *Comus* so implacably announces? And lastly is he denying
himself, the true poem of the *Apology for Smectymnuus,* the composition and pattern of the best and honourablest things? Are we to
assume that he is driven by dualisms, that at the springs of his thought
there is only inconsistency? It may be so. But there is in this passage
no hesitation, no hint that he is evading a dilemma. He considers his
proposition as self-evident; and because it cannot be logically justified,
we have to assume that it is otherwise determined, that Milton sees in
it, not an evasion of facts, but a necessary, obvious, statement of tradition.

The basis of that tradition is that the Renaissance loved action. It
was their ending end, their bedrock of finality. For Ben Jonson, even
the soul does not contemplate. It "workes" and "knowledge is the action of the soul."[23] Discipline, abstention—these are necessary, but it
does not follow from this that they are final. Freedom from wanton-

ness may be freedom for grace. But the end is not adoration—in serving God or in serving Gloriana. It is vindication, the extension of the right

> . . . to subdue
> By force, who reason for thir Law refuse,
> Right reason for thir Law, and for thir King
> Messiah . . .[24]

If the world is for Milton a "gloomy house of correction" he only transcends in order that he may transform it. There is for him no still point, no heaven of the changeless. "Nothing can be recounted justly among the causes of our happiness unless in some way it takes into consideration both that eternal life and this temporal life."[25] To ascend "above the sphery chime" one must love virtue, virtue which sallies out to meet her adversary, which is born of action and eventually begets it. Milton would not have agreed with our latest transcendentalist: "Through the clear waters of their being we look down on the tainted polluted mud of their actions, and we see how maimed, how blundering, how blind is the world of action compared with the world of being."[26] But for Milton the good is not final. It is merely the ground of a transforming militant goodness. We possess our souls of heavenly virtue not to escape, but to redeem our bodies: and at this point of emergence of knowledge into action the hierarchic values are reversed. We measure our understanding by its awareness of the changeless; we measure our utterance by its capacity to change. To say in this context that poetry is "more simple, sensuous and passionate" means that its transforming intelligence permeates even the frontiers of reality, that the security of a perfected understanding orders the scope and grandeur of its utterance. The result—one wonders if it is deliberate—is to discover virtues where Plato found defects. It may of course be accidental that Milton's founding of eloquence on wisdom resembles Plato's founding of goodness on the good:

> . . . that spirit of yours, not satisfied with this gloomy house of correction, will betake itself far and wide, until it shall have filled the world itself and far beyond with a certain divine extension of magnitude.[27]

To this one could compare:

> . . . he was good and in one that is good no envy of anything
> else ever arises. Being devoid of envy then, he desired that
> everything should be so far as possible like himself.[28]

And what Lovejoy calls the dialectic of plentitude—the giving of
existence to all possibles by goodness—does, in a sense, justify Milton's preference of poetry to rhetoric. Poetry is superior, because it is
more inclusive, because its intelligence shines into the senses, because among all the organic arts, it has least outside its area of redemption. This may seem slender evidence on which to base so considerable a thesis. Nevertheless it makes sense of a passage which has
hitherto only made sense by being wrenched from its context, and
rapturously misunderstood by Coleridge and Arnold.[29] It is the kind of
theory which could easily arise from an attempt to reconcile poet,
Platonist, and Puritan. It recognizes and is consistent with tradition
—it represents in fact the kind of critical modification which gives
tradition its relevance, and its power of survival. Most important of
all, it illuminates two problems which have hitherto been neglected
in Miltonic research: the relationship of poetry to the good life, and
the running contrast between art and nature.

Any discussion of the first must refer eventually to two passages:

> For doubtlesse that indeed according to art is most eloquent,
> which returnes and approaches neerest to nature from whence
> it came; and they expresse nature best, who in their lives least
> wander from her safe leading, which may be call'd regenerate
> reason. So that how he should be truly eloquent who is not
> withall a good man, I see not.[30]

> And long it was not after, when I was confirm'd in this
> opinion, that he who would not be frustrate of his hope to
> write well hereafter in laudable things, ought him selfe to bee
> a true Poem, that is a composition and patterne of the best
> and honourablest things; not presuming to sing high praises
> of heroick men, or famous Cities, unlesse he have in himselfe
> the experience and the practice of all that which is praise-
> worthy.[31]

These passages, when they are discussed at all, are treated as a more
elaborate version of Longinus' assertion that the poet must be a good
man. But to me they are more than a mere recapitulation, and they
can be presented as following from the argument sketched in the

Tractate. Art is most eloquent when it returns to nature. Milton deliberately says "return" where his successors would have said "follow."
You cannot return to a place you have not left. Moreover nature is
best expressed by those "who least wander from her safe leading" of
regenerate reason. Here the word "regenerate" is critical. It means,
quite inevitably, that the knowledge of Nature *demands* experience
at the level of Grace. Conversely the order of Grace is built on that of
Nature—"our understanding cannot in this body found itself, but on
sensible things." Thus the two worlds, far from being separate, demand each other as a condition of their existence. It is the possession
of knowledge, of the good, which makes possible the radiance and
creative power of goodness. Reason is not restrictive. On the contrary it liberates those powers of fecundity which are otherwise man-
gled and suppressed in chaos. By regenerating reason in yourself you
return to reason in nature, and by becoming a composition of the best
and honourablest things, you answer to and discover that harmony
of reason with the good, by which all nature is sustained and fertilized. I would emphasize "fertilized" because in ordinary usage we
think of creative energy as something opposed to restraint. Occasionally we discover that the two are not incompatible; and sometimes as
the result of a tremendous speculative effort we persuade ourselves
that the one assists the other. But Milton is bolder; and I think that
what he is saying (he never quite says it because it is an instinctive
assumption) is that fertility is made possible, and not merely assisted
by, restraint. On this point the evidence of the *De Doctrina* is instruc-
tive:

> It is objected, however, that body cannot emanate from
> spirit. I reply, much less then can body emanate from nothing.
> For spirit being the more excellent substance, virtually and
> essentially contains within itself the inferior one, as the spirit-
> ual and rational faculty contains the corporeal, that is, the
> sentient and vegetative faculty.[32]

Thus every item in the hierarchies of existence is sustained and comprehended by its superior—and the chain of causes terminates in the
First Cause. Knowledge *creates* power. Discipline *creates* abundance.
It is not simply negative, "the removal of disorder," not "confined and
cloyed with repetition of that which is prescribed." It is "the very visible shape and image of virtue,"[33] impregnating poetic activity as the
"vital virtue" of God's spirit impregnates the creation. And because

such discipline is the manifestation, the informing radiance, of the divine, it accepts no circumscriptions save those which it has created.

> . . . or whether the rules of *Aristotle* herein are strictly to be kept, or nature to be follow'd, which in them that know art, and use judgement, is no transgression, but an inriching of art.[34]

The word "inriching" should be noted carefully since it is a rare and a special word for Milton. It is used only three times in the body of his works,[35] and since one of these occasions involves an irate reference to piracy the context of the other is overwhelmingly important:

> . . . nor to be obtain'd by the invocation of Dame Memory and her Siren daughters, but by devout prayer to that eternall Spirit who can enrich with all utterance and knowledge, and sends out his Seraphim with the hallow'd fire of his Altar, to touch and purify the lips of whom he pleases; to this must be added industrious and select reading, steddy observation, insight into all seemly and generous arts and affaires, . . .[36]

The "hallowed fire" which touches Milton touched also the prophet Isaiah; and the words "enrich with all utterance and knowledge" are a transcript from I Corinthians i, 5: "That in every thing, ye are enriched by him, in all utterance, and in all knowledge." The spirit of God enriches as it purifies. The spirit of man purified, radiant and plunging into creativeness is "no transgression but an inriching of art." To follow nature simply means to follow one's disposition.[37] What is implied is not, as Mr. Lewis suggests, a hesitation between two kinds of epic, but a declaration for creative freedom.[38] This is made more likely by the fact that whenever Milton uses a nature-art antithesis he invariably synonymizes nature with abundance. To see this we have only to turn to his description of Paradise:

> Flours worthy of Paradise which not nice Art
> In Beds and curious Knots, but Nature boon
> *Powrd* forth profuse on Hill and Dale and Plaine . . .[39]

or see the same thing through the eyes of Raphael:

> Into the blissful field, through Groves of Myrhhe,
> And flouring Odours, Cassia, Nard, and Balme;
> A Wilderness of sweets; for Nature here

> Wantond as in her prime, and plaid at will
> Her Virgin Fancies, *pouring* forth more sweet,
> Wilde above Rule or Art; enormous bliss.[40]

This takes us back to the perversities of *Comus*:

> Wherefore did Nature *Powre* her bounties forth,
> With such a full and unwithdrawing hand,
> Covering the earth with odours, fruits, and flocks,
> Thronging the Seas with spawn innumerable . . .[41]

and beyond all this to the ecstasy of the Creation:

> About his Chariot numberless we *pour'd*
> Cherub and Seraph, Potentates and Thrones,
> And Vertues, winged spirits, and Chariots wing'd . . .[42]

There are of course other sanctions for this sense of richness. We can argue if we like that Milton's theory is written out for him by his overwhelming awareness of fertility.[43] We can find a precedent in Spenser's Garden of Adonis. And we can find an even more important precedent in the contrast of the Garden with the Bower of Acrasia. For, as Mr. Lewis has pointed out, the characteristic of the Bower is enervation, not activity. "There is not a kiss or an embrace in the island: only male prurience and female provocation."[44] But Milton carries the identification further. For him goodness is fertility. It is based on, it flowers from the possession of the good. The antitheses we use when we discuss his writing, the stock opposition of puritan to poet, of ascetic restraint to creative luxuriance—these do not exist at the centre of his insight. Professor Haller has seized on one aspect of this truth in his insistence that Milton's puritanism confirms rather than contradicts his poetry.[45] We have to extend this to its aesthetic correlative—that sensuousness is enriched not starved by discipline, and creative exuberance occasioned by self-denial.[46] This may not help us and perhaps it did not help Milton. Poetic inspiration is a gift capriciously bestowed and not a reward for effort, however arduous, so an "encompassing support of all the arts and sciences" may be no more to the point than a whiff of nitrous oxide. Nevertheless, in criticizing the argument we must not slip into belittling its finality. It was for Milton an "ending end." His whole life was an attempt to illustrate it. Consequently, if we are to accept the theory as erroneous, its continual practice is strangely obtuse. I cannot see that the theory is erroneous and the practice obtuse. Milton refuses to sport with Amaryllis because it is ordinary good sense to prefer Urania. His aim is decorum and not a dionysiac ecstasy. Where he goes wrong is not in his assertion that creative power depends upon self discipline (this is, in a way, obvious, for a man who has the bad taste to behave like a beast will evidently not have the good taste to write poetry), but in his vague conviction that the two are somehow proportional. The result is that each creative failure is made to point towards a new asceticism.[47] "Il Penseroso" plays with a monk's cell. The "Sixth Elegy" talks of living on herbs. But with "Lycidas" Milton is beginning to "scorn delights." And four years later the full fury of his invective is poured out on "libidinous and ignorant Poetasters." In this slowly hardening intolerance, something is generated which cuts at the roots of poetic spontaneity, and inward ripeness is denied to Milton almost because of the fervour with which he pursues it.

Such marginalia however should not distract from the essential importance of what was said by Milton. Through education, through virtue, we know God. We imitate Him and therefore His Creation. We return and approach to the Nature which is His Art. If Milton's epic programme is studied under these *dicta* we can see good reasons for his writing *Paradise Lost*. Mr. Basil Willey, I am aware, has pointed to selective influences in the climate of opinion; and Dr. Tillyard and Sir Herbert Grierson have done so too in terms of Milton's biography. But there is something else besides these converging necessities. For Milton, the creation is the perfect poem. He mentions it first among his poetic intentions, he returns to it as the matrix of his utterance. All of his eloquence is shaped by its activity. Paradise is perfected by its plenitude. Hell is its parody, the causeway from Hell its burlesque. The reverberating overtones of the Fall are chaos. The atonement is a new creation, a bringing of good out of evil. Everything that the epic says and does is suffused and controlled by this central efflorescence. The organization is of course traditional: as Thibaut de Maisières points out, it is based on Hexæmeral conventions.[48] But in my interpretation of Milton's thought I have tried to display it as answering his instincts. I have treated *Paradise Lost* as summing Milton's life, as adumbrating the dilemmas of his time, as opposing the concept of nature's spirituality to the unleashed forces of an advancing mechanism. I have tried here to visualize it as flowing from the realities which are ultimate to Milton's modes of thought. True richness is born of knowledge. The bliss of nature "wilde above Rule or Art" confirms and commemorates an intrinsic order. So too eloquence is good *because* it is passionate, because it is addressed to man in his totality, because it is "of power beside the office of a pulpit, to inbreed and cherish in a great people the seeds of vertu and publick civility, to allay the perturbations of the mind, and set the affections in right tune.[49] Milton was thinking perhaps of his "Arthuriad" when he said this. But *Paradise Lost* meets his definition more nobly. In setting Creation against the Angelic Fall, the Incarnation against the lapse of Eve and Adam, in this eternal pulsating rhythm of good out of evil, he discovers the framework which gives strength to his vision of poetry. Critics may see only deterioration between *Comus* and *Paradise Lost*. They may talk learnedly of the times and of tradition, and say that Milton "long choosing" had begun too late. But it is well to admit that he could not have done otherwise; and with the prejudice of the time moving us in other directions, we are perhaps not always competent to find out what he did.

NOTES

1. *Literary Criticism in the Renaissance* (1908).
2. *Milton's Theory of Poetry and the Fine Arts* (1924).
3. *The Rise of Puritanism* (1938), *passim*.
4. *Works* (Columbia University Press), vol. viii, pp. 131-33.
5. *Areopagitica* (*Works, ed. cit.*, vol. iv, p. 318).
6. Both resemble, e.g., the opening passage of La Primaudaye's *French Academy*; cf, also "Third Prolusion" (*Works, ed. cit.*, vol. xii, p. 171).
7. *Works, ed. cit.*, vol. xii, p. 267.
8. Haller puts the matter plainly (*op. cit.*, p. 304): "He is like Bacon in that he clearly perceives the diseases that afflict learning. He is like Bacon too in taking all knowledge for his province and in believing that knowledge is power. But the power he is hoping to gain through knowledge is not that of the scientist but that of the orator, the preacher, the poet in public life, in a word the seer and prophet."
9. *Works, ed. cit.*, vol. xii, pp. 163-4.
10. *Works, ed. cit.*, vol. iv, p. 277. M. W. Bundy ("Milton's view of Education in *Paradise Lost*," *J.E.G.P.*, XXI (1922), 127-52) has contrasted this with *Works, ed. cit.*, vol. iv, p. 280: "I call therefore a compleat and generous Education that which fits a man to perform justly, skilfully and magnanimously all the offices both private and publick of Peace and War." Raphael's commission in *Paradise Lost* comes under the second heading, Gabriel's under the first. But as

O. M. Ainsworth points out (*Milton on Education*, 1928, pp. 14-15, 42-43), the definitions are complementary: ". . . these aims, combining as they do the classical spirit with the Christian are of the essence of humanistic educational doctrine." The transition from the visible to the invisible is of course not peculiar to Puritanism and can be found, e.g. in Vives.

11. *Christian Directory* (1825 edn.), vol. i, p. 375. Elsewhere Baxter refers to Education as "God's ordinary way for the conveyance of his grace." *Reliquiæ Baxterianæ* (1696), pp. 6-7.

12. *Works, ed. cit.*, vol. iv, p. 277.

13. Foster Watson has here noticed a close following of Vive's curriculum by Milton ("A Suggested Source of Milton's Tractate 'Of Education,'" *Nineteenth Century*, 1909, pp. 607-17). Several other resemblances are summarized by Ainsworth, *ed. cit.*, p. 13. E. N. S. Thompson ("Milton's 'Of Education,'" *S.P.* XV (1918), 159-75) has however pointed out that Milton is less empirical than Vives, relying on book learning, not direct observation.

14. The strongest evidence for this, outside the Tractate, is *Paradise Lost*, V, 507-12:

> O favourable spirit, propitious guest,
> Well hast thou taught the way that might direct
> Our knowledge, and the scale of Nature set
> From center to circumference, whereon
> In contemplation of created things
> By steps we may ascend to God.

The connection between this passage and the Tractate is strengthened by the fact (pointed out by Bundy, *op. cit., passim*) that Raphael's mission is specifically educational. The idea is commonplace. A typical example can be found in *The Interlude of the Four Elements* (*Old Plays*, ed. Dodsley-Hazlitt, vol. i, p. 9). I have not had access to W. C. Curry's *Milton and the Scale of Nature* (*Stanford Univ. Studies in Lang. and Lit.*, 1941) which has no doubt something to say about it. Milton's familiarity with the Elizabethan assumptions is alluded to by E. M. Tillyard, *The Elizabethan World Picture* (1943), *passim*.

15. The word "bucolic" is not used by Milton, and is not accurately descriptive. The authors commended are Orpheus, Hesiod, Theocritus, Aratus, Nicander, Oppian, Dionysius, Lucretius, Manilius, and the rural part of Virgil.

16. J. E. Spingarn, *Critical Essays of the Seventeenth Century*, vol. ii, pp. 54-55. Milton's classification differs from that of Hobbes in that (*a*) he does not specifically mention Pastoral in the lowest division, (*b*) he lumps Comedy with Domestic Tragedy and ignores satire in

the intermediate category. That he has in mind a basic threefold division is, however, made clear by his subsequent reference to "the fitted style of lofty, mean, or lowly." This probably originates from the three styles of classical rhetoric. For an account of the degree to which the theory of rhetoric affected that of poetry in England see J. W. H. Atkins, *English Literary Criticism, The Mediæval Phase* (1943), pp. 23-8, and D. L. Clark, *Rhetoric and Poetry in the Renaissance* (1922), *passim*.

17. Spingarn, *op. cit.*, vol. i, p. 28. To this and to succeeding quotations compare Milton's encyclopaedic conception of orator and poet, *Works, ed. cit.*, vol. xii, p. 249.

18. *A Reformation of Schooles*, 1642.

19. Quoted by Haller, *op. cit.*, p. 138.

20. A. O. Lovejoy, *The Great Chain of Being* (1936), pp. 116-21.

21. *Works, ed. cit.*, vol. iv, p. 286. L. Jonas (*The Divine Science*, 1940, p. 169) argues that "perspicuously" applies to logic, "elegantly" to rhetoric, and the "fitted style of lofty, mean, or lowly" to poetry. I cannot grant this. In the first place, Milton's discrimination of poetry from rhetoric is not one of kind, but of degree of greater passionateness; in the second place the division into lofty, mean, and lowly is a commonplace of scholastic rhetoric.

22. Cicero describes the poet as "closely akin to the orator, being somewhat more restricted in rhythm, but freer in his choice of words, and in many kinds of embellishment his rival and almost his equal" (*De Orat.* i, 70). Cf. Jonson: "The *Poet* is the nearest Borderer upon the Orator, and expresseth all his virtues though he be tied more to numbers, is his equal in ornament, and above him in his strengths. Because in moving the minds of men, and stirring of affections, in which Oratory shewes and especially approves her eminence, he chiefly excells." (Ded. to *Volpone*, Spingarn, vol. i, p. 15.) Puttenham also emphasizes the power of poetry (as against prose) to move (*Elizabethan Critical Essays*, ed. G. Gregory Smith, vol. ii, pp. 8-9). For Sidney the logician and rhetorician are tied to Nature, which only the poet transcends (Gregory Smith, vol. i, p. 156). Critics of the Italian Renaissance, e.g., Savonarola, Lombardus, Varchi, differentiate in that logic proves by syllogism, rhetoric by enthymeme, poetry by example (Clark, *op. cit.*, pp. 132-4; Spingarn, *Literary Criticism in the Renaissance*, pp. 25-6). Minturno and Scaliger regard it as the business of rhetoric and poetry to move, and take it that the example is more effective than the precept.

Milton's treatment of rhetoric as ornate and graceful can be found in Hawes and Skelton, and is orthodox. But there seems no precedent for his *reasons* for exalting poetry above rhetoric. He may have thought he had found them in Longinus, but Longinus's basic distinction (*De Sub.* XV) is one of kind between the rhetorical and poetical imagination.

23. Spingarn, *op. cit.*, vol. i, p. 24.
24. *Paradise Lost*, VI, 40-3.
25. "Seventh Prolusion," *Works, ed. cit.*, vol. xii, p. 255.
26. Stephen Spender, *Life and the Poet* (London, 1942), p. 48. The reference is to Milton, Keats, and Byron.
27. "Seventh Prolusion," *Works, ed. cit.*, vol. xii, pp. 265-7.
28. *Timæus*, sections 29-30.
29. Cf. Coleridge, *Select Poetry and Prose*, ed. Stephen Potter (1930), p. 315; M. Arnold, *Essays in Criticism; Second Series* (London, 1935: New Eversley Series), p. 71; and, for a recent example, E. E. Stoll, *From Shakespeare to Joyce* (1944), p. 73.
30. "Apology for Smectymnuus," *Works, ed. cit.*, vol. iii, p. 287.
31. *Ibid.*, p. 303.
32. *Works, ed. cit.*, vol. xv, p. 25.
33. "Reason of Church Government," *Works, ed. cit.*, vol. iii, pp. 185-6.
34. *Ibid.*, p. 237.
35. The Columbia Index lists "enriching" twice and does not list "enrich."
36. "Reason of Church Government," *Works, ed. cit.*, vol. iii, p. 241.
37. The key to Milton's meaning is not, as Mr. C. S. Lewis thinks, in Tasso (*A Preface to Paradise Lost*, 1942, pp. 5-6), but in what Milton says a few lines later; ". . . if to the instinct of nature and the imboldning of art ought may be trusted. . . ." Hence "nature" in this passage is synonymous with instinctive inclination. "Imbolden" presumably means to heighten, organize, exaggerate, stress by simplification. Hence the propositions that to follow nature is to enrich one's art, and that art "imboldens" what the instinct of nature provides, are complementary.
38. See e.g. the contrast of Art with Inclination in the Garden of Adonis, *The Faerie Queene*, III, vi, 44, and Mr. Lewis's discussion of the two terms in Spenser (*The Allegory of Love*, pp. 323-30).
39. *Paradise Lost*, IV, 241-3.
40. *Paradise Lost*, V, 292-7.
41. *Comus*, 709-12.
42. *Paradise Lost*, VII, 197-9. The italics in this and the preceding quotations are mine.
43. Professor Saurat was the first to draw attention to this. See also E. M. W. Tillyard, *The Miltonic Setting*, pp. 65-72, and *Paradise Regained, The Minor Poems and Samson Agonistes*, ed. M. Y. Hughes (1937), pp. xxx ff.
44. C. S. Lewis, *The Allegory of Love*, p. 332.

45. "The essence of his *biographia literaria* is that when in the cultivation of his gifts he found his way to the poetry of the ancient world and the Renaissance, he found not distraction and escape from the Puritan urge to salvation and service, but the strongest possible confirmation" (*Op. cit.*, pp. 306-7.) Again, ". . . he never acknowledged the war between poetry and Puritanism which may be after all nothing but the reflection of our own divided souls" (*op. cit.*, p. 289).

46. One notes Mr. W. H. Auden's drift in this direction: "He [the ideal critic] will see artistic freedom and personality as dependent upon the voluntary acceptance of limitations which alone are strong enough to test the genuine intensity of the original creative impulse" (*The Intent of the Critic*, ed. D. A. Stauffer, 1941, p. 146). And compare also Arthur Barker: "The integration of the natural and the spiritual thus conceived and the perfection of the first by the second with the increase not the loss of its peculiar glory, was to be the central aim of Milton's finest work, in prose no less than in poetry; it connoted the potent balance of his special powers" (*Milton and the Puritan Dilemma*, 1942, p. 8).

47. The evidence for Milton's disappointment with his poetic development is in "How soon hath Time," the Epigraph to the 1637 edition of *Comus*, and in the first few lines of "Lycidas." It is possible to treat these as poetic gestures which have little to do with Milton's feelings, but I follow Professor Barker in thinking that this is not so. However, I cannot follow him to his conclusion that "the controversialist in Milton was born of the frustration of the poet who seemed to see in the embattled forces in the church and state the public counterpart of the powers contending in his own mind" (*op. cit.*, p. 6).

48. Maury Thibaut de Maisières, *Les Poèmes inspirés du Début de la Genèse à l'Epoque de la Renaissance* (Louvain, 1931), *passim*. Mr. Lewis in talking of Milton's "hesitation between the classical and the romantic types of epic" (*op. cit.*, p. 7) is surely neglecting this *genre*. See also G. McColley, "Paradise Lost," *Harvard Theological Review*, 1939, pp. 181-235, and G. C. Taylor, *Milton's use of Du Bartas* (1934), *passim*.

49. "Reason of Church Government," *Works, ed. cit.*, vol. iii, p. 238.

[EDITOR'S NOTE. See also Mr. Rajan's *Paradise Lost and the Seventeenth Century Reader*, 1947, reissued 1962. On the principle of variety and contrast, see H. S. V. Odgen, *JHI*, X (1949), 159-82; on Milton's poetic theory and practice, Z. S. Fink, *ES*, XXI (1939), 164-5; A. S. P. Woodhouse, *UTQ*, XIII (1943-44), 66-101; E. Sirluck, *JEGP*, LX (1961), 749-85; R. Tuve, *JEGP*, LX (1961), 209-25, and *Elizabethan and Metaphysical Imagery*, 1947; R. Daniells, *Milton, Mannerism and Baroque*,

1963; D. Bush, *MP*, LXI (1963), 204-7; P. R. Sellin, *JEGP*, LX
(1961), 104-22; J. T. Shawcross, *MLQ*, XXIV (1963), 21-30; J. M.
Steadman, *Italica*, XL (1963), 28-34; on the relation to logic and rhetoric, D. L. Clark, *Milton at St. Paul's School*, 1948; L. Howard, *HLQ*, IX
(1946), 149-73; J. B. Broadbent, *ES*, XXXVII (1956), 49-62, and *MP*,
LVI (1959), 224-42; K. Svendsen, *TSLL*, I (1959), 11-29; W. O.
Scott, *PQ*, XLII (1963), 183-9.]

HUGH N. MACLEAN

Milton's *Fair Infant*

I

Milton's critics have not until recently directed much attention to
the early poem *On the Death of a fair Infant dying of a Cough*. Tillyard's comments, while couched in terms of the poem's relation to the
rest of Milton's early work, do not develop that question in detail.
Brooks and Hardy, although they suggest some tentative patterning
in the poem, are content to dismiss the *Fair Infant* as, primarily, a
rather unsuccessful exercise in the employment of decorative metaphor.[1] Scholars of Milton's poetry before 1630 have, reasonably
enough, gravitated in one direction toward the brilliance of the *Nativity Ode,* and in another toward the developing pattern of Milton's
mind and poetic practice in the Latin elegies and occasional pieces.
Professor Allen has, however, recently shown that the *Fair Infant* reflects a theme employed by Gregory Nazianzen and Jerome: "the
pagan dies out of his glory, the Christian into his"; and he also remarks (and demonstrates) that the poem "is a vivid indication of the
poet's mature technique."[2] The present essay, which may perhaps be
regarded as a pendant to Profesor Allen's comments, suggests (by
way of extension) that the structure and imagery of the *Fair Infant*
reveal a greater degree of unity and progression than has so far been

From *ELH, A Journal of English Literary History,* XXIV (1957), 296-305.
Reprinted by permission of the author and The Johns Hopkins Press.

proposed; and (by way of addition) that the poem, with regard particularly to Milton's éffort to bring into meaningful poetical relation classical and Christian image and idea, represents a significant and intermediate stage between the relatively simple design of *Elegy III* and the elegy *On the death of the Bishop of Ely,* and the complex patterns of the *Nativity Ode.*

That Milton's personal emotions and experience are not profoundly reflected in the *Fair Infant* is generally accepted; it may perhaps be added that the complete absence of *sound* from the poem serves in itself as an outward and visible sign of Milton's state of mind when he composed the piece. In *Elegy III,* as Lancelot Andrews is received into heaven, "the blossoming earth shook with joyous sounds"; the Bishop of Ely's flight toward the stars is initiated at the call of a heavenly voice; the gods and heroes of the *Vacation Exercise* are united by the bard's "melodious harmonie," echoing "what unshorn Apollo sings/To th' touch of golden wires." But Milton celebrates the passing of Anne Phillips' child in absolute silence: all is visual in this world of mime-figures who communicate chiefly by gesture. The reference to "that high first-moving Spheare" is unaccompanied, as such passages in Milton more usually are accompanied, by a reference to the musical harmony of the "spheary chime." And the silence is all the more striking in contrast with the wealth of aural passages apparent, from an early date, in Milton's work; not to mention the relevant comments on the "solemn and divine harmonies of music" in the tractate *Of Education,* or the reference in *Ad Patrem* to his youthful introduction to music, within the family circle. Also, it is clear that in a literal sense, the *Fair Infant* is primarily an occasional poem, celebrating, in accordance with the conventions of a tradition, a relatively unimportant event in terms designed to enhance and magnify the significance of that occasion. Donne's *Anniversaries* are perhaps the most representative examples of this tradition, which (notwithstanding the strictures of Jonson) may be continuously observed in such poems as Lord Herbert of Cherbury's *Elegy over a Tomb* and Carew's *Maria Wentworth,* before it burgeons to full amplitude with Dryden's *Anne Killigrew.* The title of Milton's poem stresses its relation to the tradition.

But the poem is ambitious beyond the limits set by Brooks and Hardy, who conclude that "What [Milton] has attempted to achieve is a sort of formal statement in which the appropriate sentiments on such a death can be controlled and unified."[3] In two earlier Latin poems, *Elegy III* and the *Bishop of Ely,* Milton (as Professor Allen notes) has effectively set over against an initial stage of grief, expressed in terms of classical imagery, a final stage of Christian joy. In each poem, Christian images supersede the classical vision, but do not banish the images of classical story. An allusion to "the beloved of Cephalus" concludes the imagery of *Elegy III;* while the Bishop of Ely, at the last, speaks of his arrival before "the bright portals of Olympus." The Christian victory, so to speak, contains, and even (for its fullest effect) depends upon the continued presence of classical elements, which imaginatively take their place in the eternal scheme. It should also be observed that in neither poem is the central figure (once received into heaven) considered to be *acting* further in man's behalf. For the Bishop of Ely, "it is enough to enjoy [Paradise] forever"; while Christ bids Lancelot Andrews, "henceforth forever . . . rest from thy hard labours."

In the *Fair Infant,* the relatively simple antitheses of the two elegiac pieces are developed in terms of a more complex pattern. Milton is not attempting to control and unify merely "the appropriate sentiments on such a death"—although such an intention is continuously present. He is attempting also, within the limitations of a convention, to control and unify a body of poetic imagery reflecting his Christian and Classical heritage; to combine, in particular, classical form and imagery with "matter" of Christian significance. That the scheme of the *Nativity Ode* has not yet developed in Milton's mind is a reasonable assumption. But the *Fair Infant* finds him moving in that direction; concerned to work out an aesthetic pattern which may retain the beauty and symbolic aptness of classical story, while indicating at the same time the subordination of classical assumptions to those of the Christian dispensation. This design, worked out more completely than in *Elegy III* or the *Bishop of Ely,* is chiefly responsible for the relatively successful progression of stanzas I through IX. At the same time, the central figure of the *Fair Infant* also takes a mid-position between those of the elegies and the *Ode.* The Bishops were essentially passive; but this child is an active agent, who intercedes beyond the grave for men yet on earth, and whose role, in its most significant aspect, is "To stand 'twixt us and our deserved smart . . . ." Neither Edward King nor Charles Diodati were explicitly to be assigned so demanding a part, which could be adequately sustained, for a poet of Milton's persuasion, only by the God-man Christ. The "fair infant," certainly, cannot satisfy the extravagant demands made on her; so that the progression of image, in effect, lacks a sufficiently significant central point of reference. The subdued and rather hasty ending of the poem (which is quite unlike the peaceful and confident serenity marking the conclusions of later works) may reflect the poet's sense of failure, confirmed by exclusion of the piece from the edition of 1645. Again, it seems unlikely that Milton, when he composed the *Fair Infant*, already had in mind the pattern of the *Nativity Ode,* with its Christian and classical figures significantly ranged in relation to the Christchild; rather, problems encountered in the composition of the *Fair Infant* pointed on to a resolution, based on greater understanding and deliberate purpose, in the *Nativity Ode*. In short, the earlier poem finds Milton grappling with elements which will be successfully combined only when the fusion of poetical power and religious experience is achieved and given expression in the *Ode.*

II

Structurally, the poem falls into four divisions: two groups of three stanzas each, a third of four stanzas, and a single concluding stanza which recalls and corrects the impression created in stanza I. There are other links as well: the tenth verse is directly related to the sixth, and, in a different way, to the eleventh; while stanzas VII-IX constitute an implicit response to the first of *three* questions, or problems, posed in the sixth stanza.[4] In a general way also, of course, the poem reflects the characteristic movement of Christian elegy, progressing from a mood of grief, through a gradually amplified stage of meditation and calming reconciliation, to a final note of consolation and hope, marking the poet's recognition of the true meaning of death. But within that broad movement Milton elaborates a subtle and developing pattern.

The first three stanzas are characterized, after initial suggestions of the poet's grief, chiefly by an emphasis on incompleteness and mistake. Winter, in stanza I a merely natural personification, is drawn into a classical frame of reference by the allusion (in stanza II) to Boreas and Orithyia. But from the first, winter is an essentially foolish figure; a hasty and elderly blunderer, he is marked in the second verse by an almost pompous self-importance, emphasized by the poet's dry comment, *"He thought* it toucht his Deitie full neer. . . ." His motives are confused: "amorous" desire is involved, but more important is a bumbling insistence on the maintenance of his honour—an "honour," however, which is so only "'mongst the wanton gods."

The tedious wanderings and confident final pounce are entirely futile. Further, winter is powerless to restore colour to the poem: the fading rose-tints of the opening verse do not revive, but give place merely to "ycie-pearled" and "cold-kind" shades of bleak white, reinforcing the suggestion that winter is a clumsy killer. Again, what movement there is in these initial stanzas cannot rise above the "middle empire of the freezing aire." The natural world, that is to say, imposes a steady curb on these classical figures who seek to dominate it. The areas of imagery are strictly limited to the natural and the classical: the figures of Ovidian story, superimposed on the "infant's" natural world, are quite unable, for all their efforts, to transcend natural death. In fact, the effort to do so merely emphasizes the essential powerlessness of a classical vision in the natural world. Stanzas I-III, accordingly, are marked by negation and futility. Some other elements, not yet present, must be introduced to realize a freer and more inward condition.

Milton, however, does not at once, or abruptly, alter the direction of his poem: stanza IV still moves in the area of classical imagery. But the significant word in that stanza is "transform'd." Once again, figures from classical story descend into nature, and this time an act of creation, of a sort, is the result: "Young *Hyacinth*" is given new life, although that life is still held on the natural plane. Apollo's motivation springs, still, from a type of earthly love. But his relation to Hyacinth is evidently of a more refined quality than winter's "amorous" feelings for the "fair infant"; it is the memory of an especially close friendship which impels Apollo to perpetuate his companion's name and presence in the natural world. Colour, too, returns to the poem, in the vivid purple flower; and we are reminded (in the last line) of winter's futility, to emphasize the fact that a step forward has certainly been made. Yet, an atmosphere of uncertainty and error continues to oppress the poem; for Apollo's "unweeting hand" was, after all, in part responsible for the death he could not recall or undo. The *Metamorphoses* has made an important contribution; but there is more to be done, although the Ovidian transformation has in a sense provided the key which permits movement beyond that of the first three stanzas. A transformation freed from classical thoughtlessness or accident would seem to be indicated as the next step; and that is what centers the fifth stanza, which (for the first time) announces a movement "Above mortalitie," from natural to supra-natural planes. Nor is there any hint of error or mistake: "Heav'n" knows what it does. Death is *really* transcended, in contrast to the evasion of death by Apollo's sleight-of-hand; and "earths dark wombe," appropriately, is replaced by a "divine" (if still not altogether identifiable) brilliance.

These two stanzas (IV and V) together form the first "turning-point" of the poem, and they lead naturally to the questions of stanza VI; the answers to those questions will allow the re-entrance and fuller flowering of classical imagery. This in turn will enable the poet to move toward the Christian version of stanza IX, in which classical assumptions are clearly relegated to an inferior place; although the progression of the poem to that stage has been made largely in terms of images drawn from classical story. Accordingly, Milton permits himself to imagine a continuing doubt in regard to the *kind* of divinity which he had observed in the face of the living child. Three "problems" are now presented (in stanza VI); (a) whether the infant's soul has flown to a Christian or to a classical heaven; (b) whether or not the infant was mortal; (c) why her soul departed from the world in such haste. The first of these "problems" reflects Milton's central aesthetic concern to effect a transition of emphasis, through his poetic imagery, from classical to Christian terms, and by that process to establish the ascendancy of the latter more firmly than the relatively brisk treatment of this theme in the earlier stanzas had permitted; that transition is made in stanzas VII-IX.[5] The second "problem" also is dealt with in this area of the poem: the child's "mortality" was only that of an intermediate stage between states more than mortal. However, Milton's response to the third "problem" creates a difficulty regarding the *character* of the child's divinity, and that in turn raises doubts regarding the character and function of her mortal aspect. This third "problem" is partially answered in the ninth stanza; but an effort to complete that answer (the business of stanza X) leads to an abrupt and almost glum concluding line, after which, in the final stanza, Milton turns away.

Stanzas VII-IX, however, form a quite successful poetical unit, which has its own aesthetic pattern. The classical world provides the imagery of the seventh verse: it is suggested that the child may have been a star fallen from the ceiling of Olympus, or, perhaps, a timid goddess seeking safety from the terrors of war between Olympians and Titans. Here are only passive and negative associations; downward movement exclusively; no suggestions of colour other than the vague "sheenie Heav'n." Further, the natural world seems still in control of these classical figures: Jove puts the fallen star back in its place "in natures true behoofe"; the goddess finds in nature a haven denied her among the gods. The imagery of the succeeding stanza moves a step farther: this is the half-world of personified abstractions, on the borderland of classical story. These figures—Astraea, Peace (or Mercy),[6] and Truth—are, indeed, active; they descend "to do the world some good"; but their movement, still essentially *downward,* is not all their own, for they are "Let down" by some off-stage power. Thus their active virtue is rendered somewhat less impressive than it might have been; it is qualified and restrained; and this impression is reinforced by the imagery of the stanza, for the white robe of Truth is not made dazzling, but dimmed and shadowed by the "clowdie throne" of the last line.

Stanza IX triumphantly puts an end to these tentative conjectures. As in those earlier pivotal stanzas, Milton deliberately re-introduces vivid colouring—"the golden-winged hoast"—and now adds to it the swift sense of an unimpeded movement able to "poast . . . with speed" from heaven to earth and back again. He concludes with an explicit repudiation of the mere morality suggested by the previous stanza; this swift and shining being symbolizes, instead, heaven's purpose:

> . . . to set the hearts of men on fire
> To scorn the sordid world, and unto Heav'n aspire.

Here at length is a motivation more than natural or ethical: the Christian God has employed the child, so to speak, in the service of an other-worldly purpose. The first "problem" is, therefore, solved; and the other two apparently so.

But the tenth verse, returning to the charge, and specifically (it seems) to the third "problem," reveals Milton's continuing sense of incompleteness. The stanza begins with the question of reasons for the child's speedy departure from earth; but the lines that follow enumerate various aspects of a role not so far in the poem assigned to the child. Stanza IX had imagined her as a heavenly messenger, re-minding men of supernatural glory, and in her person symbolizing that glory, as well as its meaning for mankind. Now, however, Milton finds himself describing nothing less than a mediatrix for all men: the "fair infant" is to turn aside the pains of Hell, to cancel and banish natural evils, and to intercede with a just God in humanity's behalf.

Instead of a ministering angel, mortal for a time, then once more in
the ranks of heaven (as in the ninth verse), the "infant" has become
virtually a Redeemer; and that part is reserved for the true God-man,

> . . . the Son of Heav'ns eternal King,
> Of wedded Maid, and Virgin Mother born. . . ,

i.e. for a figure from the first both mortal and immortal in a unique
sense. Thus, the poet finds his second "problem" once again advancing
upon him. Such a figure, in this poem, is beyond Milton's intentions
and powers. Accordingly, he abandons the theme; then concludes his
poem, once more on the natural plane, with a stanza balancing the
suggestion of a wrathful God (in the tenth verse) by an admonition to
await the pleasure of a merciful God. This final stanza also restores
the mood of Christian elegy by recognizing the death of the child (in
stanza I actualized and made fearful by the poet's language: "kill'd,"
"blasted") to be no more than a "false imagin'd loss." But the difficulties encountered in stanza X, looking back to the "problems" of stanza
VI, have not been satisfactorily resolved; and the poem, accordingly,
concludes in anticlimax.

III

The *Fair Infant,* then, although a failure in some ways, appears to
represent an intermediate stage in Milton's early development. Aesthetically, it marks an advance over the relatively simple classical-
Christian antithesis of thought and image informing *Elegy III,* as
well as over the mild (but not final) rejection of a classical viewpoint
made, in Christian terms, by the *Bishop of Ely.* I do not suggest that
Milton, when he was writing the *Fair Infant,* had evolved the design
or method of attack revealed in the *Nativity Ode.* Also, there is no
question that real order and triumphant pattern, neither of which
mark the *Fair Infant,* are attained only in the poem which marks Milton's recognition of a real religious experience, competent to subordinate and control other elements. But I think it will be granted that
the *Fair Infant* finds him working, as in the *Ode,* with contrasting
areas of imagery, with shifting tones of darkness and light, with fading and appearing colour, and with movement within the pattern of
the poem, to develop and enhance the significance of his theme. Only
the later poem successfully combines these materials; but in the *Fair
Infant* Milton is becoming aware of their possibilities. The prelude to
the *Ode* takes up and re-works images present in the closing stanzas

of the *Fair Infant*, in every case transferring their significance to a higher plane; while Milton manages also to become himself a part of the design. Thus, the merely natural mother and child of stanza XI in the *Fair Infant* give place to a supra-natural pair, linking earth and heaven eternally; and the suggestion in the early poem of a fame at length cancelled by "the worlds last-end" is replaced in the *Ode* by the certainty of "perpetual peace," to be achieved by Virgin, Son, and Father in concert. Another contrast emerges in this regard: stanza X of the earlier poem suggests a figure who *turns aside* the will of God, and essentially opposes (in man's behalf) various aspects of a scheme ruled by God. But in the *Ode*, Christ (who brings "Our great redemption from above") works *"with* his Father" for the sake of all men. So the note of discord, present in spite of the poet's language in the *Fair Infant*, gives way to the harmony of the *Nativity Ode*.

And that harmony must include the poet too. Instead of a third-person account of the mother's gift, the *Ode* is Milton's own gift. No longer content merely to describe (as one describes a picture) the artificial mediatrix who, silently winging between earth and heaven, merely illustrates God's design to "set the hearts of men on fire," Milton moves personally into the scene, greeting the real Mediator who is God's design, and, as the picture becomes a speaking picture, joining his own voice

> . . . unto the Angel Quire,
> From out his secret Altar toucht with hallow'd fire.

NOTES

1. *Poems of Mr. John Milton . . .* , ed. Cleanth Brooks and J. E. Hardy (New York, 1951), p. 242.
2. Don Cameron Allen, *The Harmonious Vision: Studies in Milton's Poetry* (Baltimore, 1954), pp. 47-52.
3. *Op. cit.*, p. 242.
4. Professor Allen (*op. cit.*, p. 50) speaks of "the double question of stanza six." But the last line of this stanza in fact poses a problem which is distinct from the two proceeding it, and which is sufficiently important to be posed a second time, in the first line of stanza X.
5. Professor Allen states that this "first question is answered by avoiding it, for it is put as a rhetorical question to permit the poet to answer the second question in the negative" (*op. cit.*, p. 50). Yet the images

of stanzas VII-IX, together with the progressive pattern linking them, constitute, surely, a definite although implied answer to the first problem.

6. While the reference in the *Nativity Ode* (lines 141-144) to the descent of Truth, Justice, and Mercy, would certainly provide support for the identification of the "sweet smiling youth" in the *Fair Infant* as Mercy, and while Professor Allen, for other reasons, suggests Virtue, it seems worth mentioning that Milton in *Prolusion IV* (composed about the same time as the *Fair Infant*, on Parker's authority) has the passage: ". . . whether, for instance, Astraea was the last of the goddesses to leave the earth; for I suspect that Peace and Truth would not have abandoned even hostile mortals many ages after her." If Milton's intentions in the *Fair Infant* were in accordance with the suggestions of this essay, Peace would seem to be a more appropriate identification than Mercy, since Milton deliberately reserves the vision of a *merciful* and Christian God for the concluding verse of his poem.

[EDITOR'S NOTE. Mr. Maclean's reference in n. 6 is to W. R. Parker, *RES*, XI (1935), 276-83; and see *TLS*, December 17, 1938, p. 802. See also J. H. Hanford, *RES*, IX (1933), 312-15; H. F. Fletcher, *The Intellectual Development of John Milton*, II, 1961; and the studies of early poems cited by Miss Stapleton in the article following. Cf. J. I. Cope, *JEGP*, LXIII (1964), 660-74.]

LAURENCE STAPLETON

Milton and the New Music

In thinking of composition in a poem, as distinguished from the circumstances of the poet's writing it, the only question that matters is
what exists and acts in the lines themselves. But the kind of observation then demanded of the reader is, luckily, inexhaustible, provided
that the poem has intensity of language, or feeling, or idea: inseparable elements, varyingly combined according to the skill and interest
of the poet and not unaffected by the spirit of the age. By the spirit
of the age I mean what the poet and his associates read, heard discussed, saw about them, but equally, the expectations of the intelligent reader or listener, by which any writer will be affected whether
he sympathizes with these expectations or wishes to change them.

When the poet elects to write on a traditional theme, one that has
been practised by a number even of his own contemporaries, he at
once invites our attention to the method of his composition: what he
includes, what rejects, and whether the several parts of his poem so
interact as to become independent. In Milton's "On the Morning of
Christ's Nativity," a particularly striking example of the possibility
of such choices on the part of the poet matches the possibility of such
discoveries on the part of the reader.

Before Milton at dawn on Christmas day in 1629 began his "hum-

From *University of Toronto Quarterly*, XXIII (1953-54), 217-26. Reprinted
by permission of the author and the University of Toronto Press.

ble ode," he had no doubt read other poems about the Nativity, though which ones he may have read is largely a matter of conjecture, and of limited relevance. Images of creation as a harmony and of the music of the spheres he had encountered in ancient writers, then, fused with Christian tradition, perhaps in Tasso or in Giles Fletcher, or the ubiquitous du Bartas in Sylvester's translation. In these rhetorical excursions, there is nothing to compare with what Mr. Arthur Barker has called the "controlled complexity"[1] of the Nativity Ode. Milton obviously worked with a sense of command and of novelty in the task. He said as much, in writing to his friend Charles Diodati. But the combination of forthrightness and of reserve in the language of the poem shows it, too.

In his study of the Nativity Ode, Mr. Barker maps out its structure firmly. "The first eight stanzas . . . describe the setting of the Nativity, the next nine the angelic choir, the next nine the flight of the heathen gods. The . . . last stanza presents the scene in the stable." He finds that "the three movements each present a single modification of the simple contrast, preserved throughout the poem, between images suggesting light and harmony and images of gloom and discord." The three equal movements are held in relation "not by the repetition of a structural pattern, but by the variation of a basic pattern of imagery."[2]

While not disagreeing with, indeed valuing, Mr. Barker's analysis, it seems to me that this poem is built out of something more than the variation of a basic pattern of imagery. Fortunately, Mr. A. S. P. Woodhouse, recognizing the merit of Mr. Barker's article, at the same time adapts its critical insight to a wider purpose and leads us to approach the question of structure rather differently. He suggests that the poem has not only an "asethetic centre" (the music of the spheres) but an "intellectual core": "the effect of the Nativity, the routing of the heathen gods by Christ, is the culmination of the poem and in some sense its *intellectual* core."[3] The question then arises, how is the "aesthetic centre" of the poem related to its "intellectual core"?

Paintings of the Nativity sometimes please the beholder because of the domesticity, the familiarity provided by the setting. A barn or rough shed, a child being gazed upon by inarticulate grown-ups, animals surprised by the commotion, people of many kinds—rich and poor, sophisticated and simple: here a painter could find opportunity to engage many kinds of interest and to use all his skill in juxtapositions of colour, in painting faces, clothing, the characteristic stance of different kinds of men. Often such pictures convey a feeling of geniality, of festivity, in which the symbolism of the occasion is subordinated to the sense of human participation in it. That, I think, is the impact of The Adoration of the Magi as Jan Breughel the elder conceived it, with an animated and even humorous treatment of detail. Or of Gentile da Fabriano's more formal, more ornate, but equally crowded and humanly active presentation of the same subject. In contrast, Milton's composition strikes us instantly as uncluttered.[4] His achievement has been to reduce to a minimum the background of the scene in the manger and the birth of the child, in order to bring to life quite different aspects of the event. He is interested in presenting to us a movement in time, with a full sense of its immediate novelty and the direction of its future influence.

The separation of the first four stanzas of the poem from "The Hymn" makes this, so to speak, a poem with a frame. The Nativity Ode, for all that it may be taken as a piece of music (and about music) is a short narrative as well. As the poet invents the convention (it is perfectly possible to invent a convention) of his running to prevent the "Star-led Wisards" upon the Eastern road from arriving before him, the effect is to invite the reader to look at the scene before anything happens, to emphasize the solitude and even the emptiness of the moment. The poet's supposition and the reader's acceptance of being present, the frame as I have called it, is hypothesis. Looking into the frame of the event, then, we see at first no human witness. The time is just before dawn

> while the Heav'n, by the Suns team untrod,
> Hath took no print of the approaching light,
> And all the spangled host keep watch in squadrons bright.

As the Hymn begins, the mood of expectancy acquires content. The cold, the stillness of winter darkness (when both stillness and sound are more audible) produce and are the effect of an abeyance of nature's usual business. The "deformities" of nature (conceived by Milton as a result of the Fall of Man when "Earth felt the wound") are covered by "innocent snow." Now—and we become increasingly aware of the firstness of now—the suspension of activity, the quiet, receives substance in the sending of Peace to earth, God's "ready harbinger," able to stop the sound of battle and to arrest the conflict for power:

> The Trumpet spake not to the armed throng,
> And Kings sat still with awfull eye,
> As if they surely knew their sovran Lord was by.

Here, surely, Milton invests the New Testament promise of "peace on earth" with a particular incisiveness suited to his own vision.

I think no one has remarked how often Milton achieves a major counterpoint by contrasting two kinds of enchantment. One kind is the enchantment of good, which can evoke from man, or other beings, a higher power, a *raptus* of contemplation that is a step in the process whereby "in contemplation of created things/By steps we may ascend to God." Even characters of evil intent, like Comus or Satan, may be attracted momentarily by the power of goodness. Comus, before his vain attempt to corrupt the Lady, surprises himself in an involuntary response to her virtue. "Can any mortal mixture of Earth's mould," he asks

> Breathe such Divine inchanting ravishment?
> Sure something holy lodges in that brest
> And with these raptures moves the vocal air
> To testifie his hidd'n residence.

And Satan for an instance when he first perceives Eve alone in the garden finds his malice overawed:

> That space the Evil one abstracted stood
> From his own evil, and for the time remain
> Stupidly good. . . .

Stupidly, because his will and understanding are corrupted and he is no longer able to act in response to good; at the same time unwilling to feel its impact and unable to ignore it.

The enchantment of good Milton thinks of as an enhancement of our capacities of mind and feeling, not a deprivation, whereas the enchantment cast by evil dulls and lessens our humanity. This difference Comus notices when he compares the attraction of the Lady's song with the deceitful enchantments used by Scylla and Charybdis and by his mother Circe.[5]

> they in pleasing slumber lull'd the sense,
> And in sweet madness rob'd it of itself,
> But such a sacred, and home-felt delight,
> Such sober certainty of waking bliss
> I never heard till now.

The structure of the Nativity Ode may be looked upon, from one point of view, as an exploration of the contrast between the enchantments of deceit and the truth for which music is a sign. The descent of persuasive and decisive Peace provides for the reader an introduction to the experience of a rapt enchantment, leaning towards good. Or, to put it another way, this preparatory enchantment is incomplete because the decision that must fulfil it has not yet been dramatically announced. As before, a visual perspective leads to a more concrete awareness of the intention of the whole pattern. A calm silences even the ocean, as we are told of the legendary time close to Christmas when "Birds of Calm sit brooding on the charmed wave"—a bit of lore that only literary tradition and the incantatory sound of the verse make us accept (for otherwise how could we be convinced by scholars who tell us that the birds of calm, halcyons, were kingfishers—restless and rattling as we know them disturbed on any pond?). Nevertheless, this stretch of the poem produces a finely controlled crescendo while

> The Stars, with deep amaze,
> Stand fixt in stedfast gaze,

and the staying of the sun beyond the time of its usual rising compels in the beholder an economy of observation that perhaps we could compare to the heightening of perception one discovers in watching an eclipse.

In this manner "first light," as I believe military records still call that special time before sunrise when it is not dark, confirms the sense of an impending new event. But interest would soon be lessened if there were no human witnesses—as figures in a landscape, themselves negligible, are often needed to make the terrain more real. And when, as in the New Testament account, shepherds appear, "simply chatting in a rustic row," their natural and as it were occupational unawareness of all but essential change makes them the best listeners for the new music that at last and suddenly begins. For the shepherds are emblems of innocence in the whole idea: not devoted aspirants, not celebrants, but people in a field, expecting nothing different, therefore the more appropriately a testimony to a change that must emerge out of ordinary time. No matter how many other poets had put shepherds into a "pastoral" scene; few could, as Milton did, allow them to be present without trimmings, on the job, naturally seeing what was there, not saying anything.[6] The immensity of refer-

ence that he still has to develop in his "new music" could thus at
the outset be characterized by a fundamental simplicity in its first
appearance.

The new music: this is a phrase used by the early Christian Platonist, Clement of Alexandria, in his *Exhortation to the Greeks.* I
do not know if Milton, at twenty-one, had read this work, although
he later praises Clement.[7] Of Clement himself relatively little is
known. Probably a Greek, probably one who had been initiated into
the mysteries of Greek cults, he later became a teacher of Christianity
in Alexandria. There, as a thinker influenced by Platonism and a
man widely read in philosophy and poetry, he addressed himself, in
his *Exhortation,* to a group unwilling to break the "cake of custom,"
unready to renounce ancient superstitions for the clear truth that
Clement saw in the conception of Christ as the Logos, or Word, the
bringer to mankind of knowledge that could emancipate him from
the senseless worship of inanimate objects and the deception imposed
by the oracles and magical arts.

With at times impressive eloquence Clement describes in the *Exhortation* his hope of a new period in which mankind can achieve
a worthier faith and a truer knowledge. The word, the truth he hopes
to persuade his hearers to find in Christ, is precisely the "new music."
The Thracian Orpheus and other ancient bards were deceivers. "But
far different is my minstrel, for He has come to bring to a speedy end
the bitter slavery of the daemons that lord it over us" (p. 9). The
ancient religions, Clement argues, enslaved man. "By commemorating
deeds of violence in their religious rites" they led men to idolatry, and
by their enchantments "they have held captive in the lowest slavery
that truly noble freedom which belongs to those who are citizens
under heaven" (p. 9). Far different is the teaching of the "new
music," the discovery of the Logos in the new identity given by
Christ. To Clement this is man's hope of a faith worthy of his capacity for reason. For the Logos is reason, it is the principle of creation in the universe, which "arranged in harmonious order this great
world, yes, and the little world of man, too, body and soul together"
(p. 13). The new music, then, is not new in essence; what is new is
the opportunity given to men to perceive it. Blending biblical quotation and neo-Pythagorean doctrine Clement describes the music as
"before the morning star," since the Logos was the beginning of all
things; but, he says, "because he lately took a name . . . the Christ,
—I have called him a New Song" (p. 17).

Milton does not, like Clement, identify the new music with Christ; he describes it, like the coming of Peace, as an announcement of a change in human history. The music answers the sense of expectation now present in the shepherds:

> As all their souls in blisful rapture took:
> The Air such pleasure loth to lose,
> With thousand echo's still prolongs each heav'nly close.

It has power to repair the breach in Nature's perfection and to anticipate the fulfilment of Nature's reign, "the renovation of heaven and earth, and of all things therein," the fabric of vision set out in the Book of Revelation as Milton conceived it in his own terms. The harmony of this music is, he suggests, like the harmony of creation, "when of old the sons of morning sung." We know that the metaphors of Pythagorean thought, expressing the idea of music as number, as the measure of things, appealed greatly to thinkers of the Renaissance, not only to poets and philosophers but to scientists like Kepler as well. As a brilliant modern expositor of Greek thought has put it, in the Pythagoreans we find "an intuition which has guided the whole course of mathematical physics from its founder Pythagoras until the present day: 'The nature of things is number.' "[8] This intuition Milton associated with the mighty questions in the Book of Job: "Where wast thou when I laid the foundations of the earth? . . . Who hath laid the measure thereof, if thou knowest? or who hath stretched the line upon it? . . . When the morning stars sang together, and all the sons of God shouted for joy?" The act of creation, the bringing of order out of chaos, began, indeed constituted, the music of the spheres, and to Milton, as to Clement, was the work of the Logos. As Clement put it, "this pure song, the stay of the universe and the harmony of all things, stretching from the centre to the circumference and from the extremities to the centre, reduced this whole to harmony . . ." (p. 13).

The symbol of the music of the spheres allows Milton to achieve in the centre of his composition a masterly focus, making the present moment both revive man's lost capacity for perfection and prophesy its future realization.

> For if such holy Song
> Enwrap our fancy long,
>   Time will run back, and fetch the age of gold, . . .

> And Hell it self will pass away,
> And leave her dolorous mansions to the peering day.

A future time of perfection is conceived in terms of a past; the differentiation between Paradise and Utopia which Milton attains at the end of *Paradise Lost* is not here, and is not needed here. The accent is given to the future hope; in fact the victory of truth and justice and mercy is predicted. This, then, is the climax of anticipation; this is what is to be realized as the content, the purpose, of the moment of Christ's birth.

But to guard the poem and the realization itself from the vacuity of mere wish, Milton turns from a cosmic vision of the future to the decisiveness of its immediate effect on human history. Before the possible reconciliation of man and God, there must be a conquest of error and superstition, symbolized by the banishing of the pagan gods and the cessation of the deceitful oracles. Although "the Babe lies yet in smiling Infancy," the authority of truth demands acknowledgment: "The wakeful trump of doom must thunder through the deep." In the fight against evil that the poem now describes, the impact of Christ's presence resembles the energetic figure of Michelangelo's last judgment, or reminds us of T. S. Eliot's lines

> in the juvescence of the year
> Came Christ the tiger.[9]

In this section of the Nativity Ode we observe the conquest of what might be called negative enchantment, the enchantment of evil. In *Comus,* as in the *Odyssey,* the two brothers and their "attendant spirit," Thyrsis, are protected from the danger of Comus's enchantments by a medicinal herb, *haemony,* just as Ulysses was protected from the wiles of Circe by the herb that Hermes gave him, *moly.* But in the Nativity Ode no allegorical device is needed; the arrival of the Word of God, the possibility of human regeneration through knowledge of truth, brings in a new age when

> No nightly trance, or breathed spell
> Inspires the pale-ey'd Priest from the prophetic cell

of Apollo's shrines. One after another the jealous and cruel deities of antiquity—Ashtaroth, Moloch, Osiris—hasten into darkness. As Clement in his *Exhortation* had abjured the Greeks, worship of these gods represented an inferior stage in human existence; confronted by a religion of love and mercy, they could not survive (pp. 19, 27, 243). This conception, however unhistorical to modern minds, was echoed in early Christian writers such as Eusebius and caught the imagination of many, Spenser and Sir Thomas Browne among them, as well as Milton, who rejoiced that "the Babe could in his swaddling bands control the damned crew."

Yet if the sentence of doom pronounced against the ancient deceivers of the human spirit—"sullen Moloch" or "Libyc Ammon"—is stern, the tutelary genii of wood and grove (elsewhere favoured in Milton's imaginings) are dismissed more gently. As

> the yellow-skirted Fayes
> Fly after the Night-steeds, leaving their Moon-lov'd maze,

we are prepared for a simple transition to the coming of day in an ordinary world. With skilled economy Milton balances Christ's vanquishing of the pagan gods with the sun's banishing of the shadows of night. No part of the poem has perhaps evoked as much disagreement among critics as its ending, more often than not assailed for the amusing conceit of the "sun in bed curtained with cloudy red." In such a line, however, Milton was writing in the language of his time; moreover, he was, I think, pleasing himself by a bit of humour. For while the writer of this poem was aware of tradition, he wrote independently and with individuality of attack. The turn of every sentence shows this. If there is any comparable Nativity scene in painting, it would be, I think, Masaccio's Adoration of the Magi. However different in its details, particularly in the kinds of people he included in the scene, Masaccio's boldness and simplicity of statement cause in the beholder a "moment of astonishment."

"Life itself is a moment of astonishment"[10]—that is Paul Valéry's description of what he discovers in the state of awareness out of which, sometimes, a poem results. Everyone knows that poems which continue to be read have many possible levels of meaning. For Mr. Barker, we have seen, the pattern of the Nativity Ode is a contrast between imagery of light and imagery of darkness. This is, so to speak, one way of looking into the composition. I think we can also say that the Nativity Ode as a poem is a moment of astonishment and is about a moment of astonishment.

In the last lines we feel the inventiveness of a poet who knew how to conclude a complex structure with a pleasing coda. Channing tells us that Thoreau loved Milton for his "neatness and swing." Milton's firmness and accuracy, much underestimated by some modern poets, are always noticeable in his manner of ending—almost by understatement, but not without a strict last spin of sense and observation. For neatness and swing it would be hard to beat the ending of the Nativity Ode:

> Heaven's youngest-teemed Star
> Hath fixt her polisht Car,
>   Her sleeping Lord with Handmaid Lamp attending:
> And all about the Courtly Stable
> Bright-harnest Angels sit in order serviceable.

Order ready for service, and useful; polished, alert, the watch is kept. We are left with the attentiveness and clarity that was created for us by the opening lines, but there has been a change, a discovery. An event in time has occurred, and a poem has defined the intersection of its present with its futurity.

NOTES

1. Arthur Barker, "The Pattern of Milton's Nativity Ode," *University of Toronto Quarterly*, X (1940-41), 177. Mr. Barker briefly and efficiently characterizes the traditional patterns of idea and imagery which could have furnished Milton with a convention. He does not discuss Tasso's "Pel Presipio di nostro Signore," which, as Grierson pointed out in the Introduction to his *Metaphysical Lyrics and Poems of the Seventeenth Century* (1921), xlviii, is perhaps closer to Milton's Nativity Ode than any comparable English poem. Mr. Barker's article will, I think, remain the taking-off point for future critical discussions of the Nativity Ode. It is supplemented in some details by the comments of Cleanth Brooks and John Hardy in their introduction to the poem in *Poems of Mr. John Milton* (New York, 1952); in the main, however, their interpretation follows his analysis.
2. Barker, 173. These divisions refer to the main body of the poem, leaving apart the four introductory stanzas and the concluding stanza.
3. A. S. P. Woodhouse, "Notes on Milton's Early Development," *University of Toronto Quarterly*, XIII (1943), 92. This whole article is full of discerning observations on Milton's early verse and must be regarded as an indispensable complement to J. H. Hanford's "The Youth of Milton," in *Studies in Shakespeare, Milton and Donne*, by Members of the English Department of the University of Michigan (1925).

4. Cf. E. M. W. Tillyard, *Milton* (London, 1930), 37. Mr. Tillyard suggests that fifteenth-century Italian paintings of the Nativity "give the simplest comparison" with the *quality* of the Nativity Ode, its "homeliness, quaintness, tenderness, extravagance, and sublimity. . . ." But from the point of view of the structure of the poem, the differences are more marked than the similarity.

5. Mrs. Gretchen L. Finney, the author of valuable studies on the musical background of *Comus, Lycidas,* and *Samson Agonistes,* has also discussed the reflection in Milton's writing of the idea that music has power to move the soul to ecstasy or rapture. See her article, "Ecstasy and Music in Seventeenth Century England," *Journal of the History of Ideas,* VIII (1947), 153-86. In *Comus,* she says, "there is an illusive shift from what seems to be a purely metaphorical use of the word 'ravishment' to describe the singing of the Lady to a somewhat more literal allusion to the release of the soul in the description of Circe and the Sirens. And there follows a contrast of the two experiences which implies that while the latter dulls perception, the former has rational appeal" (p. 184). She finds that there is probably a change in Milton's attitude towards the idea of music and ecstasy, so that his use of it in *Paradise Lost* is different from the appearance of this theme in the early poems.

6. Milton describes the shepherds chatting on the lawn before they hear the music or become aware of the "globe of circular light" as the cherubim and seraphim are seen "harping in loud and solemn quire." He makes rather a point of the usualness of their mood in advance. The music overcomes them with "blissful rapture"; they are not mentioned again. This is in marked contrast to the ready-witted shepherds of the *Second Shepherd's Play* or, at the other extreme, to Crashaw's practiced pastoral singers with their hymn of studied paradoxes.

7. As "this worthy Clement, Paul's disciple" (*Reason of Church Government,* in *Columbia Milton,* III, 211). In *Of Reformation in England,* Milton had warned of "heresies . . . thick sown" in Clement's account of the early church. There are four references to Clement in the Commonplace Book, but none of these is to the *Protrepticos* (*Exhortation to the Greeks*).

Eusebius, Plutarch, and other writers down to Spenser have been mentioned as transmitters to later generations of the idea of the cessation of the oracles at the time of the birth of Christ: the idea of the music of the spheres has, of course, an even longer ancestry. Clement's linking of the two ideas in his hymn of praise to Christ as the Logos suggests a closer connection with Milton than has been noticed. Mrs. Finney in the article cited above refers to Clement as one of the early writers through whom the Pythagorean concept of cosmic harmony found its way into Christian thought and was applied to explain the creation of the world.

It does not seem to me essential to argue that Clement's *Exhortation to the Greeks* is a source for Milton's Nativity Ode, but the analogy between the pattern of ideas in the treatise and the thematic structure of the poem is too striking to be overlooked. Even though Milton might have, and undoubtedly did, encounter these ideas elsewhere, I do not know where he would have found them in this combination.

Quotations in the text are from the Loeb Classics edition: *Clement of Alexandria,* with an English translation by G. W. Butterworth (London and New York, 1919). All quotations are from the *Exhortation to the Greeks.*

8. F. M. Cornford, *The Unwritten Philosophy* (Cambridge, 1950), 20. He adds that in the Pythagorean cosmogony, "the two great principles of Nature are Light and Darkness."

9. "Gerontion." Perhaps it is worth noting that in his essay on Lancelot Andrewes, Eliot gives as examples of "flashing phrases which never desert the memory" two from Andrewes: the first, "Christ is no wildcat," then, "the word within a word, unable to speak a word." Finally he quotes the passage which he wove into his own "Journey of the Magi." See *For Lancelot Andrewes* (London, 1928), 27.

10. Paul Valéry, "Poetry and Abstract Thought," *Essays on Language and Literature* by Marcel Proust, Paul Valéry, Jean-Paul Sartre, Jean Paulhan, Francis Ponge, Brice Parain (London, 1947), 76. I owe my knowledge of this essay to Miss Marianne Moore.

[EDITOR'S NOTE. See also G. L. Finney, *Musical Backgrounds for English Literature,* [1962]; D. C. Allen, *The Harmonious Vision,* 1954; L. L. Martz, *The Poetry of Meditation,* 1954; R. Tuve, *Images and Themes in Five Poems by Milton,* 1957; J. B. Broadbent, in *The Living Milton,* ed. F. Kermode, 1961; L. Nelson, Jr., *Baroque Lyric Poetry,* 1961.]

JOHN HOLLANDER

Milton's Renewed Song

In studying some of the ways in which sixteenth- and seventeenth-century poets employed the transmitted lore of *musica speculativa*, we have occasionally drawn an implicit distinction between the operations of experience and knowledge in the treatment of music as a subject matter for poetry. In a sense, such a distinction is already drawn by the classical bifurcation of speculative and practical music; but we have seen how poetic traditions as well contributed to the separation of the experience of actual music, as one of life's varied phenomena, and the response to a philosophy of music. Occasionally, as in Crashaw's "Musicks Duell," both the musical thought and the poetic language are of such a nature as to make for a subtle blending of the two. We are able to think of the poem as treating of actual music, that is, because its ideology is close to our own, and because that notion of music as a sensual ravishment allows for the description of the contest in elaborate erotic imagery that nevertheless always keeps to details of actual musical practice. I have suggested earlier in this chapter that George Herbert's spiritual music might have had as much personal meaning, with respect to the association of actual music with both solitary contemplation and loving fraternity in his own life, as it had a very definite meaning with respect to intellectual

From *The Untuning of the Sky,* Princeton: Princeton University Press, 1961, pp. 315-31. Reprinted by permission of the author and the publisher.

history and poetic conventions. But, by and large, Renaissance poetry tends to separate speculative and practical music, combining them only in the fairly inflexible relationship of the *encomium musicae,* in which the former is introduced in order to praise the latter.

In any consideration of Milton, the split between what is learned by studying and what is known more immediately must always seem an artificial one. I mean by such a split not so much the "dissociation of thought and feeling" that has become so much of a cliché, since its introduction by T. S. Eliot a generation ago,[1] in the criticism of seventeenth-century poetry, as perhaps a distinction like that drawn even longer ago by Bertrand Russell between "knowledge by acquaintance" and "knowledge by description."[2] At any rate, Milton is thoroughly an intellectual poet (and if he is also so in our most current sense of the word, it must be added that he is certainly a type of the *engagé* intellectual: in Professor Tillyard's words, he "considered literature mainly as a species of action").[3] The corpus of his poetry is a speculative monolith; poetry was for him, among other things, an instrument for bringing to bear the thought of history, as well as some of the history of thought, upon the problems of a rich and turbulent present. And in his poetry we find knowledge, speculation, invested with the intensity of direct sensual experience.

It would be hard to say, then, whether speculative or practical music played a more fundamental role in the thoughts and commitments of even the young Milton. Much has been written of his musical background, training and interests.[4] Even more attention has been paid to the rich profusion of musical reference, both speculative and practical, in the body of his work.[5] From the oratorical exercise of his schooldays on "The Music of the Spheres" (*"De Sphaerarum Concentu"*) through the many passages of practical and theoretical musical allusion in *Paradise Lost,* Milton's vast knowledge of both the secular music of his own day and of Classical and Christian musical doctrine is amply revealed. Critics of the past thirty-five years have demonstrated the extent of that revelation. Attention has been paid primarily to the more expository treatments of Christian musical doctrine in Milton's poetry, such as "On the Morning of Christs Nativity," ll. 93-140, "Arcades," ll. 61-78, and the many sections on the music of heaven in *Paradise Lost.* It is certainly true that the greater number of such treatments and references manifest the received Christian Humanist interest in the ethical implications of the heav-

enly music, in the notion that, since the Fall, human imperfection
rather than thresholds of hearing or custom has rendered that music
inaudible.

While Milton's use of music to mean "poetry" in pastoral contexts
is almost a truism, it has not been pointed out that Milton was able to
absorb as well some of the Baroque doctrines about the rhetorical nature of music. A passage like that in Book IV of *Paradise Lost,* ll. 674-
688, in which we learn that the heavenly music is indeed audible in
heaven, "With Heav'nly touch of instrumental sounds/In full harmonic number join'd . . . ," is often commented on with reference
to Milton's use of traditional musical lore, for example. But in the
demonic games in Book II, the poetry-music-rhetoric nexus comes up
in a rather new way. After the military and athletic contests among
the fiends of Hell have been described, we are told that

> Others more mild,
> Retreated in a silent valley, sing
> With notes Angelical to many a Harp
> Thir own Heroic deeds and hapless fall
> By doom of Battle; and complain that Fate
> Free Virtue should enthrall to Force or Chance.
> Thir Song was partial, but the harmony
> (What could it less when Spirits immortal sing?)
> Suspended Hell, and took with ravishment
> The thronging audience. In discourse more sweet
> (For Eloquence the Soul, Song charms the Sense,)
> Others apart sat on a Hill retir'd,
> In thoughts more elevate, and reason'd high
> Of Providence, Foreknowledge, Will, and Fate,
> Fixt Fate, Free will, Foreknowledge absolute,
> And found no end, in wand'ring mazes lost.
>
> (II, 546-561)

No matter what the perverse import of the text of the devils' epic
song, the melody itself, partaking of the potency of the heavenly
music, remains strongly effective. The notions of word and note are
separated here in Hell; it is the doctrine which has suffered in the fall
of the rebel angels, rather than the purely musical power to charm
and move. But Milton carefully stipulates that it is the soul itself that
is affected by the "rational" powers of "Eloquence," while "Song

charms the Sense" alone and cannot, no matter how attractive, actually operate upon the highest psychic faculties. The philosophical discussions that are next described, although graceless, vagrant quests for the self-knowledge to which the fiends can never attain, must be "discourse more sweet," harmonious, and well attuned. The distinction between "Eloquence" and "Song" is certainly a step toward the later seventeenth-century bifurcation of the functions of language and music. It will be noticed that the passage moves from the epic "music" (i.e. poetry) of the games in Hell, to the musical skill retained by the fallen angels, to a contrast between this music, or even poetry-music, and actual doctrine. That the fiends can sing the wrong words to the marvellous melodies of angelic music is just another oddity of their utterly paradoxical predicament.

Nowhere in Milton, perhaps, are the affective properties of music used in a more complicated metaphoric fabric than in *Comus*. Even the passage from *Paradise Lost* mentioned above is primarily *expository* in its use of *musica speculativa* or of changes rung upon it by the exigencies of the poem's philosophic scheme. But in *Comus* the intricate combination of actual and theoretical music resonates far beyond the conventional play of masquers' identities represented by the casting of Henry Lawes, the masque's composer, as the Attendant Spirit-Thyrsis-Pan-Orpheus figure. In the first place, the Lady's song (one of a sparse five in a long and extravagant entertainment), while serving as a primary instrument in the action of the masque itself, is self-referential in two senses: it addresses itself to its own resonating effects (its echoes, here personified as the nymph Echo herself, not only a favorite pastoral figure but a favorite metaphor for the relationship of actual human music to the heavenly harmony), on the one hand; and on the other, it covertly refers to the Lady herself and her own predicament ("the lovelorn Nightingale" is taken up by the disguised Attendant Spirit's comments, ll. 566-567: "And O poor hapless Nightingale thought I,/How sweet thou sings't, . . .").[6] In the second place, from the Lady's opening remarks on the "Riot and ill manag'd Merriment" of Comus' dance, and on the fact that it is her ear which must be her "best guide now" (ll. 170-177), to the final invocation of the "Spheary chime" (l. 1021) as the summit of a purely material world surmounted by the influences of Virtue, musical figures of several sorts are employed.

But it is primarily the Lady's song that generates most of these intricacies:

SONG

Sweet Echo, sweetest Nymph that liv'st unseen
         Within thy airy shell
      By slow *Meander's* margent green,
And in the violet imbroider'd vale
      Where the love-lorn Nightingale
Nightly to thee her sad Song mourneth well.
Canst thou not tell me of a gentle Pair
      That likest thy *Narcissus* are?
            O if thou have
         Hid them in som flowry Cave,
            Tell me but where
Sweet Queen of Parly, Daughter of the Sphear,
      So maist thou be translated to the skies,
And give resounding grace to all Heav'ns Harmonies.

                                        (ll. 230-243)

This song is in some measure a hymn in praise of music itself. As actual melody, it is "inchanting ravishment" for Comus, "raptures that move the vocal air" (and here, if anywhere in the course of the poem, is the musical pun on "air" employed to enrich the terms of Comus' expression of wonder); for the Attendant Spirit, it

Rose like a stream of rich distill'd Perfumes,
And stole upon the Air, that even Silence
Was took e're she was ware, and wish't she might
Deny her nature, and be never more
Still to be so displac't. I was all eare,
And took in strains that might create a soul
Under the ribs of Death, . . .[7]

                                        (ll. 556-562)

If there is an ironic parallel between the reactions of Comus and the Spirit, it results in good measure from the transcendent power of the Lady's song; both nature's monster and the airy pastoral musician are ravished by its charms. In addressing itself to Echo, the Lady's prayer may have suggested to the audience at Ludlow Castle the echo songs, which became increasingly more frequent during the seventeenth century, and in which the echoes' repetition, by another voice or by a chorus, of an ultimate word, phrase, or even syllable, cast an intensifying or ironic light on the line of text itself. In these songs, the echo gives the lie to what produces it. There is no such betrayal here, of course, just as there is employed no such device; but the thwarted expectation of a candidly malicious "Echo" may have had in itself some effect. "Sweet Echo" is more than merely the fabled nymph. In personifying some of the characteristics of music itself, she brings persuasive eloquence to mind. Although in the first six lines, she is addressed solely as the pastoral nymph, the second section of the song entreats some higher, or at least more general, power.[8] If the Lady is praising Echo by calling her "Sweet Queen of Parly," it is in the role of eloquent, rhetorical, and governing music that she is praising her; not only is she the queen of all speech because of her resemblance to a disembodied *idea* of speech sounds, but she reigns over all "parly" in the other sense of concordant, conferential discourse as well.

Some questions have been raised as to the Christian elevation of the pagan nymph in the final lines; J. E. Hardy, in particular, points to what he feels to be some difficulty in the mind of the Lady with respect to the confusion of things Christian and pagan.[9] If we turn to the variant manuscript readings of these two final lines, however, we may be able to see how a possible addition of Christian reference may have occurred to Milton at some time during his revisions. In the manuscript version which contains the five songs and their settings (B.M. add. ms. 11518), ll. 242-243 read as follows: "So maist thou be transplanted to the skyes/& hold a Counter point to all Heav'ns Harmonies."[10] Here it is simply the pagan music of the spheres to which the nymph, lifted into the heavens in perfectly familiar Ovidian fashion, will add her music. With the substitution of "translated," and the even more revealing one of "resounding grace,"[11] the meaning of "Heav'ns Harmonies" actually changes into a reference to Christian celestial music, the singing of the angels that was troped into the Classical notion. "Grace," of course, retains its musical meaning of "ornament" or "embellishment," which "resounds" because it is still that of Echo; the Christian implications of "grace" are secondary, but extremely strong. They seem to suggest that Echo-affective music-rhetoric's powers are manifestations not of natural skill merely but of something higher; surely it is significant that the Lady herself demonstrates, in the course of her entreaty and her praise, these powers to a remarkable degree.

It has been traditional to regard these changes as representing Milton's desire to substitute "a less technical word or phrase, as if he himself saw the possible danger to his poetry from his learning."[12] That this will probably not do is evidenced by more than the fact that "grace" is, if anything, more "technical" in the language of seventeenth-century musical discourse than is "counterpoint"; as an account of what lay behind the changes, it gives no consideration to any movement toward compactness that might have been at work, or to any possible enrichment or development of the thought. It is true that after the 1629 "Ode on the Morning of Christs Nativity," Milton's diction moves away from the Metaphysical in the direction of the more discursive and expository. And while this may be said to involve a turning away from the more farfetched conceit, it in no way implies a loss of the use of the extended figure. The removal of a highly technical term could be taken only for a desire to do away with *misplaced* specificity, not with specificity itself. We shall see in a moment how important this notion is in trying to account for some of the changes in "At a Solemn Musick."

If the foregoing cursive observations on some of Milton's musical imagery have shown that it does more than expound traditional or adapted doctrine, they have also intended to suggest that stylistic considerations are here, as elsewhere, of some significance in the determination of the ways in which such imagery is to be used. "At a Solemn Musick" is most usually treated as the supremest example of Milton's exposition of *musica speculativa*. In the following discussion, we shall attempt to read it in the context of seventeenth-century attitudes toward sacred music, and also as a meditative poem involving the musical imagery of psychic tonus.

"At a Solemn Musick" is certainly a meditation, but not having the set topic, such as death, required by Professor Martz's stricter use of the term: the circumstance provoking the meditation is, or purports to be, an occasional one. The poem's movement, consequently, by no means resembles the involved "symbolic action" of the more Metaphysically oriented poem of religious contemplation; nor does the imagery involve the use of emblematic devices, the whole poem occasionally bearing the *impresa-motto* relationship to its title (as seems often to be the case with Herbert). Instead, the contemplation moves from the consideration of a concrete, mundane event through a synthesized Classical-Christian account of the universal significance of that event, to a final supplication based on that account. That the whole argument of the poem, preceding that final prayer, is handled in a single, twenty-four line sentence, and that the purely technical problem of sustaining the syntactic intensity through mazes of de-

pendent clauses and varied line-lengths is brilliantly solved in the
poem has been remarked before.[13] That the text appearing in the
1645 edition of Milton's poems is the product of arduous rewriting is
obvious from the changes in almost every line of the three successive
drafts of the poem; but many of the fundamental effects of these
changes upon the poem's final successful state seem to have been
ignored. Considerations of those emendations generally lump the can-
cellations and substitutions here with those at the end of "Sweet
Echo" in *Comus*. In the words of a frequently quoted critic, the corrections are "designed to avoid the technical musical terms which are
in the original readings, and which, as technical, might be obscure to
the general reader."[14] But let us turn here to the text itself:

> Blest pair of Sirens, pledges of Heav'ns joy,
> Sphear-born harmonious Sisters, Voice, and Vers,
> Wed your divine sounds, and mixt power employ
> Dead things with inbreath'd sense able to pierce,
5 > And to our high-rais'd phantasie present,
> That undisturbed Song of pure concent,
> Ay sung before the saphire-colour'd throne
> To him that sits thereon
> With Saintly shout and solemn Jubily,
10 > Where the bright Seraphim in burning row
> Their loud up-lifted Angel trumpets blow,
> And the Cherubick host in thousand quires
> Touch their immortal Harps of golden wires,
> With those just Spirits that wear victorious Palms,
15 > Hymns devout and holy Psalms
> Singing everlastingly;
> That we on Earth with undiscording voice
> May rightly answer that melodious noise;
> As once we did, till disproportion'd sin
20 > Jarr'd against natures chime, and with harsh din
> Broke the fair musick that all creatures made
> To their great Lord, whose love their motion sway'd
> In perfect Diapason, whilst they stood
> In first obedience, and their state of good.
25 > O may we soon again renew that Song,
> And keep in tune with Heav'n, till God ere long
> To his celestial consort us unite,
> To live with him, and sing in endles morn of light.[15]

Starting almost at the very beginning, we may notice how, in the successive versions of line 3, there is a movement from abstraction to misplaced concrete musical imagery and then to a proper balance between the two: the first reading is ". . . vine power & joynt force employ"; the second, "Mixe yor choise chords & happiest sounds employ"; and the third and final version corrects the grotesquerie of the application to words of "strings" ("chords," as well as the reading "vertical harmonic clusters," the former being the more conventional, older meaning usually employed in musical imagery in the sixteenth and seventeenth centuries). The redundancy of "power" and "force" is also removed, but the identity of voice and verse, preserved long enough for them to be "wed" rather than merely blurred, is of considerable importance. The sisterhood of music and poetry is a theme that we have observed before, and whether we are to read "Sphear-born" in the second line as "carried upon the spheres" or, like the Lady's Echo, "Daughter of the Sphear," the purely pagan cosmological compliment can be seen to be a conventional one. But from the very beginning, the Christian theme of the intimation of the heavenly music as seen in actual earthly singing appears in "pledges of Heav'ns joy";[16] and it is obvious that the invocation of the union of music and poetry will be made to signify more than merely a dual compliment, as in Barnfield's sonnet to Spenser and Dowland, in which music and poetry are sister and brother. It is just this union of "Voice, and Vers," heralded at the beginning of the poem, which some studies tend to lose sight of.

Perhaps the most significant emendation for a study of the poem's strategy, however, might be said to consist in the removal, after line 4 in the second draft, of four lines that would have tended to hasten the conclusion of the poem, and somewhat to trivialize the import. After the reference to the penetrating power of the words-music, and before the mention of the hearer's state of mind, the two sister Sirens[17] continued to be addressed:

> and whilst yor equall raptures temper'd sweet
> in high misterious holie spousall meet
> snatch us from earth a while
> us of our selves & home bred woes beguile . . .

In the first place, these lines continue the personification of music and poetry and reinforce the metaphor of wedding with an almost erotic image, the "temper'd sweet" of tuning coming under an interpretation of some mystical, quasi-sexual aura. That Milton wanted to reserve

the traditional figure of temperament and tuning for later expansion
seems obvious, and that the later section will avoid the use even of the
conventional "sweet" in favor of the more unusual "fair" (because of
the former word's frequent erotic, or at least amorous, use) seems to
suggest something of what might have contributed to these lines' un-
suitability. But it was probably the premature supplication, not a
prayer to God, but to the semi-deified Christian muses, which rang
most false; and the "snatch us from earth," after some serious consideration and fussing ("holie" replaced by "happie"; "native" for
"home bred"), had to go because of the almost hyperbolic quality of
the image, when contrasted with the more staid, but more deeply believed, prayer at the end, in which the wish is expressed only that the
human hearer-meditators may some day be brought into tune with
Heaven.

The final major emendation is also a deletion. Instead of lines 19-
25 of the final version, the earlier drafts give:

> by leaving out those harsh chromatick (later variant:
>   ill-sounding) jarres
> of sin that all our music marres
> & in our lives & in our song . . .

The tentative change from "chromatick" to "ill-sounding" was quite
possibly designed to avoid a mistakenly over-specific reading, in which
it might be assumed that Milton was arguing against the virtue of a
particular musical style, or against an association of, say, secular music
with such a style.[18] Here, "& in our lives & in our song" clearly differentiates, I think, mundane existence from the special life of religious
contemplation and prayer, and Milton seems to be using "song" much
as Herbert might. But instead of merely qualifying "rightly" in line
18, the final version of these lines includes a reference to Original
Sin, and to one of his own favorite themes of the prelapsarian audi-
bility of the celestial music. "As once we did" introduces the historical
dimension, and clearly outlines the reference of the final prayer's "O
may we soon."[19]

"That song" is referred to three times, all preceded by the same
demonstrative pronoun. The "pure concent" to which the hearers'
attentions are raised is surely, as has been pointed out,[20] the celestial
harmony, which, in Milton's synthesis of Christian and pagan themes,
is prefigured by the music of the siren-spheres just as the latter is an-
ticipated by actual earthly music. "That undisturbed Song of pure

concent" is also characterized by the "pure concent," the agreement, of its own component elements, text and melody. Milton's meditation on "solemn" music ("its music is 'solemn,'" says Leo Spitzer, "because it has the primordial and primeval aim of all Christian music: religious elation")[21] leads him almost at once to his underlying theme of the true, "rational," "eloquent" music of both Greek theory and of its adaptation in Humanist *musica speculativa;* the strength of the continually referred-to song as a perfect, functioning union of voice and verse carries over into the jar and din and discord of lines 17-24. The implication is that the ancient harmony of melody and text was broken by the act of disobedience that brought human history into lamented being, aside from the harmoniousness of the "perfet Diapason," the great octave into which all creatures were cast by the moving power of divine love. It is almost as if all created life were being figured forth as moving, singing spheres themselves: such, at any rate, is the force of "whose love their motion sway'd/In perfet Diapason." But what is finally important here is that the "fair musick that all creatures made/*To* their great Lord" (my italics) is the music of prayer, the solemn singing whose temporary reunification of the divorced music and poetry is itself moving the poet to contemplation in the poem. Prayer, since the Fall, must needs be a consciously contrived process, a work, in fact, of poetic art; it cannot be automatic and spontaneous as once it was before "disproportion'd sin/Jarr'd against natures chime." "That song" is perfect prayer, possible, in an imperfect world, only through the act of liturgical-poetical-musical devotion. The traditional lament of early Baroque musical esthetics, to the effect that the music of Classical Antiquity possessed the perfect unification of text and melody from which the corrupt modern bifurcation of musical and poetic concern was a long fall, seems to lurk behind all this as a secular counterpart of the Christian Fall. And considering Milton's Classical-Christian syntheses, one might not be too far afield in suggesting that the "celestial consort" from which all has fallen away might have involved for him the union of text and music, of rational eloquence and the cosmological operation of Christian grace, all mingled in a composite image.

The "high-rais'd phantasie" of line 4 refers, as Professor Hutton has pointed out,[22] to the imaginative faculty of the soul that meditates, in Christian Neoplatonist thought, between the body and the intellect; but he seems to miss the traditional use of "high-rais'd" to describe the psychic tonus. Although the conventional metaphor of

the tuned instrument is lacking here, the clear implication of the
"raising" (in pitch, in altitude, intension, in moral power) of the
soul, or part of it, is not. The subject of the poem is certainly as much
the public prayer of its title as it is the moralizing of the relationship
between *musica mundana* and *musica humana,* occasioned by the
hearing of some practical music. Unlike the contemplative, solitary
poetic treatment of personal prayer, "At a Solemn Musick" starts out
with the fact of a high musical service, moves from it to an account
of its effects, as we noted above, returns to the Biblical imagery of its
immediate context (and of the text of an actual anthem?), and finally
moves into the prayer for salvation. But it moves through the consciousness of a particular poet, for whom the concerns of the responsibilities of the poetic role and the poetic gifts were to become monu-
mental. The relationship of poetry to the devotion of the inner voice
can be figured in the relationship between public and private prayer,
in a way; and Milton's personal engagement in the poem may be seen
to appear in connection with this kind of comparison. The task of
the poet was in the early 1630's at Horton beginning, for Milton, to
assume a course parallel to that of the Priest-Shepherd, or, as we
might put it, to that of the sacred composer whose obligation it was
properly to unite holy text and influential music. Thus, in a sense,
"At a Solemn Musick" ranges its meditation over the condition of the
listening poet as well.[23] If the harmony of word and sound has been
soured, the composer of liturgical music can provide short moments
of sweetness during which the pure, perfect source of all sweetness
itself may be, if not glimpsed actually, then promised for an eventual
eternity. So may the poet, by employing his skill in unison with
proper intention, approach the perfection of inspired eloquence of
the Psalmist himself.

For that Psalmist, music was the epitome of holy intercourse. We
have seen how, during the middle of the seventeenth century in England, that epitomization received either qualification or change of
emphasis in its treatment by poets. Milton's combination of the praise
of music generally, in the fashion of the previous century, with the
figurative equivalence of song and prayer of the contemplative tradition, the whole finally turned to a consideration of public prayer and
public utterance (it is not so much the jarring of disproportioned
musica humana that is bemoaned, but of customs and practices),
represents to some extent a synthesis of these conventions. In "At a
Solemn Musick" Milton seems almost to be consecrating his life and

his art to a purpose figured forth as a liturgical one. Like most of its young author's subsequent productions in the next few years, it is an ambitious poem. And like them, its success seems all the more enhanced by its forward qualities.

NOTES

1. In his essay on "The Metaphysical Poets," 1921.
2. See *The Problems of Philosophy* (London, 1952), pp. 46-59.
3. E. M. W. Tillyard, *Milton* (London, 1951), p. 362.
4. Sigmund Spaeth, *Milton's Knowledge of Music* (Princeton, 1913), pp. 12-56; see also Ernest Brennecke, Jr., *John Milton the Elder and His Music* (New York, 1938); Willa McClung Evans, *Henry Lawes* (New York, 1941), pp. 79-109.
5. See Spaeth, *op. cit., passim;* Theodore Howard Banks, *Milton's Imagery* (New York, 1950), pp. 26-31; Tillyard, *Milton,* pp. 63-65, 374-379; James Hutton, "Some English Poems in Praise of Music," *English Miscellany,* II (1951), pp. 43-59; Gretchen Lee Finney, "A World of Instruments," *ELH,* XX (1953), pp. 111-116; Spitzer (Part II), pp. 335-340; Nan C. Carpenter, "The Place of Music in *L'Allegro* and *Il Penseroso,*" *University of Toronto Quarterly,* XXII (1953), pp. 354-367.
6. It seems difficult to agree with John Edward Hardy, in his essay on *Comus* in Cleanth Brooks and John Edward Hardy, *Poems of Mr. John Milton* (New York, 1951), p. 200, that the "Sweet Echo" lyric "is little more than a song to herself." It is certainly much more than that, being addressed to Echo as a figure of music's virtues of fluid ubiquity, and intended as a kind of prayer for deliverance. It is with the Lady's charming singing that both Comus' and the Attendant Spirit's affections are engaged, and the former appears ironically only in answer to the import of her text, although the fact that the music had charmed him is not ironic in the least. John Arthos, in *On "A Mask Presented at Ludlow-Castle"* (Ann Arbor, 1954), pp. 75-77, has some relevant remarks on the song in question as incantation, almost of the nature of a charm. Such is certainly its role on the literal level of action.
7. Cf. Orsino's lines in *Twelfth Night,* I, i, 8-10: "O, it came ore my eare, like the sweet sound / That breathes upon a banke of Violets; / Stealing, and giving Odour. . . ."
8. Lawes, in his original setting of the song, seems to have intended an emphasis on such a division. The opening lines form a kind of introduction; but despite the rather freely quasi-recitative style of setting, there is clear musical repetition of the musical phrase of "Canst thou

tell me" at the words "So maist thou be." Lawes was undoubtedly
suggesting some kind of conditional relationship, in his setting, between the promise of the final lines and the answering of the Lady's
plea.

9. *Op. cit.*, pp. 201-202. Hardy makes much of "translated" here, insisting (p. 201) on a sense closer to "metamorphosed" than to the obvious one of "assumption into Heaven having circumvented death";
in any case, this word is a later addition (see below), and seems to
represent an actual layer of composition in the Christian synthesis that
Milton later added. For a discussion of the possible implications of the
complimentary "Daughter of the Sphear," see Hardy, p. 201 and
Hutton, *op. cit.*, pp. 48-49.

10. For all the variant and MS. readings of *Comus* and "At a Solemn
Musick" discussed below, see *The Columbia Milton,* I, 421-425 and
502.

11. Both the Bridgewater and Trinity MSS. substitute "resounding grace"
for "counterpoint," as does the British Museum MS. But only the
latter retains "transplanted."

12. Laura E. Lockwood, "Milton's Corrections to the Minor Poems,"
Modern Language Notes, XXV (1910), p. 203. C. S. Lewis, in "A
Note on *Comus,*" *Review of English Studies,* VIII (1932), pp. 171-
172, remarks only that the original "Hould a Counterpointe" is more
"unexpected" a reading, without specifying why (although it is very
possible that he had in mind much of what has been observed here).

13. See, for example, Tillyard, *op. cit.*, pp. 63-65.

14. John S. Diekhoff, "Critical Activity of the Poetic Mind: John Milton," *PMLA,* LV (1940), p. 749. Diekhoff agrees completely with
the comment of Miss Lockwood, quoted above. See also his comments
on the emendations in "At a Solemn Musick" in "The Text of
Comus, 1634 to 1645," *PMLA,* LII (1937), pp. 709-710.

15. Text of edition of 1673. The most important variant in the printed
1645 edition is the reading of "content" for "concent" in line 6.

16. Brooks and Hardy, in their essay on "At a Solemn Musick," *op. cit.*,
pp. 117-119, read "offspring" for "pledges."

17. The Platonistic sirens who produce the actual sphere-sounds are invoked here, but their presence is reinforced by what would seem to be
Milton's covert allusion to the many allegorizations of the other Sirens
as forces of eloquence leading men not to their destruction, but toward God.

18. For "chromatick" as a stylistic designation, rather than a specific ref-
erence to harmonic or melodic texture, see John Daniel's "Chromatick
Tunes" songs, discussed above [*The Untuning of the Sky*], Chapter
IV.

19. On this see Hutton, *op. cit.*, pp. 50-51. The comments of Leo Spitzer

on the emendations here, in *op. cit.*, Part II, 337, are of most interest when they outline a specifically linguistic point, such as his intriguing remark that the deletion of earlier line 11: "loud symphonie of silver trumpets blow" may have turned on Milton's desire to rid so "Hebrew" a poem of so Greek a word as "symphonie," whether used in a Greek technical sense of *consonance,* or in a more modern sense, synonymous with "consort."

20. Particularly by Hutton, *op. cit.,* p. 49.

21. *Op. cit.,* Part II, 336.

22. *Op. cit.,* p. 49.

23. Some of the notions in this paragraph are hinted at in an unpublished Columbia University master's essay by William A. Darkey, Jr., entitled "Milton's 'At a Solemn Musick'; a Commentary" (1949), to which I am indebted for the stress it puts on the continued importance of the initial invocation throughout the poem, a point missed by many commentators. See, for example, the insistence of Clay Hunt, in *Donne's Poetry: Essays in Literary Analysis* (New Haven, 1954), p. 133, that "the harmony of the soul which Milton contemplates is primarily an emotional harmony," a point which seems somehow either trivial, or misleading in its simplistic interpretation of what Milton might have meant by *musica humana.*

[EDITOR'S NOTE. See also G. L. Finney, *Musical Backgrounds for English Poetry* [1962]; L. Spitzer, *Classical and Christian Ideas of World Harmony,* 1963; A. E. Barker, *UTQ,* X (1940-41), 167-81; A. S. P. Woodhouse, *UTQ,* XII (1943-44), 66-101; E. Sirluck, *JEGP,* LX (1961), 749-85; F. T. Prince, *The Italian Element in Milton's Verse,* 1954.]

ROSEMOND TUVE

Structural Figures of *L'Allegro* and *Il Penseroso*

There are good reasons why the images of these two poems have for centuries given pleasure to almost anyone who can read. They offer also certain sophisticated pleasures, but their first attractiveness results from the peculiarly direct and simple relation we feel in them between experience as lived through and as imagined, the experiences meanwhile typifying what is universally pleasurable and universally desired by men. Every human mind has attempted the two allegiances Milton gives shape to, has felt both their differences and their compatibility. The poems are not taken care of by saying that Milton portrays two moods, or two lives, or two men, or two days and nights, or Day and Night, or Light and Darkness; all these, assigned by critics as subjects, are instrumental. It is not possible to state the subject of either poem without using his figure or another; he portrays not pursuer or pursuit but that bodiless thing itself which the freely delighting mind or the meditative mind tirelessly seeks to ally itself with. Thence comes part of the satisfactoriness of the images; contrary to common statement, we do not tire of pleasures or of thought but of the pursuing without taking possession—and each of these

From *Images and Themes in Five Poems by Milton*, Cambridge: Harvard University Press, 1957, pp. 15-36. Copyright, 1957, by the President and Fellows of Harvard College. Reprinted by permission of the author and the publisher.

slight images stands for a lived experience in the moment when we enjoy and know the quality of that for which we ran. The mind is insatiate of "experience" thus defined. It has so little of it. We shall see presently that the secret of the images' decorum (the much-discussed problem of their generalness) lies here—where such secrets always lie, in the relation of images to poetic subject, to the *raison d'être* of the whole poem as completely as that can be grasped.

For a reader, a decision about this last matter is the final decision to make, and images help him to it. Yet the critic of images finds a description of poetic subject the most economical single statement he can begin with, a necessary and practical substitute for a full analysis of the entire sequence of images, since any reader who will try out the critic's answer to this one question will himself supply such an analysis, very like the one no critic has space for. The imagery of *L'Allegro* and *Il Penseroso* has been examined in more separate treatments, especially in recent years, than that of any of the other minor poems, and I shall mention all the important ones in one connection or another; anyone who will reread all these treatments will perceive that as soon as we can detect what each critic thinks to be the subject of the poems, we see that it not only determines how much and what parts of the imagery he notices, but that we can predict where praise and blame will fall. As is not unusual with youthful work, these poems are more implicated in the habits and aims of their period than some others of Milton's works; what follows from this is that the typical dissatisfied reader of their images is the reader (naïve or sophisticated) who cannot forbear prescribing certain poetic aims, subjects, and habits (Romantic or modern, those of a Keats or those of an Eliot) as necessary ones. For my own definition of the subjects of the poems, which is not in the least revolutionary, I would claim only that it follows the text, that it would have occurred immediately to any intelligent seventeenth-century reader trained in a grammar school, and that it will take care of every image and word, in context, in each poem.

Milton says outright what he is doing in *L'Allegro*: "And if I give thee honour due,   Mirth, admit me of thy crue"; 115 following lines honor her by showing her nature as it shines through a score of forms of "unreproved pleasures free," and his conclusion is an election or statement of allegiance: "These delights, if thou canst give,   Mirth with thee, I mean to live." Many a pastoral *débat* moves towards such a reply or choice; we are more familiar with those "praises" of Love

or of Virtue which take the related shape of "the pastoral invitation."
The poet had given his first thirty-five lines, after banishing Mirth's
opposite, to invoking her: "But com thou Goddess fair and free"—in
heaven she has her being as the Grace named Euphrosyne; men call
her "heart-easing Mirth." They have called her many similar names;
since she laps them "against eating Cares," all generations and societies of men have tried to be of her company. She is the subject of
L'Allegro.

But she is not a person; she is a personification, that is, she is a way
of talking about the absolutely not the contingently real. She is one
of those three Graces whom the mythographer Conti calls "deesses de
bienfaits," allegorized by Conti and Gyraldus and Ripa and Valeri-
anus and Cartari, "moralized" by being connected with Seneca's *De
beneficiis*, spoken of or painted as free, liberal, like Truth naked or
with untrammeled garments; and she is that one, Euphrosyne, who
especially figures Gladness, as her sisters figure splendor, brightness,
or majesty (Aglaia), and flourishing or bourgeoning (Thalia). She
is no half-intended classical tag. Behind her significancy as the major
image of Milton's poem there lies not only all that classical tradition,
long-annotated, had made of the Graces, but this tradition enriched
by the philosophising and symbol-making interpretations of neo-
Platonic Renaissance writers like Ficino and spread widely by my-
thographers and commentators. To this we must add a long literary
tradition in other tongues and in English—Spenser's vision of these
"daughters of delight" dancing upon the Acidalian mount in his pastoral book (*FQ* VI.x), Ben Jonson's numerous masques. She is the
Euphrosyne who "figures" "Chearfulnes, or gladnes" and appears
both alone and with her two sister "Charities or Graces" in Jonson's
masques and the Coronation entertainment, his "Laetitia" dressed in
flowers like Ripa's *Allegrezza*, his "Delight" who is accompanied by
Sport, Laughter, Revel, and such others. She is indeed that Dame
Gladnesse who dances with "Sir Mirthe" (*Deduit*) in the garden of
the *Romaunt of the Rose*, where all cares—Elde, and Sorowe, and
Povert—are left outside, painted on the walls without. All sins as well,
all heart-eating foes like Felonye, Vilainye, Coveitise. For the chiefest
companion of the central figure has great importance in each of Milton's twin poems, and "The Mountain Nymph, sweet Liberty," whom
Milton's Mirth leads in her right hand, is an essential element in his
conception of that free Grace, as she had been in dozens of others.[1]

This is not to say that Milton wants the "unreproved pleasures free" of his vision of delight to be like those transgressions that miraculously do not count as such, with which we are familiar in descriptions like Tasso's of the Golden Age, which Daniel translated as "A Pastorall." But such pleasures are like his "unreprovable" ones in one special respect, and he indicates it by his wish to live with Liberty *and* with Mirth—they all have the flat absence of any relation to responsibility which we sometimes call innocence. This is a primary ground of difference between the pleasures of Mirth's man and Melancholy's man, and recognition of that fact goes far to set aside the vexed question[2] of whether these two are "opposites," "contrasts," "diagonally contrasted," "balanced," "merged," and the like, whether Milton is "both" L'Allegro and Il Penseroso. What man is not? We need make no trouble about a division, no fanfare about a unification, that every man daily makes, within the bounds of his own personality. Not by the reconciling of things opposed, but by the comprehending of things different, and not in a pattern of the antitheses but in a living and experiencing mind. But "some melancholy in Milton's mirth" there is not, if we abide by his own definitions; the differences remain differences, and the Cherub Contemplation who is "first, and chiefest" companion in *Il Penseroso* breathes another air than that in which "youthful Poets dream On Summer eeves by haunted stream" or contemplate Shakespeare's plays of fancy and Jonson's learned masques and comedies. Every pleasure in each poem is a pleasure of the mind, for that is where the subjects of his two poems have their being. The emphasis upon Milton as an unusually detached spectator in a world of cheerful or of melancholy objects and events, walking solitary and observant through a day's round, results (like Dr. Johnson's phrase quoted above[3]) from seeing the subject of this poem as "Milton's mirth," not mirth. "The cheerful man's day" is just a variant of this narrowing of subject; it is one which produces requests wrongly made of the images, and judgements of them falsely based.

For the subject of *L'Allegro* is every man's Mirth, our Mirth, the very Grace herself with all she can include. Therefore its images are not individualized. Milton does not describe a life, or a day, but through images causes us to recall, imagine, and savor the exact nature of joy when it is entirely *free* of that fetter, care, which ties down the joys we actually experience in an order of reality that does not present us with essences pure. Therefore Eliot will not find here his "particular milkmaid," for this one must instead be all milkmaids who ever sang; she must even be whatever fresh singing creature, not a

milkmaid, does bring the same joy to the heart of him to whom milkmaids bring it not. The Plowman forever whistling, and the Mower
who whets his scythe, do not exist thus simplified and quintessential
in Nature, yet the fresh delight these catch for us lives in every such
one we see—see with the eyes, that is, of one admitted of Mirth's
crew. That is precisely the grace she confers. It is the first secret of
this imagery that it does not speak only of what it mentions, rather
provides a channel along which our perhaps barely similar experiences
flow straight and full to a single meaning.

A second secret is that they do this *in despite* of sorrow, like the
lark which is just one of all the creatures of earth who in these moments seem to take man into a fellowship of ease and innocence. It is
a strength of pastoral imagery, especially that bordering upon the
"pathetic fallacy," that it conveys "that mutual exchange of good will"
which has been given as one definition of the late Renaissance allegorized meaning of "the Graces."[4] Milton's landscape of lawns and
fallows, with its nibbling flocks and bare breasts of mountains, just so
sets sorrow at naught. The reasons for it are too profound to examine
here, but that which lies behind an earthly paradise archetype in
terms of mountain-flowers-trees-and-birds, and that which made men
connect freedom, the country, and holidays, long before they were
penned in cities, operates to make us walk with secure well-being
through the world of *L'Allegro*'s images.[5] We frame it meanwhile to
the shape of our own minds and experiences.

Various explanations have been given for this immediacy in the
imagery. I do not believe[6] that it results either from simplicity of outline compelling us to fill in our own detail, or from an image-tech-
nique which though it chiefly generalizes is capable also of realistic
"individualizing" when the sensibility is awakened (for example, the
dripping eaves of *Il Penseroso*). Either these are not the factors which
matter, or some other is unnoted. This can be tested by the generalized four-line figure of the Sun as king, or the genre-painting image
of the Cock with its accompanying military metaphor, ". . . with
lively din,   Scatters the rear of darkness thin" (two of the very few
uses of metaphor within single images). We are as obedient to participate in these more elaborate images as in Tillyard's cited case of
the cottage with its mere "two aged Okes." *Golden slumber* on the
"heapt *Elysian* flowres" is as "real" as the *tanned* haycock. What is
real is the experience of pleasure we have through each of them.
This experience is sporadically rather than necessarily connected

with sensuous precision. Not one of all these is individualized. They are not "individuals," unique sights seen by one man's eye, but particulars, irradiated by the "general" which they signify: a fresh and vivid joy such as we take in living itself—or could, were it but careless.

This seems to me the answer to the much-discussed "generalness" of the images of these two poems—a bad word for a great virtue. They have it because of the nature of the two subjects, and it is in no way at odds with particularity, only with individual-ity. Perhaps it is this virtue which makes natural another effect, quite as unexpected (except in rhetorical theory, which directs us to both) as this conveying of "reality" without the "realism" of portraying single objects. We have a sense that Milton has covered his subject. Turning, our "eye hath caught new pleasures"—and lo when we have walked through two or three meadows with nothing in them except a daisy here and there, and past the towers in the tufted trees and the cottage, we seem to have known all that the phrase can mean, "the pleasures of the eye." In the "Towred Cities" which break the horizon line before us we approach all those we know or imagine, and hear the "busie humm" of every festivity enjoyed in any of them; the feasts and revels so few and indistinct (to our senses) yet leave no such gaieties unincluded, just as all the innumerable variations which a lifetime can put into the phrase "the pleasures of books" are taken care of by *Il Penseroso's* little seventeenth-century list. One supposes that this sense of completeness is another result of the functioning of images when their subject is a "general" or universal, and they are in decorous relation to it.

The unindividualized character of the images is matched in the time-structure of the poems. It seems to be taken for granted by most recent writers on the imagery proper, and is necessary to the main theses of some of these, that Milton's major concern is to portray the full round of a day, the "pensive man's day" beginning with evening, but both "days" progressing straightforwardly through time and all but constituting the poems' subjects. This is surely not quite accurate. There are various *days* in *L'Allegro;* one of them lasts all through a Sunshine Holyday, when *"sometimes"* in one of the upland hamlets there is dancing in the chequer'd shade until the live-long day-light fails and the tales begin—and we do not know for sure how much of this revel we join. "Oft" the speaker listens to the hunt (he does not see, but thinks of, the way a hill still dew-covered looks *hoar*). Thereupon we hear of him *"Som time* walking" on the green hillocks over against where the sun begins his state. Nor can we certainly tell whether we are to imagine as actually attended the pomps and feasts, at court, for they not only are set in cities, but culminate in the dubious appositive, "Such sights as youthful Poets dream   On Summer eeves by haunted stream." Surely, as we should expect from "admit me . . . to live with thee," we do follow roughly through the most usual unit into which we divide the passage of time as we live it, but not nearly closely enough for this to indicate the significance of each whole poem's images, nor are the first thirty-seven and sixty-two lines, respectively, thus to be set aside as extraneous to their pattern. Actions take place both in August and June; we watch each: Phillis leaves in haste to bind the sheaves, *"Or if* the earlier season," to lead to the haycock in the meadow. The last image—the miraculous imitation of immortal verses so sung that Orpheus who hears them knows why his own music but half regained Eurydice—has no place nor time: *"And ever* against eating Cares. *Lap me* in soft Lydian Aires. . . ." Where are we? and whence, and when, does the music sound? This is not *the joyful man's day*. It is *Joy*. "And if I give thee honour due,   Mirth, admit me of thy crue."

These pleasures are of course not the "vain deluding joyes" banished at the commencement of *Il Penseroso*. Each poem begins with a banishing of the travesty of what is praised in the other, a common rhetorical device, not unrelated to the method of dialectic which is one ancestor of the Prolusions (of course) and of the whole long tradition of *débats, conflictus* wedded to eclogue, the pastoral "choice," and the like small kinds. In each case, what is banished is quite real, not the subject of the other poem seen in a different mood, or moral temper. "Loathed Melancholy," child of death and night, was (and is) the source of a serious mental condition. Serious but not solemn, both banishing-passages have the wit of contrast (with the companion poem, with the personage praised in the remainder of the exordium) and the wit of bringing out the paradoxical but quite true doubleness of that for which we have but one name.[7] For it is a Goddess, *sage* and *holy*, of *Saintly* visage—*divinest* Melancholy—who is indeed the true subject of all of *Il Penseroso*, without qualification and without apology. Her nature is very exactly delineated in it, without waste or irrelevance; the leisurely economy of the images is a primary factor in making the poem what Johnson called it, a noble effort of the imagination. Nobility is a just term for its pre-eminent character, if we make room therein for the delicacy and spacious amplitude with which a sensitive mind grasps and presents a great conception, avoiding doctrinaire rigor and awake to the hair-thin variousness with which men conceive ideas. *Melancholy* is of course not the conception we call by that name. She presents to the imaging faculty, that the understanding and heart cannot but lay hold of it and desire it, a great humanistic ideal.

It would be folly and presumption, and certainly eludes my competence, to describe with neat labels a conception which not only this poem but half a dozen moving expositions illuminate at length with ardor and care. It seems to me preferable to speak of places where those who read this essay may pursue such conceptions, usually places where Milton too had almost certainly taken fire from them. In accordance with what one begins to suspect is a universally applicable rule, an informed and deepened understanding of a poem's whole subject provides, more directly than analysis, a changed response to its images. Although Milton's poem stands to suffer more from the trivializing, than the vital mistaking, of its subject, its power and delicately touched seriousness can be so enriched by readings which go beyond what I can include here, that I shall not attempt to be more than a guidepost, nor present fully the philosophical ideas involved.

Since the publication of Panofsky and Saxl's *Dürers "Melencolia I"* in 1923, and certainly since Panofsky's *Albrecht Dürer* in 1943, it has been conveniently open to us to see much more truly certain meanings Milton's major image indubitably has, though since covered over by time and semantic change. No doubt they have been seen and pointed out in a dozen classrooms, and we have simply not got around to a special study applying new knowledge in a critical analysis of the images of *Il Penseroso,* but at any rate the only printed recognitions of a changed conception are the partial ones I mention below in specific connections. The important relevant points in Panofsky's book[8] are: that he brings to the fore the Renaissance popularity of Aristotle's *Problemata,* XXX, with its treatment of the necessary relation between melancholy and genius (philosophical, political, poetic); that he shows how Ficino was pre-eminent in revising (not inventing anew) the traditional conception of melancholy, leading the way in a humanistic glorification of the Melancholy Man as the type par excellence of the contemplative, the intellectual genius intent upon understanding hidden wisdom; and that he re-examines the connection (again traditional, but repointed) of these ideas with Saturn, the Saturnian man and the planet's influence. Knowledge of this particular strain of meaning for Melancholy was not esoteric or farfetched, and Milton could scarcely have been ignorant of writers such as Ficino, Vives, Fracastoro, Melanchthon, Bodin, Agrippa.[9] A student of mediaeval literature saw such connections with Milton's poem before these studies came out, for traditional conceptions have been modified and re-directed rather than quite changed. It still seems necessary to read some or one of the Renaissance treatments if one is to realize the artistic implications (on the level of minutiae in the images) of Milton's use of a figure like "divinest Melancholy" daughter of Saturn; exact phraseology and total impression are important when the task in hand is to recreate a symbolic figure who has lost her earlier significancy, and worse still taken on an unfitting one with numerous distractions in the form of unscrutinized associations.

This can be exemplified here. If one should choose, as accessible and widely popular in the late Renaissance, Cornelius Agrippa's *Three Books of Occult Philosophy,* one has only to read chapter 60 of Book i to learn that Saturn who governs the melancholy man is "the Author of secret contemplation," who estranged from "outward businesses" makes the mind ascend higher than these up to the knowledge of future things; that, as Aristotle says, by Melancholy "some men are made as it were divine, foretelling things to come, and some men are made Poets"; that "all men that were excellent in any Science, were for the most part melancholy."[10] It is not by chance that Milton's poem on Melancholy ends with his hope finally to "sit and rightly spell Of every Star . . . And every Herb," "Till old experience do attain To something like Prophetic strain." The word *"divinest* Melancholy" is quite accurate, so also the *rapt* soul, the *holy passion;* her visage is for good reasons "too bright To hit the *Sense of human sight"* (the intuitive *mens* is governed by melancholic Saturn, the discursive *ratio* by Jupiter, according to Ficino).[11] She of course wears Wisdom's hue which is that of the black humor,[11] and she is in truth both a daughter born to solitary Saturn by "bright-hair'd *Vesta"* (celestial pure fire, not that of Venus and Vulcan) and a patron "Saint" of those whose desire is to understand the mysteries of things, and who practise poetry as a high form of contemplative knowledge.

Milton leaves out of his conception of prophetic poetry in *Il Penseroso* none of the gentler and homelier elements we would wish poetry to retain; we walk also in known and simple places, and it is part of the unusual flexibility of his portrayal that for example the connection with dream's "lively portrature" leaves room for many visions other than those we now label prophetic. The dream which the Goddess Melancholy is asked to bring rather reveals the mysteries of Fancy than the awesome secrets of prophecy; it is to come when the noise of bees and waters entice the dewy-feather'd Sleep, and is to "Wave at his Wings in Airy stream, Of lively portrature" spread out and laid softly on the eyelids, while music "Sent by som spirit" breathes above or about. This is like those visions of which Night sings in Jonson's *Vision of Delight,* calling upon Phantasie to spread her wings and "Create of ayrie formes a streame" that will "be a waking dreame; Yet . . . fall like sleep upon their eies, Or musick in their eare." All such things are the province of a goddess of the Imagination, and there is no inconsistency.

The ways are many by which the man favored with knowledge of hidden worlds is to be brought to it, and images suggest them. Spare Fast comes (much as in *Elegy vi.* 59ff.) to bring him where he hears what the Muses tell, and he knows the groves whence the nymphs have not yet been frightened by him who uses rather than contemplates nature—the Active Man. Melancholy is a pensive *Nun* because she is a votary, and her "looks commercing with the skies" are those of the mind that searches out, rapt in contemplation, the secrets of the spheres; they are such secrets as the "deep transported mind" soars "Above the wheeling poles" to see, looking in "at Heav'ns dore," in the *Vacation Exercise* passage of similar temper and imagery. The moonlit haunts and arched walks of twilight groves are not like the appurtenances of sentimental melancholy in intent, but like those places where the "quietness and sadness" in which Saturn works open the mind "opportunely" to celestial influences (Agrippa's phrases). Light as the usual symbol for knowledge (the figure of the Cherub Contemplation is light-filled) is never felt to be in opposition to these and the other darkened images—the dim religious light, the fire-lit gloom, the shadows brown, the lamp-lit high lonely tower—because it is not the *darkness* which is operating symbolically; it is the votary's retired, solitary hiddenness, "Where no prophaner eye may look," where the mind seeing by a different light from that of Day's garish eye learns the things known to the Cosmic Mind, Melancholy's great father whom Agrippa calls "a keeper of secret things, and a shewer of them."

That musical harmony and its power should come into the imagery
is to be expected because of the closeness of all these matters to the
imagery of the cosmic harmonies. Agrippa too treats of music, marking the difference between the Lydian mode (Jupiter's, as are blood
and air[12]) and the "mixt Lydian" that belongs to Saturn and melancholy. It is quite natural that Milton moves from the imagination's
dream to yet deeper insight, from the music to which the dreamer
wakes—"Sent by som spirit to mortals good" or by the Genius of the
Wood—on to the music of that "Service high" to which the student
goes, and whose anthems clear bring, through his ear, all Heaven before his eyes. Religious music and imagery here no more surprise us
than Agrippa surprises us with "the chastity of a mind devoted to
God doth make our mind (as *Orpheus* teacheth *Museus* in the hymn
of all the gods) a perpetual temple of God." Milton's "But let my
due feet never fail . . ." is in the temper of much of Agrippa's third
book. This passage on the "studious Cloysters pale," asking the goddess Melancholy never to let him fail to walk in those strait confines
and love the vaulted chapel with its full-voiced quire and liturgical
service, is no wrenched interpolation or sudden Christianizing; neither, however, is it a mystic's experience in any proper sense, unless
we would loosely call all contemplative experience "mystical."[13]
These, like the cell and the tower, are all places where assistance to
the knowledge of hidden mysteries can come to the contemplating
mind looking upon the unknown and otherwise unknowable, and no
cleavage is assumed (in the respect here noted) between natural and
divine philosophy. Agrippa thinks of prophecies of Christ's appearance on earth, like Virgil's in the Fourth Eclogue, as coming to a
mind governed by Melancholy. The basic element which harmonizes
these varied but not inconsistent aspects of the imagery is that of
Melancholy as daughter of one whose power was over the mind's
perception of hidden cosmic harmonies, Saturn who was great, wise,
intelligent, ingenious, "of great profundity, the author of secret contemplation, impressing, or depressing great thoughts in the hearts of
men, . . . a keeper of secret things, and a shewer of them, causing
the loss, and finding of the author of life and death."

The modern researches that provide us with a better understanding
of such conceptions regnant in Milton's day give us not a new poem
but a more unified and sensitive one. Milton's diction and imagery
corroborate the connection at every point, and other similar connections have been made. The quotation from Pico with which Wood-

house illuminates the figure of the cherub Contemplation, and his analysis of the range and relevance of *Il Penseroso's* similar readings, fall directly into place; we might add Dionysius on the cherubim, that glowing order in the angelic hierarchy who reflect the very light of God's own wisdom and can transmit it to his instruments below.[14] D. C. Allen is the first critic to comment fully on the images clustered around "thrice great *Hermes*"[15]; they are entirely consonant with the materials and conceptions I have just pointed to, and I have of course intended Agrippa as convenient example rather than as special source.

Milton's references to Musaeus and Orpheus, to Hermes, and thence of course to Plato, to studies touching the after-existence of "The immortal mind" and the planet-consenting power of the elemental Daemons, make the frame of reference within which he is speaking quite clear; his imagery evokes the major figures in that group of *prisci theologi* who were thought to have foreshadowed Christian revelation. To name those who had endeavored to show this harmony (indeed even historical continuity) of thought would be to make a roster of famous Christian writers; it would include such celebrated and devout Christian apologists, known to all educated men, that Milton's similar harmonizing of pagan study with Christian worship, of Platonist with hermit, must be seen as but one more harmony among many.[16] We are left with no supersubtle inconsistencies to explain away—the complexities are instead quite intended and real —and with no oddities to excuse. The poem ends firmly, with a climactic last representative of those who taste Melancholy's pleasures in tne pursuit of wisdom; for certainly the hermit who spells out the secrets of the physical universe in his solitary cell is no concession to religiosity but the very type of the withdrawn seer who experiences the last pleasure: to know things in their causes and see into the hidden harmonies of the cosmos. The "Hairy Gown" is that of the Contemplative who is one of Saturn's children, in the pictures that illustrate that planet's influence. If Milton's hermit in his mossy cell had a caption it would be neither "romantic Middle Ages" nor "religious touch," but *Platonic Ascent;* we should read beside the herbs sprouting in the moss "philosophia naturalis," on the cell's threshold "philosophia divina" and upon its lintel *vita contemplativa.*[17]

It makes a true difficulty for us that such images no longer surround us. Readiness and pleasure in apprehending Milton's figure of Melancholy—both with ease and excitement, that is—come not from some point to be learned at second hand but from saturation in the phrasings and impressions of whole other treatments of the same fundamental ideal. The reason for this is a point about imagery, in both poems.

The major figure in each poem is, in each, the one true use of *symbol*. The structural use of symbols in a poem is not a matter of the frequent appearance in varying connections of some great element—Light or Darkness or garden or underground place—in which we are accustomed to see symbolic meanings; these appearances result from, not cause, the symbolic unity of the work. We come out with a structure of meanings, not a pattern of mentionings. Symbolism is always implicit, never explicit, for a poet like other human beings uses a symbol because there is no other way ("no earthly way," as we put it) to say what he means and all he means. Nor can we do better. Yet there is always something wrapped up—the unstatable—in that foldedness; within us, when we have taken it folds and all, it unfolds where not words but significances are the agents. It is the *latter* which make a pattern.

Language being in a sense symbolic in its very nature, and man's mind a symbolizing instrument, there are of course moments when darkness, and sunlight, and towers, and water, convey needed aspects of meaning from one man to another, by a common consent built upon centuries of shared meanings. But if a great poet—or even a young but already competent poet—is truly using elements like these for their value as symbols in his poem, time and again, this way and that, then something much more surely directed can be clearly seen to be taking place. The inescapable fact about symbols is that they are used *to symbolize something,* and verbal or object recurrence is of no symbolic import unless a connection is perceived with that to which we inescapably attend when symbols are used, the pattern of thesomething-symbolized. If a poet has such a shape or form, a pattern of the unseizable, to present, his symbols will fix our eyes upon *it,* and through them we step from understanding to understanding at his bidding, continuing in and ending with the same great basic significance that gave us our first hint and start. An eminent singleness of meaning characterizes symbols, and they end as they began, immeasurably deepened but never split up into fussy or novel equations; this we can test by thinking of any of Milton's (or another's) great uses of Light:Wisdom or Fire:Love, and many to which we can put no fitting abstraction (Garden, Shepherd) but which sit in our minds, great unverbalizable unities.

For the two conceptions to which he has given a shape Milton found the names Mirth and Melancholy, inherited names for inherited figures. Just these shapes we shall find nowhere but in these poems, and uses of light and the things of day do not symbolically reveal the form of one conception, shadows and night the other. The two personages are truly figurative in their action, the sole important *figures* of any scope, and each is the "dominant symbol" of her poem —not light nor darkness nor towers.[18] They do not themselves act out their natures, and make no allegory (lack the "continued" character of allegorical metaphors). After the habit of goddesses (or planets, or "generals"), they *govern*—and their servants display the nature of that rule and its rewards,[19] themselves constituting a praise of her they serve. Each is "in" every action or place, sight or sound, in her poem (especially in the landscapes; often these have *only* the meaning of *expressing*—sometimes quite temporarily—the universal which the goddesses *symbolize*); and Mirth's man gradually personifies the Personification, shadows forth the Grace Euphrosyne, not the other way around. This is the way metaphor acts; particulars declare significances. It is not because we look in these poems at symbols of whose force we remain quite ignorant without aid, that reading elsewhere about them makes the poems show as more exquisitely just—although there is a little of this in the case of Melancholy and the allegorized meaning of the Graces. It is rather because figurative writing is a hundred times more pleasurable when we recognize every nuance of significance.

Had we been born earlier we should have had one more help to the kind of pleasure some readers take in imagery: its perfect decorum, showing that astonishing artistry in the maker which awakens gratitude, a form of literary criticism. It is a help that the author himself had in creating the decorum.

I refer to the fact that a seventeenth-century reader recognized immediately the rhetorical structure of these two poems. By virtue of that recognition he also apprehended immediately the fitness which is the great aesthetic attribute their images exhibit; it is what has made, as Leishman says, almost every phrase memorable. Each poem is "a praise," the form of "demonstrative oration" called *encomium,* taught to every grammar-school boy according to the rules in such a handbook as Aphthonius, the one Milton probably studied. The images flow directly out of this rhetorical structure, with its usual "places," of exordium, of praise by "what kind he came of"—what na-

tion, ancestors, parents—praise by his "acts," his gifts of mind, of
countenance or quality, friends, actions.[20] It would not surprise one
who had written dozens of these praises of this or that "general," or
virtue, or personage, to find certain parallels between Milton's two
poems; I too would willingly miss this surprise for the informed
amazement of recognizing the imaginativeness and disciplined command with which imagery builds the known but natural form. This
structure had a powerful influence upon the lyric, with its related aim
of celebrating and praising. The reader who knew the structure (that
is, every educated reader of its time) would not turn the great subject
of Il Penseroso into "the pensive man's day," would take in the unity
of each poem and something of its relation to the other with a single
flash of recognition, and would understand and enjoy the very virtue
of the images which has been so much rubbed and questioned—for
long tracts of each poem consist of the rhetorical "circumstances"
which can justly and delicately limn out the unseizable through the
seizable. Where it is suitable, this can produce images of peculiar
power to catch the form of what men live for in the fleeting shapes
of how they live; it is necessary to be critically alert to the suitability.
There are good literary reasons for the omission of minor metaphors
from these poems.

Our sense that certain works will permanently charm is almost always connected with some structural excellence. The shapely perfection of L'Allegro and Il Penseroso depends most upon a central figurative conception at the heart of each, and these large formative images
have been clarified to us as modern scholarship has cleared away ob-
structions present since the early 1700's. I have not meant by this
emphasis upon modern researches and upon the importance of genre
and structure to set aside the work from Warton onward which has
annotated the images with sources and parallels. Any student of imagery who despises these cuts himself off from his main necessity:
the understanding of the words of the text, made precise only thus
through innumerable experiences with contexts. This understanding
is not always easy, given a lapse of some hundreds of years and considering certain other differences which separate a Milton from any
one of us who look at him. I have ignored some criticism, chiefly
modern, of the images of L'Allegro and Il Penseroso, which seemed
rather dedicated to the critical principle that madness in great ones
must not unwatched go. No willing student of these poems has been
able to resist them.

NOTES

1. The phrase from Natale Conti (Comes) comes from *Mythologie,* iv. 15 (Lyons, 1612); for the Jonson figures cited see Allan Gilbert, *Symbolic Persons in the Masques of Ben Jonson* (Durham, N. C., 1948), where the other mythographical writers mentioned can also be conveniently found, and for the neo-Platonic writers, E. Panofsky, *Studies in Iconology* (New York, 1939); on the trinity of Graces, aspects of the nature of the Platonized and allegorized Venus, see pp. 168-169, their nudity, pp. 155, 159. Even the definitions from handbooks used by an E.K. (in *Shepheardes Calender,* April) for his gloss on these "Goddesses of al bountie and comelines" can restore for us one significance possessed by Milton's figure—the "free liberality" surely intended to accompany the equally traditional significance of pleasures freely enjoyed with a glad mind. See Starnes and Talbert, *Classical Myth and Legend in Ren. Dictionaries* (Chapel Hill, 1955), index.

2. This point is discussed, sometimes as the central one, from Masson onward, and appears in several of the influential studies to which I refer in various connections in the ensuing pages: those by E. M. W. Tillyard (in *The Miltonic Setting,* Cambridge, 1938), by Cleanth Brooks (as it reappeared in Brooks and Hardy, *Poems of Mr. John Milton,* New York, 1951), by A. S. P. Woodhouse ("Notes on Milton's Early Development," *University of Toronto Quarterly,* XIII [1943-44], 66-101). J. H. Hanford's early study set a good many of the questions ("The Youth of Milton," in *Studies in Shakespeare, Milton, and Donne,* New York, 1925).

3. Or like Masson's Horton-bound reading of the images, to which Tillyard objects—coming close to substituting one hemmed in by undergraduate capacities and the interests of Milton's Cambridge. But we are in debt to Tillyard's essay for having made readers again look at the poems as illuminating two "generals" (howbeit, as I think, wrong ones: the Day and the Night), as well as for having recalled attention to connections with the Prolusions, which assuredly shed light on the imagery.

4. See D. G. Gordon, "Ben Jonson's Haddington Masque: The Story and the Fable," *Modern Language Review,* XLII (1947), p. 186.

5. The landscapes and birds and groves of *Il Penseroso* all point a different direction. Mere content (area providing the "vehicle") determines the nature of no image save public symbols. Innumerable niceties of language, of rhetorical scheme and rhythm, of associated story, *require* us to see a different "general" shining through *Il Penseroso*'s particulars (examples of these three ways of differentiating so-called

nature images are: "Heav'ns wide *pathles* way," 70; "Swinging slow with sullen roar," 76; Philomel, 56-64).

6. With Tillyard, or with D. C. Allen (see n. 15 below), both of whom cite the eaves image, *Il Penseroso* 129.

7. Obviously this disagrees with Tillyard's suggestion of a burlesque tone, and Brooks's of an *ironical* contrast, based on the exaggeration of the images. See note 9 for references that give evidence on the *two* melancholy's familiar to the period, also made clear in J. B. Leishman's valuable study of *"L'Allegro* and *Il Penseroso* in their Relation to Seventeenth-Century Poetry," *Essays and Studies*, 1951.

8. See the later study (2nd edition, Princeton, 1945), I, 157-171, and also *Studies in Iconology*, esp. pp. 209ff.

9. Lawrence Babb in *The Elizabethan Malady* (East Lansing, Mich., 1951) gives needed information and relates it (though briefly, pp. 178-180) to the two poems. This does not take the place of familiarity with some Renaissance treatment of the matter. G. W. Whiting's *Milton's Literary Milieu* (Chapel Hill, 1939) has some additional details, as does Leishman (n. 7 above).

10. See Book iii. ch. 38 for the gifts of Saturn (sublime contemplation and profound understanding, solidity of judgement, firm speculation) and the related explanation of receiving from the "cherubins" light of mind, power of wisdom, very high phantasies and figures, by the which we are able to contemplate even the divine things (the *cherub* Contemplation is chiefest companion of Saturn's daughter in *Il P.* 54). I have quoted J. F[reake]'s translation (London, 1651), comparing it with the Latin edition of 1533; ensuing quotations come from i. ch. 68, 66; ii. ch. 59; ii. ch. 24, 26; iii. ch. 55; ii. ch. 59.

11. See Panofsky, *Albrecht Dürer*, I, 169. Saturn, lord of those governed by this humor, was Prudentia even to Ridewall (elemented of Memory, Intelligence, and Fore-sight; citation in J. Seznec, *La survivance des dieux antiques*, London, 1940, p. 85, whose last chapter shows the accessibility and widespreadness of the usual manuals). To Macrobius, Saturn (Plotinus's Cosmic Mind) has the power of "discernment and thought" in his gift (contrasted with Jupiter's gift of power to act; see Panofsky, *Studies in Iconology*, p. 209 n.). Readers even of a book like Fraunce's *Countesse of Pembrokes Yvychurch* (1592) are to understand that Saturn affords a reaching wit and profound cogitations.

12. It would not be difficult to find connections between the "Jov-ial" man and L'Allegro, and this commonplace of the "Lydian Aires" is one of them. But Milton chose to use, in his Grace, a different symbol, chose even to close off this symbolism by ignoring what he knew from Hesiod and elsewhere—Jupiter as father of Euphrosyne; and it is a first law in the reading of images to seek out the author's *chosen*

symbolism. If we will not plow with his heifer we shall not find out his riddle. Happily a good poet, like Samson, always tells where his strength is hid. These poems do not have for subject respectively the Active and the Contemplative Man, though the contrast cannot but enter; their subjects are those pointed to by the two great central figures.

13. The ecstasies of apprehending relations and harmonies are not those of union with the divine. At least, missing all evidence of the usual mystical imagery (and not forgetting Milton's lines on the power of sacred music to dissolve with sweetness and bring visions of heaven) I should prefer to read in the whole last section something resembling Agrippa's ". . . contemplation, the free perspicacity of the minde, suspended with admiration upon the beholding of wisdom" (iii. ch. 46). Milton's symbolizing of the honor to be paid and the allegiance vowed to the intellectual and contemplative pursuit of Wisdom (with all that includes) is clear; and contemplation leads to, not is, the mystical union.

14. See also n. 10. Woodhouse's study is cited in n. 2, and the essay on the *Nativity Hymn* in the present volume [*Images and Themes in Five Poems by Milton*] gives references to Pseudo-Dionysius.

15. See ch. i. of *The Harmonious Vision* (Baltimore, 1954), esp. the quotations from the *Poimandres,* that much edited, annotated, and translated text; comments in E. C. Baldwin, *Modern Language Notes,* XXXIII (1918), 184-185, are briefer; see further *Hermetica,* ed. Walter Scott, Oxford, 1924, vols. I, IV (Allen's references are to *libellus*). A fairly good idea of the studies Il Penseroso would carry on is gained from Jonson's satire upon a "melancholic student" in *The Fortunate Isles* (printed 1624/25)—his natural affinities are with Hermes, Porphyry, Proclus, Pythagoras, Plato, Archimedes.

16. D. P. Walker cites editions, translations, commentaries, Italian Renaissance scholars, and surveys the French writers (Mornay, the Pléiade, Lefevre) in "The *Prisca Theologia* in France," *Journal of Warburg and Courtauld Institutes,* XVII (1954), 204-259. See pp. 208-210 on the *Pimandre,* which a French bishop could praise as more pious than David, Hermes being thought either to precede or to derive his wisdom from Moses.

17. See Panofsky, *Studies in Iconology,* p. 78 and Fig. 48, and notes, also p. 138. We should remember that the terrifying aspects of Saturn's influence are not to be thought of as entirely opposed to the meanings I have been indicating, but that the connection of melancholy with genius was part of a total conception as complicated when seen by earlier ages as by ourselves. There is a special tie to natural philosophy in *Il Penseroso* 173 (*experientia:* knowledge gained by experiment, trial).

18. The two discussions of symbolism in *L'Allegro* and *Il Penseroso* here referred to are those of Cleanth Brooks and D. C. Allen (cited in n. 2, n. 15). Brooks's observation of recurrences and his precision in reading are often very revealing, in this influential essay as in all his criticism. I do not think his chief interpretation can stand up, largely for the reason given in the paragraphs discussing pattern and symbols, and also because some recurrences seem to depend on noting words while ignoring clearly intended major meanings. Some of Milton's towers have symbolic force; so do some uses of light. Few poems lack such uses of language, and they do not constitute "a basic symbolism."

19. Leishman calls this "personification giving place to exemplification," but this view cuts the tie between the universal and all the particulars in which it inheres.

20. I use here F. Johnson's reprint of Rainolde's *Foundation of Rhetoric, 1563* (New York, 1945; see f. 40). But see ch. 8 of *John Milton at St. Paul's School* (New York, 1948) by D. L. Clark; he of course notes the relation I make. There is some treatment of the connections of these matters with the character of "amplifying" images especially, and with Renaissance lyric theory, in the present writer's *Elizabethan and Metaphysical Imagery* (Chicago, 1947), section 1 of ch. v.

[EDITOR'S NOTE. See also E. Tate, *MLN*, LXXVI (1961), 585-90; and on music K. Svendsen, *Explicator*, VIII (1950), Item 49, and N. C. Carpenter, *UTQ, XXII* (1952-53), 354-67.]

JOHN M. WALLACE

Milton's *Arcades*

Confronted with any masque except *Comus,* the critic is aware of a
thinness and a lack of complexity in the text and he has long concluded that the masque's major symbols cannot reside primarily in the
libretto, where they occur as hints or ciphers, but in the dramatic
event itself. In turning, quite properly, to the visual aspects of the
masque, he has, however, largely neglected the symbolism inherent
within the important person or persons to whom the masque was addressed. Myths congregate around living people no less than they do
around the classical gods and goddesses and the places they inhabited,
and in order to revive the full meaning of these expensive entertainments we should, ideally, be as conscious of the halos circumscribing
a mortal reputation as we are of the iconographical "properties" in the
actual performance.

Lady Alice, Dowager Countess of Derby, in whose honor *Arcades*
was presented, was one of the most distinguished old aristocrats of
her time. Of a good family, she was married first to Lord Strange who
later became Earl of Derby, and then to Sir Thomas Egerton who became Lord Ellesmere, Viscount Brackley, and Chancellor of England.
She was thus connected with two leading patrons of English letters,

From *Journal of English and Germanic Philology,* LVIII (1959), 627-36, with
revisions by the author. Reprinted by permission of the author and the publisher.

for Lord Strange had earned the applause of Nashe and Greene and
had given his name to a famous company of players, while Egerton
is known to have had more than eighty literary works dedicated to
him.[1] Sir William Vaughan wrote of him that he "so tendereth & fos-
tereth the professours of true wisedome that he is worthily named the
Reviver and restorer of wisedome: yes, I have heard it sundry times
blazed, that England never had the like zealous patron of scholars."[2]
The Countess' letters reveal that she took an active part in her husband's affairs, and she was also a patron in her own right. Spenser
claimed kinship with her in his dedication to *The Teares of the
Muses,* sonnets were addressed to her, Davies of Hereford acknowledged his indebtedness, Thomas Gainsford wrote an unrestrained
eulogy, Marston composed a masque for her, and an obscure poet
thanked her for kindnesses undertaken on behalf of "my late Uncle
Marm. Newton."[3] She had entertained Queen Elizabeth at Harefield
and, as Masson has summarized, "she was the relic of times already
romantic in the haze of the past, and there was, perhaps, no aged
gentlewoman then living that carried in her memory, or could suggest by her mere presence to others, a nobler series of poetic recollec-
tions."[4] Her age and her fame made her a figure whom Milton could
praise more easily for her wit than her beauty, and she lived in a
period when a long experience of life was considered to bring knowledge and not a deliberate hebetude.

In the opening song of *Arcades,* the shepherds approach the Dowager, "Sitting like a Goddes bright, / In the center of her light,"[5] and
they exclaim involuntarily that, at long last, their "solemn search hath
end." The journey from Arcadia in the warm south ends here in a
sacred and northern wood; their immediate intuition that the "sudden
blaze of Majesty" has terminated their wanderings could be compared
with the certainty which possessed the wise men when the divine star
halted over the stable at Bethlehem. The kings, however, came from
the east and it is not this Biblical journey which Milton wished the
Countess to recall. He informed her of his intention in the second
stanza when he disclosed the topos which underlay the theme of the
itinerant shepherds:

> *Fame* that her high worth to raise,
> Seem'd erst so lavish and profuse,
> We may justly now accuse
> Of detraction from her praise,

> Less than half we find exprest,
> *Envy* bid conceal the rest.

With the same words a distinguished traveler, the Queen of Sheba, had once expressed her amazement at the wisdom of Solomon: "And she said to the king, It was a true report that I heard in mine own land of thy acts and of thy wisdom. Howbeit I believed not the words, until I came, and mine eyes had seen it: and, behold, the half was not told me: thy wisdom and prosperity exceedeth the fame which I heard" (I Kings 10: 6-7). Milton has retained the full import of the queen's speech, together with its most memorable line; the enviousness of fame, which is Milton's specific addition to the Biblical verses, was a contemporary commonplace, especially in dedicatory epistles to a patron, and it happens to reoccur in Du Bartas' account of the same story. In Sylvester's translation, which is accurate, Sheba protests that, as Solomon's fame

> Excels all Kings, thy vertues passe the same:
> Thy peer-les Prayse stoops to thy Learned tongue,
> And envious bruit hath done thy Wisedome wrong.[6]

Throughout the history of the Christian church, the visitation of Sheba has been given an allegorical interpretation. "Regina Austri," wrote Isidorus, "quae venit ad audiendam sapientiam Salomonis, Ecclesia intelligitur, quae ad verbum Dei ab ultimis finibus terrae congregatur," and similar commentaries, often quoting the text which Milton used, may be found scattered among medieval exegetics. For Nolanus, Sheba represented a barbarous nation, but not barbarous in mind, which sought, "in aperto peregrina," to enter the city of the saints. Richard de Saint-Victoire described her as the soul seeking divine revelation and Henry Lok, rejecting Solomon as a prototype of Christ, interpreted her journey as a search for merely human wisdom:[7]

> If Saba queene, a iourney tooke in hand,
>   From South to North, wise Salomon to heare;
>   If humane wisedome was to her so deare,
>   That she did visit thus his holy land;
> Then do I muse why men do idle stand,
>   In pride of youth, when wit and meanes abound,
>   Their tender braines to feed with wisedome sound,
>   Far passing that this queene in trauell found.

Few Biblical figures being more familiar to the seventeenth century than Solomon, whose Song of Songs had already influenced the pastoral tradition, Milton could confidently expect that his reference would be appreciated. The Countess, old in years and wisdom, was to see herself as the female counterpart of Solomon, and she was likely to remember that the goddess of wisdom, Sapientia, had traditionally been described in the same terms of light and splendor which greeted her ears once more under the elms at Harefield.[8] In the homage of the shepherd poets she would rightly discern their intention of forsaking Arcadian pursuits in order to worship in the presence of divine philosophy. About twenty years later, Milton was to praise the Queen of Sweden in a similar version of the Sabine myth, in which Sheba has learnt her lesson and become herself another Solomon: "Henceforward, not the queen of the south alone shall be celebrated in story. The north has now also his queen, and worthy too, not merely to go and listen to that wisest king of the Jews, or to any other, should any ever more arise like him, but to be herself the heroine to be visited by others, flocking from all quarters as to the brightest pattern of royal virtue."[9]

As a goddess of sapience, the Countess would not have misunderstood Milton's references to Latona and Cybele with which the opening song concludes. They have sometimes been interpreted as a compliment to her fecundity, as not fewer than twenty of her direct descendants are known to have been living at the time. Latona, the "ever mild" and "gentlest of the goddesses" in Hesiod, is overshadowed in mythological works by the fame of her two offspring; it is probably eccentric to suppose that Apollo and Diana can be equated with the Earl of Bridgewater and his wife, although one was the daughter and the other the stepson of the Countess, but it is certain that Latona was a northern goddess, whose shrine was in the mysterious island of the Hyperboreans and associated therefore with Britain. Her birthplace was noted for the musical accomplishments of its inhabitants, and she herself was variously allegorized as the earth or the night.[10] Milton's epithet for her, "the wise Latona," appears to be an invention which would make the thematic image of wisdom wholly unambiguous, but Natale Conti provides a gloss which gives further meaning to Milton's invocation of her name. For Conti, and for George Sandys who copied him, she was a personification of that goodness and innocence ("oblivio malorum") which, in a world afflicted by calamity, hopes to arrive at the celestial beauty.[11] To read

Conti into Milton's Latona is to focus in one word the sense of pure and sacrosanct isolation which envelops her in the masque and to append the quality of virtue to the dominant concept of wisdom.

The legend of the earth-goddess Cybele, the details of which underwent many refinements at the hands of the syncretists, remained broadly consistent, and no more suitable an annotator than Diodorus Siculus can be found for her appearance in *Arcades*. Cybele, he explained, was "admired for her intelligence; for she was the first to devize the pipe of many reeds and to invent cymbals and kettledrums . . . and in addition she taught how to heal the sicknesses of both flocks and little children by means of rites of purification."[12] She was a goddess especially reverenced by shepherds for her health-giving and protective powers. Sapience is the main image in the masque and the flight from Arcadia is the main theme. The two goddesses with whom the Countess is compared are ancillary to the image, but each contributes a little toward its extension and depth.

When the Countess reposed in her seat of State, awaiting the appearance of the masquers, there could have been little doubt in her mind about the kind of compliment she was to be paid, because it had become habitual and tactful for authors to extol her wisdom; nor, if she knew the young and ambitious poet, could she have suspected him of missing a golden opportunity. If there is one fact of which we may be imaginatively, though not historically, certain, it is that Milton would eagerly have seized his chance to do a public service for a lady whom Spenser, his "sage and serious poet," had honored forty years before. When, in 1630-34, he wrote *Arcades*, Milton was no more than a subaltern in the ranks of Christian poets fighting against the Ovidian hordes; and the redoubtable Prynne, whose *Histriomastix* appeared at this time, might well have considered *Arcades* the work of the devil. The subtle transformation of pagan into Christian myth would not, however, have gone unobserved by the recipient of *The Teares of the Muses*, which is also a Christian poem in classical disguise. Spenser's piece is a long and plaintive lament on the corrupt state of English poetry, in which the nine muses wring their hands over the deplorable levity of the upper classes, who now "Despise the brood of blessed Sapience." Until patrons are reformed, poetry will continue to decline:

> It most behoves the honorable race
> Of mightie Peeres, true wisedome to sustaine,

> And with their noble countenaunce to grace
> The learned forheads, without gifts or gaine:
> Or rather learnd themselves behoves to bee;
> That is the girlond of Nobilitie.
>
> ("Clio," ll. 79-84)

The muses finally break their "learned instruments" in despair, but Spenser's dedication of the poem to Lady Strange is, by direct implication, a compliment to her exceptional wisdom; she, almost alone in a dark era, was fit to receive the tributes of a Christian poet.

If the Countess' reputation as a sponsor of reformed poetry had begun and ended with Spenser, Milton would still have taken his cue from a master whose aspirations were so similar to his own. In 1607, however, Lok addressed a sonnet to the Countess in which she figures as a star drawing its influence from "our rare goddess, wisedome's clearest light."[13] John Davies of Hereford, who described himself as her "devoted Beadsman," prefaced his *Holy Roode* with an exhortation to abandon the "Siren-pleasures" of this world, and included a flattering portrait of the Dowager:

> *But you (with* Salomon*) have erst suruaid*
> *(Nay prou'd) the value of* Earthes *deerest* Ioyes;
> *Then hardly can your Iudgement be betray'd*
> *Unlesse* sense *will not see their* felt *annoyes.*[14]

Josias Byrd, the Countess' "ever devoted chaplain," dedicated a sermon to her which took as its theme the belief that "it is more glorious, and better, to be . . . a member of the Church, then the head of a kingdome,"[15] and William Jewel offered her a work entitled *The Golden Cabinet of true Treasure: Containing the summe of Morall Philosophie* (London, 1612). It was dedicated "To the Right Honorable and most vertuous Lady, the worthy Patronesse of Learning, Alice, Countesse of Darby, &c." and he closes his epistle with sentiments to which Milton could have given his approbation: "Your Noble minde loves the substance onelie, not the outward shew; and ioyeth more in being vertuous indeed, then in seeming so: whereby you add one vertue more unto your manie others; and deserve exceedinglie to be praised, for not desiring it." The consistency with which these dedications declare her wisdom and her interest in learning, and the piety of the works themselves, suggest that the Countess, over a long period of years, was known for her activities in the Christian cause. *Arcades,* so far as we know, was the last poetic wreath to be laid at her feet and the man who inscribed it to heavenly sapience could do so with an easy conscience.

The long soliloquy by the Genius of the Wood, which forms the body of the masque, is a kind of verbal tableau in which the visiting shepherds could perceive the benefits which would accrue from their permanent residence in a new land. They are not offered a home wholly without danger, as the sacred grove is constantly threatened not only by "evil dew" and "blasting vapours chill," but by the "canker'd venom" of the eternal serpent. Their unremitting vigilance, however, would prevent these evils from establishing themselves in Christian territory. The ancestry of the shepherds, moreover, dictates their emigration: "Of famous *Arcady* ye are, and sprung / Of that renowned flood, so often sung, / Divine *Alpheus,* who by secret sluse, / Stole under Seas to meet his *Arethuse.*" The genealogy of the wanderers is itself a prophecy of their quest for divine wisdom. George Sandys gives two versions of the myth, both of which are probably fused in this passage. In one, Alpheus "signifies blots or imperfections" and Arethusa "is by interpretation Vertue"; in the other, Fulgentian, version, "Alpheus is the light of Truth, and Arethusa the excellency of equity."[16] In the image of Alpheus, therefore, Milton could discern a shepherd (or a poet) who was "divine" by right and yet blotted with the sin which would require his pilgrimage to the goddess Latona; for Arethusa, or virtue, was a stream which rose from the ocean in the island of Ortygia, and it was on this island that Latona had given birth to Apollo and Diana. The shepherd-poets, by visiting Latona in the park at Harefield, were but re-enacting the drama of their first ancestor, with the single difference that Alpheus had gone "under Seas" to Ortygia in the south, while the Arcadians had (presumably) traveled overland to a comparable island in the north. The parallel is another example of Milton's skill in transferring the Arcadian myth into a Christianized landscape.

The Genius is an appropriate person to greet the pilgrims because, like the shepherds, he is of classical or pagan origin: "For know by lot from *Jove* I am the powr / Of this fair Wood, and live in Oak'n bowr." It is from Jove, not the wise Latona, that he receives his commission "To nurse the Saplings tall, and curl the grove," but he has also found a "great Mistres . . . Whom with low reverence I adore as mine." His devotion to her—and of this the shepherds should take note—has not prevented him from practising his old arts, but he has gained the power of listening to the celestial harmony. No "grosse unpurged ear" was able to hear it, but the converted Genius now ponders the "sweet compulsion [which] doth in musick ly, / To lull the daughters of *Necessity*, / And keep unsteddy Nature to her law." The music of the spheres had once before, in Marston's "Entertainment," pealed in honor of the Dowager,[17] but Milton invoked the heavenly choir with a far deeper understanding than Marston of what his praise would imply. Only if the Countess was an image of that sapience which, in Spenser's "Hymn of Heavenly Beautie," was the loveliest attribute of God, could the genius proclaim that "such musick worthiest were to blaze / The peerles height of her immortal praise."

Arcades is, or should be, a *locus classicus* in the seventeenth-century pastoral genre, for it epitomizes the growing dissatisfaction with the Arcadian ideal. The pastoral's revival in the Renaissance had preserved within itself the seeds of its own destruction, since the Virgilian model, especially the First Eclogue, had never offered a simple idealization of country life. Common sense, also, would have instructed poets that a rural retreat devoid of sin would deprive their bucolics of all possibility of drama. The general pattern of their compromise with primitivism was a paradise in which the disruptive forces of contention, infamy, or despair had temporarily taken root, and the expulsion of these extraneous elements restored the garden to its prelapsarian state. For Milton, however, the conversion of the pagan world, not a compromise with it, was the only legitimate aim of a Christian. Dr. Hamilton has suggested that Spenser had a similar intention in writing *The Shepheardes Calender,* but if the breaking of Colin's pipes symbolizes his rejection of the pastoral mode in favor of a more dedicated life in the world, the symbolism is not as clear as it is in the final song of *Arcades*.[18] The shepherds are openly encouraged to "Bring your Flocks, and live with us" (a fine ironic inversion of the Marlovian line), and the masque closes with a succinct mythical allusion which clearly repeats the invitation. It would be better, as Du Bartas advised,[19] to sing the destruction of paganism than the praises of "th' *Arcadian* king":

> Though *Syrinx* your *Pans* Mistress were,
> Yet *Syrinx* well might wait on her.
>   Such a rural Queen
> All *Arcadia* hath not seen.

At least four distinct interpretations of Syrinx existed in the Renaissance. The first, which is not applicable to *Arcades*, believed Siringa to be the celestial harmony, and the second associated her with human music because the Greeks had given her name to an instrument. Boccaccio mentioned the first meaning sympathetically but rejected it in favor of another. Syrinx was "una opra di natura armonizata con tanto ordine, che mentre con continuo tratto è guidata a in certo, e determinato fine, ci faccia una armonia non punto differente da quella dei buoni cantori, il che è gratissimo a Iddio"; a modification of this view reappears in Bacon where the nymph is an "exact and measured" kind of discourse. Finally Phillipe de Vitry considered Syrinx to be the worldly pleasure which causes our loss of the eternal happiness, and for an anonymous poet of the fourteenth century she was "Ces delits vains et variables, / Qui sont faintis et decevables."[20] Syrinx in *Paradise Regain'd* (II, 188) is given as an example of a rare beauty whom the wiles of Satan have seduced, so Milton's own understanding of the myth would appear to combine the Boccaccian interpretation with the more sternly moral views of the medieval writers. In *Arcades*, Syrinx operates as a metaphor for the naturally melodious poet who, corrupted by the world, is exhorted to bring his talents to the throne of sapience.

To read *Arcades* in terms of a pilgrimage from the profane to the religious, from the classical south to the Christian north, from Saba to Solomon, is to make it consonant with all we know about Milton's early life and work, and his twin themes of renunciation and aspiration are nowhere better illustrated than in his first masque. Furthermore, *Arcades* shows how the persons to whom masques were directed may play an integral part in the structure of the entertainments. The central symbol of *Arcades* is the Countess, personifying heavenly wisdom, but in no part of the text is she so described. No amount of research into the history of Cybele and Latona, with whom she is tentatively compared, would yield the correct knowledge of her symbolic identity, and neither would the brightness which surrounds her, nor the celestial music overhead provide of itself sufficient evidence. But the unmistakable presence of the Sabine myth and the confirmatory facts of the Dowager's reputation, can leave no doubt of her dramatic significance. Without her the journey of the shepherds would have no more point than a picnic, and the masque no existence at all.

NOTES

1. Virgil B. Heltzel, "Sir Thomas Egerton as Patron," *HLB*, XI (February, 1948), 105-27.
2. *Ibid.*, p. 113.
3. Gainsford, *The History of Trebizond* (London, 1616); Marston, "Entertainment of Alice, Dowager-Countess of Derby," *Works,* ed. A. H. Bullen (London, 1887), III, 383-404; T. N. G. [Thomas Newton], *Atropoïon Delion, or, The death of Delia: With Teares of her Funerall* (London, 1603). For sonnets and Davies see below. The fullest account of works dedicated to the Countess occurs in David Masson, *The Life of John Milton* (London, 1881), I, 590-602 and in Thomas Heywood, *The Earle of Derby and the Verse Writers and Poets of the Sixteenth and Seventeenth Centuries,* Printed for the Chetham Society (Manchester, 1853).
4. *Life,* I, 592.
5. *Arcades* is quoted in this essay from *The Works of John Milton,* ed. F. A. Patterson *et al.* (New York, 1931), I, 72-76.
6. *Du Bartas His Devine Weekes and Workes,* trans. Josuah Sylvester (London, 1613), "The Magnificence," p. 588. Also Thomas Fuller, *Poems,* ed. Grosart (1868), p. 103.
7. Isidorus, *PL,* LXXXIII, 113; Nolanus, *PL,* LXI, 168; Richard de S-V., *PL,* CXCVI, 180; Henry Lok, *Miscellanies of the Fuller Worthies' Library,* ed. A. B. Grosart (n.p., 1871), II, 197.
8. Convenient summaries of this tradition are contained in the notes on "The Hymn of Heavenly Beautie" in *The Works of Edmund Spenser: A Variorum Edition,* ed. Edwin Greenlaw *et al.* (Baltimore, 1943) and in Joseph B. Collins, *Christian Mysticism in the Elizabethan Age* (Baltimore, 1940), pp. 215-31.
9. *A Second Defence* in *Works,* VIII, 107, 109.
10. See especially Diodorus Siculus, trans. C. H. Oldfather, Loeb Classical Library (Cambridge, Mass., 1935), II, 47; Boccaccio, *La Geneologia de gli dei de gentili,* trans. Giuseppe Betussi (Venice, 1581), Bk. IV; Vincenzo Cartari, *Imagini de gli dei delli antichi* (Padua, 1626), Section on Apollo, p. 48; Lilius Gregorius Gyraldus, *Opera Omnia* (Basel, 1696) I, 384. Daremberg, *Dictionnaire des Antiquités* (Paris, 1904) has a summary. For Latona's connection with England, see A. O. Lovejoy and G. Boas, *Primitivism and Related Ideas in Antiquity* (Baltimore, 1935), p. 307. Merritt Hughes in his ed. of Milton (New York, 1937) also annotates the "wise Latona" from Conti.
11. Conti, *Mythologiae sive explicationis fabularum libri decem* (Patavii, 1616), Bk. IX, 6; Sandys, *Ovids Metamorphosis Englished, Myth-*

ologiz'd and Represented in Figures (London, 1640), commentary on Bk. VI, p. 116.

12. Diodorus Siculus, III, 58; Gyraldus, I, 137-50, has a lengthy summary. Besides sections on Cybele or Rhea in works already cited, see Albricus, *Deorum Imaginibus Libellus* in *Auctores Mythographi Latini,* ed. A. van Staveren (Amsterdam, 1742), sect. 12; Third Vatican Mythographer in *Scriptores Rerum Mythicarum,* ed. G. H. Bode (Cellis, 1834), p. 157; Alexander Ross, *Mystagogus Poeticus* (London, 1653), pp. 375-78.

13. *Miscellanies,* ed. Grosart, p. 372.

14. *The Complete Works of John Davies of Hereford,* ed. A. B. Grosart (Edinburgh, 1878), Vol. I. Davies also dedicated *Summa Totalis* as well as a sonnet in *The Scourge of Folly* to the Countess and her husband.

15. *Loves Peerless Paragon, or The Attributes and Progresse of the Church* (Oxford, 1613), ded. epistle. After my paper had been accepted for publication, Dr. F. B. Williams of Georgetown University very kindly sent me a complete list of works dedicated to the Countess. It included the following additional titles: Barnabe Barnes, presentation verses (not dedication) in *Parthenophil and Parthenope* (1593); Thomas Anyan, *A Sermon on Act Sunday* (1612); John Whalley, *God's Plentie Feeding True Pietie* (1616); Pierre du Moulin, *A Treatise of the Knowledge of God,* trans. R. Codrington (1634).

16. *Ovid,* p. 102. D. C. Allen, "Milton's Alpheus," *MLN,* LXXI (March, 1956), 172-73 has applied the Fulgentian interpretation to lines in "Lycidas."

17. *Works,* ed. Bullen, III, 396.

18. A. C. Hamilton, "The Argument of Spenser's *Shepheardes Calender,*" *ELH,* XXIII (September, 1956), 171-82. But Milton is transforming, not rejecting, the pastoral mode.

19. "Urania," in *Workes* (1613), p. 666.

20. Boccaccio, *op. cit.,* section on Pan in Bk. I; Bacon, *De Sapientia Veterum* in *Works,* ed. Spedding, Ellis, Heath (London, 1870), VI, 714; de Vitry, *Les Oeuvres* (Reims, 1850), p. 143; *Ovide Moralisé,* ed. C. de Boer, in *Verhandelingen der Koninklijke Akademie,* New Series, Vol. XIV (Amsterdam, 1914), ll. 4053-54. Conti, Cartari, Ross, and Gyraldus associate Syrinx with human music, although Gyraldus hints at an obscure and untraceable allegory translated from the Greek by his friend A. Thilesius (*Opera,* II, 452).

[EDITOR'S NOTE. See the studies of Milton's early poems listed with the preceding essays.]

SEARS JAYNE

The Subject of Milton's Ludlow *Mask*

I

If, as Professor Adams complains, Milton's *Comus* has been "over-read,"[1] the chief reason is that we are still trying to find out what the masque means. In spite of the wide acceptance given to Professor Woodhouse's theological interpretation of the work,[2] critics keep twisting the dials, trying to sharpen the focus. The difficulty is that none of the adjustments tried so far brings the whole narrative into focus at once.

For example, a good deal of the narrative of the masque is obviously a poetic transposition of the Circe myth from the *Odyssey*,[3] but if one tries to focus the whole masque in terms of that myth, one loses sight of the two brothers and Sabrina.

Similarly, many details of the masque seem to have been dictated by the occasion for which it was written; the work makes fair sense simply as a *Masque of Parenthood*, enumerating the many ways in which the Earl has ensured the virtue of his children: by heredity, by education, by employing a bodyguard (Thyrsis),[4] and by the influence of the traditional family environment (Sabrina as Severn). But this reading, too, has defects; though it keeps the Circe myth in

From *PMLA*, LXXIV (1959), 533-43, with some revisions by the author. Reprinted by permission of the author and the Modern Language Association of America.

focus (as appropriate to the classical education of the children), it loses entirely the religious meanings of the masque.

Religious implications are unquestionably present. The Attendant Spirit is not only Thyrsis, and Mercury, but also a guardian angel. The influence of "Heaven" upon the action of the masque[5] is emphasized again and again, by the brothers, by the Lady, by the Attendant Spirit, and even by Comus. Other religious implications may be seen in the catechism to which Comus subjects the Lady (ll. 277-291), in the Lady's reference (ll. 213-215) to faith, hope, and chastity,[6] and in the unmistakable allusions to the "Father's house" as the realm of glory, on "holier" ground than Comus' palace. Indeed, the theological overtones of the masque are so impressive that the most popular current interpretation of the work sees it as an allegory of the Christian doctrine of Grace, in which the Lady (the human soul) fails to escape sensuality when she depends upon reason (haemony) in the realm of nature, but succeeds when she is assisted by Grace[7] (Sabrina).

Even this reading, however, leaves many important elements of the masque unclear. The action of the masque is not clearly divided between the two realms of nature and grace; if anything, it is divided into three realms: nature, grace, and glory. Moreover, the help afforded by Sabrina is not the only grace-like assistance given to the Lady in the masque; haemony and the Attendant Spirit also help. Finally, the theological reading does not account well for the elaborate philosophical equipage of the masque. It is this philosophical element which I believe provides the real clue to the meaning of the masque.

II

The philosophical meanings of Milton's *Mask* have not been neglected, of course, in the copious criticism of the work.[8] Both Platonism and Stoicism are present, and both have been much discussed, but usually in terms of their classical forms. Thus Milton's Platonism has usually been discussed in terms of Milton's borrowings from the dialogues of Plato.[9] What I mean to propose here is that in the Ludlow *Mask* Milton's Platonism is not classical Platonism, but Renaissance Platonism, and Milton's principal authority is not Plato, but Ficino.

The prejudices against this suggestion are extremely deep, and I must acknowledge them in some detail. For one thing, Milton nowhere in any extant work mentions Ficino or acknowledges his debt to him, whereas he cites Plato frequently. The answer to this is that just as no self-respecting modern scholar would cite Jowett in order to show that he understood Plato, though the modern scholar's view of Plato (if he is the average literary critic) is usually Jowett's, so Milton's view of Plato was probably Ficino's, though it would not have occurred to him to cite Ficino. Moreover, Milton does acknowledge his debt to Spenser,[10] especially on the subjects treated in the Ludlow *Mask,* and a debt to Spenser on these subjects is largely a debt to Ficino.

Another prejudice against thinking of Milton as a Renaissance Platonist rises from Milton's own statement in the *Apology for Smectymnuus,* where he reviews his own study of chastity as having proceeded from medieval romance, to Plato and Xenophon, to Christianity.[11] Milton's autobiographical statement, upon which most interpretations of the masque have rested heavily, seems to separate Platonism from Christianity, and to identify Platonism with the works of ancient Greeks only. But this statement does not mean that Milton went from romanticism to paganism to Christianity; it means only that he became learned in philosophy before he became learned in theology. At no stage of Milton's career would Platonism have been, for him, the non-Christian rationalist philosophy which most modern readers associate with the names "Plato" and "Xenophon."

Most modern readers are rationalists; what they know about Plato they have learned from nineteenth-century rationalists such as Jowett and Taylor, who followed Leibnitz in distinguishing Platonism from Neoplatonism as rationalism from mysticism. Twentieth-century scholarship, however, has shown that most of the crucially "mystical" doctrines of the Neoplatonists are present in the canonical dialogues of Plato himself, especially the *Parmenides* and the *Timaeus,* and that the old distinction between Platonism and Neoplatonism no longer obtains.[12] But one need not prove that Plato was a Neoplatonist in order to realize that the distinction between Platonism and Neoplatonism was not available to Milton. The Renaissance did not use the term "Neoplatonism"; neither Milton nor any other Renaissance scholar distinguished Platonism from Neoplatonism. For them there were only "Platonists," the standard view being that Plato had deliberately shrouded his meaning in images and fables and that that meaning had not been discovered until later, as Plato himself predicted it would be, by Porphyry, Proclus, Iamblichus, and the Pseudo-Dionysius.[13] Although it is usual today in literary criticism to refer to the Renaissance version of the Platonic tradition as Renaissance "Neoplatonism" (in order to indicate that the Renaissance tradition was more influenced by Plotinus than by Plato), for Milton and his contemporaries the distinctive characteristics of Platonism had nothing to do with the differences between Plato and Plotinus. The seventeenth-century reader distinguished Platonism from the other formal philosophies, such as Stoicism, Cynicism, and Aristotelianism, by two distinctive characteristics: first, it was more mythological[14] than the others, and second, it was more Christian[15] than the others.

If, instead of coming to Milton's *Mask* from the Christian doctrine of nature and grace, or from the classical doctrine of *sophrosyne,* one comes to it from the point of view of the Renaissance Platonist, one sees that for Milton Platonism, mythology, and Christianity were already completely synthesized, and that he was merely trying his hand at a technique of mythologized Christian Platonism which had been popular ever since the time of Ficino.

III

The *Mask* begins with a speech of the Attendant Spirit in which he explains the setting, the world in which the action of the masque is to take place. With this speech the reader is plunged immediately into the mythological language of Renaissance Platonism, and in order to understand the world which the Spirit describes one must translate that language.

It was Ficino who set the fashion of discussing Platonic doctrines in mythological language. The language of Ficino's *Theologia Platonica* and his other most influential works, the *Epistolae* and the *Opera Platonis* (including his commentaries on the dialogues) is a language distinctively mythological. Thus we see him in the *Epistolae* saying: "When rich and powerful Juno does not hear us . . . we must seek our help entirely from Minerva . . . For no power can lift man to the ethereal head of the universe except one which has itself sprung from the head of Jove."[16]

We know from other passages in the *Epistolae* (see fol. clxxii[v]) that Juno stands for the active life, and Minerva for the contemplative life. Through the influence of Ficino, these and other Platonic allegorizations gradually replaced the older Christian moralizations of classical mythology. This Platonized mythology became, during the revival of learning, the raw material of painters,[17] sculptors, and poets, including Spenser and Milton.

Among the more commonplace identifications of Platonic mythology is Ficino's reference to the Neoplatonic triad of the One, the Angelic Mind, and the World Soul as Uranus, Saturn, and Jupiter.[18] It is this Platonic meaning of Jupiter as the World Soul that we see in Spenser's Mutabilitie cantos, and it is this same Jupiter that we see in Milton's masque. Jupiter, in the masque, is not God, but the World Soul. Milton's reference to "high and nether Jove" (1.20) is probably not, as most editors guess, a reference to Zeus and Hades, but a technical reference to the fact that the World Soul in "Platonic" doctrine conventionally has two parts, an upper and a lower layer, which we may think of in plain language as constituting the World Body and the World Soul, respectively.[19] The general view of the relation between the World Soul (as Jove) and human affairs may be seen as far back as Cicero's exposition of Platonism in the *Academic Questions,* where he explains that the Platonists believe the world to be controlled by a World Soul, a providence watching over everything subject to its rule, including the heavenly bodies and all human affairs.[20] Ficino emphasizes the protective as well as the directive powers of Jove[21] and explains that his influence upon human affairs is accomplished by means of daemons, which "mix agreeably and eagerly in the governing of lower things, but especially of human affairs, and from this friendly service they all seem good; but some Platonists and Christian theologians claim that there are also bad daemons . . . The good daemons, our protectors, Dionysius the Areopagite usually calls by the name angels, the governors of the lower world, and this differs little from the interpretation of Plato" (*Commentary on the Symposium,* p. 185).

This is the background of the Attendant Spirit in Milton's *Mask;* he is referred to consistently in the Trinity MS as a "daemon," or "guardian daemon," and we should think of him in the poem not as an angel from St. Peter's heaven, but as a Platonic airy spirit, carrying out the last stage in the process of emanation from God to the outermost circle of the World Soul. Moreover, we may associate Jupiter with the astrological functions of the World Soul. According to Ficino the various planets can be referred to in terms of their specific kinds of influence: "Attending to this process are the several kinds of daemons, mediaries between heavenly beings and men. Jupiter gives us the power of governing and ruling through the service of Jovian daemons."[22] This aspect of Jove, Jove as governor, is one of the associations which contributes to the flattery of the new President of Wales in Milton's *Mask*.

But for Milton, as for Ficino, another kind of association with the name Jupiter was more important than the astrological one. In the Christian column of his mythology Ficino equates Jove with divine providence, communicated to man through the services of Mercury, that is the angels (*Epistolae,* fol. clxxii^{r-v}). Divine providence is distinguished by the Platonists from natural providence, in the same way that Christian theologians distinguished between the orders of nature and grace.[23] In Ficino divine providence is normally represented by Jove and natural providence by Prometheus (*Epistolae,* fols. iii^r and xli^v).

In the Ludlow *Mask* Milton adopts the distinction between divine and natural providence, and he uses Jove, as Ficino does, to represent divine providence. But the Prometheus myth did not suit his purposes for natural providence, so he used a different myth for that, a myth suggested by another Platonist, Petrus Calanna.[24] In Calanna's version, natural providence is represented by Neptune, whose authority in myth is always subordinate to and corresponds with the authority of Jove. In making everything in his masque take place in the realm of Neptune, Milton refers not only to England's insularity, but also to the philosophical relationship between the realm of natural providence (Neptune) and that of divine providence (Jupiter). Since natural providence cannot conflict with divine providence, everything that happens in Neptune's realm happens under Jove's jurisdiction as well. The correspondence between the two realms is emphasized in the masque in several ways. The Attendant Spirit, for example, says in the epilogue that his route back to heaven lies by way of the ocean, and he is able to summon the river goddess, Sabrina. Moreover, the Attendant Spirit and Comus are paralleled in great detail; the Attendant Spirit does not stay to defeat Comus when he sees the girl in his clutches, nor does he himself attack Comus with the haemony. Comus, as one agent of natural providence, argues quite rightly that his functions are natural, that is, they are possible within the realm of natural providence: but a soul's rejection of him is also equally "natural."[25] The alternative which is put before the Lady is not a choice between natural and unnatural, but between two equally natural courses; the other victims of Comus have all chosen the fleshly alternative, but the Lady chooses the course which preserves more fully her freedom, her capacity ultimately to throw off the chains of the body and return to God. Her choice is made with the sanction of divine providence, but also, because she is still in the flesh, with the sanction of natural providence.

Thus, insofar as the masque deals at all with the problem of nature and grace, it seems to me to deal with it not in the terms of Christian theology alone, as Mr. Woodhouse has suggested, but also in terms of the mythology of Christian Platonism, as a relation between the realms of divine and natural providence.

An analogous case in the masque is the background of the light imagery. One could argue that Milton shows the action of the poem as taking place in the dark because in the Renaissance table of correspondences between the four elements and the four times of day the element of water, in whose realm the action occurs, corresponds with the night part of the daily cycle; one could also argue that Milton's treatment of light imagery is essentially Christian, with backgrounds in James i.17, Dante, and elsewhere. Both of these explanations are doubtless correct, but in the masque they melt connotatively into the syncretism of Christian Platonism.[26] It was inevitable in a Platonic allegory that the relation between God and the physical world should be expressed in terms of light imagery, with God, as the sun, at the center of the universe, and all physical things at the outer extremities, in varying degrees of darkness. Critics who wish to read the Ludlow masque as an allegory of nature and grace have sometimes been disturbed by the fact that the darkness of the realm of nature at the beginning of the masque does not give way to the light of grace at the end. The explanation, I believe, lies in the fact that the masque is not primarily about nature and grace, but about the soul's achievement of Platonic *castitas*. The fact that it is still dark at the end of the poem merely indicates that the whole action of the achievement of chastity takes place in the realm of natural providence, that is, while the soul is still in the body. To understand what Milton's concept of *chastity* involves, we must return to the second important characteristic of Renaissance Platonism; it was not only more mythologized than other philosophies, but also more Christianized.

IV

The correspondence between Platonism and Christianity for Renaissance thinkers centered in the fact that both doctrines appeared to give identical accounts of the ascending and descending relations between God and man. The details of the correspondence, including the identification of the Platonic Good, or One, with the Christian God, were worked out by Ficino, and English theologians from Colet onwards continually used Platonic language and myth to revitalize the Christian account. The standard view may be illustrated in this passage from Ficino:

> The soul originally lived contentedly in the presence of God; then, because of its desire for love of the body, it fell into the body and joined with the body, where it was swamped with forgetfulness and with the ignorance whence all evil springs. This physical world reflects the nature of that divine world, presenting to us visibilia by which we may surmise the nature of the invisible world. The soul is easily excited to a desire for heaven because it is naturally inclined in that direction. But even sunk as it is in a gross body, the soul can still escape the effects of the body. It eventually remembers truer things, recalling its proper nature and its natural seat; recognizing the baseness of the body and loathing it, the soul seeks to return to heaven, where it enjoys nectar and ambrosia, that is the knowledge and enjoyment of God. Stimulated by memory, the soul seeks and finds its wings again; it rouses itself from its dead body, it awakes from its sleep, it emerges from the river Lethe and straining the long-unused wings of its goodness and wisdom it flies back to heaven.[27]

Thus Christian "Platonism" saw human life in three stages: 1. the descent of the soul from heaven into the prison of the flesh; 2. the struggle of the soul against the demands of the flesh; and 3. the return of the victorious soul to heaven. It is the second stage, of course, which most interests Milton. The distinctive thing about the soul in that stage, according to Ficino's account,[28] is its intermediary position between the physical and spiritual worlds; it is capable of looking both ways, drawn both by love of the body and by love of God, both by the centrifugal force of the emanating process and by the centripetal force of the returning process in the cosmic breathing. In order to return to God, the soul must at some moment in its existence turn from love of the flesh to love of God; there must be in the life of the soul, that is, some turning point, some moment at which the soul reverses the emphasis, between its twin affections, from physical to spiritual and begins the return part of the *"circuitus spiritualis."* Ficino lists seven ways in which this turning point of rejection of the flesh, withdrawal of the soul from the material world, may be accomplished before physical death: among these are dreams, visions, poetic trance, religious trance, and chastity[29] (that is, willed rejection of bodily sense and desire). Thus chastity is not so much a condition as a particular event, the achievement of a turning point in the history of the soul.[30]

The means by which the soul achieves chastity can be understood only in terms of an analysis of the nature of the soul. Ficino's view of the soul is that it is equipped for its distinctive median position between the physical and the spiritual by having two parts: a lower soul consisting of the appetitive and irascible passions, and an upper soul consisting not merely of reason, but also of an additional part called the mind (*mens angelicus*). The function of the reason, as in Plato, is to control the lower parts of the soul; the function of the *mens* is to preserve the vision or memory of divinity which the soul brings with it from its life before this incarnation and which provides the means by which the soul finds its way back to God. In order to achieve chastity, or release from the bondage of the flesh, the reason part of the soul must first conquer the passions, but this alone is not enough; in order to escape its prison of the flesh the soul must not only free itself of the influence of the passions, through reason, but also, through the *mens,* remember its own previous purely spiritual (chaste) state and so be led by the *mens*[31] away from the flesh and back toward God. Reason makes the change possible by eliminating the pull on the soul from the flesh, but the soul would remain stationary if the *mens* did not exert a counter-pull back toward God.

This is the nature of the *act* of chastity in terms of Ficino's exposition of the nature of the soul. A useful illustration of the idea in Renaissance allegorical painting is a painting of Bandinelli entitled "The Combat of Ratio and Libido,"[32] which shows a battle between two armies of Roman deities, one representing reason and the other representing the passions. In the clouds above stands a female figure, *Mens,* the remaining part of the Ficinian soul, waiting to lead the soul to heaven as soon as reason has conquered the passions. It is this particular conception of the soul and of chastity, I believe, which Milton allegorizes in the Ludlow *Mask.*

V

Milton divides the narrative action[33] of the masque into three scenes corresponding to the three motions of the soul, descending, stopped, and ascending. We first see the soul moving away from God in the physical world subject to the demands of the flesh. Second we see the soul halt its downward (or outward) motion using reason and philosophy to reach the point of no motion, the "hinge" of its career; third we see it with the help of the *mens* begin its upward (or inward) motion away from the flesh and back toward God. The human soul is represented in the poem not merely by the Lady, but jointly by the Lady and Sabrina; the Lady represents the Reason, and Sabrina represents the *mens*.

In the first scene, of 658 lines, Reason is shown wandering in the dark wood of physical existence, where the principal danger is that she may succumb to either the appetitive or the irascible passions; this is what the Younger Brother means in referring to "the direful grasp / Of Savage hunger or of Savage heat" (ll. 357-358). As it turns out, the Lady is subjected to both kinds of passion, but in reverse order. Under the influence (the magic dust) of her physical nature (Comus), the Lady is first subjected to the "irascible" passion of fear, by means of which Comus lures her to his palace, and then to all the "appetitive" passions at once, as Comus attempts to seduce her.

In the second scene, of only 300 lines, the heroine is shown immobilized in a chair in the enchanter's palace. The seat in which Comus forces the lady to sit may be interpreted as the seat of forgetfulness (Arthos, p. 46) in which the soul sits during its sojourn in the body, but the soul is still, in Platonism, as in Christian theology, free to reject the body. The important significance of the immobility of the Lady in the palace of Comus as opposed to her former mobility under his influence in the forest is that whereas in the forest she accepted him, in the palace she has rejected his desires, and this rejection results in her being paralyzed. Her paralysis represents the point of stopped motion in the emanation of the soul away from God toward the flesh.

As a matter of fact, the Lady is paralyzed in two stages. So long as she merely rejects Comus' attentions, she is merely fastened to the chair; thus innate human reason,[34] uninstructed, is able temporarily to reject the passions, but the Lady can still move enough to accept or reject Comus' cup, as the unassisted reason is still subject to temptation. Only when Comus has been banished by the haemony, that is, when reason is fortified by philosophical knowledge, does the soul banish temptation entirely; at the same time the departing Comus waves his wand and paralyzes the Lady completely, symbolizing the fact that only in this final rejection, both rational and philosophical, does the soul lose entirely its motion toward the flesh.

In the explanation just given I have identified haemony with philosophy. The standard Renaissance allegorization of moly in the Circe myth was reason, the power by which Odysseus conquered sensuality. Milton says that haemony is more efficacious than the moly of Odysseus. By this I think Milton means that though the uninstructed reason can control passion on any individual occasion, permanent protection is afforded only by philosophical training, adding principle to practice. The background of this distinction between reason and philosophy as the two states in the pursuit of temperance is to be found not in Ficino but in Poliziano.[35] In his introduction to Plato's *Charmides*,[36] Poliziano explains that the ultimate object of all human life is sapience, or the knowledge of God; indeed this is what is meant by philosophy, or love of wisdom;[37] but the pursuit of sapience is too esoteric an occupation for the rude and unlettered masses. The soul must have rejected sensation before it can acquire philosophical insight: "Only when a farmer has completely cleared fields of roots and briars may he then at last begin to sow his seed; in the same way, only when a man has cast out of his soul all desires . . . using the fire and sword of self-discipline, may he then receive into his purged soul the true seed [of philosophy]. Only then will that seed, unhampered by the choking weeds and thorns of burgeoning desire, grow to maturity and bear the fruit of happiness" (*Opera*, pp. 297-298).

Thus, according to Poliziano, the two steps toward the regeneration of the soul are first, temperance and second, philosophical instruction. That instruction, according to Poliziano, and the Platonists generally, is always given by means of symbols. The "prisci theologi," from Orpheus and Homer to Plato, always shrouded their teachings in myths and fables, to protect the sanctity of the truth against the irreverent barbarism of the unworthy. As an illustration of this principle Poliziano cites the myth of Circe and Ulysses and explains the allegorical meaning of the herb *moly,* which Mercury brought to Ulysses, as divine philosophy.

In the *Mask* Milton has borrowed Poliziano's idea and invented a new name, haemony, for the herb which transcends moly, as philosophy transcends reason. Haemony, then, represents Christian philosophical knowledge, divine philosophy,[38] which assists in the rescue of the girl. The brothers are used in the poem only to explain by their discourse the meaning of the herb which they later bring to the assistance of their sister. That is, their function in the masque is not so much narrative as expository. Between them they expound the philosophical idealist's attitude toward chastity: the Elder Brother representing the idealist's faith in the superiority and inviolability of the soul, and the Younger Brother representing the patience which the idealist must necessarily exercise; the element of patience, stressed by the Attendant Spirit at the end of the masque, though commonly associated with Stoicism, is emphasized by many Christian Platonists, including Ficino and Colet (*Epistolae,* fol. cix[r]). The Lady, as reason exercising temperance, takes the first step of the soul toward the achievement of chastity by herself. The Brothers, with the haemony representing philosophical education, take the second step. The exigencies of Milton's structure require that he expound through the dialogue of the Brothers the nature of the philosophy (haemony) before it appears in the narrative, and this fact tends to confuse the reader, but the *narrative* sequence is the same as the allegorical sequence; the Lady's rejection of Comus by reasoned choice precedes her defense against him by philosophical idealism and patience.

The link between haemony and philosophy in the masque is suggested not only by the function of the Brothers, but also by several other details. Like philosophy, for example, the haemony is said to have been provided by a human being:

> a certain Shepherd Lad
> Of small regard to see to, yet well skill'd
> In every virtuous plant and healing herb
> That spreads her verdant leaf to th'morning ray.
> He lov'd me well, and often would beg me sing,
> Which when I did, he on the tender grass
> Would sit, and hearken even unto ecstasy,
> And in requital ope his leathern scrip,
> And show me simples of a thousand names.
> Telling their strange and vigorous faculties;
>
> (ll. 619-628)

Since the speaker is Lawes, it is tempting to see in the Shepherd Lad a reference to Milton himself in his relation to Lawes: he admiring

Lawes' musicianship, and Lawes being impressed with Milton's academic learning; certainly Milton's learning in the poems is well described in the reference to "a thousand names." A further indication
that Milton is following Poliziano in using haemony to represent divine philosophy is the fact that as philosophy was regarded as rightly
and necessarily esoteric, not available to the uninitiated, so the Attendant Spirit says of haemony that it is

> Unknown and like esteem'd, and the dull swain
> Treads on it daily with his clouted shoon
>
> (ll. 634-635)

Those who see haemony as Christian grace or Christ's atonement
argue that haemony represents a power superior to that of the Attendant Spirit since the Attendant Spirit says it has protected him and
that he received it from a shepherd. But the Spirit is there speaking
in his disguise as shepherd. As an agent of divine providence he is
merely making up this account with perhaps an indirect reference to
Milton's having contributed to the philosophical education of the
boys.

With the help of philosophical knowledge, then, the soul is able to
prevent further temptation by the passions or, in Neoplatonic terms,
it ceases to look outward and away from God in the direction of the
body; but it does not make the actual turn in the *circuitus spiritualis*
back toward God except by the action of the *mens*, or mind, that part
of the soul which is the spark of divinity in it, that part in which is
lodged the memory of God from the previous life of the soul before its
present incarnation.

In the action of the poem this final stage in the achievement of
"chastity" is represented by Sabrina's restoring of motion to the paralyzed girl. In both Christian and Platonic doctrine, as in common
sense, one of the distinctive attributes of life is voluntary, "original"
motion (i.e. uncaused motion). The standard view is expressed in the
Dream of Scipio, where Cicero says that the eternality of God is
shown by the fact that he is the first mover of the world. Similarly
the soul must be immortal since it is the mover of the body; "whatsoever is moved of itself," says Cicero, "is eternal."[39] In showing the
mind as causing the motion of the body, Milton was dramatizing the
basic relation between soul and body as it was understood by the Platonists.[40]

The distinctive characteristics of the *mens* part of the soul are its immateriality, its immortality, and its memory. Like the *mens*, Sabrina is both immaterial and immortal. Her immateriality she herself indicates:

> Thus I set my printless feet
> O'er the Cowslip's Velvet head,
> That bends not as I tread.
>
> (ll. 897-899)

Her immortality is pointed out by the Attendant Spirit, who explains that Sabrina has achieved chastity at an earlier stage of her existence, at which time, having demonstrated herself as "sincerely" chaste by plunging into a river, she was given over to the daughters of Nereus

> to imbathe
> In nectar'd lavers strew'd with Asphodel,
> And through the porch and inlet of each sense
> Dropt in Ambrosial Oils till she reviv'd
> And underwent a quick immortal change,
> Made Goddess of the River.
>
> (ll. 837-842)

The religious character of Sabrina's experience is suggested by the references to nectar and ambrosia, which, in Platonic mythology, meant respectively knowledge and enjoyment of God. Sabrina knows how to turn the soul toward God primarily because she remembers having done it before; the soul is able to turn toward God because it retains a memory of God from having gone through the process of achieving chastity in a previous incarnation. The nature of that process is described by the Elder Brother in terms which make the parallel with Sabrina unmistakable:

> So dear to Heav'n is Saintly chastity
> That when a soul is found sincerely so,
> A thousand liveried Angels lackey her,[41]
> Driving far off each thing of sin and guilt,
> And in clear dream and solemn vision
> Tell her of things no gross ear can hear,
> Till oft converse with heav'nly habitants
> Begin to cast a beam on th'outward shape,
> The unpolluted temple of the mind,

And turns it by degrees to the soul's essence,
Till all be made immortal . . .

(ll. 453-463)

This account not only recapitulates Sabrina's career; it also forecasts
the Lady's career: the Attendant Spirit ("liveried Angel") drives off
Comus (thing of sin and guilt), whereupon Sabrina tells the Lady
"of things no gross ear can hear," applying the salve of memory to
rid the soul of its *oblivio* and remind it of the divinity it has forgotten.
In reminding the soul of its home with God, the *mens* acts as agent
of God, but it is an agency working through the process of natural
providence; thus Sabrina is shown as an agent (goddess) of Neptune.
If, in Sabrina, God is stooping to assist the human soul, that stooping
is done through the normal machinery of natural providence, seen in
the fact that the soul by nature includes a *mens,* or spark of divine
memory, among its parts. Thus, when the Younger Brother asks:
"What hidden strength / Unless the strength of Heav'n, if you mean
that" (ll. 417-418), the elder Brother replies, "I mean that too" (that
is, the assistance of divine providence, or grace), "but yet a hidden
strength" (that is, a provision of natural providence), "which if
Heav'n gave it, may be term'd her own" (ll. 418-419). Thus Sabrina, though Heaven gave her to the Lady, may be termed the
Lady's own, as may all the natural powers of the soul. Sabrina does
not represent the supernatural power of Grace, but a natural power;
as goddess of the river she is an agent of Neptune, or a power provided by natural providence, with the permission and instrumentality
of divine providence. The achievement of the chastity which Milton
is talking about is the soul's achievement, not God's.[42] Milton's emphasis is, like that of Ficino, humanistic rather than Augustinian.

In the last scene of Milton's masque, only 65 lines long, the heroine
is shown returning to her own home, and being restored to her parents. We are not shown in detail how the girl gets back to her parents
after being released; Milton is not interested, as the medieval mystics were, in the specific steps by which the soul rises to God after
achieving the turning point of chastity. We are shown in the masque
only the last step of the process, the arrival of the children at their
home. Lest the suggested identification of the Earl with God get out
of hand, Milton quickly shifts attention to a more emblematic statement of the idea in the Attendant Spirit's description of his own return to heaven and the nature of that heaven. Like the imagery of the

rest of the poem, the imagery of the Attendant Spirit's description is
dominantly Platonic; Milton depends heavily upon myths already exploited by Spenser in the *Faerie Queene* (III, xii), borrowing the figures of Cupid and Psyche and the Garden of Adonis; to these he adds
further the Platonized imagery of the Garden of the Hesperides. The
Attendant Spirit invites particular attention to the symbolic language
of his description of the Platonic heaven, "List mortals if your ears be
true" (l. 997). He does not mean to emphasize his remarks as a recapitulation of the earlier action of the masque.[43] Except for the last
six lines, the epilogue serves rather to describe the third and last stage
in the Platonic history of the soul.

Only in the last six lines of the masque does the Attendant Spirit
look back over the meaning of the work as a whole. There, as the divine agent who has supervised the whole thing, he says, in effect: "if
you wish to know what I have tried to show in this masque, it is that
the way to get to heaven is by being virtuous in this world, and also
that God helps us along in that process."

> Mortals that would follow me,
> Love virtue, she alone is free,
> She can teach ye how to climb
> Higher than the Sphery chime;
> Or if Virtue feeble were,
> Heav'n itself would stoop to her.
> (ll. 1018-1023)

This, for the Ludlow audience, would have been enough, but it was
not enough for Milton himself. What Milton meant by "Virtue" in
the Attendant Spirit's speech was a particular concept: the Platonic
concept of *castitas*. The masque, with its three-step narrative and its
philosophical framework, is a detailed allegorical analysis of the way
in which "Virtue" enables the soul to get to heaven, that is, the way
in which the soul achieves its turning to God.

VI

In developing the case for this interpretation of the masque, I have
not extended it to accommodate detailed discussion of the major images and themes of the masque, but these, too, fit the case. There is
the Platonized Circe myth, brought in to support the function of reason in chastity; there is the Platonized Sabrina myth (Platonized be-

fore Milton, incidentally, by Fletcher), brought in to support the supra-rational function of the will-intellect in chastity; there is the imagery of light, the imagery of water, the imagery of motion, and, throughout, the Platonized mythology of Jove, Neptune, and Cupid, all coordinated in a Platonic Masque of Chastity.

It is true that the concept of chastity which I have suggested for the masque is a complex and esoteric one, but it was not too esoteric to serve as subject for many allegorical paintings and sculptures of the period, and it is a subject which would have appealed to the intellectual pride as well as to the moral sense of the young Milton.

It may be objected that Milton does not use allegory in this way in any other known work of his. This is true, but I think Milton was trapped into allegory by his inexperience and the nature of the subject. Many critics have observed that Milton makes his masque bear a heavier burden than most masques of the period bear;[44] the demands of the subject forced him to ignore many of the conventions of the typical masque. Milton's difficulty lay in the fact that the doctrine of chastity which he chose to expound was not so much a state of being as a complex act of will; he had therefore to depend mainly upon the technique of allegorical narrative rather than upon the less rigorous technique of emblematic suggestion used in most masques of the period. In undertaking the assignment, Milton had undertaken to serve three masters: the masque form, the occasion, and his own philosophical idea. In the end the only one of the three he respected, and the one to whom he sacrificed both of the others, was philosophy; the philosophical idea rules the masque from beginning to end, except for one unimportant detail—the title.

Even if Milton had named his subject in the title of the work, I imagine that very few in the Ludlow audience, or even in the cast (perhaps, as I have suggested, only Lawes himself, who had been given the "simples" by his "shepherd" friend Milton) would have recognized the esoteric concept which Milton had in mind in combining the familiar Circe myth with the unfamiliar Sabrina myth. By entitling it simply *A Mask Performed at Ludlow Castle,* he kept the focus where, for that audience, it belonged, not on chastity, but on the glorification of the Earl and his family. As in his early poem, however, "On the Death of a Fair Infant," which Milton wrote not for the bereaved mother, but for prospective admirers of Milton, so in the Ludlow *Mask,* Milton seems to have been writing not for the audience addressed so much as for the learned world in general. For that larger audience I think he was writing not *A Mask Performed at Ludlow Castle,* but a Platonic *Masque of Chastity.*

NOTES

1. Robert M. Adams, *Ikon: John Milton and the Modern Critics* (Ithaca, 1955), p. 1. All of the modern readings except those of Miss Tuve, Mr. Madsen, and Mr. Whiting, noted below, are neatly summarized in M. Y. Hughes' Odyssey edition of the masque in *Complete Poems and Selected Prose* (New York, 1957). Professor Woodhouse has called to my attention a short essay on *Comus* in a rare volume published privately by the author, John A. Himes, *Miltonic Enigmas* (Gettysburg, Penn., 1921).

2. A. S. P. Woodhouse, "The Argument in Milton's *Comus*," *UTQ,* XI (1941), 47-71, and *"Comus* Once More," *UTQ,* XIX (1950), 218-223.

3. Rosamond Tuve, "Image, Form, and Theme in *A Mask," Images and Themes in Five Poems by Milton* (Cambridge, Mass., 1957), pp. 112-161. Miss Tuve suggests (p. 116) that the Circe myth is the "great hinge" on which the meaning of the masque turns.

4. The emphasis upon Lawes' participation in the masque is particularly strong. See especially ll. 84-87, where Lawes assumes the likeness of a Swain

> That to the service of this house belongs,
> Who with his soft Pipe and smooth-dittied Song
> Well knows to still the wild winds when they roar.

and ll. 494-496, where the Elder Brother describes Lawes again:

> Whose artful strains have oft delay'd
> The huddling brook to hear his madrigal,
> And sweeten'd every musk rose of the dale.

5. The Younger Brother exclaims, "Heav'n keep my sister!" (l. 486). The Elder Brother says, "Heav'n be for us." (l. 489). The Lady explains to Comus that he cannot hurt her even though for the moment "Heav'n sees good" that she remain helpless (l. 665). The Attendant Spirit observes to the parents that "Heav'n hath timely tri'd their youth" (l. 970) and even Comus says, "It were a journey like the path to Heav'n To help you find them" (ll. 303-304).

6. It should be said in defense of Milton's use of the trinity of faith, hope, and chastity, that it was a commonplace in Renaissance Platonic allegory. In the soul's progress to God every step which the soul takes closer to God is also a step further away from the flesh which it has repudiated. Thus *chastity* is legitimately equated with *charity* as a

negative part of the process of love of God. Christian painters often identified love with chastity. See *Wind, Pagan Mysteries.* Milton himself, in *Apology for Smectymnuus,* also identifies the process of chastity with the process of love.

7. The two emphases of the Christian relation between man and God are expressed in the two sayings: "God helps those who help themselves," and "No one rises to heaven except those whom God himself raises" (John vi.44). Mr. Woodhouse sees Milton as preferring the latter emphasis; in my reading Milton prefers the former. This is not to say, of course, that Mr. Woodhouse denies the necessity of virtue to grace in Milton's theology.

8. Among the most vigorous defenders of the philosophical interpretation of the masque (emphasizing the conflict between reason and passion) see J. C. Maxwell, "The Pseudo-Problem of Comus," *CJ,* I (1948), 376-380; A. E. Dyson, "The Interpretation of Comus," *Essays and Studies,* n.s., VIII (1955), 89-114; and John Arthos, *On A Mask Presented at Ludlow Castle* (Ann Arbor, 1954).

9. See the three major works on the relations between Milton and Plato: Herbert Agar, *Milton and Plato* (Princeton, 1928); Irene Samuel, *Plato and Milton* (Ithaca, 1947); and J. S. Harrison, *Platonism in English Poetry* (New York, 1903). Since this article was written, Professor Arthos has published an essay suggesting Ficino's Commentary on the *Charmides* as "the source and explanation of Milton's meaning" in *A Mask.* My own conclusions about Milton's debt to this and other works of Ficino were reached independently and differ a good deal from those of Professor Arthos, but I should certainly endorse most of what he has to say. See John Arthos, "Milton, Ficino, and the *Charmides,*" *Studies in the Renaissance,* VI (1959), 261-274.

10. In *Areopagitica,* Hughes ed., pp. 728-729, and in the *Mask* itself, l. 822.

11. *Apology for Smectymnuus,* Hughes ed., p. 694: Thus, from the laureate fraternity of poets, riper years and the ceaseless round of study and reading led me to the shady spaces of philosophy, but chiefly to the divine volumes of Plato and his equal, Xenophon: where, if I should tell ye what I learnt of chastity and love (I mean that which is truly so, whose charming cup is only virtue, which she bears in her hand to those who are worthy—the rest are cheated with a thick intoxicating potion which a certain sorceress, the abuser of love's name, carries about) and how the first and chiefest office of love begins and ends in the soul, producing those happy twins of her divine generation, knowledge and virtue—with such abstracted sublimities as these, it might be worth your listening, readers . . .

12. See, for example, P. Merlan, *From Platonism to Neoplatonism* (Hague, 1953).

13. See Ficino, *Epistolae*, fol. vi^r, for a clear statement of the standard view.

14. For the mythologizing process see Jean Seznec's *The Survival of the Pagan Gods* (New York, 1953); Douglas Bush, *Mythology and the Renaissance Tradition* (Minneapolis, 1932); and especially André Chastel, *Ficin et l'art* (Geneva, 1954).

15. Ficino's *Theologia Platonica* was the standard treatment in the 16th and 17th centuries of the identity of the Christian and Platonic theologies. See Nesca Robb, *Neoplatonism of the Italian Renaissance* (London, 1935), though she, too, perpetuates the 19th-century view of Neoplatonism.

16. Ficino, *Epistolae*, fol. xciv^r: Ubi nos dives potensque Iuno non audit . . . Totum igitur auxilium, Salvine, nostrum nobis est a Minerva petendum . . . Nempe solum id numen ad ethereum mundi caput hominem potest atollere quod ipso summi Iovis est capite natum.

17. On Platonic iconography the standard authority is still Panofsky's *Studies in Iconology;* but see also now Edgar Wind, *Pagan Mysteries in the Renaissance* (New Haven, 1958). For Michelangelo see Panofsky, ch. vi and Ch. de Tolnay, *Werk und Weltbild des Michelangelo* (Zurich, 1949), ch. ii. For Botticelli see Wind and E. H. Gombrich, "Botticelli's Mythologies," *Journal of the Warburg and Courtauld Institutes,* VIII (1945), 7-60.

18. The identification is borrowed by Ficino from Plotinus, *Enneads,* IV, iv, 9-10. See Ficino's *Commentary on the Symposium,* tr. S. Jayne, *Univ. of Missouri Studies,* XIX (1944), pp. 127-128, 180. See also Ficino, *Epistolae,* fol. iv^v: "nam mundi totius animum saepenumero iovem platonici nuncupant."

19. Cf. the medieval distinction between *natura naturans* and *natura naturata,* and see Ficino, *Commentary on the Symposium,* pp. 136-137.

20. Cicero, *Academic Questions,* tr. C. D. Yonge (London 1853), p. 15.

21. Interea nota priscos sacerdotes consuevisse in sacris tertiam libationis pateram Iovi servatori praecipue consecrare: ut declararent principia, media, fines omnium, ut in legibus Plato refert, sub Iovis providentia disponi atque servari. (Commentary on the *Charmides* in *Platonis Opera* [Lyons, 1590], p. 767, col. 2G.)

22. Ficino, *Commentary on the Symposium,* p. 187. On daemons see also Ficino, *Epistolae,* fol. cxlviii^r, ff.

23. Renaissance Platonists often recognized the Christian distinction, but in terms of three realms, not two: the realms of nature, grace, and glory, corresponding to Plotinus' triad of the World Soul, the Angelic

Mind, and the One. Francesco Vieri, in *Compendio della Dottrina di Platone* (Florence, 1577), fol. b6ᵛ, for example, classifies all the dialogues of Plato in three groups according as they deal with each of these realms. Other Platonists distinguished between the realm of divine providence and the realm of natural providence as between the upper and the lower halves of the World Soul (the outermost circle of divine emanation). The essential difference between the realms is that the realm of natural providence involves corporeal substance, whereas that of divine providence does not; the realm of natural providence is the realm in which divine law takes the form of natural law. The two realms correspond roughly to the Christian realms of nature and grace.

24. Nunc vero quia Sacerdotium est nostrum Philosophandi genus, ad Neptunum recurrimus, providentiae naturalis Symbolum, et generationis typum. Est quoque Neptunus, ut nostri sub aenigmate effigunt, aquarum numen, ergo a naturali providentia est, et Neptuno aquarum Praeside, . . . [corresponding to Athena, who represents divine providence, or sapience, because sprung from the mind of God.] Petrus Calanna, *Philosophia seniorum . . . de mundo animarum et corporum.* (Panormi, 1599) (Copy in Bodleian), p. 103.

25. A different way of looking at the nature problem in the masque may be seen in William G. Madsen, "The Idea of Nature in Milton's Poetry," *Three Studies in the Renaissance* (New Haven, 1958), pp. 185-218.

26. The fullest Renaissance analysis of the sun-moon metaphor in Platonic terms is Ficino's short work, *De Sole et Lumine;* see also his *Epistolae,* fols. lxiiʳ, xlviiiʳ, and clxxxviiᵛ. A partial exposition of the Platonic significance of the light imagery in the poem is given by Miss Tuve (*Five Poems,* pp. 146-151).

27. Ficino, *Epistolae,* fol. iiiᵛ; the text is my translation of a Latin marginal paraphrase by John Colet. See S. Jayne, *John Colet and Marsilio Ficino* (Oxford, 1963), pp. 89-90.

28. For an account in English, see P. O. Kristeller, *The Philosophy of Marsilio Ficino* (New York, 1944), pp. 171-199, 235-288. The fullest account of this particular aspect of Ficino's philosophy is Walter Dress, *Die Mystik des Marsilio Ficino* (Berlin, 1929). The relevant sections in Ficino's own works are in the *Theologia Platonica* XIII. 2 (*Opera,* pp. 289-290): see also *Commentary on Symposium,* pp. 158-159.

29. *Theologia Platonica,* XIII, 2 (*Opera,* p. 292).

30. An analogous relation between act and process may be seen in the relation between vow and condition in Meister Eckhart's principle of poverty as a form of renouncing the world for God.

31. Although this doctrine sounds extremely dégagé, like most of the

ideas of Plato and Plotinus, it rests on an empirical observation; in this case, the observation that our minds can wander away from the circumstances of the present into another world. See Joseph Katz, *The Philosophy of Plotinus* (New York, 1950), p. xxiii. Ficino elsewhere refers to the same part of the soul as the "eye" of the soul. See Commentary on the *Symposium*, p. 189. See also Plotinus, *Enneads*, IV, iv, 43. "Only the soul that is concentrated within itself on the world of Mind" can be proof against sorcery. Quoted by John Arthos in *A Mask* (Ann Arbor, 1954), p. 75.

32. An engraving based on the original is reproduced by E. Panofsky, *Studies in Iconology*, Plate LVIII; I follow Panofsky's analysis of the work (pp. 148-150) which is borne out by the inscription on the engraving. The engraving is also reproduced by Jean Seznec in *The Survival of the Pagan Gods*, p. 113.

33. My discussion is based upon the 1637 text of the work in the edition of Merritt Hughes (New York, 1957) but I have taken into account the textual variations among all of the extant MSS and printed versions as well as the studies of those variants by Mr. C. S. Lewis (*RES*, VIII [1932], 170-176) and Mr. J. Diekhoff (*PMLA*, LII [1937], 705-727). None of the alterations in the poem between the Trinity MS. and the final edition in Milton's lifetime alters the meaning of the poem which I have proposed.

34. The function of innate reason in conquering the passions as the necessary first step in the three-step process is also stated in Ficino's commentary on the *Charmides, Platonis opera*, p. 767, col. 2B-C:

. . . quo fit ut temperantia opus sit in primis: per quam expulsa perturbationum caligine mens facta cernior, divini solis lumine abunde circunfundatur: unde sapientiam primo recuperet: deinde prudentiam adipiscatur. (2B)

. . . tum per ipsam temperantiae ideam innatam menti, humanam intelliget temperantiam . . . Accedit ad haec: quod in hoc precepto significat neminem nisi temperatum de temperantia loqui ad persuadendum vel debere vel posse. (2C)

35. Angelo Poliziano (1454-94) was the littérateur of the Platonic Academy at Florence and tutor of the children of Lorenzo de Medici. On Poliziano see, in English, W. Parr Greswell, *Memoirs of Angelus Politianus* (Manchester, 1805), pp. 1-151. His part in the mythologizing of Platonism is best described in A. Chastel, *Ficin et l'Art*, especially pp. 141 ff. Poliziano's most influential single work, so far as Platonic iconography is concerned, is his *La Giostra di Giuliano*.

36. The *Charmides*, Plato's only dialogue on temperance, would have been especially important to Milton in preparing a masque on chastity, not merely because of the relation of the virtues, but because, as Ficino says in his own commentary on the dialogue: "Socrates' aim in

this dialogue is to persuade everyone to follow a life of temperance, but he wants to convince three kinds of people especially, The Young, The Noble, and The Beautiful." (Studium Socratis in hoc dialogo est, omnes quidem ad temperantiam cohortari. Tres vero praecipue, scilicet adolescentes, et nobiles atque pulchros.) *Platonis opera,* p. 767, col. 1C.

Milton would undoubtedly have read not only Ficino's commentary on the *Charmides,* but also Poliziano's preface to the dialogue. That preface, in the form of a Latin letter to Lorenzo de Medici, was written to introduce Poliziano's translation of the dialogue. He did not complete the translation, but the text of his preface and the completed fragment of translation were published in his *Opera* (Lyons, 1546), II, 293-299.

37. This is the standard definition of philosophy in the period. See, for example, Francisco de Vieri, *Libro in quo a calumniis detractorum Philosophia defenditur* (Rome, 1586): "Philosophy is nothing else but the love of wisdom"; But the true wisdom is God himself (fol. a2r).

38. The term *haemony* has many specifically Christian connotations which seem to fit it for identification with Christian Grace, but it does not fit in that meaning in the masque as a whole. The standard exposition of the Christian meanings of haemony is that of E. S. Le-Comte, "New Light on the 'Haemony' Passage in Comus," *PQ,* XXI (1942), 283-298. J. A. Himes (*Miltonic Enigmas,* [Gettysburg, Penn., 1921] pp. 11-19) identifies the "shepherd lad" as St. Paul, moly as labor, and haemony as the cross. See John Steadman, "Milton's Haemony: Etymology and Allegory," *PMLA,* LXXVII (1962), 200-207.

39. Cicero, *Paradoxa Stoicorum, Scipio hys Dreame,* tr. Thomas Newton (London, 1569), STC 5314, fols. vi^r—vii^r.

40. Cf. Ficino's Commentary on the *Charmides,* p. 767, col. 2E-F: "Atque Avicenna sequutus Platonicos, et Hippocratem, probat animum ex ipsa sui natura adeo materiam omnem exuperare, ut cum primum in seipsum fuerit restitutus, possit elementa mundi mira quadam virtute movere; atque habere in corpora quaevis imperium: quo fit, ut multo magis possit in proprium . . . (2F) Declaratur et mira potestas animi; a quo omnia tam bona, quam mala in corpus defluant: et quo volente corpus servari valeat incorruptum."

41. Cf. the interesting parallel in Ficino's commentary on the *Charmides,* p. 767, col. 1H: "Tanta vero est excellentia temperantiae, ut et eam omnes in operibus suis observent elegantes, et ipsius virtute non solum corpus sub luna quodlibet, verum etiam caelum ipsum universumque servetur."

42. For those who want to see the conflict in the masque as a conflict

between Comus and Sabrina, a morality-play struggle for the passive and inert figure of Everywoman, there are innumerable fascinating overtones available: Sabrina's victory can represent the triumph not merely of good over evil, but of sea over land, female over male, object over subject, beauty over desire for beauty, passivity over activity, the eternal feminine over the eternal masculine, etc. But the narrative hardly supports such an interpretation. The charms of Comus and the charms of Sabrina are equally natural powers; the one in the world, the other in the soul. The real issue in the poem is the issue of chastity, the conflict between love of the body and love of God.

43. The recapitulation theory is part of Professor Woodhouse's exposition of the masque.

44. The standard account of English masques is still that of Enid Welsford, *The Court Masque* (Cambridge, 1927). Miss Tuve (*Five Poems,* pp. 112-121) makes several helpful suggestions about the importance of reading Milton's *Mask* as a masque. For the reverse view see Don Cameron Allen, "Milton's *Comus* as a Failure in Artistic Compromise," *ELH,* XVI (1949), 104-119, and *The Harmonious Vision* (Baltimore, 1954), 29-40. A useful discussion of Milton's debt to Jonson's masques is G. W. Whiting, *"Comus,* Jonson, and the Critics" in *Milton and This Pendant World* (Austin, 1958), pp. 3-28.

[EDITOR'S NOTE. For other comment see F. Bruser, *SP,* 44 (1947), 625-644; D. Wilkinson, *EIC,* X (1960), 32-43; J. Arthos, *MLN,* 76 (1961), 321-4, and *Anglia,* LXXIX (1961), 204-13; T. Wheeler, in *Studies in Honor of J. C. Hodges and A. Thaler,* ed. R. B. Davis, 1961; J. B. Broadbent, *Milton's "Comus,"* 1962; on the Attendant Spirit, M. Lloyd, *N&Q,* VII (1960), 421-3; on music, G. L. Finney, *Musical Backgrounds for English Literature,* [1962]; on *A Mask* and Shakespeare, E. Seaton, *E&S,* XXXI (1946), 68-80, J. M. Major, *SQ,* X (1959), 177-83; for another view of its relation to the court masque, G. F. Sensabaugh, *SP,* XLI (1944), 233-49; on the text, J. T. Shawcross, *PBSA,* LIV (1960), 38-56; for some productions, A. Gossman and G. W. Whiting, *RES,* XI (1960), 56-60, C. Shattuck, *JEGP,* LX (1961), 123-40.]

JON S. LAWRY

"Eager Thought": Dialectic in *Lycidas*

Despite its sovereign status among English elegies and within English poetry in general, two strictures upon *Lycidas* continue in some degree to shadow the poem: the one would hold with Dr. Johnson that its pastoral apparatus is a flaw in terms both of art and of personal expression; the other would agree with G. Wilson Knight[1] that the work lacks order or unity. Both strictures have become increasingly untenable in the light of one type of study which has helped to make reavailable the form and power of the pastoral elegy in itself,[2] and of another type which has marked the structural[3] and affective[4] unity of Milton's poem. Yet some readers still may feel that Milton sets cool pastoral against impassioned personal outcry, and will consider the two modes of expression to be in direct conflict. Milton editors and critics therefore will continue to face the question of unity in *Lycidas*. Recently Douglas Bush and Merritt Y. Hughes,[5] for example, delivered defenses of the poem in the course of registering adverse charges made against it.

We may however take an additional step toward reconciling the supposedly antagonistic modes of statement in *Lycidas* by considering the poem as in part a dialectical process, in the Hegelian sense: the initial dogmatic proposition (thesis) is opposed by a skeptical sec-

From *PMLA*, LXXVII (1962), 27-32. Reprinted by permission of the author and the Modern Language Association of America.

ond (antithesis); from their encounter there arises a third statement, one of mystic certainty (synthesis). Within *Lycidas*, the major subject of this process is poetry itself. The timeless, serene, and objective attitudes of pastoral, impassioned only in formal artistic imitation of loss, are opposed by the skeptical affronts of death, temporal corruption, and several failures of consolation, all of which are impassioned in and through actual experience. However, each of these two modes of awareness or response is found to be incomplete in the course of the work, and a consummate statement, greater than either but partaking of both, gradually evolves. Put another way, the general issue is that of the possibility of poetry and, more particularly, of Christian poetry. Within the *données* of *Lycidas*, the attitudes and materials of the pastoral sequences are held to be *ideally* poetic—ideal in both the popular and the philosophic sense, being both the personal preference of the speaker and also an imaginative construct. They are also elements in a traditionalized and almost impersonal "poetic" response to death.[6] But the "digressions" enforce actuality upon this ideal, threatening to destroy it exactly as actuality had destroyed Edward King. That the apparently destructive argument of actuality has also been cast in poetry is, of course, an indication that its force is limited, and that poetry will prove its power even within the supposedly hostile hold of actuality. However, the resolution of these seeming opposites —pastoral *vs.* local engagement, timeless poetry *vs.* experience, art *vs.* actuality—produces a reconstituted possibility of poetry which in part grows out of the formerly opposed modes, *both* of which have seemed, whether by impotence or by antagonistic assault, to signal the defeat of poetry.

Such a process seems to me demonstrably present in *Lycidas*. However, it is in one sense misleading to describe the poem as dialectical, for it does not follow partitioned steps within a triadic strategy, nor, of course, is its method primarily ratiocinative. It is triumphantly a poem, not discourse; its procedures are affective and histrionic, not argumentative. Not only are potentialities of synthesis lodged in the early stages of the poem, but also pastoral details appear in the digressions and pressures of actuality in the pastoral sections, thereby suggesting in another way the immense reconciliation which is to come. As Arthur Barker has shown (see n.3), the elegy should be read as a triple suite of related thematic developments; it follows that the total statement will be present by suggestion or implication in each of the three sections. Also, it is of course necessary to recognize that actual-

ity is not finally considered to be alien to poetry, even though in particular segments of *Lycidas* it is presented as an agency of defeat for
both poet and poetry. In short, neither the occasional concentration
upon divisive particulars nor the use of a Hegelian analogy in the following discussion should be taken as evidence of true contrarieties
within the poem, for the whole purpose of the study is to adduce the
opposite.

From the viewpoint of its dialectic (or almost any other viewpoint,
for that matter), the poem is not about Edward King, save as the conditions of his life and death intersect the ideal pastoral attitude in *Lycidas*. Nor, by the same token, is it primarily about John Milton. Instead, it is about poetry and the poet, generally conceived, and of the
conditions impelled by existence upon the poet and his works. It is
with this concern that the dialectical process begins. On the one
hand, King's death (and the death of any person, but especially of
any poet) is objective material for poetic expression, the "ideal" form
of which is the pastoral elegy. The conditions of poetry are so far
"pure," any real sense of loss having been transmuted into the beautiful imitation of such a sense. The poet to this point is involved only
as singer; his commitment is a "melodious tear."[7] But on the other
hand, the death of the individual poet, King, implies the real death
of the poet generally and the consequent death of poetry. Melodious
artistic lament—the essential concern of which is neither King nor
Milton but the expression itself within the formal determinations of
the genre—is confronted by the anguished recognition of real physical
loss, of defeated promise, and of corrupt society. Lament veers sharply
away from the provinces of "pure" art as the vulnerable poet himself
and his equally vulnerable creations become its subject.

Our sense of what that "pure" poetry is, of what materials evoked
it, and of how the poet was conceived to stand in relation to actuality,
may be enhanced by looking briefly to the twin poems "L'Allegro"
and "Il Penseroso." In those poems, the poet is in effect a recording
agent, sympathetic to the world but detached from it, an observer who
converts what he sees into formal beauty. To him, the world is a pageant for supply. His poetry and thought will to some extent respond
in mood and form to the sensations which he receives, but as a man
he will remain uninvolved, whether seen or unseen by the world. In
both poems the speaker at last attends or attains the purity of music,
the art form most distant from direct involvement with experience.[8]
Poetry, whenever it appears as subject within the poems, is considered

to be imaginative, almost dream-like: allegory, romance, classic and Elizabethan drama, all received purely as delight to sense and thought —"such sights as youthful Poets dream / On Summer eves by haunted stream," or "Forests, and enchantments drear, / Where more is meant than meets the ear." Even the entrance into the "busy hum of men" is made distant and imaginative: the hum is that of a medieval chivalric court, not the court of James or Charles. The generally pastoral mode of these poems, if extended to the elegy, seems to indicate fairly exactly the attitude toward "pure" poetry in *Lycidas*. By its means King and seventeenth-century England can be received in the objective and melodious mode of pastoral beauty, negating or transforming reality much as did Orpheus in the twin poems, who through melody might almost set free Eurydice and make "Hell grant what Love did seek."[9]

Lycidas begins within the pastoral mode of "L'Allegro" and "Il Penseroso," in which objective—"pure"—elegiac lament is possible.[10] The apology for premature entry into demanding poetry is in part conventional, and vestiges of the pastoral possibility remain in the description of the elegy as a "melodious tear." But the apology becomes somewhat more than conventional, and other than pastoral, by the nature of the protest against too early exercise of poetry. King's untimely death *forces* expression. By implication, reality, with its conditions of death and unripeness, stands opposed to the evergreen laurel, myrtle, and ivy symbolic of poetry, which are "never sere." Experiential intensity repeatedly breaks into the conventional apology in oxymoron and paradox: "Sad occasion *dear*," "melodious *tear*."[11] Divergent attitudes at once appear as conventional, objective lament is opposed by the real loss of a real man. The occasion is "dear" poetically, "sad" actually; even more precisely, the occasion is "dear" both in the sense of occasioning a purely poetic token of affection and in the sense of exacting, at great cost, personal grief from the speaker. Similarly, an actual "tear" obeys the demand of existence, but in the pastoral attitude the tear as poetic lament may be "melodious." The initial announcement of the poem—"*Lycidas* is dead"—also looks both to the reality of death and to imaginative pastoral beauty by the use of an "unreal," transmutative name. The name "Lycidas," that is, can objectify Edward King into the unaffecting; his actual death can receive no such distancing.

The pastoral convention is maintained in the invocation to the muses, but a dominating point of opposition is again reached in the

immediate connection of the lost Lycidas with poetry ("he knew /
Himself to sing, and build the lofty rhyme"). Lament for Lycidas will
necessitate lament for poetry—by implication, for the very poetry of
the present elegist. Such association of the dead poet with the living
appears more fully in the speaker's hope for a like memorial:

> So may some gentle Muse
> With lucky words favor my destin'd Urn,
> And as he passes turn,
> And bid fair peace be to my sable shroud.

The term "lucky words" at this point in the poem reflects (with perhaps a shade of irony) a pastoral objectivity, but it is opposed at once
by the term "destin'd Urn," which reverberates with the same recognition of loss—including loss of poetry—as had the earlier notice of the
death of Lycidas. In memory, pastoral reasserts itself by objectifying
Cambridge into a scene like those in "L'Allegro," but that scene is
at once swept away by the heavy real change inflicted by actuality.
The sense of the loss of Lycidas, partially held off again for a time
by conventional pastoral images of desolated nature—which, however,
bear their own grim sense of mortality—returns strongly with "Such,
Lycidas, thy loss to Shepherd's ear": again the threat of reality to poetry overcomes the pastoral attitude.

Ensuing conventional appeals to pastoral deities are intersected by
the same sense of destruction, and for a time the pastoral convention
is nearly surrendered. The saving pastoral nymphs are gone, particularly from the nearly objective British scene: they were not where the
Druids lie, nor on Mona, nor at the Dee. The pastoral attitude and
legendary British subjects (which in the twin poems lent imaginative
delight) are alien to the real scene, and would be in any case helpless
before actuality: "Had ye been there— . . . what could that have
done?" The materials of "pure" poetry seem useless or unuseable,
denied by death.

This unwilling but progressive surrender of the pastoral attitude
moves directly from the recognition that Orpheus' voice, too, was
stopped in death, to the first alleged "digression," that concerning the
certain defeat of the "slighted Shepherd's trade" by the "blind *Fury*
with th'abhorred shears." The speaker recognizes a double defeat of
poetry and of the honorable fame due the poet: inattention from a
corrupt world, which sports with Amaryllis in the shade,[12] and destruction in death. A hint of the possible reconciliation of "pure" po-

etry with existence is made by Phoebus:[13] praise of poetry and of the poet is not so much denied by reality as lodged elsewhere than in the world. Both poet and poetry must be considered *sub specie aeternitatis,* within the "artifice of eternity." For the first time in the poem, synthesis—in the partly disclosed theme of resurrection and right judgment—tentatively reveals itself.

However, Phoebus' lofty and not immediately comforting statement is left suspended as the poem returns to pastoral conventions ("now my Oat proceeds"), which have already shown themselves unequal to the thrust of reality. The pastoral world, through Triton and other water-figures, is found innocent of Lycidas' death by water, but was, however, impotent to prevent it. Reality, in "that fatal and perfidious Bark,"[14] is *necessarily* "guilty"; Atropos' abhorred shears again glint savagely across the pastoral scene. Then suddenly St. Peter,[15] a water-figure for the moment alien to the pastoral world, appears, shivering the helpless pastoral scene completely for the time. Like the progression from Orpheus to the poet in the first "digression," the movement from Camus to St. Peter in the second is logical in terms of imagery, but, like the earlier progression, it intersects and contradicts the whole pastoral framework. St. Peter speaks not through the imaginative and beautiful pastoral convention but through stern theological "realities," judging the contemporary physical reality. His sweeping condemnation of the false clergy takes sharp note of the death of Lycidas, the true poet-priest who should have been spared. The synthesis will insist that he *has* been "spared," of course, but for the moment false poets and false priests, alive whereas Lycidas is dead, define the apparent nature of reality (Atropos' shears and the corrupt world's inattention still dominate the speaker's vision). Although the "two-handed engine," beyond human time, will somehow restore justice, little mitigation is offered for the present, in which poetry and pastoral seem futile to prevent, to transcend, or to express reality (pastoral conventions do not appear directly in the "digressions"; the original "ideal" form cannot yet cope with seemingly antithetical materials). However, the second note of synthesis has been lodged, and a transformation of the pastoral attitude now begins. Transferred into Christian application, gradually adopting the Christian iconology of the shepherd as poet-priest, the pastoral materials can move into and beyond formerly antagonistic reality. Triton, helpless before the destructive wave, will be transformed into Christ, the saviour who walks the waves, stills them, and makes them baptismal.

Such a change within pastoral is distantly figured as the poem returns from the second "digression" to the pastoral mode: the stream of Alpheus, shrunken by the "dread voice" of St. Peter, returns to fullness. Now for the preceding pastoral return, "Arethuse" had been the vehicle. The mythical Alpheus and Arethusa, by metamorphosis removed from the antagonisms of life into water seeking mysterious union, are in themselves a principle of reconciliation or synthesis. Furthermore, Alpheus—in "Arcades" called "divine"—in himself suggests the dialectic of the poem. Criminally involved in reality, he was granted a sea-change whereby he became material for pastoral beauty (through association with Theocritus); he also may be included among the symbols of reconciliation, suggesting in his effort for union with Arethusa the "unexpressive nuptial Song" which is to come.[16] The poem proceeds now in a mood of relative serenity, as if both real corruption and the apparent powerlessness of the pastoral were largely overcome.

Before the final synthesis is reached, however, there appears the lapidary flower section, in which pastoral impotence, if alleviated, is yet present. As Wayne Shumaker has shown (see n. 4), these memorial flowers bring color and a lightening of the grimmest sense of death; yet they offer only illusory ease and "false surmise" against the reality of loss. But "false surmise" looks ahead, as well, to the evident physical reality—the terrifying picture of King's body "hurl'd" or hidden in the destructive sea.[17] That reality, too, begins to undergo a transformation, somewhat in the manner of the metamorphosis of Alpheus, for King's body also may mysteriously visit the bottom of the world or sleep within the protective (though physically unavailing) sight of Michael. The two attitudes of the poem here meet: pastoral poetry in and of itself is weak before the onslaught of actuality, but actuality itself gradually has been discovered to rest within a vastly larger aspect, that of eternity. The confrontation of the two modes, each of which has revealed weakness and incompleteness, together with the emergent Christianizing of both, permits the poem to move with certain confidence beyond the last eddy of doubt, in which both attitudes were caught in the suspense of "false surmise" and were thereby made ready for the reconciliation which follows.

The full architectural turn from "Lycidas is dead," and the fully achieved synthesis of modes, is announced with "Lycidas your sorrow is not dead, / Sunk though he be beneath the wat'ry floor." All the water images, formerly given to sterility, the unbearable reality of drowning, or to the impotence of pastoral beauty (save, of course, in the prophetic use of the "pastor" St. Peter on Galilee and of "divine" Alpheus seeking union across the abysses of ocean), now unite to present resurrection.[18] The seemingly dying Day-Star sinks in order to rise, just as Christ, who also triumphed over the waves and made them benign, "died" to a greater life. Lycidas now is offered in place of death by water the waters of baptismal anointment, and in place of a dirge the joy of the "unexpressive nuptial Song." The full choir of heaven takes the tears from his—and the speaker's—eyes, resolving the "melodious tear" into celebration. Lycidas in his way becomes transformed from victim to saviour, like Christ;[19] he is delivered beyond the lament either of pastoral or of reality.

There is a full return to pastoral convention at the end of the elegy, but that convention now has been shot through with Christian illumination. The "Swain" at the close is the poet in full command of both pastoral and actuality through the emergence of their transforming and reconciling third. The "tender stops" of pastoral are directed now to the celebration of resurrection, to Lycidas within the union of Christ and his church. The formerly agonized reception of reality now is altered as a higher vision leads the speaker into "eager thought." The resolved poet-priest, comfortably observing the day-star repeating the cycle of loss and return, serenely anticipates not loss of life and poetry but, for both, "Tomorrow . . . fresh Woods, and Pastures new." "Pastures" puts the final stamp upon the synthesis, for the reference can be "pastoral" in the sense of poetry and at the same time "pastoral" in the sense of a Christian pastorate, because poet and priest, singer and Christian song, have been united.[20]

Our study of the poem has at times carried the discussion beyond its established limits as Christian materials appeared. We may then recapitulate the terms of its argument. *Lycidas* begins with pastoral conventions which represent an ideal attitude toward poetry and the poet: melodious song produced by an uninvolved observer of the world, both song and singer being free of time and the passions of experience. Within this framework, the death of King might have remained nothing more than object for beautiful though somber lyrical imitation. But because King was a poet, his death impels reality upon poetry and the poet. Reality at first is felt to be wholly antagonistic, anti-poetic: men are corrupt and inattentive, death destroys the poet, false poets and false priests live whereas the true die. Thereafter a synthesis slowly emerges. The pastoral gains potency as Christian iconology is joined to it. Temporal reality is revealed in a far different light as Christian judgment and Christian confidence in resurrection bring corruption to account and death into increased life. The fully satisfied Christian "Swain" of the conclusion retains the pastoral beauty of "pure" poetry, but has through Christianity found for it new modes of powerful awareness; Theocritus has assumed the harp of David. Poetry will henceforth use any materials, bestow upon them the beauty of song, and find them in all ways glorious. The poet may now confront, receive, and finally surmount experience, combining pastoral or "pure" beauty with his expression of experienced realities; for those realities, seen within God's eternally Real purposes, are materials for holy song. Such reconciliation of song and existence is found repeatedly in the later Milton, where again the seeming antagonisms of poetry and personal experience are wrought into serene unity, almost as an extension of the imagery and dialectic of *Lycidas*:

> Thee *Sion* and the flow'ry Brooks beneath
> That wash thy hallow'd feet, and warbling flow,
> Nightly I visit: nor sometimes forget
> Those other two equall'd with me in Fate,
> So were I equall'd with them in renown,
> Blind *Thamyris* and blind *Mæonides*,
> And *Tiresias* and *Phineus* Prophets old.
> Then feed on thoughts, that voluntary move
> Harmonious numbers.
>
> (*PL*. III, 30-38)

NOTES

1. *The Burning Oracle* (London, New York, and Toronto, 1939), p. 70.
2. Notably James Holly Hanford, "The Pastoral Elegy and Milton's *Lycidas*," *PMLA*, XXV (1910), 403-47, and A. S. P. Woodhouse, "Milton's Pastoral Monodies," in *Studies in Honour of Gilbert Norwood*, ed. Mary E. White (Toronto, 1952), pp. 261-278. These general studies have been supplemented with others that consider particular pastoral elements, such as that of the Orpheus legend in pastoral by Caroline W. Mayerson, "The Orpheus Image in *Lycidas*," *PMLA*, LXIV (1949), 189-207, and that of the tradition of *consolatio* by Don Cameron Allen, *The Harmonious Vision* (Baltimore,

1954), pp. 43-58. An extensive appreciation of Milton's use of pastoral appears in Rosemond Tuve, *Images & Themes in Five Poems by Milton* (Cambridge, Mass., 1957), pp. 76-111.

3. The classic statement is that of Arthur Barker within his study "The Pattern of Milton's *Nativity Ode*," *Univ. of Toronto Quarterly*, X (1940-41), 167-181. See also Woodhouse, "Monodies," pp. 273-277; Allen, *Vision*, pp. 63-70; and J. Milton French, "The Digressions in Milton's 'Lycidas,'" *SP*, L (1953), 485-490.

4. See Wayne Shumaker, "Flowerets and Sounding Seas: A Study of the Affective Structure of *Lycidas*," *PMLA*, LXVI (1951), 485-494; John Edward Hardy, "Reconsiderations: I. *Lycidas*," *Kenyon Review*, VII (1945), 99-113; and Richard P. Adams, "The Archetypal Pattern of Death and Rebirth in Milton's *Lycidas*," *PMLA*, LXIV (1949), 183-188.

5. Douglas Bush, *Mythology and the Renaissance Tradition in English Poetry* (New York, 1957—copyright 1932), pp. 263-264; Merritt Y. Hughes, in his edition of Milton's *Complete Poems and Major Prose* (New York, 1957), p. 116. (The quotations from Milton which appear in the present study are taken from the Hughes edition.)

6. Masson's comments upon this point are suggestive: he held that *Lycidas* is a "lyric of lamentation, rendered more shadowy and impersonal by being distanced into the form of a narrative and descriptive phantasy" (*The Life of John Milton*, Cambridge, 1895, I, 611). He missed, however, the powerful immediacy of the so-called digressions and of the conclusion.

7. "It is the pastoral tradition that allows *Lycidas* to be a lament for the death of Poetry": Tuve, *Images & Themes*, p. 93. One should probably add that the cause for lament runs exactly counter to the poetry which expresses the lament; that is, fear of the death of poetry is discovered in the nonpastoral sections of *Lycidas* rather than in the ideally poetic pastoral areas. Only the impotence of pastoral—not pastoral itself—makes company with the fear that poetry, like the poet, will die.

8. Allen, *Vision*, pp. 4-19, terms the poet in the twin poems "as lonely as God," sharing His "stasis"; he finds the slumber invoked to be a "poetic sleep filled with 'strange, mysterious dreams'"; and he describes the active movement into music at the close of "Il Penseroso" as a marriage of verse and music in which "common experience fades away but the music continues." Something of the same use of music appears in *Lycidas*, but, until the very end, only in the pastoral sections: the Muses "sweep the string," an "Oaten Flute" was used lovingly by both Lycidas and the speaker, and the Heaven eventually perceived resounds to the "unexpressive nuptial Song." Else-

where, discordant experience and wretched worldly pipings mar the pastoral harmonies, for in this poem the speaker is heavily involved with reality direct.

9. Continually drawn to the Orpheus myth, Milton in *Lycidas* looks to the brutal death of Orpheus; his awareness that the melodious singer who controverts reality later must become its victim is another measure of the pressure of actuality in the poem. However, Orpheus later should be recalled in the resurrection assigned to Lycidas, for Orpheus also mystically triumphed over water. The Orpheus myth lies close to the heart of the dialectic in *Lycidas*. See further Mayerson, "The Orpheus Image," and Allen, *Vision*, pp. 62-63. Allen notes analogies which permit the association of King and Milton not only with Orpheus but with Christ.

10. Mayerson, "The Orpheus Image," p. 204: "The pastoral landscape represents the serene world of the poet's desire; the turbulent ocean is a symbol of the disorder which circumstance and self-analysis have revealed."

11. These oppositions are total, in one sense, as the poem opens. The poet is a voice for dispassionate melody, but is also a man personally involved in loss, if only by projection to his own death. But the very telescoping of these oppositions into grammatically interdependent terms forecasts the unity which will be wrought from seemingly discrete attitudes, much as the metaphysical conceit could yoke seeming opposites; much as "two eyes make one in sight."

12. The speaker, too, is for the moment despairingly drawn toward the world's satisfaction with fleshpots or with amatory verse. If the conditions of existence truly destroy the poet through either death or inattention, poetic surrender or suicide seems inevitable.

13. The reconciliation implied by Phoebus and by his counsel is made doubly strong if, as Michael Lloyd asserts in "The Fatal Bark," *MLN*, LXXV (1960), 103-109, Phoebus is to be firmly associated with the "day-star" of the conclusion and with Christ. Cleanth Brooks and John Edward Hardy, however, hold the answer of Phoebus to be of little comfort (*Poems of Mr. John Milton*, London, 1957, p. 179, n. 5).

14. Michael Lloyd, "The Fatal Bark," pp. 103-105, identifies the "bark" with man born in sin: "The curses with which it is rigged are those which Adam brought on man, among them subjection to death." The analogy, if perhaps fanciful, nevertheless offers reinforcement to the sense that actuality is guilty, if considered only within its own terms.

15. Ralph E. Hone, "'The Pilot of the *Galilean* Lake,'" *SP*, LVI (1959), 55-61, argues that Christ, not St. Peter, is alluded to as the

Judge in this section. However, his position should be weighed with studies which develop the conventional interpretation, such as those of John M. Steadman, "St. Peter and Ecclesiastical Satire: Milton, Dante, and 'La rappresentazione del dì del giudizio,'" *N&Q*, V, n. s. (1958), 141-142, and Malcolm Mackenzie Ross, "Milton and the Protestant Aesthetic: the Early Poems," *Univ. of Toronto Quarterly,* XVII (1947), 359.

16. D. C. Allen, "Milton's Alpheus," *MLN*, LXXI (1956), 172-173, cites the figurative meaning assigned to Alpheus and Arethusa by Bishop Fulgentius, adding that the allusion at this point in the poem might "remind the good priest of the virtues of the river and the fount, and also . . . suggest to them that they, too, could flow through an ocean of evil and corruption without being tainted."

17. "False surmise" is lodged in a thoroughly ambiguous position in the poem, from which multiple references are possible, even necessary: that the flower section offers false comfort, that a "Laureate Hearse" for the corpse can never be hoped for, that the speculations about King's physical whereabouts are not aware of their own connotations (which will lead toward the resurrection statement), and that the lament is unjustified—for the poem will swing almost immediately to "Weep no more, woeful Shepherds." Perhaps we can best say that *all* the partial attitudes, still awaiting the triumphant reconciliation, are involved in "false surmise."

18. The poem may also justify the argument that another water-image has throughout held the terms of reconciliation. The Olympian or Parnassian "sacred well . . . beneath the seat of *Jove*" transcends both actuality and pastoral, for Jove is potentially a synonym for God —who guarantees right judgment upon the poet's life and poetry. In terms of Christian poetry, Jove-Jehovah produces, justifies, and rewards. To a lesser extent, Phoebus also guarantees poetry by Christianizing its conditions and rewards. The both Grecian and more than Grecian "sacred well" reflects in brief measure much of the argument of the poem: the union of Christianity with pastoral, the transformation of physical reality through the lens of divinity, and the eternal reconciliation offered by the resurrection theme.

19. Michael Lloyd, "The Fatal Bark," 104-105, holds instead that St. Michael's Mount is also Paradise, and that the good man, redeemed by grace through Christ, looks homeward to either Eden or Heaven. I am more inclined to take "Genius of the shore" in its traditional reading, but to recognize the analogue with Christ who, through death, offers salvation. Lycidas at least offers the lesser "salvation" of the works (including Christian song) that he performed in life, and of the exemplary image of his own resurrection.

20. I am indebted to Professor Alfred H. Marks for the suggestion that "Pastures new" may indicate both new pastoral and a newly-accepted Christian pastorate, thereby confirming again the synthesis which has been achieved. I am not persuaded that the final lines forecast a leavetaking of minor poetic forms and of pastoral. Rather, they seem to me to indicate continuing future use and *expansion* of traditional poetic forms with Christian materials.

[EDITOR'S NOTE. See also J. C. Ransom in *The World's Body*, 1938, and M. C. Battestin, *CE*, XVII (1955-56), 223-8; R. Wallerstein in *English Institute Essays*, 1948, and *Studies in Seventeenth-Century Poetic*, 1950; D. Daiches in *A Study of Literature*, 1948; H. N. Frye, *University of North Carolina Studies in Comparative Literature*, No. 23 (1959), 44-55; R. L. Brett, *Reason and Imagination*, 1959; G. S. Fraser in *The Living Milton*, ed. F. Kermode, 1961; L. Nelson, Jr., *Baroque Lyric Poetry*, 1961; M. Lloyd, *EIC*, XI (1961), 390-402; M. H. Abrams in *Varieties of Literary Experience*, ed. S. Burnshaw, 1961; W. G. Madsen, *SEL*, 3 (1963), 1-7; for the verse and rhyme, F. T. Prince, *The Italian Element in Milton's Verse*, 1954; G. L. Finney, *Musical Backgrounds for English Literature*, [1962]; Ants Oras, *MP*, LII (1954), 12-22; for explanation of biblical, classical, medieval allusions, G. R. Coffman, *ELH*, 3 (1936), 101-13; E. L. Brooke, *N&Q*, III (1956), 67-8; H. F. Robins, *RES*, V (1954), 25-30; J. F. Steadman, *N&Q*, V (1958), 141-2; W. B. Hunter, Jr., *MLN* LXV (1950), 544; on the text, J. T. Shawcross, *PBSA*, LVI (1962), 317-31. A number of essays on the poem have been collected in *Milton's "Lycidas": The Tradition and the Poem*, ed. C. A. Patrides, 1961.]

MACON CHEEK

Of Two Sonnets of Milton

In his tractate "Of Education" Milton concludes his survey of "the studies wherein our noble and our gentle youth ought to bestow their time, in a disciplinary way" with the following statement as summary of the method of study he would have them pursue: "In which methodical course it is so supposed they must proceed by the steady pace of learning onward, as at convenient times, for memory's sake, to retire back into the middle ward, and sometimes into the rear of what they have been taught, until they have confirmed and solidly united the whole body of their perfected knowledge, like the last embattling of a Roman legion."[1] To push ever forward, and yet to retire periodically backwards, in order thus to consolidate the new into the old, to integrate the old into the new, and thereby to achieve a unity as well as a firm and solid foundation of mind—such was the way that he proposed for his prospective scholars and governours; and such apparently was the way that he himself followed, not in his studies and period of preparation alone, but likewise afterwards in his life and in his works. And one result of this method was to give a remarkable unity to the entire corpus of his poetry, so that the basic Miltonic point of view, although it grew and unfolded, never changed funda-

From *Renaissance Papers,* Columbia: University of South Carolina Press, 1956, 82-91. Reprinted by permission of the Executors of the Estate of the late Macon Cheek and the publishers.

mentally; so that, for example, his deepest conception of the poet as a prophetic voice whose lips breathe Jove, as enunciated already in a poem composed when he was one-and-twenty,[2] was still essentially his conception when he composed his great epic; or so that, to cite here only one example other, the true Miltonic style was suggested already in occasional lines of "The Nativity Ode and Hymn," and sustained at length through an entire piece, albeit a brief one, in the sonorous diapason titled "At a Solemn Music,"[3] which is usually regarded as belonging at the beginning of his Horton period, and as having been composed therefore when he was about twenty-five.

In smaller details of idea, style, and even phraseology anticipations of his later and more mature works are to be found in his early ones, or to reverse it, the later not infrequently hark back to and echo the earlier, thus integrating the earliest sometimes into the latest, and so consolidating the whole into a kind of oneness. Thus in the "In Quintum Novembris,"[4] a miniature Latin epic written during his eighteenth year, appear already in outline the basic concepts of Satan's character as these are to be developed at full length in *Paradise Lost*, while some of the very phrases as translated from the Latin into English carry over from the early piece into the epic. In another Latin poem, "In Obitum Praesulis Wintoniensis,"[5] written also during his eighteenth year, the order in which death attacks the various forms of life, assaulting first the flowers and plants, next the birds and animals, and finally man, is precisely the same order as is emphasised in *Paradise Lost*,[6] when after the fall of Adam and Eve death for the first time enters into the created universe. "The Hymn on the Morning of Christ's Nativity"[7] contains a catalogue of pagan deities which closely resembles, not alone in the names of the deities selected, and in the pagan religions represented, but in some of its more minute details of description as well, the catalogue or roll-call of such deities in Book I of *Paradise Lost*;[8] while a passage in Book XII[9] of the epic reads almost like an argument or brief synopsis of the Christmas poem of 1629. The famous passage on fame in "Lycidas,"[10] which suggests first the classical definition of fame as immortality among men to be achieved through some great work here, and then redefines it on the more spiritual and Christian level as approval by God hereafter, contains to all intents and purposes the same definition as Satan gives and the same redefinition as Christ responds in the series of temptations in *Paradise Regained*.[11] And finally, to conclude a list of citations which might of themselves be drawn out into a small essay, in

"Comus" the agent of evil, the name-character of the piece, in describing his method of assault upon the virtuous, and his technique of temptation, describes admirably well the method and technique which Satan employs in *Paradise Lost*:

> I under fair pretence of friendly ends,[12]
> And well plac't words of glozing courtesie
> Baited with reasons not unplausible
> Wind me into the easie-hearted man,
> And hugg him into snares;

and perhaps no lines in all *Paradise Lost* embody quite so accurately and so tersely, as do these from the masque, the final result of evil upon the agent of evil as the epic conceives it:

> But evil on it self shall back recoyl,[13]
> And mix no more with goodness, when at last
> Gather'd like scum, and setl'd to it self
> It shall be in eternal restless change
> Self-fed, and self-consum'd.

An excellent example of this underlying unity of Milton's thinking is to be found in a striking similarity in sequence of ideas and images which either inform or lie behind two of his autobiographical sonnets, when these are considered together, and at the same time in relation to the letter which accompanied and interpreted the earlier of them. Both these sonnets were written at critical periods of his life, at moments which must have seemed to him turning-points in his career, and moments therefore which asked both a retrospective view back over the past and a prospective one forth into the future; a summing-up and account-taking, as it were, of the way so far travelled, and a chart, whether of modest hope or of patient resignation, for that still to be travelled. The first, "On Having Arrived at the Age of Twenty-three," was written on or about December 9, 1631, his twenty-third birthday, and thus some eight months before he was to round off his education at Cambridge;[14] and so bring to a conclusion the first stage of his life, that of youth and preparation, with the necessity of beginning a second, that of young manhood and a profession. It was inserted into a letter to a friend, otherwise unidentified, who had expressed some anxiety over young Milton's prolonged lingering amid the cloistered seclusion of books and his seeming reluctance to adventure forth into the struggle of life; or to his ap-

pointed labour in his Master's vineyard, as the imagery of the letter
would have it, and along with the letter it served as an answer to the
friend's anxious chiding. The other, that "On his Blindness," if the
date of composition traditionally assigned it be the correct one, was
written approximately one-and-twenty years later, some time around
1652,[15] that is, and soon after the total loss of his eyesight—an event
which considerably more than graduation from Cambridge ended one
phase of his life and required that he readjust himself as best he
might to another and much more difficult one. And though there
was no letter to accompany it, and no prose commentary to elucidate
either it or the circumstances under which it was written, it is a noteworthy fact that the imagery and contents of the sonnet of 1652 are
in certain important aspects closely in accord with those of the letter
of 1631, in fact, more closely so than are those of the sonnet enclosed
within that letter—a fact which not only argues the close unity of
Milton's thinking, but which may throw considerable light on the
later poem.

Although several commentators, such as Pattison,[16] Smart,[17] and
Verity,[18] for example, have noted minor resemblances between the
two poems, no one heretofore has compared them in detail; nor apparently has anyone discussed the remarkable similarity between the
sequence of images and connotations which appear in the early letter
and reappear in the sonnet of more than twenty years later. In order
to examine the poems comparatively, and both in the light of the letter, it is necessary first to examine the letter, which is in essence, as
Milton says, an account to his friend "of this my tardie moving," and
while not a "set apologie" an attempted explanation thereof. A major
part of its body is devoted: first, to a refutation of the charge that it is
an overly great love of learning which inactivates him and detains
him from setting forth in some useful profession; second, to a summary of the four several motivations which in any normal young
man would militate against such inactivity and studious retirement
for its own sake; and third, to a modest justification of himself on the
ground that his delay is occasioned not by idle and unprofitable absorption in learning as an end in itself, but rather by a fixed purpose
to come to his life's work, which he feels is to be a high and dedicated
one, well and fully prepared. But this argument of its main body is
enclosed within an introduction and a conclusion which cite three
gospel passages, and these citations form the foundation whereon the
argument of the letter rests: the one, that in the introduction, being

the passage from the *Gospel of John*[19] which warns to labour while it is yet day, since the night comes soon wherein no man can labour; and the other two, both in the conclusion, being, first, the parable from the *Gospel of Matthew*[20] of the servant who buried his one talent, and, second, the parable from *Matthew*[21] also of the labourers who coming late to work in the vineyard received none the less the same reward as those who came early.

Now the sonnet, "On Having Arrived at the Age of Twenty-three," aside from its general reference to "the Great Taskmaster" which is vaguely applicable to any of the three, refers directly to no one of these passages. Only of the third and last, that of the labourers come late into the vineyard, does it carry any more obvious echo; and this only when the idea is reversed from that of the reward to the later-comer to that of assurance that the labourer, however delayed may be his coming, will still come, and with God's assistance will labour

> in strictest measure even[22]
> To that same lot, however mean, or high,
> Toward which Time leads me, and the will of Heav'n.

There is nowhere in it any mention of the vineyard, of the light, or of the talent, the basic imagery which informs it being indeed of a quite different nature: that of the octave centred in the image of time as a subtle thief stealing with hasty wing on the garden of youth, which has as yet brought forth no bud or blossom; and that of the sestet merely of some abstract lot, not figuratively expressed, and a pledge on the part of the poet to strive toward the fulfillment of that lot. The poem is a brief essay in critical self-examination, both retrospective and prospective—the former in its octave which meditates on the swift passing away of his youth and his failure so far to produce aught of worth or note; the latter in its sestet which with a proud humility forecasts the accomplishment, if God will, of some such work. It is thus a piece which combines the "tempus fugit" theme, so familiar to Renaissance poetry, with the theme of personal dedication, so natural to Milton; and aside from its high seriousness and the high sense of religious dedication at its end has little reference to the several themes suggested by the several scriptural quotations in the letter.

When one turns, however, to the sonnet "On his Blindness," subjecting it to the same careful scrutiny, and comparing its contents with those of the letter of 1631, and specifically with the three citations from the *New Testament* there quoted, one discovers: first, that the imagery informing this sonnet is almost wholly scriptural; and, second, that this imagery is drawn largely from the several gospel passages cited in the letter. As for two of these passages—that of labouring while it is yet light since darkness comes on apace, and that of burying the one talent and being rebuked by the Master upon His return—there can be no doubt that they are both embedded in Milton's poem, in fact, intricately interwoven with one another there to form the argument of its octave, as even a cursory reading will show:

> When I consider how my light is spent,
>   E're half my days, in this dark world and wide,
>   And that one Talent which is death to hide,
> Lodg'd with me useless, though my Soul more bent
> To serve therewith my Maker and present
> My true account, least he returning chide,
> Doth God exact day-labour, light deny'd
> I fondly ask

And so to consider first the "light" image and its connotations. The passage from John to which the letter refers, and almost as indubitably so the sonnet, when taken in its full context, reads as follows: "And as Jesus passed by, he saw a man which was blind from his birth. And his disciples asked him, saying, 'Master, who did sin, this man, or his parents, that he was born blind?' Jesus answered, 'Neither hath this man sinned, nor his parents; but that the work of God should be made manifest in him. I must work the works of him that sent me, while it is day; the night cometh when no man can work. As long as I am in the world, I am the light of the world.' When he had spoken, he spat on the ground, and made clay of the spittle, and he anointed the eyes of the blind man with the clay, and said unto him, 'Go wash in the pool of Siloam,' (which is by interpretation 'Sent'). He went his way therefore, and washed and came seeing."[23] In this passage John is apparently using the idea of light in three senses: first, as the physical light of day, and by metaphor it would seem of life; second, as the spiritual light which is Christ, and which in Him is come to enlighten the world; and third, as the communication by the spiritual Light of the physical light, and thereby the restoration of sight, which is a kind of light, to the blind, who moves in darkness. The reference in Milton's letter forms a part of the greeting to his friend, who is haled "as a good watch man to admonish that the

howres of the night pass on (for so I call my life as yet obscure, &
unserviceable to mankind) & that the day with me is at hand wherein
Christ commands all to labour while there is light."[24] Here both night
and light are obviously used in a figurative sense, night meaning a
barren and unproductive life, obscure and unserviceable to one's fellowmen, and day with its light that period of creative and productive
life wherein Christ commands all to labour in service to humanity,
and, as the sentence following suggests, in order "that God should be
honoured in everyone."

The reference as used in the sonnet forms, as it were, the outer
frame of the octave, extending through its first two lines, interrupted
through its next four, and then picked up and carried through its last
two; the reference to the parable of the buried talent being inserted in
between and constituting lines three through six, as a careful reading
will reveal. Here light is used in several senses, in all the three perhaps that John associated with it, and in addition certainly in that
which Milton in his letter gave it. Thus the light that is spent means
first of all the vision that is lost, which loss, as his Samson was later to
phrase it, leaves man so afflicted

> As in the land of darkness yet in light[25]
> To live a life half dead, a living death
> And buried; but O yet more miserable!
> My self, my Sepulcher, a moving grave.

But as the question, "Doth God exact day-labour, light deny'd?"
makes clear, it means also the physical light of day that is now
through blindness denied, that light of day in which man performs
the work appointed him of God, and without which his world is a
perpetual night wherein no man can labour. And since the work appointed him, this day-labour, is called by John, when the labourer is
Christ, the bringing of light into the world; and by Milton, when the
labourer is a dedicated man, the working of some noble service for
humanity—it is quite likely that when he conceived the octave of this
impassioned sonnet Milton had both these meanings in mind as well.
For he conceived of the poet as a light-bringer also, although on an
infinitely lower scale, of course, than the Son of God, and such a
poem as he himself hoped to write as among the supreme services a
man could accomplish for his fellowmen. So in this context it seems
rather futile to argue whether the "light" means the light of the physical eye, the light of the physical sun, the spiritual light within man,

or the visible working and manifestation of this inner and spiritual light in a creative life, since as Milton used the word in various other places it carried all these meanings—and so one may argue well may here; especially when one remembers that while writing the sonnet he was only recently blind, that his poetry from the "Fifth Latin Elegy" through *Samson Agonistes* reveals him to have been almost Greek in his devotion to the sun, that he regarded light either as the primal quality or as the prime creation of God, and that he constantly associated light with his own creative faculty.

Embedded within the "light" reference is that of the one talent "lodg'd with me useless"; and since the Matthew parable[26] is too long to permit quotation in full and too familiar to warrant such, suffice it for the present purpose to examine Milton's letter reference and his later use of it in the poem, comparing the two. In concluding his discussion of those ambitions, hopes, cares, and necessities of life which militate against a too studious retirement, he reminds the friend of the letter: "The Love of Learning, as it is the pursuit of something good, it would sooner follow the more excellent & supreme good knowne and praesented, and so be quickly diverted from the emptie & fantastick chase of shadows & notions, to the solid good flowing from due & tymely obedience to that command of the gospell set out by the seasing of him that hid the talent."[27] Here devotion to learning is justified as a means to that solid good, a wise and intelligent life, that is, which will know to follow the divine injunction, and in obedience to it cultivate, enrich, and increase the talent that is granted to its fullest, rather than bury it away, and when the day of reckoning comes have even the one talent seized. In the sonnet the talent has not been seized, for Milton, the servant to whom it was given, had proved himself a faithful one,

> my soul more bent
> To serve therewith my Maker and present
> My true account;

and the talent remained lodged with him, but lodged useless, inasmuch as the daylight in which he might have cultivated it had been changed into "cloud instead and everduring dark,"[28] and the talent, as it were, thus buried alive; and since to hide it is death, he has come to comprehend that state of living-death which he was to describe so poignantly in the words of Samson:

> Scarce half I seem to live, dead more than half:[29]
> O dark, dark, dark amid the blaze of noon,
> Irrevocably dark, total eclipse,
> Without all hope of day.

As compared with most men Milton was assuredly a man of many talents, and that he chose to associate himself with the servant of one talent can be explained, in part perhaps, as Newton suggests,[30] by his modesty, but more satisfactorily by the fact that of his many gifts he must have valued one so highly that in comparison with it all the rest shrank into insignificance, and in the cultivation of this one seemed to centre his very life and reason for living. From the time of his youth, it would seem, he had liked to think of himself as a labourer in the vineyard of his Lord, and his labour there was to be the writing of great poetry, of poetry written both for the service of man and to the glory of God. And now suddenly in his forty-fourth year, and irrevocably and beyond renewal, he found the God-given light vanished and the awful darkness come upon him: the light that had vanished being the loss of his vision, it is true, but at the same time much more —for in the momentary anguish in which the sonnet was written it meant, as chief among those other losses aforementioned, the loss of his ability to fulfill the chief aim of his life, the writing of the great poem, and thus of necessity the burying of the one talent. And having taken away the wherewithal toward its fulfillment, the outer light of day whereby he might cultivate and bring to fruition the inner light of the divine poem, would the Keeper of the vineyard, would the Master who from the days of his youth had imposed upon him the necessity of writing this poem, still exact "day-labour, light deny'd" and demand of him the talent utilised when the gift of utilising it had been removed?

So are two of the scriptural passages of the letter of 1631 obviously incorporated into the sonnet of 1652, or rather so do they form the very framework on which its octave is built and the matter out of which it is built; while its sestet, like that of the sonnet, "On Having Arrived at the Age of Twenty-three," though it does not in detail employ the imagery of the third scriptural passage of the letter, that of the late-comers into the vineyard, yet breathes the spirit of it, going even farther than the earlier poem, to say

> They also serve who only stand and wait.

And at two highly critical moments of his life, spaced more than a score of years apart, to find so close a sequence of thoughts and images running in Milton's mind argues, as I have suggested, a remarkable unity in his thinking, a unity which might be illustrated by a number of other examples; and at the same time, as I have also tried to show, the ideas and images of the letter of his youth go a considerable way toward clarifying the sonnet of his middle years.

NOTES

1. *The Works of John Milton.* (New York: Columbia University Press, 1931). "Of Education," vol. IV, p. 287.
2. *Ibid.* "Elegia Sexta," vol. I, pp. 206-15.
3. *Ibid.* "At a Solemn Musick," vol. I, pp. 27-28. (Cf. F. T. Prince, *The Italian Element in Milton's Verse,* Oxford: Clarendon Press, 1954, p. 65.)
4. *Ibid.* "In Quintum Novembris," vol. I, pp. 236-55.
5. *Ibid.* "Elegia Tertia," (11. 15-30), vol. I, p. 180.
6. *Ibid. Paradise Lost,* X, 602-9.
7. *Ibid.* "On the Morning of Christ's Nativity," (11. 173-220), vol. I, pp. 8-10.
8. *Ibid., Paradise Lost,* I, 381-520.
9. *Ibid. Paradise Lost,* XII, 356-371.
10. *Ibid.* "Lycidas," (11. 64-84), vol. I, p. 79.
11. *Ibid. Paradise Regained,* III, 22-108; IV, 221-363.
12. *Ibid. Comus* (11. 160-64), vol. I, p. 91.
13. *Ibid. Comus* (11. 592-96), vol. I, p. 107.
14. David Masson, *The Life of John Milton in Connexion with the History of His Time.* (London: MacMillan, 1881), vol. I, pp. 325-27.
15. *Ibid.* Vol. V, pp. 237-40. (Masson dates the sonnet 1655, but it is more commonly dated 1652; cf., for example, Tillyard, Milton, p. 189).
16. *Milton's Sonnets,* edited by Mark Pattison. (London: 1883), pp. 96-98; 204-6.
17. *The Sonnets of John Milton,* edited by John S. Smart (Glasgow: 1921).
18. *Milton's Sonnets,* edited by A. W. Verity. (Cambridge University Press: 1916), pp. 32; 67-69.
19. *Gospel of John,* IX, 4.
20. *Gospel of Matthew,* XXV, 14-30.
21. *Gospel of Matthew,* XX, 1-16.

22. *Columbia Milton.* "On Having Arrived at the Age of Twenty-three," vol. I, p. 60.
23. *Gospel of John,* IX, 1-7.
24. *Columbia Milton.* "Letter to a Friend," vol. XII, p. 320.
25. *Ibid. Samson Agonistes* (11. 99-102).
26. *Gospel of Matthew,* XXV, 14-30.
27. *Columbia Milton,* "Letter to a Friend," vol. XII, p. 324.
28. *Ibid. Paradise Lost,* III, 45.
29. *Ibid. Samson Agonistes* (11. 79-82).
30. *Milton's Poems,* edited by Thomas Newton. (London: 1749), vol. III, p. 531.

[EDITOR'S NOTE. See also J. H. Hanford, *MP,* XVIII (1921), 475-83, and *University of Michigan Publications; Language and Literature,* I (1925), 89-173; W. R. Parker, *RES,* XI (1935), 276-83; A. S. P. Woodhouse, *UTQ,* XIII (1943-44), 66-101; K. Svendsen, *Explicator,* VII (1949), Item 53; R. M. Smith, *MLN,* LX (1945), 394-8; D. C. Dorian, *Explicator,* VIII (1949), Item 10 and X (1951), Item 16; M. Kelley, *MP,* LIV (1956), 20-25; W. R. Parker, *PMLA,* LXXIII (1958), 196-200; J. T. Shawcross, *JEGP,* LVIII (1959), 29-38; H. F. Robins, *RES,* VII (1956), 360-66; J. L. Jackson and W. E. Weese, *MLN,* LXXII (1957), 91-3; F. Pyle, *RES,* LIX (1958), 376-87; R. L. Slakey, *ELH,* XXVIII (1960), 122-30; A. Gossman and G. W. Whiting, *RES,* XII (1961), 364-70; T. Stoehr, *ES,* XLV (1964), 289-301; on Milton's blindness, E. G. Brown, *Milton's Blindness,* 1934; W. B. Hunter, Jr., *JHM,* XVII (1962), 333-41.]

THOMAS WHEELER

Milton's Twenty-third Sonnet

For almost three hundred years editors and critics had assumed that
Milton's last sonnet obviously referred to his second wife, Katherine
Woodcock. Since William Riley Parker's article, "Milton's Last Sonnet,"[1] a considerable controversy has arisen concerning the identity of
the "late espoused Saint." Parker's chief contention is that the reference to "Purification in the old Law" applies only to Mary Powell,
who died three days after the birth of Deborah. Katherine Woodcock
lived well beyond the sixty-six days prescribed by Leviticus xii, 2-5.
Parker interprets the *as* in line 5 to mean *like* and argues that it
would be nonsense to speak of Katherine as like one purified since,
according to the law, she was purified. Supposing that the "once
more" in line 7 indicates that Milton had seen the face of his de-
ceased wife, Parker argues that Katherine cannot be the subject of
the poem because Milton had never seen her.

Attempting to refute Parker's argument, Fitzroy Pyle[2] points out
that the "once more" is meant to contrast with the dream vision: that
in Heaven Milton will see Katherine "without restraint." Pyle interprets "embrace" to mean "kiss" and supposes that the dream ended
because, as the veiled figure began to put aside the veil to kiss Milton,
he was unable to visualize the face about to be revealed. Following

From *Studies in Philology*, LVIII (1961), 510-15. Reprinted by permission of
the author and The University of North Carolina Press.

another line of argument, Charles Dahlberg[3] notes that the sonnet is in the hand of Jeremy Picard, an amanuensis whose earliest work cannot be dated before January 14, 1657/8. Parker, in rebuttal, denies that "embrace" means "kiss," and asserts that for several reasons the fact that Picard transcribed the poem is irrelevant to the whole argument.[4] Edward LeComte concludes that the emphasis on purity and purification indicates that Katherine is the subject, since her name is derived from the Greek "katharos," meaning "pure."[5]

There is one matter on which all these scholars agree: that Milton is writing about either Mary Powell or Katherine Woodcock. Only Leo Spitzer proposes that the "late espoused Saint" is not a real person at all but an ideal figure like Dante's *donna angelicata*.[6] Spitzer's hypothesis has one advantage: it obviates the rather sterile argument over which wife Milton is referring to. And it puts the problem of interpretation in the proper perspective. That is, it seeks to interpret the poem not on the basis of historical fact, as if it were an obituary notice, but in the light of what we know of Milton's mind.

But Spitzer is unconvincing in his interpretation simply because the poem obviously does refer to historical fact. Why else would Milton so carefully refer to "childbed taint"? He must have had either Mary Powell or Katherine Woodcock in mind. So the discussion seems to come back to the same dreary question: who was that wife John Milton dreamed about?

I would like to suggest an interpretation of the sonnet which combines Spitzer's approach with the biographical method but avoids the pitfalls of both. It is an interpretation which makes irrelevant the question of which wife Milton is concerned with and at the same time provides an insight into the workings of Milton's mind.

To begin with, it will be wise to accept Milton's dream as a real dream. But one ought to remember that Milton was under no obligation to tell the literal truth in his sonnets. Plenty of sonnets and other lyrics in the Renaissance are simply imaginative poems having no relation whatsoever to the literal, biographical truth. If a poet had to fall in love to write love poetry, if he had to be in love at the time he wrote it, and if the only truth of his lyric was an absolute correspondence with his experience, then we must find ourselves confronted with a parcel of love-sick men who incidentally can express themselves in verse, not a group of poets—makers—who, in writing love poetry, were deeply concerned with a poetic tradition springing from Ovid, Catullus, Petrarch, and others. How many mistresses did Herrick have? Who was Donne in bed with besides that flea? And who is that lovely Italian girl that Milton worshipped from afar in his early sonnets? Obviously, Milton's dream might be purely a piece of fiction.

But I think that for very good reasons it is prudent to assume that Milton's dream was substantially what he said it was. For one thing, no one can ever prove that it was not. For another, Milton was not writing on a traditional theme and imitating established models. Even more convincing, however, is Milton's usual practice in his sonnets: his blindness, the massacre of the Waldensians, the victories of Fairfax, the problems that confronted Cromwell—these were hardly figments of Milton's imagination. His later sonnets are sober, predominantly serious, and factual.

Having accepted the sonnet as a substantially accurate record of a dream, we find ourselves again confronted with the question: who is the veiled figure? Perhaps we might best answer this question by asking some others. Who is Lycidas? Who is the Lady in *Comus*? Who, in sonnet XIII, is Henry Lawes? Who, in sonnet XVII, is Sir Harry Vane, the younger? One might answer that they are all real people—that Lycidas is Edward King, that the Lady is the daughter of the Earl of Bridgewater, that Lawes and Vane are simply Lawes and Vane. But Milton does not see them as real people. Edward King is the good shepherd in his dual role of poet and pastor. The Lady in *Comus* is virtue; since she is above temptation, she is hardly a human being. Vane and Lawes are idealized figures. Milton's habitual practice in writing about real people is to present them in idealized forms. He sees in them the embodiment of learning, piety, chastity, wisdom, or whatever. This is not to say that the real person is lost altogether. Edward King was a poet of sorts, Lawes a great musician, Vane an important leader, and one would hardly wish to cast aspersions upon the chastity of the Earl's daughter. But Milton raises these real people above the level of reality and makes them symbols of his own ideals.

To say that Milton was an idealist is hardly original. His idealism is everywhere evident in his work. What could be more idealistic than his proposed academy? The whole argument of *Areopagitica* is based on the idealistic notion that truth will always defeat falsehood in free and open combat. In the two defenses of the English people Milton idealizes the virtue and accomplishments of his countrymen. And, in a supreme burst of idealism, in the *Ready and Easy Way to Establish a Free Commonwealth*, Milton recommends a form of government to be administered by men whom he naïvely supposes to be invulnerable to graft, partisan pressures, and the corruption to which great power usually leads.

I suggest that sonnet XXIII is best interpreted if we remember this facet of Milton's mind. He is writing primarily about loss—the almost insufferable loss of a beloved woman. It seems unlikely that Mary Powell, from whom he sought a divorce, could be the subject of his longing. And if he meant Katherine Woodcock, then he was wrong about "purification in the old Law," a possibility which one ought to keep in mind. But even if Milton did refer to Katherine and did make a mistake in referring to the Mosaic law, the figure presented in the poem is clearly idealized. She

> Came vested all in white, pure as her mind:
> Her face was vail'd, yet to my fancied sight,
> Love, sweetness, goodness, in her person shin'd
> So clear, as in no face with more delight.

This is not Katherine Woodcock; it is an ideal in the mind of John Milton. Regardless of whether the poem got its start in an actual dream or not, it represents what every dream represents: the shaping of reality by the mind. It is not Mary Powell or Katherine that Milton longs for; it is that "apt and cheerful conversation of man with woman" that he never found. It is the kind of Paradise depicted in the Garden: Eve, beautiful, womanly, and submissive; Adam whispering to Eve

>   Awake
> My fairest, my espous'd, my latest found,
> Heavens last best gift, my ever new delight . . .

and Eve answering

> O Sole in whom my thoughts find all repose,
> My Glorie, my Perfection. . . .

The poignant grief of the sonnet reminds one of Satan's anguish as he beholds the nuptial bliss of Adam and Eve.

> Sight hateful, sight tormenting! thus these two
> Imparadis't in one anothers arms
> The happier *Eden,* shall enjoy thir fill
> Of bliss on bliss, while I to Hell am thrust,
> Where neither joy nor love, but fierce desire,

> Among our other torments not the least,
> Still unfulfill'd with pain of longing pines.

Even more to the point is another dream, narrated in *Paradise Lost*, a dream which is obviously fictitious, yet so much like sonnet XXIII that one can hardly believe that Milton wrote without the sonnet in mind. Adam is telling Raphael about the creation of Eve.

> The Rib he formd and fashond with his hands;
> Under his forming hands a Creature grew,
> Manlike, but different sex, so lovly faire
> That what seemd fair in all the World, seemd now
> Mean, or in her summd up, in her contain
> And in her looks, which from that time infus'd
> Sweetness into my heart, unfelt before,
> And into all things from her Aire inspir'd
> The spirit of love and amorous delight.
> She disappeerd, and left me dark, I wak'd
> To find her, or for ever to deplore
> Her loss, and other pleasures all abjure.

It is no *donna angelicata* of Dante that Milton dreams of but the very image in his mind of a paradise which, like Adam, he sought but never found.[7]

This interpretation of the sonnet has two distinct advantages. First, it makes unnecessary a controversy which adds nothing to our understanding and appreciation of the sonnet. To any sensitive reader the important fact about the poem is the sense of almost unutterable loneliness and the suffocating isolation of the man whose day is night. It makes no difference who he is talking about. The Mary Powell-Katherine Woodcock argument is, no pun intended, a blind alley.

But one might wish to see in this sonnet something of its author's mind. The interpretation I suggest has this second advantage. It connects this poem with the mind of Milton as we see it in many of his other works and deepens our response to the pathos of Milton's situation: for he has nowhere to live but in his mind, and he has not even the remembrance of an ideal marriage, only the ideal itself which he cannot seize in the midst of his darkness. No other poem shows us so poignantly Milton's sense of isolation. Not even *Samson Agonistes* carries the power of this brief lyric, for Samson will know a last moment of triumph but John Milton will live out his life in darkness.

Finally I think we see in sonnet XXIII one other aspect of Milton's mind: his tendency to dramatize himself. The man who, in the *Second Defense,* saw himself surveying "as if from a towering height, the far extended tracts of sea and land and innumerable crowds of spectators betraying in their looks the liveliest interest and sensations most congenial with [his] own," now sees himself alone, lonely, and in the dark. And while it is prudent, as I have said, to assume that Milton's dream was substantially as he described it, the dream is almost too dramatic, too good a subject for a sonnet. Regardless of what has been said about the sonnet "On the Late Massacre in Piemont," it seems to me that sonnet XXIII is the most compellingly powerful of all Milton's lyrics. May it not be that to dramatize his loneliness and sense of loss Milton has improved upon his dream? Has he not in the magnificent compression of the sestet showed himself to be still the poet, the maker, raising his experience above the level of prosaic reality to the regions of charmed song?

NOTES

1. William R. Parker, "Milton's Last Sonnet," *RES,* XXI (1945), 235-238.
2. Fitzroy Pyle, "Milton's Sonnet on His 'Late-Espoused Saint,'" *RES,* XXV (1949), 57-60.
3. Addendum to Pyle's article.
4. William R. Parker, "Milton's Last Sonnet Again," *RES,* N.S. II (1951), 147-152.
5. Edward S. Le Comte, "The Veiled Face of Milton's Wife," *N&Q,* CXCIX (1954), 245-246.
6. Leo Spitzer, "Understanding Milton," *Hopkins Review,* IV (Summer 1951), 17-25. [EDITOR'S NOTE. Reprinted in *Essays on English and American Literature,* by Leo Spitzer, (Princeton: Princeton University Press, 1962).]
7. Perhaps this is why the figure is veiled: she represents an ideal which Milton has never seen on earth but which he certainly expects to see in Heaven.

[EDITOR'S NOTE. See also R. M. Frye, *N&Q,* CXCIV (1949), 321; J. T. Shawcross, *N&Q,* III (1956), 204-4; T. B. Stroup, *PQ,* XXXIX (1960), 125-6.]

ARTHUR E. BARKER

Structural Pattern in *Paradise Lost*

Milton, as Professor Thompson has said, "realized that form is determined not by rule or precedent but by the thought to be expressed.
Hence he adapted the pattern of the epic to his own ends, and wrote
as a creative artist."[1]

From its opening invocation *Paradise Lost* invites attention to this
process of adaptation and transcendence. The initial statement of the
threefold subject (disobedience and woe, till restoration) immediately
suggests specific comparison with the opening statement of the *Aeneid*
(Troy fall and wandering, till the new city be founded). This suggestion is reinforced periodically throughout; so also is the opening
invocation's adventurous claim to no middle flight above the Aonian
mount, no mere description of the loss and restoration of an earthly
city. And one of the chief pleasures of the student of Milton has always been to watch, under the guidance of skilled commentators from
Addison to Professor Thompson, how Milton expressively modifies
the conventions and the pattern of epic to suit the meanings of his
theme.

So guided, most of us readily agree with Addison's observation that
Paradise Lost does not fall short "of the *Iliad* or *Aeneid* in the beauties

From "Studies in Milton: Essays in Memory of Elbert N. S. Thompson,"
Philological Quarterly, XXVIII (1949), 17-30. Reprinted by permission of the
publisher.

which are essential to that kind of writing"; and it is to be hoped that the tradition so established may somehow be continued in spite of the difficulties of increasing unfamiliarity with Milton's classical models. The process of adaptation was in fact one of Milton's chief instruments of expression. Each of his important poems assumes as one of its points of departure a tradition of interpretation and a convention of form, and in each of them successful communication depends very largely on a recognition of likeness as the basis for expressive variation. Nor is this the case merely with conventional detail. It may be doubted whether the total force of *Paradise Lost* can ever be felt by a reader who does not recognize how its total pattern reproduces while modifying and modifies while reproducing the total pattern of the *Aeneid*.

It is not difficult to win from a modern reader half of this recognition. But when one has shown that the *Aeneid* has indeed a significant structural pattern—six Odyssean books of wandering balanced by six Achillean books of war and establishment, three distinct movements of four books each, six groups of two books apiece, with the structural weight so made to fall on a series of prophecies of glory to be won from apparent failure—when one has indicated by simple arithmetic the controlling structural pattern of Virgil's epic and has turned to Milton's awareness of it, one is almost certain to be met by the complaint that Milton does not imitate it adequately. Before long one is likely to find oneself dealing, like Professor Thompson on another occasion,[2] with the implications of Addison's remark that the tenth book of *Paradise Lost* "is like the last act of a well-constructed tragedy, in which all who had a part in it are drawn up before the audience, and represented under those circumstances in which the determination of the action has placed them." Are not the succeeding books, it is asked, superfluous, or at any rate (as Addison notes) "not generally reckoned among the most shining books of the poem"? And does not this mean, among other things, that Milton's imitation of the Virgilian pattern is inadequate?

It is difficult to convince a modern reader that Milton's intention was not merely to copy but to adapt the Virgilian pattern, to use the classical models as bases for variations which would assist in the expression of the Christian theme. The paradox of the Christian theme is itself difficult enough to express convincingly. Milton already found it so. But it is perhaps just here that the comparison and contrast with Virgil may be of most effect. We have at any rate a suggestive point of contrast in the attitudes of the two poets towards their work. The Roman poet on his death-bed, we are told, gave direction that his beautifully patterned epic should be burned; the blind Milton, in the year of his death, produced a "revised and augmented" edition of his poem, correcting errors in spelling and punctuation and even tinkering with its division into books in order to change what the title-page of 1667 had described as "a poem written in ten books" into "a poem in twelve books." This tinkering is Milton's last recorded comment on his poem.

II

At first sight this change in numeration seems of little moment. Editors usually draw our attention to the fact that, by the simple process of dividing roughly in half the two longest of his 1667 books, Milton accomplished a redivision ever since regarded as perfectly just. The change involved no shifting about of material whatsoever, and only the slightest of additions. Four lines were added at the beginning of the new book VIII to provide the appearance of a new departure; they indicate, it is said, no change in direction; our first parent is merely represented as guilty of a momentary lapse of attention in the middle of Raphael's lecture. Similarly, five lines were added for the beginning of the new book XII (and the Argument was slightly revised); Michael is merely made to pause for a moment in his partially illustrated address, "betwixt the world destroy'd and world restor'd." That is all. Milton has perceived that a poem which invites comparison with the ancient epics, and particularly with Virgil, ought to have twelve books, not ten.

It seems a strangely retarded perception. Someone should ask at least for once the eminently simple-minded question. "What cause . . . ?"

With almost any other poet, though blind, this question might well be left unasked. English Renaissance poetry is a major field of bibliographical activity because of infinitely numerous revisions of more extensive importance than this. Yet the meticulousness with which the blind Milton revised *Paradise Lost* for the 1674 edition, with the absence of any other major changes of any kind, suggests the desirability of contemplating even this shred of evidence as to the author's intention in a poem so vast and variously interpreted. And there are two characteristics of Milton's major poems which suggest that the question may not be unprofitable. One is his habit of using a conventional form as a point of departure; the other his architectonic skill. Both depend in considerable measure for their success on simple clarity in the initial massing and division of material.

The effect of balance more or less characteristic of any work of art frequently arrives in Milton at a mathematical plainness almost suggestive of the counting of lines. We need not suppose that his muse worked quite so mechanically or laid so lowly a burden on herself; but Milton's mind operated at ease only when he perceived in or imposed on his material a precise mathematical division of some sort. No doubt such precision gave him a much-needed sense of security and control. At any rate, it is certainly a fact (of which I once tried to make something . . .) that much of the force of the "Hymn" of the *Nativity Ode* and also of *Lycidas* is derived from the modulation of three equally and precisely balanced movements, similar in figurative (or structural) pattern, yet evolving a cumulative effect through variation. At the other end of Milton's career, *Samson Agonistes,* it is well known, consists of five perfectly regular and almost mathematically equal "acts," each reproducing and developing towards its completion the basic pattern of trial and triumph in defeat. Milton did not always reach such precision. The genre of *Comus* could perhaps hardly have sustained such rigorous definition as is possible in other forms, though its much revised structure deserves closer analysis from this point of view; implicit in *Paradise Regained* there is such a structural pattern, though handled in a way unusual with Milton. But it is obvious that this simple effect of balance was of importance to him, and one can sometimes watch him striving to impose a pattern of exact balance where none perhaps existed. A large example (upon which I have commented at length elsewhere) is to be seen in his attempt in *Defensio Secunda* in 1654 to see in his controversial activity a consistent threefold pattern; in the 1640's, he says, he perceived that there were three species of liberty; the chronological blocks of his prose deal with them in an orderly and (it is implied) predetermined sequence. It is curious that a mind so bent on well-balanced hinging should feel it desirable to change the book divisions of its major production after a seven-year interval.

The habit of taking as an expressive point of departure some traditionally fixed or even highly conventionalized form (sonnet, masque, elegy, epic, tragedy), and the instinctive habit of dealing with poetic material in clearly defined and precisely balanced blocks held together and given extension by their reproduction of some basic pattern, are not of course merely Miltonic habits. They are only more obvious in him than they are generally in the poetic art of the Renaissance—or of any highly conscious creative period. They contribute to one of the uses of poetry which was of the utmost importance to him. As Professor Woodhouse and Professor Tillyard among others have indicated, Milton's major poems seem to have performed a cathartic function for the poet himself: each seems in its creation a process whereby the poet resolves a paralysing tension. This is obvious in the cases of *Lycidas* and *Samson Agonistes;* and, properly handled, the obvious need not divert us for long from the poem to the poet. It would seem that in moments of tension Milton found a secure point of departure in the fixity of some traditional form (and, of course, though it is not in question here, some traditional complex of ideas), and that the precise balancing of blocks of poetic material afforded him a secure and regularized channel within which to resolve the tension by the working out of variations.

Does this generalization hold for *Paradise Lost* as well as for *Lycidas* and *Samson Agonistes?* If one's first (though not one's final) observation about "a true poem" is that it is "a composition and pattern," why did Milton in 1674 find himself dissatisfied with the composition and pattern implied by the division of the material of *Paradise Lost* into ten books? Is it possible that the simple redivision into twelve books ("differently disposed," as Edward Philips tells us, ". . . by his own hand, that is by his own appointment") indicates that the process of resolution had not quite clarified itself when Milton published the poem in 1667, that subsequently he saw in it a pattern which the ten-book division tended to obscure?

III

The original ten-book division immediately suggests comparison with the drama. It inevitably recalls Davenant's projected structure for *Gondibert.* It also implies that the structure of *Paradise Lost* owes much to the neo-classical theory, formulated by the Italians and of great force among Milton's English predecessors, which closely associated the tragic and the epic forms and resulted in a long series of abortive five-act epic experiments.[3] The relation of Milton's theory to this tradition deserves closer attention; the redivision of *Paradise Lost* seems at first to suggest that he never quite made up his mind as to whether "the rules of Aristotle herein are strictly to be kept, or nature to be followed. . . ."

However that may be, the 1667 edition of *Paradise Lost* presents a firmly organized five-act epic, perfectly exemplifying what were thought to be the Aristotelian requirements for structure. It successfully achieves what Sidney had earlier attempted, and it certainly out-Gondiberts Davenant. Its plot is seen at a glance to consist of five "acts" (with appropriate "scenes"), and the cumulative effect of these acts is exactly what Davenant said it should be.

Act I presents Satan's revival in Hell, and the council's sketching out of the plot against man with Satan's voyage to the universe; books 1 and 2. (Throughout, in order to reduce the exposition to the very nadir of *simplesse*, Arabic numerals will be used to indicate the books of 1667, Roman for those of 1674.) Act II, having opened with a scene in Heaven firmly focussed on the curve of Satan's flight, carries him to earth and leads to his first attempt to put the plot in operation; books 3 and 4. Act III, with that freedom which is one of the recognized advantages of epic, returns us in actual time to events in the past, the war in Heaven and Satan's defeat; books 5 and 6. In terms of formal development—the subject of actual and apparent time is far too complex for attention here—it gives a decided turn to the plot's development: Satan is twice temporarily defeated. Act IV is the crucial act. It consists of books 7 and 8: book 7, Raphael's account of the Creation and the colloquy on astronomy and woman, now known to us as books VII and VIII; and book 8, the book of the Fall, known to us as book IX. This act decisively changes the direction of the action: Satan has at last succeeded; and this "counterturn" is confirmed by the final act, books 9 and 10. Act V presents the immediate consequences of the Fall (book 9, now known to us as X), and the scriptural vision of misery, Michael's prophecy, with the expulsion from Paradise (book 10, now known to us as XI and XII).

The ideal formal requirements for five-act epic set forth in the Preface to *Gondibert* could hardly be more adequately fulfilled. Says Davenant:

> The first *Act* is the general preparative, by rendring the chiefest characters of persons, and ending with something that looks like an obscure promise of design. [So in *Paradise Lost* Satan, and the first sketch of the design against man which provides the poem with its plot.] The second begins with an introducement of new persons [God, the Son, the angels], so finishes all the characters [Adam and Eve], and ends with some little performance of that design which was promis'd at the parting of

the first *Act* [Satan inducing Eve's dream of evil]. The third makes a visible correspondence in the underwalks, or lesser intrigues, of persons [Satan's conflict with God], and ends with an ample turn of the main design and expectation of new [Satan's temporary defeat in Heaven, from which, as we know, he has already partially recovered]. The fourth, ever having occasion to be the longest [so indeed it certainly is in *Paradise Lost,* 1667] gives a notorious turn to all the underwalks [the Creation], and a counterturn to that main design which chang'd in the third [Satan's successful achievement of man's fall]. The fifth begins with an intire diversion of the main and dependent Plotts [the penitence of Adam and Eve, the Son's intercession, Satan's return to hell—though perhaps here alone Milton faults in his design], then makes the general correspondence of the persons more discernible [Michael's implied commentary on the action], and ends with an easy untying [in *Paradise Lost,* uneasy tying?], of those particular knots which made a contexture of the whole, leaving such satisfaction of probabilities with the Spectator as may perswade him that neither Fortune in the fate of Persons, nor the Writer in the Representment, have been unnatural or exorbitant.[4]

It seems a pity that the Satanic interpreters of *Paradise Lost* have not generally been familiar with the five-act epic theory, or with Davenant's preface, or with the 1667 edition, when such satisfaction of probabilities might have been theirs. For the implications of the ten-book division of the poem are too plain to need much comment. The five-act structural emphasis comes down heavily on the crucial fourth act: Satan's successful counterturning of God's creative design when man's fall is accomplished. The "main design," artfully left doubtful at the end of the first two acts, and given a "turn" at the end of the third, receives its definitive pattern through the counterturn at the end of the fourth (book 8, or IX). What follows in the final act, the vision of unending earthly misery and the expulsion from Paradise, serves only to make clear the pattern of woe which makes the contexture of the whole.

Was it Milton's aim in the redivision of the poem in 1674 to shift this weight of emphasis from the book of the Fall, and so to offset the not merely dramatic but tragic implications of the counterturn in what looked like Act IV? The redivision does not change the actual struc-

ture of his poem in any way. Does it, however, by suggesting a different structural pattern, bring out implications muted in the earlier
division?

IV

A poem is not, in spite of Davenant and neo-classicism, a "building";
it moves in time, it does not stand in space. Yet a poet may not un-
justifiably say, with Davenant, "you may next please, having examined the substance, to take a view of the form, and observe if I have
methodically and with discretion disposed of the materials. . . ."
Under some circumstances he may even be justified in imitating some
of the architectural tricks, so popular in the seventeenth century,
whereby an appearance of considerable extension is given to an un-
avoidably narrow edifice.

If the term "baroque" is applicable to Milton, it can certainly be
used to describe the most obvious effect he achieved by turning books
7 and 10 into books VII and VIII and books XI and XII. Did he
remember at this point, one wonders, the baroque illusion which off-
sets the narrowness of the Laudian chapel at Peterhouse (where flowing curves along the short horizontal much extend the facade) or the
great curve of the collonade of St. Peter's? However that may be, the
effect of the redivision in this respect is no mere illusion. It gives to
the material of his poem following the defeat of Satan in Heaven an
appearance of extension equal to its actual original weight in number
of lines. The total number of lines in the last four books of the original poem is some three hundred—but *only* some three hundred—less
than that of the first six books. The division of this material into six
books gives the poem the just balance demanded by the treatment its
theme has received. It is the ten-book division which, in this respect,
is an illusion. Is the five-act pattern an illusion also?

The division into twelve more than modifies the five-act scheme.
By presenting an arrangement reminiscent of Virgil's it induces a
pattern of emphasis very different from that examined in the preceding section. Obviously the twelve books of 1674 fall into six groups
of two books each. The first three groups remain as they were, with
the decision of the action left temporarily in the balance. But the
fourth group now presents, not the Creation and Fall (7 and 8), but
the Creation and Adam's progressive understanding of his situation
through his colloquy with Raphael (old 7 become VII and VIII). The
fifth group now presents in combination Adam's fall and penitence

(the second half of old Act IV with the first half of old Act V; old 8 and 9, new IX and X). And the sixth the vision of human misery, and Michael's prophecy of the Messiah with the expulsion (old 10 become XI and XII).

The shift in grouping is so simple, involving as it does mere numbering, that the importance of the result may pass unrecognized. The mind of a responsive reader does rest, consciously or unconsciously, at the end of each book of a long poem, and at the end of each pair. The reader is induced so to rest in *Paradise Lost* by the invocations and the new departures in subject matter in the first three pairs of the poem. This rhythm will be continued to the end. In the 1667 arrangement the mind will come to rest on the Fall and the expulsion; looking backward, it will see its rests at the ends of the first three groups as premonitions of these events. In the 1674 version, it will come to rest on Adam's understanding of his situation (and of love), reached under Raphael's direction, on the contrition of Adam and Eve and their hope of mercy, and consequently on the Messianic prophecy of final victory as well as on the expulsion from Paradise.

As one looks back over a poem in which the rests have come as they do in the 1674 division, one sees that the structural stress has throughout fallen with increasing weight on the foreshadowings of the Son's ultimate triumph, on the operations of the divine mercy and love. It is here that *Paradise Lost* reproduces while modifying the large structural pattern of the *Aeneid*, with its steadily repeated prophecies of Roman glory. The correspondence is not exact. How could it be? But the expressive reminiscence is clear in 1674, as it was not in 1667. Indeed, whereas the prophecy sounded most clearly by Virgil at the end of books two (Creusa), four (Mercury), six (the Sibyl), and eight (Vulcan), dies away in the fury of the struggle with Turnus, the prophetic note of *Paradise Lost* swells from the ambiguity of Satan's view from the steps that link Heaven and Earth, and of the scales seen aloft, through the victory of the Son in Heaven to Michael's final prophecy. Moreover, in the new pattern, implications lost in the tragic structure of 1667, are underlined for the memory. One example must suffice. We are in error when we see the discourse on love at the end of book VIII and of the fourth group merely as prelude to and motivation for the Fall; it is also prelude to man's restoration and to the reconciliation of Adam and Eve at the end of book X and of group five. Adam in fact falls in imagination when he speaks wildly of Eve's beauty in book VIII; he is restored to sanity by the intervention of Raphael before the book ends. When at the end of the next two-book group we come to rest on the reconciliation of Adam and Eve, we shall look back across the Fall, not so much to Adam's imaginative lapse as to the sanity Raphael taught. And we shall look forward to Adam's restoration to something more than mere sanity at the end of the two-book group to come.

Such is Milton's discretion in the new disposition of his materials. The purpose of the redivision is to reduce the structural emphasis on the Fall of man and to increase the emphasis on his restoration. And this shift in emphasis is underlined by other structural effects of the redivision which combine to shift onward the poem's centre of gravity.

V

The ten books of 1667 will divide in but two ways: into five "acts" and into two blocks of five. The twelve books of 1674 (such is the force of simple arithmetic) divide in three ways.

Like the *Aeneid*, the *Paradise Lost* of 1674 consists of three movements of four books apiece. As with the "Hymn" of the *Nativity Ode* and with *Lycidas*, the three movements develop variations on a basic pattern. Virgil's first movement of four books turns upon Dido (and Creusa); his second carries Aeneas from Carthage to the moment when Turnus is about to attack, by way of the Sibyl; his third describes the war with the Latins. No correspondence to this pattern of three large and equally balanced movements is suggested by the ten-book division of 1667. In 1674 the three movements are clearly defined: one turns upon Satan, one upon the Son, one upon Man. The curve of the first is defined by Satan, reviving and frustrated, of the second by the Son as avenging justice and as creative love, of the third by Adam's fall and restoration. The rests at the ends of the first two movements fall upon the scales seen in heaven and on the delicate balance of Adam's original perfection, of the third on the balance to be made up at the last.

Each of these movements pauses and turns, as do Virgil's, upon its centre. It is not merely the direction of Satan's actual flight which changes between books III and IV; the apparent revival which has brought him to the verge of heaven's light now becomes a clear process of degeneration marked by God's comments, Satan's soliloquy, and his discomfiture in the garden. So the second turns with the Son from avenging justice to creation. So the third turns from sin through penance towards regeneration.

However one looks at the structure of *Paradise Lost* in its new division, attention is focussed firmly on one point, variously indicated from different angles. The ten-book division presents a five-act structure, and that structure is tragic. Its centre, if it has one, lies between books 5 and 6; that is to say, in the midst of the War in Heaven, with evil at its most arrogant height. But that centre is an illusion which obscures the halving of the poem by actual number of lines. The redivision of 1674 presents a poem which in structural pattern, however viewed, hangs self-balanced on its centre. That centre is between books VI and VII, with evil on the one hand frustrated, and on the other creation and recreation. Every structural subdivision in the poem is so aimed.

Is the new absent-mindedness of our first parent, one wonders, after all so insignificant, as he

> Thought him still speaking, still stood fixt to hear;
> Then as new wak't thus gratefully repli'd . . . ;

or Michael's medial pause? And is it wholly a flight of fancy to see the simple redivision as changing a tragic pattern into the three-fold pattern of a divine comedy, underlining the intention expressed in the opening invocation by throwing into clearer relief the adaptation and modification of the Virgilian pattern?

Yet it would not be true to say that by the simple act of redivision Milton has repudiated the theory of the five-act epic. Five acts can still be readily discerned in the 1674 poem, though they are not the same as those of 1667. Milton makes no sacrifices; to be "still closing up truth to truth" is for him the golden rule in epic structure as well as in theology and arithmetic. The first two "acts" remain unchanged: books I and II, Satan's revival and the sketching out of the plot; books III and IV, his arrival in Paradise and the failure of his first attempt. But Act III is no longer simply books V and VI, the war in heaven and Satan's defeat; it is now the whole of Raphael's reminiscential narrative, with the commentary, books V to VIII, in the actual time-scheme of the poem one day. Act IV is now books IX and X, the Fall and its consequences ending in penitence, in the actual time-scheme one more day, while Act V has become books XI and XII (old 10), man's misery and redemption or, in terms of Adam himself, the process of regeneration, the work of but another day.

In this dramatic scheme the new Act III provides a most "ample turn of the main design and expectation of new," but the turn is no longer in Satan's temporary defeat at the hands of avenging justice; it is in the operations of creative love as it acts purposefully, and in Adam's progressive recognition of its meaning. Act IV, still the crucial act, no longer gives "a counterturn to that main design which changed in the third," for its end is no longer Satan's success but man's penitence and reconciliation; it therefore underlines the turn of Act III and prepares for the final victory to be prophesied in Act V.

The dramatic and epic structural patterns are thus brought into exact alignment by the simple redivision of 1674. *Paradise Lost* is in fact the consummate example of five-act epic structure. Its author's final tinkering clarified its beautifully coherent epic pattern on the Virgilian model and adjusted its drama to leave with the reader a much deeper "satisfaction of probabilities."

VI

Did Milton succeed through this redivision in changing "those notes" to epic? That is another question. It is with structural pattern that we have been directly concerned throughout, and with intention as it expresses itself in structural emphasis, not with execution. We have indeed been dealing with an imitation of an imitation several times removed, and with the shadow of a fictional skeleton. The substance (and indeed the actual shape) of the fiction remained quite unchanged in 1674. But the change does alter the light in which it appears, and may suggest that it is at once less questionable and more questionable than has sometimes been thought.

Milton, it is clear, was by no means unaware of what has been called "the unconscious meaning" of *Paradise Lost*. It may be that in 1667 he was not quite aware of it, or that for some reason or other he was then much inclined towards it; it is certainly emphasized by his having written in ten books. But the 1674 renumbering indicates his consciousness of Satan's power over the poem, and (if it was not simply a trivial toying) the new disposition was meant to strengthen Satan's chains. Its motive was to shift the poem's emphasis and its centre in a way that would point more clearly to its stated intention. *Paradise Lost* was always meant to be a poem whose beginning is disobedience, which middle is woe, and whose ultimate end is restoration. It may be that the intention was clouded in 1667, or that Milton's view of restoration was obscured. The 1674 revision is at any rate an effort to clarify the poem's ways.

It is also clear that Milton's control over his vast material never wavered, though he may not always have been clear as to what he was doing or had done with it. He renumbers his books; he does not change his argument. The masses have been set in their places, though they have not been properly identified. And yet one must pause. If the disposition of the masses was patient of a tragic pattern of structural interpretation in 1667, the unmoved masses remain patient of it after the tinkering of 1674. If they were patient of a Virgilian patterning in 1674, they were already so in 1667. No amount of arithmetical ingenuity can obscure this fact. One must read both poems and see both patterns, for the two patterns suspend the theme between the horns of a paradox. This is the chief function of its structure.

Among the Miltonic virtues we have lately been taught to question —from organ music and amplifying imagery to simple honesty—architectonic skill is not yet numbered. Every interpreter, of whatever colour, will allude to it, even if it be only of purpose to imply in passing that this is a virtue typical of rigid Puritan neoclassicism. Both the devoted enthusiast and the iconoclast underline his claims to consistency and therewith his claim to having raised his great argument to a solid architectural height. The enthusiast would see him as a noble Colossus, last of some titanic race of Renaissance poets, towering in splendidly integrated certainty above the New Atlantis and the mutable flood engulfing it. The iconoclast chooses to see him either as inflexibly imposing his rigorous and suffocating will on paradise, or as hypocritically pretending to an assurance which nevertheless only reveals the confusion of his motives. Milton has, to be sure, himself invited such interpretations; but it might be better if we ignored them and saw him more often (as Carlyle saw a lesser poet) as one "carrying a bit of chaos about him . . . which he is manufacturing into cosmos." He is not profitably to be identified with any of these monsters of our distraught imagination—or of his own.

Nor are his great poems, for all their regularity of structure, to be regarded as rigidly static compositions of the architectural order appropriate to Victorian tombs and monuments. They are works of poetic art, the pattern of their evolution in time beginning usually as a reminiscence of some pattern established in the past, and nearly always controlled by easily recognizable structural balance, but always in process of development through conflict and resolution towards a harmony which is dynamic because it is the result of tension released in a creative act. This harmony they by no means always perfectly achieve, less frequently than Milton himself wished to believe. Nor need they so achieve it. They do not represent or express or entomb an unutterable perfection; they indicate a direction in which perfection may be achieved. At their best they pause, like Michael, betwixt a world destroyed and world restored; and the creative act for poet and reader often comes afterwards, while the poem is "thought . . . still speaking," like Raphael.

Paradise Lost (Professor Bush has made one certain) is to be regarded as no mausoleum of decayed classicism. It is rather to be read as a metaphor of spiritual evolution. Its structural pattern is neither rigidly fixed nor shifted; it is shifting. The firmness with which Milton defines his structural blocks serves chiefly to sustain the Christian paradox on which the metaphor is hinged. It would seem that in the redivision of 1674 Milton underlines the direction of the shifting. Whatever the cause, it indicates what Professor Thompson himself has so well illustrated: he remained intent on the perfect adaptation of the pattern to the end.

NOTES

1. *Essays on Milton*, 1914, pp. 83-4.
2. "For *Paradise Lost*, XI-XII," *Philological Quarterly*, XXII (1943), 376-82.
3. On this theory before Milton, see R. H. Perkinson, "The Epic in Five Acts," *Studies in Philology*, XLIII (1946), 465-81.
4. *Critical Essays of the Seventeenth Century*, ed. Spingarn, II, 17-18.

[EDITOR'S NOTE. For other comments on the structure and patterns of *Paradise Lost*, see E. E. Stoll, *UTQ*, III (1933-34), 3-16; B. Rajan, *"Paradise Lost" and the Seventeenth Century Reader*, 1947; A. S. P. Woodhouse, *UTQ*, XXII (1952-53), 109-27; R. Colie, *JWCI*, XXIII (1960), 127-38; J. B. Stroup, *TSL*, VI (1961), 71-5; H. F. Robins, *JEGP*, LX (1961), 699-711; O. B. Hardison, Jr., *The Enduring Monument*, 1962; on classical models and principles, C. M. Bowra, *From Virgil to Milton*, 1945; D. Bush, *CJ*, XLVII (1952), 178-82, 203-4; J. Richardson, *CL*, XVI (1962), 321-31; K. Svendsen, *PQ*, XXVIII (1949), 185-206; J. M. Steadman, *SN*, XXXI (1959), 159-73; on the dramatic element, J. H. Hanford, *SP*, XIV (1917), 178-95; R. Durr, *JAAC*, XIII (1955), 520-26; D. Knight, *SAQ*, 63 (1964), 44-59.]

DOUGLAS BUSH

Paradise Lost in Our Time:
Religious and Ethical Principles

Since *Paradise Lost* is so commonly regarded as a pictorial tapestry or musical score with an unfortunate basis of dead and repellent ideas, I said that we would look at those ideas. In attempting to describe, not the complex body of Milton's thought, but a few central principles, I do not mean to imply that *Paradise Lost* should be read as a theological or philosophic treatise; nor do I mean that, as a poem, it can now be read in the same spirit in which it was composed—one would not make that claim for the works of Homer or Virgil or Dante or Shakespeare. But I do mean that the quality of Milton's poetry is inseparable from his vision of life, and that his vision of life, in its essentials, remains significant, whatever the changes in our ways of thought—and indeed to a large measure because these have changed so much. *Paradise Lost* may be a dilapidated museum with a few fine exhibits scattered along the mouldy shelves, or it may be a temple of religious thought and feeling of which the modern reader has lost the key. At the present time we have a multitude of serious minor poets, who mirror the supposedly overwhelming complexities of the modern world, but we do not hear any voice of heroic magnitude proclaiming that good is good and evil evil, that man is a religious and moral being

From *"Paradise Lost" in Our Time*, Ithaca: Cornell University Press, 1945, pp. 29-57. Copyright, 1945, by Cornell University. Reprinted by permission of the author and Cornell University Press.

in a religious and moral universe, and that the destiny of the race depends upon the individual soul. To be moved by the poetic presentation of such elementary convictions is to enjoy the experience which all great poetry gives, and it is also, perhaps, to be rid of some factitious complexities.

There is small need to emphasize Milton's conception of the high office of the poet-priest. No other poet of the Renaissance held that traditional conception with such exalted religious fervor. To recall one of his many passages on the subject, in 1641-1642, when he realized that he must defer the great poem of which he had dreamed, he set it apart not only from the amorous and complimentary verse of contemporary cavaliers but from the epics of the great pagans who had lacked the illumination of Christian faith. What he planned was

> a work not to be raised from the heat of youth, or the vapors of wine; like that which flows at waste from the pen of some vulgar amorist, or the trencher fury of a rhyming parasite; nor to be obtained by the invocation of dame memory and her siren daughters, but by devout prayer to that eternal Spirit, who can enrich with all utterance and knowledge, and sends out his seraphim, with the hallowed fire of his altar, to touch and purify the lips of whom he pleases.

That is the kind of poet we are dealing with. The critics who are always talking of Milton's pride and egotism—though they never furnish evidence—would doubtless regard this as a good specimen. It is, on the contrary, an eloquent example of his deeply religious humility.

It may be admitted at the start that the main principles of Milton's religious philosophy, while familiar to students of Renaissance thought, are no longer part of the general heritage and need to be reconstructed and revivified in the mind of the reader. But if that suggests that Milton's poems suffer from a special liability, we should remember that even the popular dramatist Shakespeare builds on fundamental ideas which have largely vanished from the modern consciousness and must be reconstructed for full and proper comprehension of the plays. Further, it might be said that, different as Shakespeare and Milton were, their central beliefs and assumptions were similar; the two were infinitely nearer to each other than either is to us. If Milton's religious outlook was puerile or worse, so was Shakespeare's.

We heard Lord David Cecil's complaint that Milton was not really a religious poet because he was a philosopher rather than a devotee. Leaving Milton out of account, we have a sufficient answer to the critic's implied definition of religion in recalling that the Christ of the New Testament was a philosopher rather than a devotee. However, Lord David may be said to have bumped upon a central fact, that Milton was one of the philosophic minds which in all centuries, and not least in the seventeenth, have been the main strength of Christianity. To Milton and many of his philosophic contemporaries we might apply some words of Mr. Eliot's written with reference to the present:

> The Idea of a Christian Society is one which we can accept or reject; but if we are to accept it, we must treat Christianity with a great deal more *intellectual* respect than is our wont; we must treat it as being for the individual a matter primarily of thought and not of feeling. The consequences of such an attitude are too serious to be acceptable to everybody: for when the Christian faith is not only felt, but thought, it has practical results which may be inconvenient.[1]

The kind of intellectual and thoughtful attitude which Mr. Eliot stresses as a modern need is for him and others a prime reason for disliking Milton—although we might expect moderns to have at least as much respect for Milton's independence as for Donne's conventional orthodoxy. Moreover, Milton was through most of his career inspired, even more than other Puritans, by a vision of the holy community which makes Mr. Eliot's idea of a Christian society, high and earnest as that is, look a little pallid.

We are not concerned here with Milton's treatment of contemporary problems of religious, civil, and political liberty. The general principles from which his ideas sprang are most familiar in the two pamphlets of 1644, *Of Education* and *Areopagitica,* and most mature and explicit in the large Latin treatise on Christian doctrine; over this last Milton worked for many years in an effort both to clarify his own beliefs and also, apparently, to construct a platform on which Protestants in general could unite. We shall observe only a few things in the three works which have an especially important bearing upon the late poems.

The letter on education, looked at horizontally, takes its place with other Puritan pamphlets attacking traditional scholastic studies and modes of teaching and urging practical and empirical reforms. Looked at vertically, the letter appears as one of the last in the long series of Renaissance tracts expounding the educational theory of Christian humanism. Although, like other progressive Puritans, Milton gives a considerable space to science, the main body of material is the ancient classics. These provide much of the necessary literature of knowledge and they nourish all human capacities, especially the faculty of moral choice which leads to rational virtue. But Milton makes it very clear that the highest natural wisdom of the pagans is a subordinate auxiliary of the Bible, that it lacks the special inspiration and final authority of Christian faith and precept. He gives two definitions of education and both are typical of European humanism. The more familiar one is this: "I call therefore a complete and generous education, that which fits a man to perform justly, skilfully, and magnanimously all the offices, both private and public, of peace and war." The less familiar but even more truly Miltonic one is this: "The end then of learning is to repair the ruins of our first parents by regaining to know God aright, and out of that knowledge to love him, to imitate him, to be like him, as we may the nearest by possessing our souls of true virtue, which being united to the heavenly grace of faith, makes up the highest perfection." That is rather remote from the modern educationist's talk about adaptation to environment.

Those who have absorbed the kind of education described in this letter are worthy to enjoy, and must not be deprived of, the kind of liberty described in *Areopagitica*. This most famous of Milton's pamphlets, which attracted no attention in its own day, has long been regarded as one of the few great declarations of civil liberty in the language. There is no need of rehearsing the arguments, sublime or satirical, but I must read some central passages of force and beauty which recall the spirit of those days of confident idealism and partly anticipate the ethical theme of *Paradise Lost*:

> I cannot praise a fugitive and cloistered virtue unexercised and unbreathed, that never sallies out and sees her adversary, but slinks out of the race, where that immortal garland is to be run for, not without dust and heat. Assuredly we bring not innocence into the world, we bring impurity much rather; that which purifies us is trial, and trial is by what is contrary. That virtue therefore which is but a youngling in the contemplation of evil, and knows not the utmost that vice promises to her followers, and rejects it, is but a blank virtue, not a pure; her

whiteness is but an excremental whiteness; which was the reason why our sage and serious poet Spenser, (whom I dare be known to think a better teacher than Scotus or Aquinas,) describing true temperance under the person of Guion, brings him in with his palmer through the cave of Mammon, and the bower of earthly bliss, that he might see and know, and yet abstain. . . .

Many there be that complain of divine Providence for suffering Adam to transgress. Foolish tongues! when God gave him reason, he gave him freedom to choose, for reason is but choosing; he had been else a mere artificial Adam, such an Adam as he is in the motions. We ourselves esteem not of that obedience, or love, or gift, which is of force; God therefore left him free, set before him a provoking object ever almost in his eyes; herein consisted his merit, herein the right of his reward, the praise of his abstinence. Wherefore did he create passions within us, pleasures round about us, but that these rightly tempered are the very ingredients of virtue? . . .

This justifies the high providence of God, who, though he command us temperance, justice, continence, yet pours out before us even to a profuseness all desirable things, and gives us minds that can wander beyond all limit and satiety.

The general argument of *Areopagitica* is in accord with the ideals of progressive Puritanism, and it is besides everywhere enlarged and enriched by its author's classical culture and humane breadth of view. But two things are not always remembered by libertarians who associate Milton with the principle of complete freedom of speech. One is that his passionate faith in the right of discussion, the power of truth, and the dignity and freedom of individual man carries with it the religious responsibility of individual discipline. The second is that, while maintaining a broad measure of freedom and tolerance, Milton does not leave without safeguards the fundamental and unquestionable bases of religion and morality, and does not object to judicious censorship of dangerous books after publication. If we are disappointed by that, let us remember that the modern right of free speech is in no small degree the result of general scepticism about absolute truth and authority, a kind of scepticism almost unknown in Milton's time and country.

The source and sanction of Milton's ideas of freedom was the

Reformation doctrine of Christian liberty, of which he was in seventeenth-century England the greatest among many exponents.[2] This conception is set forth fully in the treatise on Christian doctrine and briefly near the end of *Paradise Lost*, and it is more or less explicit or implicit in nearly all his mature writings. In a word, the Mosaic law was not only positive and truly religious and moral but also restrictive, arbitrary, and ceremonial; it was a precise external code imposed upon man. When Christ came, the Mosaic law was abrogated for the law of the gospel. With his soul illuminated by a new revelation, man was released from his involuntary subjection to the Mosaic law and became, through divine grace and his own insight and effort, a free agent, a self-directing son of God. Regenerate man is in fact freed from dependence upon and allegiance to all external authorities and institutions. The seeds of revolution latent in this Protestant individualism are obvious. Properly understood, of course, the doctrine does not make man irresponsible; it vastly heightens his responsibility to God. Over and over again Milton repeats that liberty is not license, that true liberty can be enjoyed only by the wise and good—and they, as he was driven more and more to recognize, are a minority of mankind.

With this dynamic and individualistic, yet very exacting, principle of Christian liberty is bound up another cardinal principle, that of "right reason," *recta ratio*. This Stoic concept had so long been a part of Christian thought that its origin could be half-forgotten, but it revealed its classical character, when set against evangelical Christianity, in its emphasis on divine and human reason. The concept was the basic element of Christian humanism in all ages, and in seventeenth-century England Milton was again its greatest exponent, along with the group of Cambridge Platonists.

Right reason is not merely reason in our sense of the word; it is not a dry light, a nonmoral instrument of inquiry. Neither is it simply the religious conscience. It is a kind of rational and philosophic conscience which distinguishes man from the beasts and which links man with man and with God. This faculty was implanted by God in all men, Christian and heathen alike, as a guide to truth and conduct. Though its effectual workings may be obscured by sin, it makes man, in his degree, like God; it enables him, within limits, to understand the purposes of a God who is perfect reason as well as perfect justice, goodness, and love. Hence the ancient pagans, to whom the evangelical Christian is indifferent or hostile, are for the Christian humanist men who achieved very positive steps toward ultimate truth and virtue.

Though even the highest pagan wisdom, like Plato's, was the product of only the natural reason, and must be fortified and illuminated by Christian revelation and love, that natural reason was itself a divine gift and it sought the true light. Since all truth is one, since man and the universe and God are rational, the human reason is an ally, not an enemy, of Christianity. Thus the Christian father Lactantius, quoting Cicero's assertion that morality is founded on the eternal law of right reason written in every human heart, could exclaim that the utterance was well-nigh inspired. Thus Erasmus could declare that there were perhaps more saints than those named in the calendar and could add that unforgettable phrase, "*Sancte Socrates, ora pro nobis.*" Thus Hooker, whose first book is such a magnificent picture of the reign of law and reason in the universe and in the mind of God and man, could affirm: "The general and perpetual voice of men is as the sentence of God himself. For that which all men have at all times learned, Nature herself must needs have taught; and God being the author of Nature, her voice is but his instrument." Thus Jeremy Taylor, who so constantly quoted the ancients, could say that the "Christian Religion in all its moral parts is nothing else but the Law of Nature, and great Reason." Thus Benjamin Whichcote, the seminal mind of Cambridge Platonism, reinterpreted, and established as the sign manual of the group, the biblical phrase "The spirit of man is the candle of the Lord," and insisted that right reason is found wherever true faith is found, that

> To go against Reason, is to go against God: it is the self same thing, to do that which the Reason of the Case doth require; and that which God Himself doth appoint: Reason is the Divine Governor of Man's Life; it is the very Voice of God.

And thus Milton, to cite only one utterance, maintains that the unwritten law of God

> is no other than that law of nature given originally to Adam, and of which a certain remnant, or imperfect illumination, still dwells in the hearts of all mankind; which, in the regenerate, under the influence of the Holy Spirit, is daily tending towards a renewal of its primitive brightness.

Some elements in this concept of right reason may be dwelt upon a little longer, with special reference to the Cambridge Platonists, since there are so many affinities between them and Milton. One is the divine unity and order of the world and the divine unity of all truth, natural and supernatural. Another is a degree of optimism based on that belief and on belief in the essential goodness of man, a belief very different from the Augustinian, Lutheran, Calvinist, and Hobbesian belief in natural depravity. But this optimism was held very firmly in check by a Christian consciousness of human frailty and sin and the need of grace, and was very different from the scientific and sentimental optimism which was soon to submerge it. Thirdly, in spite of an occasional strain of mysticism, the Cambridge Platonists, like Milton, opposed irrational "enthusiasm" and emphasized the active Christian life lived in a world of evil, the rational and ethical imitation of Christ. Finally, to go no further, the doctrine of right reason predicates certain absolute values of good and evil, reason and unreason. Right reason does not turn away from nature as evil, still less does it set up nature against "artificial" restraints of religion and morality. Both attitudes would be impossible because God and nature are one—which does not mean a pantheistic confusion of creation with the Creator and an irreligious worship of life and flux. What we do have is a fundamental opposition to Calvinism on the one hand and naturalism on the other. The great Elizabethan Calvinist, William Perkins, believing in an arbitrary and inscrutable God, could say that His will "itself is an absolute rule both of justice and reason," so that what He wills "thereupon becomes reasonable and just." And at the other extreme Hobbes affirms that man calls good and evil whatever he seeks to possess or avoid, since there is nothing simply and absolutely good or evil. But for men like Hooker and Taylor and the Cambridge Platonists and Milton, the spirit of man and the revealed word of God together proclaim unshakable absolutes which God Himself, if He could be imagined as having the desire, could not change.

I have stressed this great, central, and traditional doctrine of right reason partly because the anti-Miltonists have evidently never heard of it. To quote Mr. Murry again, since his remarks are both typical and explicit, Milton's "apparent peculiarity is that he is overweeningly confident in the natural man, or at least in the natural reason of man . . . and primarily in his own reason." Presumably Mr. Murry and the others would not complain that Hooker and Taylor and the Cambridge Platonists have an overweening confidence in the natural reason of man, and especially in their own reason, but Milton's exaltation of the religious and ethical concept of right reason becomes evidence of his personal and irreligious pride and egotism! It is a rather quaint fact that the charges our theologians bring against Milton's religious "rationalism" are essentially the same as those brought against Whichcote by his quondam tutor, the Calvinist Anthony Tuckney.

Without going into theological and philosophical subtleties we may observe how these ideas are embodied in *Paradise Lost*, and we may look first at the principal object of censure, the Deity. Many persons find that Deity harshly legal, tyrannical, and repellent, and would apparently prefer, and think Milton should have preferred, a Browningesque Deity who was all Love and nothing else, an infinitely vague and amiable grandfather. As a matter of plain fact, Milton does continually stress the prime power of love in God and man; his avowed theme, the assertion of Eternal Providence, means the assertion of eternal love. But Milton's religion, like that of most great writers and thinkers of his age, was not merely emotional and was never soft. His philosophic mind as well as his imagination and emotions required and responded to a partly philosophic Deity. Hebrew and Christian faith of course supplied the main outlines of an omnipotent and omniscient Creator and Sustainer of the world, a just and merciful Judge and Father. With this are fused other concepts, Platonic, Aristotelian, and Stoic, and, since Milton, like other men, retained something of the Calvinistic temper, we may add the allied idea of absolute sovereignty which was central in Calvinism. But there we come to a point where distinctions are needed and are not always made. Even Sir Herbert Grierson can say that in *Paradise Lost* "the will of God, however arbitrary it may appear, is to be obeyed. *That* is reasonable. Heaven is a totalitarian state."[3] *That* remark is a partial summary of the Calvinistic doctrine—witness William Perkins—which it was Milton's object to repudiate. Milton's position might be summed up in two aphorisms of Whichcote's:

> Right and Just is determined, not by the Arbitrary pleasure of him that has Power over us; but by the Nature and Reason of Things.
>
> God does not, because of his Omnipotency, deal Arbitrarily with us; but according to Right, and Reason: and whatever he does, is therefore Accountable; because Reasonable.

The absolute sovereignty of Milton's God, then, is not the arbitrary and tyrannous sovereignty of absolute will, it is the sovereignty of right reason and the law of nature, a sovereignty comprehended by the uncorrupted right reason of man and accepted not as servitude but as the condition of true freedom. "To follow God and to follow right Reason," says Whichcote, "is all one." God means not only infinite power and infinite love, but rational and natural order in the universe, in society, and above all in the soul of man. Those three realms are all united in the doctrine of the great chain of being which had through many centuries been the framework of man's theocentric view of the world. The hierarchic principle of order and degree linked together all animate beings and inanimate things, God, angels, man, animals, plants, and stones. In giving man his place in that descending or ascending order, cosmic and social, it also gave hierarchic order to man's own faculties and values. Thus while the doctrine provided a metaphysical philosophy, it was far more religious and ethical than scientific. The whole world, visible and invisible, is a divine harmony, as Milton is always proclaiming (often in musical terms), and disturbance of that harmony is at once a sin and a violation of nature. "The ways and dealings of God with his Creatures," to quote Whichcote again, "are all Accountable in a way of Reason; but Sinners vary from the Reason of things; and take upon them to Over-rule what is settled and established from Eternity."

Artistically, no doubt, it would have been better if Milton had relied upon his power of suggestion—

> Dark with excessive bright thy skirts appear—

and had not made God a speaking character. Both Divine Reason and Divine Father, in becoming a supreme speaker and actor in an epic, inevitably—though not invariably—become less divine. Whether or not the poet shared our uneasiness, he had a problem. His plan required the denial of Calvinistic determinism and the assertion of man's free will and God's providential justice, love, and grace, and the most authoritative mouthpiece for such doctrines might well seem to be God Himself.

But, whatever the occasional defects in presentation, Milton's concept of God appears more rigorous and forbidding to sentimentalists than it does to people who understand the exalted passion for rational and righteous order which inspired many religious thinkers from Aeschylus and Plato to Spinoza, and which was more or less shared, to go no further than Milton's immediate inheritance and background, by serious writers from Spenser, Hooker, and Shakespeare to the supposedly irreligious Hobbes. Even our few quotations from religious writers, especially Whichcote (whose extant sermons, by the way, apparently date from the Restoration period), might give pause to those who complain of a peculiar hard rationality and lack of "mystery" in Milton's religion. A good many modern critics, in their comments on Milton's Deity, only echo the most unreliable of theologians, Satan. Indeed it would be interesting to hear, from those who abhor the theology of *Paradise Lost,* in what essential respects it differed from the theology of the seventeenth-century Anglican divines. Moreover, while there is of course a gulf between the mind of Milton and the mind of Professor Whitehead, one might ask if such sentences as these, from the great modern metaphysician, do not touch some fundamentals of Milton's thought:

> God is the one systematic, complete fact, which is the antecedent ground conditioning every creative act. . . .
>
> The kingdom of heaven is not the isolation of good from evil. It is the overcoming of evil by good. . . .
>
> Every event on its finer side introduces God into the world. Through it his ideal vision is given a base in actual fact to which He provides the ideal consequent, as a factor saving the world from the self-destruction of evil. . . .
>
> He transcends the temporal world, because He is an actual fact in the nature of things. He is not there as derivative from the world; He is the actual fact from which the other formative elements cannot be torn apart.
>
> But equally it stands in his nature that He is the realization of the ideal conceptual harmony by reason of which there is an actual process in the total universe—an evolving world which is actual because there is order.[4]

Milton's Christ, as the Son of Milton's God, has incurred partly similar censure.[5] (In *Paradise Regained,* by the way, Christ is much less Lord David Cecil's "austere, unsympathetic classical philosopher" than a humble servant of God looking always for divine guidance.)[6] The anti-Trinitarian view of Christ's inferiority to the Father we may ignore, since this heresy, though distinct in the treatise, was not apparent enough in the poem to be observed by generations of devout readers, and since it is not important for us anyhow, except as an example of Milton's independent thinking. With all his emphasis on reason and moral choice, he is thoroughly orthodox in making Christ the incarnation of divine love and the atonement the great manifestation of that love. So Christ, "in whom the fulness dwells of love divine," the one heavenly being who will undertake the sacrificial mission to earth, is everywhere contrasted with the infernal being whose errand on earth is inspired by pride, hatred, and revenge. But whereas in evangelical Christianity, whether in gospel hymns or the poems of Donne, Christ means "the blood of the Lamb shed for me," for Milton as for other Christian humanists Christ is also, in Jeremy Taylor's phrase, "the great exemplar," or, in the words of Whichcote, "the principle of divine life within us, as well as a Saviour without us." Christ is, therefore, along with His other attributes, virtually identified with right reason. The rebel angels

> reason for thir Law refuse,
> Right reason for thir Law, and for thir King
> Messiah, who by right of merit Reigns.

Thus the Mediator and Redeemer represents not only divine love but the divine beauty of order in the soul and in the world. And the irresistible power of order, truth, and right is splendidly symbolized in the picture of Christ on the third day of battle:

> forth rush'd with whirl-wind sound
> The Chariot of Paternal Deity,
> Flashing thick flames . . .
> He onward came, far off his coming shone.

Finally, as we should expect, Christ is the Logos of Neo-platonic Christianity and the executive agent of God both in subduing rebellion and in creating the universe and man in accordance with "his great Idea."

The supreme manifestation of right reason is God Himself, and what God is in the world, the macrocosm, reason is in the soul of man, the microcosm. This ethical psychology, the sovereignty of the reason and will over the irrational passions and appetites, may seem very naïve in our day, when psychologists pull habits out of rats, but it was through many centuries the working faith of men not inferior to us in experience, intelligence, and vision; and it was admirably restated a few years ago by Walter Lippmann as a creed which modern man must strive to recover. As it appears in more or less Christianized form in the humanistic tradition, it has a varying Platonic, Aristotelian, or Stoic emphasis. Some English representatives are Spenser and Daniel, Chapman and Greville and Jonson. Although Christian Stoicism is strong in Milton as it is in many men of his time, the strongest emphasis and coloring are Platonic. One could cite many proofs of the Platonic strain in the basic texture of Milton's thought and feeling, but perhaps it is enough to recall the two definitions of education quoted already. The second, which some people would label Puritan, is especially close to the Plato who described the life of the true philosopher as "assimilation to God."

In *Paradise Lost* Milton's justification of the ways of God to men turns on two poles. One, the divine love and grace which once made, and continue to make, regeneration possible, belongs to all Christianity. The other, man's rational freedom of moral choice, belongs more particularly to the tradition of Christian humanism. Just now we are concerned with the latter. Some critics have made much of the arbitrary "tabu" which Adam and Eve transgress and which, they think, deprives Milton's fable of serious interest. Certainly Milton neither could nor would have got rid of the biblical tabu, but, without regarding the story as we regard it, he in every way transformed its primitive scale of values so as to make the experience of Adam and Eve a universal example of the trials and weaknesses of every man and every woman. The story had long been interpreted in terms of ancient ethical dualism (among such interpreters in Milton's own time were Sir Thomas Browne, Henry More, and Thomas Traherne), and Milton's elaboration was both traditional and original. As we shall see more fully later, Eve falls through weakness of reason, Adam through weakness of will, and both violate, not merely a tabu, but the order of nature. When they have sinned, their souls are an unnatural chaos of contending passions:

> For Understanding rul'd not, and the Will
> Heard not her lore, both in subjection now
> To sensual Appetite, who from beneath
> Usurping over sovran Reason claim'd
> Superior sway.

It must be emphasized again that this sovereignty of reason is always presented as the wholly natural order, not, as naturalistic thought would have it, an unnatural restraint, and that it is the overthrow of that sovereignty which is unnatural—a thoroughly Socratic doctrine, by the way.[7]

This is all obvious enough, and one could give an outline of *Paradise Lost* which would make the poem appear, on the ethical plane, as only an application of such ideas of rational liberty as were set forth in Milton's early prose. In comparison with Genesis, Milton's treatment of Adam and Eve is decidedly humanistic and rational, and as such it may not be thought contemptible, even in times when the Bible and Plato have given place to Freud. But what makes, or should make, a stronger appeal is a vital modification of that rational humanism which comes from the soul of an older and sadder and wiser Milton. To put it in the broadest and simplest way, for the author of *Paradise Lost* the great root of all man's sin and evil is pride, his great need is religious humility. The prohibition of the tree of knowledge is not a mere tabu, it is a test of religious humility, faith, and obedience. In his theological treatise Milton gave a list of the many and various kinds of sin involved in the fall, and the list ended with "presumption in aspiring to divine attributes, fraud in the means employed to attain the object, pride, and arrogance." Sir Herbert Grierson, in developing the view already recorded, that God is the arbitrary ruler of a totalitarian state, says that some use might have been made of the idea of presumption, "But there is no hint of the kind in *Paradise Lost*."[8] Although Sir Herbert's words seem plain enough, one can hardly believe that one understands them, since pride and presumption are Milton's whole theme.

We shall be looking at the characters and drama later, but we may here glance briefly through the poem and see the main lines on which Milton interprets or reinterprets his fable. The first few books show, dramatically, the great embodiment of pride and presumption defeated but still aspiring to equality with God. The middle books are occupied with the visit of the archangel Raphael, through whom Adam and Eve are given various and repeated warnings, direct and indirect. Very significantly, as Mr. Tillyard observes in his *Elizabethan World Picture* (1943), the first piece of instruction Raphael imparts is an exposition of the great chain of being, the principle of hierarchic order which we noticed a while ago. Then comes the angel's long account of Satan's rebellion against that order and of the war and chaos which symbolize pride and presumption running amuck. In contrast with that, there follows the account of Creation, the establishment of divine order and harmony.

By degrees we descend from the cosmic to the human, and warnings against presumption become more direct. In the eighth book we have a scientific discourse prompted by Adam's curiosity about the workings of the universe in which he finds himself. (It was unfortu-

nate that at this point Eve, who as the first sinner was especially in
need of counsel, should have obeyed feminine decorum and have left
the gentlemen to their high masculine converse; her expectation of
receiving a later digest from her husband was not adequately fulfilled.) Raphael explains the alternative theories of a geocentric and
heliocentric world and related problems, but Milton's interest is not in
astronomy itself, it is in the cautions with which the angel begins and
ends, and with which Adam agrees:

> Solicit not thy thoughts with matters hid,
> Leave them to God above, him serve and fear. . . .
>
> But apt the Mind or Fancy is to rove
> Uncheckt, and of her roving is no end;
> Till warn'd, or by experience taught, she learn
> That not to know at large of things remote
> From use, obscure and subtle, but to know
> That which before us lies in daily life,
> Is the prime Wisdom; what is more is fume,
> Or emptiness, or fond impertinence,
> And renders us in things that most concern
> Unpractis'd, unprepar'd, and still to seek.

Milton is not attacking science as such. In *Paradise Lost* he pays tribute to "the Tuscan artist," Galileo, whom he had celebrated in *Areopagitica* as a martyr to truth. And there is better though indirect evidence in what everyone knows, that Milton's imagination responds,
as no other English poet's has responded with equal power, to the conception of infinite space. His words here, then, are not a fundamental-
ist and obscurantist attack on science any more than Christ's dispar-
agement of Greek culture in *Paradise Regained* represents a barbarous
hostility to the classics. In both cases Milton is simply asserting, with
an earnestness born of ripened insight, his lifelong hierarchy of values;
and his stress on temperance in knowledge, on the proper place and
limits of human inquiry, can be paralleled in many other writers of
the century, among them Dr. John Donne. There had been in the
younger Milton a Baconian strain, which is conspicuous in the letter
on education, but it had always been much less central than the ethical and religious. In *The Reason of Church Government* (1641-
1642), for instance, he had characteristically distinguished between
"that knowledge that rests in the contemplation of natural causes and

dimensions, which must needs be a lower wisdom, as the object is low," and "the only high valuable wisdom," the knowledge of God and the ultimate ends of human life. With advancing years and increasing realization of the weakness of the human reason and will, Milton has come more and more to exalt the knowledge, love, and imitation of God and to fear scientific speculation or Greek philosophy or anything else which may obscure or distort man's vision and nourish irreligious pride in his own mind and powers.[9] As he says in the first chapter of the *Christian Doctrine,* "obedience and love are always the best guides to knowledge." "Every man," Thomas à Kempis had said, "naturally desires to know, but of what value is knowledge without the fear of God?"

Astronomical curiosity is only the most obvious example of vain presumption, and when we come to the drama of the fall the motive is generalized. Pride aspiring beyond human limits and human needs, the desire for power through knowledge, is the one motive steadily appealed to throughout Satan's temptation of Eve—in his plan of attack, in the dream he puts into her mind, in his successful dialogue with her, in her soliloquies before and after her sin, and in her subsequent persuading of Adam. If we want any further proof that the theme of *Paradise Lost* is the conflict between human pride and religious humility, we have it in the most significant place, the conclusion. After the archangel Michael has unfolded to Adam the sinful history of the human race, Adam is reconciled to the loss of Eden by the consciousness that he may gain a new Eden within his own soul:

> Greatly instructed I shall hence depart,
> Greatly in peace of thought, and have my fill
> Of knowledge, what this Vessel can contain;
> Beyond which was my folly to aspire.
> Henceforth I learn, that to obey is best,
> And love with fear the only God, to walk
> As in his presence, ever to observe
> His providence, and on him sole depend,
> Merciful over all his works, with good
> Still overcoming evil, and by small
> Accomplishing great things, by things deem'd weak
> Subverting worldly strong, and worldly wise
> By simply meek; that suffering for Truth's sake
> Is fortitude to highest victory,

> And to the faithful Death the Gate of Life;
> Taught this by his example whom I now
> Acknowledge my Redeemer ever blest.

And Michael replies with a last reminder of the gulf which separates merely human and scientific knowledge and worldly power from the true knowledge and power that are within:

> This having learnt, thou hast attain'd the sum
> Of wisdom; hope no higher, though all the Stars
> Thou knew'st by name, and all th' ethereal Powers,
> All secrets of the deep, all Nature's works,
> Or works of God in Heav'n, Air, Earth, or Sea,
> And all the riches of this World enjoy'dst,
> And all the rule, one Empire; only add
> Deeds to thy knowledge answerable, add Faith,
> Add Virtue, Patience, Temperance, add Love,
> By name to come call'd Charity, the soul
> Of all the rest: then wilt thou not be loath
> To leave this Paradise, but shalt possess
> A paradise within thee, happier far.

This is the message of the poet who, according to Mr. Murry, is "completely emancipated from the humility of religious faith";[10] who, according to Mr. Leavis, "offers as ultimate for our worship mere brute assertive will"; who, according to Lord David Cecil, lacked the Christian sensibility, did not live by faith, scorned hope, was indisposed to charity, and regarded pride not as a vice but as the mark of a superior nature. If there is in English verse any truer or more deeply felt summary of Christ's teaching than Milton's lines, I do not recall it. Certainly there is no equivalent in the "first" among English Christian poets, John Donne.

Critics who see only one Milton, and him not very clearly, make that disagreeable and unchanging Milton the author of the major poems. They seem to think that, like the younger Pitt, "he never grew, he was cast," and cast in a mould of humanistic arrogance and self-sufficiency. So far as this view is founded on private intuition and the studious ignoring of his works, there is no way to meet it. So far as it is founded on evidence, it seems to be a very hasty and superficial reaction to the ardent and militant optimism which inspired Milton's efforts to forward the great revolution. The author of the early pamphlets was on fire with hope and confidence in the complete and immediate regeneration of England and in time of the world. This pamphleteer and prophet was assuredly religious, if the Hebrew prophets were religious, but he was then on the rising and winning side; his personal faith had not been tested, and in his prose writings it was partly submerged in his public themes. But the Milton of *Paradise Lost* and the later poems had undergone a long series of disillusionments. He had lost faith in bishops, king, parliament, people, army, even Cromwell. And then, while *Paradise Lost* was being composed, came the Restoration. His twenty years of service to the good old cause, his eyesight, all his hopes, were gone. At moments he was tempted to despair even of God's providence. But in spite of many defeats he was not conquered,

> though fall'n on evil days,
> On evil days though fall'n, and evil tongues;
> In darkness, and with dangers compast round,
> And solitude.

What emerged now, in his last poems, was a more truly religious faith, not attached to and partly dependent upon dreams of a new era, but founded only upon God and the soul of individual man. Milton has not abandoned the principles of Christian liberty and right reason, because these are fundamental, but he has a new understanding of the divine nature and of human nature. The aggressive reformer has arrived at the full realization that "in His will is our peace." That is the one great text of his last three poems.

The evolution of Milton's thought and feeling, the deepening of his spiritual insight, makes him very much our contemporary. If he were as actively present to our minds as he should be, modern writers would have been pointing to the megalomaniac Satan and his destructive energy as a superlative prophetic picture of the world conquerors of our time. The word "prophetic" is not used, to be sure, in a literal sense; but neither is the parallel merely fortuitous. For the traditional motives which, with Milton's special coloring and emphasis, led to the sin of Satan and Adam and Eve, are the essential motives which have been seen at the root of the sickness of our civilization. One could not begin to catalogue the modern authors, not only philosophic but semipopular, who have been analyzing the rise and the downfall of the so-called "Renaissance man." (The term "Renaissance" in this connection is, I think, partly a misnomer, because the central Renaissance tradition was predominantly Christian, but there is no doubt concerning the rebellious mentality and movement so designated, that is, secular, self-sufficient, optimistic "liberalism.") These modern authors, looking back from the present chaos over the last three centuries, have, like Milton, seen man's undoing in his irreligious human pride. It was in Milton's own age that advanced minds in Europe generally, even if not irreligious themselves, made the first thorough break with the religious world view and religious ethics of the Middle Ages and antiquity and inaugurated the scientific naturalism and scientific *hybris* of modern times. Milton's own career might be called a partial epitome of that long cycle; if he began with a measure of "humanistic" self-sufficiency, he ended with repudiating it. In *Paradise Lost*, setting fundamental motives in the clear relief of an ancient author, Milton showed the will to power, public and private, intellectual presumption, and egoistic desire, seeking their ends through force and fraud and overthrowing the divine and natural order in the world and in the soul. He surveyed a world going through pride to destruction and issued a serious call to a devout and holy life.

The same words, however inadequate for both poems, might be used of *The Waste Land*, the nearest thing we have to a modern *Paradise Lost*. And are not those critics who dismiss Milton's purpose and theme and substance inclined to demand more of him than they do of other poets? Has not *The Waste Land*, with all the advantages of contemporaneity, suffered much the same fate as *Paradise Lost*? We are thrilled by its magical phrases and rhythms, we track down the sources of allusions, and we place the work in the poet's religious development, but has it actually counted very much in our own? Has it in the least shaken our natural pride and led us to repentance, or does any critic call it a failure because it has not? And is not its "message" as much "out of date" as Milton's? But Mr. Eliot, except as a technician, stands apart from the modern movement, and the modern temper has been formed largely by writers who have attained a foggy pinnacle beyond good and evil. That is one prime reason for reading Milton. We need the shock of encountering a poet to whom good and evil are distinct realities, a poet who has a much-tried but invincible belief in a divine order and in man's divine heritage and responsibility, who sees in human life an eternal contest between irreligious pride and religious humility.

NOTES

1. *The Idea of a Christian Society* (London: Faber and Faber, 1939), p. 8; (New York: Harcourt, Brace, 1940), pp. 4-5.

2. See A. S. P. Woodhouse's "Milton, Puritanism, and Liberty," *University of Toronto Quarterly*, IV (1935), 483-513, and *Puritanism and Liberty* (London: Dent, 1938), and Arthur Barker's fuller development of these ideas in his *Milton and the Puritan Dilemma* (Toronto: University of Toronto Press, 1942).

3. *Milton & Wordsworth* (Cambridge University Press; New York: Macmillan, 1937), p. 117.

4. A. N. Whitehead, *Religion in the Making* (New York: Macmillan, 1926), pp. 154 ff.

5. In *The Fortunes of Falstaff* (Cambridge University Press, 1943; New York: Macmillan, 1944, p. 23), Professor Dover Wilson, speaking of the frequent modern failure to appreciate Prince Hal and Henry V as the ideal king, observes parallel misunderstandings in Miltonic criticism, and remarks that Milton's Son of God has been charged with priggishness no less freely than Shakespeare's son of Bolingbroke.

6. Milton's emphasis on Christ's constant faith and humble obedience is shown by Warner G. Rice, "*Paradise Regained*," *Papers of the Michigan Academy of Science, Arts and Letters*, XXII (1937), 493-503.

7. Cf. Whichcote, Aphorism 814: "It is contrary to the order of things; for Will and Affections to go before Understanding and Judgment. It is natural, that Will should follow; and that Understanding should go before."

8. *Milton & Wordsworth* (Cambridge University Press; New York: Macmillan, 1937), p. 117.

9. It might be observed that the phrase in *Areopagitica*, "minds that can wander beyond all limit and satiety," a phrase used there with recognition of the dangers latent in the exercise of God's great gift, is echoed in *Paradise Lost* (II, 146-48) by the perverter of reason, Belial.

10. *Studies in Keats New and Old* (London: Oxford University Press, 1939), p. 110.

[EDITOR'S NOTE. The author gives the following references in an earlier chapter: Lord David Cecil, in *The Oxford Book of Christian Verse*, 1940, xvii, xxi-xxii; T. S. Eliot, in *Essays and Studies by Members of the English Association*, XXI (1936), 32-40, and *Selected Essays, 1917-1932,*

1932, 132-3, and *The Classics and the Man of Letters,* 1942; Middleton Murry, *Studies in Keats New and Old,* 2nd ed., 1939, 110, 121-2; F. R. Leavis, *Revaluations,* 1936, 58. See also Mr. Bush's *The Renaissance and English Humanism,* Toronto, 1939; *Science and English Poetry,* 1950; and *English Literature in the Earlier Seventeenth Century,* rev. ed., 1962; G. McColley, *"Paradise Lost": An Account of Its Growth,* 1940; J. S. Diekhoff, *Milton's "Paradise Lost": A Commentary on the Argument,* 1946; B. Rajan, *"Paradise Lost" and the Seventeenth Century Reader,* 1947; I. Samuel, *Milton and Plato,* 1947; M. H. Nicolson, *The Breaking of the Circle,* 1950, rev. 1960; A. Stein, *Answerable Style,* 1953; A. S. P. Woodhouse, *Milton the Poet,* 1955; K. Svendsen, *Milton and Science,* 1956; H. M. Schultz, *Milton and Forbidden Knowledge,* 1957; G. W. Whiting, *Milton and This Pendant World,* 1958; B. O. Kurth, *Milton and Christian Heroism,* 1959; R. M. Frye, *God, Man, and Satan,* 1960; J. B. Broadbent, *Some Graver Subject,* 1960; R. Hoopes, *Right Reason in the Renaissance,* 1962; J. H. Summers, *The Muses Method,* 1962; B. A. Wright, *Milton's "Paradise Lost,"* 1962; A. E. Barker, in *Essays in English Literature . . . Presented to A. S. P. Woodhouse,* ed. M. MacLure and F. W. Watt, 1964.

D. C. ALLEN

Milton and the Descent to Light

I

Though the English Protestants of the seventeenth century were, to their ultimate spiritual distress, so devoted to the literal interpretation of the Bible that they considered it the primary and superior reading, their affection for the letter and the historical sense did not prevent them from searching the text for types and allegories. This practice, of course, bore the taint of popery and hindered the full powers of the *fides divina;* yet it often yielded excellent results and enabled one to skirt the marsh of a troublesome passage. Though not addicted to the allegorical method, Milton was no stranger to it. He might scorn Amaryllis and Neaera, but he could spend an occasional moment of leisure with what Luther called "these whores of allegory." The latter books of *Paradise Lost* and the tragedy of *Samson* proved that he was quite a talented typologist, who could find foreshadowings of the great Advocate of Grace in the biographical records of the advocates of the Law. More than this, Milton, unlike many of his contemporaries who were inclined to be universal in their analogical researches, made fine discriminations between types because he believed in what we might now call "typological evolution."

From "Milton Studies in Honor of Harris Francis Fletcher," *Journal of English and Germanic Philology*, LX (1961), 614-30. Reprinted by permission of the author and the publisher.

An example of Milton's interpretative discretion is his refusal to accept—although in this he was contrary to theological opinion—the patriarch Aaron as a full type of Christ. He contended that this first priest simply adumbrated the priestly offices of Jesus.[1] When he came to this conclusion, Milton was flatly correcting the assertions of the Anglican prelates; but on another similar occasion he was mentally flexible enough to correct himself.[2] Since he also believed in a dynamic typology that changed as the sacred history was unrolled, he was quick to admit that symbols valid before the Law[3] were afterwards worthless.[4] He could also insist on the gradual revelation of types and symbols because he believed that the thunder and trumpets' "clang" on Mt. Sinai proclaimed, among other things, a new form of typology and established Moses, who was, in a guarded sense, "the Divine Mediator" and "the type of the Law,"[5] as a master typologist. This evaluation had more than human worth because it was Jehovah who instructed Moses so that he could teach this mode of interpretation to men.

> Ordaine them Lawes; part such as appertaine
> To civil Justice, part religious Rites
> Of sacrifice, informing them by types
> And shadowes, of that destind Seed to bruise
> The Serpent, by what meanes he shall achieve
> Mankinds deliverance.
>
> (P.L., XII, 230-35)

These words are placed in the mouth of the Archangel Michael, who at this moment is manipulating the magic lantern of holy shadows and who is also an experienced exegete skilled in all four senses. Shortly after speaking this gloss, he announces that the main purpose of the Old Testament is to prepare the sons of Adam for a "better Cov'nant, disciplin'd / From shadowie Types to Truth, from Flesh to Spirit" (XII, 302-303). The mighty angel thus suggests that man can ascend (as humbled Adam has ascended from the Vale of Despond to the Mount of the Visions of God) from the darkness of sin and ignorance into the light of truth, from the shadow of type and symbol into the white blaze of the eternal literal.

It must be confessed that typology, even at its finest, is little more than hindsight prophecy; it points surely to the Advent, but it is best understood when the Word is made Flesh. Allegory—a game that even Jehovah plays[6]—is, in Milton's somewhat reluctant opinion, a possible form of revealed knowledge. This knowledge may be useful in some instances and not in others. When, for example, Moses urges the Israelites not to plow with an ox and an ass, Milton, who has been searching Deuteronomy for divorce evidence, perceives that the Hebrew lawgiver has the Miltons in mind,[7] an interpretation that speaks better for a sense of mystery than for a sense of humor. In his poetry Milton uses allegory with somewhat better artistry than a modern reader might imagine. An illustration of this skill appears when he shows Satan, orbiting in space and viewing the margin of Heaven and the angelic ladder of which "Each stair mysteriously was meant" (III, 516). By reminding us that Jacob's ladder had allegorical force, Milton prepares us for Raphael's subsequent description of the *scala perfectionis*, "the common gloss of theologians." There is likewise poetic irony resident in the fact that Satan, who is totally without hope, is permitted to see what will be interpreted as Adam's way of assuming angelic nature.

In general Milton probably defined allegory as a downward descent of knowledge, a revealing of suprarational information that enabled the humble learner to ascend. Raphael's well-known comment on his account of the celestial battles (V, 570-76; VI, 893-96) and Milton's open admission that he can only accept the six days of Creation allegorically (VII, 176-79) make the Miltonic conception of allegory plain. For the poet, allegory is the only means of communication between a superior mind aware of grand principles, such as the enduring war between Good and Evil, and a lesser mind incapable of higher mathematics. It is essentially a form of revelation, or, as Vaughan would put it, "a candle tin'd at the Sun."

To burnish this observation, I should like to point to events within the confines of the epic that could be called an allegory about allegory. This sacred fiction begins to be written in Book II when Satan, leaving Hell for Eden, retains, except for his momentary ventures into several forms of symbolic wildlife, the literalness of satanship, never putting on the ruddy complexion, the horns, hoof, and tail by which he was recognized in the allegorical world. The celestial messengers, however, are real creatures and stay feathered and decorous so that Adam, unlike his sons, does not "entertain angels unawares." It is otherwise with Satan's strange relative, Death. At first he "seems" to be crowned and to shake his ghastly dart; actually, he is a vast black shadow, formless, not "Distinguishable in member, joynt, or limb, / Or substance" (II, 668-69). He is by no means the symbolic person

who writes the dreary colophon to all human stories or who is stonily
portrayed in ecclesiastical monuments. Once he has crossed his bridge
into our world, he is better known. Although he is "not mounted yet
/ On his pale horse," we are familiar with his "vaste unhide-bound
Corps" and we understand his hearty hunger for whatever "the Sithe"
of his companion Time "mowes down" (X, 588-606). The bridge between the two worlds is a convention of infernal histories; but in
Paradise Lost, it could also be called the Bridge of Allegory.

There is no doubt that at times Milton read the Scriptures for
meanings other than the literal one, but he also was aware, thanks to
a long tradition, that the pagans had a glimmer of Christian truth.
Their lamp was scantily fueled and the wick smoked, but with proper
adjustments it could be made to give off a "pale religious light." It
took almost four centuries to light this lamp in the Church; the pagan
philosophers and their idolatrous legends had first to be suppressed.
Then, taking over the methods of the same heathen brethren, the
Christian scholars began searching the mythology for physical, moral,
and spiritual notions that had been bequeathed to men by the sons of
Noah. The moral commentaries of Bishops Fulgentius and Eustathius
on pagan literature encouraged others to unshell these truths, and in
Renaissance England Chapman, Bacon, Reynolds, Sandys, Ross, and
Boys searched the pagans for what had been better revealed in the
Bible or was narrated in the Books of Creation. All of them were infected to some degree with the current confidence in a universal philosophical system, a disease nourished by earlier mystagogues such as
Ficino, Pico della Mirandola, and Agostino Steuchio, and best known
to us in the fine clinical case of Theophilus Gale. Given the virulence
of the epidemic, we are, consequently, not surprised when the daemon
from "the threshold of Jove's Court" touches on it.

> Ile tell ye, 'tis not vain or fabulous
> (Though so esteem'd by shallow ignorance)
> What the sage Poets taught by th' heavenly Muse,
> Storied of old in high immortal verse
> Of dire *Chimaeras* and enchanted Isles,
> And rifted Rocks whose entrance leads to Hell,
> For such there be, but unbelief is blind.
>   (*Comus,* ll. 512-18)

After reading this speech in *Comus,* we understand why the mythological remembrances in *Paradise Lost* are sometimes more than orna-

mental, why their submerged moral or spiritual meanings enable them to consort with and support the braver Christian myths. The multi-colored phoenix, first underwritten by Clement of Rome as a Christ symbol, adorns Milton's own adventual allegory: the descent of Raphael through the air, "a *Phoenix*, gaz'd by all" (V, 272). Eden, expressed in vegetable grandeur, is quickly seared with evil foreboding when Milton likens it to the meadows of Enna, those sinister fields "where *Proserpin* gath'ring flow'rs / Herself a fairer Flow'r by gloomy *Dis* / Was gather'd" (IV, 269-71). When Milton compares Adam and Eve to Deucalion and Pyrrha (XI, 8-14), even we do not need a whole series of pious mythologizers to make the point; and foolish Pandora hardly needs the testimony of a Father as old as Tertullian[8] to inform us that she is the pagan half-memory of silly Eve (IV, 712-19). Milton is quite conventional in permitting pagan legend to lend its soft biceps to Christian power. His method of searching for metaphoric support in heathen culture also enables him to stand aside from the other characters of the epic and act as a commentator on the pre-Christian world from the vantage point of a postclassical man. Among the various pagan figures with whom Milton plants his poetry, two rise above the rest; they are the poet-theologian Orpheus and the demigod Hercules. Both are attractive to him because of their Christian meaning.

From the flats of the first *Prolusion* through the latter ranges of *Paradise Lost*, Milton accents the legend of Orpheus in a way that suggests self-identification. The Greek hero was praised in antiquity and by men of later ages for softening the human heart and turning it through his higher magic to the useful and the good.[9] Christian as these achievements were, Orpheus, as Milton knew, enlarged them by singing of Chaos and Old Night and by teaching Musaeus the reality of the one God. St. Augustine, a Father beloved by Milton when he agreed with him, complained that Orpheus' theology was very poor stuff;[10] but other primitive theologians from Athenagoras onward hailed the Greek as unique among the unelect in explaining divine matters as a Christian would.[11] There is, as I have said, little doubt that Milton thought of the murdered poet as one of his own grave predecessors, and this view was probably enhanced by that of the Christian mythologists who described Orpheus as a pagan type of Christ.[12]

Clement of Alexandria is the first to bring both harrowers of Hell together, although his comments are actually an angry rejection of pagan complaints about Christian imitativeness. He brands the Christian doctrines of Orpheus as spurious and mocks the alleged majesty of his songs; then he turns with a "not so my singer" (ἀλλ' οὐ τοιόσδε ὁ ὁδὸς ὁ ἐμός) to praise the new Orpheus, who tamed the lions of wrath, the swine of gluttony, the wolves of rapine.[13] Religious Eusebius makes a similar comparison in a more kindly fashion:

> The Saviour of men through the instrument of the human body which he united to his divinity shows himself all saving and blessing, as Greek Orpheus who by the skillful playing of his lyre tamed and subdued wild animals. The Greeks, I say, sang of his miracles and believed that the inspired accents of the divine poet not only affected animals but also trees who left their places at his singing to follow him. So is the voice of our Redeemer, a voice filled with divine wisdom which cures all evil received in the hearts of men.[14]

The history of Orpheus as a pagan type of Christ can be traced for many centuries;[15] by Milton's time it was such a part of the symbolic fabric of Christianity that one had only to think of "lyre" to say "cross." It is, for example, Orpheus who comes into John Donne's mind when he writes in "Goodfriday," "Could I behold those hands which span the Poles, / And tune all spheares at once, peirc'd with those holes?" This is the occasional image of Christ on the lyre, but the open comparison is conventionally stated for us by Giles Fletcher:

> Who doth not see drown'd in Deucalion's name
> (When earth his men, and sea had lost his shore)
> Old Noah; and in Nisus lock, the fame
> Of Sampson yet alive; and long before
> In Phaethon's, mine owne fall I deplore:
> But he that conquer'd hell, to fetch againe
> His virgin widowe, by a serpent slaine,
> Another Orpheus was the dreaming poets feigne.[16]

Thus Christians hallowed Orpheus for his half-success as a saviour of men and for his frustrated attempt to lead a soul out of Hell's darkness.

Tatian, in his *Oration Against the Greeks,* had argued that Orpheus and Hercules were the same person;[17] Milton would hardly say this, though he found in the demigod foreshadowings of both Samson and Christ. His admission of the Christian Hercules to his pantheon begins with the "Nativity Ode," where we are shown the infant Jesus "in his swaddling bands" ready to control the snaky Typhon and the rest of "the damned crew." It is Hercules, too, who is praised in *The Tenure of Kings* for his suppression of tyrants,[18] a superb Miltonic exploit; and he is recalled in the twenty-third sonnet for his rescue of Alcestis from the dark floor of Hell. He was, of course, attractive to Christians for other reasons. Begotten by Jove of a mortal woman, he early chose the right path, eschewing "the broad way and the green"; and, according to the almost Christian Seneca, "Jove's great son" devoted his whole life, in the best Stoic manner, to the conquest of his passions and the suppression of vice.[19] His major exploits were against the forces of darkness. We first hear of him in the *Iliad* (V, 397) as he strikes Hades with his "swift arrow" to leave him in anguish among the dead. No wonder that he thrice descended into Hell with somewhat better fortunes than those of Orpheus.

When Milton read the Orphic poems, he read the one that praises Hercules as a human saviour, but the comparison between Christ and Hercules, like the comparison between Christ and Orpheus, had been made before Milton's birth. "Ipse Christus verus fuit Hercules, qui per vitam aerumnosam omnia monstra superavit et edomuit."[20] The analogy was firmly established across the Channel, where Hercules Gallus was a stern rival of Francus, by d'Aubigne's *L'Hercule Chrestien*,[21] a moral prose on the labors Christianly read. This book inspired the *Hercule Chrestien*[22] of Ronsard, who advises his reader to swim a little below his surface:

> Mais ou est l'oeil, tant soit-il aveugle,
> Ou est l'esprit, tant soit-il desreigle,
> S'il veut un peu mes paroles comprendre,
> Que par raison je ne luy face entendre,
> Que la plus-part des choses qu'on escrit
> De Hercule, est deve a un seul Jesuschrist.

Chaplain Ross, a good Scot, can put it bluntly: "Our blessed Saviour is the true Hercules."[23]

There is little question that these two pagan Christ-types were congenial to Milton not only for their Christian grace notes but for their reflection of Miltonic ideals. Both heroes were received in the "sweet Societies / That sing, and singing in their glory move," because, as Boethius made clear,[24] they early chose the proper ascent to Heaven. Their accomplishments and their exploits were the sort that Milton himself might read in his own book of hope. But there is more to it than this. Hercules and Orpheus were types—not so good as Moses or Enoch, of course—of the strong Son of God and the Singer of the New Song. The event in their story that tied the hard knot of analogy was their descent into the darkness, their triumphs or half-triumphs in Hell, and their return into the light and, eventually, to the holy summits. In this process of descent and ascent, of entering the dark to find the light, the two halves of the coin of allegory were united.

II

The visual imagery of *Paradise Lost*, as I suggested some years ago, depends to some extent on verbs of rising and falling, of descent and ascent, and on contrasts between light and darkness. These modes of expression coil about the demands of the central theme as the serpent coils about the forbidden tree so that we may be urged to abandon the horizontal movement of human history for the vertical motion of the spiritual life, the dark nothingness of ignorance and evil for the light of ultimate truth and reality. The descent of Milton into the darkness of Hell before he rises to the great "Globe of circular light" is a sound Christian rescript. "Descend," says St. Augustine, "that you may ascend." "Descende ut ascendas, humiliare ut exalteris."[25] Christ's double descent—first into the flesh and then into the dark Saturday of Hell—furnished those who humbled themselves with a map of Christian progress. One goes down in humility into the dark so that one may ascend in triumph to the light. Satan and his squires know this course well enough to pervert it.

When the black tyrant, who has been "Hurl'd headlong" down, addresses his companions, he pretends, contrary to fact, that the descent was voluntary and a preparation for ascension. "From this descent / Celestial Virtues rising, will appear / More glorious and more dread than from no fall" (II, 14-16). Satan's prideful qualification is enough to make the word *rising* ironic; but his falsehood is not only believed but seconded by the deluded Moloch, who describes with desperate wit the millions that "longing wait / The Signal to ascend" and boastfully asserts "That in our proper motion we ascend / Up to our native seat: descent and fall / To us is adverse" (II, 55-77). Moloch's knowledge is no better than his grammar, for he, like his fellows, has gone about it the wrong way. He has already ascended in pride; been guilty of a "sursum cor contra Dominum,"[26] and so he has "frozen and fallen like a flake of snow."[27] The literature of the

Church knows all these phrases for the fate of the prideful aspirant; it tells us that those who descend in humility arise to those heights, "Unde Satan elatus cecidit, fidelis homo sublevatus ascendat."[28] The humble ascend to the light; the proud enter the depths, the "caligo tenebrarum densissima."[29] For those in hope of seeing the light that Satan truly detests, the road is easily followed, because both roads, as Bernard of Clairvaux puts it, are the same:

> The same steps lead up to the throne and down; the same road leads to the city and from it; one door is the entrance of the house and the exit; Jacob saw the angels ascending and descending on the same ladder. What does all this mean? Simply that if you desire to return to truth, you do not have to seek a new way which you do not know, but the known way by which you descended. Retracing your steps, you may ascend in humility by the same path which you descended in pride.[30]

Augustine's descent in humility is paralleled by Bernard's descent in pride, because both are dark ways that lead upward to the light. Had Milton's Adam been humble in obedience, he would have ascended, as Raphael, who had read the Church Fathers,[31] made plain (V, 490-505). But Adam sacrificed his prospects of angelic perfection for the immediate rewards of romantic love; even then, however, his subsequent humility guarantees his ascension. The demons also talk of ascending, but "self-tempted," they are secure in their fall. The bitter pride and the prideful unrepentance that governs them is embossed by Satan in his soul-revealing soliloquy:

> O foul descent! that I who erst contended
> With Gods to sit the highest, am now constrain'd
> Into a Beast, and mixt with bestial slime,
> This essence to incarnate and imbrute,
> That to the hight of Deitie aspir'd:
> But what will not Ambition and Revenge
> Descend to? who aspires must down as low
> As high he soar'd . . . .
>
> (IX, 163-70)

Satan, in other words, knows the rules. In time his legions will rise far enough to occupy the middle air, but they will not advance into the "precincts of light." Depth and dark are really their "native seat."

Their master is very honest about this, admitting, as he returns from the grand seduction, that he finds descent "through darkness" an easy road (X, 393-98).

It is darkness, as well as descent, even though it is "darkness visible" that plagues the newcomers to Hades. They sit in the gloom, as Gregory the Great tells us, "inwardly dark amidst the everlasting darkness of damnation."[32] Behind them are "the happy Realms of Light" (I, 85), which they have exchanged for a dreary plain, "void of light" (I, 180). Once they were famed as God's "Bright-harness'd Angels"; now they spend their time plotting how to "affront" God's holy light "with thir darkness" (I, 389-91), confounding "Heav'n's purest Light" "with blackest Insurrection" (II, 136-37). In alternate moments they console themselves with foolish or violent plans for an escape to light (II, 220, 376-78), but Satan, who has read the sixth book of the *Aeneid,* reminds them that "Long is the way / And hard, that out of Hell leads up to Light" (II, 432-33). In Satan's church— and theology informs us that he has one—this might be called the diabolique of darkness; the counter-Church opposes to this opaqueness the sublime metaphysic of light.

We need not scratch through the Bible or the smaller gravel of the theologians to find the moral interpretation of the blackness of Hell, of the mind of evil, or what Milton's Jehovah calls the "dark designs." The Christian conscience is fully aware of the dark symbols. Ignorance, sin and sinner, damnation, Hell and its provost are festooned with black against a midnight ground, and the speculations of Beatus Jung are seldom required to expound the Christian tradition. Opposed to this night of negation is what might be called the *tenebrae in bono* which is consonant with the descent in humility and is explained by the divine darkness that even Mammon knows.

> This deep world
> Of darkness do we dread? How oft amidst
> Thick clouds and dark doth Heav'n's all-ruling Sire
> Choose to reside, his Glory unobscur'd,
> And with the Majesty of darkness round
> Covers his Throne; from whence deep thunders roar
> Must'ring thir rage, and Heav'n resembles Hell?
> As he our Darkness, cannot we his Light
> Imitate when we please?
>
> (II, 262-70)

If these were not English devils, we would put this down to conscious humor; but the absence of jest is proclaimed when Pandaemonium is lighted with sputtering gas lamps that badly imitate Heaven's essential light. The dark with which God mantles himself is as different from Hell-dark as Hell-fire is from Heaven's blazing cressets. Moses, who ascended Mt. Sinai to enter the dark folds of God's light, could lecture the swart Mammon in hermeneutics.

Though Orpheus and Hercules enter the dark and arise to the light, the basic Christian idea of the dark god in the divine night is a totally different concept. For the ancients, light was the essence of existence and the sun shone in their temples, bathing the clear gods in bright gold. Death was the greatest of horrors, not because it deprived one of limb and motion but rather because it extinguished the mortal world of light. Dying Antigone weeps because never again will she see the holy light (ll. 879-80), and her lamentation is heard again and again in Greek tragedy.[33] Light was life, and it was also wisdom. For Plato φῶς is the means by which men who live in the realm of shadow almost place their hands on the unknown and unknowable.[34] The Roman stoics soothed themselves with the same consolation of light; hence Seneca can remind the suffering Helvia that "The gleams of night" enable one to commune with celestial beings and keep one's mind "always directed toward the sight of kindred things above."[35] The Christians, too, saw Jehovah as a bright God, the Father of Lights, and in his human manifestation, the *Lux Mundi*;[36] but they also knew him as a god in darkness,[37] assuming his cloak of clouds.[38] The figure of a darkened god visible only in the soul's night demanded an explanatory inscription on the entablature.

The Christian doctrine of the light in darkness begins when Philo Judaeus, the stepfather of exegesis, interpreted Exodus 20:21. The broad cloud on Mt. Sinai, he writes, is the allegory of Moses' attempt to understand the invisible and incorporeal nature of Jehovah;[39] it is also, in a more general sense, the symbolic exposition of the process by which the contemplative mind tries to comprehend the immaterial.[40] More than a century later, Roman Plotinus compared man's perception of common experience to wandering through the statues of the gods that crowd the outskirts of a temple.[41] The luminous soul has, truly enough, descended into darkness[42] when it has entered the flesh, but it still provides an inner light.[43] Once it has reached its limit this light is also changed into an obscurity;[44] but this limit does not blind the inner sight by which one may ascend to the light in the shadows (ἐλλαμψις ἡ εἰς το σκοτος), the spiritual habitation which is the goal of the wise.[45] Philo, accounting for the experience of Moses, and Plotinus, elaborating on the light metaphysic of Plato, offered to western man an esoteric explanation of divine light: it hides itself in the dark and one must enter the cloud to find it.

Milton, who had only the rudimentary chronology of his age to guide him, would probably think of Plato as a contemporary of Moses. He would certainly accept the Pseudo-Dionysius, the great exponent of this philosophy, as the disciple of St. Paul and the coeval of Philo. He would, consequently, assign all these similar doctrines to the first Christian era. The facts, as we now know and as I intend to relate them, were otherwise, and it is Gregory of Nyssa, whom Milton was reading before he wrote An Apology, who was the precursor of the Areopagite and who brought this doctrine into the fold of the Church. Gregory invented the poignant oxymoron "bright darkness" (λαμπρός γνόφος),[46] a trope that haunts the rhetoric of mystics ever afterward. In his Life of Moses he is troubled by the god who first showed himself in light and then in a dark shroud. He sought and found a solution for this strangeness. The Logos is first seen as light, but as one ascends, it becomes dark because one realizes that it surpasses ordinary knowledge and is separated from mortal comprehension by the tenebrae.[47] This is why Moses first saw God as light. Becoming more perfect in understanding by putting aside false knowledge of the divine, he passed from the primary light of the Logos, which dissipates impiety, into the divine dark. In this night, his mind, rejecting "the simple aspects of things," was fixed in a stasis of contemplation so that here he saw the true light where God is.[48] In this way Gregory wrote out the Christian explanations of the dark experience which the person who called himself Dionysius would some centuries later make an intrinsic part of Christian knowledge.

The light metaphysic of the Pseudo-Dionysius also owes much to Origen's doctrine of the double vision obtained through the eyes of the sense and the eyes of the mind. In order that the external eyes of men may be blinded, Origen writes, and that the inner eyes may see, Christ endured the humility of incarnation. By this descent, he, who healed the blind by miracle, blinded our external eyes so that he could cure our inner sight.[49] The Pseudo-Dionysius begins his Mystical Theology with the request that he may be allowed to ascend to those oracles where the mysteries of theology are seen in a darkness brighter than light.[50] He yearns to enter the "divine darkness" (θειος γνόφος),[51] where the human handicap of seeing and being seen is removed and all forms of external perception are blinded in the sacred darkness that is inaccessible light.[52] For him the *tenebrae* is a ἀγνωσία; and when the searcher has arrived at its limits, which are complete negation, he will see at last without veils.[53] The Pseudo-Dionysius supports this doctrine with the example of Moses, who penetrated into "the cloud of unknowing" by closing his human eyes to all the vanities of mortal knowledge.[54] Moses, it is true, did not see God's face but only the divine place;[55] nonetheless, his intellectual eyes, like those of the supercelestial Intelligences and Seraphim,[56] were cleansed of the "mass of obscurity."[57]

After the tenth century the vogue of the Pseudo-Dionysius and his doctrine was enormous. Hilduin, John Scot, Hincmar, Radebert, John of Salisbury, Sarrazin, Hugo of St. Victor, Albert the Great, and St. Thomas found spiritual fascination in his writings.[58] The excitement of the Middle Ages was shared by the members of the Florentine Academy, by Ficino, who translated the Areopagite and wrote his own *De Lumine,* and by Pico della Mirandola, who discovered in the Pseudo-Dionysius a fellow exotic. But the light metaphysic of this fifth-century Greek was particularly illuminating to those who followed the upward mystic road, to John of the Cross, Ruusbroec, Tauler, and Suso, all of whom walked the way marked out by Richard of St. Victor[59] and St. Bonaventura. The manuals of the latter saint are rubricated with the paradoxical notion that to see one must become blind: "Excaecatio est summa illuminatio." One must search, says Bonaventura, for the night of light, but only those who have found it know what it is.

> Jacob's ladder is placed on these three levels, the top reaching Heaven and so is Solomon's throne where sits the king wise and in peace, lovable as the most precious husband and most desirable. Upon him the angels desire to look and the love of holy souls yearns for him just as the stag seeks fountains of water. Hither in the manner of fire, our spirit is made skillful by a most fervent desire for the ascent but is carried by a wise ignorance beyond itself into darkness and delight so that it not only says with the bride: "We will run after thee to the odor of thy ointments," but also sings with the prophet: "and night shall be my light in my pleasure." What this nocturnal and delightful illumination is no one knows unless he tries it,

and unless grace is given divinely no one tries it; and no one is given it unless he trains himself for it.[60]

The same mode of expression is found in Dante, who like Virgil and Milton descended into Hell, who went into the dark in order to see the light. The poetic allegory comes at the beginning when Dante leaves the forest of this world and having endured the night with piety prepares to enter the dark downward path so that he may ascend to the triple circle of final illumination.

> Ma poi ch'io fui al piè d'un colle giunto,
> Là dove terminava quella valle
> Che m'avea di paura il cor compunto,
> Guardai in alto, e vidi le sue spalle
> Vestite già de' raggi del pianeta
> Che mena dritto altrui per ogni calle.
> Allor fu la paura un poco queta
> Che nel lago del cor m'era durata
> La notte ch' io passai con tanta pièta.
>
> (I, 13-21)

Milton's poetic realization of the themes of descent and ascent, of the necessity of entering the dark in order to see the light, of the descent of light itself so that men may see, and of the inner eye that knows only when the exterior sight is gone, is constantly before us as we read him. These themes were carried to exorbitant excess by the mystics, but we must remember that in spite of the emphasis given them by this nervous faith they have a simple Christian provenience. It is in the plain sense, which seems nowadays to be extravagant, that Milton puts them to use. The descent of humility comes before us as early as the "Nativity Ode" when we are told how the Son of God forsook the "Courts of everlasting Day" to choose "with us a darksome House of mortal Clay." The same theme comes forward again when Christ is assured that he will not degrade his nature "by descending" to assume that of man. "Therefore thy Humiliation shall exalt / With thee thy Manhood also to this Throne" (*P.L.*, III, 303-14). On the human level the poet seeking perfection rises from the day of "L'Allegro" and enters the night, "the high lonely Tow'r," of "Il Penseroso." Thus he, too, enters the dark, as Moses did, in order to reach the dawn and the "Prophetic strain." As Milton leaves the light of the first poem that reveals only the "aspects of things," Orpheus lifts his

head, but in the night of the second he hears the singing of both
Orpheus and his son Musaeus. It is in darkness, too, that fallen Adam
descends so that the day of fleshly surrender can be followed by the
night of remorse and humility; through this course, the father of men
ascends to God, first, in prayer and, then, in vision.

The theme of the inner eyes, so comforting to the blind man, makes
its appearance as early as the *Second Defence*,[61] where Milton compares his blindness with his opponent's spiritual dark: "mine keeps
from my view only the colored surfaces of things, while it leaves me
at liberty to contemplate the beauty and stability of virtue and truth."
Samson Agonistes, if it is the last work, almost depends on this idea.
At the bottom of despair Samson, "a moving grave," doubts that "light
is in the Soul" (l. 92) and sees only "double darkness nigh at hand"
(l. 593). But Samson's night becomes day when in the complete negation of himself he yields humbly to the "rousing motions in me"
(l. 1382); then the Semichorus can sing:

> But he though blind of sight,
> Despis'd and thought extinguish'd quite,
> With inward eyes illuminated
> His fiery virtue rous'd
> From under ashes into sudden flame.
>
> (ll. 1687-91)

We must turn, however, to *Paradise Lost,* and especially to two of its
invocations, to find all of this in flower.

The epic opens with the great address recalling Moses' ascent from
the low vale to the summit of Sinai to enter the clouded light that
awaits him. The experience of "that Shepherd, who first taught the
chosen Seed" reminds Milton of the brook of Siloa which flowed into
Siloam's pool, "fast by the Oracle of God," where Christ healed the
blind man, curing at once both the inward and the exterior eyes. The
types of both Old and New Testament are then personally read as the
poet prays for the ascent toward light. "What in me is dark / Illu-
mine, what is low raise and support; / That to the highth of this great
Argument. . . ." Prayer is itself the humble act, a preface to Milton's
descent into the dark underground of Satan's province.

It is possible that Milton begins in Hell because he who met Casella
"in the milder shades of Purgatory" began there. There is, however, a
difference between the two poets and their purposes. Dante enters
Hell (although the allegorical process of conversion and Christian

education is a reader's requirement) because the literal demanded it.
Milton's descent is an artistic voluntary. In a moral sense Dante descends that he may ascend; he enters the dark to find the light. In doing so he takes Milton by the hand, but the reason is doctrinal rather
than poetic. Having explored the dark bottom of pride, Milton rises
toward the light. The preface to Book III recounts this ascension:

> Thee I revisit now with bolder wing,
> Escap't the *Stygian* Pool, though long detained
> In that obscure sojourn, while in my flight
> Through utter and through middle darkness borne
> With other notes than to th'*Orphean* Lyre
> I sung of *Chaos* and *Eternal Night*,
> Taught by the heav'nly Muse to venture down
> The dark descent, and up to reascend,
> Though hard and rare.
>
> (III, 13-21)

Milton, like Moses, sees the "Holy Light," but like the great type of
the Redeemer he must descend to his "Native Element." Light, however, is given the inner eye, and, like Vaughan's Nicodemus, he can
"at mid-night speak with the Sun!" It is more than sixteen hundred
years after the typified event; yet the English poet joins himself to
the procession, heathen and Christian, of those who acted in the great
allegory of faith, who descended to ascend, who entered the darkness
to see the light.

NOTES

1. *Church Government, Works* (New York, 1931-38), III, 202-205;
   hereafter I shall cite only volume and page.
2. *Hirelings,* VI, 55, 58; *Christian Doctrine,* XIV, 311.
3. *Christian Doctrine,* XVI, 191.
4. *Ibid.,* XVI, 197.
5. *Ibid.,* XVI, 111.
6. *Ibid.,* XV, 145.
7. *Doctrine and Discipline,* III, 419; *Colasterion,* IV, 265.
8. *Liber de Corona, Patrologia Latina,* II, 85.
9. J. Wirl, *Orpheus in der englischen Literatur* (Vienna and Leipzig,
   1913). Milton's orphic imagery has been studied by Caroline Mayerson, "The Orpheus Image in Lycidas," *PMLA,* LXIV (1949), 189-

207. The Columbia *Index* may be consulted for Milton's references to Orpheus.

10. *Contra Faustum, PL,* XLII, 282; *De Civitate,* XVIII, 14.

11. *Legatio pro Christianis, Patrologia Graeca,* VI, 928.

12. Fulgentius, *Philosophi Mythologiarum libri tres* (Basel, 1536), pp. 77-79; Berchorius, *Metamorphosis Ovidiana Moraliter* (s.l., 1509), fol. lxxiii; Boccaccio, *Della Genealogia degli Dei,* tr. Betussi (Venice, 1585), p. 87; dell'Anguillara and Horologgi, *Le Metamorphosi* (Venice, 1584), pp. 357, 387; Comes, *Mythologiae* (Padua, 1616), pp. 401-402, 548; Ross, *Mystagogus Poeticus* (London, 1648), pp. 334-37.

13. *Cohortatio ad Gentes, PG,* VIII, 56-57.

14. *Panegyric to Constantine, PG,* XX, 1409.

15. Lampridius informs us in his life of Alexander Severus (a work cited by Milton in *Of Reformation*) that this Emperor erected shrines to Abraham, Christ, and Orpheus: see *Historiae Augustæ Scriptores* (Frankfurt, 1588), II, 214. Antonio Bosio has a chapter on why Christians compared Orpheus and Christ in *Roma Sotterano* (Rome, 1630). For an account of the Orpheus-Christ metaphor in Spanish literature see Pablo Cabanas, *El Mito de Orfeo en la literatura Española* (Madrid, 1948), pp. 153-76.

16. *The Poetical Works,* ed. F. Boas (Cambridge, Eng., 1908), I, 59-60. One of the earliest English comparisons is found in Gavin Douglas: see *Poetical Works,* ed. Small (Edinburgh, 1874), II, 18. Wither objects to these comparisons in *A Preparation to the Psalter,* 1619 (Spenser Society, 1884), pp. 77-78.

17. *PG,* VI, 885.

18. *Op. cit.,* V, 19; for other references to Hercules see the Columbia *Index.* The Samson-Hercules-Christ identification is explored by Krouse, *Milton's Samson and the Christian Tradition* (Princeton, 1949), pp. 44-45.

19. *Dial.,* II, 2, 2; see also Apuleius, *Florida,* 14, and Servius on *Aeneid,* VI, 119-23. The moral mythologers who read Christ into Orpheus also found the same connections between Christ and Hercules: see Fulgentius, pp. 32, 39-42; Boccaccio, pp. 210-14; Gyraldus, *Hercules,* in *Opera* (Leyden, 1696), I, 571-98; Alciati, *Emblemata* (Leyden, 1593), pp. 50-54, 505-508; Valeriano, *Hieroglyphica* (Basel, 1556), fols, 23ᵛ, 109ᵛ, 247ᵛ, 386; Comes, pp. 372-74.

20. G. Budé, *De Asse et partibus* (Paris, 1532), p. lxix.

21. *Oeuvres,* ed. Reaume and de Caussade (Paris, 1877), II, 226-31. Annibal Caro writes the Duchess of Castro: "Sotto il misterio d'Ercole si dinota Cristo, il quale estrinse il vizio, come Ercole uccise Cacco" (*Lettere Familiari* [Padua 1763], I, 253).

22. *Oeuvres,* ed. Vaganay (Paris, 1924), VI, 137-45.

23. *Op. cit.,* p. 169.

24. *Consolations,* III, met. 12; IV, met. 7.

25. *Sermo* CCXCVII, *PL,* XXXIX, 2313-14; *Confessiones,* IV, 12; *De Civitate,* VII, 33; *Enarratio in Psalmos, PL,* XXXVII, 1596-1600, 1606.

26. *Sermo* XXV, *PL,* XXXVIII, 168.

27. *In Job, PL,* XXXIV, 875.

28. Cassiodorus, *Exposition in Psalter, PL,* LXX, 1036.

29. Anselm, *Liber de Similitudinibus, PL,* CLIX, 664-65.

30. *De Gradibus Humilitatis,* ed. Burch (Cambridge, Mass., 1940), p. 176.

31. For patristic comments on the perfectibility of an unfallen Adam, see Hugo of St. Victor, *De Vanitate Mundi, PL,* CLXXVI, 723; St. Thomas, *Summa,* I, Q.102, a.4; Pico della Mirandola, *De Hominis Dignitate,* ed. Garin (Florence, 1942), pp. 104, 106; J. Donne, *Sermons,* ed. Potter and Simpson (Berkeley, Calif., 1953-60), II, 123, VII, 108.

32. *In Ezechielem, PL,* LXXVI, 1290.

33. See also Sophocles, *Aias,* 854-65, *Oedipus Col.,* 1549-51, and Euripides, *Iph. Aul.,* 1281-82, 1506-1509.

34. *Republic,* VI, 508-509, VII, 518; *Phaedo,* 99; see J. Stenzel, "Der Begriff der Erleuchtung bei Platon," *Die Antike,* II (1926), 235-37.

35. *Ad Helviam,* VIII, 5-6; see also Plutarch, *De Genio Soc.,* 590 B.

36. Psalms 36:9, 104:2; Wisdom, 7:21-25; I Timothy 6:16; I John 1:5.

37. Exodus 20:21, II Chronicles 6:1, II Samuel 22:12, Psalms 18:11-12, 97:2, Job 22:14.

38. Ezekiel 1:4, Revelation 1:7.

39. *Vita Mosis,* I, 28.

40. *De Poster. Caini,* 5.

41. *Enneads,* VI, 9, 11, 8-22.

42. *Ibid.,* IV, 3, 9, 23-29.

43. *Ibid.,* V, 3, 17, 27-37.

44. *Ibid.,* IV, 3, 9, 23-26.

45. *Ibid.,* II, 9, 12, 31; I, 6, 9, 22-24; see M. de Corte, "Plotin et la nuit de l'esprit," *Études Carmélitaines,* II (1938), 102-15.

46. *In Cantica Canticorum, PG,* XLIV, 1000-1001. It should be noted that Tertullian prior to his polemic against Montanism describes an "obumbratio mentis" as a preface to divine knowledge; see *Ad Marcion, PL,* II, 413, and *De Anima,* ed. Waszink (Amsterdam, 1947), p. 62 and notes. Ambrose considers the *tenebrae* as a requirement of the prophetic state: *De Abraham, PL,* XIV, 484.

47. *Op. cit., PG,* XLIV, 376-77.

48. *In Cantica, ibid.,* 1001.

49. *Contra Celsum, PG,* XI, 1476.

50. *Op. cit., PG,* III, 997.

51. *Ibid.,* 1000.

52. *Epistolae, ibid.,* 1073.

53. *T.M., ibid.,* 1000-1001.

54. *Ibid.,* 1001.

55. *Ibid.,* 1000.

56. *De Coelesti Hierarchia, ibid.,* 205.

57. *De Divinis Nominibus, ibid.,* 700-701; see H. C. Peuch, "La Ténèbre mystique chez le Pseudo-Denys," *Études Carmélitaines,* II (1938), 33-53.

58. P. G. Théry, "Denys au moyen age," *Études Carmélitaines,* II (1938), 68-74.

59. *Benjamin Minor, PL,* CXCVI, 52.

60. *Breviloquium, Opera Omnia* (Florence, 1891), V, 260.

61. *Op. cit.,* VIII, 71.

[EDITOR'S NOTE. See also Mr. Allen's *Harmonious Vision,* 1954; *The Legend of Noah,* 1949, and *PMLA,* LXXI (1956), 404-5; D. Bush, *Mythology and the Renaissance Tradition,* 1932, revised 1963; I. G. Mac-Caffrey, *"Paradise Lost" as Myth,* 1959; J. I. Cope, *The Metaphoric Structure of "Paradise Lost,"* 1962, and *ELH,* XXVI (1959), 372-95; A. R. Cirillo, *ELH,* XXIX (1962), 372-95.]

C. S. LEWIS

Satan

le genti dolorosi
C'hanno perduto il ben de l'intelletto
DANTE.

Before considering the character of Milton's Satan it may be desirable to remove an ambiguity by noticing that Jane Austen's Miss Bates could be described either as a very entertaining or a very tedious person. If we said the first, we should mean that the author's portrait of her entertains us while we read; if we said the second, we should mean that it does so by being the portrait of a person whom the other people in *Emma* find tedious and whose like we also should find tedious in real life. For it is a very old critical discovery that the imitation in art of unpleasing objects may be a pleasing imitation. In the same way, the proposition that Milton's Satan is a magnificent character may bear two senses. It may mean that Milton's presentation of him is a magnificent poetical achievement which engages the attention and excites the admiration of the reader. On the other hand, it may mean that the real being (if any) whom Milton is depicting, or any real being like Satan if there were one, or a real human being in so far as he resembles Milton's Satan, is or ought to be an object of

From *A Preface to "Paradise Lost,"* London: Oxford University Press, 1942, pp. 92-100; Oxford Paperbacks, 1960, pp. 94-103. Reprinted by permission of the Clarendon Press, Oxford.

admiration and sympathy, conscious or unconscious, on the part of the poet or his readers or both. The first, so far as I know, has never till modern times been denied; the second, never affirmed before the times of Blake and Shelley—for when Dryden said that Satan was Milton's "hero" he meant something quite different. It is, in my opinion, wholly erroneous. In saying this I have, however, trespassed beyond the bounds of purely literary criticism. In what follows, therefore, I shall not labour directly to convert those who admire Satan, but only to make a little clearer what it is they are admiring. That Milton could not have shared their admiration will then, I hope, need no argument.

The main difficulty is that any real exposition of the Satanic character and the Satanic predicament is likely to provoke the question "Do you, then, regard *Paradise Lost* as a comic poem?" To this I answer, No; but only those will fully understand it who see that it might have been a comic poem. Milton has chosen to treat the Satanic predicament in the epic form and has therefore subordinated the absurdity of Satan to the misery which he suffers and inflicts. Another author, Meredith, has treated it as comedy with consequent subordination of its tragic elements. But *The Egoist* remains, none the less, a pendant to *Paradise Lost,* and just as Meredith cannot exclude all pathos from Sir Willoughby, so Milton cannot exclude all absurdity from Satan, and does not even wish to do so. That is the explanation of the Divine laughter in *Paradise Lost* which has offended some readers. There is a real offence in it because Milton has imprudently made his Divine Persons so anthropomorphic that their laughter arouses legitimately hostile reactions in us—as though we were dealing with an ordinary conflict of wills in which the winner ought not to ridicule the loser. But it is a mistake to demand that Satan, any more than Sir Willoughby, should be able to rant and posture through the whole universe without, sooner or later, awaking the comic spirit. The whole nature of reality would have to be altered in order to give him such immunity, and it is not alterable. At that precise point where Satan or Sir Willoughby meets something real, laughter *must* arise, just as steam must when water meets fire. And no one was less likely than Milton to be ignorant of this necessity. We know from his prose works that he believed everything detestable to be, in the long run, also ridiculous; and mere Christianity commits every Christian to believing that "the Devil is (in the long run) an ass."

What the Satanic predicament consists in is made clear, as Mr.

Williams points out, by Satan himself. On his own showing he is suffering from a "sense of injur'd merit" (I, 98). This is a well known state of mind which we can all study in domestic animals, children, film-stars, politicians, or minor poets; and perhaps nearer home. Many critics have a curious partiality for it in literature, but I do not know that any one admires it in life. When it appears, unable to hurt, in a jealous dog or a spoiled child, it is usually laughed at. When it appears armed with the force of millions on the political stage, it escapes ridicule only by being more mischievous. And the cause from which the Sense of Injured Merit arose in Satan's mind—once more I follow Mr. Williams—is also clear. "He thought himself impaired" (V, 662). He thought himself impaired because Messiah had been pronounced Head of the Angels. These are the "wrongs" which Shelley described as "beyond measure." A being superior to himself in kind, by whom he himself had been created—a being far above him in the natural hierarchy—had been preferred to him in honour by an authority whose right to do so was not disputable, and in a fashion which, as Abdiel points out, constituted a compliment to the angels rather than a slight (V, 823-43). No one had in fact done anything to Satan; he was not hungry, nor over-tasked, nor removed from his place, nor shunned, nor hated—he only thought himself impaired. In the midst of a world of light and love, of song and feast and dance, he could find nothing to think of more interesting than his own prestige. And his own prestige, it must be noted, had and could have no other grounds than those which he refused to admit for the superior prestige of Messiah. Superiority in kind, or Divine appointment, or both—on what else could his own exalted position depend? Hence his revolt is entangled in contradictions from the very outset, and he cannot even raise the banner of liberty and equality without admitting in a tell-tale parenthesis that "Orders and Degrees Jarr not with liberty" (V, 789). He wants hierarchy and does not want hierarchy. Throughout the poem he is engaged in sawing off the branch he is sitting on, not only in the quasi-political sense already indicated, but in a deeper sense still, since a creature revolting against a creator is revolting against the source of his own powers—including even his power to revolt. Hence the strife is most accurately described as "Heav'n ruining from Heav'n" (VI, 868), for only in so far as he also is "Heaven" —diseased, perverted, twisted, but still a native of Heaven—does Satan exist at all. It is like the scent of a flower trying to destroy the flower. As a consequence the same rebellion which means misery for the feelings and corruption for the will, means Nonsense for the intellect.

Mr. Williams has reminded us in unforgettable words that "Hell is inaccurate," and has drawn attention to the fact that Satan lies about every subject he mentions in *Paradise Lost*. But I do not know whether we can distinguish his conscious lies from the blindness which he has almost willingly imposed on himself. When, at the very beginning of his insurrection, he tells Beelzebub that Messiah is going to make a tour "through all the Hierarchies . . . and give Laws" (V, 688-90) I suppose he may still know that he is lying; and similarly when he tells his followers that "all this haste of midnight march" (V, 774) had been ordered in honour of their new "Head." But when in Book I he claims that the "terror of his arm" had put God in doubt of "his empire," I am not quite certain. It is, of course, mere folly. There never had been any war between Satan and God, only between Satan and Michael; but it is possible that he now believes his own propaganda. When in Book X he makes to his peers the useless boast that Chaos had attempted to oppose his journey "protesting Fate supreame" (480) he may really, by then, have persuaded himself that this was true; for far earlier in his career he has become more a Lie than a Liar, a personified self-contradiction.

This doom of Nonsense—almost, in Pope's sense, of Dulness—is brought out in two scenes. The first is his debate with Abdiel in Book V. Here Satan attempts to maintain the heresy which is at the root of his whole predicament—the doctrine that he is a self-existent being, not a derived being, a creature. Now, of course, the property of a self-existent being is that it can understand its own existence; it is *causa sui*. The quality of a created being is that it just finds itself existing, it knows not how nor why. Yet at the same time, if a creature is silly enough to try to prove that it was not created, what is more natural than for it to say, "Well, I wasn't there to see it being done"? Yet what more futile, since in thus admitting ignorance of its own beginnings it proves that those beginnings lay outside itself? Satan falls instantly into this trap (850 et seq.)—as indeed he cannot help doing—and produces as proof of his self-existence what is really its disproof. But even this is not Nonsense enough. Uneasily shifting on the bed of Nonsense which he has made for himself, he then throws out the happy idea that "fatal course" really produced him, and finally, with a triumphant air, the theory that he sprouted from the soil like a vegetable. Thus, in twenty lines, the being too proud to admit derivation from God, has come to rejoice in believing that he

"just grew" like Topsy or a turnip. The second passage is his speech
from the throne in Book II. The blindness here displayed reminds one
of Napoleon's utterance after his fall, "I wonder what Wellington will
do now?—he will never be content to become a private citizen again."
Just as Napoleon was incapable of conceiving, I do not say the virtues,
but even the temptations, of an ordinarily honest man in a tolerably
stable commonwealth, so Satan in this speech shows complete inability to conceive any state of mind but the infernal. His argument assumes as axiomatic that in any world where there is any good to be
envied, subjects will envy their sovereign. The only exception is Hell,
for there, since there is no good to be had, the sovereign cannot have
more of it, and therefore cannot be envied. Hence he concludes that
the infernal monarchy has a stability which the celestial lacks. That
the obedient angels might love to obey is an idea which cannot cross
his mind even as a hypothesis. But even within this invincible ignorance contradiction breaks out; for Satan makes this ludicrous proposition a reason for hoping ultimate victory. He does not, apparently,
notice that every approach to victory must take away the grounds on
which victory is hoped. A stability based on perfect misery, and therefore diminishing with each alleviation of that misery, is held out as
something likely to assist in removing the misery altogether (II,
11-43).

What we see in Satan is the horrible co-existence of a subtle and
incessant intellectual activity with an incapacity to understand anything. This doom he has brought upon himself; in order to avoid seeing one thing he has, almost voluntarily, incapacitated himself from
seeing at all. And thus, throughout the poem, all his torments come,
in a sense, at his own bidding, and the Divine judgement might have
been expressed in the words "*thy* will be done." He says "Evil be
thou my good" (which includes "Nonsense be thou my sense") and
his prayer is granted. It is by his own will that he revolts; but not by
his own will that Revolt itself tears its way in agony out of his head
and becomes a being separable from himself, capable of enchanting
him (II, 749-66) and bearing him unexpected and unwelcome progeny. By his own will he becomes a serpent in Book IX; in Book X he
is a serpent whether he will or no. This progressive degradation, of
which he himself is vividly aware, is carefully marked in the poem.
He begins by fighting for "liberty," however misconceived; but almost
at once sinks to fighting for "Honour, Dominion, glorie, and renoune"
(VI, 422). Defeated in this, he sinks to that great design which makes

the main subject of the poem—the design of ruining two creatures who had never done him any harm, no longer in the serious hope of victory, but only to annoy the Enemy whom he cannot directly attack. (The coward in Beaumont and Fletcher's play, not daring to fight a duel, decided to go home and beat his servants.) This brings him as a spy into the universe, and soon not even a political spy, but a mere peeping Tom leering and writhing in prurience as he overlooks the privacy of two lovers, and there described, almost for the first time in the poem, not as the fallen Archangel or Hell's dread Emperor, but simply as "the Devil" (IV, 502)—the salacious grotesque, half bogey and half buffoon, of popular tradition. From hero to general, from general to politician, from politician to secret service agent, and thence to a thing that peers in at bedroom or bathroom windows, and thence to a toad, and finally to a snake—such is the progress of Satan. This progress, misunderstood, has given rise to the belief that Milton began by making Satan more glorious than he intended and then, too late, attempted to rectify the error. But such an unerring picture of the "sense of injured merit" in its actual operations upon character cannot have come about by blundering and accident. We need not doubt that it was the poet's intention to be fair to evil, to give it a run for its money—to show it *first* at the height, with all its rants and melodrama and "Godlike imitated state" about it, and *then* to trace what actually becomes of such self-intoxication when it encounters reality. Fortunately we happen to know that the terrible soliloquy in Book IV (32-113) was conceived and in part composed before the first two books. It was from this conception that Milton started and when he put the most specious aspects of Satan at the very beginning of his poem he was relying on two predispositions in the minds of his readers, which in that age, would have guarded them from our later misunderstanding. Men still believed that there really was such a person as Satan, and that he was a liar. The poet did not foresee that his work would one day meet the disarming simplicity of critics who take for gospel things said by the father of falsehood in public speeches to his troops.

It remains, of course, true that Satan is the best drawn of Milton's characters. The reason is not hard to find. Of the major characters whom Milton attempted he is incomparably the easiest to draw. Set a hundred poets to tell the same story and in ninety of the resulting poems Satan will be the best character. In all but a few writers the "good" characters are the least successful, and every one who has ever tried to make even the humblest story ought to know why. To make a character worse than oneself it is only necessary to release imaginatively from control some of the bad passions which, in real life, are always straining at the leash; the Satan, the Iago, the Becky Sharp, within each of us, is always there and only too ready, the moment the leash is slipped, to come out and have in our books that holiday we try to deny them in our lives. But if you try to draw a character better than yourself, all you can do is to take the best moments you have had and to imagine them prolonged and more consistently embodied in action. But the real high virtues which we do not possess at all, we cannot depict except in a purely external fashion. We do not really know what it feels like to be a man much better than ourselves. His whole inner landscape is one we have never seen, and when we guess it we blunder. It is in their "good" characters that novelists make, unawares, the most shocking self-revelations. Heaven understands Hell and Hell does not understand Heaven, and all of us, in our measure, share the Satanic, or at least the Napoleonic, blindness. To project ourselves into a wicked character, we have only to stop doing something, and something that we are already tired of doing; to project ourselves into a good one we have to do what we cannot and become what we are not. Hence all that is said about Milton's "sympathy" with Satan, his expression in Satan of his own pride, malice, folly, misery, and lust, is true in a sense, but not in a sense peculiar to Milton. The Satan in Milton enables him to draw the character well just as the Satan in us enables us to receive it. Not as Milton, but as man, he has trodden the burning marl, pursued vain war with heaven, and turned aside with leer malign. A fallen man *is* very like a fallen angel. That, indeed, is one of the things which prevents the Satanic predicament from becoming comic. It is too near us; and doubtless Milton expected all readers to perceive that in the long run either the Satanic predicament or else the delighted obedience of Messiah, of Abdiel, of Adam, and of Eve, must be their own. It is therefore right to say that Milton has put much of himself into Satan; but it is unwarrantable to conclude that he was pleased with that part of himself or expected us to be pleased. Because he was, like the rest of us, damnable, it does not follow that he was, like Satan, damned.

Yet even the "good" characters in *Paradise Lost* are not so unsuccessful that a man who takes the poem seriously will doubt whether, in real life, Adam or Satan would be the better company. Observe their conversation. Adam talks about God, the Forbidden Tree, sleep, the difference between beast and man, his plans for the morrow, the stars, and the angels. He discusses dreams and clouds, the sun, the moon, and the planets, the winds, and the birds. He relates his own creation and celebrates the beauty and majesty of Eve. Now listen to Satan: in Book I at line 83 he starts to address Beelzebub; by line 94 he is stating his own position and telling Beelzebub about his "fixt mind" and "injured merit." At line 241 he starts off again, this time to give his impressions of Hell: by line 252 he is stating his own position and assuring us (untruly) that he is "still the same." At line 622 he begins to harangue his followers; by line 635 he is drawing attention to the excellence of his public conduct. Book II opens with his speech from the throne; before we have had eight lines he is lecturing the assembly on his right to leadership. He meets Sin—and states his position. He sees the Sun; it makes him think of his own position. He spies on the human lovers; and states his position. In Book IX he journeys round the whole earth; it reminds him of his own position. The point need not be laboured. Adam, though locally confined to a small park on a small planet, has interests that embrace "all the choir of heaven and all the furniture of earth." Satan has been in the Heaven of Heavens and in the abyss of Hell, and surveyed all that lies between them, and in that whole immensity has found only one thing that interests Satan. It may be said that Adam's situation made it easier for him, than for Satan, to let his mind roam. But that is just the point. Satan's monomaniac concern with himself and his supposed rights and wrongs is a necessity of the Satanic predicament. Certainly, he has no choice. He has chosen to have no choice. He has wished to "be himself," and to be in himself and for himself, and his wish has been granted. The Hell he carries with him is, in one sense, a Hell of infinite boredom. Satan, like Miss Bates, is interesting to read about; but Milton makes plain the blank uninterestingness of *being* Satan.

To admire Satan, then, is to give one's vote not only for a world of misery, but also for a world of lies and propaganda, of wishful thinking, of incessant autobiography. Yet the choice is possible. Hardly a day passes without some slight movement towards it in each one of us. That is what makes *Paradise Lost* so serious a poem. The thing is possible, and the exposure of it is resented. Where *Paradise Lost* is not loved, it is deeply hated. As Keats said more rightly than he knew, "there is death" in Milton. We have all skirted the Satanic island closely enough to have motives for wishing to evade the full impact of the poem. For, I repeat, the thing is possible; and after a certain

point it is prized. Sir Willoughby may be unhappy, but he *wants* to
go on being Sir Willoughby. Satan *wants* to go on being Satan. That
is the real meaning of his choice "Better to reign in Hell, than serve in
Heav'n." Some, to the very end, will think this a fine thing to say;
others will think that it fails to be roaring farce only because it spells
agony. On the level of literary criticism the matter cannot be argued
further. Each to his taste.

NOTE

[EDITOR'S NOTE. For Dryden's comment on Satan, see *Essays of John
Dryden*, ed. W. P. Ker, 1900, II, 165, and for those of Blake and Shelley,
Milton Criticism: Selections from Four Centuries, ed. J. Thorpe, 1950.
Charles Williams discussed Milton in the introduction to *The English
Poems*, World's Classics, 1940, and *The English Poetic Mind*, 1932. For
various views of Milton's Satan, see A. E. Barker, *UTQ*, XI (1941-42),
421-36; R. M. Adams, *Ikon: John Milton and His Modern Critics*, 1955;
A. J. Waldock, *"Paradise Lost" and Its Critics*, 1947; M. M. Mahood,
Poetry and Humanism, 1950; A. Stein, *PMLA*, LXV (1950), 221-31;
R. J. Zwi Werblowsky, *Lucifer and Prometheus*, 1952; D. R. Howard,
Renaissance Papers, 1954, 11-23; J. B. Broadbent, *ELH*, XXI (1954),
161-92; E. Schanzer, *UTQ*, XXIV (1954-55), 136-45; M. Y. Hughes,
MP, LIV (1956), 80-94; J. M. Steadman, *MLR*, LII (1957), 181-5,
and *JEGP*, LIX (1960), 640-54; J. E. Duncan, *HLQ* (1957), 127-36;
J. I. Cope, *MLN*, LXXIII (1958), 9-11; C. A. Patrides, *MLN*, LXXIII
(1958), 257-60; F. Manly, *MLN*, LXXVI (1961), 110-16; C. A. Huckabay, *SN*, XXXIII (1961), 96-102; I. Samuel, *MP*, LIX (1962), 239-
47; R. E. Fox, *RES*, XIII (1962), 30-39, and *NS*, 1962, 389-95; R. B.
Waddington, *TSLL*, IV (1962), 390-98; A. B. Chambers, *JEGP* LXII
(1963), 280-87, and *RN*, XVI (1963), 98-101.]

HELEN GARDNER

Milton's "Satan" and the Theme of Damnation
in Elizabethan Tragedy

We are all familiar with the progeny of Milton's Satan and the effort
of most recent criticism has been directed towards clearing the Satan
of Milton's poem from his associations with the Promethean rebel of
romantic tradition. But the question whether Satan had any ancestors
has hardly been raised, or has been dismissed by reference to the devil
of popular tradition, or by an allusion to the heroic figure of the Old
English *Genesis B.* The late Mr. Charles Williams, in an essay on
Milton which seems likely to become a classic, and Mr. C. S. Lewis,
building, as he delighted to own, on Mr. Williams, destroyed, one
hopes for ever, the notion that Satan had grounds for his rebellion.[1]
But when we have agreed that Satan's "wrongs" which "exceed all
measure" exist only in Shelley's generous imagination, and that it is
easier to draw a bad character than a good, and have assented to the
statement that Satan's career is a steady progress from bad to worse
and ends with his complete deformity, we still have no explanation of
why the Romantic critics stood *Paradise Lost* on its head, or why the
"common reader" finds the imaginative impact of the first books so
much more powerful than that of the last, or why, as one re-reads the
poem, the exposure of Satan's malice and meanness seems curiously

From *English Studies,* N.S. I (1948), 46-66. Published by John Murray (Publishers) Ltd., London. Reprinted by permission of the author and The English
Association.

irrelevant. There remains always, untouched by the argument, the image of enormous pain and eternal loss. It is out of key with the close of the poem, which does not drive it from our memory, nor absorb it.

"From hero to general, from general to politician, from politician to secret service agent, and thence to a thing that peers in at bedroom or bathroom windows, and thence to a toad, and finally to a snake—such is the progress of Satan," writes Mr. Lewis, and he rightly declares that there is no question of Milton's beginning by making Satan too glorious and then, too late, attempting to rectify the error. "Such an unerring picture of 'the sense of injured merit' in its actual operations upon character cannot have come about by blundering and accident." We can parallel this account of the career of Satan, but not from Iago and Becky Sharp, whom Mr. Lewis cites as examples of bad characters who are more interesting than their virtuous opposites. From a brave and loyal general, to a treacherous murderer, to a hirer of assassins, to an employer of spies, to a butcher, to a coward, to a thing with no feeling for anything but itself, to a monster and a "hell-hound": that is a summary of the career of Macbeth. From a proud philosopher, master of all human knowledge, to a trickster, to a slave of phantoms, to a cowering wretch: that is a brief sketch of the progress of Dr. Faustus. With varying use of mythological machinery, this theme of the deforming of a creature in its origin bright and good, by its own willed persistence in acts against its own nature, is handled by Shakespeare and Marlowe, and with great power, but in a purely naturalistic setting, by Middleton and Rowley in *The Changeling*. It is on the tragic stage that we find the idea of damnation in English literature before *Paradise Lost*. "Satan," writes Mr. Williams, "is the Image of personal clamour for personal independence." He is in rebellion against "the essential fact of things." The same can be said of Faustus, of Macbeth, and of Beatrice-Joanna, and it is particularly interesting to notice that in *Macbeth* and *The Changeling* the dramatists have altered their sources to bring out the full implications of the theme.

The devil was a comic character in the medieval drama; in the Elizabethan period he virtually disappears in his own person from the greater plays. But what Mr. Lewis calls "the Satanic predicament" is there, and it appears in the tragic, not the comic mode of vision. The terrible distinction between devils and men in popular theology lay in the irreversibility of the fall of the angels. Unlike men the fallen angels were incapable of repentance and so for them there was no pardon. As Donne puts it: "To those that fell, can appertaine no reconciliation; no more then to those that die in their sins; for *Quod homini mors, Angelis casus;* The fall of the Angels wrought upon them, as the death of a man does upon him; They are both equally incapable of change to better."[2] Donne recognizes that some of the Fathers thought that "the devill retaining still his faculty of free will, is therefore capable of repentance, and so of benefit by this comming of Christ";[3] but this is exactly the point which Aquinas denies and Donne assents to his view. Aquinas decides that the fallen angels cannot repent, since, though they know the beginnings of penitence in fear, their free-will is perverted: "Quid-quid in eis est naturale, totum est bonum et ad bonum inclinans, sed liberum arbitrium in eis est in malo obstinatum; et quia motus virtutis et vitii non sequitur inclinationem naturae, sed magis motum liberi arbitrii; ideo non oportet, quamvis naturaliter inclinentur ad bonum, quod motus virtutis in eis sit, vel esse possit."[4] In the tragic world of Faustus and Macbeth we find presented to us in human terms this incapacity for change to a better state. It never occurs to us that Macbeth will turn back, or indeed that he can; and though Marlowe, in this more merciful, as he is always more metaphysical, than Shakespeare, keeps before us the fact of Faustus's humanity by the urgings of the Good Angel, yet to the Good Angel's "Faustus, repent; yet God will pity thee," comes at once the Bad Angel's response: "Thou art a spirit;[5] God cannot pity thee"; and to Faustus's

> Who buzzeth in mine ears, I am a spirit?
> Be I a devil, yet God may pity me;
> Yea, God will pity me, if I repent.

comes the confident statement of the Bad Angel: "Ay, but Faustus never shall repent"; to which Faustus gives a despairing assent: "My heart is harden'd, I cannot repent."[6]

In the three plays mentioned, along with this incapacity for change to a better state, or repentance, go two other closely related ideas. The initial act is an act against nature, it is a primal sin, in that it contradicts the "essential fact of things," and its author knows that it does so. It is not an act committed by mistake; it is not an error of judgment, it is an error of will. The act is unnatural and so are its results; it deforms the nature which performs it. The second idea is the irony of retributive justice. The act is performed for an imagined good, which appears so infinitely desirable that the conditions for its supposed satisfaction are accepted; but a rigorous necessity reigns and sees to it that though the conditions are exacted literally, the desire is only granted ironically, and this is inevitable, since the desire is for something forbidden by the very nature of man. . . .[7]

It is not suggested that there is any direct relation between these three plays, in the sense that one was inspired by the others; nor is it suggested that when Milton drew his Satan he had these great tragic figures in mind. What is suggested is that Satan belongs to their company, and if we ask where the idea of damnation was handled with seriousness and intensity in English literature before Milton, we can only reply: on the tragic stage. Satan is, of course, a character in an epic, and he is in no sense the hero of the epic as a whole. But he is a figure of heroic magnitude and heroic energy, and he is developed by Milton with dramatic emphasis and dramatic intensity. He is shown, to begin with, engaged in heroic and stupendous enterprises, and again and again in moments of dramatic clash; rousing his supine followers, awaiting his moment in the great debate, confronted with Sin and Death and Chaos itself, flinging taunt for taunt at his angelic adversaries. But most strikingly he is presented to us by the means by which the great Elizabethan dramatists commended their tragic heroes to our hearts and imaginations: by soliloquy. Milton gives to Satan no less than five long soliloquies in Eden, three in the fourth book and two in the ninth.[8] In them he reveals to us "the hot Hell that alwayes in him burnes," and recalls again and again

> the bitter memorie
> Of what he was, what is, and what must be
> Worse.

It is in them that the quality which makes Satan a tragic figure appears most strikingly, and it is the quality Mr. Lewis makes weightiest against him: his egoism.

"Satan's monomaniac concern with himself and his supposed rights and wrongs is a necessity of the Satanic predicament," says Mr. Lewis. The same is true of the great tragic heroes of Shakespeare, and this capacity of theirs to expose relentlessly the full horror of their situations is just what makes them the heroes of their plays.[9] The predicament of Claudius is direr than Hamlet's, but Shakespeare pays little attention to it; Malcolm is the righteous avenger of a horrible crime, but the sympathy we feel for him we take for granted. We are held enthralled instead by the voice of Hamlet, defining for us his "bad dreams" or that of Macbeth telling us of solitude. If we are to complain that wherever he goes, and whatever he sees, Satan finds nothing of interest but himself, and to compare him unfavourably with Adam, who can converse on topics of general interest such as the stars, what should we say of Lear, who finds in the majesty of the storm or the misery of the naked beggarman only fresh incentives to talk about the unkindness of his daughters? If we can say of a speech of Satan's that "it fails to be roaring farce only because it spells agony," we can say the same of Macbeth, complaining at the close of a career of murderous egoism that he has no friends, or of Beatrice-Joanna, "a woman dipp'd in blood" talking of modesty. Satan is an egoist and Satan is a comic character in exactly the same way as Hamlet, Macbeth, Othello, and Lear are egoists and comic characters. "O gull! O dolt!" cries Emilia to Othello. We do not pity him the less because we assent.

The critical problem of *Paradise Lost* seems to me to lie here. We are concerned with Satan in a way that is quite different from the way we are concerned with Adam and Eve. In Mr. Lewis's treatment this is quite clear. He uses all his skill to make us regard Satan as a despicable human being, discussing him in terms of "children, filmstars, politicians, or minor poets"; but he uses equal skill to make us realize we must not regard Adam in this way. If he is right, as I think he is, in pressing a distinction between our attitudes to the two figures, he poses an acute problem for the reader of *Paradise Lost*, and appears to convict Milton of the artistic failure involved in a mixture of kinds.

The distinction I feel I would express in rather different terms. Adam and Eve are representative figures, and the act they perform is a great symbolic act. The plucking of the apple is not in itself imaginatively powerful; its power over us springs from its very triviality; the meaning and the consequences are so much greater than the image of a hand stretched out to pluck the fruit. The temptation and fall of Eve is profound in its psychological analysis, but it lacks the shock of dramatic situation. As Mr. Lewis says: "The whole thing is so quick, each new element of folly, malice, and corruption enters so unobtrusively, so naturally, that it is hard to realize we have been watching the genesis of murder. We expect something more like Lady Macbeth's 'unsex me here.'" In other words the situation is not dramatically exploited, lingered on. The scenes between Adam and Eve are deeply human, but they lack the terror, and the dreadful exaggeration of tragedy. The quarrel is only too sadly life-like, but it does not appal us, as does the spectacle of Othello striking Desdemona. In the ninth book and the books that follow, Milton is tracing with insight, with humanity and with humility the process in man through sin to repentance. The progress is steady and ordered; what is said is fully adequate to the situation, appropriate but not astounding. But Satan's defiance of God is not expressed by a symbolic gesture; in his rebellion the act and its meaning are one. And in the earlier books, and indeed wherever Satan appears, what is said goes beyond the necessities of the narrative, because Milton was writing as a tragic artist obsessed by his imagination of a particular experience, and exploring it with the maximum intensity. The experience might be called "exclusion." Wherever he goes, whatever he looks at, Satan is perpetually conscious of this. His exclusion is self-willed, as is the exclusion of Faustus, Macbeth and Beatrice-Joanna. Like them he gazes on a heaven he cannot enter; like them he is in the end deformed; like them he remains in the memory with all the stubborn objectivity of the tragic.

If it can be accepted that Satan as he is conceived and presented to us is a tragic figure, it is possible to suggest another explanation for the Romantic misconception of the poem than a dislike of Milton's theology. The early nineteenth century was greatly concerned it would seem with tragic experience; its great poets wanted to be "miserable and mighty poets of the human heart." All of them attempted to write tragedy, but, with the possible exception of *The Cenci,* they produced nothing that is admitted to be fully tragic. It was also a period remarkable for penetrating and subtle Shakespearian criticism, but for a criticism which lost a sense of the play in its discussion of the psychology of the characters, and which tended to minimize in the tragic heroes the very thing that made them tragic and not pathetic, the evil in them. In the criticism of the period Hamlet is "a sweet prince," Lear "a man more sinned against than sinning." Hamlet's savagery and Lear's appalling rages are overlooked. Lamb turned from the stage because he could not bear the cruel comedy of *King Lear,* nor the sight of Desdemona in Othello's arms. Realized intensely in the mind, divorced from his action in the play, the tragic hero was reshaped. It is of the essence of tragedy that it forces us to look at what we normally do not care to look at, and have not invented for ourselves.[10] The failure either to write or to appreciate tragedy in the Romantic period springs from the same cause: the Romantic poets' pre-occupation with themselves, and their lack of capacity to submit themselves to the "mystery of things." The famous passage in which

Keats defined Shakespeare's quality as "Negative Capability" goes to the root of the matter. But "Negative Capability" is as necessary to the spectator and critic of tragedy as to its creator. The tragic is destroyed when we identify the hero with ourselves. Just as the Romantic critics tended to see the heroes of Shakespeare's tragedies as more admirable, more tender, more purely pathetic than they are, so feeling Satan's kinship with the tragic hero they sentimentalized him and made him conform to their limited conception of tragedy. Because he was to be pitied, they minimized the evil in him, inventing wrongs to explain and excuse it.[11]

The present age is also not an age of great tragic writing, though there are some signs of a revival of the tragic spirit. Its best poetry is symbolic, and its criticism, in reviving for us the medieval tradition of allegory, tends towards an allegorical interpretation of all art. Mr. Lewis, in exposing Shelley's misconceptions, has inverted the Romantic attitude, for the effect of his chapter on Satan is to make us feel that because Satan is wicked, and wicked with no excuse, he is not to be pitied, but is to be hated and despised. Shelley saw in Satan the indomitable rebel against unjust tyranny, and while regretting the "taints" in his character excused them. Mr. Lewis, who thinks more harshly of himself and of human nature than Shelley did, exposes Satan with all the energy and argumentative zeal which we used to hear our European Service employing in denouncing the lies of Goebbels and revealing the true nature of the promises of Hitler. Both Shelley's passionate sympathy and Mr. Lewis's invective derive from the same fundamental attitude: "It is we who are Satan." As often happens with plural statements, this is a merely verbal extension of the singular; that is to say it is infected by an egoism that distorts the proper function of the tragic. When we contemplate the lost Archangel, we should not be seeing ourselves in heroic postures defying tyrants, nor weighing up our chances of ending in Hell, any more than, while we watch the progress of Lear, we should be thinking how ungrateful other people are to us for our goodness to them, or resolving to think before we speak next time. Though Shelley and Mr. Lewis are on different sides, they agree in taking sides. Neither of them accepts the complexity of the emotion which Satan arouses.

The tragic is something outside ourselves which we contemplate with awe and pity. Aristotle began the perversion of tragic theory when he suggested that the terror we feel is a terror that the same fate may befall us. Aristotle was a philosopher and a moralist, and, like many of his kind since, wanted to make tragedy safe and useful. But tragedy does not exist to provide us with horrid warnings. "Pity," said Stephen Dedalus, expanding the cryptic Aristotelian formula, "is the feeling which arrests the mind in the presence of whatsoever is grave and constant in human sufferings and unites it with the human sufferer. Terror is the feeling which arrests the mind in the presence of whatsoever is grave and constant in human sufferings and unites it with the secret cause."[12] We accept the justice by which the tragic hero is destroyed. Indeed if it were not for the justice we should have no pity for him. The acceptance of the justice makes possible the pity, and the pity calls for the justice without which it would turn to loathing. But the cause must be secret in tragedy; it must be felt within the facts exposed; what is hateful in the tragic world is that Eternal Law should argue.

The unity of tragedy is destroyed if the critic makes himself either the champion of the hero or the advocate of Eternal Law. Tragedy "arrests the mind" as the sufferings of others do, but as our own do not. But in life the arrest is short, for we are involved in the necessity of action. As spectators of tragedy we are released from our perpetual burden of asking ourselves what we ought to do. To use tragedy either as a moral example or as a moral warning is to destroy the glory of tragedy, the power it has to release us from ourselves by arousing in us the sense of magnitude and the sense of awe. Wordsworth, the most untragic of great poets, saw something of the nature of tragedy when he wrote,

> Suffering is permanent, obscure and dark,
> And shares the nature of infinity.

Tragedy may present us with a "false infinite" but it has that nature. It is permanent "with such permanence as time has." Like the rock in Mr. Eliot's *The Dry Salvages,*

> Waves wash over it, fogs conceal it;
> On a halcyon day it is merely a monument,
> In navigable weather it is always a seamark
> To lay a sudden course by: but in the sombre season
> Or the sudden fury, is what it always was.

The figure of Satan has this imperishable significance. If he is not the heroic rebel of Shelley's imagination, neither is he merely an "unerring picture of the 'sense of injur'd merit' in its actual operations upon character."

But if Mr. Lewis's view seems like an inversion of Shelley's, Mr. Williams's is not very unlike Blake's. What Blake perceived in *Paradise Lost* was a radical dualism, which was perhaps the inevitable effect of treating the myth in epic form. Among the many difficulties inherent in the subject was the difficulty of knowing how much to include in the direct action and how much to put into relations. It was impossible for Milton to begin where his tragedy *Adam Unparadised* was to have begun, in Paradise; the direct action would have been insufficient to fill the epic form. Even as it is, *Paradise Lost* is overweighted with relations. Epic tradition forbade him to begin at the beginning with the exaltation of the Son. Possibly his decision to begin with the moment when Satan lifts his head from the burning waves was inevitable once he had decided against the dramatic form in which he first conceived the subject. But the effect of beginning there, and of the whole of the "Prologue in Hell" is to make the action of the poem seem to originate in Hell, and to make the acts of Heaven seem only the response called out by the energies of Hell. However much Milton contradicts this later and asserts the overriding Will, the structure and design of his poem contradict and fight against his intention. The parallel, so often praised, between the silence in Hell, and the silence in Heaven reinforces the feeling of dualism, since *contraria sunt aequalia,* and Satan and the Son seem balanced against each other, as Blake saw them to be, while the priority of the scene in Hell seems to make Heaven parody Hell rather than Hell Heaven. Mr. Williams's statement that "the Son is the Image of Derivation in Love, and Satan is the Image of personal clamour for personal independence" is not unlike Blake's assertion of "the contraries from which spring what the religious call good and evil." It suggests at least that Milton made Satan too important in the scheme of his poem.

Perhaps the problem which *Paradise Lost* presents to the critic has its origin in Milton's own change of mind over the form in which he was to write his masterpiece. He first chose the subject of the Fall of Man as suited to a tragedy, and we know that he not only planned the disposition of his material in dramatic form, but actually began the writing. His draft *Adam Unparadised* provides Lucifer with two soliloquies: in the first he was to "bemoan himself" and "seek revenge upon man"; in the second he was to appear "relating and consulting on what he had done to the destruction of man." The first soliloquy was therefore to have been mainly expository, and in the second Lucifer was to take over the duty of the classical messenger and relate the catastrophe. The strict concentration of classical tragedy would have prevented Lucifer from usurping on the main interest, and his predicament, however much he "bemoaned himself," would have been subordinated to the whole design. Why Milton changed his mind we do not know, and he set himself a problem of extraordinary difficulty in choosing to treat this particular subject in epic form. He had somehow to fill the large epic structure, and it is difficult to see how else he could have done it than by expanding Satan's rôle. But it is possible that he turned away from tragedy because his interest had radiated out from the true centre of the action, the Fall itself, and his imagination demanded the larger freedom of the epic. Certainly the fact that Phillips remembered seeing the opening lines of Satan's first soliloquy as part of the projected tragedy suggests that Milton's conception of Satan began to form early, and it may have been that the writing of this first soliloquy showed Milton that the tragic form would not allow him to develop his conception as fully as he wished to. But whether the decision to begin his poem with Satan in Hell was simply the inevitable result of enlarging his action to make it sufficient for an epic, or whether it was Milton's interest in Satan that led him to abandon tragedy for epic, and he therefore naturally began with Satan, the figure of Satan, originally conceived dramatically, is developed dramatically throughout, and Milton expended his creative energies and his full imaginative power in exploring the fact of perversity within a single heroic figure. In this, as in much else, he is what we loosely call an Elizabethan, sacrificing simplicity of effect and strength of design to imaginative opportunity; creating the last great tragic figure in our literature and destroying the unity of his poem in doing so. The dualism which Blake found in the poem's thought, and which in Mr. Williams's analysis seems to dictate its design, is certainly there in its manner. The strong emotions of pity and terror do not mix well with the interest, sympathy and "admiration" which we feel for the heroes of what Mr. Lewis has called "the secondary epic," and, with the possible exception of Hazlitt, no critic of note has done justice to both Satan and Adam as artistic creations. The subject demanded an "infernal Serpent"; instead Milton has given us "a lost Archangel." There would be no difficulty if Satan were simply an Iago; the difficulty arises because he is a Macbeth.

NOTES

1. See *The English Poems of Milton*, with a preface by Charles Williams, (World's Classics) 1940, and C. S. Lewis, *A Preface to Paradise Lost*, 1942.

2. *LXXX Sermons*, 1640, p. 9. A recent reading of Donne's *Sermons* for another purpose has impressed upon me how often Donne provides the comment of a theologian or a moralist upon the tragedies of his contemporaries.

3. *Ibid.*, p. 66.

4. *S.T.*, Supplement, Q. XVI, Art. 3.

5. *Spirit* here as elsewhere in the play means evil spirit, or devil.

6. All quotations from *Dr. Faustus* are from the edition of Dr. F. S. Boas, 1932. The point that Faustus is presented to us as incapable of real repentance, though like the devils he knows the beginnings of penitence in fear and "believes and trembles," is obscured if we accept, as Dr. Boas does, the suggestion of Mr. H. T. Baker (*Modern Language Notes*, vol. XXI, pp. 86-7) and transfer to Faustus the close of the Old Man's speech in Act v, scene i (p. 161). In this most touching scene the Old Man makes a last appeal to Faustus to remember his humanity:

> Though thou hast now offended like a man,
> Do not persever in it like a devil;
> Yet, yet, thou hast an amiable soul,
> If sin by custom grow not into nature.

7. Donne supplies us with a comment on the "omnipotence" of Faustus, the "kingship" of Macbeth and the "marriage" of Beatrice-Joanna, when he says: "For small wages, and ill-paid pensions we serve him (Satan); and lest any man should flatter and delude himselfe, in saying, I have my wages, and my reward before hand, my pleasures in this life, the punishment, (if ever) not till the next, The Apostle destroyes that dreame, with that question of confusion, *What fruit had you then in those things, of which you are now ashamed?* Certainly sin is not a gainfull way; . . . fruitlesness, unprofitableness before, shame and dishoner after." *LXXX Sermons*, p. 65. [EDITOR'S NOTE. In the pages omitted here, Miss Gardner discusses Faustus, Macbeth, and Beatrice-Joanna, in the plays instanced above.]

8. In spite of the explanatory and anticipatory element in these soliloquies, their general effect, particularly in the two longest, IV, 32-113 and IX, 99-178, is quite different from the effect of the soliloquies of villains such as Richard III or Iago. In them we are conscious of activity of intellect and atrophy of feeling; here, as in the soliloquies of

Hamlet or Macbeth, the plans announced are less important than the analysis of the hero's predicament.

9. Henry James puts this well in the preface to *The Princess Casamassima*, London, 1921, p. viii. "This in fact I have ever found rather terribly the point—that the figures in any picture, the agents in any drama, are interesting only in proportion as they feel their respective situations; since the consciousness, on their part, of the complication exhibited forms for us their link of connection with it. But there are degrees of feeling—the muffled, the faint, the just sufficient, the barely intelligent, as we may say; and the acute, the intense, the complete, in a word—the power to be finely aware and richly responsible. It is those moved in this latter fashion who "get most" out of all that happens to them and who in so doing enable us, as readers of their record, as participators by a fond attention, also to get most. Their being finely aware—as Hamlet and Lear, say, are finely aware— *makes* absolutely the intensity of their adventure, gives the maximum of sense to what befalls them."

10. It may be suggested that the success of *The Cenci,* compared with other tragedies of the period, is partly due to the fact that the story was not invented by Shelley. He plainly felt some of the "superstitious horror" which he tells us the story still aroused in Italy, and was fascinated by the portrait of Beatrice.

11. In the preface to *Prometheus Unbound,* Shelley compared Satan with Prometheus and declared that Prometheus is the "more poetical character" since he is "exempt from the taints of ambition, envy, revenge, and a desire for personal aggrandisement, which, in the Hero of *Paradise Lost,* interfere with the interest." He thought that the character of Satan "engenders in the mind a pernicious casuistry which leads us to weigh his faults with his wrongs, and to excuse the former because the latter exceed all measure." When he wrote the preface to *The Cenci,* Shelley had abandoned the notion that moral perfection made a character poetically interesting, and acknowledged that if Beatrice had been "wiser and better" she would not have been a tragic character, but he speaks again of the "casuistry" by which we try to justify what she does, while feeling that it needs justification. When he compared Milton's God and his Devil in *A Defence of Poetry,* Shelley declared Satan was morally superior on the grounds that his situation and his wrongs excused in him the revengefulness which is hateful in his triumphant Adversary. In all these passages one can see Shelley's feeling that the Hero is a person whose side we take. The theme of a nature warped by suffering injustice, and repaying crime with crime, is certainly tragic when handled with seriousness and moral integrity as in *The Cenci,* though

it slides all too easily into the sentimental absurdities of the Byronic outcast, and it is always in danger of shallowness. It is the tragic formula of an age which does not believe in original sin, and thinks of evil as not bred in the heart, but caused by circumstances.

12. James Joyce, *A Portrait of the Artist as a Young Man*, chapter v.

[EDITOR's NOTE. Miss Gardner's interpretation of *Paradise Lost* is further developed in her forthcoming volume in the series of Alexander Lectures, University of Toronto. See the items listed with the preceding essay; and on some other literary models see W. Blissett, *JHI*, XVIII (1957), 221-32; R. M. Bottwood, *CJ*, XLVII (1952), 183-6; E. E. Kellett, *London Quarterly and Holborn Review*, CLXIV (1939), 88-99.]

A. B. CHAMBERS

Wisdom at One Entrance Quite Shut Out: *Paradise Lost*, III, 1-55

From the invocation to the third book of *Paradise Lost* we learn that
there are two kinds of light. The first is physical, the "off-spring of
Heav'n first born" (III, 1);[1] the second is "Celestial light" (51), an
"Eternal . . . beam" which is "Coeternal" with God himself (2).
So also, there are the eyes of the body and the eyes of the mind; Milton's blindness deprives him of the one, but by means of the other
he may yet "see and tell / Of things invisible to mortal sight" (54-55).
The rhetorical function of this argument is to establish Milton as a
divinely inspired poet, able to understand and explain the actions of
God himself.[2] The rhetorical proof turns upon three related topics, all
rich in traditional significance: the metaphysics of light, the purpose
of mortal vision, and the symbolism of the eyes of the soul. The first of
these has attracted considerable attention;[3] the latter two, no less important, have not.

Having made his address to light, Milton recalls that its physical
form is now denied him, even as it was of old to Thamyris, Homer,
Tiresias and Phineas (35-36). At least one of these ancient figures
might well have provided Milton's early readers with a clue as to what
course the succeeding lines would take, for Pico had said that Pallas—
the Wisdom of God—closed the eyes of Tiresias' body, but "she opened

From *Philological Quarterly*, XLII (1963), 114-19. Reprinted by permission of
the author and the publisher.

the eyes of his mind."[4] Milton will presently reach this conclusion concerning himself. First he will explore the purpose of the body's eyes and lament their loss.

> Thus with the Year
> Seasons return, but not to me returns
> Day, or the sweet approach of Ev'n or Morn,
> Or sight of vernal bloom, or Summer's Rose,
> Or flocks, or herds, or human face divine;
> But cloud instead, and ever-during dark
> Surrounds me, from the cheerful ways of men
> Cut off, and for the Book of knowledge fair
> Presented with a Universal blanc
> Of Nature's works to mee expung'd and ras'd,
> And wisdom at one entrance quite shut out.
>
> (40-50)

The first lines of this passage may suggest that the source of Milton's sorrow is the fact that nature's beauty—the vernal bloom, the summer rose—is no longer available to him. The final lines make it clear that the cause of sorrow is in fact Milton's deprivation of the Book of Nature, a volume which told the Middle Ages and Renaissance much about its divine Author. And if nature was commonly thought to be a book of "knowledge fair," the chief means of reading its pages was often said to be the vision of the mortal eye. "Of all the senses," wrote Aristotle in beginning the *Metaphysics,* "sight best helps us to know things."[5] Bacon agreed. The *Novum Organum* tells us that "perceptions" lead to "true notions and axioms," and—mentioning what Bacon calls "Instances of the Door or Gate"—goes on to remark that "sight has the chief office in giving information."[6] Bernard Sylvestris approaches Milton's gate of wisdom yet more closely, for he refers specifically to a number of those natural objects from which Milton apparently believes that knowledge is to be gained: the seasons, the day and night, the herds and the sylvan beast.[7]

It seems probable to me, however, that the eye of Milton's memory was upon none of these works but upon the account given by Bernard's mentor. Plato too had spoken of the value of mortal sight, and in the person of Timaeus he gave the philosophical justification for its value. At the same time he managed to mention most of those aspects of nature imaginatively observed and described by Milton's lines:

The sight of day and night, of months and the revolving years, of equinox and solstice, has caused the invention of number and bestowed on us the notion of time and the study of the nature of the world; whence we have derived all philosophy, than which no greater boon has ever come or shall come to mortal man as a gift from heaven. This, then, I call the greatest benefit of eyesight; why harp upon all those things of less importance, for which one who loves not wisdom, if he were deprived of the sight of them, might "lament with idle moan"? For our part, rather let us speak of eyesight as the cause of this benefit, for these ends: the god invented and gave us vision in order that we might observe the circuits of intelligence in the heaven and profit by them for the revolutions of our own thought, which are akin to them, though ours be troubled and they are unperturbed; and that, by learning to know them and acquiring the power to compute them rightly according to nature, we might reproduce the perfectly unerring revolutions of the god and reduce to settled order the wandering motions in ourselves.[8]

For Plato, it is "day and night"; for Milton, "Ev'n and Morn." By the one we are referred to "months and the revolving years"; by the other, to "the Year" and the "return" of the "Seasons." Here there is "equinox and solstice"; there, "vernal bloom and Summer Rose." Plato derives "all philosophy," that great "boon," from eyesight, and Milton refers to it as a means of achieving "knowledge fair" and "wisdom." Plato and Milton, lovers alike of wisdom though in their separate ways, reach similar conclusions in still another important respect. Neither will "harp on those things of less importance," nor will Milton, "though deprived of the sight of them," "lament with idle moan." Rather he will replace lamentation with prayer and move beyond pathos to triumphant hope. If wisdom is at *one* entrance quite shut out, then

> So much the rather thou Celestial light
> Shine inward, and the mind through all her powers
> Irradiate, there plant eyes, all mist from thence
> Purge and disperse, that I may see and tell
> Of things invisible to mortal sight.
>
>   (51-55)

In turning to the eyes of the mind, Milton probably remembers not one precedent but many, for the powers of the spiritual eye were widely praised. Some had believed that the soul, no less than the face, possessed two eyes. For the *Theologia Germanica* and for Boehme, one eye looked to eternity and one to time; for Gregory, one to the contemplative life, one to the active.[9] John of Salisbury discovered no fewer than three eyes by which man sees: the eye of the flesh, which views the world; the eye of reason, which beholds the soul; and the eye of contemplation, which looks to God.[10] Most men were content, like Pico, to distinguish merely two kinds of sight:

> Sight is twofold, corporeal and spiritual; the first is that of Sense, the other the intellectual Faculty; by which we agree with Angels; this *Platonists* call Sight, the corporeal being only an Image of this. So *Aristotle, Intellect is that to the Soul which Sight is to the Body.* Hence is *Minerva* (Wisdom) by *Homer* called γλαυχῶπις Bright-ey'd. With this Sight *Moses,* St. Paul, and other Saints, beheld the Face of God; this Divines call *intellectual, intuitive Cognition, the beatifical Vision, the Reward of the Righteous.*[11]

Relevant also to Milton's lines are two other related beliefs. The first states that God himself is an eye, and it may add that He is the eye of the human mind.[12] The second develops a parallel between physical and spiritual light by saying that what the eye is for man, so the sun is for the world; moreover, the spiritual light of God supports them both. Albinus, the middle Platonist, thus tells us that

> The sun is related to things seeing and seen, for while it is not sight itself, it allows the one to see and the other to be seen; the First Intellect is related in the same way to the intellect within our soul and to intelligible things, for while it is not knowledge itself, it allows the one to know and the other to be known, and thus brings to light (φωτίζων —"illuminating") the truth concerning intelligible things.[13]

When Milton prays that celestial light may irradiate his mind, clearly he depends on traditions rather more specific than the one which identifies God with light, for behind him stands an elaborate development of the internal connections between the kinds of vision, the purposes of sight, and the means by which both bodily and mental eyes perceive.

These topics provide the means whereby Milton elevates himself
and his reader from the first and second books' contemplation of infernal regions to the third books contemplation of empyrean heights.
The elevation is progressive: having begun with the "utter darkness"
(III, 16) of hell in book I, Milton moves upward with Satan to the
"middle" darkness (III, 16) of chaos in book II, and thence to Satan
upon "this pendant world" (II, 1052); ascending to the realm of
physical light, he ends by looking with the mental eye to God, "High
Thron'd above all highth" (III, 58). And there we learn that God
too looks forth with two kinds of sight. With the one, He

> bent down his Eye
> His own works and their works at once to view.
>
> (58-59)

Because of the other, "the Sanctities of Heaven . . . from his sight
receiv'd / Beatitude past utterance" (60-62). Here the separate
strands of the tradition unite, for at this highest of levels it is no
longer possible to distinguish between physical and spiritual light,
between the eyes of the body and those of the mind, between vision
and wisdom and beatitude. They are all one.

The meaning of the images employed in the invocation to book III
is logically completed only by later parts of *Paradise Lost,* for book IX
inverts these images of sight by showing that while vision may be an
important source of wisdom, it can be also an entrance for folly and
sin. Pointing to the forbidden fruit, Satan argues to Eve that

> in the day
> Ye eat thereof, your Eyes that seem so clear,
> Yet are but dim, shall perfectly be then
> Op'n'd and clear'd.
>
> (IX, 705-08)

The fruit "solicited" Eve's "longing eye" (743), for it seemed "Fair
to the eye . . . Of virtue to make wise" (777-78). It is, argues fallen
Eve to Adam, "of Divine effect / To open Eyes" (865-66), and Adam
notes that it was "coveting to Eye" (923). But the lamentable effect
of "op'n'd Eyes" (985) is for Adam "to cast lascivious Eyes" (1014)
and for Eve, "whose Eye darted contagious Fire" (1036), to respond.[14] The twofold means of gaining wisdom, of illuminating the
eye and irradiating the mind, goes totally awry. Adam and Eve, true,

"Soon found thir Eyes how op'n'd"; but they found also "thir minds / How dark'n'd" (1053-54).[15] That "dim suffusion" (III, 26) of Milton's blindness thus becomes a darkening of the eyes of the soul, and that mental "mist" which he prayed God to "purge and disperse" here finds its source in original sin. In the moment of the fall, Adam and Eve distort the eyes of the body and close the eyes of the mind. In a moment of grace, the epic poet—like those prophets and poets of old—of necessity forsakes the body's gate of wisdom in order to open an entrance into the soul.

NOTES

1. Quotations are from *Paradise Lost,* ed. Merritt Y. Hughes (New York, 1935).

2. John S. Diekhoff, "The Function of the Prologue in *Paradise Lost,*" *PMLA,* LVII (1942), 697-704 (also in *Milton's Paradise Lost* [London, 1958], pp. 13-27).

3. In addition to Hughes' notes, see William B. Hunter, Jr., "The Meaning of 'Holy Light' in *Paradise Lost,* III," *MLN,* LXXIV (1959), 589-92 and, for more general discussion of light in *Paradise Lost,* Don Cameron Allen, *The Harmonious Vision* (Johns Hopkins Press, 1954), pp. 95-109. Not specifically concerned with Milton but valuable for background are J. A. Mazzeo's "Light Metaphysics, Dante's 'Convivio' and the Letter to Can Grande della Scala," *Traditio,* XIV (1958), 191-229 and Clemens Bäumker's study of Witelo, *Beiträge z. Ges. d. Phil. d. Mittelalters,* IX, part 2 (Münster, 1908), 357-467.

4. *A Platonick Discourse . . . in Explication of . . . Benevieni,* trans. Thomas Stanley, *The History of Philosophy,* 4th ed. (London, 1743), p. 213; for the Italian, see *De hominis dignitate,* ed. Eugenio Garin (Florence, 1942), p. 529.

5. *Metaphysics,* I.i (980A).

6. *Novum Organum,* II, 38 and 39, *Philosophical Works,* ed. J. M. Robertson (London, 1905), pp. 350-51.

7. *De mundi universitate,* ed. Carl Barach and Johann Wrobel (Innsbruck, 1876), pp. 55-56. See also Robert Fludd, *De philosophia Moysaica* (Gouda, 1638), fols. 6^v-8^r for similar ideas, and see Marjorie Nicolson, *Newton Demands the Muse* (Princeton University Press, 1946), pp. 82, 151 for the importance of sight in the eighteenth century.

8. *Timaeus,* 47 A-C. I have used Cornford's translation (*Plato's Cosmology* [London, 1952], pp. 157-58). See also *Timaeus,* 39B and

Chalcidius, *Platonis Timaeus interprete Chalcidio cum eiusdem commentario,* ed. Johann Wrobel (Leipzig, 1876), paragraph 264.

9. The *Theologia Germanica* (VII) and Boehme (*Dialogue of the Supersensual Life,* II) are noted by C. A. Bennett, *A Philosophical Study of Mysticism* (Yale University Press, 1931), p. 46; for Gregory, see *Moralia in Job, PL,* LXXV, 762.

10. *De Septem septenis, PL,* CXCIX, 963.

11. *A Platonick Discourse* (Stanley, p. 210; Garin, pp. 497-98). See also Origen, *Contra Celsum, PG,* XI, 1476-77; Pico, *Heptaplus,* V, 1 (Garin, p. 288); Bruno, *Concerning the Cause, Principle and One,* III, trans. Sidney Greenberg as an appendix to *The Infinite in Giordano Bruno* (New York, 1950), p. 130; Chapman, *Hymnus in Cynthiam,* 444-46.

12. See Nicolas of Cusa, *De visione Dei,* VIII, trans. Emma Salter (London, 1928), p. 37, and *Hermetica,* ed. and trans. Walter Scott (Oxford, 1924), I, 251.

13. *Epitome,* X, 5, ed. Pierre Louis (Paris, 1945), p. 61. Albinus very probably was thinking of Plato, *Republic,* VI (508), as perhaps was Leone Ebreo, *Diologhi d'amore,* III, ed. Santino Caramella (Bari, 1929), p. 184. For more general correspondences between the eye, the sun, and God, see Macrobius. *Saturnalia,* I, xxi (Apud Jacobum Stoer, 1597), p. 368; Epiphanius, *Adversus haereses, PG,* XLI, 205; Ambrose, *Hexaemeron, PL,* XIV, 201; Bernard Sylvestris, pp. 66-67; Kepler, *Harmonices mundi libri V,* V, 10, *Opera omnia,* ed. Christian Frisch (Frankfurt, 1874), V, 324; Alexander Ross, *Mystagogus poeticus,* 2nd ed. (London, 1648), pp. 342-43. The eye is sometimes an emblem for God: see Edgar Wind, *Pagan Mysteries in the Renaissance* (Yale University Press, 1958), pp. 166-68.

14. Clearly, Milton makes use of the theory that the eye puts forth an internal fire by which it sees, for not only does Eve's eye dart contagious fire, but Milton's eye was "quenched" (III, 25). See Plato, *Timaeus,* 45B-D and Plutarch, *De placitis philosophorum,* IV, xiii.

15. Milton's repeated reference to eyes in book IX represents, of course, a development of his Biblical text (Gen. iii, 5), but it too has a tradition behind it. M. C. Bradbrook, *The School of Night* (Cambridge University Press, 1936), pp. 68 and 182, refers to Heraclitus, Seneca, and Chapman. (AUTHOR'S ADDITIONAL NOTE. Barbara K. Lewalski, "Structure and the Symbolism of Vision in Michael's Prophecy, *Paradise Lost,* Books XI-XII," *PQ,* XLII (1963), 26-7, has discussed the significance of the temporary restoration of Adam's vision by Michael. The important passage, for my purposes, is XI, 411-15: "but to nobler sights / Michael from Adam's eyes the film remov'd / Which that

false Fruit that promis'd clearer sight / Had bred; then purg'd with Euphrasy and Rue / The visual Nerve, for he had much to see.)

[EDITOR's NOTE. For the various prologues in *Paradise Lost,* see J. S. Diekhoff, *PMLA,* LVII (1952), 697-704; and on Milton's inspiration, L. Langdon, *Milton's Theory of Poetry and Fine Art,* 1925; J. H. Hanford, *UTQ,* (1938-39), 403-19; J. I. Cope, *MP,* LV (1957), 6-10; G. W. Whiting and A. Gossman, *SP,* LVIII (1962), 193-205; A. D. Ferry, *Milton's Epic Voice,* 1963; J. M. Steadman, *Neophil.,* XLVII (1963), 61-73; H. F. Robins, *If This Be Heresy,* 1963; W. B. Hunter, Jr., *Rice Institute Pamphlet,* XLVI, No. 4 (1960), 1-4, and *SEL,* IV (1964), 35-42; M. Y. Hughes, *SEL,* IV (1964), 1-34.]

MAURICE KELLEY

The Theological Dogma of *Paradise Lost,* III, 173-202

In Milton's attempt to justify the ways of God to men, perhaps no passage in *Paradise Lost* is more important than Book III, 173-202, for in these lines Milton expounds his doctrine of predestination and its concordance with the mercy, grace, and wisdom of God. To the average reader, however, the passage offers considerable difficulty; and it is indeed surprising, in view of the importance and the obscurity of this portion of the epic, that editors and scholars have done so little to clarify the doctrine of these thirty lines. Newton[1] contented himself with asserting that the views there expounded were Calvinistic, and Todd followed Newton. Sumner,[2] without comment, showed a parallelism between portions of the passage and Milton's *De doctrina,* a document which is uncompromisingly Arminian. Brydges, however, repeated Newton's observation; and Barber[3] argued at some length for a Calvinistic interpretation. Verity, on the other hand, seemed to agree with Sumner, but dismissed the matter with a single sentence: "The doctrine of predestination here alluded to is discussed at some length in the Christian Doctrine, I, 4." Masson, Browne, and Moody, in turn, ignored the matter. Such disagreement, therefore, would seem to justify an attempt to throw more light on the passage by determining the precise doctrine that Milton there advances and the

From *PMLA,* LII (1937), 75-9. Reprinted by permission of the author and the Modern Language Association of America.

relation of that doctrine to the view on predestination advanced in the *De doctrina*.

Comparison of the passage under discussion with the symbols of the Reformed Church reveals that the lines do not expound a Calvinistic doctrine. According to *Paradise Lost*, the possibility of election results from the grace of God, but the enjoyment of this possibility requires the volition of man.

> Man shall not quite be lost, but sav'd who will,
> Yet not of will in him, but grace in me
> Freely voutsaft
>
> (III, 173-75)

In Calvinism, this gratuitous election likewise results solely from the pleasure of God, but the individual is powerless to contribute in any way to his own salvation.

> Those of mankind that are predestinated unto life, God, before the foundation of the world was laid, according to his eternal and immutable purpose, and the secret counsel and good pleasure of his will, hath chosen in Christ unto everlasting glory, out of his mere free grace and love, without any foresight of faith or good works, or perseverance in either of them, or any other thing in the creature, as conditions, or causes moving him thereunto; and all to the praise of his glorious grace.[4]

According to *Paradise Lost*, reprobation is a matter of man's determination, for each has the opportunity to repent and be saved.

> The rest shall hear me call, and oft be warnd
> Thir sinful state, and to appease betimes
> Th' incensed Deitie while offerd grace
> Invites
>
> (III, 185-88)

The Calvinist, however, grants man no such opportunity.

> The rest of mankind, God was pleased, according to the unsearchable counsel of his own will, whereby he extendeth or withholdeth mercy as he pleaseth, for the glory of his sovereign power over his creatures, to pass by, and to ordain them to dishonor and wrath for their sin, to the praise of his glorious justice.[5]

Thus between the doctrine of *Paradise Lost* and of Calvinism exist essential differences: in the epic, election and reprobation both depend upon man's cooperation; in Calvinism, God alone determines these matters, and man is powerless to cooperate in the salvation of his own soul. The beliefs, therefore, are not identical.

Paradise Lost, however, does accord with the Arminianism of the *De doctrina,* which argues that God elects men to everlasting life on the condition of faith and repentance, and rejects only those who refuse to believe and repent. Thus,

> Man shall not quite be lost, but sav'd who will,
> Yet not of will in him, but grace in me
> Freely voutsaft; . . .

The principal special decree of God relating to Man is termed predestination, whereby God in pity to mankind, though foreseeing that they would fall of their own accord, predestinated to eternal salvation before the foundation of the world those who should believe and continue in the faith; for a manifestation of the glory of his mercy, grace, and wisdom, according to his purpose in Christ.[6]

Hence the Father is often called *our saviour,* inasmuch as it is by his eternal counsel and grace alone that we are saved.[7]

>   . . . once more I will renew
> His lapsed powers, though forfeit and enthrall'd
> By sin to foul exorbitant desires; . . .

When, however, God determined to restore mankind, he also without doubt decreed that the liberty of will which they had lost should be at least partially regained, which was but reasonable.[8]

> Upheld by me, yet once more he shall stand
> On even ground against his mortal foe,
> By me upheld, that he may know how frail
> His fall'n condition is, and to me ow
> All his deliv'rance, and to none but me.

For a manifestation of the glory of his mercy, grace, and wisdom. This is the chief end of predestination.[9]

> Some I have chosen of peculiar grace
> Elect above the rest; so is my will:[10]

> The rest shall hear me call, and oft be warnd
> Thir sinful state, and to appease betimes
> Th' incensed Deitie while offerd grace
> Invites; for I will cleer thir senses dark,
> What may suffice, and soft'n stonie hearts
> To pray, repent, and bring obedience due.

Seeing, then, that God has predestinated from eternity all those who should believe and continue in the faith, it follows that none can be reprobated, except they do not believe or continue in the faith . . .[11]

If then God reject none but the disobedient and unbelieving, he undoubtedly gives grace to all, if not in equal measure, at least sufficient for attaining knowledge of the truth and final salvation.[12]

> To prayer, repentance, and obedience due,
> Though but endevord with sincere intent,
> Mine eare shall not be slow, mine eye not shut.

But even if there be any decree of reprobation, Scripture everywhere declares, that as election is established and confirmed by faith, so reprobation is rescinded by repentance.[13]

> And I will place within them as a guide
> My Umpire Conscience, whom if they will hear,
> Light after light well us'd they shall attain,
> And to the end persisting, safe arrive.

And, lastly, the gift of reason has been implanted in all, by which they may of themselves resist bad desires, so that no one can complain of, or allege in excuse, the depravity of his own nature compared with that of others.[14]

> This my long suffrance and my day of grace
> They who neglect and scorn, shall never taste;
> But hard be hard'nd, blind be blinded more,
> That they may stumble on, and deeper fall;
> And none but such from mercy I exclude.

As this change [renovation] is of the nature of an effect produced on man, and an answer, as it were, to the call of God, it is sometimes spoken of under the metaphor . . . of tasting.[15]

. . . in the matter of sin God's providence finds its exercise . . . in impelling sinners to the commission of sin, in hardening their hearts, and in blinding their understandings.[16]

. . . it is not the human heart in a state of innocence and purity, and repugnance to evil, that is induced by him to act wickedly and deceitfully; but after it has conceived sin, and when it is about to bring forth, he, in his character of sovereign disposer of all things, inclines and biasses it in this or that direction, or towards this or that object.[17]

. . . he does not produce these effects [hardening the heart and blinding the understanding] by infusing an evil disposition, but on the contrary by employing such just and kind methods, as ought rather to soften the hearts of sinners than harden them. First, by his long suffering . . . The hardening of the heart, therefore, is usually the last punishment inflicted on inveterate wickedness and unbelief in this life.[18]

. . . no one is excluded by any decree of God from the pale of repentance and eternal salvation, unless it be after the contempt and rejection of grace, and that at a very late hour.[19]

Two lines remain:

> Some I have chosen of peculiar grace
> Elect above the rest; so is my will.

Since the rest of the passage under discussion agrees with the Arminianism of the De doctrina, these two lines may be interpreted in accordance with the treatise. Election, says Milton, is general rather than particular: Peter is chosen not because he is Peter but because he is a believer.[20] "Some," then, refers to the believers; and the "rest,"[21] as the following lines indicate, are the unbelievers. "Chosen" is to be interpreted as "elected"; "of" as "because of"; "peculiar" as "that which belongs to one to the exclusion of others"; "grace" is to be taken in its technical sense as "the free and unmerited love of God for mankind." Interpreted thus, the passage accords with its context, and may be paraphrased thus: "because of the free and unmerited love which I have for mankind, I have elected the believers, who, unlike the unbelievers, are destined to salvation." Considered by themselves, the two lines are by no means clear, and are capable of a Calvinistic interpretation; but considered in their context and in relation to the *De doctrina,* it becomes evident that the two lines express an Arminian view in perfect accord with the systematic theology that Milton was writing at about the same time that he must have dictated this part of the epic.

NOTES

1. Unless otherwise indicated, all references in this paragraph are to notes on *Paradise Lost,* III, 183-84.
2. *The Prose Works of John Milton,* Bohn Library, IV, 43 ff.
3. *Bibliotheca Sacra,* XVI (1859), 557 ff; XVII (1860), 1 ff.
4. *Westminster Confession,* III, 5.
5. *Ibid.,* III, 7.
6. *The Prose Works of John Milton,* Bohn Library, IV, 43. [EDITOR'S NOTE. Cf. *Works* (New York: Columbia University Press, 1931-38), XIV, 91.] See also *Paradise Lost,* III, 302; XII, 425-26.
7. *Prose Works,* IV, 285. [*Works,* XV, 255.]
8. *Ibid.,* IV, 61. [*Works,* XIV, 135.]
9. *Ibid.,* IV, 48. [*Works,* XIV, 103.]
10. An interpretation of this passage will be offered below.
11. *Ibid.,* IV, 64. [*Works,* XIV, 141.]
12. *Ibid.,* IV, 66. [*Works,* XIV, 147.]
13. *Ibid.,* IV, 65. [*Works,* XIV, 145.]
14. *Ibid.,* IV, 59. [*Works,* XIV, 131.] Milton equates conscience and reason. See IV, 15 [*Works,* XIV, 29] and *P.L.,* IX, 351-352; XII, 82-90.
15. *Ibid.,* IV, 323. [*Works,* XV, 355.]
16. *Ibid.,* IV, 201. [*Works,* XV, 69.]
17. *Ibid.,* IV, 203. [*Works,* XV, 73.]
18. *Prose Works,* IV, 207. [*Works,* XV, 81.]
19. *Ibid.,* IV, 70. [*Works,* XIV, 157.]
20. *Ibid.,* IV, 49. [*Works,* XIV, 107.]
21. If one did not hesitate to push matters too far, he might suggest that Milton's use of *rest* rather than the correlative *others* was due to the following comment: "So Matt. xx. 16 'many be called, but few chosen' only signifies that they which believe are few" (*Prose Works,* IV, 54). [*Works,* XIV, 117.]

[EDITOR'S NOTE. See also Mr. Kelley's *This Great Argument: A Study of Milton's "De Doctrina Christiana" as a Gloss upon "Paradise Lost,"* 1941; R. M. Frye, *God, Man, and Satan,* 1960; C. A. Patrides, *PMLA,* LXXIV (1959), 7-13; B. G. Lumpkin, *SP,* XLIV (1947), 56-68; T. S. K. Scott-Craig, *HLQ,* XVII (1953), 1-15; J. M. Steadman, *JWCI,* XXII (1959), 88-105.]

IRENE SAMUEL

The Dialogue in Heaven: A Reconsideration of *Paradise Lost*, III, 1-417

When Douglas Bush and C. S. Lewis—not to name readers as disparate in time and temperament as Pope, Blake, and Shaw—find the God of *Paradise Lost* unattractive, it may be ill-advised to attempt the justification of Milton's ways with Heaven. Even the excellent refutation of the Satanist position in John S. Diekhoff's book on *Paradise Lost* ignores rather than answers, perhaps quite properly, those who have objected to Milton's God as not so much a tyrant as a wooden bore.[1] My paper is addressed to such readers and to any others who are willing to start from the assumption that Milton may have known what he was about in the first half of Book III as surely as in Books I and II. I put it thus because objections have generally turned on the first episode in Heaven and have rather consistently echoed Pope's quip that "God the Father turns a school-divine." I wish to argue that we have mistakenly read the scene as a mere presentation of doctrinal assertions conveniently divided between the Father and the Son, and that to take it thus is to forget both how highly Milton prized poetic economy[2] and how central he made this episode to the action of his whole poem. For may not the trouble be that we have incautiously misconstrued as dogma what Milton in-

From *PMLA*, LXXII (1957), 601-11. Reprinted by permission of the author and the Modern Language Association of America.

tended as drama? In short, the failure may be not in the scene but in our reading of it.

Milton, we know, thought mere presentation of testimony of "very little power for proof" even in logical argument: "testimony affirms or denies that a thing is so and brings about that I believe; it does not prove, it does not teach, it does not cause me to know or understand why things are so, unless it also brings forward reasons."[3] How unlikely then that he would have rested the poetic argument of *Paradise Lost,* turning as it must on this very scene in Heaven, on the mere testimony of theological statement or on his own mere assertion that these statements are made by personages named God and the Son. Surely we do more wisely to assume that Milton intended the statements in the scene to demonstrate that the persons involved are recognizably God, the creator of the universe, and the Son, his "word, wisdom, and effectual might."

The meaning of the council in Heaven starts before either person speaks, since it depends in large part on the continuity of the poetic fabric: the obvious contrasts with Hell indicate how we are to regard Heaven.[4] Thus, for example, the invocation of light in the opening lines of Book III at once helps to establish Milton's God as the cosmic principle, the source of ordered nature, partly because we have seen Hell's darkness filled with unnatural perversions and monstrosities. We are impelled by the lines to mark such contrasts, though we ought also to note the near-absurdity of the word "contrast"; it suits Satan's pretensions well enough, but hardly suggests that what he opposes is the entire universe. We have to bear in mind from the first that we could predict nothing of Milton's God and Heaven by simply inverting his Satan and Hell, though we are expected to learn much by observing their differences.

What we learn, to begin with, is that, unfortunately for Satan, the God of *Paradise Lost* is not merely another being on whose pattern he can model his rebel state, but Total Being, *the* Primal Energy, *the* Voice of Reason, *the* Moral Law that makes possible a moral cosmos as surely as the laws of physics make possible a physical cosmos. He is *the* Creator who by intention brings into being others who act of themselves, and consequently *the* Intelligence that comprehends the universe. Significantly enough, his first act in the poem is to bend "down his [omniscient] eye, / His own works and their works at once to view." To try to read the dialogue that follows without allowing the first speaker his full nature would indeed make nonsense of the scene.[5]

But as soon as we take Milton's God as Being, infinitely beyond all created beings, the scene has dramatic point. The near tonelessness of his first speech at once proves itself the right tone. It has offended readers because they assume that the "I" who speaks is or should be a person like other persons. The flat statement of fact, past, present, and future, the calm analysis and judgment of deeds and principles— these naturally strike the ear that has heard Satan's ringing utterance as cold and impersonal. They should. For the omniscient voice of the omnipotent moral law speaks simply what is. Here is no orator using rhetoric to persuade, but the nature of things expounding itself in order to present fact and principle unadorned.[6]

Clearly Milton uses that toneless voice of the moral law to destroy immediately the straw figure of a gloating, tyrannical victor that Satan and his followers had conjured up in Books I and II. More important, he uses it to afford the Son opportunity for his impassioned reply. And this we must mark emphatically before turning to what either says: the Father in dialogue with the Son is not listening to an echo, but encouraging the distinctive tones of a quite different voice. To take the difference as showing the amiability of the Son at the expense of the cold, rigorous Father is to mistake Milton's point. The compassion, love, and grace we are asked to observe in the Son (ll. 140-142) are emphatically equated with the substantial expression of the invisible Godhead (ll. 138-140): the Son's compassionate tone is made possible by the passionless logic of the Father.[7]

We may now turn to what is said, noting briefly that it is said in the presence of the assembled angels, for all to hear, though the opening words are directed to the Son. God states that man will fall, expounds the doctrine of free will, observes a difference between the rebellion of Satan's crew and the disobedience of man, uses past, present, and future tenses interchangeably, announces his intention of mercy to man, and ends as though the final word had been spoken. The Son, unbidden, answers; and what he answers, though put most respectfully, sounds remarkably unlike mere assent:

> O Father, gracious was that word which clos'd
> Thy sovran sentence, that Man should find grace. . . .
> For should Man finally be lost, should Man
> Thy creature late so lov'd, thy youngest Son
> Fall circumvented thus by fraud, though join'd
> With his own folly? . . .

> Or shall the Adversary thus obtain
> His end, and frustrate thine, shall he fulfil
> His malice, and thy goodness bring to naught . . .
> . . . or wilt thou thyself
> Abolish thy Creation, and unmake,
> For him, what for thy glory thou hast made?
> So should thy goodness and thy greatness both
> Be question'd and blasphem'd without defence.

Put any such figure as Satan feigned to rebel against in the place of the Godhead here, and what the Son says would surely win him the most crushing reply. Unlike the "yes man" Satan had made of Beelzebub by the time he dared to make his second speech in Hell, the Son *argues*: "That be from thee far, / That far be from thee, Father." In Milton's Heaven the independent being speaks his own mind, not what he thinks another would like to hear.[8]

And that independent voice turns out to be precisely what this other does like to hear. When the voice of the moral law resumes to congratulate its interlocutor, it briefly adopts a tone of praise:

> O Son, in whom my Soul hath chief delight . . .
> All hast thou spok'n as my thoughts are, all
> As my Eternal purpose hath decreed:
> Man shall not quite be lost. . . .

Now the eternal purpose, though the same as in the first speech, can reveal another aspect that the Son's answer has brought into prominence. The new statement of the moral law proceeds, again with the cold logic of "thus it is and thus must be," to redefine the future of man:

> But yet all is not done . . .
> Die hee or Justice must; unless for him
> Some other able, and as willing, pay
> The rigid satisfaction, death for death.

Thus the question is raised,

> Say, Heav'nly Powers, where shall we find such love,
> Which of ye shall be mortal to redeem
> Man's mortal crime, and just th' unjust to save,
> Dwells in all Heaven charity so dear?

These are the first words directly addressed to the angels, a synthesis that combines with the immutable moral law the Son's opposing love. But to the angelic ear it apparently sounds no less harsh than the original statement and no less final: "all the Heav'nly Quire stood mute." The question and the moment of silence inevitably remind us of the council in Hell when Beelzebub proposed the voyage to Earth and asked who dared go (II, 402-426). But the resemblance underscores the difference.

In Hell the stage was in every way set. All the ceremonious preliminaries, the trumpet proclaiming a solemn council, the call summoning the worthiest of each band, the signal dividing nobility from commoners, all served to prepare these admitted to the inner chamber for the lofty tone in which Satan asked their advice. In marked contrast, the council in Heaven starts without fanfare, in every possible way in the open. It takes place outdoors and in the presence of "all the Sanctities of Heaven." Though no one's presence has been commanded, any one who wishes may hear. (Uriel, Gabriel, and Gabriel's troop are notably absent for reasons of dramatic necessity.) Without a word of preface, presumably on the spur of the occasion, God speaks, and as if with the utmost finality. He does not pretend to seek advice, but calls attention to Satan loose in the world, and announces what will follow.

In Hell, after Satan's explicit request, three of his followers offer two distinct plans. But just as the second is about to win unanimous approval (II, 284-298), Beelzebub intervenes to propose as his own, and win acceptance for, what is in fact Satan's plan, stated piecemeal in Book I (ll. 120-122, 162-165, 650-656). The proposal calls for the selection of a spy; and Beelzebub makes it, evidently as Satan planned, stressing the risk involved with the clear purpose of frightening off every one but Satan (II, 378-385). When Satan then offers to go, he is the actor taking his cue in a scene he had written for himself. It is a magnificent moment designed to show his magnificent courage. And if he almost spoils it for his deluded audience with his final words, "This enterprise / None shall partake with me," he saves his pose by at once moving offstage.

What of the monarch Satan thought to emulate?[9] God makes no pretense of willingness to collect opinions on an open question. Yet he immediately sanctions and adopts the view presented by the Son, incorporating it into his new statement and modifying his first so that a task emerges. Without urgency or emphasis, he names the task. And it needs only to be named, for it involves not risk or danger but what to angelic ears must sound like annihilation. The grand opportunity— "Which of ye will be mortal to redeem / Man's mortal crime?"—presumably means utter abolition of being. But this is a prospect that even in Hell only the brutal Moloch could regard with equanimity; this is the very penalty that the Son could not bear to think the Father intended for fallen man.

Little wonder that "none appeared / . . . that durst upon his own head draw / The deadly forfeiture." Yet these are no cowardly puppets dependent on constant approval and reassurance from God. Every angel we later meet acts on his own responsibility without running to the Godhead for advice: thus Uriel counsels what seems a young angel (III, 681-735), then copes with what has proved an escaped devil (IV, 124-130 and 555 ff.); the lesser Ithuriel and Zephon meet Satan's taunts (IV, 820-856); Gabriel confronts him (IV, 877 ff.); Abdiel stands against him and all his forces (V, 804 ff.); and the loyal angels wage their war against the rebels, all on their own momentum. That is indeed the most striking characteristic of Milton's angels, the independence with which they demonstrate the lie of Satan's talk about their harp-playing servility (IV, 942-945; VI, 166-170).

But what is now involved is presumably a certainty. The speaker is omniscient; none of his hearers is. Milton thought the point worth making at some length in his *Christian Doctrine*. "The good angels do not look into all the secret things of God," he asserted (I, ix; Columbia ed., XV, 107) after arguing that "Even the Son . . . knows not all things absolutely" (I, v; XIV, 317), since "the attributes of divinity belong to the Father alone" (XIV, 227), and the first of the divine attributes listed is omniscience.[10] Here too omniscience is God's alone. His hearers are confident of his goodness, but they cannot fully know what is in his mind. That is what gives the Son's offer its great dramatic value. The Son cannot know any more than others at the council that the task named does not mean annihilation. The moment of silence includes his silence to underscore the clear enormity of the solution. When after that moment's hesitation he offers to die for man, he does not know that the death he undertakes will not be final; he *trusts* that the omnipotence whose goodness he does know will not permit injustice.

Again he answers what he has heard: "Father, thy word is past, man shall find grace; / And shall not grace find means?" But his an-

swer is far more than the offer of his life for man's. Again he responds
to the unalterable law out of his own nature, now out of his bound-
less trust:

> I shall not long
> Lie vanquisht; thou hast giv'n me to possess
> Life in myself for ever, by thee I live,
> Though now to Death I yield, and am his due
> All that of me can die, yet that debt paid,
> Thou wilt not leave me in the loathsome grave
> His prey . . .
> But I shall rise Victorious.

What the Son speaks is no assurance privately communicated nor any
prescience bestowed uniquely on him. To read his speech so would
destroy its meaning, the point of the scene in Heaven, and much of
the system of values on which the whole poem rests. All that the Son
says of his eventual triumph over death comes from nothing but a
perfect confidence in the nature of the Godhead. He does not fore-
know any part of his ressurection, the harrowing of Hell, or the re-
union of Heaven and Earth at Doomsday. His lines can only mean
that, knowing the omnipotence and perfect benevolence of the Father, he can not believe that his sacrifice of himself will have a different kind of issue. And in fact he does not name the details of his victory as God, again approving and adopting all that he has said, will
presently name them.

For the moment his words hang unconfirmed as he "attends the
will / Of his great Father." He has not pronounced that will. And
the angels too attend, "what this might mean, and whither tend /
Wond'ring." If they still wonder so should the reader; the outcome of
the dialogue is as yet uncertain, the last word not yet spoken.

The final speech of God, reconciling the immutable moral law and
the Son's trusting offer, the proposed vicarious atonement and the
Son's hope of victory, does indeed transcend both. For one thing, we
immediately note that the Father's voice, so cold and logically formal
in stating fact and principle, can adopt a tone more warm and loving
even than the Son's when a deed is to be praised, a reassurance given.
The warmth in God's tone began, we noted, in the first five lines of
his second speech where he applauded the Son's answer (ll. 168-172),
but was at once lost in the severe abstractions that followed. Now in
the third and last of God's speeches the warmth is unmistakably dom-

inant, a warmth toward the Son that embraces the humanity he will share. For the Son there is rapturous delight and praise, and by no cosmic pathetic fallacy, but because Milton evidently thinks rapturous praise in the nature of the moral law when it sanctions what is praiseworthy. Even more important, each of the Son's hopeful phrases is caught up into a detailed affirmation: as he trusted it would be thus it shall be, and each time with something affirmed beyond what he had hoped.

He had said "Account me man" as the equivalent of "on me let thine anger fall." Now God promises that it shall be so—and more: "Their nature also to thy nature join / And be thyself man among men on earth, / . . . Be thou in Adam's room / The head of all mankind." He had said, "I for his sake will leave / Thy bosom, and this glory next to thee / Freely put off." Now God promises: "Nor shalt thou by descending to assume / Man's nature, lessen or degrade thine own. . . . / Thy humiliation shall exalt / With thee thy manhood also to this throne." He had said, "By thee raised I [shall] ruin all my foes . . . and return, / Father, to see thy face." Now God promises: "Here shalt thou sit incarnate, here shalt reign / Both God and Man . . . / Anointed universal king; all power / I give thee, reign for ever." He had hoped, "Wrath shall be no more / Thenceforth, but in thy presence joy entire." Now God assures him: "The world shall burn, and from her ashes spring / New Heaven and Earth, wherein the just shall dwell / And . . . / See golden days . . . / With Joy and Love triumphing and fair Truth."[11]

But the climactic element in God's final utterance is that it shifts the emphasis of the discussion from the subject initially proposed, the redemption of man, which now becomes secondary, to a new theme, the exaltation of the Son. That this is finally the major theme we know both from the expansion given it in God's final speech with its emphatic ending,

> But all ye Gods,
> Adore him, who to compass all this dies,
> Adore the Son, and *honour him as me;*

and from the hymn of praise with which the angels at once, rightly grasping all they have heard, meet the command.

The dialogue, for all its brevity, for all its use of the familiar and expected, has moved from its presumably fixed beginning to an unforeseen end. Where the corresponding scene in Hell made a stately progress to a foregone conclusion, proceeding with all possible solemnity from Satan's plan to Satan's plan, though it had to run a course more tortuous even than Belial's speech, the quick, terse, unplanned scene in Heaven arrives by tremendous leaps at a resolution unimaginable except to Omniscience at the outset. The "high decree unchangeable" has been radically altered, not of course in its unalterable essence, but in its application to man's destiny. The cold logic of the moral law has confirmed the Son's compassion, incorporated that compassion into the administration of the decree, and exalted it into the virtue most to be honored in the universe. What has made possible the changed application of the law has been raised by the law itself to an importance equal to its own. The role of the Son in the dialogue has elicited a resolution worlds removed from the initial prediction. And beyond working out a plan for man's redemption, the dialogue of the council in Heaven has shown in dramatic process the Son's growth to what the Father himself calls virtual equality.

And again we mark the contrasts of Hell. Before the council there Satan had been supreme, and through the council he affirmed his supremacy, establishing his power and prestige beyond the need of such arguments as he had opened the session with. Before the scene in Heaven the Son had already had a notable career: as first born and "only begotten"—the one creature produced directly by the creator; then as the instrument of the creation of the angels—the point Satan disputed with Abdiel (V, 835-837 and 853-863); then as appointed head of all the angels, his second "begetting"[12]—the occasion of Satan's offended pride. Next he had the power of God transferred to him for the purpose of ending the war in Heaven (VI, 710 ff.) and yet again for the creation of the new universe (VII, 163-166 and 192-196). The first two of these steps are alluded to, the rest we hear of later in Raphael's account to Adam. The whole career is neatly summed up in the angel's song of praise (III, 372 ff.) with which the scene here ends.

We witness directly only the final elevation of the Son, and for the meaning of *Paradise Lost* it is of moment that we should directly witness it, since it is the great contrast to the process by which Satan—and Eve and Adam after him—fell. In his opening pronouncement God had said:

> Freely they stood who stood, and fell who fell.
> Not free, what proof could they have giv'n sincere

Of true allegiance, constant Faith or Love,
Where only what they needs must do, appear'd,
Not what they would? what praise could they receive?
What pleasure I from such obedience paid,
When Will and Reason (Reason also is choice)
Useless and vain, of freedom both despoil'd,
Made passive both, had serv'd necessity,
Not mee.

There the doctrine as major premise of a syllogism condemning the fallen sounded harsh. Here we see its obverse. Freely the Son makes his choice of word and deed; and if the choice has been foreknown, foreknowledge had no influence on his virtue. What praise is given to the right choice freely made, what pleasure taken in it by the moral law, we again see in Book VI in the reception of Abdiel. But we must know the happy meaning of the law of free will at the very time that we first hear it expounded in its unhappy significance for man.

Without the freedom which permits rebel angel and man to err the full wisdom and compassion of the Son would be impossible. This is not to argue for a "fortunate fall" any more than for explicit Arian doctrine as essential to the meaning of *Paradise Lost*. Doubtless Milton's Arianism made it possible for him to handle the council in Heaven as a dramatic dialogue between distinct speakers more easily, with less conflict between what he saw as dramatically desirable and what he felt as doctrinally correct,[13] than a Trinitarian might. Doubtless too his conviction of man's ultimate redemption permitted him to think that man's *culpa* proves ultimately *felix* despite the cost of that dearly bought felicity. But the doctrinal heart of the scene is neither Arianism nor the *felix culpa*, but free will, central to Milton's thought everywhere, not in *Areopagitica* alone, nor only where it makes for tragedy in *Paradise Lost*. Here in the first scene in Heaven the same principle makes for all that we consider desirable in a universe.

Moreover what happens in the dialogue in Book III is analogous to what might have happened in Book IX. If Eve had her moment when she might, like Abdiel, have caught the liar in his lie, Adam had his when he might, like the Son, have risked himself to redeem Eve. He himself recounts to Raphael in Book VIII what independent assertion of his mind and will to his maker had won for him. What his making a like assertion in like confidence might have won for fallen Eve we cannot know since he does not make it. But it is worth observing that tragedies stem from alternatives ignored as well as choices made. A trust comparable to—on however lower a level than—the Son's and a self-abnegation willing to risk whatever was to be risked demanded only Adam's faith that the benevolence he had always known would remain benevolent, and the whole application of the moral law might have changed as the Son's choice changes it. What Adam, perfect and therefore "able," could have done for Eve remains unfortunately outside the action. But Eve was not irredeemably lost, as Adam at once concluded in his immediate assumption of a hostile universe. So much is clear from what follows for fallen Eve and Adam both. It is specifically clarified in advance by the dialogue of the Son with the Father. The trust that confronts and by confronting changes "Die hee or justice must" into "Thy humiliation shall exalt / With thee thy manhood also to this throne" is a possibility at some level for every being in the universe Milton established in *Paradise Lost*. His success in establishing it is no less remarkable in the swift dialogue in Heaven than in the poem that hinges on that brief scene.

NOTES

1. Cf. *English Literature in the Earlier Seventeenth Century* (London, 1946), p. 381, and *A Preface to Paradise Lost* (London, 1942), p. 126; and see *Milton's Paradise Lost* (New York, 1948), chs. v and vi.
2. The popular word now is "strategy," though one may still prefer the metaphor of the productive household to the metaphor of the destructive battlefield. Milton, at any rate, used the term "economy," explaining it in the Preface to *Samson Agonistes* as "such . . . disposition of the fable as may stand best with verisimilitude and decorum." For what he meant by "decorum," "verisimilitude," and "economy" the reader should consult Ida Langdon, *Milton's Theory of Poetry and Fine Art*, Cornell Stud. in Eng., No. 8 (New Haven, 1924).
3. *Logic*, I, 32, trans. A. H. Gilbert, *The Works of John Milton*, Columbia ed., XI, 283. My references to Milton's prose are to the volume and page numbers of this edition. For *Paradise Lost* I have used the edition by Merritt Y. Hughes (New York, 1935), but have normalized some spellings for the quotations incorporated into my own prose.
4. Ernest Schanzer has collected a number of such parallels in "Milton's Hell Revisited," *UTQ*, XXIV (1955), 136-145. My notion of these contrasts is that Milton used his augmented treatment of Hell to make possible an abbreviated treatment of Heaven. Thus, for example, because Hell is finally summed up as "a universe of death" where "all life dies, death lives," and Death in fact is king (as he claims [II, 698-699] and his crown proves [II, 673]), we recognize more imme-

diately that Heaven is the realm of vitality and indeed of nature, without any hammering at the point. And thus in turn the list of the beauties of nature from which blindness has cut the poet off (III, 40-50) can suggest to us that Milton's God is the God of Nature long before we meet the phrase "God and Nature bid the same" (VI, 176). Or again, because we have noted the incestuous monstrosities, ugly contention, and even uglier agreement between Satan, his perfect image Sin, and their only begotten son Death, the whole dialogue in Heaven between the Father and *his* only begotten Son, who is his perfect image, takes on added meaning.

5. Lewis shows that Milton keeps to "the great central tradition" of Christian doctrine throughout *P.L.* (pp. 81-91). But Lewis, it occurs to me, makes heavier theological demands on the reader than Milton ever suggests in the poem.

6. Milton, of course, knew the ancient distinction between what is appropriate in persuasion and in exposition. Cf. Aristotle, *Rhetoric,* trans. Lane Cooper, III, 1404a: "Strict justice, of course, would lead us, in speaking, to seek no more than that we should avoid paining the hearer without alluring him; the case should, in justice, be fought on the strength of the facts alone, so that all else besides demonstration of fact is superfluous. . . . No one uses them [the devices of style] in teaching mathematics." And see Plato, *Phaedrus,* especially 263.

7. It will be evident that I fully agree with Maurice Kelley that "no indecision is present in *Paradise Lost,* III" (*This Great Argument,* Princeton, 1941, p. 34) and even that nothing Milton says in *P.L.* conflicts with his *Christian Doctrine.* But is there any evidence that Milton wanted his reader to adopt, or so much as recognize, the Arianism implicit in Bk. III? Any reduction of the drama of the council-scene to exposition of doctrine surely distorts Milton's intent.

8. Milton clearly knew the traditional treatment of the dispute in Heaven on this very theme of man's condemnation or salvation, so that he would feel no suggestion of impiety in attributing vigorous argument for opposing views to the participants in such a celestial *débat.* See Hope Traver, *The Four Daughters of God,* Bryn Mawr Coll. Monographs, No. 6 (Bryn Mawr, 1907), for the history of this popular mediaeval theme from the Hebrew *Midrash* to the Renaissance. Miss Traver observes that Milton "knew a number of the versions of the allegory" (p. 146) and that it "would have reached crowning expression in English drama" if he had carried out the plan of the Cambridge Manuscripts (p. 143). I am indebted to Professor Merritt Y. Hughes for calling my attention to the relevance of Miss Traver's work to my thesis. Milton with his true epic touch reassigns

the old arguments of mercy and justice, along with some decidedly new arguments, to the Son of God, transmutes the *débat* into a dialogue, uses what he had assimilated from Homeric scenes on high Olympos, and creates an episode central to *P.L.*

9. Need we cite evidence of Satan's attempts at "Godlike imitated state?" Perhaps the most interesting are the echoes in V, 772, and throughout Bks. I and II of God's words in V, 600-601; the most obvious, the palace on the mount in V, 756-766, and the throne in II, 1-5, to be compared with God's in III, 58; the most significant the sudden self-revelation in X, 444-450, with its almost ludicrous effort to duplicate the effect of God described in III, 375-382.

10. Note that when Michael is to give Adam knowledge of the future Milton makes clear twice over that Michael's prophecy has to be allowed him by Omniscience: "reveal / To Adam what shall come in future days, / As I shall thee enlighten" (XI, 113-115); and "So both ascend / In the visions of God," where "of God" must mean "provided by God" (XI, 376-377).

11. The phrase "joy and love," emphatically repeated in the first reference to Eden (III, 67-68), recurs here to make us doubly sure that the atonement will re-establish true Paradise; for the phrase is virtually the leitmotiv of Eden. See IV, 519, VI, 94, VIII, 621; and cf. the anticipations in *Comus*, ll. 1010-11, and *Lycidas*, l. 177. The excellent collection of Milton's repeated phrases by Edward S. Le Comte, *Yet Once More* (New York, 1953), to my mind, offers no adequate explanation of Milton's intended repetitions.

12. For the dual meaning of "beget" in the Son's career see *Christian Doctrine*, I, v (Columbia ed., XIV, 181-91), and the expositions of John S. Diekhoff and Maurice Kelley.

13. I am indebted for my phrasing here to Professor Hoxie N. Fairchild, whose critical comments on my argument have, I trust, helped me to avoid theological pitfalls. (AUTHOR'S ADDITIONAL NOTE. After the work of Hunter, Adamson, Patrides, and Robins, I would no longer use the term Arianism at all in description of Milton's doctrine.)

[EDITOR'S NOTE. See W. B. Hunter, Jr., *HTR*, LII (1959), 9-35, and LVII (1964), 353-65, *JHI*, XXI (1960), 349-69; J. H. Adamson, *HTR*, LIII (1960), 269-76; C. A. Patrides, *JHI*, XXV (1964), 423-9, and *JEGP*, LXIV (1965), 29-34; H. F. Robins, *If This Be Heresy*, 1963; M. Kelley, *HTR*, LIV (1961), 195-205; E. Creeth, *MLN*, LXXVI (1961), 696-700; J. E. Parish, *SP*, LVI (1959), 619-25; D. W. D. Dixon, *Papers of the Michigan Academy of Science, Arts, and Letters*, XXXVI (1950; published 1952), 275-81.]

WILLIAM G. MADSEN

Earth the Shadow of Heaven: Typological Symbolism in *Paradise Lost*

> what surmounts the reach
> Of human sense, I shall delineate so,
> By lik'ning spiritual to corporal forms,
> As may express them best, though what if Earth
> Be but the shadow of Heav'n, and things therein
> Each to other like, more than on Earth is thought?
> —*Paradise Lost*, V, 571-576

In prefacing his account of the war in heaven with these words, Raphael is saying that it will be not allegorical or merely metaphoric, but analogical; that although he will have to use the language of accommodation in order to convey his meaning at all, still there may be (he puts the statement in a subordinate clause and in the interrogative mood) a relationship between earth and heaven, between the physical and the spiritual, which is inherent in the nature of things. After Raphael finishes his narrative, Adam denies that earth is the shadow of heaven:

> Great things, and full of wonder in our ears,
> Far differing from this World, thou hast reveal'd
> Divine Interpreter . . .
>
> (VII, 70-72)

From *PMLA*, LXXV (1960), 519-26. Reprinted by permission of the author and the Modern Language Association of America. Portions of this paper were read at the December 1959 meeting of the Modern Language Association.

Adam is right. There is nothing whatever in the world as he knew it that is like the war in heaven. What did Raphael mean when he said that earth may be the shadow of heaven?

Recent commentators without exception have interpreted this phrase in a Neoplatonic sense. "Though the conception of earth as the shadow of heaven has been traced to various sources," say Hughes in his latest edition, "it stems from Plato's doctrine of the universe as formed on a divine and eternal model, and from Cicero's interpretation of it (in *Timaeus ex Platone* ii, 39-41) as implying that "the world which we see is a simulacrum of an eternal one.' "[1] It is my contention that this interpretation is mistaken; that Milton is using "shadow" here not in its Platonic or Neoplatonic sense but in its familiar Christian sense of "foreshadowing" or "adumbration"; and that the symbolism of *Paradise Lost* is typological rather than Platonic.

I

As Hughes's quotation from Cicero suggests, it is mainly to the *Timaeu* : that Plato's followers owe the conception of the visible world as an image, reflection, likeness, or shadow of an eternal world, but the word "shadow" itself is not used in this dialogue. In the *Republic*, however, "shadow" is a key word in the well-known analogies of the Line and the Cave. In trying to explain to his listeners how the philosopher must rise above even a knowledge of virtues like justice and temperance to a knowledge of the good, Socrates asks them to imagine a line divided into two parts, with each of the parts further subdivided. The two main divisions of the line correspond, one to the visible realm, the other to the intelligible, and the subdivisions in each main division are compared in respect to their clearness and want of clearness. The lowest subdivision of the visible consists of images (*eikonas*). "And by images I mean, in the first place, shadows (*skias*), and in the second place, reflections in water and in solid, smooth and polished bodies and the like" (510 A). The higher subdivision of the visible comprises the actual things—animals, artifacts, etc.—of which these are the images or shadows. Corresponding to these two classes of objects are two faculties of the mind; the lower is *eikasia*, or "perception of shadows," the higher is *pistis*, usually translated "faith" or "conviction." The two subdivisions of the intelligible are related analogously. Corresponding to shadows in the visible realm is the realm of mathematical entities, and corresponding to the faculty of *eikasia* is *dianoia*, "understanding." Corresponding to the higher realm of the visible is the realm of the *archai* or Forms, which are apprehended by *noēsis*, "reason." Although Plato does say that sense objects are copies or images of Forms, the main point of the analogy of the Line is to distinguish between *dianoia* and *noēsis*, and the distinction between shadows and physical objects is introduced primarily by way of illustration.

In the allegory of the Cave immediately following, Socrates suggests a more graphic analogy of the same relationship. Imagine, he says, a cave in which human beings have been living all their lives facing the back wall, their heads chained so that they cannot turn around. Behind them is a parapet, and behind the parapet and above it is a fire. Some men are walking behind the parapet holding up over it statues and figures of animals made of wood and stone and other materials. The fire casts shadows (*skias*) of these statues on the wall of the cave, which is all these human beings have ever seen and which of course to them is reality. Now suppose, he continues, that one of the prisoners is dragged out of the cave into the sunlight. He would at first be dazzled by the light. Gradually his eyes would grow accustomed to it, first looking on shadows (*skias*) and reflections of things in the water, then at the things themselves, then at the moon and stars at night, and finally at the sun itself, which to Socrates symbolizes the Good. Socrates goes on to explain that in the allegory the cave is the world of sight, the fire is the light of the physical sun, and the journey out of the cave is "the ascent of the soul into the intellectual world" (517 B).

In the *Timaeus*, then, we have the conception of the visible or sensible world as a copy or image of the invisible or intelligible; in the *Republic* we have the term "shadow" applied analogously to the things of the sensible world. In the current of thought in late antiquity loosely referred to as Neoplatonism, the conception of the *Timaeus* and the term "shadow" from the *Republic* are fused, as in the following passage from Plotinus:

> He that has the strength, let him arise and withdraw into himself, foregoing all that is known by the eyes, turning away for ever from the material beauty that once made his joy. When he perceives those shapes of grace that show in body, let him not pursue: he must know them for copies, vestiges, shadows, and hasten away towards That they tell of. For if anyone follow what is like a beautiful shape playing over water—is there

not a myth telling in symbol of such a dupe, how he sank into
the depths of the current and was swept away to nothingness?
So too, one that is held by material beauty and will not break
free shall be precipitated, not in body but in Soul, down to the
dark depths loathed of the Intellective-Being, where, blind
even in the Lower-World, he shall have commerce only with
shadows, there as here. (I, 6, 8).

These are metaphors in Plotinus, doubtless, like his comparison of
God to light, to which the metaphor of shadow is obviously related.
With the Gnostics, however, we are not sure what is metaphor and
what is literal statement, at least if Irenaeus is to be trusted. Whatever
may have been the intention of the Gnostics themselves when they
said that this world was but an image and shadow of the world above,
Irenaeus chose to take them literally:

> If, again, they declare that these things [below] are a shadow
> of those [above], as some of them are bold enough to maintain,
> so that in this respect they are images, then it will be necessary
> for them to allow that those things which are above are pos-
> sessed of bodies. For those bodies which are above do cast a
> shadow, but spiritual substances do not, since they can in no
> degree darken others. . . . If, however, they maintain that
> the shadow spoken of does not exist as being produced by the
> shade of [those above], but simply in this respect, that [the
> things below] are far separated from those [above], they will
> then charge the light of their Father with weakness and in-
> sufficiency, as if it cannot extend so far as these things, but
> fails to fill that which is empty, and to dispel the shadow, and
> that when no one is offering any hindrance.[2]

In spite of its association with Gnosticism and Irenaeus' attempt to
reduce it to absurdity, the conception of the world as shadow continued to occupy a central position in Christian Neoplatonism, partly
perhaps because of such statements in the Old Testament as David's
"our days on the earth are as a shadow, and there is none abiding"
(I Chron. xxix. 15). Be that as it may, we find the idea in St. Bonaventure, Nicholas of Cusa, Pico della Mirandola, and Ficino. Even in
so stoutly orthodox a work as Thomas Wilson's *A Christian Dictionary* the word "shadow" is defined as "This whole world, and the things
thereof. Psalm 39, 6, and 73, 20. Rom. 12, 2. 1 Cor. 7, 31. 1 Ioh. 2, 17.

Being but as shadowes of heavenly and true happinesse."[3] Indeed, the notion was so commonplace in the Renaissance that Lambertus Danaeus, like Irenaeus, found it necessary to warn the orthodox. He had probably been reading Irenaeus as well as Nicholas of Cusa and the Italian Neoplatonists, for he attributes the idea that earthly realities are but shadows both to Plato and to Valentinian the Gnostic, against whom Irenaeus had directed much of his polemic. Like Irenaeus, Danaeus takes the metaphor literally:

> But what absurdities and inconveniences doe followe that opinion, marke. For they muste needes confesse that those thinges, these heauenly *ideae* and Patterns, whereof, by their Doctrine, these earthly things are shadowes, too bee bodies, which is an absurd thing. Neither can a bodily thing be an image of thinges that are meere spirituall. Moreouer, all this whole most beutifull woorke of GOD, which is called the worlde, shalbee a fantasie, and a meere dreame, and not that thing which we suppose it to be: which is blasphemous.[4]

But the metaphor was too vigorous to be demolished like this, and the phrase continued to appear in writers of a Platonizing tendency like Valentine Weigelius, Sir Henry Vane, and Peter Sterry,[5] not to mention Blake, Shelley, Coleridge, the Transcendentalists, and even Arthur Symons almost in our own day.[6] "Shadow" was a favorite word with Peter Sterry, and since it has been (erroneously) asserted that his thought has affinities with Milton's, I will bring this aspect of my discussion to a close with a quotation from him:

> Thus is the Soule, or Spirit of every man all the World to Him. The world with all Varietie of things in it, his owne body with all it's parts, & changes are himselfe, his owne Soule, or Spirit springing up from it's owne ffountaine within itselfe into all those fformes, & Images of things, which it seeth, heareth, smelleth, tasts, feeles, imagineth, or understandeth. In the supreame, & inward part of itselfe it conteineth all fformes of things in their Originall, Eternall, Glorious Truths, & substances. In it's lower, & more outward part, which is still itselfe, & within itselfe it bringeth forth itselfe sportingly into a shadowie ffigure of itselfe & in this shadowie ffigure into innumerable shadowes, & ffigures of those glorious fformes in it's superior part. This shadowie ffigure is that, which wee call this

world, & the body. The Soule often looking upon this, like Narcissus upon his owne fface in the ffountaine, forgets it to be itselfe, forgets that itselfe is the fface, the shadow, & the ffountaine, so it falls into a fond Love of itselfe in it's owne shadowie ffigure of itselfe. So it languisheth, & dys becoming only a Shadow of itselfe, in which itselfe with all it's superior, and true Glories ly buried.[7]

II

We have now to look at the word "shadow" in its other meaning of foreshadowing, adumbration, or, to use the technical language of biblical interpretation, type. This was, indeed, a much more common use of the word in the seventeenth century than the Neoplatonic meaning we have been discussing. It appears, for example, in the titles of Christopher Harvey's *Synagogue: or the Shadow of the Temple* (1640) and William Guild's popular handbook of types of Christ, MOSES VNUAILED: OR THOSE FIGVRES WHICH SERVED VNTO *the patterne and shaddow of heauenly things* (1620). Examples abound in the religious literature of the time, and it would be pointless to multiply them. The interesting question for us is how the word "shadow" came to have this specifically Chrisitan meaning, and what connection, if any, there is between this and the Neoplatonic conception.

The word *skia* occurs three times in the New Testament in the sense of type or foreshadowing:

> Let no man therefore judge you in meat, or in drink, or in respect of an holyday, or of the new moon, or of the sabbath days:
> Which are a shadow of things to come; but the body is of Christ. (Col. ii.16-17)

> Now of the things which we have spoken this is the sum: We have such an high priest, who is set on the right hand of the throne of the Majesty in the heavens;
> A minister of the sanctuary, and of the true tabernacle, which the Lord pitched, and not man.
> For every high priest is ordained to offer gifts and sacrifices: wherefore it is of necessity that this man have somewhat also to offer.
> For if he were on earth, he should not be a priest, seeing that there are priests that offer gifts according to the law:

Who serve unto the example and shadow of heavenly things, as Moses was admonished of God when he was about to make the tabernacle: for, See, saith he, that thou make all things according to the pattern shewed to thee in the mount. (Heb. viii.1-5).

For the law having a shadow of good things to come, and not the very image of the things, can never with those sacrifices which they offered year by year continually make the comers thereunto perfect. (Heb. x.1)

These are not the only typological passages in the New Testament, of course, but they are the only ones in which the word *skia* is used. What metaphor did Paul in Colossians and the author of Hebrews have in mind? Sixteenth and seventeenth century commentators took "shadow" here to mean either "shadow cast by a body" or "silhouette or outline, as in painting." In both cases we have to do with a simple analogy of proportion: as type is to antitype, so is the shadow to the body or substance, or the first draft of a picture to the finished painting. Calvin, with his usual clarity, distinguishes between the analogies in Colossians ii. 17 and Hebrews x. 1.

> *For the law hauing the shadow, &c*] He borrows this similitude from the art of painting: for he takes this word *shadow* in this place, otherwise than it is taken, Col. 2. 17. where S. *Paul* calles the old ceremonies, shadows, because they had not the very substance of the things in them, which they did represent. But the Apostle saith here, they were like rude draughts, which are but the shadows of the liuely painting. For painters are wont to drawe that which they purpose to counterfeit or represent with a cole, before they set on the liuely colors with the pensill. The Apostle then puts this difference betweene the law and the Gospell: to wit, that that which at this day is drawne and painted with fresh and liuely colours, was onely shadowed out vnder the law by a rude or grosse draught.[8]

David Dickson and William Jones make use of both analogies in commenting on Hebrews x. 1.

> The revealing of Christ, and his Benefites, vnder the Gospell, and vnder the Lawe, differ as farre in measure of light, as the shadowe of a thing, and the lyuelie image thereof, drawne

with all the lineamentes. For, they sawe Christ, and Righteous-nesse, and aeternall Lyfe through him, as those which are in the house see the shadowe of a man comming, before hee enter within the doores: but, wee, with open face, beholde in the Gospell, as in a Mirrour, Christ's Glorie shyning; Christ, in the preaching of his word, crucified before our Eyes, as it were, and bringing with him Lyfe, and Immortalitie, to light.[9]

So in the Law they had a sight of *Christ*, yet it was darkly in a shadow. Wee have the very expresse forme and image of *Christ*, with all his benefits: they had *Christ* in an obscure pic-ture drawne at the first in darke lines: wee have him as in a lively picture graced with most lightsome and excellent col-ours.[10]

Recent commentators, however, have seen in these passages in He-brews the Platonic doctrine of the world as image or copy. The author of Hebrews, says Alexander C. Purdy in *The Interpreter's Bible*, "is controlled by a two-story view of reality: on the ground floor the shadowy, transient, fugitive events and institutions; in the upper story the permanent, perfect realm of reality." And again, "The idea of a realm of reality over against the shadowy realm presented by our senses is clearly Platonic, but, of course, this does not mean that our author had read Plato or that he was a philosopher like Plato. It means that his Christian convictions are presented in the atmosphere of Platonic idealism."[11] If the author of Hebrews was the first, he was certainly not the last to present his Christian convictions in the atmos-phere of Platonic idealism. In spite of the historic association between Christianity and the Attic Moses, however, there is a fundamental op-position between these two world-views that is already apparent in Hebrews. It is the opposition between the historical, eschatological spirit of Christianity implicit in the phrase "shadow of good things to come," and the non-historical, ontological spirit of Platonism. A typi-cal Platonizing Jew like Philo saw in the Old Testament not the progressive revelation of God's purpose in the types and shadows of the Old Law, but rather allegories of subjective moral and religious experience or of Platonic archetypes. For the Gnostics Christ is not a Redeemer but an Illuminator; He is a Neoplatonic intermediary be-tween the intelligible and the sensible realms rather than an actor in the divine drama of salvation.[12] The Epistle to the Hebrews, on the other hand, is profoundly eschatological. The author's gaze, as Father Prat has said, "is constantly turned towards the future, and the events of Jewish history are the book in which he reads the destiny of the heavenly Jerusalem, unchangeable and eternal."[13] Or as a recent Protestant scholar has said, for the author of Hebrews "what lies between heaven and earth, God and man, is not the difference between the phenomena of sense-perception and pure being, but the difference between holiness and sin."[14]

The scholarly controversy over the philosophical orientation of Hebrews presents in its most striking form the radical divergence of meaning and implication inherent in the word "shadow" itself. The Platonist who says that earth is the shadow of heaven is saying (among other things) that history has no meaning. Things on earth have meanings, no doubt, but the meanings, if I may so express it, are static. It is not in their dynamic relationships with each other, as events in history, that earthly things have meaning; it is rather in their analogical relationships or their physical properties, and the world is a kind of symbolic pageant or emblem. On the other hand, the Christian who says that earth is the shadow (that is, foreshadowing) of heaven is asserting the validity of history. The world is a stage on which the drama of salvation is enacted, and earthly things have meaning primarily in the context of history.[15] In Platonic and Neoplatonic thought man's nature is defined by the rational categories of Being and Becoming, the intelligible and the sensible; his immersion in the meaningless cycle of time is a misfortune, and the duty of man is to become a philosopher and thereby escape from the world. In Christian thought man is defined primarily by moral categories, and the Platonic distinction between the intelligible and the sensible is replaced by the Christian distinction between the Creator and His creation; man's immersion in time is the condition of his salvation, and the duty of man is to become a saint and thereby redeem the world.

III

In the Garden before the Fall Adam exists, as it were, outside of history, exempt from the limitations of time. There is of course movement in Adam's universe, as Joseph Summers has shown,[16] but it is Platonic cyclic movement, not Christian linear movement. It is the "Grateful vicissitude" of the "perpetual round" of light and darkness (VI, 6-8). There is no real change in Paradise, there is only "interchange" (IX, 115). Even Raphael's speculation (in one of his few references to the future) about the destiny of unfallen man is Neoplatonic:[17]

> time may come when men
> With Angels may participate, and find
> No inconvenient Diet, nor too light Fare:
> And from these corporal nutriments perhaps
> Your bodies may at last turn all to spirit,
> Improv'd by tract of time, and wing'd ascend
> Ethereal, as wee, or may at choice
> Here or in Heav'nly Paradises dwell.
>
> (V, 493-500)

This is the familiar Neoplatonic doctrine of the vertical ascent through the scale of being, not the horizontal journey through "tract of time" that fallen mankind will have to make.

"All teems with symbol," said Plotinus,[18] and this apparently Neoplatonic garden is indeed a forest of symbols, but paradoxically they are typological and prophetic, not Platonic; they speak of what lies ahead, not what lies above; they are a shadow of things to come.

The rivers of Paradise, for example, do not stand for the four cardinal virtues, as they do in Henry More's allegorical interpretation,[19] which is quite in the Platonizing manner of Philo Judaeus, but in their movements they foreshadow the Fall and man's subsequent wanderings:

> Southward through *Eden* went a River large,
> Nor chang'd his course, but through the shaggy hill
> Pass'd underneath ingulft, for God had thrown
> That Mountain as his Garden mould high rais'd
> Upon the rapid current, which through veins
> Of porous Earth with kindly thirst up-drawn,
> Rose a fresh Fountain, and with many a rill
> Water'd the Garden; thence united fell
> Down the steep glade, and met the nether Flood,
> Which from his darksome passage now appears,
> And now divided into four main Streams,
> Runs diverse, wand'ring many a famous Realm
> And Country whereof here needs no account.
>
> (IV, 223-235)

The trees "weep"; the serpent, even before Satan enters him, "of his fatal guile / Gave proof unheeded"; the "steep wilderness" on the side of the mount of Paradise foreshadows the wilderness of this world to which Adam and Eve must descend after their trespass; Eve's dream is prophetic, and Adam wakes from his to find "all real, as the dream / Had lively shadow'd" (VIII, 310-311). One of the most interesting examples of typological symbolism in the Garden is Eve's recital to Adam of how in her first moments of existence she gazed at her own image in the water. She would have pined with vain desire till now, she says, if a voice had not thus warned her:

> What thou seest,
> What there thou seest fair Creature is thyself,
> With thee it came and goes: but follow me,
> And I will bring thee where no shadow stays
> Thy coming, and thy soft imbraces, hee
> Whose image thou art . . .
> (IV, 467-472)

She followed the voice, but she thought Adam less fair than the "smooth wat'ry image" and turned away from him. You called me back, she tells him, and

> thy gentle hand
> Seiz'd mine, I yielded, and from that time see
> How beauty is excell'd by manly grace
> And wisdom, which alone is truly fair.
> (IV, 488-491)

When Adam explains to Eve that manly grace and wisdom are to physical beauty what the physical reality is to its shadow, he is drawing the obvious lesson from Eve's experience. But there is another meaning that entirely escapes Adam. There is a foreshadowing as well as a shadow here, and it is a foreshadowing of Adam's own sin (not of Eve's, as is so often said).[20] When he determines to throw in his lot with Eve, he is preferring the physical shadow to the moral substance. He has seen his image in her, just as Satan saw his image in Sin, and he turns from God to Eve, as Eve had turned from Adam to her own shadow in the water.

After the Fall a further typological significance of Paradise is revealed. "See Father," says Christ after Adam and Eve have repented,

> See Father, what first fruits on Earth are sprung
> From thy implanted Grace in Man, these Sighs
> And Prayers, which in this Golden Censer, mixt
> With Incense, I thy Priest before thee bring,
> Fruits of more pleasing savor from thy seed
> Sown with contrition in his heart, than those
> Which his own hand manuring all the Trees
> Of Paradise could have produc't, ere fall'n
> From innocence.
>
> (XI, 22-30)

It was a human act, performed at the beginning of history, that made it possible for Christ to use language in this way. Only by an act of sin that destroyed the Garden could the Garden come to be seen as a type of the spiritual life. Adam could not know that his cultivation of the Garden was a shadow of things to come.

If the Garden foreshadowed the Fall of man, the Wilderness fore-shadows his restoration in Christ, though it is now in the laws and ceremonies instituted by God rather than in the book of nature that man's future may be read by those who have eyes to see. The law was given to the Jews, Michael explains to Adam,

> With purpose to resign them in full time
> Up to a better Cov'nant, disciplin'd
> From shadowy Types to Truth, from Flesh to Spirit,
> From imposition of strict Laws, to free
> Acceptance of large Grace, from servile fear
> To filial, works of Law to works of Faith.
>
> (XII, 301-306)

With the coming of Christ all types are abolished; the shadow gives way to the substance. "All corporeal resemblances of inward holiness and beauty are now past," said Milton in attacking the liturgy and the hierarchy of the Anglican church.[21] The only temple is the upright heart and pure, and the natural types of the Garden and the cere-monial types of the Wilderness are fulfilled spiritually in the minds and hearts of Christians. We are confronted here with a paradox. In so far as the Old Testament contained the shadow of things to come and the New Testament the substance, the new dispensation has more validity, more meaning, than the old. From another point of view, however, human history before the coming of Christ has a

meaning that history after His coming cannot possibly have; before
Christ the world is charged with the grandeur of God's symbolic,
typological drama; after Christ we have Michael's dreary vision of a
world apparently emptied of significance and given over to Satan.
What, we might ask, is the meaning of life on this earth now, in this
last age of the world's history?

It is a difficult question to answer. Malcolm Ross for one thinks
there is no meaning. Milton's God, he says bluntly, has abandoned
history.[22] Milton did not always think so, Ross points out. In the early
days of his revolutionary enthusiasm he could look forward to the
Coming of the "eternal and shortly expected King,"[23] and he could
couch his expectation in the familiar terms of the Exodus typology:

> O perfect and accomplish thy glorious acts! for men may leave
> their works unfinished, but thou art a God, thy nature is per-
> fection: shouldst thou bring us thus far onward from Egypt to
> destroy us in this wilderness, though we deserve it, yet thy
> great name would suffer in the rejoicing of thine enemies, and
> the deluded hope of all thy servant. When thou hast settled
> peace in the church, and righteous judgment in the kingdom,
> then shall all thy saints address their voices of joy and triumph
> to thee, standing on the shore of that Red Sea into which our
> enemies had almost driven us.[24]

The young Milton's faith that God would not allow His name to suffer in the rejoicing of His enemies finds its parallel in Adam's confidence that God would not carry out His threat of death

>   lest the Adversary
> Triumph and say; Fickle their State whom God
> Most Favors, who can please him long? Mee first
> He ruin'd, now Mankind; whom will he next?
> Matter of scorn, not to be given the Foe.
>   (IX, 947-951)

But God did sentence Adam to death, and He did allow His English
to return to the fleshpots of Egypt. With the restoration of Charles II
it would seem, as Ross wittily remarks, that God had changed His
mind.[25]

But I do not think that this is the way Milton saw it. The attitude
with which the mature Milton confronted the "contrived corridors
and issues" of history, especially the failure of the Commonwealth, is
dramatically realized, it seems to me, in Raphael's account of the war

in heaven. The purpose of Raphael's narrative is not merely to demonstrate to Adam the consequences of disobedience; a recital of the first two books of *Paradise Lost* would have been a much more effective means to that end. Nor is its purpose to reveal that there is a Platonic idea of war in heaven, of which mere earthly wars are an imperfect embodiment.[26] Milton, I venture to say, is not really interested in the particulars—if there were any particulars—of Satan's first battle with God. What he is interested in, and what he wants his readers to be interested in, is Raphael's *account* of that war, which is a different matter. And Raphael's account is not a moral allegory, nor is it primarily a metaphorical description of what happened a long time ago in heaven.[27] It is a shadow of things to come, and more particularly it is a shadow of this last age of the world and of the Second Coming of Christ.[28]

For the world is not only a waste wilderness in which the spiritual Eden is re-created in the minds of the regenerate, it is also a battlefield, the scene of "th' invisible exploits / Of warring Spirits" (v. 565-566). Recent critics have elucidated for us some of the moral meanings that the war in heaven can have: obedience to the will of God, discipline, freedom of choice. In my opinion, however, the principal lesson that Raphael's narrative inculcates is the lesson of patience, the virtue with which the Christian confronts the perplexities of history. It is among the most difficult of virtues to practice, as difficult for Milton as it was for some of the good angels. If the youthful Milton had taken part in the war in heaven, he would have fervently assented with Abdiel:

> O Heav'n! that such resemblance of the Highest
> Should yet remain, where faith and realty
> Remain not; wherefore should not strength and might
> There fail where Virtue fails, or weakest prove
> Where boldest; though to sight unconquerable?
> His puissance, trusting in th' Almighty's aid,
> I mean to try, whose Reason I have tri'd
> Unsound and false; nor is it aught but just,
> That he who in debate of Truth hath won,
> Should win in Arms, in both disputes alike
> Victor; though brutish that contest and foul,
> When Reason hath to deal with force, yet so
> Most reason is that Reason overcome.
>
> (VI, 114-126)

If it were only true, history would offer no perplexities, and God's purposes could be read in the rise and fall of empires. And when Abdiel's "noble stroke" sent Satan back recoiling, one can imagine the youthful Milton in the very forefront of the angelic host, filled with "Presage of Victory and fierce desire / Of Battle" (VI, 201-202), just as he had been in the forefront of those who saw in the Puritan Revolution a presage of the Millennium. But Abdiel was wrong: his reason did not overcome Satan's might, and the first blow struck against evil did not end the war. From the reader's point of view the outcome of the struggle is never in doubt because he is privileged to see it under the aspect of eternity. This vision is not granted to the angelic participants, however, and after their "forc't rout" by Satan's cannon, the good angels "stood /A while in trouble" (VI, 633-634). For them the outcome hangs in the balance for two long days (and a day is to God as a thousand years), and the war would have gone on forever had not God intervened in His good time. The war in heaven lasts until Christ appears to drive the rebel angels into Hell, and the world goes on "To good malignant, to bad men benign," until Christ shall come at last "to dissolve / Satan with his perverted World" (XII, 538, 546-547), because patience is the exercise of saints. Nor is patience a kind of spiritual setting-up exercise arbitrarily imposed on us by God. Patience is necessary because we are creatures living in a world we did not create and immersed in a time-process which is the fulfillment of a purpose not our own. We must act, assuredly. We must put on the whole armor of God and wrestle against principalities and the rulers of darkness, as the good angels did, but we must abide the time. Whatever else the restoration of Charles II meant to Milton, it did not mean that God had changed His mind and abandoned history. The typological meaning of Paradise was not revealed until it had been destroyed, nor the meaning of the Old Testament dispensation until it had been abrogated. So too the meaning of this last age will be fully revealed when Christ's mystical body has grown to its full stature and the righteous have entered into the state of "perfect glorification."[29] Meanwhile we live in a time that is intersected by eternity, and our actions on earth are shadows of heaven—or of hell.[30]

NOTES

1. *John Milton: Complete Poems and Major Prose* (New York, 1957), p. 315. All quotations from Milton's poetry are from this edition. The

Neoplatonic interpretation of Raphael's lines appears also in James H. Hanford, *A Milton Handbook* (New York, 1946), p. 205, and in his edition of the poetry; in M. M. Mahood, *Poetry and Humanism* (New Haven, 1950), p. 204; in Paul Shorey, *Platonism Ancient and Modern* (Berkeley, Calif., 1938), pp. 41-42, 184; and in all the annotated modern editions of *Paradise Lost* that I have seen.

2. Irenaeus, *Against Heresies,* II viii, 1-2, in *The Ante-Nicene Fathers,* ed. Alexander Roberts and James Donaldson (Grand Rapids, Mich., 1953), I, 368.

3. Etienne Gilson, *The Philosophy of St. Bonaventure,* trans. Dom Illtyd Trethowan and F. J. Sheed (New York, 1938), pp. 210-212 and p. 515, n. 10; Nicolas Cusanus, *Of Learned Ignorance,* trans. Fr. Germain Heron (London, 1954), pp. 150 and 158 (III. vii. and III. x); Pico della Mirandola, *Heptaplus,* in Edisione Nazionale Dei Classici Del Pensiero Italiano, I (Firense, 1942), 184; Ficino, *Epistolae* (*Opera,* Basle, 1573), I, 659, quoted in Nesca Robb, *Neoplatonism of the Italian Renaissance* (London, 1935), p. 87; Thomas Wilson, *A Christian Dictionary* (London, 1612), s. v.

4. *The Wonderfull Workmanship of the World* (London, 1578), p. 24a.

5. Valentine Weigelius, Astrologie *Theologized* (London, 1649), pp. 45-46. On Vane see R. M. Jones, *Spiritual Reformers in the 16th and 17th Centuries* (London, 1914), p. 276. On Sterry see below, n. 7.

6. Blake, *Jerusalem,* 77; Shelley, *Prometheus, Unbound,* II, iii.11-16; Coleridge, "The Destiny of Nations," vv. 12-25; *The Complete Essays and Other Writings of Ralph Waldo Emerson,* ed. Brooks Atkinson (Modern Library ed.), pp. 216, 284, and passim; Arthur Symons, *The Symbolist Movement in Literature* (Dutton Everyman Paperback ed., 1958), pp. 95-96.

7. Vivian De Sola Pinto, *Peter Sterry: Platonist and Puritan* (Cambridge: University Press, 1934), pp. 161-162.

8. *A Commentarie on the Whole Epistle to the Hebrewes. . . . *Translated Ovt of French . . . (London, 1605), pp. 200-201. Professor Walter MacKellar has called my attention to the gloss on "shadow" in *Hebrews* x: 1 in the *Geneva Bible*: "which was as it were the first draught and purtrait of the lieuly paterne to come."

9. David Dickson, *A Short Explanation of Paul to the Hebrewes* (Aberdeene, 1635), p. 197.

10. William Jones, *A Commentary Vpon the Epistles of Saint Paul to Philemon and to the Hebrewes* (London, 1635), p. 383.

11. *The Interpreter's Bible* (New York, 1955), XI, 583-584, 585. See also E. C. Rust, *The Christian Understanding of History* (London,

1947), pp. 174-178. Arndt & Gingrich's *A Greek-English Lexicon of the New Testament* (Chicago, 1952) defines *skia* as "2. shadow, foreshadowing (in contrast to reality)" and cites parallels from Philo Judaeus that are decidedly Platonic in implication. None of the modern commentaries or lexicons that I have consulted makes use of the analogy from painting. That the word was so used in ancient times is attested by Liddell and Scott: "'III. 1. shadow in painting 2. silhouette, profile."

12. I am indebted here to C. K. Barrett, "The Eschatology of the Epistle to the Hebrews," in *The Background of the New Testament and Its Eschatology*, ed. W. D. Davies and D. Daube (Cambridge: University Press, 1946).

13. Fernand Prat, S. J., *The Theology of Saint Paul*, trans. from the 11th French ed., by John L. Stoddard (Westminster, Md., 1926), I, 361.

14. Barrett, p. 388 (see n. 12).

15. See Emile Brehier, *The Philosophy of Plotinus*, trans. Joseph Thomas (Chicago, 1958), pp. 17-18.

16. "'Grateful Vicissitude' in *Paradise Lost*," *PMLA*, LXIX (March 1954), 251-264.

17. This passage is more fully discussed in my monograph, "The Idea of Nature in Milton's Poetry," in *Three Studies in the Renaissance*, Yale Studies in English, 138 (New Haven, 1958), pp. 235-237. In "The Fortunate Fall in *Paradise Lost*," *MLN*, LXXIV (1959), 103-105, I discuss its relationship to Milton's Christian view of man's ultimate destiny.

18. *Enneads*, II, iii, 7.

19. *Conjectura Cabbalistica* (London, 1653), p. 38.

20. I cannot agree with Mrs. Bell (*PMLA*, LXVIII (Sept. 1953), 871) that this episode reveals a "dainty vanity" in Eve. Her image is physically the most beautiful thing she has seen, that is all. This natural attraction to the beautiful has nothing to do with vanity. Eve's fall is perhaps dramatically foreshadowed in her initial failure (a failure of intelligence) to distinguish between the higher good (Adam's inward beauty) and the lower good (her physical beauty). The difference between dramatic foreshadowing (an oft-noted feature of Milton's narrative technique) and typological foreshadowing is that the significance of a type is not revealed until it has been fulfilled in the antitype.

21. *The Reason of Church Government*, II, ii, in Frank Allen Patterson (ed.), *The Student's Milton* (New York, 1941), p. 528.

22. Malcolm M. Ross, *Poetry and Dogma* (New Brunswick, N.J., 1954), p. 106.

23. *Of Reformation*, in Patterson, p. 469.

24. *Animadversions,* in Patterson, p. 493. There is an interesting study of the Exodus typology in early Christian thought in Jean Daniélou, *Sacramentum Futuri* (Paris, 1950), pp. 131-200.

25. Ross, p. 106.

26. James H. Hanford, "Milton and the Art of War," *SP,* XVIII (1921), 232-66.

27. It is difficult to describe Raphael's mode of discourse in the critical terms available to us. It differs from allegory in that the first term is not a fiction; it differs from ordinary metaphorical discourse in that we cannot test the validity of the metaphor by pointing behind it to the reality which is being described. It is obviously not meant to be literally true; on the other hand, Milton would certainly claim for it more than "imaginative" or "poetic" truth. It is because of the impossibility of looking behind the narrative to the actual conflict in heaven (whatever its nature) that I have regarded its significance as primarily (though not exclusively) typological, that is, oriented toward the future.

Milton perhaps would have claimed for his own narrative in *Paradise Lost* the same kind of relation to reality that Raphael's has. It is very unlikely that "Milton actually believed that he was adding historic details to the Scriptures," as William J. Grace maintains ("Orthodoxy and Aesthetic Method in *Paradise Lost* and the *Divine Comedy,*" CL, I (1949), 174). Grace sets up a false antithesis between Milton's "attempt to present the facts of history at first hand" and Dante's "more veiled and indirect allegorical method." Milton's mode of discourse, like Raphael's, lies somewhere between these two extremes. But this is matter for another discussion.

28. For evidence that Ezekiel's vision, which Milton incorporates in his description of Christ's rout of the rebel angels, was regarded as a foreshadowing of Christ's recreation of the universe on the Last Day, see J. H. Adamson, "The War in Heaven: Milton's Version of the *Merkabah,*" *JEGP,* LVII (1958), 690-703.

29. *Christian Doctrine,* I. xxxiii, in Patterson, pp. 1046-8.

[EDITOR'S NOTE. On Milton's theory of biblical interpretation and the principle of accommodation, see also H. R. MacCallum, *UTQ,* XXXI (1961-62), 397-415; C. A. Patrides, *TSLL,* V (1963), 58-63; J. M. Steadman, *PMLA,* LXXVIII (1963), 36-9; A. B. Chambers, *HLQ,* XXVI (1963), 381-2; J. H. Sims, *The Bible in Milton's Epics,* 1962; on Plato's theory of mimesis, see J. A. Philip, *Transactions and Proceedings of the American Philological Association,* XCII (1961), 453-68.]

ARNOLD STEIN

Milton's War in Heaven—An Extended Metaphor

I

If the war in heaven is approached as Milton's fulfilment of his epic obligations, if we regard it as a realistic war to be taken quite seriously, then we cannot escape Dr. Johnson's verdict that the "confusion of spirit and matter" fills the whole narrative with "incongruity." How can we believe in the fiction of a raging battle in which immortal spirits uncomplainingly confine themselves in hindering armor and, in between verbal debates, use material weapons that lessen their might? But suppose the material action of the war does not exist for its literal and independent meaning, but is instead part of a complex metaphor? That is the view that this study proposes taking.

We are told before the narrative begins that it will be metaphorical:

> what surmounts the reach
> Of human sense, I shall delineate so,

From *ELH* (*English Literary History*), XVIII (1951), 201-20. This article appears as a chapter of Mr. Stein's *Answerable Style: Essays on "Paradise Lost,"* Minneapolis: the University of Minnesota Press, 1953. Copyright, 1953, by the University of Minnesota. Reprinted by permission of the author; and the University of Minnesota Press; and Appleton-Century-Crofts, publisher of the Frank A. Patterson edition of *Milton's Complete Poems,* © copyright 1930, 1933, by Frank Allen Patterson, quoted by Mr. Stein.

By lik'ning spiritual to corporal forms,
As may express them best.

(V, 571 ff.)

But still, this is preceded by what seems to be an echo of Aeneas'
polite prologue to Dido (which would anticipate a direct historical
tale), and it is followed by Raphael's enigmatic questioning of the
metaphor:

though what if Earth
Be but the shaddow of Heav'n, and things therein
Each to other like, more than on earth is thought?

Presumably, though, the metaphor has not been discredited but further qualified, for when he concludes his account Raphael emphasizes
the metaphorical point of view again: "Thus measuring things in
Heav'n by things on Earth / At thy request." In between, besides the
constant indirect touches more significant to fallen than to unfallen
man, there have been some deliberate gestures towards the understanding of the immediate audience—some of them charming in their
thoughtfulness (like grandfather translating remote events into terms
of grandchild's familiar experience). When God's legions march forth
upon the air, it is as when all the birds came summoned "to receive /
Thir names of thee." When heaven resounds, all the earth, "had
Earth bin then," "had to her Center shook." When Michael and
Satan meet, it is as if nature's concord should break and two opposing
planets clash. But this, the deliberate framework of metaphor, does
not take us far, though it invites us to build on the angel's hint.

From the opening of Book I the war in heaven seems more than a
simple, finished event. In the invocation we have the authorized formal side presented—the war was ambitious, impious, proud, vain, and
resulting in ruin. Satan's first speech implies that there was another
side—even after we have partly discounted the personal tones of the
defeated leader who speaks of the good old lost cause, "hazard in the
Glorious Enterprize." That too is a formal side, presented by the losing actor in the drama. Then Satan goes on, to reveal, before he can
pull himself together in defiance, something more:

into what Pit thou seest
From what highth fal'n, so much the stronger provd
He with his Thunder: and till then who knew
The force of those dire Arms?

(I, 91 ff.)

A little later the surprise has been bolstered with a kind of indignation:

> but still his strength conceal'd,
> Which tempted our attempt, and wrought our fall.
>
> (I, 641 ff.)

We soon learn that we cannot get answers in hell, but we begin to see certain questions, and the possibility that their answers may appear when we see the dramatic presentation of the rebellion. For one thing, Satan's "innumerable force" receives a definite tally later—it is only one third of the angels. And this fact will look different when we learn that God opposes the enemy force with an equal number only, and then puts a fixed limit on the individual strength of the contestants, and then sends only the Son against the rebels, and with His strength limited too. Satan puts so much store on his having shaken the throne of God, against "His utmost power"—"Who from the terrour of this Arm so late / Doubted his Empire"—that we begin to wait for the actual presentation of the conflict. In his long soliloquy at the beginning of Book IV, though Satan tells us much, he answers none of the questions he has raised in our minds about the war. His silence is no doubt a commentary—so complete a fact requires no mention, once the forensic necessity has been removed—but we cannot know this at the time.

The clash with Gabriel at the end of Book IV provides us with a sudden new viewpoint—it will prove to be true anticipation of what happens in the battles, even though we cannot know this yet. For the first time, with Satan present, an actor on the scene, we see him entirely from the outside; and the external view is one of complete ridicule. It is Gabriel's

> O loss of one in Heav'n to judge of wise,
> Since Satan fell, whom follie overthrew.
>
> (IV, 904 f.)

The dominating spirit of the encounter, on both sides, is that of scornful ridicule. Gabriel's most telling point is directed at Satan's *discipline*. The fight itself never takes place because Satan, in spite of his blind defiance, has been forced by experience to recognize that ultimate *strength* is external. He obeys God's sign, even though he has just been defying, with words, God's chariot once more. Gabriel's final comment brings the three themes together again—strength, ridicule, discipline:

> Satan, I know thy strength, and thou knowst mine,
> Neither our own but giv'n; what follie then
> To boast what Arms can doe, since thine no more
> Then Heav'n permits, nor mine.
>
> (IV, 1006 ff.)

Perhaps this sounds like a piece of ceremonial tournament chivalry—at least to our merely human understanding. If so, it may be because the ceremony is made of symbolic gestures that are founded upon truth. It is not ceremony to Gabriel, but direct truth, the truth of innocent inexperience that has not (according to Satan's taunt) tried evil. And Satan has experienced that truth.

Within the larger framework of the angel's narration to Adam there is another major framework that governs our perspective of the rebellion. The dominant mood of the war is like nothing so much as a scherzo, a kind of great diabolical scherzo, like some of Beethoven's—with more than human laughter, too elevated, and comprehensive, and reverberating not to be terribly funny. God sets the mood when he comments to the Son on the budding rebellion:

> Neerly it now concernes us to be sure
> Of our Omnipotence, and with what Arms
> We mean to hold what anciently we claim
> Of Deitie or Empire. . . .
> Let us advise, and to this hazard draw
> With speed what force is left, and all imploy
> In our defence, lest unawares we lose
> This our high place, our Sanctuarie, our Hill.
>
> (V, 721 ff.)

The Son, as usual, reflects the Father's meaning:

> Mightie Father, thou thy foes
> Justly hast in derision, and secure
> Laugh'st at thir vain designes and tumults vain.
>
> (V, 734 ff.)

Throughout the serious events of the foreground, in the spacious North, the great laugh, omniscient and uncircumscribed, cannot fail to be heard.

Before proceeding to the more central ridicule, and to some of the significant reverberations, it is worth noting how much of the battle is conducted in terms of external ridicule. In one sense, at least, the conflict is between God's mockery and Satan's. Anticipations of this begin early. We have already noted the "till then who knew / The force of those dire Arms" and the "tempted our attempt." There is the suggestive mockery (that is meant to do more than perform its immediate practical function) when Satan rouses his fellow fallen from the burning lake:

> or have ye chos'n this place
> After the toyl of Battel to repose
> Your wearied vertue, for the ease you find
> To slumber here, as in the Vales of Heav'n?
> Or in this abject posture have ye sworn
> To adore the Conquerour?
>
> (I, 318 ff.)

We have testimony from the other fallen angels that ridicule was an important attitude in the conflict. Moloch remembers

> When the fierce Foe hung on our brok'n Rear
> Insulting, and pursu'd.
>
> (II, 78 f.)

(This is not literally accurate, but it has a symbolic truth: which makes it interesting. Or if Moloch is mostly remembering what happened to him in a small skirmish, when he fled bellowing (VI, 362), that makes an interesting, and true synechdoche.) To the extent that the conflict still exists, ridicule continues to be an active attitude. Belial's precise verb, in a context where any sort of resounding phrase might have been expected, touches metaphorically the symbolic situation. God's legions scout far and wide, he says, "Scorning surprize." (II, 134.) And God himself "All these our motions vain, sees and derides." (II, 191.) And Belial, for good measure, introduces his own God-like imitated perspective of irony:

> I laugh, when those who at the Spear are bold
> And vent'rous, if that fail them, shrink and fear
> What yet they know must follow, to endure
> Exile, or ignominy, or bonds, or pain,
> The sentence of thir Conquerour.
>
> (II, 204 ff.)

Still concerning ourselves with external ridicule, let us look at the scenes in Heaven, for the beginnings of the attitude we have been exploring. From the start it is not only God who mocks, though God omnisciently sets the mood first. There are, of course, the formal flytings traditional in literary battles, but these do more than provide the usual variety and relief. They are part of the complex structure of ridicule, the most external part of which consists in the frequent repetition of words denoting scorn, scoffing, laughter, deriding, contempt, disdain, vanity, and folly. The words reflect deeds, for besides the verbal abuse there is great laughter and counter-laughter in heaven. The laughter is symbolic action, but there is also real action that produces real laughter by the participants, besides the action that is intended to induce laughter in the reader.

If we think of the main events on their physical level alone (the other levels will make their significant comic additions), we shall see how consistent the line of ridicule is, and how close it approaches at times to what is almost a kind of epic farce. Satan's wound by the sword of Michael renders him physically ridiculous for the first time. His imbruting himself as a cormorant, as lion, as tiger; the more telling view of him, not *as* a toad, but without so much as the dignity of definition, merely the suggestive "Squat like a Toad"; the indirect view of his leaping into Paradise like a wolf or a thief—these views are less ridiculous through physical emphasis than they are through what is involved mentally and morally. (The fact that Satan later complains, as if for the first time, when he has to imbrute himself as a snake, helps bear this out.) The wounding by Michael is parallel to Satan's first being exposed to complete ridicule by Gabriel—the Satan whom folly overthrew. Gabriel's ridicule is psychological, with physical overtones; Satan wounded is physically ridiculous, with psychological overtones. . . . The situation is physical, but we know Satan and his proclamation that the mind governs place—*is* place. Any physical discomfiture that he suffers will be most keenly felt in his mind. And though the material wound will heal without apparent scar, because of the vital nature of his "liquid texture," we are left to draw our own conclusions about the mental wound. We remember him "Gnashing for anguish and despite and shame." In physical terms alone this makes no sense—which is of course true of the whole war. But the physical is part of the metaphorical view (the narrator's, to begin with) that always has non-physical as well as physical meanings. Even when the climax of defeat is reached and the physical metaphor becomes reality, it is a reality that surpasses the physical through the agency of the physical. But that is to look too far ahead.

In one important scene (that we must later return to, on another level) the good angels are also exposed to physical ridicule, "Angel on Arch-Angel rowl'd" by the shot from Satan's cannon. The situation, with all its details, is quite unsparing:

> Foule dissipation follow'd and forc't rout;
> Nor serv'd it to relax thir serried files.
> What should they do? if on they rusht, repulse
> Repeated, and indecent overthrow
> Doubl'd, would render them yet more despis'd,
> And to thir foes a laughter; for in view
> Stood rankt of Seraphim another row
> In posture to displode thir second tire
> Of thunder: back defeated to return
> They worse abhorr'd. Satan beheld thir plight,
> And to his Mates thus in derision call'd.
> (VI, 598 ff.)

The physical ridicule is capped by verbal derision as Satan and Belial vie with each other at word play. Then the physical comes back, in what at the moment seems to be the climax of the war, the battle of the landscape.

It is epic comedy, even on its physical level—elevated to the epic by magnificent imaginative power, made comic by controlled excess.

> From thir foundations loosning to and fro
> They pluckt the seated Hills with all thir load.
> Rocks, Waters, Woods, and by the shaggie tops
> Up lifting bore them in thir hands: Amaze,
> Be sure, and terrour seis'd the rebel Host,
> When coming towards them so dread they saw
> The bottom of the Mountains upward turn'd,
> Till on those cursed Engins triple-row
> They saw them whelmd, and all thir confidence
> Under the weight of Mountains buried deep,
> Themselves invaded next, and on thir heads
> Main Promontories flung, which in the Air
> Came shadowing.
> (VI, 643 ff.)

Part of the comic effect is in Milton's carefully interrupting the view-point at the crucial moment. We have the huge, comprehensive de-tails of the rocks, waters, woods; and then the gigantic niceness of the detail that pictures the mountains, pulled up by the tops, coming bot-tom side up towards them (apparently in a slow arc, the way a shot is put). In between, we are forced to look away, to separate ourselves from the action, and see it as spectator, not as participator—"Amaze, / Be sure, and terrour. . . ."

The scene reaches its height when the rebels reply in kind:

> So Hills amid the Air encounterd Hills
> Hurl'd to and fro with jaculation dire,
> That under ground they fought in dismal shade;
> Infernal noise; Warr seem'd a civil Game
> To this uproar.
>
> (IV, 664 ff.)

Surely it is naïve to think Milton straining for grandeur in this pas-sage. That is to read this as if it were the sort of humorless exaggeration that Statius and Lucan can assault the reader with. The cumulative ridicule will not permit our doing so. Besides, the effect that Milton achieves is the effect of strain. Things have now been pushed to the utmost, beyond which all heaven might have "gone to wrack." If we do not regard this as humorless grandeur, we may suspect "jaculation" of being the kind of exaggerated word that is calculated to embarrass the exaggeration, after the manner more familiar in mock epic. The fighting underground, which Milton may have picked up from Sta-tius, and improved upon, is not presented as straight grandeur, but as both grand and grotesque. We cannot ignore the controlling effect of "infernal," here suddenly introduced to echo Satan's threat of making a hell of heaven, and to anticipate "Heav'n ruining from Heav'n." It is the approach to chaos, the result of the violence that heaven cannot brook, the strain to the point of cracking. But this is to move away from the physical level, which is our immediate concern. If we have been following the line of ridicule correctly so far, we are probably right in suspecting that the excess in this passage is laughing at an object: it is a materialistic concept of *might*. But to see what this means we must go on.

In the grand finale of physical ridicule the rebels are again ex-posed to laughter by the interrupted point of view. The chariot of God rides over the "Shields and Helmes, and helmed heads" of the prostrate possessors,

That wish'd the Mountains now might be again
Thrown on them as a shelter from his ire.

(VI, 842 f.)

The Son checks His strength, not wishing to destroy but only to "root" them out of heaven. He raises up the overthrown (to heap new ridicule upon them):

and as a Heard
Of Goats or timerous flock together throngd
Drove them before him Thunder-struck, pursu'd
With terrors and with furies to the bounds
And Chrystall wall of Heav'n, which op'ning wide,
Rowld inward, and a spacious Gap disclos'd
Into the wastful Deep; the monstrous sight
Strook them with horror backward, but far worse
Urg'd them behind; headlong themselves they threw
Down from the verge of Heav'n, Eternal wrauth
Burnt after them to the bottomless pit.

(VI, 856 ff.)

Never do they appear so ridiculous, not even as a timorous flock, as when they are caught isolated between the before and the behind.

The scene itself is magnificent and superhuman as an expression of wrath and physical force. But the violence that the rebels naïvely set in motion returns to deprive them of all superhuman grandeur, and then of merely human dignity (if man had been then). They descend, as in a series of explosions, the scale of creation. Though they have enough will to throw themselves down, as a herd of animals, they have been *rooted* out. (And *will*, it must be noted, was believed to go further down the scale of being, as in Donne's "Nocturnall"; "Yea plants, yea stones detest, / And love.") It is "Heav'n ruining from Heav'n"—which seems to suggest the descent of spirit to matter, and of matter to the unformed matter of chaos, even to a kind of sub-chaos:

confounded *Chaos* roard,
And felt tenfold confusion in thir fall
Through his wilde Anarchie, so huge a rout
Incumberd him with ruin.

(VI, 871 ff.)

This is to be understood metaphorically, as the climax of their physical humiliation. It does not last, any more than their later mass metamorphosis into serpents, with which this is parallel. But it is a punishment, on the material level, for the material nature of their sin. If they regain their form in hell, that is because they regain free will (which has been interrupted by divine wrath). Spirits, we remember, "Cannot but by annihilating die." Incidentally, Bacon says the same thing about matter: "Annihilation and absolute Destruction cannot be effected but by the Omnipotency of God." Bacon's remarks on the cyclical behavior of matter may explain what is happening to the rebel angels. In their struggle to escape God's wrath they may be co-operating, or more, in the transformation. Matter, Bacon says (in commenting on the myth of Proteus, in *The Wisdom of the Ancients*), "being thus caught in the straits of Necessity, doth change and turn herself into divers strange Forms and Shapes of Things, so that at length (by fetching a Circuit as it were) she comes to a Period, and (if the force continue) betakes herself to her former Being."

II

It is time to find a better term for what has been called *external* and *physical*. The ridicule on this level, as the last part of the discussion indicated, has its real (i.e. metaphorical) meaning in reference to the *material*—the lowest stage in the familiar scale of matter, mind, and spirit. In spite of an arbitrary attempt to isolate the material level, it has been implicit, and sometimes explicit, that this level has its metaphorical meaning in reference to the other levels. As we proceed, the interrelationships will become more apparent and more complex. But first, with the perspective we have gained, let us look at the material level again.

"Our puissance is our own," Satan declares to Abdiel. It constitutes a denial of values outside the self and an assertion of the materialistic value of might. Raphael provides us with a choral commentary when he declines to name some of the rebel angels and their deeds, "In might though wondrous and in Acts of Warr":

> For strength from Truth divided and from Just,
> Illaudable, naught merits but dispraise
> And ignominie.
>
> (VI, 381 ff.)

Might, elevated to an absolute, proves an impostor in the divine comedy once it comes face to face with the direct expression of God's will. The rebels must be taught in terms of the value they hold, and so they "learn, as likes them, to despise / God and *Messiah* his annointed King." The issue is formulated by the Son when he declares his reason for the solitary contest against the rebels:

> That they may have thir wish, to trie with mee
> In Battel which the stronger proves, they all,
> Or I alone against them, since by strength
> They measure all, of other excellence
> Not emulous, nor care who them excells.
>   (VI, 818 ff.)

As prelude to their materialistic punishment by the descent through chaos, the trampled rebels have their strength withered, their "wonted vigour" drained; they are left "Exhausted, spiritless."

But they sin against reason too, and so we may expect to find, on this second level, a pattern of ridicule running parallel to that on the materialistic level. It is still a conflict, however—Satan's ridicule of the mind matched against God's. As in hell, Satan is a great master of forensic irony. His opening speech for war, like the speech raising his followers from the burning lake, uses verbal ridicule as if it were a lash—reversing, as it were, the nervous process by making the mind tell the flesh that it hurts:

> Thrones, Dominations, Princedomes, Vertues, Powers,
> If these magnific Titles yet remain
> Not meerly titular, since by Decree
> Another now hath to himself ingross't
> All Power, and us eclipst under the name
> Of King anointed, for whom all this haste
> Of midnight march, and hurried meeting here,
> This onely to consult how we may best
> With what may be devis'd of honours new
> Receive him coming to receive from us
> Knee-tribute yet unpaid, prostration vile,
> Too much to one, but double how endur'd,
> To one and to his image now proclaim'd?
>   (V, 772 ff.)

Though we are most likely to think of Satan as a figure of pride and unconquerable will, it is apparent that one of his views of himself, a public view, is as a master of reason. And he can make an appeal in the name of reason with no less assurance than in the name of freedom. After the opening ridicule, intended to soften up his audience by submitting them to what practically amounts to physical pressure, he moves to the next stage, that of preparing them intellectually for the final stage, spiritual rebellion that will complete the circle by expressing itself in physical rebellion. It is significant that what Satan offers is an appeal to reason rather than a demonstration, an appeal either in the form of loaded question or loaded statement:

> But what if better counsels might erect
> Our minds and teach us to cast off this Yoke?
> > ye will not, if I trust
> To know ye right, or if we know your selves. . . .
> Who can in reason then or right assume
> Monarchie over such as live by right
> His equals, if in power and splendor less,
> In freedome equal?

But if Satan considers himself a master of reason, it seems to be in a public way, for purposes of appeal, or debate, or ridicule. Actually, he seems to distinguish between the reason and what are to him the higher functions of the mind. Reason is the most important means of destroying reason, and it is a major weapon of the intellectual cynic. When Satan calls Abdiel "seditious Angel," he is relishing his own humor; but he is also, shrewd relativist that he is, undermining the possibility of judgment. Look, he is saying, if I am a rebel, so are you; and if you look at it logically, one sin is pretty much like another. Similarly, in the formal debate with Abdiel, Satan, by way of introducing his heresy of self-generation, accuses Abdiel of heresy. Satan's argument is an interesting demonstration of his attitude towards reason:

> > who saw
> When this creation was? rememberst thou
> Thy making, while the Maker gave thee being?
> We know no time when we were not as now;
> Know none before us, self-begot, self-rais'd

By our own quick'ning power, when fatal course
Had circl'd his full Orbe.

(V, 856 ff.)

He is ridiculing the possibility of knowledge for Abdiel by setting the
fixed limits of knowledge within the self. If Abdiel was not there it
did not happen. If we do not know it then it is not so. And seeing is
believing. At least that is the limit to which reason can be stretched
for the opponent's mystery; it is strangely different when Satan announces his own version of the miracle of creation.

Satan, of course, renders himself ridiculous by his argument. As
Mr. C. S. Lewis has commented, Satan both loses in dignity and
produces just the evidence to prove that he was not self-created. It
might be added that for the God he has rejected he must supply (besides the deity of self) an external power, Chance or Fate, that is related to, and perhaps dependent upon still another power, Time. One
may observe that intellectually, more than physically, Satan performs
the office of rendering himself ridiculous, and with a minimum of external assistance. This happens when his materialistic bent of mind
leads him to interpret having lasted one day of battle as proof of God's
fallibility and non-omniscience. Since his position is often that of an
opportunist, when he has to rationalize it he exposes himself.

But there is a certain amount of intellectual ridicule that is externally administered. For instance, a remark like this, which deliberately presents physical ridicule in terms of intellectual ridicule:

that to be less than Gods
Disdain'd, but meaner thoughts learnd in thir flight.

(VI, 366 f.)

The two levels are joined again when the rebels are driven out of
heaven; for we remember the initial slogan of freedom, later exalted
to dominion, as they leave indiscriminately "together throngd," with
even their own orders and degrees (which "Jarr not with liberty") beyond their concern. To be more accurate this ridicule is not really administered externally. It is pointed up, by a kind of choral commentary, but it is already there, dramatically earned when the intellectual
presumptions of the rebels work out their conflict with reality. This is
true of the most important commentary on the intellectual ridiculous-
ness of the rebels. It is the Son's remark before he unlooses the Father's indignation, and it goes to the very core of the rebels' position,

to expose its essential incongruity—"mee they have despis'd, / Yet envied." They have envied His elevation, though by merit, and envied it in terms of might and in terms of scorn. The external ridicule only exposes what is internal, what in the course of dramatic action works its way out.

This is perhaps a convenient place to look back for a moment at Dr. Johnson's criticism, with which this study began. Milton, it is plain, like the metaphysical poets, and like other Renaissance writers, and like twentieth-century writers, has a much less restricted taste for incongruity than has Dr. Johnson. Milton, no less than Shakespeare or Donne, but in his own way, has a comprehensive taste for incongruity, which he can control and resolve into his larger structure. The "confusion of spirit and matter" that Johnson deplored is controlled confusion, the dramatic working out of what Satan ignorantly set in motion.

But this is to jump a stage, for what we are supposed to be considering still is the second level, that of mind. To pick up the thread again, what is ridiculous about Satan's mind mostly reveals itself by what he says and how, and by what he does. If his chief use of reason is to destroy the authority of the reason, it is with no intention of destroying the authority of the mind. The mind is of great importance to Satan—the mind is its own place—but that is because the mind has other faculties besides that of reason.

Satan's analysis of the first day's battle reveals a significant part of his attitude towards the mind. We endured some disadvantage, he admits, and pain, though as soon as we came to *know* that evil we were able to be superior to it by despising it. Our "Empyreal forme" is superior to wounds, which close and heal by our own native vigor. The remedy of evil is as small as it is easy. Perhaps "more valid Armes," more violent weapons will gain us superiority over our foes, or at least remove the odds they enjoyed, since there is no essential difference between us in nature.

> if other hidden cause
> Left them Superiour, while we can preserve
> Unhurt our mindes, and understanding sound,
> Due search and consultation will disclose.
>
> (VI, 442 ff.)

It is mind over matter, that is, the unconquerable will over material evil. It is also spiritual form that seems to be most prized for its ability to resist, in a kind of material way, the material damage of wounds. The mind must be preserved unhurt, like the spiritual form, so that it can search out material means to gain a material superiority. It is mind over matter but limited to matter, turned downwards to gain superiority on a lower plane, and running the risk of adjusting to the plane upon which it has chosen to work out its destiny.

In battle Satan's only moral quality is courage, a partial virtue that has no moral value independent of other virtues. His chief rational qualities are strength of will and inventive ingenuity. The invention of artillery is a symbolic act, a characteristic achievement of Satan's mind (as Sin is), an achievement that exhibits Satan's great mastery over the material, and implies a reciprocal relationship between his mind and matter. Compared with him, his followers (apparently even Mammon) are superficial, surveying only the "bright surface" of things, with no "mind" for the materials underneath. But the significance of Satan's symbolic demonstration of mind over matter is not limited to himself; his act turns what has been a war conducted under discipline fatally towards chaos. To prevent general chaos, and to control the motion downwards now inevitably begun, God's wrath must intervene, suspending free will so that heaven can ruin from heaven. To understand what is involved we must look at the key problem of discipline.

Satan's revolt is, among other things, a break in discipline. The best commentary comes from the encounter between Satan and Gabriel at the end of Book IV, an encounter, as we have observed, that provides an important commentary on the major themes of the war in heaven. Gabriel says

> Was this your discipline and faith ingag'd,
> Your military obedience, to dissolve
> Allegeance to th'acknowledg'd Power supream?
>   (IV, 954 ff.)

Whatever else it is, the break in discipline is a rational sin too, for Satan sets the stage for his revolt by depending upon the discipline upwards of his inferiors, the while he is himself rejecting the discipline that he owes upwards. His sin requires that his own allegiance be downwards rather than upwards for the external support necessary to any rational creature within the moral universe.

Milton's treatment of free will makes discipline a part of the rational soul (which traditionally comprehended both the understanding and the will). God requires obedience, but obedience freely given, an expression of the understanding carried out by the will. Adam's thoughts after having been created seem to be a demonstration of the reason (apparently natural reason) moving towards obedience:

> how came I thus, how here?
> Not of my self; by some great Maker then,
> In goodness and in power praeeminent;
> Tell me, how may I know him, how adore,
> From whom I have that thus I move and live,
> And feel that I am happier then I know.
>
> (VIII, 277 ff.)

Obedience must be freely given, but God helps His creatures perfect their wills. Ceremonies provide occasion in heaven, as on the day that "brings forth" heaven's Great Year, when the hosts are called by "Imperial summons." The orders and degrees provide every creature with opportunities for exercising his discipline: only God has no superior. Besides, the doing of disciplinary tasks is itself a ceremony in heaven. We remember that Raphael was sent on a ceremonial expedition to the gates of hell, and so was absent the day Adam was created:

> But us he sends upon his high behests
> For state, as Sovran King, and to enure
> Our prompt obedience.
>
> (VIII, 238 ff.)

The Son, whose obedience is perfect, says that to obey the Father is "happiness entire." He says this as He assumes power on the third day of battle, in order to fulfil the divine will: only in this fulfilment does He have glory and exaltation. Meanwhile, the role of the loyal angels has been on a lower scale of fulfilment, closer to the performance of duty through the acceptance of discipline. Their service, which has been fearless and faithful, is accepted by God. This they are told by the Son; presumably their service includes, though unmentioned, the ridicule they suffered before Satan's cannon. (Abdiel had endured ridicule and "Universal reproach, far worse to beare / Then violence.") This physical ridicule, we must remember, is directly due to their arms; unarmed, Raphael comments, they could, as spirits, easily have evaded Satan's material missiles.

Why the arms? They make no literal sense, as Dr. Johnson readily

saw, but they make the same kind of symbolic sense that the whole
war makes. Are not the arms part of the limiting discipline, part of
the ceremony of perfecting the will? Do not the arms limit the material might of both sides, to add to the limit which God has already
providently set in order to prevent destruction? Actually, both sides
are inconvenienced by their arms; for when the rebels are pinned under the mountains their armor helps trap them, crushing and bruising
their "substance." For all his ingenuity, it does not occur to General
Satan that his troops are really more powerful without the accepted
discipline of their arms. The strategic lesson is learned only after Satan introduces a secret weapon that violates the code which he appears to be accepting and in fact partly is, though through ignorance.
"Rage" prompts the loyal angels to counter-invention, which is superior to Satan's invention—perhaps because it breaks from the discipline altogether and returns more completely to fundamental material
force. But it leads simply towards chaos, the destruction, not of the
enemy, but of heaven. (There are literary overtones, for good measure, of Zeus' battle against the mountain-wielding forces of destruction, the Giants—in the hymn celebrating the creation Satan's rebels
are significantly referred to as "the Giant Angels.") Finally, when the
discipline has broken down, God suspends free will and intervenes:

> Warr wearied hath perform'd what Warr can do,
> And to disorder'd rage let loose the reines.
>
> (VI, 695 f.)

But even the Chariot of God proceeds within the limits of discipline.
It shakes all heaven—except the throne of God. And the Son checks
half His strength, in order not to destroy.

There is plenty of evidence of Milton's personal interest in the
problem of discipline; one pertinent outside commentary may be
found in *Paradise Regained*, when Christ answers Satan's argument
that God seeks glory. Christ replies that God made all only to show
goodness freely; but, having done so, justly expects thanks:

> The slightest, easiest, readiest recompence
> From them who could return him nothing else,
> And not returning that would likeliest render
> Contempt instead, dishonour, obloquy.
>
> (III, 128 ff.)

This is a version of traditional Elizabethan political philosophy, quite as applicable to the social structure or to the church structure (though Milton personally breaks with some of the implications). It is firmly based upon hierarchy; the discipline of order and degree expresses a philosophical view rather than mere etiquette, a philosophical view that regards order as possible only through discipline and therefore regards chaos as the logical alternative to discipline. Ulysses' great speech on "degree," in *Troilus and Cressida,* traces the steps leading to mere power and will and self-consuming appetite that finally ends in chaos. It is a significant commentary, but even more important for the circumstances under consideration is a pragmatic analysis by Bacon from his interpretation of the myth of Orpheus. The myth is an image of philosophy—when Orpheus' music appeases the infernal powers it represents natural philosophy, when it attracts the beasts and trees it represents "Moral or Civil Discipline." Natural philosophy, Bacon says, with pointed wryness, is seldom or never attained:

> And therefore Philosophy, hardly able to produce so excellent an Effect, in a pensive Humour (and not without cause), busies herself about Human Objects, and by Persuasion and Eloquence, insinuating the love of Virtue, Equity, and Concord in the Minds of Men, draws Multitudes of People to a Society, makes them subject to Laws, obedient to Government, and forgetful of their unbridled Affections, whilst they give Ear to Precepts, and submit themselves to Discipline; whence follows the building of Houses, erecting of Towns, planting of Fields and Orchards with Trees, and the like; insomuch that it would not be amiss to say, that even thereby Stones and Woods were called together and settled in Order. . . . Tumults and Seditions and Wars arise; in the midst of which Hurly-burlies, first Laws are silent, Men return to the pravity of their Natures; Fields and Towns are wasted and depopulated; and then (if their Fury continue) Learning and Philosophy must needs be dismembered; so that a few Fragments only, and in some Places, will be found like the scattered Boards of Shipwreck, so as a barbarous Age must follow.

The material sin is punished most completely during the war, and in a material way. The sins against mind and spirit receive their full punishment only over a longer period of time; the punishment is also in kind, by internal development, through degeneration. But the material is the thread that runs through the other two levels, for Raphael's basic metaphor was to express divine happenings by likening spiritual to corporeal forms. For the critic trying to express what happens in the poem perhaps another metaphor may be used, that of the circle, which is a traditional symbol of the divine; but if the circle expresses the impostor divine, it is a symbol of moral irony and the ridiculous.

The break in discipline presumes completeness within the circle of self. When Satan declares that his puissance is his own, he is denying the possibility of a source of power external to himself. He is also referring inward, to self, for moral sanction, rather than outward. He is declaring that he is, or can be, at the top of the hierarchy, the one uncircumscribed circle. If he is not right, then he has tried to ascend the scale of creation by an internal willing of self God. The orthodox method of ascent, as Raphael tells Adam, is by being nearer or tending nearer to God; which means rising towards a purer resignation in His will, which is always external to the creature.

To make self an impostor god means trying to possess the power of spirit by means of matter. One might almost say by grace of matter, for the elevation of self to godhead may require taking matter into a partnership of deity. Not that matter is without worth—the concept of a scale of creation implies the value of matter and the possibility of ascent. Milton himself is very firm on the indivisibility of flesh and spirit. Raphael's metaphor of spiritual in corporeal form is also a way of explaining, by an earthly analogue in terms of matter, what is otherwise unexplainable in human terms—the hierarchy of spirit which works upward by merit, that closest to God being "more spiritous." Matter, both real and metaphorical, does not lack dignity. But Satan confounds the material with the external; in his search for power external to himself he turns to the material which he thinks he can master with his mind, and so make part of his own puissance. The invention of artillery is an attempt to usurp ultimate moral might by means of matter:

> eternal might
> To match with thir inventions they presum'd
> So easie, and of his Thunder made a scorn.
>   (VI, 630 ff.)

It is setting matter against spirit by means of mind. And matter that can ascend by spirit can also descend, if spirit breaks its discipline and tends further from the source of its informing power.

Ultimate moral law and ultimate force *are* external, but to be confused with material force only by the morally perverted. Through free will, if God allows an equal contest and sends only one third of His angels against the rebel third, perverse will can cause a deadlock that requires the intervention of external power. But the external power fulfils moral law and only completes the circle that has been ignorantly set in motion.

NOTE

[EDITOR'S NOTE. See also A. H. Gilbert, *MP*, XL (1942), 19-42; A. Williams, *SP*, XLII (1945), 253-68; D. Taylor, Jr., *TSE*, III (1952), 69-72; E. H. Emerson, *MLN*, LXIX (1954), 399-402; C. Herbert, *Renaissance Papers*, 1956, 92-101; G. W. Whiting, *N&Q*, CLXIII (1932), 384-6, and *SP*, LX (1963), 214-26.]

GEORGE WILLIAMSON

The Education of Adam

When Milton decided to make the Fall of Man "doctrinal and exemplary to a nation" by "teaching over the whole book of sanctity and
virtue," we may be sure that he wanted to make his teaching effective. But too often his teaching in *Paradise Lost* has seemed tedious to
the reader, especially after the brilliance of the opening action. Indeed, for several books the story suspends that action to the point
of seriously abating the epic suspense. Was this a consequence of following the principle of beginning *in medias res*? Or was it the result
of Milton's epic strategy?

The suspense could not turn on the uncertainty of the outcome, but
rather must turn upon the interpretation of the Fall. Why Adam
would fall, not how, alone gave scope to the poet. For Milton was
limited as the Greek dramatists were limited, free only to interpret a
known story. In making it "doctrinal and exemplary" he could develop tension in the story only in terms of its characters, their motives, and their moral behavior. The impressiveness of Satan is Milton's tribute not only to the power of evil but also to the glory of
moral warfare. The education of Adam must prepare him for his ordeal as well as the reader for its significance. Thus his education
seems both intrinsic and extrinsic to the plot; doctrine and example

From *Modern Philology*, LXI (1963), 96-109. Reprinted by permission of
the author and the publisher.

unite in the epic strategy. If the education of Adam teaches over "the whole book of sanctity and virtue," it also includes "all the instances of example" necessary for his instruction. In Milton's strategy the didactic element is intended both to motivate and to amplify the tragic consequences of the fall of man. At the same time it must leave man with more hope than Satan was able to muster after the fall of the angels. This is achieved by the ambiguity of the so-called "fortunate fall," which Satan inverts in Hell (II, 14-17).

I

In the Argument prefixed to Book I of *Paradise Lost* we read: "Which action past over, the Poem hasts into the midst of things, presenting Satan with his Angels now fallen into Hell." The action past over is Satan's revolt from God and expulsion from Heaven, or "the prime cause" of man's fall from obedience. The ensuing action depends upon Satan's report of a prophecy in Heaven about "a new World and new kind of Creature to be created." This report introduces the story of man as sequel to the fall of the angels. And this conjunction of the two stories necessitates the "relations" of Books V to VIII, which suspend the seduction of man and prepare for his loss of Paradise. Moreover, for the education of Adam these relations narrate both the "action past over" and the creation of "a new World and new kind of Creature." At the same time they explore the potentialities of human nature which the Fall will exhibit.

Then in Book IX the action which joins the two stories is resumed and carried to its tragic consequence. The education of Adam, however, as well as the ultimate significance of his story, requires the further relations—or vision and relation—of the last two books. His education serves first as the dramatic preparation for the catastrophe and then as the moral extension of its consequences. Thus the education of Adam becomes both a structural element in the epic plot and a didactic element in the meaning of *Paradise Lost*. If his education is carried on by relations, his catastrophe belongs to the main action; but without the relations his catastrophe would be lacking in what Dryden called concernment. Since the relations are narrated between the beginning and end of the main action, they naturally raise questions about their dramatic function. To answer that their function is doctrinal is to beg the poetic question. Moreover, Milton's insistence on the freedom of moral choice subordinates his doctrine to character and the agency of plot.

Of course the creation of "a new World and new kind of Creature" introduced Sir Thomas Browne's other book of divinity, Nature. It added what Bacon called "the book of God's works" to "the book of God's word," and it taught the same lesson. When a man, says Bacon's *Advancement of Learning,* "seeth the dependence of causes, and the works of Providence; then, according to the allegory of the poets, he will easily believe that the highest link of nature's chain must needs be tied to the foot of Jupiter's chair." Sir Thomas Browne found the first Cause of Common Errors in the common infirmity of Human Nature, and so directed an inquiry into the reasons for the Fall of Man. Milton was also concerned with the relations between the two kinds of learning.

In *Paradise Lost* Milton followed the aim and principle of education which he set forth in *Of Education.* First the aim:

> The end then of learning is to repair the ruins of our first parents by regaining to know God aright, and out of that knowledge to love him, to imitate him, to be like him, as we may the nearest by possessing our souls of true virtue, which being united to the heavenly grace of faith makes up the highest perfection.

But, as Donne explained in his *Second Anniversarie,* the mind of man limits his method of learning:

> But because our understanding cannot in this body found itself but on sensible things, nor arrive so clearly to the knowledge of God and things invisible as by orderly conning over the visible and inferior creature, the same method is necessarily to be followed in all discreet teaching.

For Milton, however, this principle finally rested upon his so-called materialism as set forth in Paradise Lost (V, 469 ff.). Patrick Hume, Milton's first annotator, explained this materialism as the consequence of Scripture and the Scale of Nature or chain of being. Hume calls this "a real visible Ladder" which "leads us by *Steps in Contemplation of Created Things up to God,* the Invisible Creator of all Things." This is why Raphael's concrete approach to Adam's instruction is something more than a pedagogic fiction. For Milton it was not an allegory of the poets that tied the highest link of nature's chain to the foot of Jupiter's chair, but neither did nature yield the highest wisdom; as *The Reason of Church Government* (II) said, "the contemplation of natural causes and dimensions . . . must needs be a lower wisdom, as the object is low." Although Bacon could also deceive Uriel, the study of God's works became for him a way to acquire power; for Milton it could also lead to the sin of pride.

Before Satan alights on the World in Book III, Milton presents the theological scheme that is basic to the drama of his poem. Although animated in presentation, it is expository in nature and hence not dramatic in purpose or feeling. As dignified exposition rather than debate, it lacks the intensity of the Council in Hell, but it gives intensity to the consequences of that Council. God as the *deus ex machina* plays a role of expositor rather than manipulator. Man's fate will turn on the idea (ll. 100 ff.) that rational liberty makes obedience a manifestation of love; God cannot compel service.

By the close of Book IV Satan's plan of temptation has been formed and his action, "tempting her in a dream," has been interrupted by the guardian angels. This plan centers on the "fatal Tree," the only sign of their obedience left (ll. 522 ff.):

> Hence I will excite thir minds
> With more desire to know, and to reject
> Envious commands, invented with designe
> To keep them low whom knowledge might exalt
> Equal with Gods; aspiring to be such,
> They taste and die.

Already the first epic relation of matter not covered by the action proper (ll. 440 ff.) has revealed Eve's vanity, which opens her to the temptation of pride. Now she reveals a desire to know by her question about the moon and stars (ll. 657-58):

> But wherfore all night long shine these, for whom
> This glorious sight, when sleep hath shut all eyes?

Her question implies the need for admiration and is turned to flattery by Satan in her dream. But Adam replies that light is necessary for life and that God is not dependent on man for praise. When Satan's action is interrupted, the outlines of the temptation are clear; but his action has to be suspended both for the education of Adam and for the preparation of the audience. While the didactic purpose is being served, dramatic tension is developed by our growing insight into Adam and Eve.

If the tree of knowledge gives Satan the grounds of temptation, Eve

first directs speculation toward the heavens. Both the reply of Adam
and the dream inspired by Satan suggest the involvement of pride in
Eve's question. Thus when Raphael is sent to prepare Adam for his
trial, the reader is prepared to follow and interpret Adam's response to
the lessons of the "action past over" and to the "new World and new
kind of Creature." The path of temptation has been defined enough
to arouse the reader's apprehension.

II

Book V opens with Adam and Eve's first experience of evil and the
beginning of trouble in the form of Eve's dream. This anticipates the
tragic temptation in its essentials, but it also reflects and alters her past
experience. First she thought her seducer's voice that of Adam, and its
question related to her question of the night, that the moon and stars
shone "in vain, / If none regard." And then its flattery harmonized
with her own first experience of vanity (ll. 44-47):

> Heav'n wakes with all his eyes,
> Whom to behold but thee, Natures desire,
> In whose sight all things joy, with ravishment
> Attracted by thy beauty still to gaze.

Adam had exhibited this capacity while Eve was still dreaming. Now
he explains her dream as a manifestation of evil created out of past experience by faculties usually subordinate to reason (ll. 114-16):

> Som such resemblances methinks I find
> Of our last Eevnings talk, in this thy dream,
> But with addition strange.

Now both are troubled and their trouble finds expression in a prayer
for help (ll. 205 ff.). And so God sends Raphael to fulfil the providence expressed in Book III, chiefly by recounting the "action past
over." As "the sociable Spirit" he is most sympathetic to Adam's deepest need, and so enables Milton to explore the human condition.

For Milton the prodigality of nature provides not only a manifestation of God's providence but also a constant trial of temperance. This
topic motivates the encounter between Comus and the Lady; it becomes the field of trial to which Adam is related in *Areopagitica*; it
supports much of the education of Adam in human nature. It is manifest in the Garden of Eden and in the preparations to entertain Raphael. The angelic supper provides the occasion for Raphael to satisfy

Adam's desire to know by explaining the scale of Nature by which matter works up to spirit (as in *Comus*). Its importance is emphasized by Adam (ll. 508 ff.):

> Well hast thou taught the way that might direct
> Our knowledge, and the scale of Nature set
> From center to circumference, whereon
> In contemplation of created things
> By steps we may ascend to God.

This is the principle of education set forth in Milton's tract of that name; it may also lead to undue aspiration. But Raphael had imposed a condition on man's future that worries Adam: "What meant that caution joind, *if ye be found / Obedient?*" Raphael explains that our service of God must be voluntary, the effect of love, not of necessity, if it is to be acceptable. As in *Areopagitica* freedom of will is a necessary condition of virtue as of love. Adam's desire to hear more of what "Hath past in Heav'n" gives Raphael the opportunity to exemplify the meaning of obedience, which Milton has translated into love.

But first Raphael lays down the assumption of his teaching (ll. 571 ff.):

> what surmounts the reach
> Of human sense, I shall delineate so,
> By lik'ning spiritual to corporal forms,
> As may express them best.

It is the assumption found in *Of Education*, but Raphael extends it to express a possibility which he had already suggested in his comparison of man and angel:

> though what if Earth
> Be but the shaddow of Heav'n, and things therein
> Each to other like, more then on earth is thought?

Now the action past over becomes a great lesson in obedience to God, and a graphic answer to Adam's question (ll. 514 ff.):

> can wee want obedience then
> To him, or possibly his love desert
> Who formd us from the dust, and plac'd us here
> Full to the utmost measure of what bliss
> Human desires can seek or apprehend?

The human situation is related to the trial of virtue in *Areopagitica*: "This justifies the high providence of God, who, though he command us temperance, justice, continence, yet pours out before us, even to a profuseness, all desirable things, and gives us minds that can wander beyond all limit and satiety." And Belial reminds us how easily our minds succumb to romantic aspiration:

> for who would loose
> Though full of pain, this intellectual being,
> Those thoughts that wander through Eternity?

How such a desertion could happen is exemplified by the revolt in Heaven, with Satan as the great model of disobedience and Abdiel as the great model of obedience, one whom pride alienates from God and one who cannot "his love desert." The emphasis on love in *Paradise Lost* belongs to the emphasis on the social nature of man and the bonds that produce society or relate man to the good. By love he may ascend the scale of being as well as descend it by lust. Thus "the sociable Spirit" Raphael becomes the best interpreter of the human condition. As the proud Spirit Satan represents the perversion of virtue and his followers the more negative sins; together they animate the sins that produce alienation from God.

Book VI reveals the significance of Abdiel's stand: Abdiel is an example of the moral courage that enables one to stand against evil. He embodies Milton's favorite moral doctrines; his example corrects the argument in Hell that force is stronger than reason. Here "the easier conquest" is that of force, the necessity of the fallen Angels, "who reason for thir Law refuse." Yet force does not and cannot resolve the war with evil; for Milton believed that force can curb or punish evil, but only reason can conquer it. Comus, we may recall, could neither force nor persuade virtue. Adam is taught that God and Nature (reason) both bid us follow virtue: to serve vice is to be enslaved (ll. 174 ff.). Evil is born of disobedience and produces violence and war (ll. 262 ff.). When the war in Heaven degenerates into a primitive battle of Titans, uncontrolled force threatens Heaven with ruin, and shows that "Warr wearied hath perform'd what Warr can do." When Christ drives out the forces of evil, for Heaven "Brooks not the works of violence and Warr," Christ manifests the punishment of God rather than the triumph of force. And so Adam learns "By terrible Example the reward / Of disobedience"; learns about the first cause of his story (ll. 900 ff.):

> *Satan,* hee who envies now thy state,
> Who now is plotting how he may seduce
> Thee also from obedience, that with him
> Bereavd of happiness thou maist partake
> His punishment, Eternal miserie.

We know that at best this tragic consequence may be shortened but not escaped. And since this mitigation is theological rather than dramatic, our concern has to center in the troubles of the human characters.

Book VII deals with the Creation which is God's answer to Satan's revolt, and which makes possible the conclusion of the Conclave in Hell. But its revelation is motivated by Adam's human nature:

> Led on, yet sinless, with desire to know
> What neerer might concern him,

he returns to his early curiosity about the world (ll. 84 ff.):

> Deign to descend now lower, and relate
> What may no less perhaps availe us known,
> How first began this Heav'n which we behold
> Distant so high, with moving Fires adornd.

Possibly that "perhaps" intimates doubt on Milton's part, but for the reader it continues the revelation of human nature upon which our concern must be founded. Here Milton's imagination returns to his Native Element (ll. 23 ff.):

> Standing on Earth, not rapt above the Pole,
> More safe I sing with mortal voice, unchang'd
> To hoarce or mute, though fall'n on evil dayes,
> On evil dayes though fall'n, and evil tongues;
> In darkness, and with dangers compast round,
> And solitude.

And every detail of his own fallen state brings new sympathy to his voice and new understanding to his theme.

Adam disclaims any intention to seek forbidden knowledge, but offers the same excuse that Satan addressed to Uriel (ll. 95-97):

> not to explore the secrets aske
> Of his Eternal Empire, but the more
> To magnifie his works, the more we know.

Bacon in answering the Divines in his *Advancement of Learning* not only distinguished between philosophy and revelation but used St. Paul to distinguish between pride and charity as ends of knowledge. Although he thought the study of nature ought to produce wonder with respect to God, it should not be limited: "To conclude therefore, let no man upon a weak conceit of sobriety or an ill-applied moderation think or maintain, that a man can search too far, or be too well studied in the book of God's word, or in the book of God's works; divinity or philosophy." Milton, however, would impose some restraint in line with St. Paul's charge that "Knowledge puffeth up" (ll. 126 ff.):

> But Knowledge is as food, and needs no less
> Her Temperance over Appetite, to know
> In measure what the mind may well contain,
> Oppresses else with Surfet, and soon turns
> Wisdom to Folly, as Nourishment to Winde.

Thus Milton's "conceit of sobriety" connects the spiritual and the material.

Creation culminates in the new creature man, "self-knowing," made in the image of God, brought into (ll. 538 ff.)

> This Garden, planted with the Trees of God,
> Delectable both to behold and taste;
> And freely all thir pleasant fruit for food
> Gave thee, all sorts are here that all th'Earth yeelds,
> Varietie without end; but of the Tree
> Which tasted works knowledge of Good and Evil,
> Thou mai'st not; in the day thou eat'st, thou di'st;
> Death is the penaltie impos'd, beware,
> And govern well thy appetite, least sin
> Surprise thee, and her black attendant Death.

Milton has already established the metaphorical range of "appetite" and now he translates the test of obedience into a test of temperance. The penalty imposed is the main one, death, without mention of the contingent ones of "all our woe, / With loss of *Eden*." This omission leaves open an extension of the tragic consequences which may become significant. Book VII ends with a limited invitation to Adam's curiosity: "if else thou seek'st / Aught, not surpassing human measure, say."

Book VIII centers on man, and human nature is put into sharp focus. Here we are initiated more specifically into grounds for the fall of man. On Adam's thirst for knowledge the Argument is suggestive: "Adam inquires concerning celestial Motions, is doubtfully answer'd, and exhorted to search rather things more worthy of knowledg." His question merely extends the question raised by Eve and altered in her dream, but this repetition also enhances its significance. Adam's concern about celestial motions no doubt exceeds sobriety, but it is related to the prodigality argument of Comus, for he finds excess in the macrocosm and wonders (ll. 26 ff.)

> How Nature wise and frugal could commit
> Such disproportions, with superfluous hand
> So many nobler Bodies to create,
> Greater so manifold to this one use,
> For aught appears . . .

This disproportion of means to end seems to Adam wasteful, but his implied moral challenges the wisdom of nature rather than temperance. The prodigality of nature serves more than one purpose in *Paradise Lost*.

Milton's treatment of Eve at this juncture is worth notice. When she perceives Adam "Entring on studious thoughts abstruse," and departs to her gardening, Milton saves her from condescension (ll. 48 ff.):

> Yet went she not, as not with such discourse
> Delighted, or not capable her eare
> Of what was high.

If this makes Eve worthy of being Adam's helpmeet, her preference for Adam rounds out Milton's view of marriage:

> hee, she knew would intermix
> Grateful digressions, and solve high dispute
> With conjugal Caresses, from his Lip
> Not Words alone pleas'd her.

The importance of Eve to Adam turned the words, "and solve high dispute / With conjugal Caresses," into irony at the Fall.

Raphael's reply to Adam's question is intended to discourage Adam's curiosity. Positively Raphael uses the occasion to point a lesson in values; negatively he uses the conflicts between the Ptolemaic and

Copernican systems to point the futility of such knowledge. He concludes by warning Adam not to aspire too high (ll. 173-74): "be lowlie wise: / Think onely what concernes thee and thy being." In acquiescing Adam seems to join Eve: "nor with perplexing thoughts / To interrupt the sweet of Life." Yet as he surrenders what Belial would not lose, "Those thoughts that wander through Eternity," he admits (l. 188), "But apte the Mind or Fancie is to roave," and hence it must be taught that the prime wisdom is "That which before us lies in daily life." But Adam was not ready to understand Donne's conclusion to his satiric *Progress of the Soul* when he says, "wonder with me, why"

> most of those arts, whence our lives are blest,
> By cursed *Cain's* race invented be,
> And blest *Seth* vexed us with Astronomy.

Although Adam is willing to change the subject and speak of useful knowledge, he does not surrender his curiosity (ll. 200-202):

> whence haply mention may arise
> Of something not unseasonable to ask
> By sufferance, and thy wonted favour deign'd

And so, prompted by an even deeper need, he tells his story in order to detain Raphael. Beginning as a subterfuge it culminates in the revelation of his craving for rational society. In exploring the problem of solitude Milton lays the basis for Adam's fall. After his creation Adam also dreams of the tempting fruit, but wakes in time to be warned by God about the pledge of obedience. In pronouncing the penalty of death God adds what the Angel omitted (ll. 331-33):

> From that day mortal, and this happie State
> Shalt loose, expell'd from hence into a World
> Of woe and sorrow.

Then in "the Garden of bliss" Adam discovers a deficiency in his relation to the animals (l. 354): "but in these / I found not what me thought I wanted still." And so after thanking God for his bounty, he presumes to object:

> In solitude
> What happiness, who can enjoy alone,
> Or all enjoying, what contentment find?

For he cannot find rational society among the animals (ll. 389-92):

> Of fellowship I speak
> Such as I seek, fit to participate
> All rational delight, wherein the brute
> Cannot be human consort.

Of course all this is a trial in self-knowledge, for God "Knew it not good for Man to be alone," and so creates his "other self." In his sleep Adam sees a ravishing vision, and as he wakens Milton projects her importance to Adam (ll. 478-80):

> She disappeerd, and left me dark, I wak'd
> To find her, or for ever to deplore
> Her loss, and other pleasures all abjure.

Although Eve brings his "Storie to the sum of earthly bliss," she presents a new problem in self-knowledge (ll. 530 ff.):

> here passion first I felt,
> Commotion strange, in all enjoyments else
> Superior and unmov'd, here onely weake
> Against the charm of Beauties powerful glance.

But this father of Samson has his own explanation: nature again used more than she needed:

> Or Nature faild in mee, and left some part
> Not proof enough such Object to sustain,
> Or from my side subducting, took perhaps
> More then enough; at least on her bestow'd
> Too much of Ornament, in outward shew
> Elaborate, of inward less exact.

Now Adam finds disproportion in the microcosm: reason is not equal to passion, so that higher faculties seem inferior to lower, and beauty makes wisdom look like folly.

Raphael gives the same answer as before to Adam's charge against nature: "Accuse not Nature." Wisdom is not to be doubted but obeyed; otherwise he will lose the sense of proportion, and make false judgments, take the seeming good for the real good. As with celestial motions, Raphael argues that "Bright inferrs not Excellence," but that Eve was "Made so adorn for thy delight the more, / So awful, that with honour thou maist love." He tells Adam that physical desire is shared by the animals, and is not worthy to subdue (ll. 585 ff.)

> The Soule of Man, or passion in him move.
> What higher in her societie thou findst
> Attractive, human, rational, love still;
> In loving thou dost well, in passion not,
> Wherein true Love consists not.

Thus Adam's weakness is rebuked as Raphael proceeds to give love a Platonic bias:

>   love refines
> The thoughts, and heart enlarges, hath his seat
> In Reason, and is judicious, is the scale
> By which to heav'nly Love thou maist ascend,
> Not sunk in carnal pleasure, for which cause
> Among the Beasts no Mate for thee was found.

This scale, in effect, connects human and divine love.

By this rebuke Adam is "half abash't" and hastens to disclaim any delight (ll. 597-99)

> In procreation common to all kindes
> (Though higher of the genial Bed by far,
> And with mysterious reverence I deem).

If Adam seems reluctant to leave the *lectus genialis,* he none the less describes the feminine ways and signs of union that attract but do not subject. Indeed the unabashed half of Adam insists that Raphael ascend the scale to heavenly love and report on its relation to the sense of touch. Whereupon Raphael blushed "Celestial rosie red, Loves proper hue," and answered (ll. 620-21):

> Let it suffice thee that thou know'st
> Us happie, and without Love no happiness.

If Adam learned no more about angelic love than that it did not leave the physical entirely behind, he did get a strong reaffirmation of love, which Raphael incorporated into his parting advice:

> Be strong, live happie, and love, but first of all
> Him whom to love is to obey, and keep
> His great command; take heed least Passion sway

> Thy Judgement to do aught, which else free Will
> Would not admit; thine and of all thy Sons
> The weal or woe in thee is plac't; beware.

This sums up Adam's predicament. His fundamental weakness is born out of the greatest human need, relief from solitude. If there is no happiness without love, Adam's position between God and woman will become a tragic dilemma and as full of ambiguity as the so-called fortunate fall.

III

In Book IX the tragic action is resumed. All the preparations have been made, and Milton must now change the notes to tragic. For him the argument is "Not less but more Heroic then the wrauth / Of stern Achilles." He declares that he was

> Not sedulous by Nature to indite
> Warrs, hitherto the onely Argument
> Heroic deem'd, chief maistrie to dissect
> With long and tedious havoc fabl'd Knights
> In Battels feign'd; the better fortitude
> Of Patience and Heroic Martyrdom
> Unsung.

This is the fortitude of his early thought which he came to know better through blindness.

Satan's eulogy of the Earth (ll. 99 ff.) magnifies our sense of Adam's bliss while it expands Satan's motives for revenge upon Adam. The luxuriance of the Garden in turn becomes Eve's excuse to Adam for the separation of their labors. Adam replies that God has not imposed labor upon them strictly (ll. 242-43). Although "solitude sometimes is best societie," he fears the attempt of Satan upon her; for he is uncertain (ll. 261 ff.)

> Whether his first design be to withdraw
> Our fealtie from God, or to disturb
> Conjugal Love, then which perhaps no bliss
> Enjoy'd by us excites his envie more.

Adam thinks in terms of his dilemma. Notice how Milton weaves his themes of prodigality, labor, solitude, society, love, into his preparation for the Fall.

This is how the Argument phrases the beginning of Eve's defection: "Eve loath to be thought not circumspect or firm enough, urges her going apart, the rather desirous to make tryal of her strength." In Book IV Satan had sought to arouse discontent and inordinate desires in Eve; now she seems to exhibit overconfidence rather than strength, and to argue "Vertue unassaid" into tempting evil through pride. Adam answers Eve in the vein of *Comus* that man is (ll. 348 ff.)

> Secure from outward force; within himself
> The danger lies, yet lies within his power:
> Against his will he can receave no harme.
> But God left free the Will, for what obeyes
> Reason is free, and Reason he made right
> But bid her well beware, and still erect,
> Least by some faire appeering good surpris'd
> She dictate false, and missinforme the Will
> To do what God expressly hath forbid.

Adam is now perfect in his lesson: Will is free when it obeys reason, not the passions; but reason can be deceived, and so he warns against deception. But if Eve's will cannot be persuaded, Adam can only say, "Go; for thy stay, not free, absents thee more." The potentialities of their separation—their tragedy on the human level—are all in that line.

Satan's seduction of Eve (ll. 532 ff.) appeals to her original experience of self-awareness and translates her effect upon Adam into general flattery. But when Eve repeats the command of God, Satan questions their pride of place, the penalty of God, and even His omnipotence. When Eve is seduced by rational deception, desire, and appetite, she reduces the prohibition to that of knowledge and its potentialities. Finally she puts aside the temptation to keep this boon to herself out of love for Adam (ll. 832-33):

> So dear I love him, that with him all deaths
> I could endure, without him live no life.

The Argument describes Adam's reception of her fall in these words: "Adam at first amaz'd, but perceiving her lost, resolves through vehemence of love to perish with her; and extenuating the trespass, eats also of the Fruit." But in the poem when she tells Adam she has eaten of the fruit and its effects are not as they have been told, Adam (ll. 890 ff.)

> Astonied stood and Blank, while horror chill
> Ran through his veins, and all his joynts relax'd;
> From his slack hand the Garland wreath'd for *Eve*
> Down drop'd, and all the faded Roses shed.

Thus the effect of her fall passes through Adam and his flowers, and continues into his cry of pain:

> How art thou lost, how on a sudden lost,
> Defac't, deflourd, and now to Death devote?

And then the first want that he knew in Paradise undoes him (ll. 906 ff.):

> And mee with thee hath ruind, for with thee
> Certain my resolution is to Die;
> How can I live without thee, how forgoe
> Thy sweet Converse and Love so dearly joyn'd,
> To live again in these wilde Woods forlorn?

In that last line her loss already transforms Paradise.

   Then Adam extenuates the trespass by arguments like those of Eve and Satan (ll. 921 ff.). Neither one as yet suspects Satan in the Serpent. Eve takes Adam's resolution as a trial of love or separation (ll. 975-76):

> This happie trial of thy Love, which else
> So eminently never had bin known.

This is the Happy Fall on the human level. Adam fell (ll. 998-99)

> Against his better knowledge, not deceav'd,
> But fondly overcome with Femal charm.

For he chose "to incurr / Divine displeasure for her sake, or Death." And the fall first betrays itself in their love: "in Lust they burne." In terms of *The Doctrine and Discipline of Divorce* (IV) their rational burning sinks into sensual burning and they experience shame. Reason and Will fall into subjection to sensual appetite, and high passions begin to separate them and alienate their love.

   Both the ethos and the magnitude of the original tragedy of love remove it from romantic descendants like *All for Love, or the World Well Lost.* Milton's eloquent gloss on St. Paul's "burning" is fundamental to the human drama of *Paradise Lost*:

What is it then but that desire which God put into Adam in Paradise, before he knew the sin of incontinence; that desire which God saw it was not good that man should be left alone to burn in; the desire and longing to put off an unkindly solitariness by uniting another body, but not without a fit soul to his, in the cheerful society of wedlock? Which if it were so needful before the fall, when man was much more perfect in himself, how much more is it needful now against all the sorrows and casualties of this life, to have an intimate and speaking help, a ready and reviving associate in marriage? Whereof who misses, by chancing on a mute and spiritless mate, remains more alone than before, and in a burning less to be contained than that which is fleshly, and more to be considered; as being more deeply rooted even in the faultless innocence of nature.

Thus solitude or loneliness becomes the basic affliction of human life.

In Book X, before man's Redeemer prepares to mitigate his doom, we are reminded that man's fall was also a test of faith. Now since obedience is love, the appearance of Adam and Eve is revealing (ll. 111 ff.):

> Love was not in thir looks, either to God
> Or to each other, but apparent guilt,
> And shame, and perturbation, and despaire,
> Anger, and obstinacie, and hate, and guile.

Adam blames Eve and is rebuked by Christ; Eve admits her guilt. Man's redemption is concealed in the enigmatic judgment of Satan. Man is to live with pain and sorrow, and eat by the sweat of labor; his death is postponed. Sin and death prepare to extend their reign over the new world. Satan returns to Hell triumphant, only to experience a degradation of form corresponding to his degradation of soul (like Comus's rout) and to become a victim of his own deception.

In his lament (ll. 720 ff.) Adam complains against Providence, yearns for death as an escape, fears that death may be "endless miserie," is torn by the dilemma of the fallen angels. Finally he admits his guilt, and both desires and fears the punishment (ll. 837-39):

> Thus what thou desir'st,
> And what thou fearst, alike destroyes all hope
> Of refuge . . .

His bitter tirade against Eve ends with some general reflections on the misfortunes of love for later men, including Milton. While Adam seeks to shift the blame, Eve strikes the note of true repentance and craves forgiveness; she is ready to bear the punishment for both. Eve's penitence softens Adam, and he professes (ll. 952 ff.)

> If Prayers
> Could alter high Decrees, I to that place
> Would speed before thee, and be louder heard,
> That on my head all might be visited,
> Thy frailtie and infirmer Sex forgiv'n . . .

Adam, however, had exhibited himself as somewhat less firm before his outburst against Eve. His wisdom is more evident when he urges that they strive

> In offices of Love, how we may light'n
> Each others burden in our share of woe;
> Since this days Death denounc't, if ought I see,
> Will prove no sudden, but a slow-pac't evill,
> A long days dying to augment our paine,
> And to our Seed (O hapless Seed!) deriv'd.

Adam's lament is enough to show us how the postponement of death may add to their tragic suffering. This extension of woe prompts Eve to suggest that they remain childless or seek death, Belial's "sad cure." But Adam finds a safer resolution when he realizes that Satan was in the Serpent and that God's sentence depends upon Eve's "Seed." He concludes (ll. 1043 ff.) that Eve's course

> cuts us off from hope, and savours onely
> Rancor and pride, impatience and despite,
> Reluctance against God and his just yoke
> Laid on our Necks.

This is not "the better fortitude / Of Patience and Heroic Martyrdom."

Instead of "immediate dissolution" their doom now has brought them pain in childbirth and the curse of labor, neither the worst of misfortunes. In contrast to Book IX this one ends with the cessation of mutual blame and the beginning of sincere repentance as they

> Repairing where he judg'd them prostrate fell
> Before him reverent, and both confess'd
> Humbly thir faults, and pardon beg'd . . .

Although the Fall threatened to alienate Adam and Eve from each other as well as from God, their moral drama—at least as a mode of "prevenient Grace"—prepared them for divine reconciliation. But the final blow has not yet fallen.

IV

In Book XI God adds the final consequence of man's fall, the loss of Eden. Nature's Law, which Adam has twice criticized, forbids him (ll. 48-52) "longer in that Paradise to dwell," for "Those pure immortal Elements. . . . Eject him tainted now." As God explains, man now finds himself in a new dilemma:

> I at first with two fair gifts
> Created him endowed, with Happiness
> And Immortalitie: that fondly lost,
> This other serv'd but to eternize woe;
> Till I provided Death; so Death becomes
> His final remedie . . .

Now Adam has to learn the meaning of "all our woe," for which sin is the cause and death the relief. Michael, the warrior of Heaven, is sent to exile Adam and Eve; and if they are patient, to dismiss them, "though sorrowing, yet in peace." Eve expresses the state of mind upon which their banishment is to fall (ll. 179-80):

> What can be toilsom in these pleasant Walkes?
> Here let us live, though in fall'n state, content.

Thus exile is to continue the undiminished tragic note: on the human side by Eve, on the theological side by Adam.

If the Vision shows Adam that his exile is not from God, it also shows him that his exile is to a world of sin and death. Indeed the Vision is like a great Morality teaching patience. The operation of original sin introduces the "shapes of death," the wages of sin. After the spectacle of Cain and Abel, Adam cries (l. 462), "But have I now seen Death?" Then Adam learns that temperance leads to painless death. The next spectacle shows what Donne calls "those arts, whence our lives are blest," culminating in "A Beavie of fair Women." This scene pleases Adam (ll. 594 ff.):

> Those were of hate and death, or pain much worse,
> Here Nature seems fulfilled in all her ends.

If these lines emphasize the morality nature of the episodes, Adam's response suggests the original Adam: "Female charm" still "attach'd the heart / Of *Adam*" and earned him another rebuke. For Adam has seen "the Tents / Of wickedness," of Cain's race, who for Donne also were inventors "Of Arts that polish Life." After the next scene Adam, in tears, learns that he has seen War, and Michael stresses the theme of heroic patience by saying (ll. 685-86):

> For in those dayes Might onely shall be admir'd,
> And Valour and Heroic Vertu call'd.

Then a scene of luxury and riot multiplies vice until the Deluge, and Adam exclaims (ll. 759-62):

>   better had I
> Liv'd ignorant of future, so had borne
> My part of evil onely, each dayes lot
> Anough to bear.

Thus Adam learns the burden of "all our woe" as he learns the meaning of death. But the last scene also taught him a lesson about his hope for peace (ll. 779-80):

> But I was farr deceav'd; for now I see
> Peace to corrupt no less then Warr to waste.

If this corruption suggests Belial, Noah as "the onely Son of light / In a dark Age" suggests Abdiel and becomes the means to grace (ll. 886 ff.):

> Such grace shall one just Man find in his sight,
> That he relents, not to blot out mankind . . .

Thus "one just Man" brings "peace from God" and revives Adam by the assurance "that Man shall live." But the assurance of "one greater Man" is still unrevealed.

To this revelation Book XII proceeds. To Adam it is another world in more than one sense:

> Thus thou hast seen one World begin and end;
> And Man as from a second stock proceed.
> Much thou hast yet to see, but I perceave
> Thy mortal sight to faile; objects divine
> Must needs impaire and wearie human sense.

Such matter is beyond Adam's ken and so it is narrated. First Michael represents the origin of tyranny in Nimrod, and extends the doctrine of rational liberty to show how tyranny from without may enslave one who is enthralled by tyranny within. After the extension of tyranny from ethics to politics, Michael epitomizes (ll. 105 ff.):

> Thus will this latter, as the former World,
> Still tend from bad to worse . . .

until God withdraws his presence to "one peculiar Nation," and makes faithful Abraham the promise of a messiah (ll. 147 ff.):

> This ponder, that all Nations of the Earth
> ⸱ Shall in his Seed be blessed; by that Seed
> Is meant thy great deliverer, who shall bruise
> The Serpents head; whereof to thee anon
> Plainlier shall be reveald.

This revelation proceeds by various types of Christ, as sin did by the shapes of death, until Adam understands "Why our great expectation should be call'd / The seed of Woman," but not how the prophecy is to be fulfilled. Finally Adam learns that Christ will save man from death (ll. 394 ff.)

> Not by destroying Satan, but his works
> In thee and in thy Seed: nor can this be,
> But by fulfilling that which thou didst want,
> Obedience to the Law of God, impos'd
> On penaltie of death, and suffering death,
> The penaltie to thy transgression due,
> And due to theirs which out of thine will grow:
> So onely can high Justice rest appaid.

This is the supreme example of "Patience and Heroic Martyrdom" instead of the duel of force which Adam expected. But it is also the supreme example of love:

> The Law of God exact he shall fulfill
> Both by obedience and by love, though love
> Alone fulfill the Law.

This is the New Testament abridgement of the Law for which Donne is thankful in Holy Sonnet XVI, and this is the sacrifice which elicits Adam's wonder at the paradox of his fall—or at God (ll. 470-71)

> That all this good of evil shall produce,
> And evil turn to good.

When Adam asks about the fate of the faithful after Christ ascends to Heaven, Michael returns to the course of original sin, which does not exempt the church but ends with the last judgment (ll. 537 ff.):

> so shall the World goe on,
> To good malignant, to bad men benigne,
> Under her own waight groaning, till the day
> Appeer of respiration to the just,
> And vengeance to the wicked, at return
> Of him so lately promiss'd to thy aid . . .

History had finally taught Milton not to expect in this world "that good men may enjoy the freedom which they merit and the bad the curb which they need."

In Adam's summary of what he has learned from Michael we should notice the repetition of the heroic theme which Milton stated before the Fall (ll. 569 ff.):

> that suffering for Truths sake
> Is fortitude to highest victorie,
> And to the faithful Death the Gate of Life;
> Taught this by his example whom I now
> Acknowledge my Redeemer ever blest.

Thus to the faithful death becomes the gate of life. Michael replies that Adam has now acquired wisdom rather than the knowledge he
                                                    onely add
sought, but adds a further injunction (ll. 581 ff.):

> Deeds to thy knowledge answerable, add Faith,
> Add Vertue, Patience, Temperance, add Love,

> By name to come call'd Charitie, the soul
> Of all the rest: then wilt thou not be loath
> To leave this Paradise, but shalt possess
> A Paradise within thee, happier farr.

Wisdom is not enough, one must add works, and works answerable to the virtues that summarize this wisdom; then the mind will have created a new Paradise instead of the one lost. Meanwhile Eve has been "composed to meek submission" in a dream, unlike the effect of her earlier dream.

Michael's instruction plays a role similar to that of Raphael's, except that it ends with the wisdom necessary for the world and a happy ending. The purpose of the last two books is to unfold the consequences of the Fall—again as moral preparation, but this time for the loss of Eden and happiness, though with the ultimate hope of a happy ending. Both books bring home the meaning of Adam's doom or judgment, which he has not understood, and both prepare him for new trials. They develop the tragedy of his loss of Eden or happiness, not least by giving perspective to that loss. Adam's new awareness adds to his martyrdom as much as to his ultimate hope. Finally, these revelations themselves become a trial of patience for his dismissal from Eden.

Adam and Eve depart in mingled hope and sadness:

> They looking back, all th' Eastern side beheld
> Of Paradise, so late thir happie seat,
> Wav'd over by that flaming Brand, the Gate
> With dreadful Faces throng'd and fierie Armes.

The aspect of justice is obvious in this scene, but it does not inhibit grief:

> Som natural tears they drop'd, but wip'd them soon;
> The World was all before them, where to choose
> Thir place of rest, and Providence thir guide:
> They hand in hand with wandring steps and slow,
> Through *Eden* took thir solitarie way.

This prospect, "The World was all before them," could bring no quickening to Adam's heart, and though Providence was their guide, their steps were wandering and slow. The last two lines epitomize their tragedy; "their solitary way" touches a basic human need, emphasizes their loss of society, which Adam feared might include God, and describes their exile to an alien world alone but mutually supported. Thus Adam enters upon the life of Everyman in a world of woe, where he must prove himself. We must not forget that the action of the poem ends with paradise lost, and that the "relations" of the poem are subordinate to that action and its characters.

NOTE

[EDITOR's NOTE. On Paradise see C. M. Coffin, *ELH*, XXIX (1962), 1-18; F. Manly, *MLN*, LXXVI (1961), 398-403; H. Schultz, *Milton and Forbidden Knowledge*, 1955; R. M. Frye, *SRen*, II (1955), 148-59; R. H. West, *Milton and the Angels*, 1955; J. B. Broadbent, *MP*, LI (1954), 160-67; J. H. Summers, *PMLA*, LXVII (1954), 251-61; A. Stein, *Admirable Style*, 1953; E. M. W. Tillyard, *Studies in Milton*, 1951; I. Samuel, *PMLA*, LXIV (1949), 708-23, and *JEGP*, LXIII (1964), 441-9; W. Haller, *ELH*, XIII (1946), 79-87; W. and M. Haller, *HLQ*, V (1942), 235-72; on Eve, M. A. N. Radzinowicz in *Reason and the Imagination*, ed. J. A. Mazzeo, 1962; D. D. Miller, *JEGP*, LXI (1962), 542-7; D. A. Day, *TSLL*, III (1961), 369-81; D. C. Allen, *MLN*, LXXV (1960), 108-9; W. B. Hunter, Jr., *ELH*, XIII (1946), 255-65, and *MLQ*, IX (1948), 255-65.]

H. V. S. OGDEN

The Crisis of *Paradise Lost* Reconsidered

Six years ago Dr. E. M. W. Tillyard's "The Crisis of *Paradise Lost*" appeared, and more recently Mrs. Millicent Bell's "The Fallacy of the Fall in *Paradise Lost*" has followed.[1] Both offer an intepretation of the poem based on the fact that Adam and Eve are not "perfect" before the Fall. From this premise Dr. Tillyard and Mrs. Bell develop theories about the structure of the poem which are not, I think, tenable, in spite of some valuable insights which their essays contain. Stated broadly, their thesis is that Adam and Eve are really "fallen" before the Fall, that consequently the Fall itself is not the crisis of the poem, but that instead the regeneration of Adam and Eve in Book X is the culminating event around which the poem is organized. I shall try to show that Adam and Eve, though not perfect before the Fall, are by no means already "fallen," that the Fall is the central theological event in the poem, and that it is likewise the climax of the narrative.

I

Dr. Tillyard's interpretation rests in the first place on the assumption that according to the "bare story" and to Milton's theological belief,

From *Philological Quarterly*, XXXVI (1957), 1-19. Reprinted by permission of the author and the publisher.

Adam and Eve were innocent and sinless and therefore perfect until the moment of eating the apple. Secondly, it rests on the valid premise that in the poem Adam and Eve are imperfect before the Fall; witness the episodes of Eve's dream, Adam's confession of an idealizing love for Eve in Book VIII, and the separation of the two at the beginning of Book IX. There is then, he argues, a discrepancy between narrative and belief, and he holds that the discrepancy is the result of Milton's need to "present in ample narrative the transition from a state of innocence to a state of sin" (p. 10). A handling of the change from innocence to sin with the abruptness called for by Milton's alleged theological belief "would have been sudden and violent and would have carried no conviction." So Milton gives us a different handling: "Instead he resorts to some faking: perfectly legitimate in a poem, yet faking nevertheless. He anticipates the Fall by attributing to Eve and Adam feelings which though nominally felt in the state of innocence are actually not compatible with it" (pp. 10-11).

It would be difficult and unrewarding to argue the validity of the assumptions about Milton and about poetry which underlie the conception of faking. And it is not at all necessary, since there is no discrepancy between Milton's real belief and the narrative. Milton is no more faking than St. Augustine was in the *City of God:*

> Our first parents fell into open disobedience because already they were secretly corrupted; for the evil act had never been done had not an evil will preceded it. And what is the origin of our evil will but pride? For "pride is the beginning of sin." And what is pride but the craving for undue exaltation? and this is undue exaltation, when the soul abandons Him to whom it ought to cleave as its end, and becomes a kind of end to itself. This happens when it becomes its own satisfaction. And it does so when it falls away from that unchangeable good which ought to satisfy it more than itself. This falling away is spontaneous; for if the will had remained steadfast in the love of that higher and changeless good by which it was illumined to intelligence and kindled into love, it would not have turned away to find satisfaction in itself, and so become frigid and benighted; the woman would not have believed the serpent spoke the truth, nor would the man have preferred the request of his wife to the command of God, nor have supposed that it was a venial transgression to cleave to the partner of his life even

in a partnership of sin. The wicked deed, then . . . was committed by persons who were already wicked.[2]

The issue of faking depends on what the terms *sinless* and *innocent* mean. For Dr. Tillyard they mean *perfect,* though he does not use this word. What is needed is some such distinction as that which St. Augustine makes between the evil will which precedes the act and the evil act itself. As a glance at the concordance shows, Milton repeatedly says that Adam and Eve are *sinless, innocent, upright,* and *pure* before the Fall. Dr. Tillyard himself points out that Eve is called *sinless* as late as IX, 659 ("To whom thus *Eve* yet sinless"), when she has already been led by Satan to the Tree. Clearly Milton does not mean by these terms that Adam and Eve are perfect. He does mean that although they are liable to temptation and although their wills may be attracted to what the temptation offers, they are innocent and upright, sinless and pure, until their conscious minds yield and they commit the act of disobedience. Dr. Tillyard quotes the crucial passage (V, 117-119) relevant to this (from Adam's reassuring statement to Eve after her dream), but apparently denies its application. Eve consciously rejects (or seems to do so) the evil which Satan (and Satan alone) has poured into her mind: "but O how glad I wak'd to find this but a dream!" Thus she remains sinless and innocent. That is, she remains free to reject evil in the future, and specifically to reject the germ of temptation which Satan has left in her "fancy." And so she remains free to attain that degree of true self-knowledge and of knowledge of the divine order and its creator which would constitute her perfecting, i.e. her confirmation in love of and obedience to God which is the purpose of the testing process. As we read the episode, we readily see the dream both as narrative foreshadowing of the Fall and as a psychological step toward it. If, however, Eve had availed herself of her unimpaired freedom and rejected the explicit temptation in Book IX, we would see the dream as a step in Satan's defeat and in Eve's spiritual growth. So with Adam's inordinate love of Eve; the subsequent event determines our perspective. Dr. Tillyard assumes (p. 12) that innocence and experience are incompatible opposites in the poem; but experience could have strengthened innocence and confirmed rectitude as readily as in the event it destroyed them. The great significance of the Fall is that it is not reversible by human effort or action. Up until the overt act, Adam and Eve could have changed their minds. But once the evil act had sealed the evil will, Man could only be redeemed by Christ's Incarnation and Crucifixion. If Milton meant what he repeatedly said (e.g. I, 2-3; III, 92-95; IX, 5-13) and what all Christians have believed, the Fall was the great moral turning-point for Adam and Eve and for human history as well. We shall consider below whether it is the turning-point, i.e. the "crisis," of the narrative.

Mrs. Bell finds no faking in *Paradise Lost,* since she believes that the handling of the narrative reveals Milton's "real" beliefs as opposed to his stated views. (The faking, presumably, is in the *De doctrina Christiana.*) Her argument runs as follows. The Fall is causeless, because perfect beings could have no motive to fall. According to the "myth" and to theological opinion (including Milton's), unfallen Adam and Eve represent the "absoluteness of perfection" (p. 863). Since Milton could not find a cause for the Fall and since he wholly accepted the Bible account, he unwittingly took psychological causes from Fallen Man and used them in depicting the supposedly unfallen couple in the development leading up to the Fall. Adam and Eve, she says, came to the formal temptation in Book IX "mature in the possession of every passion" (p. 876); in them on that occasion "human nature is shown in its full complexity of motivation" (p. 873). Consequently the Fall is only apparent. "There is, in effect, no longer a Fall as the Bible plot presents it—there is, possibly, no longer a Fall at all" (p. 867). It follows that the Fall cannot be the climax of the poem; instead the climax comes with the reconciliation of Adam and Eve in Book X.

What evidence does Mrs. Bell offer that Adam and Eve were perfect before the Fall? Three pages of Mr. Arnold Williams's *The Common Expositor* are cited;[3] on these three pages one finds what various commentators said about the extent of Adam's knowledge, especially about his knowledge as demonstrated in naming the animals, and the upshot is that "some commentators were as anxious to whittle down the sum of Adam's knowledge as apparently the early hexamerists had been to augment it." This is all irrelevant to Adam's moral perfection. The part of Mr. Williams's book which is relevant is the summary of what commentators said on Genesis I, xxvii: "So God created man in his own image." Here if anywhere one would expect the commentators to assert man's original absolute perfection; Mr. Williams does not record that any of them do.[4] Mrs. Bell's second reference is to Mr. Merritt Hughes's introduction to his edition of *Paradise Lost.*[5] Here one finds quoted a passage from Joseph Glanvill's *Vanity of*

Dogmatizing, in which Glanvill says that God furnished Adam "with all those accomplishments which his specifick capacity could contain" and in which he goes on to expatiate on Adam's excellences. Mr. Hughes's conclusions are that Milton shared "this general conception" with Glanvill, although "he certainly did not follow Glanvill in his amazing claims about 'the circumference of our Protoplast's senses.'" He also says, as Mrs. Bell points out: "In contrast with speculation about Adam like Glanvill's, Milton imagined his Adam a very human sort of person in Eden." Nor does her third reference, Milton's *De doctrina Christiana,* substantiate the claim for perfection. Book I, chapter vii, is cited as a whole. There are only two short passages in chapter vii which are directly relevant:

> We may understand from other passages of Scripture, that when God infused the breath of life into man, what man thereby received was not a portion of God's essence, or a participation of the divine nature, but that measure of the divine virtue or influence, which was commensurate to the capabilities of the recipient.
>
> Man being formed after the image of God, it followed as a necessary consequence that he should be endued with natural wisdom, holiness, and righteousness. Gen. i, 27. . . . Certainly without extraordinary wisdom he could not have given names to the whole animal creation with such sudden intelligence. Gen. ii, 20.[6]

Nothing that is said here means that Adam was created perfect. A longer passage at the beginning of Book I, chapter x, contains statements which further define Milton's conception of Man's original excellence:

> With regard to that which relates to man in his state of rectitude, God, having placed him in the garden of Eden, and furnished him with whatever was calculated to make life happy, commanded him, as a test of his obedience, to refrain from eating of the single tree of knowledge of good and evil . . . .
> For since it was the disposition of man to do what was right, as a being naturally good and holy, it was not necessary that he should be bound by the obligation of a covenant to perform that to which he was of himself inclined . . . .
> Seeing, however, that man was made in the image of God,

and had the whole law of nature so implanted and innate in him, that he needed no precept to enforce its observance, it follows, that if he received any additional commands, whether respecting the tree of knowledge, or the institution of marriage, these commands formed no part of the law of nature, which is sufficient of itself to teach whatever is agreeable to right reason, that is to say, whatever is intrinsically good.[7]

These passages sum up half of Milton's belief about Adam's state before the Fall, and there is nothing in them which means that Adam was perfect in an absolute sense. The other half (so to speak) of Milton's belief, and this is what Mrs. Bell's and Dr. Tillyard's theories lead them to ignore, is stated briefly near the beginning of chapter xi of Book I of the De doctrina Christiana:

This sin originated, first, in the instigation of the devil, as is clear from the narrative in Gen. iii and from 1 John iii.8. "he that committeth sin is of the devil, for the devil sinneth from the beginning." Secondly, in the liability to fall with which man was created, whereby he, as the devil had done before him, "abode not in the truth," John viii.44. nor "kept his first estate, but left his own habitation," Jude 6.[8]

According to the treatise, then, the original state of rectitude included the liability to sin. This is clear in another passage, in which the term *perfection* is used of the unfallen state:

. . . God preserves neither angels, nor men, nor any other part of the creation absolutely, but always with reference to the condition of his decree. For he preserves mankind, since their spontaneous fall, and all other things with them, only so far as regards their existence, and not as regards their primitive perfection.[9]

That is, the original perfection of fallen creatures was not an absolute perfection; they were liable to a "spontaneous fall" [*sua sponte lapsos*]. As Miss Ruth Mohl has shown, Milton always conceives of perfection in the De doctrina Christiana as relative, that is, as admitting of degrees.[10]

But what of the poem itself? The basic passage is in God's first speech in Book III: "I made him just and right, Sufficient to have stood, though free to fall" (ll. 98-99), and the following lines, in which God speaks of the angels but (by clear implication) of Adam also. The term *perfect* is used of Adam twice in the poem, both times by Raphael in warning speeches (V, 524, and VIII, 642) and both times very clearly in a qualified sense, meaning perfectly able to make the right choice, i.e. "sufficient to have stood." The context makes this quite clear, and there is nothing in *Paradise Lost* to justify the conviction that the fable of that poem is founded on the "donnée of Man's inconceivable perfection" (p. 868).

Because of her concept of pre-lapsarian perfection, Mrs. Bell is led to ask: what cause could bring about a change from such a state? With her premise, there can be but one answer: none. Hence Milton, she goes on to argue, imputed to Adam and Eve the feelings and motives of fallen man. Milton was unaware of what he was about, because of his unquestioning faith in the authority of Scripture; he fell into a "confusion of cause with result" (p. 864). The confusion is not Milton's. The causes of the Fall, as Milton stated them in a passage quoted above, lay in Satan's "instigation" and in Adam's and Eve's "liability" to fall. This, however, is not the answer wanted; the question really is, what were the psychological causes of the Fall? Mrs. Bell's answer to this question is quite right (though not her further inference): there was no psychological cause. Adam's and Eve's state was such that they were free to choose; that is, they were free from causal influence, from all cause-effect sequences. This is what St. Augustine means (in the passage quoted above) by saying "This falling away is spontaneous."[11] This is what Milton means in referring to their "spontaneous fall" in the *De doctrina Christiana*. This is what he had meant in a passage written many years earlier, in *The Doctrine and Discipline of Divorce,* where he says that "man's own freewill self-corrupted is the adequate and sufficient cause of his disobedience *besides* [i.e. outside of] *Fate*."[12] But it does not follow that because Milton held the Fall to be causeless, he attributed any or all imperfections to Man before the Fall, so that Man came to the Temptation in Book IX "already fallen" (p. 878).

With the demand that the poem present us with a plausible psychological description of the change from innocence to the fallen state no one will disagree. And Milton has given it to us, largely in those passages which Dr. Tillyard and Mrs. Bell point to: Eve's seeing her reflection in the water (IV, 460-466), Eve's account of her dream (V, 28-128), Raphael's warning to Adam against the pursuit of improper knowledge (VIII, 1-202), Adam's confession of a tendency toward inordinate love of Eve (VIII, 521-617), and the separation scene at the beginning of Book IX.[13] The issue is whether they are right in finding in these passages evidences of "feelings which though nominally felt in the state of innocence are actually not compatible with it" and of an unfallen Man who is "congenitally Man as we know him, subject to temptations and excesses."[14] Assuming the liberty of reading into Adam's and Eve's behavior before the Fall whatever motives and feelings he wishes, Dr. Tillyard does not hesitate to "attribute to Milton's treatment of Adam's and Eve's psychology a subtlety not usually allowed" (p. 14), e.g. "the pair were still in the honeymoon stage, and the last thing Eve really wanted was to be separated even for a morning from her lover. So she lays a mild trap for Adam. . . . Adam, after the manner of men when sleepy or not at their best, falls into the trap. . . ." Mrs. Bell's account of the episode is similar: "Provoked by the barbs beneath her 'sweet austere composure' and 'accent sweet,' he finally does go more penetratingly into the dangers . . . , but it is really too late—Eve has managed to arouse in herself a small head of willful steam. And Adam, at the very climax of his most forceful argument, suddeny collapses—perhaps, though Milton doesn't tells us so, it is the look on her face which is responsible."

Fortunately Mr. Arnold Stein's recent analysis of the steps leading up to the Fall makes a detailed consideration unnecessary here.[15] Where Dr. Tillyard and Mrs. Bell find imperfection, Mr. Stein finds what he calls *gestures*. The metaphor makes all the difference, since it implies (what Mr. Stein also makes explicit) that there is a distinction between the liability to sin and the commission, between potentiality and actuality, between the beginnings of an evil will and the completion of an evil act. The gestures involve Eve's tentative self-love and Adam's tentative inordinate love of Eve; though both of these are closely connected with their attitudes toward knowledge, there are no other sins foreshadowed.[16] Where Mrs. Bell finds Milton guilty of "blurring the transition from innocence to experience" (p. 867), Mr. Stein shows us how carefully Milton has worked out the complicated process and how deliberately he has chosen his images to reveal the inner nature of Adam's and Eve's spiritual testing and fall.[17] The gestures are steps in the testing process, steps toward trial and temptation, but not necessarily steps toward sin.[18] Only in the explicit temptation of Book IX do Adam's and Eve's conscious minds contemplate the positive choice of a forbidden "good"; consequently they first sin here. The eating of the fruit is an external act overtly breaking the prohibition, and it is consequently irreversible. The inner developments which, temporally and in terms of narrative discourse, lead up to the overt act, are reversible; the mind is "its own place," a place of freedom until it (of itself) surrenders its autonomy.

II

If the Fall is the great moral and theological turning-point of the poem, is it likewise the narrative climax? Is it, to use Sir Walter Raleigh's metaphor, the point from which the whole plot "radiates," so that "there is not an incident, hardly a line of the poem . . . but leads backwards or forwards to those central lines in the Ninth Book"? If we find, upon examination, that everything in the poem before the Fall points toward that event and that everything after it proceeds from it and looks back to it, and if it appears further that the reconciliation of Adam and Eve and their partial regeneration in Book X is not even the climactic event of the narrative after the Fall, much less the event around which the whole poem is organized, our question will have been sufficiently answered in the affirmative.

Why then does the poem begin with Satan's awakening in Hell? Because that is, in fact, the beginning of "the instigation of the devil." The story of the Fall of Man begins when Satan collects his forces and organizes his campaign against Mankind. The earlier events, to be related in Books V-VIII, create the necessary antecedent conditions for the Temptation and Fall, but they are not an integral part of those events. Beginning with Satan's recovery, the flow of narrative from Book I on into Book V is unbroken; the account of the Council in Heaven, simultaneous with the events it discusses, is no interruption. As a result of this straight sweep of narrative, the poet creates suspense. Not surprise, which depends on our ignorance of what is to come, but the suspense of all great epic and tragic poetry, where, knowing the nature of the outcome, we see disaster loom up and envelop the hero. Though we cherish hope, we are gripped less by uncertainty than by fear—and then by pity. Satan revives, collects his host, decides upon revenge, escapes from Hell, ascends through Chaos, comes to the Universe, to the Earth, to Eden, to Paradise, to Adam and Eve. Each step brings him closer to his intended prey and heightens the sense of impending danger.

A consequence of beginning the poem in Hell is that Adam and Eve are kept off the stage. If our concern for them is to be paramount, we must no lose sight of them. The poet, therefore, repeatedly reminds us that this is a poem about the Fall, that Adam and Eve are the victims of a malignant assault, and that our welfare is involved in theirs. He alludes to man and to human suffering repeatedly in Book I: even the catalogue of Fallen Angels contains indirect reminders of the human misery which the Fall will entail. He refers directly to the Fall itself, not only in the opening lines (I, 1-4 and 28-33) but again in line 219. But most important is the series of references to Man beginning with Satan's disclosure, ironically ambiguous, that he knows of a new "generation" (I, 651-653). Next Beelzebub, in the climactic speech of the Council in Hell, names Man specifically and outlines the whole program of attack (II, 345-385). Then Satan communicates to Sin and Death his mission against the "race of upstart creatures," and Death grins a "ghastly smile, to hear His famine should be filled." And at the end of Book II (1023-1033), the poet himself reminds us of the coming triumph of Sin and Death over Man. The suspense created is the product of Satan's character, of his actual progress, and of his assertions of intent, combined with the poet's foretelling his coming success.

The scene in Heaven which follows establishes the framework within which the whole action takes place. From mankind's point of view, God's severity is the proper response to Satan's campaign; his sternness is an aspect of Man's hope. More than this, the poet uses God's severity to heighten our sense of Christ's love. His justice is the occasion of Christ's mercy, and God is severe precisely in order to give Christ's love the opportunity to manifest itself resplendently. The Father and the Son exhibit a conscious mutual deference; the pattern of their speeches is like that of a dance, a dance expressing perfect love. Moreover, the clear contrast between Satan and Christ here further exalts Christ's glory.

Central as Christ is to Milton's theology, however, the poem is about Adam and Eve, and the scene in Heaven, like the preceding scenes in Hell, is so handled as to focus our attention on Man (see III, 64-69) and on the Fall (III, 92). In Books I and II Man was seen as Satan's intended prey. Now he is seen in his role of chooser; he is not necessarily the victim, he is the doer. Everything, we learn from the divine colloquy, depends on Man's choice. He is, in fact, the central concern of the divine interlocutors; each of their speeches, from God's first declaration of Man's imminent trial to Christ's promise of offered salvation, turns directly on Man's fate. Thus the continuity of the narrative and the growing suspense of Satan's campaign are not interrupted.

We return, in consequence, to the account of Satan's progress with an established sense of the central position of Man in this story. Satan meets Uriel in the Sun, and expresses an "unspeakable desire" to see and know all of God's new creation, "but chiefly Man"; he dwells on Man for some twelve lines (III, 663-674). Uriel's reply, which begins with a statement of the proper attitude toward the knowledge of God's creation, ends with a clear direction to Paradise: "That spot to which I point is *Paradise,* Adams abode" (III, 733-734). For the first time in the poem Adam is named, and, ominously, he is named to Satan.

The building of suspense continues in Book IV, where Milton alternates the moods of hope and fear as he gives the stage alternately to Adam and Eve and to Satan. Satan's campaign now takes on its final form: "I will excite their Minds With more desire to know, and to reject Envious commands" (IV, 522-524). The book ends with hope predominant in the clash between Satan and Gabriel. The encounter makes clear to Satan (and to us) the limitations of his campaign. In Book II Beelzebub had hoped to lay waste or conquer the new Creation by force (II, 362-370); in Book III (90-92) God had implied that force would be forbidden and in Book V (242-243) he will say so directly. God's purpose being to test Adam's and Eve's obedience, he will permit no infringement of free choice. Satan and Gabriel confront each other, and, recognizing Gabriel's superior power, manifest in the trappings of war and revealed in the image of the heavenly scales, Satan flees. Again the action is directed to the coming temptation and Fall.

Eve's account of her dream, with which Book V opens, reveals her potential weakness. Eve has been the victim of an assault none the less real because it is mental not physical. We readers have already learned that Gabriel protects Adam and Eve where they cannot protect themselves. The dream, and especially the innocent placid quality of Adam's reassurance to Eve (V, 95-128) and of the prayer which follows (V, 153-208), make clear that they are in urgent need of the information which we have, that they must be warned of the campaign now launched against them. Neither of them is aware of the existence of Fallen Angels, much less of the presence of an enemy in Paradise. Consequently the main narrative function of the long middle portion of the poem, from Book V, 219, to the end of Book VI, and in part on to the end of Book VIII, is the warning and admonishment of Adam and Eve. Throughout this middle portion we are never allowed to lose sight of the human pair. Till now our fears have been aroused chiefly through Satan's threats; from now on they arise mainly from friendly warnings. Every time Adam is warned, we remember that the warning is to be in vain. Like Satan's speeches, they point to the Fall.

Raphael does not utter his first warning until he has suggested the nature of Man's future if Adam remains obedient (V, 496-503). The climactic warning comes at the end of Book VI. Only then does Adam learn of Satan's presence in Paradise:

> . . . he who envies now thy state,
> Who now is plotting how he may seduce
> Thee also from obedience . . . .
>
> (VI, 900-902)

What follows is the account of the Creation, and though the pull of hope and fear is somewhat relaxed, we are not allowed to lose our sense of coming disaster. The account begins with a passage of direct foreshadowing (VII, 40-50), and Raphael not only reasserts the prohibition against eating the fruit of the Tree of Knowledge (VII, 542-47) but also hints again of Man's happy future if he does not fall (VII, 630-32). In Book VIII the tension is gradually heightened. Its opening, presenting the discussion of the solar system and of the proper kind of knowledge, reveals a significant change in Adam's state of mind. Heretofore his requests to Raphael for information had been altogether such as Raphael approved. Now Adam questions the wisdom of Divine order:

> . . . in all thir [i.e. the heavenly bodies'] vast survey
> Useless besides, reasoning I oft admire,
> How Nature wise and frugal could commit
> Such disproportions, with superfluous hand
> So many nobler Bodies to create . . . .
>
> (VIII, 24-28)

Raphael warns Adam against the spiritual error underlying this attitude (VIII, 61-128), and Adam accepts the rebuke, but we are prepared for further revelations of weakness. This we meet in Adam's own account of his potentially inordinate love of Eve, first intimated in lines 471-477 and explicitly stated in lines 546-559. Thus Book VIII begins the intensification of suspense which is to culminate in Book IX.

Though we have not been allowed to forget Satan in Books VII and VIII, he has not been present in the action. Now at the beginning of Book IX we encounter him directly, and our awareness of his presence remains through the whole episode of Adam's and Eve's separation. His attack on Eve's fancy has come to infect her will; we realize the Fall itself is imminent. Adam, however, shows little of his potential desire for improper knowledge or inordinate love which he has betrayed in Book VIII. His last speech to Eve (IX, 343-375) states the proper attitude toward knowledge and shows a right understanding of his present external situation. But when he says that "within himself The danger lies, yet lies within his power," he suggests that he does not really understand his own inner state of mind; he has grasped the principle but not its full implication for himself. The explicit emphasis, however, is on Eve's more developed inordinacy and on her greater vulnerability.

In handling the Fall itself, Milton is confronted with a difficult narrative problem, that of the complex climax. He must tell of Eve's fall, show how it leads up to Adam's fall, and then relate Adam's fall so that it will not be repetition or anti-climax. It is as though Homer were committed to telling how Achilles killed two Hectors in one day; or as though Othello were made to kill Desdemona and then another woman equally essential to the plot. Broadly speaking Milton's solution is to proceed from mounting fear, to present dismay, to pity. He makes Eve's temptation and fall the climax of our fear, just as it is the climax of Satan's campaign. Satan attacks Eve's mind directly, and speech by speech the dreadful anticipation mounts. When Eve eats the fruit, our suspense is relaxed as our fear gives way to dismay.

In leading up to Adam's fall, Milton does nothing to build suspense anew; he does not work upon our hopes and fears as to Adam's coming decision. Eve's soliloquy (IX, 795-833) reveals the present evil, the rapid falling off from her former love, the effect of disobedience and false knowledge on her mind. Her speech to Adam (IX, 856-885) can only add to our sense of present dismay. Moreover Milton does nothing to evoke our pity until the brief description of the grief-stricken Adam (IX, 888-895); then the effect is overwhelming. Adam's soliloquy (IX, 896-916), uttered to himself after hearing out Eve's speech, is the great climax of dismay and pity to which the long preparation of suspense has led us. Its economy is tremendous. Adam voices the pity and sorrow which we in our lesser degree feel, even while he reveals his yielding state of mind in terms of his pity for Eve. His pity here is a reflection of his inordinate love and ultimately of his misdirected knowledge. But it is also much more than that, because his love for Eve is more than merely inordinate love. That is what it will become (briefly) after the Fall, but for the moment, all potentially inordinate developments to the contrary notwithstanding, Adam's love for Eve is what remains of their unfallen union. Adam's choice seems to him to be one between obedience to God and love of Eve; this is a choice between two such goods as are beyond easy conception, and his predicament seems tragic. And in the choice of Eve there seems to be an element of nobility, for Adam makes his choice in the knowledge of a loyalty forsaken and a penalty incurred. The tragic note is enforced by the two underlying ironies: Adam chooses to save his relationship to Eve, but her choice has already made their unfallen union irredeemable—at least by anything that Adam can do; and secondly, the Eve he chooses is partly the false image of Eve he has created in his mind. As Adam reveals his love and pity and sense of tragic doom in his inward utterance, our dismay and sorrow mount to the highest level of intensity in the poem. But in his following speech (IX, 921-959) he begins to lose his tragic stature. We know that he says what he says not because he thinks it is true but because he knows it will please Eve, and we include him in our pity as he utters sentiments which are intellectually invalid and which reveal the working of his false knowledge and his inordinate love.

The poem has now reached its great turning-point; the mortal sin has been completed:

> Earth trembl'd from her entrails, as again
> In pangs, and Nature gave a second groan,
> Skie lowr'd, and muttering Thunder, some sad drops
> Wept at compleating of the mortal Sin
> Original . . . .
>
> (IX, 1000-1004)

The forward drive of the narrative no longer comes from our dread of a coming event but from our concern with the results of the Fall and from our desire for Adam's and Eve's reconciliation with God. There is anticipation here, but we look forward not to a catastrophe but to final peace. The immediate effects of the Fall (not its continuation) and God's first counter-measures are related in the remainder of Book IX and Book X, the remote and ultimately more important effects and counter-measures in Books XI and XII. The first effect on Adam and Eve themselves may be called the transmutation of the spirit to flesh (the opposite process to that which Raphael had described in V, 496-99). From spiritual union they fall to physical union (IX, 1011-1145), and their ensuing quarrel is the measure of their loss.

Book X begins with the reception of the Fall in Heaven. God speaks, reasserting the principle of freedom and the irreversibility of the Fall, and sends Christ to impose judgment. The judgments bring home their guilt to both Adam and Eve, and are thus the prelude to their redemption. Without conviction of guilt there can be no repentance; the judgment itself is part of God's mercy. The judgment of the serpent is "oracular," and all three judgments, since they raise questions that Adam and Eve need answered, call for and look forward to the exposition of the future in Books XI and XII.

The process of the regeneration of Adam and Eve, which begins with the judgment, culminates at the end of Book XII. The first result of the judgment, however, is that Adam is in complete misery. He is cut off from God and anticipates nothing but a future of "endless woes" for himself and his posterity. His long speech (X, 720-844) shows that he needs to know of the possibility of establishing a new relationship with God and of participating in God's great plan of salvation. In addition the speech reveals that Adam accepts the justice of the judgment. (In this respect the speech is in pointed contrast to Satan's parallel utterance in Book IX, 33-113.) Adam admits God's justice and is therefore eligible (though he does not know it) for divine help. This is immediately given:

> . . . for from the Mercie-seat above
> Prevenient Grace descending had remov'd
> The stonie from thir hearts. . . .
>
> (XI, 2-4)

These lines are the poet's comment on the action of this part of Book X; they may serve as a corrective to Dr. Tillyard's conception: "And what issues out of it all? Something that initially looks like bathos: two ordinary human beings in despair, divided, and then coming together in ordinary human decency" (p. 43). God's grace comes to both, but is manifest first in Eve. She is in the presence of her hierarchical superior and can ask for help and forgiveness directly. Adam, however, has cut himself off from God's presence, and is not yet ready to turn to God in prayer. Instead he turns upon Eve and reviles her and womankind, giving expression (in part) to his sense of overwhelming loss in the deterioration of their relationship. What we must remember here is not Mary Powell (that is fatal!), but their unfallen relationship in Books IV and V. The denunciation (X, 867-908) is Eve's present test of obedience. This time her loyalty to Adam stands unshaken, and building upon it she brings him in turn to manifest the workings of God's grace in forgiving her. For Dr. Tillyard, their reconciliation is not only the climax of the episode but of the whole poem: "For all the importance of the penitence, it is on the reconciliation that the fullest structural emphasis falls: in it Milton seems to have centered the most intimate significance of his poem. He has, in the actual poem, in his manipulation of his poetic material, carefully led everything up to this reconciliation" (p. 42). Nothing which Dr. Tillyard has adduced demonstrates this thesis nor the anthropocentric premise underlying it. Actually the reconciliation here is not even the climax of the episode, since Adam's and Eve's relationship to each other is less important than (and is dependent upon) their relationship to God. The prayer with which Book X ends is the climax of the episode, but the episode itself is only part of the larger line of narrative which began with the Fall and which culminates at the end of the poem.

Adam and Eve pray in repentance, but they do not yet understand God's ways to Man nor Christ's offer of salvation. Until they understand these things and until they know the answers to the questions raised in Christ's judgments and in Adam's speeches at the end of Book X, their earthly redemption will be partial. They will understand neither the scope of the disaster they have caused, nor the meaning of the Incarnation, the Resurrection, the New Law, and the Last Day. Above all, being ignorant of Christ's love and sacrifice, they will lack the great examplar of obedience. The new knowledge which they are about to be given compensates for the right knowledge which they threw away and redeems them from the false knowledge which they tried to get. Without the confirmation of renewed obedience based on this knowledge, Adam and Eve will not achieve that mood of reconciliation and of peace with which the poem, both for them and for us, must close.

Book XI continues the process of establishing Man's new and more

distant relationship to God, a relationship of which the ejection from
Paradise is the symbol. The opening scene in Heaven (XI, 14-125),
recalling the parallel scene in Book III, again shows God's justice as
the occasion of Christ's love, though now, in view of Adam's and
Eve's repentance, God's tone is milder. Michael's speeches, so much
less intimate than Raphael's though evincing an equal concern for
Adam's and Eve's welfare, exhibit the estrangement while they fore-
tell the coming salvation. Beginning with the murder of Abel and the
Cave of Death, Adam's vision of human history up to the Flood
brings home to him the misery he has caused. He sees the results of
the Fall stretching out into the future, in order that he may comprehend the significance of the prophecy which follows in Book XII.

The handling of human history in the vision in Book XI is relatively full; the pace is adapted both to the purpose of teaching Adam
the results of the Fall and to his interest in his more immediate posterity. In the prophecy in Book XII the pace is accelerated, partly
perhaps in accommodation to Adam's personal remoteness from the
events but mainly to focus his mind on the great steps of the process
which begins with the Old Law. The Crucifixion, the Resurrection,
the Last Judgment are the climactic events of the prophecy, but they
are related economically. This is a poem about Adam and Eve, not
about Christ. Michael ends the account of these events with a triumphant statement of future bliss:

> . . . to reward
> His faithful, and receave them into bliss
> Whether in Heav'n or Earth, for then the Earth
> Shall be all Paradise, far happier place
> Then this of *Eden,* and far happier daies.
> (XII, 461-465)

Happier for whom? Not for the Fallen Angels, nor yet for the ma-
jority of mankind, but for those who are saved. And at what cost?
Milton has emphasized Christ's sacrifice repeatedly, and though he
does not stress Christ's passion, he does not ignore it (XII, 411-415).
Adam's response to this speech is his enthusiastic ejaculation of the
Paradox of the Fortunate Fall. This must be read in its context, where
it is dramatically appropriate. Having been shown the misery he has
caused, Adam has suddenly been told that for some there will be
salvation and eternal happiness and that God's ways are just and
merciful. His outburst is partly relief, partly amazement, partly love.

And it must be insisted (as Professor Lovejoy himself has remarked)[19] that Adam does not assert that the Fall was fortunate; he says he is in doubt:

> . . . full of doubt I stand,
> Whether I should repent me now of sin
> By mee done and occasiond, or rejoyce
> Much more, that much more good thereof shall spring,
> To God more glory, more good will to Men
> From God, and over wrauth grace shall abound.
>
> (XII, 473-478)

Clearly the "much more good" that is to ensue is God's goodness, and Adam's only cause for rejoicing is that his sin will have been the occasion and opportunity for God's goodness. There is nothing here which states or implies that Man's lot is or will be better than if Adam and Eve had not fallen. Presumably Adam's doubt is allayed in the sobering account which follows, as Michael's recital exhibits the dominance of evil in human affairs from the time of the early Christian Church until the Last Day.

Michael's last prophetic speech ends with his second declaration of the eternity of bliss for the saved, and Adam responds with his majestic assertion of the principle of obedience (XII, 553-573). This is the consummation of Adam's earthly regeneration which began in Book X; only now has he the knowledge of Christ in whom his faith is to center, and only now has he the great exemplar of obedience and love which he is to follow. This is abundantly clear in Michael's next speech. If Adam learns the lesson of proper knowledge and obedience, Michael says, and if he adds faith, virtue, patience, temperance, and love "the soul of all the rest,"

> *then* wilt thou not be loath
> To leave this Paradise, but shalt possess
> A Paradise within thee, happier far.
>
> (XII, 585-587)

It is sometimes, apparently, assumed that these lines mean that Adam will be happier after leaving the Garden of Eden than he was in it before the Fall. Michael's comparison, however, looks back to Adam's speech in Book IX, 296-333, where Adam had mourned the necessity of leaving "this happy place, our sweet Recess." Michael had then answered him with the partial consolation that God is everywhere (ll. 335-369). Now he can offer much greater comfort, and he tells Adam that by faith in Christ and hope for the second coming of Christ and love of God, he can win a happiness which will be far greater than the happiness of continued residence after the Fall in the Garden of Eden. These are the terms of Michael's comparison, and there is nothing to justify the imputation of an easy optimism, monistic or otherwise, to this final passage. The mood is one of mingled sadness and resolution, not at all that of Mrs. Bell's "triumphant victory which is the only possible 'prosperous outcome'" (p. 881). On the contrary Michael's last words are sobering:

> That ye may live, which will be many dayes,
> Both in one Faith unanimous though sad,
> With cause for evils past, yet much more cheer'd
> With meditation on the happie end.
>
> (XII, 602-605)

Present regret for the sin committed, firm resolution for future obedience, hope for future salvation: these are the main components of the complex mood in which the Father and the Mother of Mankind take their way from Paradise in dignity and peace.

NOTES

1. In *Studies in Milton* (London, 1951) and *PMLA,* LXVIII (1953), 863-883.
2. *The City of God,* Book XIV, chapter xiii, trans. Marcus Dods (Edinburgh, 1878), II, 25-26. Mrs. Bell cites this passage and much of the rest of this chapter of *The City of God* in her exchange with Mr. Wayne Shumaker in *PMLA,* LXX (1955), 1185-1203, which appeared over a year after this article was written. Her claim that Milton consciously accepted this chapter (p. 1195) is quite contradictory to her earlier insistence that Milton regarded Adam and Eve as perfect before the Fall. St. Augustine here imputes a greater corruption of will to Adam and Eve before the Fall than Milton does. Milton was, after all, Arminian rather than Augustinian.
3. (Chapel Hill, 1948), pp. 80-82.
4. Pp. 72-74.
5. (New York, 1953), pp. xxxiv-xxxv.
6. *Works of John Milton* (New York, 1933), XV, 39 and 53.
7. *Ibid.,* pp. 113-117.
8. *Ibid.,* p. 181.

9. *Ibid.*, p. 59.

10. Ruth Mohl, *Studies in Spenser, Milton and the Theory of Monarchy* (New York, 1949 [republished, 1962]), pp. 125-126. Two passages in Milton's *Doctrine and Discipline of Divorce* (in Works, III, 441 and 456-457) explicitly refer to the perfection of Adam and Eve before the Fall. The former makes it quite clear that the perfection Milton had in mind was a relative one.

11. Cf. *The City of God*, Book XII, chapter vi, where Augustine analyses the causelessness of the fall of the angels.

12. In *Works*, III, 441.

13. Professor Maurice Kelley listed the main steps of Adam's growing imperfection in *This Great Argument* (Princeton, 1941), p. 149. I cannot agree with Professor Kelley that Milton has "so portrayed Adam that his fall is a foregone and inevitable conclusion."

14. Tillyard, p. 11, and Bell, p. 873.

15. In *Answerable Style* (Minneapolis, 1953), pp. 75-108.

16. Building mainly on the passage in the *De doctrina Christiana* (*Works*, XV, 181-183) beginning "For what sin can be named, which was not included in this one act?," Mrs. Bell develops the notion that Adam was totally depraved before the Fall. She fails to distinguish between the will preceding the act, the act itself, and the results of the act. Milton says that the act included, among many other sins, the sin of parricide; he means that the act resulted in parricide. Adam was not tempted to commit parricide, nor did he have any desire to do so. So with most of the sins in Milton's formidable list, which he compiled to convince his readers of what Mrs. Bell denies, i.e. the importance of the Fall.

17. The one disagreement I have with Mr. Stein's interpretation of this episode is that already stated by Mr. Cleanth Brooks in the *Kenyon Review*, XV (Autumn, 1954), 654-656.

18. *Answerable Style*, pp. 82-83.

19. A. O. Lovejoy, "Milton and the Paradox of the Fortunate Fall," *Essays in the History of Ideas* (Baltimore, 1948), p. 282.

[EDITOR's NOTE. See also W. Schumaker, *PMLA*, LXX (1955), 1185-7, 1197-1302; M. Bell, *PMLA*, LXX (1955), 1187-92; J. M. Steadman, *JHI*, XXI (1960), 180-97; J. Peter, *A Critique of "Paradise Lost,"* 1960; E. I. Marilla, *Essays and Studies in English Language and Literature: Upsala*, XV (1953); M. Bertschinger, *ES*, XXXIII (1950), 49-64; J. S. Diekhoff, *MLN*, V (1944), 429-34; J. H. Hanford, *SP*, XV (1918), 176-94.]

KESTER SVENDSEN

Adam's Soliloquy in Book X of *Paradise Lost*

I wish to discuss this soliloquy as a dramatic monologue, not only for
what it reveals of Adam but *as* a revelation of Adam, as a monologue.
I wish also to show something of its structural relationship to the rest
of the poem. I am concerned with the logic of the passage as a drama-
tization and as a part of a long narrative poem.

Adam's soliloquy is the longest single speech in *Paradise Lost*, ex-
cluding, of course, the narratives by Raphael and Michael, which are
not proper speeches at all in the dramatic sense of the word. One is
surprised to find so little about this soliloquy in Milton scholarship
and criticism. It has been annotated, to be sure; and the echoes of
Shakespeare, biblical material, Greek philosophy, theological disputation, and scholasticism have been remarked by the editors. Some
attention has been paid the dramatic function of these hundred and
twenty-four lines (X, 720-844), but very little analysis has been
brought to bear upon the soliloquy as a poetic structure within the
framework of the epic. In many ways this is the most significant single passage in the poem; and, if the suggestions advanced in this paper
prove valid, the soliloquy will be seen not only as a most important
stage in the development of Adam's character but as a partial justification for the eleventh and twelfth books, which have often been criticized as padding.

From *College English*, X (1949), 366-70. Reprinted by permission of the
author and the National Council of Teachers of English.

In the first place, Adam's soliloquy is a tragic recognition scene, obligatory to the plot. The debate in Hell, as has been remarked, bears very little relation to the action of the poem; but this debate of Adam with his conscience is a necessary result of the Fall and the prelude to his emotional maturity. The psychological experience of the soliloquy is a catharsis as a process of discovery; as Adam learns more about himself, he purges off the grosser corruption of his will. But the total experience is one of creation rather than excretion. The purging is only a preliminary to growth, the growth of Adam's faith in God, a faith that he lost when he yielded to Eve and regains only after Eve has taught him that his deity is a God of mercy as well as of justice. But at the conclusion of the soliloquy Adam is in the depths of despair; his tortured acceptance of God's justice leaves him finally flat upon the ground. Only after he has listened to Eve's prayers does he realize that God will listen to his.

The soliloquy is also the great justification scene of the poem. This is the place where the promise in the opening lines of Book I is made good. Adam must recognize his guilt and accept it as just; he must also receive Eve as a partner in his guilt, not merely as Satan's partner in evil. The strategy of the passage is debate: Adam divides against himself; reason struggles with passion; he calls up excuses and evasions, only to argue them down, his reason gradually emerging to keep him honest. Yet the process is not merely logical; if it were, the dramatic features would be lost in a desert of theological disputation. One can perceive an emotional, as well as an intellectual, progress in Adam's situation. He moves from despair and grief to resentment, to uncertainty, to fear and horror, to desperate irony, and finally, to terror. His last state before Eve's appearance is one of pathos, self-consciously expressed by Adam when he says that the groves and dales were accustomed to "farr other Song" than the present lament.

This is one of the loneliest scenes in literature. Adam is completely isolated, alienated from God on account of his sin and from Eve because he cannot at this stage consider her as anything but an instrument of Satan. Even the animals glare at him as they pass. Hidden in gloomiest shade, Adam moves in a spiritual darkness as well. He has nowhere to turn and no one to turn to except his conscience. His sense of guilt is his only companion, and he wrestles with it as with an adversary.

Adam begins with a consciously ironic contrast between his present and former state. "O miserable of happie . . . mee . . . now becom / Accurst of blessed." The antithesis in the opening lines strengthens the conflict and promotes the reader's awareness of the division, which is the major method of the soliloquy. That Adam is still in the grip of pride appears from his concern, at first, not for posterity but for what posterity will say of him. Later his concern is genuine, and when he answers one question with another, "What if thy Son / Prove disobedient, and reprov'd, retort, / Wherefore didst thou beget me," the analogy shows that posterity sticks in his mind, and the reader is prepared for a return to the theme.

Adam's consciousness of the contrast between his innocence and his guilt reaches a little peak of grief when he apostrophizes the lost Eden, and then shifts abruptly to resentment, addressing his creator with a presumption that reveals the evil of pride and corrupt will still at work in him: "O fleeting joyes / Of Paradise, dear bought with lasting woes. / Did I request thee, Maker, from my Clay, / To mould me Man?" It is this repeated shift in subject or point of view that helps to keep the soliloquy fluid and active, as well as to convey the confusion and conflict in Adam's mind. After tortured argument, he accepts the justice as well as the superiority of God and says: "Be it so, for I submit, his doom is fair." He reaches a calm that is broken immediately by his uncertainty about the delay of death's stroke. He still does not understand the nature of his punishment because he is too obsessed with his own anguish. The pain is chiefly in his mind, and, until it is purged of some of its carnal fear and insecurity, the mind will be darkened. The doubts that assail him, provoked by his sin, are, however, evidence of an active mind. Adam is on his way back intellectually, though he is still floundering in emotional upheaval. Morbidly he debates with himself the death of the soul with the body and concludes: "All of me then shall die." But this decision does not diminish his growing awareness of "endlesse miserie," his feeling that his whole existence will but repeat the conditions of his present chaos. Now his concern for posterity becomes unselfish; he wishes not so much to avoid the curses of those he addresses as his sons as, in ironical language, to waste the patrimony on himself. It is consistent with the psychological experience here that this genuine concern should lead Adam to another rebellious question against God's justice: "Why should all mankind / For one mans fault thus guiltless be condemn'd, / If guiltless?" The rebellion dissipates under honest self-criticism as he realizes that what he desires and what he fears alike destroy all hope of refuge. He concludes, despairingly: "O

Conscience, into what Abyss of fears / And horrors hast thou driv'n me; out of which / I find no way, from deep to deeper plung'd!"

It was still daylight when Adam began his struggle with conscience. Now it is night, a night different from others because his sense of guilt represents all things with double terror. He curses his creation now, not his creator, imagining in his weakened judgment that he can separate the act from the actor. As he laments the different song to which the hills and dales once made answer, Eve approaches, and, to judge from Adam's savage outburst, she startles him. Except for one side glance, Adam has not thought of Eve in the preceding lines of the soliloquy. Now the full force of his despair and frustration is visited upon her as a tangible form of them and is then extended to all womankind. In his anger he challenges God for his motive in creating woman. Finally, he generalizes about marriage in a way that seems ridiculous, in view of his inexperience with reluctant parents or rival lovers:

> Or whom he wishes most shall seldom gain
> Through her perverseness, but shall see her gaind
> By a farr worse, or if she love, withheld
> By Parents, or his happiest choice too late
> Shall meet, alreadie linkt and Wedlock-bound
> To a fell Adversarie, his hate or shame:
> Which infinite calamitie shall cause
> To Humane life, and houshold peace confound.

The editors remark upon this passage only that it is Milton's recollection of his own unhappy experience with Mary Powell or his interest in a Miss Davis. In view of Adam's inexperience, one may suppose that this had seemed the best explanation for the presence of the lines. Dramatically considered, however, the lines make good sense without reference to Mary Powell. Adam's generalizations are ridiculous, and properly so. The effect of such a speech is to suggest both lack of judgment in Adam and his ripeness for persuasion by Eve. He moves from the particular to the general; he is blustering, generalizing from a single example which his own experience will not even support, much less confirm. I do not speak of Milton's intentions in the matter. I speak only of the dramatic figure Adam cuts as he makes these remarks, a ridiculous figure perfectly appropriate to his disorganized and weakened spirit. A comparable effect on the reader occurs earlier when Adam describes himself as more miserable than any example past or future. The reader's awareness of Adam's ignorance of future examples tends to persuade him all the more of Adam's distraught condition.

It is in the next speech that Eve teaches Adam what he could not learn in his soliloquy; for she rouses his pity by offering to take all the punishment on herself. She thus teaches him mercy as a feature of his superiority to her; and his faith in God's mercy wakens from that moment. Before this he has been concerned only with the justification of God and with his own miserable lot. Now his faith grows, and he looks to God for mercy. In this sense Adam is just beginning to believe in a complete God, a God of love and mercy as well as a God of power and justice.

As to the structure of the soliloquy, three themes dominate: Adam, his immortality, and death, death feared and invited, with the latter two moving the first, Adam, toward a climax of despair. The strategy of the passage is dialectic—on the one hand, the sense of emotional deformity and turmoil, produced in part by the abrupt changes in subject and tone, not to speak of the many contrasts, broken lines, and the high proportion of double caesuras. Contrasting to this feeling of turmoil and chaos is the binding and unifying effect produced by the repetition of ideas, words, and even sounds. The twin themes of immortality and death are reflected constantly in the synonyms and figures throughout. Adam speaks of *lasting woes, endless woes, living Death, wrath without end,* and so on. Similarly, the words *death* or *dies* and *curse* run like dark threads through the fabric of the passage. The three themes—Adam, immortality, and death—unite in a climax in the despairing cry, "both death and I / Am found Eternal." The singular verb expresses Adam's terrified identification of himself with his punishment as a single everlasting entity.

A further unification appears from the presence in the soliloquy, in their usual order, of what the theologians, including Milton, called the "four degrees of death." The first degree is all those evils which lead to death and which came into the world upon the Fall of man, the most important of which are guiltiness and the terrors of conscience. The second degree is spiritual death, which is the obscuring of right reason. The third is the death of the body and soul, the very conclusion which Adam himself reaches. The fourth degree—and this, too, realized within the soliloquy—is death eternal, the punishment of the damned.

It should be remarked here that the mortalist heresy, which is identified with Milton as well as with Adam because of its appearance in *De doctrina Christiana* is, dramatically considered, really one of the evasions that Adam abjures near the end of the soliloquy. Adam tries to comfort himself by saying, "All of me then shall die," but soon abandons that notion, as he realizes that none of him will ever die.

In addition to the repetition of ideas and words indicated above, there is in the passage a very interesting use of sound. It is full of the harsh sounds which Chard Powers Smith, in analyzing Shakespeare's poetry, has described as those which give strength and fiber to English verse. For a single illustration, the *k*-sounds in such words as *becom, accurst, request, Maker, clay, concur'd, darkness, corporeal,* and *clod* contribute, unobstrusively but unmistakably, to the emphasis upon Adam's agony.

The organic relationship of this passage to the rest of the poem can now, I think, be demonstrated structurally as well as psychologically. Thus, when Adam and Eve sinned, the discord moved from them out into the cosmos, producing directly the external effects of the Fall. Just before the soliloquy opens, the movement is comparable but reversed. The movement now is from the circumference to the center. As they are mentioned in this passage, first come the alterations in the stars and planets; then the winds and the change in the skies; then discord in animals is described; and, finally, Adam also in chaos.

> these were from without
> The growing miseries, which Adam saw
> Alreadie in part, though hid in gloomiest shade,
> To sorrow abandond, but worse felt within.

The effects of the Fall move back upon him, and that fact is further suggested by what Adam says of his curses:

> all from mee
> Shall with a fierce reflux on mee redound,
> On mee as on thir natural center light
> Heavie, though in thir place.

This reversal of movement effects a relation between the organization of the preceding events and the organization of this passage.

The relation of the soliloquy to the events of the last two books is not structural in this same way, but it is no less organic. The Adam in Books XI and XII acts like the Adam of Book X and does so in part because of what happens in the soliloquy. The one grows out of the other. It is not simply that the instructed Adam moves from the despair of the soliloquy to a realization of his opportunities and responsibilities. All through his soliloquy, as he twists and turns under the lash of his conscience, Adam clutches at evasions or jumps to conclusions, only to correct himself under the prodding of his slowly emerging reason. The process is continued in the visions, which are a kind of education by induction. Michael shows him death and tells him of senility, and Adam says: "Henceforth I flie not Death, nor would prolong / Life much." Michael corrects him: "Nor love thy Life, nor hate." Again, Adam sees the bevy of fair women and thinks Nature fulfilled in their beauty. Michael rebukes him: "Judg not what is best / By pleasure." After the lecture Adam shifts his ground and has to be corrected again. He says: "Still I see the tenor of Mans woe / Holds on the same, from Woman to begin." Michael replies: "From Mans effeminate slackness it begins." One of the effects of the original sin and of the despair into which Adam fell is this impulsiveness, this impaired judgment. It is not merely that these corrections by Michael provide some suggestion of dramatic conflict in what would otherwise be, as far as Michael and Adam are concerned, straight exposition. They are also, and more importantly, the appropriate psychological effect of Adam's experience in the soliloquy, and they tie that section to the experience of Books XI and XII.

The device of the debate within the soliloquy is paralleled by the debate within the dialogue. The one is not only related to the other but arises out of it as a feature of Adam's character. The relationship strengthens the sense of structural unity and necessity in the poem as a whole and, in this effect, justifies, dramatically at least, the last two books. The practice is continued to the very end of the poem, with Michael's final modification. After Adam exclaims in satisfaction that he has learned his lesson, Michael commends him but again qualifies his enthusiasm:

> onely add
> Deeds to thy knowledge answerable, add Faith,
> Add Vertue, Patience, Temperance, add Love,
> By name to come call'd Charitie, the soul
> Of all the rest: then wilt thou not be loath
> To leave this Paradise, but shalt possess
> A Paradise within thee, happier farr.

NOTE

[EDITOR'S NOTE. See also J. Buxton, *RES,* XV (1964), 52-3; I. Samuel, *PMLA,* LXXVIII (1963), 449-51; J. M. Steadman, *SP,* LIX (1962), 201-10; M. C. Pecheux, *PMLA,* LXXV (1960), 359-66; B. A. Wright, *RES,* X (1959), 62-3 and *Milton's "Paradise Lost,"* 1962; J. E. Parish, *JEGP,* LVIII (1959), 241-7.]

WILLIAM H. MARSHALL

Paradise Lost:
Felix Culpa and the Problem of Structure

In the twelfth book of *Paradise Lost,* Adam, now enlightened by Michael concerning the consequences of the Fall and the regeneration of Man through the sacrifice of the Son of God, exclaims:

> O goodness infinite, goodness immense!
> That all this good of evil shall produce,
> And evil turn to good; more wonderful
> Then that by which creation first brought forth
> Light out of darkness! full of doubt I stand,
> Whether I should repent me now of sin
> By mee done and occasiond, or rejoyce
> Much more, that much more good thereof shall spring,
> To God more glory, more good will to Men
> From God, and over wrauth grace shall abound.
>
> (XII, 470-78)

The parallel occurs in *Christian Doctrine* (Chapter XIV): "The Restoration of Man is the act whereby man, being delivered from sin and death by God the Father through Jesus Christ, is raised to a far more excellent state of grace and glory than that from which he had fallen."[1] These citations offer a beginning for any discussion of Mil-

From *Modern Language Notes,* LXXVI (1961), 15-20. Reprinted by permission of the author and the Johns Hopkins Press.

ton's use—essential, it would seem—in *Paradise Lost* of the Paradox of the Fortunate Fall. Surprisingly perhaps, an awareness of the full significance of the Paradox in Milton's poem has been slow to develop, even since the publication of *Christian Doctrine,* and from the body of more recent criticism of this aspect of *Paradise Lost* the disagreement among the critics becomes most readily apparent.[2] This fact would ordinarily emphasize the power of the poem to evoke individual response to a complex structure of symbols and ideas, and in fact such is the case with much else in *Paradise Lost,* but the confusion caused by the meaning and structural function of the theme of *felix culpa* in the poem carries at least implications of a kind of failure on Milton's part. This would appear to be inevitable in terms of the nature and function of what we call didactic literature, that which contains a meaning that is ultimately ethical. In its intellectual content *Paradise Lost* is such a work, for the intention behind it and its ethical significance are Christian.

But this meaning, that Man shall be redeemed through the sacrifice of the Son of God, emerges from the poem in two ways—by the explicit statement of the poet, of God, and finally of Michael in the last two books; and by implication in the action which appears to bring Satan's victory. It is not my intention to present still another analysis of the action of *Paradise Lost,* but it is perhaps worthwhile to point out *again* several significant, though self-evident, aspects of the poem.

Through the first nine and a half books the method is dominantly that of irony, of which we—who are conditioned by the poet's assertion that Satanic "malice serv'd but to bring forth/Infinite goodness" (I, 217-18) and God's promise that "Man therefore shall find grace,/ The other none" (III, 131-32)—are constantly aware. The balance, though delicate, is precisely maintained between the explicit action in the poem clearly leading to the Fall of Man and the implicit meaning that Man, though about to fall and to become helpless, shall be saved by the Son. We accept this and seek for the ironic implications in Satan's every act and speech, and though in time Satan triumphs over Man, actively and dramatically, we know that this triumph is temporary. This knowledge allows us to find much of the tension and therefore much of the power in the poem. What we grasp from the recognition of the irony gives emotional emphasis to the intellectual meaning of the work, of which the irony itself has been the principal instrument. In the ninth book occurs that moment toward which the action of the poem has been working. A kind of catharsis is achieved, and if anything remains of the central action of the Fall itself, it is merely to give dramatic emphasis, by Satan's return to hell in the tenth book, to the irony which has been implicit in the action leading to his apparent victory.[3]

In the last two books of *Paradise Lost* there is left, within the frame of the dramatic structure of the poem, only the dénouement, the passing of Adam and Eve from the Garden. But they must go forth with hope; at least a limited understanding on Adam's part of the nature of Man's redemption is essential for the fulfillment of divine purpose, so that an explicit and complete revelation to Adam of what is the intellectual meaning of the poem must follow. The promise of redemption is ironically implicit in Adam's misunderstanding of the nature of death in God's decree that if Adam and Eve transgress they must die (VII, 544), but Adam's mind must be cleared of this, and the significance of all that has happened, of which we are already aware, must be brought to him. But in having Michael explain to Adam, the poet necessarily shifts his emphasis as he moves from the dramatic and emotional to the intellectual climax of the poem,[4] that point in the twelfth book at which Adam comprehends the way of Man's redemption and asks the paradoxical question. But the emotional force of the action and of our recognition of the ironic and real meaning of the poem has been spent, so that Adam's excited expression of happiness at the promise of redemption becomes, from the point of view of dramatic structure, an anticlimax. The belief that aesthetically the dramatic climax of the poem, at which Eve seeks one kind of knowledge, and the intellectual climax, at which Adam is given quite another kind of knowledge, *should* be reconciled has inspired much of the writing about what is ultimately the intellectual meaning of the poem, the Paradox of the Fortunate Fall. But the proposition that they *can be* reconciled—that Milton's subject, "Mans First Disobedience" (I, 1), can be made to coincide fully with his purpose, to "justifie the wayes of God to men" (I, 26)—lies at the heart of the matter.[5]

Paradise Lost is constructed upon two systems, one dramatic and the other intellectual. During the first nine and a half books the action is explicitly concerned with Milton's subject, working itself through the climax in the Fall to the scene of Satan's return to hell; hereafter, however, the intellectual system, which has been largely implied before, becomes overt, directly expressing Milton's purpose, and, except for the passing from the Garden, the action exists within the sequence of images that Michael sets before Adam. The first phase of the poem is anthropocentric, for the struggle between Satan and Man fills the foreground, but the second is theocentric and conceptual, concerned with the resolution of the conflict between the forces of Good and those of Evil. Here, quite simply, lies the basis of the problem of the hero of *Paradise Lost*, whether it is Satan or Adam (or in the place of Adam, the Son of God). In the first part of the poem Satan is, if not the protagonist, the center of attention, the instigator of action; in the second part Adam is the object of instruction. Satan is nearly always active in the poem, just as Adam is almost consistently passive. But the poem itself is primarily a narrative, telling of the Fall of Man, and the movement of action toward the climax of the Fall carries its most obvious emotional force. Satan, the chief actor, must appear stronger than Adam, and in terms of the meaning of the poem, ironically implicit in the action, he must be a worthy opponent of the Deity; hence, as most critics have recognized, Satan becomes a towering figure and wins a kind of emotional support, even empathy perhaps, for the part that he plays.[6] But aside from this reaction there is that which springs from the other side of our ambivalence toward Satan and is achieved through our recognition of the ironic position that Satan fills. This develops emotional intensity to the point at which Satan's position is dramatized in the scene of his return to hell, in response to which our intellectual comprehension and emotional acceptance of the action become, for the moment, fused. The meaning of *Paradise Lost* is paradoxical, and to this point the method of revealing it has been that of irony. We accept the meaning largely because we feel that we know more than Satan does, and it is not until it is spelled out to Adam outside of the central structure of narrative and we must subject its paradox to logical analysis that it ceases to move us.[7]

That *Paradise Lost* is by intention a poem embodying a system of belief leading ultimately to an ethical position renders it a didactic work, for didacticism would seem to be first a matter of intention. But the didactic effects here are intellectual rather than dramatic. They demand that our emotional reaction to the story be subordinated to our intellectual response to the explicit assertion in the final books of the Paradox of the Fortunate Fall.[8] This we cannot do, for it involves repudiation, rather than subordination, of what we have felt during the first nine and a half books, so that the didactic aspect of *Paradise Lost*, as opposed to the dramatic aspect in this particular instance, is hardly successful.

Apparently the intention of some who have written about the poem has been to make the didactic aspect successful, or—as in the case of Mrs. Bell's assertion that Adam and Eve are fallen from the start or Mr. Ogden's suggestion that Adam's enunciation of the Paradox is not to be taken as a serious expression of anything other than his own emotional state at the time—to make meaning primary though it would appear to be a meaning unlike what the author of *Christian Doctrine* intended in his poem. But the emotional acceptance of the meaning must emerge from the action, and this it does through irony, though only in part. In the action leading to the Fall of Man we foresee and emotionally anticipate the destruction of Satan; but only through the explanation of the poet, of God, and of Michael do we know of Man's redemption. The final Fall of Satan, ironically present in the account of the Fall of Man, does not carry with it as emotionally forceful the implication that Man shall be made regenerate.

NOTES

1. *The Works of John Milton*, ed. Frank Allen Patterson *et al.* (New York, 1933), XV, 251.
2. For more recent comment, see John Erskine, "The Theme of Death in *Paradise Lost*," *PMLA*, XXXII (1917), 573-82; Cecil A. Moore, "The Conclusion of *Paradise Lost*," *PMLA*, XXXVI (1921), 1-34; Allan H. Gilbert, "The Problem of Evil in *Paradise Lost*," *JEGP*, XXII (1923), 175-94; Denis Saurat, *Milton: Man and Thinker* (New York, 1925), p. 131; John Diekhoff, *Milton's Paradise Lost: A Commentary on the Argument* (New York, 1946), p. 131; B. Rajan, *Paradise Lost and the Seventeenth Century Reader* (New York, 1948), p. 45; Millicent Bell, "The Fallacy of the Fall in *Paradise Lost*," *PMLA*, LXVIII (1953), 863-83; *PMLA*, LXX (1955), 1187-97, 1203; Wayne Shumaker, "The Fallacy of the Fall in *Paradise Lost*," *PMLA*, LXX (1955), 1185-87, 1197-1202; H. V. S. Ogden, "The Crisis of *Paradise Lost* Reconsidered," *PQ*, XXXVI (1957), 1-19; William Madsen, "The Fortunate Fall in *Paradise Lost*," *MLN*, LXXIV (1959), 103-5.
3. In terms of this function of the scene in hell, the observation of A. J. A. Waldock (*Paradise Lost and Its Critics* [Cambridge, England, 1947], pp. 91-92) is very much to the point, that the technique

of the poet—to raise Satan to expectation of success "and then to dash him down"—is "*exactly* that of the comic cartoon."

4. It is significant that Raphael's account of the Creation and of the rebellion of Satan exists as part of both the dramatic and the intellectual development of the poem, but Michael's explanation is almost exclusively part of the intellectual.

5. James Holly Hanford (*John Milton, Englishman* [New York, 1949], p. 201) does not think that they can be reconciled: "No defeat of Satan can outweigh the earlier manifestations of his transparent will; no promise to Adam of a moral Paradise within can counterbalance the tragic ruin of his innocence. The conclusion of *Paradise Lost* is a contradiction of its beginning."

6. See Saurat, p. 219; Maud Bodkin, *Archetypal Patterns in Poetry* (New York, 1958), pp. 224-39.

7. These conclusions at least recall what Cleanth Brooks (*The Well Wrought Urn* [New York, 1957], pp. 17-18) has asserted, specifically about the meaning of Donne's "The Canonization" but generally about "almost any insight important enough to warrant a great poem," that the only way open to the poet is that of paradox: "More direct methods may be tempting, but all of them enfeeble and distort what is to be said."

8. Cf. the distinction made by E. M. W. Tillyard (*Milton* [London, 1949], pp. 257-88) between "the conscious meaning" and "the unconscious meaning" in *Paradise Lost*.

[EDITOR'S NOTE. For other views and further references, see the two following essays, by Sasek and Hughes.]

LAWRENCE A. SASEK

The Drama of *Paradise Lost,* Books XI and XII

Since the eighteenth century, critics have given the conclusion of
Paradise Lost very little appreciative attention; they have either ignored the last two books, or written patronizingly about them, or criticized them adversely. One recent opinion, typical of even a fairly
sympathetic reader of Milton's poetry, is that the two final books have
no "dramatic significance" or "energy" and constitute "a languid
movement" toward the conclusion.[1] To admirers of Satan, the final
dialogue of Adam and Michael merely continues the poetic deterioration that began as early as Book III. Readers more sensitive to the
drama of temptation are likely to stop reading with attentive appreciation after the reconciliation of Adam and Eve in Book X and to
respond thereafter only to a few beautifully-phrased moral precepts
in Michael's advice to Adam, besides, of course, the final twenty-five
lines, in which the cataclysmic image of the gate of Paradise, crowded
with avenging Angels and lighted by the flaming sword, gradually
fades away, to be replaced by the quiet movement of the epic conclusion, describing in simple words the mood of Adam and Eve at their
departure into the world of sorrow. In numerous studies of the structure, diction, and imagery of *Paradise Lost,* scholars dismiss the last

From *Studies in English Renaissance Literature,* ed. W. F. McNeir; *Louisiana
State University Studies: Humanities Series,* No. 12 (1962), 181-96, 235. Reprinted by permission of the author and the Louisiana State University Press.

two books with a discussion of the possible reasons for a decline in poetic power, a decline usually assumed without an attempt at demonstration.

To some extent, the universality of the negative reaction to the last two books is its own justification. But not entirely. The revival of enthusiasm for Donne's poetry after more than a century of neglect is one of several available examples of factors in critical appreciation that sometimes unjustly decree long disfavor to unique poetic achievements. Two such factors are misreading and reading with prejudice owing to the preponderance of adverse opinion, which, in literary criticism as well as in politics, sustains a band-wagon psychology. These factors may well have caused the final two books to suffer continual, undeserved neglect or, at least, lack of properly attentive reading. More careful attention may not lead to discovery of outstanding verbal merits in them, but it may quite possibly restore to them something of the force they might logically be expected to have as the concluding sixth part of the epic. Fairly recent efforts at explanation have brought about new appreciation of the drama of Adam and Eve's dissension and reconciliation,[2] and we should, before accepting the theory of Milton's lapse in creative ability at the end of his story, try to explain the content and style of his conclusion as the result of a deliberate working out of his epic plan. One such attempt was made by E. N. S. Thompson, but it apparently failed to influence critical opinion appreciably. Affirming the importance of the final two books in the development of Milton's epic theme, he emphasized the poetic effectiveness of some of Milton's scenes from biblical history;[3] but he apparently failed to convince critics that the last two books were more than a necessary but uninspired conclusion, attaining the poetic intensity of the preceding books only in isolated passages.

Paradoxically, the last two books may have been misread because of the general knowledge of the traditional epic device that Milton was there adapting. Before the decline of classical studies, comparison of the shields of Aeneas and Achilles was a schoolboy exercise that few potential students of Milton escaped and that predisposed them to dismiss Milton's biblical paraphrase as merely an instance of his adherence to epic tradition. Their interpretation influenced even readers who are hardly familiar with these passages of the *Iliad* and *Aeneid* in translation. Perhaps the conclusion of *Paradise Lost* suffers most from having an element in common with the *Aeneid*: a presen-

tation by the poet of the course of history following and arising from
the events of his main action. If considered a mere adaptation of the
vision of the future that Virgil described on the shield of Aeneas
(*Aeneid* VIII, 626-728), the vision seen by Adam seems diffuse and
over-extended. The future glory of Rome is presented by Virgil in
slightly more than one hundred lines, whereas Michael's exposition
of the future occupies about 1,100 lines. In a similar way, the scenes
that Milton modeled on Homer's description of the shield of Achilles (*Iliad* XVIII, 478-608) may lead the reader to attribute the same
function to the passages in *Paradise Lost* that their analogues have in
the *Iliad*. The result is a distortion of Milton's meaning and a disregard of the organic functions of the passages in his epic. What is
needed, then, is more emphasis on the differences and unique qualities in Milton's use of a traditional epic device.

Milton's debt, in his final books, to the predecessors whom he mentioned in *The Reason of Church Government* (1641-1642) is obvious, but more superficial than is generally realized. From Homer
he imitated a few scenes. From Virgil and Tasso (*La Gerusalemme
Liberata*, Canto XVII) came the basic notion of a glimpse of the future, including portrayals of the illustrious descendants of the hero.
From Tasso, perhaps, came the idea of a commentator. But one cannot
be sure how directly the line of influence reached *Paradise Lost*, for
Milton was obviously familiar with the use made of these epic models
by Du Bartas, in whose *La Sepmaine* Adam is given a revelation of
the future by the Archangel Michael. The similarities in Du Bartas'
and Milton's presentations of biblical history extend from specific
scenes to the general situation, including the removal of Eve from
the scene while the Archangel speaks with Adam.[4]

In both epic poems the relevant passages have one function in common: they enlarge the scope of the action. In the *Iliad* the scenes on
the shield of Achilles provide a background for the fighting before
the gates of Troy; they place the Trojan war in perspective with all
of life by showing men at work and at play, in the pursuits of peace
as well as of war. That they are intended to present the world as a
whole, the cosmic setting of the epic conflict, is clear enough from
the fact that the river Oceanus, the sea, which the Greeks believed
to encircle the whole habitable world, is engraved around the rim of
the shield. The shield of Aeneas extends the *Aeneid* in time; scenes
from Roman history and portraits of illustrious Romans place the
action of the *Aeneid* in perspective with the whole history of Rome,

which, to Virgil and the Romans, was the entire civilized world. The shield of Rinaldo is less comprehensive, but it does extend the significance of the action of *La Gerusalemme Liberata* to Tasso's times, by presenting the illustrious ancestry of the house of Este. In both *La Sepmaine* and *Paradise Lost*, Michael unfolds to Adam a world history which concretely relates the story of the fall to universal history.

But the differences between Milton's biblical pageant and the analogous epic scenes of his predecessors are fundamental. Homer, Virgil, and Tasso used essentially descriptive techniques. The scenes in the *Iliad* are of men in action, but they are presented as pictures on a shield, without narrative quality in themselves and without narrative funtion in the *Iliad*. Virgil took from Homer the basic device of pictures on a shield, but gave it an even more static quality, in that many of his pictures are merely portraits. Only when the history of Rome is brought to the battle of Actium are scenes of action recounted. The shield of Rinaldo is occupied solely by portraits of Rinaldo's illustrious progeny, a pedigree of the House of Este; stories are told about the figures on the shield, but they are merely commentaries on the portraits and form no narrative sequence. In the *Aeneid* and the *Gerusalemme Liberata*, as in the *Iliad*, the actions on the shield are at most dynamic pictures and have no narrative connection with the action of the epic. At most, the shields send their owners into action with a greater awareness of the significance of their deeds.

Like his predecessor Du Bartas, Milton adapted the epic device by substituting for the shield a coherent narrative sequence. Milton's vision and narrative, his adaptations of the epic device, modify the course of his main plot and are, in fact, an integral part of it, a logical conclusion or outcome of preceding events and a necessary link between them and his ultimate conclusion. But Milton went further than Du Bartas in adding a dramatic quality to the traditional devices. The *Sepmaine* contains no dramatic dialogue; the angel's narration proceeds without interruption, and Adam's reaction is given in one consecutive discourse. However, throughout the vision of Milton's Book XI and Michael's narrative in Book XII, the voice of Adam keeps breaking into the story: questioning, sorrowing, rejoicing. Instead of a mere historical pageant we have a dialogue in which the incidents narrated are selected for their effect on Adam. The angel's tone and mood change with those of his interlocutor. Constantly, three elements—Michael's mission, the story of biblical events, and Adam's state of mind—are linked by cause and effect relationships.

The last two books of *Paradise Lost* thus become a study of Adam's development from horror at the thought of leaving Paradise, to shame and despair at the consequences of his sin, to a final understanding of and reconciliation with God's purpose. Adam gradually attains the state of mind indicated by God when he orders Michael to send him from Paradise "though sorrowing, yet in peace." And it is on the process by which Adam attains his new, final insight that the attention of the reader should be directed, if the last two books are to be appreciated for their due significance as the end of the drama of sin and promise in *Paradise Lost*. The biblical scenes mean far less in themselves than do their counterparts in the earlier epics.

The organic function of the last two books in the development of Milton's theme has been affirmed by James H. Hanford; however, he stopped with the scene portraying the death of Abel, which, he noted, was the final crisis of the loss of Paradise, for in it death entered the story, excepting by allegory, for the first time.[5] But mere physical death is not the end of the tale, and all that Adam is to learn and to suffer vicariously in the last two books is organic to the poem if we accept Milton's first statement of his argument at face value. Consistently with epic tradition he summarized his theme in the opening lines of the epic: it is to be the story "Of Mans First Disobedience, and the Fruit / Of that Forbidden Tree."[6] By the end of Book X, man's first disobedience has been narrated in full, but the "fruit" is yet to be described, if we take the word in its inevitable double sense as not only the physical object, but also the result of the action revolving about the forbidden tree; the "fruit" or fruition of the disobedience is revealed to Adam in the last two books.

Some of the results of sin are shown in Books IX and X, in the familiar passages telling of Satan's humiliation and of the physical change in the created world, but mainly in Adam and Eve's mutual recriminations and final reconciliation and penitence. At the beginning of Book XI, while the son intercedes at the throne of the Father for the repentants, Adam and Eve find comfort in their new reconciliation with each other and with God, taking pleasure especially in the foretold victory of Eve's descendants over Satan. Eve, whose words always reveal less spirituality than Adam's, takes pleasure in the familiar environment of Paradise. But her words fall ironically upon the reader's ear, since they have been preceded by the Father's injunction to Michael to expel Adam and Eve from Paradise. The task of Michael embraces the whole dramatic problem that must be resolved in the last two books. The reasons given for the expulsion are several, and those most commonly noted by readers are the theological arguments that, in themselves, provide no adequate justification of the last two books. Adam and Eve are held to be unfit inhabitants of Paradise because, corrupted by sin, they cannot reside among pure elements. Nor can they be given an opportunity to eat of the tree of life and so become immortal in their corruption. However sound the theological principles expressed in the symbolic argument may be, they are not dramatically effective, for the reader has been made aware of the repentance of Adam and Eve and of their profession of obedience to the divine will. Another reason for the expulsion is more significant, although sometimes overlooked: God notes that Adam's action since the eating of the fruit, action dramatically presented in the epic, makes him unfit to live in Paradise. His fallen nature is not only an abstract theological concept; it is portrayed in his behavior. In spite of his repentance, evident in his manner while he repents is the fact that his heart is "variable and vain"; his repentance is caused by grace won for him by the son (XI, 90-93). The very joy of Adam and Eve at the beginning of Book XI is thus a sign of instability, while Eve's pleasure in the physical environment shows excessive regard for the material, a degree of spiritual blindness. By implication, Michael's task is, in part, to help Adam achieve stability and to give both Adam and Eve a deeper understanding of their sin and a more sober perception of their hopes. Explicitly, Michael is to send Adam and Eve, who are now in a foolish, unjustified state of self-confidence, from Paradise "though sorrowing, yet in peace" (XI, 117), in a state of mind more consistent with their present human lot. To do so, Michael must make Adam apprehend, both intellectually and emotionally, the nature of their sin and cause him to accept the expulsion as just, yet not destroy hope. To achieve his end, Michael must reconcile, in Adam's awareness, justice with divine mercy. His task is to fulfill conclusively Milton's announced intention in *Paradise Lost*: to "justifie the wayes of God to men." Noteworthy is the statement that throughout his discourse with Adam, Michael is to have divine inspiration; he is to be enlightened by God (XI, 115). In one sense, the divine inspiration is Milton's credo concerning the truth of the Bible; but, dramatically, it suggests that his words are of unique importance, since they come more directly from God than Raphael's earlier discourses.

Michael's procedure is to announce the dread sentence of expul-

sion abruptly, prefacing it only with the encouraging promise that
Adam will have time to repent and so escape Death. Milton here uses
the device of epic iteration, by having Michael repeat the sentence
verbatim, as if to emphasize it. Thereafter, the whole trend of Michael's discourse with Adam is to mitigate its harshness, but his opening words are appropriate to his military dress; he repeats the command like a soldier under definite orders. Adam, who had forebodings
of unwelcome news when he saw Michael approach, is "Heart-strook
with chilling gripe of sorrow" (XI, 264) and unable to speak. Consistently with dramatic decorum, then, Milton has Adam receive his
sentence silently, leaving to the woman the commentary, a lamentation that she can utter without impropriety. Although Adam weeps
later in the discourse, it is for the misfortunes of others, not because
of his immediate, personal tragedy. But Eve greets the news as "worse
then of Death" (XI, 268) and speaks a touching lament for the loss
of Paradise. In chivalric manner, the angel gives Eve what words of
comfort he can, pointing out that she is in duty bound to follow her
husband, and that her home, her Paradise, is wherever he dwells. The
suggestion that human companionship will mitigate the rigors of life
outside Paradise revives Adam's spirits also. Adam's words contrast
sharply with Eve's preceding lament; instead of commenting on the
material loss, the loss of Paradise, he reveals the proper mood of a
penitent, the spiritually-oriented awareness that the greatest punishment and cause of sorrow will be loss of the presence of God and of
the chance to serve Him. Adam's speech, then, reveals his moral attitude, contrasts his character and preoccupations with Eve's, and, in
addition, motivates Michael's next words. In answer to Adam's question concerning where he can find God if he is removed from Paradise, Michael explains the reasons for the biblical résumé that is to
follow. He will show Adam what will befall his offspring so that
Adam can learn a vital lesson: "so shalt thou lead / Safest thy life,
and best prepar'd endure / Thy mortal passage when it comes" (XI,
364-366). That the ensuing action will constitute a moral lesson is
clear enough; there is no doubt of its didactic function. But it has
been introduced dramatically, and from Adam's varied moods thus
far, one can expect that the succeeding revelations will also have a
dramatic effect upon him.

From an objective, critical perspective, the purpose of the vision
and narrative is not only biblical paraphrase for its own sake, nor
merely the instruction and education of the reader, but also the satis-

faction of the reader's curiosity concerning the final condition of Adam, the state of mind and soul in which Adam will leave Paradise. Milton preaches, insofar as he does so, dramatically, through his characters. The reader is to follow and learn from the vision by observing its effect on Adam. Whether or not the intention is successfully fulfilled cannot be determined until we learn to read the passage without preconceptions of its purpose and quality. That a mere poetic résumé of biblical history is not intended is clear enough from the principles of selection Milton followed. His inclusion of specific passages is best explained by a consecutive study of their effect on Adam throughout the two books. His omissions may be illustrated by one example, noted long ago by Warburton. The sins of the Israelites, their rebellions during their wanderings in the desert, are omitted, although, as Warburton noted, some incidents "would have afforded noble imagery."[7] But they would merely have duplicated impressions of evil which Adam had already received, and at this point Michael's speech was designed to comfort Adam by showing his descendants reaching the promised land. Hence, although the biblical story of the wandering in the desert is full of setbacks, such as the incidents of the golden calf and the rebellion of Korah, Dathan, and Abiram (Numbers 16), in Michael's account only the establishment of the Mosaic laws is included. Studies which might, in themselves, have provided good subjects for poetry are omitted as inappropriate to the dramatic function of the narrative and inconsistent with its immediate dramatic purpose.

To set the stage for the vision that Adam must be shown, Michael takes him to a hilltop, from which, apparently, the whole world is visible. The succeeding catalogue of place names (XI, 388-411) could, perhaps, be justified as a tour de force of versification and sound effects, but it also plays a vital part in the story; it enlarges the scope of action from the terrestrial Paradise to the whole known world. A vast stage is set for the playing of the biblical drama, for the portrayal of the causes of Adam's succeeding emotions and utterances. At first the large stage seems to dwarf Adam's significance by reducing the relative importance of Paradise, which for several books has been the locale of all the action; yet, paradoxically, his stature is enlarged from that of one inhabitant of an isolated Paradise to that of the grand progenitor of the whole world of men. His emotions and speeches are now in counterpoise not merely with Eve's but with the vast, panoramic scenes of biblical history.

The first biblical scene shown by Michael is the murder of Abel. Hanford has called this "the true climax of the story of the fall,"[8] but this estimate of its importance may be an exaggeration. The scene, however, is dramatically significant in that it shows to Adam for the first time the repugnant aspect of the physical death that his sin has brought into the future experience of himself and his descendants. Death, which has heretofore been a dread notion, now becomes a clearly apprehended experience. The sight shocks Adam, but at this point in his education he seems more distressed by the physical pain than by the moral evil of murder. "Is this the way / I must return to native dust?" (XI, 462-463) is his ultimate query. Michael, in answer, intensifies the horror of the vision by showing a picture of the lazar house, with its inmates in the throes of various maladies. Why Milton enlarged the number of diseases listed from eleven in the first edition to seventeen in the second can only be conjectured, but possible reasons are that he was striving for a more representative, and hence more comprehensive, list of human ills and that he was trying to provide a stronger motivation for Adam's violent reaction. Having seen death in its manifold horrors, Adam loses composure: "compassion quell'd / His best of Man," and he weeps (XI, 496-497). But consistently with Milton's development of Adam's psychology, the fit of grief changes to a question of God's ways: should not man, made in "Th'Image of God" (XI, 508) be free of deformities? When Michael explains briefly that sin has debased man's nature, Adam, with the words "I yield it just" (XI, 526), accepts, in effect, a justification of the doctrine of original sin. But, still concerned mainly with physical death, Adam asks if there is a more pleasant way to die. He is reconciled to his mortal end by Michael's account of the death of a temperate man. But, because he has been developed consistently as a dramatic character instead of a mere symbol in a didactic discourse, he reacts too strongly; he seems almost eager for death. By comparison with what he had feared a moment earlier, a mild and benign death now seems welcome. Only after this dramatic action and reaction is he given a properly balanced view by the Archangel: "Nor love thy Life, nor hate; but what thou livst / Live well, how long or short permit to Heav'n" (XI, 553-554).

With line 555 begins a new sequence of visions, designed to teach Adam to recognize evil in various forms. The lesson is necessary because so far, even when Adam saw evil in the murder of Abel, he has been impressed primarily by its physical horror. He has yet to learn that evil may have a bewitchingly pleasing aspect. The first scene of Adam's second lesson is an analogue of Achilles' shield in that it shows the occupations of men at peace: practicing mechanical arts and enjoying music, love, and festivity; but Milton put a similar scene to very different use. Adam, blind to the signs of vanity and lust, reveals his ignorance by showing pleasure in the vision, declaring that "Here Nature seems fulfilld in all her ends" (XI, 602). Thus he motivates the necessary instructions from Michael; the explanation that the busy, ostensibly happy cities are the abodes of evil. Adam's reaction is characteristic; as he did after the fall, he attributes the evil to women, and Michael echoes Raphael's early warning (VIII, 561-594) as he places the blame on "Mans effeminate slackness" in allowing himself to be seduced despite his superior wisdom (XI, 634). The dialogue thus reaffirms the early admonition of Raphael and resolves conclusively the mutual recriminations of Eve and Adam immediately after their fall. The peaceful scene is supplemented by a vision of warfare, from which one solitary man, Enoch, is rescued by divine intervention. From the pictures of men at peace and war, Adam receives the lesson that the arts of men, which seem fair from the outside, are full of evil within and ever ready to erupt into war. The just man has little chance to sway the world by his own eloquence or virtue. Earthly codes of fame and honor are explicitly repudiated as empty of virtue.

Beginning with line 712, Adam is again shown a world living at peace. The outwardly pleasant scene appears to be redundant, but as it leads to the deluge, Adam learns a new lesson. He has already seen the pervasiveness of evil, the small influence of goodness among men, and the concern of God for the just; but he is now shown as well God's punishment for sin. In other words, divine justice is here vindicated. In the last half of Book XI, Adam has progressed emotionally from his dismay at the disguises of evil and at its pervasiveness to rejoicing in the endurance of the just and in God's protection and care of the faithful; now the covenant of God with Noah, the agreement never to destroy the world, ends Adam's uncertainty about the mortal future of his descendants. At the end of Book XI, he has seen death and evil; he has learned that the pains of death may be mitigated and that evil, although deceptive in appearance, may be avoided; and he has achieved a balanced perspective of the evil and good in man's nature. The vision is not joyful, but it permits hope, and Adam seems ready to face his natural life, the consequences of his natural acts, calmly and hopefully.

As is well known, Book X of the first edition of *Paradise Lost* included the books numbered XI and XII in the second and subsequent editions. The only textual change made by Milton at the point of division of Books XI and XII was the addition of five lines at the beginning of the new Book XII, saying that Michael had "paus'd / Betwixt the world destroy'd and world restor'd." He then resumed his narration. The change can be explained by the disproportionate length of the former Book X and by other structural considerations.[9] The point at which Milton chose to begin the new book can be accounted for partly by Michael's implication that the world was beginning anew (XII, 7). Another explanation is provided by the change in Michael's method of presentation of biblical history at this point; heretofore he has shown Adam visions, and hereafter he will merely narrate events. This change in technique, however, raises more questions than it answers; for one must wonder why Milton abandoned the vision at this point. The professed dramatic reason is apt enough; one can readily accept Michael's statement that Adam's "mortal sight" was beginning "to faile" (XII, 9), but it is far from inevitable or conclusive. Aesthetic variety seems to be an inadequate reason, since the reader could go on imagining visions without boredom; in fact, the visions are more imaginative and vivid than the succeeding narration. And Milton's technique in Book XI was flexible enough to allow him to present such diverse scenes as the strife of Cain and Abel, a broad panorama of biblical life, the rescue of Enoch, and the deluge.

A logical explanation of the change in technique may be found in the dramatic relationship of Michael and Adam, which, after the deluge has been shown, enters a new phase. Visions of events were needed to teach Adam the appearance of death, of good and evil actions, and of God's rewards and punishments. When these pictures have been apprehended, Adam has to achieve an intellectual understanding of God's scheme of salvation, including the nature of moral virtue, of the incarnation, and of redemption. At the moment, Adam is yet unaware of the immediate causes of sin among men, of the moral discipline needed to avoid it, and of the basis for hope of salvation. He must be instructed in theological doctrine; and Milton, thinking perhaps of the duty of the preacher, poet, and prophet, who lacks the power of evoking physical visions, causes Michael to adopt the technique of the pulpit. Significantly, Adam's last question in the epic concerns the duty and fate of the clergy (XII, 480 ff.). Furthermore, in Book XI Adam learned lessons which, although new to an inhabitant of Paradise, were familiar enough to Milton's public. The succeeding instructions are aimed more directly, although still through Adam, at Milton's readers.

Michael's first story is of Nimrod and ends in the building of the Tower of Babel. Adam's reaction to it shows a developing conscience, a growing knowledge of moral right, as he denounces the usurpation of power by one man over another (XII, 63-78). But Michael must point out to Adam the reasons for tyranny, which is a consequence of Adam's sin, and the justice of God in permitting evil to exist. The lesson may be topical in part, but Milton was certainly aware, as his readers must be, that it could be topical in any age, not in seventeenth-century England alone. The most important reason for Milton's choice of this episode is that it provides a needed lesson at this stage in Adam's spiritual development.

The second story of Book XII provides an introduction to theology, as Michael recounts the election of the chosen people, the reign of the patriarch Abraham, the exodus of the Jews, and their history up to the conquest of Canaan. Here for the first time Adam becomes aware of the full extent of divine mercy; he realizes that his descendants will be shown greater favor than they have merited (XII, 276-279). But, in accordance with his fallen "variable" nature, he becomes overly-optimistic, assuming that the successes of the Jews represent the conclusion of the history of his earthly descendants. He must be recalled by Michael to awareness of sin among the Jews; and their history is carried to the appearance of the Redeemer in the line of David. Again, Adam is too much pleased, and consistently with his human intellect and with the prophecies that have been given him earlier, he now pictures Christ defeating the serpent in a physical contest. The pretext is thus furnished for Michael's exposition of the doctrine of redemption and of the importance of works of faith and love. The second cardinal virtue, hope, is in a sense the theme of all the discourses of Michael. The biblical history ends with the triumphant apocalyptic vision of the final judgment and the conquest of death.

Adam has now been brought from his first despair at the thought of death, through a succession of hopes and fears, to a comprehension of the final victory of good over evil. Remembering the alternation of his overly-optimistic and ultrapessimistic reactions, one is not surprised at his comment, "full of doubt I stand, / Whether I should repent me now of sin / By mee done and occasiond, or rejoyce / Much more, that much more good thereof shall spring" (XII, 473-476). And one should be reluctant to attribute to Milton any notion of the *felix culpa,* at least without severe qualification.[10] Adam's speech does not express a reasoned theological view of the consequences of sin; read dramatically, it expresses his emotional reaction to news of the final triumph of good, after he has several times been on the verge of despair. The tale of misery that has preceded the final triumph and the tale of postbiblical human history that Michael has yet to unfold, both contradict any argument that the fall was "fortunate." Furthermore, as Diekhoff has indicated, it is beside the point to say that the saints will eventually reach a higher level of bliss than Adam enjoyed in Paradise, for Raphael had explained to Adam that his state in Paradise was not static or terminal.[11] If he had remained faithful, he might gradually have achieved an angelic nature (V, 493-503). Now the happy outcome is reserved for a few among many and must be reached through the pain and misery described in Books XI and XII. Although the victory of good separates *Paradise Lost* in mood from the classical tragedies of Greece, it does not, on the other hand, make the poem exactly a divine comedy, if we consider Adam, as man, the principal character. The truth is that Adam is both Lear and Edgar, both Hamlet and Fortinbras, and we cannot forget the defeat of the one while we take comfort in the reassertion of order represented by the other. Although Milton affirms the happiness of the saints, he portrays vividly the expulsion of Adam from Paradise.

Moreover, the words that suggest the concept of *felix culpa* are not Adam's final comment on the human predicament. Following his outburst of joy, he asks Michael what guides the just will have in their earthly pilgrimage, and the answer is a pessimistic survey of the history of the Christian era, including the grim summary and prediction: "so shall the World goe on, / To good malignant, to bad men benigne" (XII, 537-538). Adam's response, and his final word, is hopeful but almost stoic in its resignation to suffering; he sums up his lesson with the words "Henceforth I learne, that to obey is best" (XII, 561) and "suffering for Truths sake / Is fortitude to highest victorie / And to the faithful Death the Gate of Life" (XII, 569-571). Michael's approval of Adam's words is clear enough when he calls them "the summe / of wisdome" (XII, 575-576). He suggests only adding deeds and virtues to knowledge (XII, 581-585).

The long dialogue then concludes with words that, like the preceding, may have universal, didactic application, but that are inextricably
part of the dramatic situation. Several lines refer to the approach of
the angelic guards, who are to escort Adam and Eve from Paradise.
But before and after announcing to Adam that the time for departure
has come, the Angel speaks words of comfort, which also could be
misinterpreted if taken out of context. The statement, "then wilt thou
not be loath / To leave this Paradise, but shalt possess / A paradise
within thee, happier farr" (XII, 585-587), may seem, at superficial
glance, to be a confirmation of Satan's theological principle: "The
mind is its own place" (I, 254); but in context, Michael is merely saying that Adam will be happier with a good conscience outside Paradise than he would be with a bad conscience within Paradise. No
comparison is made with his early state of innocence in Paradise;
Michael's word is a logical concluding speech for a mission the purpose of which was to expel Adam and Eve, against their inclination,
from Paradise and to prevent despair. Likewise, the angel's very last
words, concluding the dialogue which began in Book XI, emphasize
the causes for optimism: "ye may live, . . . though sad, / With cause
for evils past, yet much more cheer'd / With meditation on the happie
end" (XII, 602-605). The cheerfulness is relative because the statement is dramatic, because it merely translates into dramatic discourse
appropriate to the specific scene God's direction to send Adam and
Eve forth "though sorrowing, yet in peace."

The last two books of *Paradise Lost* therefore present a drama in
which the character of Adam is molded into an example of Christian
fortitude. They dramatize the final stage in Adam's development,
which has proceeded from innocence, through sin, through reconciliation with God, to a full knowledge and acceptance of the justice of
God's judgment—in other words, to a condition in which Adam and
his descendants will be able to make their way through sorrow and
evil to final redemption. Many readers will prefer the elevated tone
of the early books, but whoever appreciates the human drama of
Books IX and X should also be aware that in the last books Milton has
consistently developed this drama of sin and repentance to a theologically consistent and psychologically valid conclusion. He has developed the psychology of Adam as painstakingly, meticulously, and carefully as he explored the psychology of Adam and Eve during their sin
and its immediate sequel. At each stage of Michael's revelation,
Adam's emotional reactions and utterances are determined by his pre-

vious knowledge and emotional condition. From the ignorant, erring inhabitant of an unworldly paradise, he develops into the first man, as we know man, setting out for the imperfect world of our experience. The poetic problems that Milton faced in portraying this development were as formidable as those he surmounted earlier in the epic, and the last two books, if read with constant awareness of the dramatic situation, should receive more respect than they are generally given.

NOTES

1. R. M. Adams, *Ikon* (Ithaca, N. Y., 1955), pp. 125-127, 207. These views may be compared with the strictures of J. B. Broadbent, *Some Graver Subject: an Essay on "Paradise Lost"* (London, 1960), pp. 269-298.

2. See E. M. W. Tillyard, *The English Epic and Its Background* (London, 1954), p. 437; and Kester Svendsen, *Milton and Science* (Cambridge, Mass., 1956), pp. 105-112.

3. "For Paradise Lost, XI-XII," *PQ*, XXII (1943), 376-382.

4. See George Coffin Taylor, *Milton's Use of Du Bartas* (Cambridge, Mass., 1934), pp. 112-124.

5. "The Dramatic Element in *Paradise Lost*," *SP*, XIV (1917), 185.

6. All citations from *Paradise Lost* are to *The Works of John Milton*, Frank A. Patterson, *et al.*, eds., 18 vols. (New York, 1931-1938).

7. *The Poetical Works of John Milton*, Henry John Todd, ed., 4 vols. (London, 1852), II, 531.

8. "The Dramatic Element in *Paradise Lost*, p. 185.

9. For a thorough discussion of Milton's change from an epic of ten books to one of twelve books, see Arthur Barker, "Structural Pattern in *Paradise Lost*," *PQ*, XXVIII (1949), 17-30.

10. The argument for Milton's adoption of the notion of the "fortunate fall" is made at length by Arthur O. Lovejoy, "Milton and the Paradox of the Fortunate Fall," *ELH*, IV (1937), 161-179.

11. John S. Diekhoff, *Milton's Paradise Lost* (New York, 1946), pp. 130-131. See also H. S. Ogden, "The Crisis of *Paradise Lost* Reconsidered," *PQ*, XXXVI (1957), 17-19.

[EDITOR'S NOTE. See also H. R. MacCallum, in *Essays in English Literature . . . Presented to A. S. P. Woodhouse*, ed. M. MacLure and F. W. Watt, 1964; L. L. Martz, *The Paradise Within*, 1964; B. K. Lewalski, *PQ*, XLII (1963), 25-35; D. Taylor, Jr., *TSE*, X (1960), 51-82; J. M. Steadman, *SP*, LVI (1959), 214-25; F. T. Prince, *E&S*, XI (1958), 38-52; J. E. Parish, *Rice Institute Pamphlet*, XL, No. 40 (1954), 1-24.]

MERRITT Y. HUGHES

Some Illustrators of Milton:
The Expulsion from Paradise

In a recent article Professor Kester Svendsen[1] has reproduced John
Martin's treatment of the expulsion of Adam and Eve from Eden together with Fuseli's painting of "the beauty and gorgeous nudity of
Adam and Eve [to] imply, as does their posture, a relation physically
and spiritually that of lovers, not leavers." The purpose is to give
Martin's handling of the scene the rank that it deserves among romantic depictions of the closing scene in *Paradise Lost*. His dark landscape with the distant dinosaur, the deep perspective of a river flowing away from the crags which the handfasted couple are descending,
and the stag and the lion which represent "the solitude and the violence that await in the world," are described by Svendsen as both
symbolizing humanity's future scientific conquests and perpetuating
a symbolism traditional among Milton's illustrators. The serpent slid-
ing away from Eve as she looks back toward the vague radiance behind her is mentioned, though the dog looking up at Adam is not;
and in the writhing limbs of the dead trees in the lowest foreground
Svendsen sees a symbol both of "arms agonized in supplication, the
coils of the serpent, and by an inescapable association, the tree of
redemption."[2] Though, if they could read Svendsen's explication of

From "Milton Studies in Honor of Harris Francis Fletcher," *Journal of English
and Germanic Philology*, LX (1961), 670-79. Reprinted by permission of the
author and the publisher.

the painting, both Milton and Martin might be surprised by the triple symbolism which he sees in the writhen tree, they might well be happy in Svendsen's recognition of the painter's creation of a new myth emergent from the old one in the poem.

The case for the illustrator as a catalyst in the precipitation of a traditional myth in whose development the poem behind his illustration may be but a stage, can be made very strong. Indeed, the case may be defended as a reasonable extension of T. S. Eliot's critical doctrine and practice. In Svendsen's hands it becomes a touchstone to identify the few great illustrators of Milton among the many who have been recognized by Collins Baker.[3] In the list which ends at 1850 Svendsen finds only three whose interpretations of the Expulsion from Eden deserve reproduction in his article, and of the three he seems to regard Blake's as the finest, if not the most interesting. Its stylization of the lightning, the fig leaves, the thorns and thistles seems to him to enhance the mystery in the brooding eyes of Blake's mounted cherubim. Though Michael's foot is not quite on the head of the serpent, the uplifted faces of Adam and Eve are full of sweetness and of something like chastened confidence. The ambivalence in the conception seems to Svendsen to express the personal view of the Fall which Blake declared in *Milton* and the *Four Zoas,* and yet "his Expulsion Scene is faithful in fact (the clasped hands) as it is creatively free."[4] Full of symbolism though the packed canvas is, it is true to the moment imagined by Milton when

> In either hand the hast'ning Angel caught
> Our ling'ring Parents, and to th'Eastern Gate
> Led them direct, and down the cliff as fast
> To the subjected Plain.[5]

The ambivalence in Milton's closing scene has been magnificently shown by Svendsen elsewhere[6] in a study which lays great stress upon the final distich of the poem:

> They hand in hand with wand'ring steps and slow,
> Through *Eden* took thir solitary way.

In most of the happy scenes in the Garden of Eden their hands were clasped—at their first appearance in the story, when Satan sees them "hand in hand,"

> the loveliest pair
> That ever since in love's imbraces met"—[7]

and even in their dispute before the Fall, which ends when, as Eve turns away, "from her Husbands hand her hand / Soft she with-drew."[8] Their departure from Eden is a final confirmation of their original handfasting. If Bentley was right in taking "solitary" to indi-cate simply that Michael has finally left them alone together, their isolation is perhaps more than compensated by their re-established confidence and communion. If Bentley's reading is accepted, their solitude, which consists in the absence of their visible angel escort, is unreal, for they know what we are told in the preceding distich:

> The World was all before them, where to choose
> Thir place of rest, and Providence thir guide.

The tone of the four closing lines of the poem can be variously heard by readers of different temperaments and backgrounds. It can vary with the multiple meanings which can be given to the word *solitary*. For a theologically knowledgeable and concerned reader, the word will imply the end of direct intercourse between the banished couple and God. A flippant commentator may read the lines as mean-ing that the exiles are to be congratulated—now that their stern escort has vanished—upon being "alone at last." A sanguine optimist may regard their solitude as an invitation to their hearts to vibrate to the iron string of self-confidence. A non-Christian Existentialist may re-gard it as a statement of the perennial challenge of life to realistic analysis and intelligent assumption of responsibility. A Christian Exis-tentialist may—like Professor Frye[9]—read the entire movement toward the climax of the poem as a fulfillment of God's declaration in Book III, 196-97:

> Light after light well us'd they shall attain,
> And to the end persisting, safe arrive.

The ambivalence in the final paragraph of *Paradise Lost* depends—as Svendsen says[10]—upon the view that the individual reader takes of the *felix culpa*,[11] and of Adam's response to Michael's declaration that in the fullness of time "the Earth / Shall all be Paradise, far happier place / Than this of Eden":

> O goodness infinite, goodness immense!
> That all this good of evil shall produce,
> And evil turn to good; more wonderful
> Than that which by creation first brought forth

> Light out of darkness! full of doubt I stand,
> Whether I should repent me now of sin
> By mee done and occasion'd, or rejoice
> Much more . . ."[12]

Among the illustrators Blake stands out as most distinctly interpreting the Expulsion in terms of redemption and possible joy. In the
stance and expressions of his Adam and Eve there is lyric feeling such
as J. B. Broadbent denies[13] to the treatment of the theme of "the Fortunate Fall" by Michael in his essentially theological exposition of it
to Adam. He even denies it (by implication) to Adam's outburst of
praise to "goodness infinite." Actually, it is hard to sever theology from
lyric feeling in the ballad stanzas which he quotes as the natural habi-
tat of the doctrine, for even there it is on account of Adam's sin, "As
clerkis fyndyn wretyn in here book," that "we mown syngyn, 'deo
gracias.'" Broadbent represents a prevailing opinion which is made
the basis of William H. Marshall's analysis[14] of *Paradise Lost* as "constructed upon two systems, one dramatic and the other intellectual,"
the former packing its "most obvious emotional force" in the movement leading up to Satan's triumph in Book IX, and the other emerging only in the ironies of his defeat in Book X and of Michael's prophecy of his ultimate downfall in Book XII.

The truth in Marshall's depreciation of the last two books of *Paradise Lost* need not blind us to their value either as theology or as
dramatic epic. In the situation resulting from Michael's exposition of
God's purpose

> to reward
> His faithful, and receive them into bliss,
> Whether in Heav'n or Earth, for then the Earth
> Shall all be Paradise, far happier place
> Than this of Eden, and far happier days—[15]

as Ogden points out[16]—Adam's burst of praise for "goodness infinite"
is a dramatically appropriate ebullition of relief, amazement, and love.
It is more appropriate if we adopt William G. Madsen's suggestion[17]
that "the Incarnation involves not the lowering of Christ's nature to
the level of human nature, but the exaltation of human nature to
mystical union with God." In the movement of the poem as a whole
Adam's outburst is still more appropriate if we accept John M. Steadman's view[18] that a deliberate and powerful Aristotelian epic recognition is involved in his last speech ending in his confession of faith

> that suffering for Truth's sake
> Is fortitude to highest victory
> And to the faithful Death the Gate of Life;
> Taught this by his example whom I now
> Acknowledge my Redeemer ever blest.[19]

To Christian readers—at least to those familiar with the epic theory of the seventeenth century—the Fall might indeed seem fortunate enough to inspire an illustration even more solemnly symbolic of redemptive joy than Blake's drawing. To those readers Addison might well have seemed justified in his inclination to drop the two last lines of the poem on the ground that they "renew in the mind of the reader that anguish which was pretty well laid by" the promise in the distich just preceding that Providence would be their guide as they sought rest in a world which was "all before them where to choose." In the climate of religious feeling which prevailed when Bentley published his edition of *Paradise Lost* in 1732 there may have been many assenters to his view[20] that the closing distich "contradicts the poet's own scheme" because he has told us "That Adam, upon hearing Michael's predictions, was even 'surcharged with joy,' ver. 372; was 'replete with joy and wonder,' ver. 468; was in doubt, whether he should 'repent of' or 'rejoice in his fall,' ver. 475; was 'in great peace of thought,' ver. 558; and Eve herself 'not sad,' but 'full of consolation,' ver. 620." Though Pearce and Newton dissented vigorously from Addison and Bentley for literary reasons, the latter's reasons for regarding Milton's closing distich as inconsistent with Adam's surcharge of joy seem valid now to Broadbent[21] and Frank Kermode.[22]

Yet in spite of knowing that Bentley was right, as Broadbent puts it, "in demonstrating that the dénouement [of the return of 'long wandered man / Safe to eternal Paradise of rest'] is not amenable to what precedes, cannot be drawn dramatically out of Book XII despite the theological bonds," both he and Kermode see the ambivalence of the Fortunate Fall as clearly as Svendsen does. *If*, says Kermode, "Milton's 'scheme' was simply to show that everything would come out right in the end, and that this should keenly please both Adam and ourselves, Bentley is not at all silly here; or, if he is, so are the modern commentators who, supported by all that is now known about the topic *felix culpa*, tend to read the poem in a rather similar way." But Kermode suspects that some modern commentators have gone astray.

Though he names no one, the heads which Kermode's cap best fits are John Erskine's and John Crowe Ransom's. From the suggestion[23] that "Adam is proud" and properly proud in response to what may seem to an obtuse reader to be the "demoralizing comfort" of Michael's revelation of God's purposes, Erskine went on to draw a picture of Adam and Eve "in excellent spirits," leaving a tiresome Paradise with "nothing but zest" for "the world as a scene of action" such as Milton's "renaissance spirit" admired. Or, as Ransom finds, God has set his clever and adventurous creatures in "an infinitely tangled wilderness of a world which would be far more seductive presently to them than their idyllic bower."[24] Erskine and Ransom differ from Bentley only in missing the inconsistency between his view of the Expulsion and the closing lines of *Paradise Lost* in their unmistakable correspondence with God's commission to Michael in Book XI (117):

> So send them forth, though sorrowing, yet in peace.

And Kermode points out[25] that Bentley also forgot[26] God's command to Michael and its relevance to the mood of Adam and Eve as they leave Paradise.

About the rightness of that mood disagreement is no longer possible. It is the result of an evolution in culture and in poetry which Professor Kurth traces[27] through the literature leading up to *Paradise Lost* and through the poem itself to the confrontation of the Christian hero in the last two books by "the grim reality of evil . . . and suffering of human life." It is the expression of what Professor Gilbert has called[28] "the virtue developed by the contest with evil [which] justifies the presence of evil." If with C. M. Bowra[29] we prefer to look at it in simple human terms as "the confidence and courage in which men should set out on the undoubted perils of life," it is still the same, for it is the basis of what he calls the "inimitable close" of the poem. Whether Adam misunderstands the Fall is of no importance, for his mood would not change if he could know that in heaven God had solemnly declared to the angels that he would have been

> Happier, had it suffic'd him to have known
> Good by itself, and Evil not at all.[30]

Though Professor Taylor regards these words as an "explicit denial—coming from God, Milton's ultimate Spokesman in the poem—that the Fall was in any way a fortunate occurrence,"[31] we may be sure that Milton did not intend any *hybris* to be read into Adam's view of the event. With Professor Diekoff[32] we must remember that Adam's

Medina's illustration of the Expulsion from The Earthly Paradise, for Tonson's edition of *Paradise Lost,* 1688. From the copy in the Folger Shakespeare Library.

(Ed.^{ne} Alinari) P.^e 2.ª N.º 7768. ROMA—Vaticano, Loggie di Raffaello. Adamo ed Eva scacciati dal Paradiso Terrestre. (Raffaello e Guilio Romano.) Alinari Photo.

(Ed.ne Alinari) N.º 3846. FIRENZE—Chiesa del Carmine. Adamo ed
Eva Scacciati dal Paradiso Terreste. (Masaccio) Alinari Photo.

This illustration, from the 1613 edition of Andreini's *L'Adamo*, which Voltaire declared to have been the inspiration for *Paradise Lost*, confirms the conclusion that Milton's expulsion scene was a deliberate break with tradition. From the copy in the Folger Shakespeare Library.

view of the fall is no less explicit when he says to Michael: "full of doubt I stand / Whether I should repent . . . or rejoice / Much more. . . ."[33] Our speculations about the *felix culpa* in itself, or in Milton's view of it, or in Adam's, may all be subject to the limitation which A. J. A. Waldock[34] compared to Heisenberg's "Uncertainty principle" in physics—to something in the nature of the concept itself which makes it immensurable under scrutiny. What is important is that Adam's conception of it, and God's as interpreted to Adam by Michael, should have brought *Paradise Lost* to what Waldock could call its "inimitable close."

The rightness of the close no longer needs defense. Its importance as an artistic achievement and also as marking a long step forward in thought about man's proper attitude toward his situation in life, is best understood in the iconographical context. Milton's recreation of the myth of the Fall and its consequences was an achievement greater than that which Svendsen sees in Martin's treatment of the Expulsion from Eden. The measure of Milton's accomplishment in the last three books of his epic, and especially in the closing scene of Book XII, can be taken by comparing its closing lines with the treatment of the scene by his first illustrator, John Baptist Medina. His story has been told by Miss Helen Gardner,[35] and his illustrations of Tonson's edition of *Paradise Lost* in 1688 have been described by her and assessed as a genuine attempt at interpretation of the poem which deserves some respect and attention. Her accounts of several of his illustrations for the first ten books of the poem justify her estimate of their value, but she acknowledges that his treatment of the Expulsion from Paradise is "a sad disappointment." Her explanation for the failure is the fact "that the subject was too familiar, and that Medina, instead of studying his author, was content with a bad imitation of Raphael's 'Expulsion' in the Loggia, itself derived from Masaccio's fresco in the Carmine in Florence." The lack of intrinsic value in both Medina's picture and that by Raphael (with the help of Julio Romano) marks their documentary importance as transcripts of a traditional conception of the woe becoming to the couple being evicted from Paradise— woe which is foreign to the mood of Milton's ending of his poem.

Woe is the theme of Masaccio's much better painting, and there is nothing in the pose or features of his Michael that clearly suggests anything like divine compassion. The uplifted sword in the angel's hand is a sword of justice, compelling obedience of a different kind from that which Milton's couple have learned to pay to their guide.

Masaccio's Adam has a dignity which neither Raphael nor Medina seems to have thought of giving to their male figures. Masaccio's Eve's face is a study in pure anguish, but neither of his figures moves with the contemptible animal fright that makes the Eve disgusting in the paintings by Raphael and Medina. If Milton saw Raphael's picture in the Vatican (as he probably did not), it could hardly have interested him for more than a moment. Nor can he have been interested in the illustration of the Expulsion in Andreini's *L'Adamo* (in the lavishly illustrated first edition by Bordoni, Milan, 1613), which represents Michael as pursuing the terrified exiles with his flaming sword lifted and ready to strike. If during his visits in Florence he saw Masaccio's obscurely placed painting, he may have carried its memory away to react morally against it—partly because its artistic merit made it unforgettable.

It was a long time before illustrators of Milton's expulsion scene could treat Adam and Eve as anything but studies in anguish or despair fleeing from the archangel's sword. So they appear in the headpiece to the Twelfth Book of *Paradise Lost* in the beautiful edition of the poem which was "Printed for Jacob Tonson, at *Shakespear's Head in the Strand*," in 1720. So, in a rather languid way, they survive in Gustave Doré's engraving of the scene.[36] Blake was the first artist to conceive Milton's Expulsion with hope and love in the faces of Adam and Eve, and an unarmed Michael leading them by the hands, as Milton has him do.

In the twentieth century it might be expected that illustration of Milton's Expulsion scene would follow the course which John Martin first explored in 1827. With John Erskine's new Adam and Eve in his essay on "The Theme of Death in *Paradise Lost*" as models a painter might create two figures for whom the Fall would obviously be inconceivable in any terms but Fortune. But in perhaps the most expressive modern treatment of the Expulsion, that in the edition of *Paradise Lost. A Poem in Twelve Books* which was published in London by the Cresset Press in 1931, death and not Fortune or Power is the theme. The very dark woodcut shows Adam and Eve close-up, nude, with hands clasped, but with averted faces. Adam's expression is wretched, resentful, and baffled. He is twentieth-century man, miserable in a hostile universe. Nothing more remote from the physical grace and dignity of Masaccio's Adam could be imagined. Beside him Eve covers her face with her free left arm. Her gesture is sheer terror, for a skeleton thrusts his jaws over her shoulder in an effort to bite her

cheek. The Miltonic warrant for her escort in the place of Michael—
if any—may be found in speeches like Adam's rhetorical demand to
know "Why is life giv'n / To be thus wrested from us?" After gathering several such passages of poignant protest against death to support
his thesis, Kermode declares[37] that *"Paradise Lost* is a poem about
death, and about pleasure and its impairment."* Kermode is not ap-
peased by Milton's treatment of death as a release "from the great
wound the senses have suffered," nor by his gratification of the senses
for a while with the flowers and fruits of the Earthly Paradise, or with
the perfumes and ethereal light of heaven. For Kermode, the great
paradox of *Paradise Lost* is not the Fall but "the paradox of Eve as de-
stroyer and giver of life."[38] The poem can be so read, and in our time
that reading may make Michael give way to the skeleton as escort for
Adam and Eve when they leave Paradise to choose their place of rest
with no thought that Providence can be their guide.

The spirit of the symbolism in the other *de luxe* edition of our
time[39] is similar, but it goes further than the Cresset edition in strip-
ping Adam and Eve of their supernatural guidance. The woodcut at
the end of Book XII is a horizontal panel showing them with hands
clasped, stumbling forward without escort of any kind. Between them
is a child's version of a serpent. Beside Adam is a half-crouching dog.
Around them and hemming them in are four colossal faces, two
menacing and two averted, with horrent locks. Since a fragment of
Milton's Biblical myth survives in the serpent, one wonders whether
the four faces are modern versions of the "dreadful Faces" and "fiery
Arms"[40] of the Biblical seraphim who guard the gate of Paradise and
watch Milton's Adam and Eve as they retreat. Or are they a modern
reminiscence of the four mounted angels in the background of Blake's
Expulsion? Behind the four hostile or threatening faces a still more
enormous face fixes its expressionless eyes on the backs of the harassed
human couple. Its expression is obscured by two swords crossed in
front of it. Cosmic violence and indifference usurp the place of the
Providence under whose guidance Milton's Adam and Eve were left
by Michael to pursue what once seemed like a "solitary way."

NOTES

1. "John Martin and the Expulsion Scene in *Paradise Lost," Studies in
   English Literature,* 1500-1900, I (1961), 63-74.
2. "John Martin and the Expulsion Scene," p. 71.

3. C. H. Collins Baker, "Some Illustrators of Milton's *Paradise Lost* (1688-1850)," *Library*, 5th ser., III (1948), 1-21, 101-19.

4. "John Martin and the Expulsion Scene," p. 70.

5. *P.L.*, XII, 637-40.

6. *Milton and Science* (Cambridge, Mass., 1956), pp. 107-13. Cf. Stanley B. Greenfield's note on *Paradise Lost*, XII, 629-32 in *Expl.*, XII (1961), item 57.

7. *P.L.*, IV, 321-22.

8. *P.L.*, IX, 385-86.

9. Roland Mushat Frye, *God, Man and Satan: Patterns of Christian Thought and Life in Paradise Lost, Pilgrim's Progress, and the Great Theologians* (Princeton, 1960), p. 113.

10. *Milton and Science*, p. 106.

11. In *"Paradise Lost: Felix Culpa* and the Problem of Structure," *MLN*, LXXVI (1961), 15-20, William H. Marshall lists previous treatments as follows (p. 16): John Erskine, "The Theme of Death in *Paradise Lost*," *PMLA*, XXXII (1917), 573-82; Cecil A. Moore, "The Conclusion of *Paradise Lost*," *PMLA*, XXXVI (1921), 1-34; Allan H. Gilbert, "The Problem of Evil in *Paradise Lost*," *JEGP*, XXII (1923), 175-94; Denis Saurat, *Milton: Man and Thinker* (1925), p. 131; John S. Diekhoff, *Milton's "Paradise Lost: A Commentary on the Argument* (New York, 1946), p. 131; B. Rajan, *Paradise Lost & the Seventeenth Century Reader* (London, 1947), p. 45; Millicent Bell, "The Fallacy of the Fall in *Paradise Lost*," *PMLA*, LXVIII (1953), 863-83, and LXX (1955), 1187-97; Wayne Shumaker, "The Fallacy of the Fall in *Paradise Lost*," *PMLA*, LXX (1955), 1185-87, 1197-1202; H. S. V. Ogden, "The Crisis of *Paradise Lost* Reconsidered," *PQ*, XXXVI (1957), 1-19; William G. Madsen, "The Fortunate Fall in *Paradise Lost*," *MLN*, LXXIV (1959), 103-105. To this list must be added the study by Dick Taylor, Jr., "Milton and the Paradox of the Fortunate Fall Once More," *Tulane Studies in English*, IX (1959), 35-52, and the discussions of the Fortunate Fall by J. B. Broadbent in *Some Graver Subject: An Essay on Paradise Lost* (London, 1960), pp. 282-86, and by Frank Kermode, "Adam Unparadised," in *The Living Milton* (London, 1960), pp. 116-24.

12. *P.L.* XII, 469-76.

13. *Some Graver Subject*, p. 282.

14. *"Paradise Lost: Felix Culpa* and the Problem of Structure," pp. 18-19.

15. *P.L.*, XII, 461-65.

16. "The Crisis of *Paradise Lost* Reconsidered," p. 18.

17. "The Fortunate Fall in *Paradise Lost*," pp. 104-105.

18. *Studia Neophilologica*, XXXI (1959), 159-73.

19. *P.L.*, XII, 569-74.

20. Bentley is quoted from Henry John Todd's variorum edition of *The Poetical Works of John Milton* (London, 1801), III, 465-66.

21. *Some Graver Subject*, p. 286.

22. *The Living Milton*, p. 102.

23. John Erskine, "The Theme of Death in *Paradise Lost*," pp. 573-82. The quoted phrases are from pp. 578 and 581.

24. John Crowe Ransom, "The Idea of a Literary Anthropologist and What He Might Say of the *Paradise Lost* of Milton," *Kenyon Review*, XXI (1959), 137.

25. *The Living Milton*, p. 102.

26. Ants Oras, in *Milton's Editors and Commentators from Patrick Hume to Henry John Todd (1695-1801)* (Dorpat, 1931), p. 51, agrees with J. W. Mackail that "Bentley's notes . . . prove that the task was carried out in a hurry, and that much of the work in its final form may have been dictated."

27. Burton O. Kurth, *Milton and Christian Heroism: Biblical Epic Themes and Forms in Seventeenth Century England* (Berkeley and Los Angeles, 1959), p. 127.

28. "The Problem of Evil in *Paradise Lost*," p. 188.

29. *From Virgil to Milton* (London, 1948), p. 210.

30. *P.L.*, XI, 88-89.

31. "Milton and the Paradox of the Fortunate Fall Once More," p. 51.

32. *Milton's "Paradise Lost": A Commentary on the Argument*, p. 131.

33. *P.L.*, XII, 473-75. The full passage is quoted above.

34. *Paradise Lost and Its Critics* (Cambridge, Eng., 1947), pp. 145-46.

35. "Milton's First Illustrator," *Essays and Studies*, new ser., IX (1956), 27-38.

36. *Milton's "Paradise Lost,"* illustrated by Gustave Doré (New York, 1885), plate 50, opp. p. 312.

37. *The Living Milton*, p. 121.

38. *The Living Milton*, p. 120.

39. *Paradise Lost. A Poem by John Milton. The Text of the First Edition Prepared for Press by J. Isaacs and Printed at the Golden Cockerel Press* ([London], 1937).

40. *P.L.*, XII, 644.

DONALD R. PEARCE

The Style of Milton's Epic

> *That diction, on the other hand, is lofty and raised above the*
> *commonplace which employs unusual words. By unusual, I*
> *mean strange (or rare) words, metaphysical, lengthened—any-*
> *thing in short that differs from the normal idiom. . . . For by*
> *deviating in exceptional cases from the normal idiom the lan-*
> *guage will gain distinction. . . . (Aristotle, Poetics XXII)*

Mr. E. M. W. Tillyard, discussing Milton's later style in *The Mil-*
tonic Setting, is at some pains to deny the charge "so commonly
brought against Milton, that of forsaking common English speech
and of hardening into a remote grandeur." "The main peculiarities or
heightenings of Milton's style in *Paradise Lost* are quite unlatin," he
writes, and where obvious latinisms are found, many of them "could
be good English idiom just as well." One of the notable features of
Milton's later style, he goes on to say, is its drive toward simplicity:
"Milton reacted against the riot of verbiage that makes the Elizabe-
thans and Jacobeans so exhilarating . . . [and] tried to extract the
utmost of significance from simple words like *fair* or *joy* or *strive*."
Thus, if a good deal of the supposed latinization in *Paradise Lost*
"turns out to be English after all, the charge of remoteness or of

From *The Yale Review*, LII (1963), 427-44. Copyright, 1963, by Yale University. Reprinted by permission of the author and the publisher.

368

using English words like a dead language loses much of its support."

Mr. Tillyard has made a spirited and novel defense of Milton's "englishness," though these brief quotations do it less than justice; but in one respect it seems to me as unsatisfactory as it is unexpected. It is unexpected because if there is one thing which it might be supposed a professional Miltonist would prize above anything else in Milton, it would be precisely the "remote grandeur" of his style, its complete and utter artificiality. Even Dr. Johnson, who with one part of his mind thought the diction of *Paradise Lost* merely pretentious— "a Babylonish dialect," formed on the "perverse and pedantic principle of using English words with a foreign idiom"—could not conceal his delight in its rhetorical grandeur, and on the same page with his disapproval we find him exclaiming "criticism sinks in admiration!" It was Addison's opinion that Milton had to deviate from "the common forms and ordinary phrases of speech" to achieve sublimity—a colloquial sublimity being for him a contradiction in terms. Addison was, I think, perfectly correct; and I therefore strongly question whether by attempting to minimize the Latin element in Milton's style in favor of its "englishness" Mr. Tillyard is not giving away with his left hand more than he can ever hope to get back with his right. Indeed, it is when one sets out to relate the diction of *Paradise Lost* to "the norm of the common tongue" that one notices a precisely opposite effect, viz. that the norm behind Milton lies in the *uncommon* tongue, in the learned body of formal prose, theological, philosophical, forensic, descending from medieval and classic literary tradition, with which from his youth onward, as cloistered scholar and as public servant, Milton was thoroughly familiar. *Paradise Lost* displays the virtues of great prose.

Wordsworth appears to have been the first critic to comment on the prose element in Milton's verse. In a famous passage in the Preface to *Lyrical Ballads*, while insisting on the essential identity of the language of prose and the language of metrical composition he makes reference to Milton as follows: ". . . some of the most interesting parts of the best poems will be found to be strictly the language of prose when prose is well written. The truth of this assertion might be demonstrated by innumerable passages from almost all of the poetical writings, even of Milton himself." A few years later, we find Hazlitt making a similar point: "That approximation to the severity of impassioned prose which has been made an objection to Milton's poetry, and which is chiefly to be met with in these bitter invectives, is one of its greatest excellences." He is referring to the debates in Hell in Book II of *Paradise Lost,* presumably to lines like the following, where the prose ordering of the language unmistakably imitates the mode of classical oratory:

> But, first, whom shall we send
> In search of this new World? whom shall we find
> Sufficient? who shall tempt with wandering feet
> The dark, unbottomed, infinite Abyss,
> And through the palpable obscure find out
> His uncouth way, or spread his airy flight,
> Upborne with indefatigable wings
> Over the vast abrupt, ere he arrive
> The happy Isle? What strength, what art, can then
> Suffice, or what evasion bear him safe. . . .

There is not much here to remind one of the "norm of common speech." Rather than any vernacular that ever existed, what these verses are drawing on is the highly literate "norm" of the classical oration, impassioned, calculated, artificial down to its last syllable. To see this point more clearly, let us place beside the Milton a comparable passage from Shakespeare's *Troilus and Cressida,* where the norm of common speech truly does underlie and inform the diction of the verses:

> *Agamemnon:*   Princes,
> What grief hath set the jaundice on your cheeks?
> The ample proposition that hope makes
> In all designs begun on earth below
> Fails in the promis'd largeness: checks and disasters
> Grow in the veins of actions highest rear'd;
> As knots, by the conflux of meeting sap,
> Infect the sound pine and divert his grain
> Tortive and errant from his course of growth.
> Nor, princes, is it matter new to us
> That we come short of our suppose so far
> That after seven years' siege yet Troy walls stand;
> Sith every action that hath gone before,
> Whereof we have record, trial did draw
> Bias and thwart, not answering the aim,
> And that unbodied figure of the thought
> That gave't surmised shape. . . .

Beside Milton's formal cadences, Shakespeare's lines seem virtually ad-libbed, the figures loose, repetitious, expedient, as in the dramatic circumstances they perhaps ought to be; for Agamemnon is not, like Beelzebub, addressing an assembly of fallen angels in Hell, but only a group of his officers and friends in a tent. Still, even allowing for that, the diction of the passage is unschooled, inelegant, and "noisy" in ways not arising from either character or occasion. The noise is in the form itself; in the exigencies of the theatrical art as Shakespeare conceived it. What do we actually learn in this passage? We learn that large hopes are always getting disappointed (3-5), because disappointments always intervene (5-9), so we ought not to be too disappointed (10-12), because the record shows that hopes are always getting disappointed (13-17). The redundance thunders on throughout the rest of the scene with familiar Elizabethan extravagance and energy. Lines like

> . . . trial did draw
> Bias and thwart, not answering the aim
> And that unbodied figure of the thought
> That gave't surmised shape. . . .

are surely "actor's lines," and not very far from rant. The throwaway element in them is obviously large. The norm behind Agamemnon's words, behind a great deal of Shakespeare for that matter, being of necessity colloquial, is simply insufficiently austere for certain things.

Nothing could be further from Milton's stylistic practice than these colloquial verses of Shakespeare. And one of the things I am going to claim is that the "remote grandeur" of Milton's language in *Paradise Lost* originates in the formalities of classic prose—a scholastic discipline of thought and word and word-order that deeply pervades the entire poem, infiltrating even the tenderest lyrical passage, to stiffen it as with gold brocade:

> But neither breath of Morn, when she ascends
> With charm of earliest birds; nor rising Sun
> On this delightful land; nor herb, fruit, flowers
> Glistering with dew; nor fragrance after showers;
> Nor grateful evening mild, nor silent Night,
> With this her solemn bird, nor walk by Moon
> Or glittering starlight, without thee is sweet. . . .

The careful graduation of the sense here, the lucidity of statement, the choice economy of diction, the logical word order, the chaste and clear verbal music, all exhibit traditional strengths of efficient prose. Though "domestic Eve" is speaking, it is only her vocabulary that comes from "common speech"; the classic formality and graciousness of her phrasing turns what she says into a kind of delicate oratory. Again, at the poem's crisis, when Eve plucks the forbidden fruit, Milton writes:

> So saying, her rash hand in evil hour
> Forth reaching to the Fruit, she plucked, she eat.
> Earth felt the wound, and Nature from her seat,
> Sighing through all her Works, gave signs of woe
> That all was lost.

The clarity of the verbal linkages, the direct registering of the events, the severe suppression of figure, surely refer the art of the passage to prosaic norms. We are not very far, in fact, from the objective language of the laboratory report. The phrases lock together with finality, and make an irreversible word order for the irreversible moral action.

Take an elaborate instance, Satan's address to Uriel in Book III. Satan has broken out of Hell and is cruising in the vicinity of the "world." Uncertain which of several "shining orbs" is the planet he seeks, he asks Uriel, the Solar angel, to direct him. The question is so skillfully put that Uriel has no suspicion at the moment that he is being deceived:

> "Uriel! for thou of those seven Spirits that stand
> In sight of God's high Throne, gloriously bright,
> The first art wont his great authentic will
> Interpreter through highest Heaven to bring,
> Where all his Sons thy Embassy attend,
> And here art likeliest by supreme decree
> Like honour to obtain, and as his Eye
> To visit oft this new Creation round—
> Unspeakable desire to see and know
> All these his wondrous works, but chiefly Man,
> His chief delight and favour, him for whom
> All these his works so wondrous he ordained,
> Hath brought me from the Choirs of Cherubim
> Alone thus wandering. Brightest Seraph, tell
> In which of all these shining orbs hath Man

His fixed seat—or fixed seat hath none,
But all these shining Orbs his choice to dwell—
That I may find him, and with secret gaze
Or open admiration him behold
On whom the great Creator hath bestowed
Worlds, and on whom hath all these graces poured;
That both in him and all things, as is meet
The Universal Maker we may praise;
Who justly hath driven out his Rebel Foes
To deepest Hell, and, to repair that loss
Created this new happy Race of Men
To serve him better: wise are all his ways!"

The skills of near pedantry required to read these lines with enjoyment and understanding are clearly such as are unlikely to come from one's experience with the common tongue, or even from general English poetic tradition. The careful interior structuring of the passage, the managed series of subordinations, nudged into line at the right instants by the reappearing primary sense, conform to a tradition of trained prosaic eloquence, in which the art of effectively disposing the members of a complex sentence among its main rhetorical elements has attained a high level of accomplishment. The formal scheme of the passage is reducible to something like: "Uriel . . . of those Seven Spirits, the first . . . Chiefly man has brought me. . . . Brightest Seraph, tell in which . . . that I may find . . . and behold . . . that we may praise. . . ." Reducing to essentials, we arrive at the bare *"Uriel . . . tell,"* which, deftly concealed behind twenty-six lines of camouflaging rhetoric, cuts across the whole passage like a command. The lines display exquisite prosaic skills that descend to the Renaissance from traditional oratory and diplomacy, an eloquence which Milton learned at school, and as Cromwell's Secretary for Foreign Tongues applied in the public service for twenty years.

The fact that before he began to devote himself to the composition of *Paradise Lost* Milton had spent most of the previous two decades composing documents of state and other tracts, and philosophic or polemical treatises, many of them in Latin, has never received as much attention as it deserves from students of Milton, at least as it bears on the linguistic practices of his great poem. He wrote an immense amount of prose during that long period, all of it notable for clarity, passion, and strength, some of it as accomplished as any that has ever been written in English, or that may ever be again. But the rhetorical and substantial connections between that prose and his later verse are so close that we are, in fact, undoubtedly justified in discovering the stylistic model of *Paradise Lost* in the "tradition" of Milton's own prose writings rather than in foreign epics, or classical precedents such as Virgil's *Aeneid.* One may be quite emphatic about this. There is not only far less structural resemblance between Milton's poem and the *Aeneid,* in particular, than is often claimed (for example, by C. S. Lewis); there is more often than not no real similarity to be observed at all between the sweetly-jointed Virgilian line and the pedantic brilliance of Milton's verse. John Crowe Ransom was, I think, right in arguing several years ago that it is in the early *Lycidas* (1637) that Milton showed his final mastery of the Virgilian manner, and that in the case of *Paradise Lost* "the great departure from the epical substance of Virgil makes it needful to depart from the poetic tone." Mr. Ransom drops the subject at this point; but I think we can supply the demonstration, using the prose tradition as our main resource.

The distance between the poetical style of *Lycidas* and that of *Paradise Lost* is "measured" by the intervening twenty years' discipline of prose. Virgil—that is to say, pastoral sweetness of tone, choice dignity of epithet and phrase, lyric ornateness generally—died for Milton with the shepherd poet of *Lycidas;* as, in fact, did Milton's youthful Italianate muse, for the poem is a kind of self-epitaph. What followed were the years of public prose during which the epic style was gradually prepared and cast:

> How happy were it for this frail, and as it may be truly called mortal life of man, since all earthly things, which have the name of good and convenient in our daily use, are withal so cumbersome and full of trouble, if knowledge, yet which is the best and lightsomest possession of the mind, were, as the common saying is, no burden; and that what it wanted of being a load to any part of the body, it did not with a heavy advantage overlay upon the spirit! For not to speak of that knowledge that rests in the contemplation of natural causes and dimensions, which must needs be a lower wisdom, as the object is low, certain it is that he who hath obtained in more than the scantest measure to know anything distinctly of God,

and of his true worship; and what is infallibly good and happy in the state of man's life, what in itself evil and miserable, though vulgarly not so esteemed; he that hath obtained to know this, the only high valuable wisdom indeed, remembering also that God, even to a strictness, requires the improvement of these his entrusted gifts, cannot but sustain a sorer burden of mind, and more pressing, than any supportable toil or weight which the body can labour under, how and in what manner he shall dispose and employ those sums of knowledge and illumination, which God hath sent him into this world to trade with.

This magnificent paragraph, from *The Reason of Church Government,* amply displays Milton's skills as a writer of prose, and suggests its relation to the dynamics of his later verse. The passage is not only rhetorically strong; it also possesses great formal elegance. Each of the half-dozen eddying qualifications helps to produce and distribute the thought, keeping it fittingly complex yet everywhere articulate and sharp; the carefully placed subordinations, the tasteful suspensions, "breathe" with the progress of the argument; and while the whole paragraph is a model of dignified discourse, the individual phrases, weighty taken singly, by some minor miracle of handling almost dance their way into the reader's mind. It is a vanished art, and its last poetical practice went into the making of Milton's later style.

Books like *The Christian Doctrine, The Reason of Church Government, Areopagitica,* though probably never so intended by Milton, when read alongside *Paradise Lost* resemble exercises in philosophic definition, theological exegesis, historical and political critique and, in short, appear as stylistic *rehearsals* for the performance of a poem he had not yet written. And as one looks at them from this point of view, it is impossible, I think, not to be impressed, as scholars like Maurice Kelley and Arthur Sewell have been, by Milton's encyclopedic preparation for *Paradise Lost,* by the orderliness of his thought and of his vision of the world, and by the beauty of that order; or without coming to realize how closely he had examined and defined main points of philosophy, science, and Christian doctrine. Words like "Nature," "God," "Matter," "Angel," "Spirit," all of which were soon to become key terms in *Paradise Lost,* one finds him ranging and defining in his prose with a lexicographer's care, with the result that no casual meanings were left clinging to them: they had become a firm and coherent *terminology*, capable of supporting an action of whatever massiveness he cared to mount on it.

Classic eloquence, then, served Milton in two main ways in *Paradise Lost*. First, it provided a continuous rhetorical device of *alienation*, imparting an aloofness to the whole action, so that the reader is at no time in any danger of ignoring the decisive *distance* between his natural, daily self and those splendid events and persons. Second, it assured Milton maximum precision of utterance—for ancient eloquence tolerated no busy Elizabethan blurring of syntax, image, and idea. What he had made was a prosodic engine, or better, a *measure*, of unparalleled sweetness and austerity, formal and remote but full of grace, an instrument by which the poem's complex cosmology, theology, history, and myth, always shading off into each other at best, could be manipulated with continuous and fastidious precision.

Precision in the use of the key terms is, in fact, what ultimately gives the verse of *Paradise Lost* its characteristic lucidity and force. Definite in the essentials, the details purified themselves. Prosaic virtues of clarity, order, strict definition, working from line to line, adjusting clause to clause, word to word, are the real source of that classic "finish," a clear hardness of texture, which everywhere distinguishes the Miltonic line from any other—a quality scarcely to be seen again in English poetry except, though with a difference, in the work of Alexander Pope, who had also defined his terms. Thus, when Milton says, to quote the crucial lines again:

> So saying, her rash hand in evil hour
> Forth reaching to the Fruit, she plucked, she eat.
> Earth felt the wound, and Nature from her seat
> Sighing through all her Works gave signs of woe
> That all was lost. . . .

he knows exactly what he means by the general term "Nature," and so does the reader, because Milton consistently employs the term in ways conforming to a firm definition. "Nature" has the following exact meanings in *Paradise Lost* (I draw from *The Christian Doctrine*): the art of God; that part of physical creation contained within the Primum Mobile; hence the system known as the World, lying between Chaos (the realm of unformed matter) and the Empyrean (the realm of pure Spirit); manifesting, as Milton phrases it, "that general law which is the origin of everything, and under which everything acts." As an operative term in the poem, it is carefully marked off from neighboring terms like Chaos, Hell, Limbo, Matter, Fate, Heaven, Sin, Reason, as each of these terms is marked off from the others. Thus, in the case of the lines just quoted, Milton shows himself as interested in the metaphysical as in the dramatic situation. We learn not just that Eve has sinned by violating the prohibition of the garden, but also the exact extent of the reverberation of her deed. And not only that, but also what her deed did *not* affect, and was, in fact, "systematically" incapable of affecting.

A good deal, therefore, of what might look like stiffness or schoolmasterly pedantry in Milton is actually a relentless, nuclear certainty, penetrating from the philosophic to the rhetorical to the grammatical details of the text. And this is why imitation of Milton, as the eighteenth and nineteenth centuries amply demonstrated, was almost always bad; for it was mainly imitation of effects without causes. Milton had no real followers in verse. What was not copiable was the achieved clarity of his thought; but that precisely was the generative principle of his style. His positive stylistic influence upon our literature really appears to descend by another route than the poetic, viz. by way of the prose tradition. The true inheritors of Milton's eloquence were prose writers like Burke, Gibbon, Newman, Arnold. *Paradise Lost,* it is tempting to assert, inaugurates and presides over our "Age of Prose and Reason."

As prosaic clarity in the key terms of a work fosters coherence in the details, ambiguity at those points produces inconsistent imagery, disheveled phrasing, reliance upon mere sonority. When Thompson writes, Miltonizing:

> Nature! great parent! whose unceasing hand
> Rolls round the seasons of the changeful year,
> How mighty, how majestic, are thy works!
> With what a pleasing dread they swell the soul,
> That sees astonished! and astonished sings!
> Ye too, ye winds! That now begin to blow
> With boisterous sweep, I raise my voice to you. . . .

it is perfectly clear that however much the roll of the verses may recall Milton, the terms "Nature," "parent," and "works" are being used without Miltonic rigor. Nature as "nurse" is implicit in the imagery of the first two lines; the next three induce a vaguely regal image; in lines six and seven the winds are apparently conceived of as somehow different from either Nature or her "works." While it is true that Thompson was simply not the poet Milton was in anything, it is also true that an undisciplined ambiguity in his use of general terms is one of the reasons why he was not. And though the passage may not present Thompson at his best—he is capable of more grace and weight—it is a fair passage, and shows clearly what is true of imitators of Milton generally—that they relied far more upon chancy verbal resonance for poetical effectiveness than Milton himself ever did.

The reputation for "sonority" has haunted Milton for over a century; it is time it was dismissed. Actually, Milton's verse is frequently more hushed, less dependent upon the listener's eardrums, less concerned with making mere popular gestures of sound, than any other in English. This is perfectly consonant with trained and eloquent prosaic tradition. C. S. Lewis once compared the Milton of *Paradise Lost* to a man performing a rite. The comparison is just; for at bottom the poem is all ritual language, all a delphic artifice, in some deep sense *spellbound:*

> . . . and shoals
> Of Fish that, with their fins and shining scales,
> Glide under the green wave in sculls that oft
> Bank the mid-sea. Part, single or with mate,
> Graze the sea-weed, their pasture, and through groves
> Of coral stray, or, sporting with quick glance,
> Show to the sun their waved coats dropped with gold,
> Or, in their pearly shells at ease, attend
> Moist nutriment, or under rocks their food
> In jointed armour watch. . . .

The charm of these lines—they seem to me inexhaustibly charming—comes from a *special silence among the images* rather than from any real or imagined sonority of language: fish "that with their fins and shining scales / Glide under the green wave in sculls," caught and fixed forever in the silent act of disappearing "under the green wave" to their completely fishy world: it is a perfectly magical and silent image. To find sonority in lines like these would be to look for something that is not there. The lines are, in fact, silent because of the sanctity of the thought. The fish, the clams, the crustaceans are named, described, with pure, motiveless objectivity. Milton makes no attempt to speak through them, or incorporate them into some philosophy, as by contrast Wordsworth habitually does with natural objects. He does not want to *use* them. He leaves them chastely alone in their creature existence, to the greater glory of God:

> . . . on smooth the seal
> And bended dolphins play: part, huge of bulk,
> Wallowing unwieldy, enormous in their gait,
> Tempest the ocean. There leviathan,
> Hugest of living creatures, on the deep
> Stretched like a promontory, sleeps or swims,
> And seems a moving land, and at his gills
> Draws in, and at his trunk spouts out, a sea.
> Meanwhile the tepid caves, and fens, and shores,
> Their brood as numerous hatch from the egg, that soon,
> Bursting with kindly rupture, forth disclosed
> Their callow young; but feathered soon and fledge
> They summed their pens, and, soaring the air sublime,
> With clang despised the ground, under a cloud
> In prospect. . . .

The passage continues in this gracious way for another hundred lines, to close in a remarkable—almost waddling—imitation of primordial motility:

> Earth in her rich attire
> Consummate lovely smiled; air, water, earth,
> By fowl, fish, beast, was flown, was swum, was walked,
> Frequent; and of the sixth Day yet remained. . . .

Nowhere throughout does the cliché of Miltonic "sonority" apply. When Milton describes how Eden's fig tree formed

> a pillared shade
> High overarched, and echoing walks between

it is the pictured stillness in the lines, not any verbal resonance, that strikes us. The image is that of pastoral aracades gulfed in some large, dreamlike silence, punctuated by intermittent footsteps. It is a piece of soundless phantasy. In the same way, the effectiveness of the lines

> till Morn
> Waked by the circling Hours, with rosy hand
> Unbarred the gates of light

lies in their mysteriousness. We are charmed not because of their resonance, but by a totally different quality that pervades them like a scent, a quality for which Milton has been more often censured than praised: their exquisite pedantry. This is a quality that directly derives from the literary traditions of formal classic prose.

When Dr. Johnson called the style of *Paradise Lost* "pedantic," he was far from intending to be complimentary. But I am satisfied with the word, partly for polemical reasons; it sums up what I would call the poem's *studied elegance,* something less prized in current literary taste than it once was. To call Milton's verse pedantic, or studiously elegant, amounts to pretty much the same thing; for what one is really paying tribute to is an underlying gravity of purpose, of professional craftsmanship, which on every page of his work distinguishes Milton from all other poets writing in English. Milton is so much the professional, in fact, that he makes most English poets look a little like gifted amateurs by contrast. One feels the need of a phrase like "the practice of literature" when discussing him. For the language of *Paradise Lost* is an eminently studied, eminently professional thing, carefully built up out of the choicest elements and practices of ancient and modern languages, from the Bible and from what he called "the mother dialect," to form an instrument of a most subtle and pedantic perfection. A reader of Milton who possesses any degree of literary sophistication at all is sure, therefore, to experience, as he will with no other English poet, a connoisseur's pleasure, which is that of being constantly aware of moving among rarities, among treasured specimens of the literary art.

One form Milton's "pedantry" takes is an abundant use of ornate classical simile and allusion. A good deal has been written about these rhetorical features of his work, but mostly by way of explication; not much has actually been said about the stylistic operation of the allusions and similes in the poem. The established view is that they are "happy digressions," charming ornaments that (as Professor J. H. Hanford says) provided Milton "with a welcome means of pouring forth the treasures of his mind." Mr. Hanford remarks on something more illuminating, but does not develop it: "The key to this habit," he says, "is in part at least, Milton's passion for scholarly completeness." This is perfectly true. When Milton alludes to something in Ovid or in Virgil he does so with chapter-and-verse exactness. And the effect of this "habit" is obviously to limit connotation and increase the clarity of image or idea.

But if we examine them more closely, it soon becomes apparent that some other principle than "scholarly completeness" is at work to give

these similes and allusions that beads-on-a-string look which they exhibit page after page throughout the poem. For one thing, the component parts of the similes (necessarily of the allusions) are seen to
come invariably not from the order of nature but from the order of art,
from, as Mr. Hanford correctly observes, myth, legend, romance,
technical arts, and from other literatures. Even the famous comparison of Satan's shield to the disc of the full moon as seen in Galileo's telescope is properly not an exception to this; for the astronomical
moon in 1670 was still a most "romantic" object, a place of fabulous
conjecture, not a physical cinder as for us.

This practice of Milton's did not escape the scholarly eye of Dr.
Johnson, but he had nothing good to say for it: "The Garden of
Eden," he writes, "brings to his mind the vale of Enna where Prosperine was gathering flowers. Satan makes his way through fighting
elements like Argo between the Cyanes rocks, or Ulysses between the
two Sicilian whirlpools when he shunned Charybdis on the larboard."
To Johnson, little more is going on in such passages than a somewhat
glib schoolboy association of ideas, and he hurries to agree with Dryden that Milton "saw nature through the spectacles of books." It is a
brilliant comment; and, of course, entirely just. Milton did see the
world through the spectacles of books, the world of *Paradise Lost* at
any rate, and it is very much to the point to notice that this is, in fact,
the way he saw it. To be somewhat more explicit, we could say that
regularly throughout *Paradise Lost* a person, image, or event in Milton's narrative will be presented in terms of person, image, or event in
other works of art or literature. That is what seeing nature "through
the spectacles of books" literally means. But there is more to say about
it. Any act of comparison affords dual perspectives on an object. Such
doubling is not just esthetic, or descriptive, however; it is ultimately
ontological. A comparison invokes another level of being as well as of
fact. The reality, then, which Milton invokes by employing images,
similes, and allusions carefully drawn from literature rather than
"life" is not that of the raw and random order of nature but that of
the ideal and definitive order of art.

We need not doubt that Milton intended this with all the conscien-
tiousness he put into everything else in *Paradise Lost*. We must try,
though, to decide why he did as he did. I think we can be quite sure
that his purpose in strewing the text of *Paradise Lost* with classical
similes and allusions was not merely to furnish himself with opportunities to "pour forth the treasures of his mind" in an access of schol-

arly self-indulgence. On the contrary, the effect of all that elegant scholarship was rather to *seal his poem off in imaginative literature,* to insulate it against "life" in the untransmuted, "natural" and historical sense, at all points enclosing thought and image with a protective lacquer of "art," and by so doing to increase the sheer indestructibility of his poem by increasing the element of pure artifice in it. Again and again, allusion to a choice incident or moment in past literature or art communicates an esoteric brilliance to the lines, and endows them with a reflected and nostalgic grace. Repentant Adam and Eve are compared not to objects of nature, or even to persons in later history, but to grave figures in Ovidian mythology; their prayers ascend to God by an elaborate Homeric "machinery":

> Yet their port
> Not of mean suitors; nor important less
> Seemed their petition, than when th' ancient pair
> In fables old, less ancient yet than these,
> Deucalion and chaste Pyrrha, to restore
> The race of mankind drowned, before the shrine
> Of Themis stood devout. To Heaven their prayers
> Flew up, nor missed the way, by envious winds
> Blown vagabond or frustrate: in they passed
> Dimensionless through heavenly doors; then, clad
> With incense, where the golden altar fumed,
> By their great Intercessor, came in sight
> Before the Father's throne.

This particular extract points up a further characteristic of Milton's handling of classical allusions worth our pondering on, i.e. his tendency to be a trifle overspecific, to dwell on them a bit more than the poetic occasion seems, often, to require. (Is this perhaps what gives the impression of "pouring forth the treasures"?) It is not enough to justify these small excesses by seeing them as graceful cadenzas scattered throughout the poem for embellishment and charm. Something far less incidental than embellishment seems to be taking place. In the reference to Orpheus and his fate at the opening of Book VII, for example, one notices how Milton lingers over the allusion, as if unwilling to break it off:

> But drive far off the barbarous dissonance
> Of Bacchus and his revellers, the race

> Of that wild rout that tore the Thracian bard
> In Rhodope, where woods and rocks had ears
> To rapture, till the savage clamour drowned
> Both harp and voice; nor could the Muse defend
> Her son, So fail not thou who thee implores;
> For thou art heavenly, she an empty dream.

Or consider this handling of the Hercules allusion during the description of the "Olympic Games" in Hell:

> Others, with vast Typhoean rage, more fell,
> Rend up both rocks and hills, and ride the air
> In whirlwind; Hell scarce holds the wild uproar:—
> As when Alcides, from Oechalia crowned
> With conquest, felt th' envenomed robe, and tore
> Through pain up by the roots Thessalian pines,
> And Lichas from the top of Oeta threw
> Into th' Euboic sea.

The allusion here to the death-anguish of Hercules (Alcides), though in itself precise, and tightly written, certainly seems to get more attention than the context calls for. It is not completely clear, in fact, why Hercules' pain is gone into at all, unless perhaps to suggest the joylessness of the neurotic pleasures of Hell. There is an even better example in the famous lines describing Hephaestas' fall from Olympus. (Hephaestas is the architect of Pandemonium; but Milton makes it abundantly clear that he has a classic past as well):

> Nor was his name unheard or unadored
> In ancient Greece; and in Ausonian Land
> Men called him Mulciber. And how he fell
> From Heaven they fabled, thrown by angry Jove
> Sheer o'er the crystal battlements: from morn
> To noon he fell, from noon to dewy eve,
> A summer's day, and with the setting sun
> Dropt from the zenith, like a falling star,
> On Lemnos, th' Aegaean isle.

In all these instances, as in others that could be cited, one detects the intentness, or obsessiveness, with which Milton touches the materials of classical antiquity. There is surely more than a tinge of self-consciousness at these points, as if some feat were being accomplished against odds, as if, indeed, Milton knew in his bones that he was writing the last poem in England, or in Europe for that matter, to employ Greek and Roman antiquity passionately, that is to say, soberly, without irony, sentimentality, or false notes. (In less than one hundred years, we may recall, Pope was to write *The Rape of the Lock* and *The Dunciad*.) Hence Milton's slight overemphasis at these points, his tendency to care too much; for at some level of his imagination he must have been aware that the classic world—even for a poet like himself, who was also a professional scholar—was already irretrievably lost and gone—indeed, like the Paradise of his poem. He compares Eve to Prosperine in the field of Enna

> gathering flowers
> Herself a fairer flower by gloomy Dis
> Was gathered—which cost Ceres all that pain
> To seek her through the world

and one's ear instinctively hovers a moment over the charmed "all *that* pain," so full of nostalgia and valediction. The Biblical matter did not evoke this tender tone from him—it was reserved always for the Greek, the pagan, the mythic. The *Lycidas* vein, we may say, had to the end, like the Gulf Stream in the ocean, maintained a clear tonal privacy in the midst of the harsher Christian materials.

W. B. Yeats was of the opinion that Milton's task in writing *Paradise Lost* was fundamentally impossible. He had, Yeats felt, attempted to return to the "synthesis of the Sistine Chapel" after the sacred and profane elements in our culture, after the classical and modern worlds, had fallen apart. Michelangelo had been able to paint Greek sages and doctors of the church, Roman sibyls and Hebrew prophets on the same ceiling, and give them "apparent equality." Precisely such cultural unity was denied Milton; and his sense of the impossibility of attaining it is reflected, one may conclude, in those poignant allusions to the classic past scattered like pools throughout his poem. It seems likely, too, that in spite of his claim that the song was unpremeditated, the obvious care with which each word, each phrase, each construction is oratorically placed, or rather poised, in the whole grave structure of the poem is ample witness of the "impossibility" of Milton's task. For to take that kind of pains could only mean that there was something peculiarly intractable in the very essence of the subject, which he sought to control by formally inspecting the credentials of every word he used.

NOTE

[EDITOR'S NOTE. On Milton's language, see R. M. Lumiansky, *MLN*, LV, (1940), 591-4; T. S. Eliot, *What Is a Classic?* 1945; H. Darbishire, *E&S*, X (1957), 31-52; C. L. Wrenn, in *Studies in English Literature*, ed. S. Korninger, 1958; on style, J. Whaler, *Counterpoint and Symbol*, 1951; E. S. LeComte, *Verbal and Psychological Pattern in Milton*, 1954; B. Groom, *The Diction of Poetry from Spenser to Bridges*, 1956; A. Stein, *Answerable Style*, 1953; C. Ricks, *Milton's Grand Style*, 1963.]

GEOFFREY HARTMAN

Milton's Counterplot

Milton's description of the building of Pandemonium ends with a reference to the architect, Mammon, also known to the ancient world as Mulciber:

>   and how he fell
> From Heav'n, they fabl'd, thrown by angry *Jove*
> Sheer o'er the Crystal Battlements: from Morn
> To Noon he fell, from Noon to dewy Eve,
> A Summer's day; and with the setting Sun
> Dropt from the Zenith like a falling Star,
> On *Lemnos* th'Ægaean Isle
>
> >   (*Paradise Lost*, I, 740-6).

These verses stand out from a brilliant text as still more brilliant; or emerge from this text, which repeats on several levels the theme of quick or erring or mock activity, marked by a strange mood of calm, as if the narrative's burning wheel had suddenly disclosed a jewelled bearing. Their subject is a Fall, and it has been suggested that Milton's imagination was caught by the anticipation in the Mulciber story of a myth which stands at the center of his epic. Why the "caught" imagination should respond with a pastoral image, evoking a fall grad-

From *ELH* (*English Literary History*), XXV (1958), 1-12. Reprinted by permission of the author and The Johns Hopkins Press.

ual and cool like the dying of a summer's day, and the sudden, no less aesthetically distant, dropping down of the star, is not explained. One recalls, without difficulty, similar moments of relief or distancing, especially in the cosmic fret of the first books: the comparison of angel forms lying entranced on the inflamed sea with autumnal leaves on Vallombrosa's shady brooks, or the simile of springtime bees and of the dreaming peasant at the end of Book I, or the applause following Mammon's speech in Book II, likened to lulling if hoarse cadence of winds after a storm, or even the appearance to Satan of the world, when he has crossed Chaos and arrives with torn tackle in full view of this golden-chained star of smallest magnitude.

The evident purpose of the Mulciber story is to help prick inflated Pandemonium, and together with the lines that follow, to emphasize that Mammon's building is as shaky as its architect. This fits in well with the plot of the first two books, a description of the satanic host's effort to build on hell. But the verses on Mulciber also disclose, through their almost decorative character, a second plot, simultaneously expressed with the first, and which may be called the counterplot. Its hidden presence is responsible for the contrapuntal effects of the inserted fable.

The reader will not fail to recognize in Milton's account of the progress of Mulciber's fall the parody of a biblical rhythm: "And the evening and the morning were the (first) day." The thought of creation is present to Milton, somehow associated with this fall. Moreover, the picture of *angry* Jove blends with and gives way to that of *crystal* battlements, and the imperturbability of the summer's day through which the angel drops:

> from Morn
> To Noon he fell, from Noon to dewy Eve,
> A Summer's day;

while in the last part of his descent an image of splendor and effortlessness outshines that of anger or ignominy:

> and with the setting Sun
> Dropt from the Zenith like a falling Star.

In context, of course, this depiction is condemned as mere fabling, and there is nothing splendid or aloof in the way Milton retells the story:

> thus they relate,
> Erring; for he with his rebellious rout
> Fell long before; nor aught avail'd him now
> To have built in Heav'n high Tow'rs; nor did he scape
> By all his Engines, but was headlong sent
> With his industrious crew to build in hell.
>
> (746-51)

Yet for a moment, while moving in the charmed land of pagan fable, away from the more literal truth in which he seeks supremacy over all fable, Milton reveals the overwhelming, if not autonomous drive of his imagination. Mulciber draws to himself a rhythm reminiscent of the account of the world's creation, and his story suggests both God and the creation undisturbed (Crystal Battlements . . . dewy Eve) by a fall which is said to occur later than the creation, yet actually preceded it. Here, surely, is a primary instance of Milton's automatically involving the idea of creation with that of the Fall. But further, and more fundamental, is the feeling of the text that God's anger is not anger at all, rather calm prescience, which sees that no fall will ultimately disturb the creation, whether Mulciber's fabled or Satan's real or Adam's universal Fall.

Milton's feeling for this divine imperturbability, for God's omnipotent knowledge that the creation will outlive death and sin, when expressed in such an indirect manner, may be characterized as the counterplot. For it does not often work on the reader as independent theme or subplot, but lodges in the vital parts of the overt action, emerging from it like good from evil. The root-feeling (if feeling is the proper word) for imperturbable providence radiates from many levels of the text. It has been given numerous interpretations in the history of criticism, the best perhaps, though impressionistic, by Coleridge: "Milton is the deity of prescience: he stands *ab extra* and drives a fiery chariot and four, making the horses feel the iron curb which holds them in." Satan's fixed mind and high disdain are perverted reflectors of this same cold passion, but doomed to perish in the restlessness of hell, and its compulsive gospel of the community of damnation. So deep-working is this spirit of the "glassy, cool, translucent wave," already invoked in *Comus,* that other poets find hard to resist it, and, like Wordsworth, seek to attain similar virtuosity in expressing "central peace, subsisting at the heart Of endless agitation." Milton's control is such, that even in the first dramatic account of Satan's expulsion, he makes the steady flame of God's act predominate over the theme of effort, anger, and vengefulness: in the following verses "Ethereal Sky" corresponds to the "Crystal Battlements" of Mulciber's fall, and the image of a projectile powerfully but steadily thrust forth (evoked in part by the immediate duplication of stress, letter and rhythmic patterns) recreates the imperturbability of that other, summer space:

> Him the Almightly Power
> Hurl'd headlong flaming from th'Ethereal Sky
> With hideous ruin and combustion down
> To bottomless perdition, there to dwell
> In Adamantine Chains and penal Fire . . . .
>
> (44-8)

One of the major means of realizing the counterplot is the simile. Throughout *Paradise Lost,* and eminently in the first two books, Milton has to bring the terrible sublime home to the reader's imagination. It would appear that he can only do this by way of analogy. Yet Milton rarely uses straight analogy, in which the observer and observed remain, relative to each other, on the same plane. Indeed, his finest effects are to employ magnifying and diminishing similes. Satan's shield, for example, is described as hanging on his shoulder like the moon, viewed through Galileo's telescope from Fiesole or in Valdarno (I, 284-91). The rich, elaborate pattern of such similes has often been noted and variously explained. Certain details, however, may be reconsidered.

The similes, first of all, not only magnify or diminish the doings in hell, but invariably put them at a distance. Just as the "Tuscan Artist" sees the moon through his telescope, so the artist of *Paradise Lost* shows hell at considerable remove, through a medium which, while it clarifies, also intervenes between reader and object. Milton varies points-of-view shifting in space and time so skilfully, that our sense of the reality of hell, of its power vis-a-vis man or God, never remains secure. Spirits, we know, can assume any shape they please; and Milton, like Spenser, uses this imaginative axiom to destroy the idea of the simple location of good and evil in the spiritual combat. But despite the insecurity, the abyss momentarily glimpsed under simple event, Milton's main effort in the first books is to make us believe in Satan as a real and terrible agent, yet never as an irresistible power. No doubt at all of Satan's influence: his success is writ large in religious history:

which may also be one reason for the epic enumeration of demonic names and place-names in Book I. Nevertheless, even as we are closest to Satan, presented with the hottest view of hell's present and future appeal, all suggestion of irresistible influence must be expunged, if Milton's two means of divine justification, man's free will and God's foreknowledge of the creation's triumph, are to win consent.

These two dominant concepts, expressed through the counterplot, shed a calm and often cold radiance over all of *Paradise Lost,* issuing equally from the heart of faith and the center of self-determination. The similes must persuade us that man was and is "sufficient to have stood, though free to fall" (III, 99), that his reason and will, however fiercely tempted and besieged, stand on a pinnacle as firm and precarious as that on which the Christ of *Paradise Regained* (IV, 541 ff) suffers his last, greatest, archetypal temptation. They must show the persistence, in the depth of danger, passion or evil, of imperturable reason, of a power working *ab extra.*

This they accomplish in several ways. They are, for example, marked by an emphasis on place names. It is the *Tuscan* artist who views the moon (Satan's shield) from the top of *Fesole* or in *Valdarno* through his optic glass, while he searches for new Lands, Rivers, Mountains on the spotty globe. Do not the place names serve to anchor this observer, and set him off from the vastness and vagueness of hell, its unnamed and restless geography, as well as from his attempt to leave the earth and rise by science above the lunar world? A recital of names is, of course, not reassuring of itself: no comfort accrues in hearing Moloch associated with *Rabba, Argob, Basan, Arnon,* or sinful Solomon with *Hinnom, Tophet, Gehenna* (I, 397-405). The point is that these places were once neutral, innocent of bloody or holy associations; it is man who has made them what they are, made the proper name a fearful or a hopeful sign (cf. XI, 836-39). Will Valdarno and Fiesole become such by-words as Tophet and Gehenna? At the moment they are still hieroglyphs, words whose ultimate meaning is in the balance. They suggest the inviolate shelter of the created world rather than the incursions of a demonic world. Yet we sense that, if Galileo uses the shelter and Ark of this world to dream of other worlds, paying optical rites to the moon, Fiesole, Valdarno, even Vallombrosa may yield to the tug of a demonic interpretation and soon become a part of hell's unprotected marl.

Though the figure of the observer *ab extra* is striking in Milton's evocation of Galileo, it becomes more subtly patent in a simile a few lines further on, which tells how the angel forms lay entranced on hell's inflamed sea

> Thick as Autumnal Leaves that strow the Brooks
> In *Vallombrosa*, where th'Etrurian shades
> High overarch"t imbrow'r; or scatter'd sedge
> Afloat, when with fierce winds *Orion* arm'd
> Hath vext the Red-Sea Coast, whose waves o'erthrew
> *Busiris* and his *Memphian* Chivalry,
> While with perfidious hatred they pursu'd
> The sojourners of *Goshen,* who beheld
> From the safe shore thir floating Carcasses
> And broken Chariot Wheels. . . .
>
> (302-11)

A finer modulation of aesthetic distance can hardly be found: we start at the point of maximum contrast, with the angels prostrate on the lake, in a region "vaulted with fire" (298), viewed as leaves fallen seasonally on a sheltered brook vaulted by shade; go next to the image of sea-weed scattered by storm, and finally, without break of focus, to the Israelites watching "from the safe shore" the floating bodies and parts of their pursuers. And, as in music, where one theme fading, another emerges to its place, while the image of calm and natural death changes to that of violent and supernatural destruction, the figure of the observer *ab extra* becomes explicit, substituting for the original glimpse of inviolable peace.

Could the counterplot be clearer? A simile intended to sharpen our view of the innumerable stunned host of hell, just before it is roused by Satan, at the same time sharpens our sense of the imperturbable order of the creation, and of the coming storm, and of the survival of man through providence and his safe-shored will. Satan, standing clear of the rout, prepares to vex his legions to new evil:

> on the Beach
> Of that inflamed Sea, he stood and call'd
> His Legions, Angel Forms, who lay intrans't
> Thick as Autumnal Leaves . . .

but the scenes the poet himself calls up mimic hell's defeat before Satan's voice is fully heard, and whatever sought to destroy the calm of autumnal leaves lies lifeless as scattered sedge. The continuity of the similes hinges on the middle image of Orion, which sketches both Satan's power to rouse the fallen host and God's power to scatter and destroy it. In this "plot counterplot" the hand of Satan is not ultimately distinguishable from the will of God.

A further instance, more complex still, is found at the end of Book I. Milton compares the host gathered in the gates of Pandemonium to bees at springtime (768 ff). The wonder of this incongruity has been preserved by many explanations. It is clearly a simile which, like others we have adduced, diminishes hell while it magnifies creation. The bees are fruitful, and their existence in the teeth of Satan drowns out the sonorous *hiss* of hell. Their "straw-built Citadel" will survive "bossy" Pandemonium. As Dr. Johnson kicking the stone kicks all excessive idealism, so Milton's bees rub their balm against all excessive demonism. But the irony may not end there. Are the devils not those bees who bring food out of the eater, sweetness out of the strong (Judges 15: 5-19)?

It may also be more than a coincidence that the most famous in this genre of similes describes the bustle of the Carthaginians as seen by storm-exiled Aeneas (*Aeneid* I, 430-40). Enveloped in a cloud by his divine mother, Aeneas looks down from the top of a hill onto a people busily building their city like a swarm of bees at summer's return, and is forced to cry: "O fortunati, quorum iam moenia surgunt!" —o fortunate people, whose walls are already rising! Then Vergil, as if to dispel any impression of despair, adds: *mirabile dictu,* a wonder! Aeneas walks among the Carthaginians made invisible by divine gift.

Here the counterplot thickens, and we behold one of Milton's amazing transpositions of classical texts. Aeneas strives to found Rome, which will outlast Carthage. The bees building in Vergil's text intimate a spirit of creativity seasonally renewed and independent of the particular civilization. The bees in Milton's text represent the same privilege and promise. Aeneas wrapped in the cloud is the observer *ab extra,* the person on the shore, and his impatient cry is of one who desires to build a civilization beyond decay, perhaps even beyond the wrath of the gods. An emergent, as yet invisible figure in Milton's text shares the hero's cry: he has seen Mammon and his troop build Pandemonium, Satan's band swarm triumphant about their citadel: despite this, can the walls of creation outlive Satan as Rome the ancient world?

All this would be putative or extrinsic if based solely on the simile of the bees. For this simile, like the middle image of Orion vexing the Red Sea, is indeterminate in its implications, a kind of visual pivot in a series of images which act in sequence and once more reveal the counterplot. Its indeterminacy is comparable to Milton's previously mentioned use of proper nouns, and his overall stylistic use of the *pivot*, by means of which images and words are made to refer both backwards and forwards, giving the verse period an unusual balance and flexibility. The series in question begins with the trooping to Pandemonium, and we now give the entire modulation which moves through several similes:

> all access was throng'd, the Gates
> And Porches wide, but chief the spacious Hall
> (Though like a cover'd field, where Champions bold
> Wont ride in arm'd, and at the Soldan's chair
> Defi'd the best of *Paynim* chivalry
> To mortal combat or career with Lance)
> Thick swarm'd, both on the ground and in the air,
> Brusht with the hiss of rustling wings. As Bees
> In spring time, when the Sun with *Taurus* rides,
> Pour forth thir populous youth about the Hive
> In clusters; they among fresh dews and flowers
> Fly to and fro, or on the smoothed Plank,
> The suburb of thir Straw-built Citadel
> New rubb'd with Balm, expatiate and confer
> Thir State affairs. So thick the aery crowd
> Swarm'd and were strait'n'd; till the Signal giv'n,
> Behold a wonder! they but now who seem'd
> In bigness to surpass Earth's Giant Sons
> Now less than smallest Dwarfs, in narrow room
> Throng numberless, like that Pigmean Race
> Beyond the *Indian* Mount, or Faery Elves,
> Whose midnight Revels, by a Forest side
> Or Fountain some belated Peasant sees,
> Or dreams he sees, while over-head the Moon
> Sits Arbitress, and nearer to the Earth
> Wheels her pale course, they on thir mirth and dance
> Intent, with jocund Music charm his ear;
> At once with joy and fear his heart rebounds.
>
> (761-88)

The very images which marshall the legions of hell to our view reveal simultaneously that the issue of Satan's triumph or defeat, his real or mock power, is in the hand of a *secret arbiter,* whether God and divine prescience or man and free will. In the first simile the observer *ab extra* is the Soldan, who as a type of Satan overshadows the outcome of the combat between pagan and Christian warriors in the "cover'd field." The second simile is indeterminate in tenor, except that it diminishes the satanic thousands, blending them and their warlike intents with a picture of natural, peaceful creativity, Sun and Taurus presiding in place of the Soldan. "Behold a wonder!" echoes the *mirabile dictu* of Vergil's story, and prepares the coming of a divine observer. The mighty host is seen to shrink to the size of Pigmies (the third simile), and we know that these, the "small infantry," as Milton had called them with a pun reflecting the double perspective of the first books, can be overshadowed by Cranes (575-6). The verse period then carries us still further from the main action as the diminished devils are also compared to Faery Elves glimpsed at their midnight revels by some belated Peasant. From the presence and pomp of hell we have slowly slipped into a pastoral.

Yet does not this static moment hide an inner combat more real than that for which hell is preparing? It is midnight, the pivot between day and day, and in the Peasant's mind a similar point of balance seems to obtain. He is not fully certain of the significance or even reality of the Fairy ring. Like Aeneas in Hades, who glimpses the shade of Dido (*Aeneid* VI, 450-5), he "sees, Or dreams he sees" something barely distinguishable from the pallid dark, obscure as the new moon through clouds. What an intensity of calm is here, reflecting a mind balanced on the critical pivot, as a point of stillness is reached at greatest remove from the threats and reverberations of hell! But even as the man stands uncertain, the image of the moon overhead becomes intense, it has sat there all the time as arbiter, now wheels closer to the earth, and the Peasant's heart rebounds with a secret intuition bringing at once joy and fear.

The moon, clearly, is a last transformation of the image of the observer *ab extra,* Soldan, Sun and Taurus, Peasant. What was a type of Satan overshadowing the outcome of the real or spiritual combat is converted into a presentment of the individual's naive and autonomous power of discrimination, his free reason, secretly linked with a superior influence, as the moon overhead. The figure of the firmly placed observer culminates in that of the secret arbiter. Yet this moon is not an unambiguous symbol of the secret arbiter. A feeling of the moon's uncertain, changeable nature—incorruptible yet spotty, waxing and waning (I, 284-291; II, 659-666; see also "mooned horns," IV, 978, quoted below)— is subtly present. It reflects this series of images in which the poet constantly suggests, destroys and recreates the idea of an imperturbably transcendent discrimination. The moon that "Sits Arbitress" seems to complete the counterplot, but is only the imperfect sign of a figure not revealed till Book IV. Thus the whole cycle of to and fro, big and small, Pigmies or Elves, seeing or dreaming, far and near, joy and fear, this uneasy flux of couplets, alternatives and reversals, is continued when we learn, in the final lines of Book I, that far within Pandemonium, perhaps as far from consciousness as hell is from the thoughts of the Peasant or demonic power from the jocund, if intent music of the fairy revelers, Satan and the greatest of his Lords sit in their own, unreduced dimensions.

We meet the Peasant once more in *Paradise Lost,* and in a simile which seems to want to outdo the apparent incongruity of all others. At the end of Book IV, Gabriel and his files confront Satan apprehended squatting in Paradise, a toad at the ear of Eve. A heroically contemptuous exchange follows, and Satan's taunts finally so incense the Angel Squadron that they

> Turn'd fiery red, sharp'ning in mooned horns
> Thir Phalanx, and began to hem him round
> With ported Spears, as thick as when a field
> Of *Ceres* ripe for harvest waving bends
> Her bearded Grove of ears, which way the wind
> Sways them; the careful Plowman doubting stands
> Lest on the threshing floor his hopeful sheaves
> Prove chaff. On th'other side *Satan* alarm'd
> Collecting all his might dilated stood,
> Like *Teneriff* or *Atlas* unremov'd:
> His stature reacht the Sky, and on his Crest
> Sat horror Plum'd; nor wanted in his grasp
> What seem'd both Spear and Shield: now dreadful deeds
> Might have ensu'd, nor only Paradise
> In this commotion, but the Starry Cope
> Of Heav'n perhaps, or all the Elements
> At least had gone to rack, disturb'd and torn
> With violence of this conflict, had not soon
> Th'Eternal to prevent such horrid fray
> Hung forth in Heav'n his golden Scales, yet seen

> Betwixt *Astrea* and the *Scorpion* sign,
> Wherein all things created first he weigh'd,
> The pendulous round Earth with balanc'd Air
> In counterpoise, now ponders all events,
> Battles and Realms . . .
>
> (978-1002)

The question of Satan's power does not appear to be academic, at least not at first. The simile which, on previous occasions, pretended to illustrate hell's greatness but actually diminished hell and magnified the creation, is used here just as effectively against heaven. Milton, by dilating Satan, and distancing the spears of the angel phalanx as ears ready for reaping, creates the impression of a balance of power between heaven and hell. Yet the image which remains in control is neither of Satan nor of the Angels but of the wheatfield, first as its bearded ears bend with the wind, then as contemplated by the Plowman. Here the counterplot achieves its most consummate form. *Paradise Lost* was written not for the sake of heaven or hell but for the sake of the creation. What is all the fuss about if not to preserve the "self-balanc't" earth? The center around which and to which all actions turn is whether man can stand though free to fall, whether man and the world can survive their autonomy. The issue may not therefore be determined on the supernatural level by the direct clash of heaven and hell, only by these two arbiters: man's free will, and God's foreknowledge. The ripe grain sways in the wind, so does the mind which has tended it. Between ripeness and ripeness gathered falls the wind, the threshing floor, the labour of ancient *ears,* the question of the relation of God's will and man's will. The ears appear to be at the mercy of the wind, what about the thoughts, the "hopeful sheaves" of the Plowman? The fate of the world lies between Gabriel and Satan, but also between the wind and the ripe ears, but also between man and his thoughts. Finally God, supreme arbiter, overbalances the balance with the same pair of golden scales (suspended yet between Virgin and Scorpion) in which the balanced earth weighed at its first creation.

NOTE

[EDITOR'S NOTE. Milton's similes are discussed in most of the studies listed with the first article on *Paradise Lost* in this volume, and from various points of view by J. Whaler, *MP*, XXVIII (1931), 313-27, and *PMLA*, XLVII (1932), 534-53; L. D. Lerner, *EIC*, IV (1954), 297-308; K. Widmer, *ELH*, XXV (1958), 258-69; D. Bush, *JEGP*, LX (1961), 631-40; D. P. Harding, *Milton and Ovid*, 1946, *JEGP*, LX (1961), 664-69, and *The Club of Hercules*, 1962; C. Ricks, *Milton's Grand Style*, 1963.]

ALBERT COOK

Milton's Abstract Music

The poets of the recent past have often wanted their personal rhythms to resemble the spoken language, or a prose not too far from cultivated speech. The bias if strong enough can lead to the rejection of blank verse itself as improper to American English. But one need not go so far as William Carlos Williams in pleading for the primacy of speech in a personal voice in order to feel cool towards Milton, whose verse is easily recognized as based on some personal rhythm quite remote from speech (or so he may seem to us; to Dr. Johnson, Milton's blank verse was too close to the spoken language, verse for the eye). Milton's imperious lulling of diction and syntax towards Latin has been pondered and assessed; since sound and sense wed indissolubly in a poem, we should expect to find, fusing Milton's invented sense, some general harmonics of sound beyond Bridges' discrimination of his syllabic laws or Arnold Stein's subtle analysis of tone colour in *Paradise Lost*.

A speaking voice will give varying emphasis to the accents of verse, and an accomplished poet will orchestrate these variations:

> It is the *cause*, it is the *cause*, my *soul*; . . .

The second "cause," rising against Othello's attempt to stifle it by logically needless repetition, will be emphasized over the first "cause," as

From *University of Toronto Quarterly*, XXIX (1959-60), 370-85. Reprinted by permission of the author and the University of Toronto Press.

both over "soul," though these three accents stand out against (and gain firmness by contrast with) the indecision in the hovering accent on the first "it" and the second "is."

The dramatic setting of this line, and the mastery of Shakespeare, enlivens the play among these accents beyond the pattern of the metre, in which all the accents are theoretically equivalent (or at least patterned more regularly than speech rhythms allow). Yet normally, in fact almost always, one can distinguish one major accent, and often three "more important" accents, in a line of verse:

> Bare *ruin'd* choirs where late the sweet birds sang. . . .
> [Possibly "bare" or "choirs," depending on interpretation.]

> Thoughts that do often lie too *deep* for tears. . . .

> Or suck'd on *coun*try pleasures, childishly. . . .

> Like a patient *e*therized upon a table. . . .

> In the gloom the gold *g*athers the light against it. . . .
> [Possibly "against," or even "gloom."]

It is a great mark of Milton's rhythm that, contrary to the practice of almost any other verse writers in English, including his own imitators in the eighteenth and nineteenth centuries, Milton carries his verse so far away from speech that one can seldom find in *Paradise Lost* a line where only three of the accents stand out over the other two, and never, I believe, a line in which one can distinguish a single major accent alone.

> *Who first seduc'd* them to that *fowl revolt?*
> The in*f*ernal Serpent; *he* it was, whose *guile*
> Stird up with *E*nvy and R*e*venge, dec*eiv'd*
> The *M*other of Man*kinde*, what time his *Pride*
> Had *cast* him *out* from *Heav'n*, with *all* his *Host*
> Of *R*ebel *A*ngels, by whose aid as*p*iring
> To *set* him*self* in *Glory above* his *Peers,*
> He *trust*ed to have equal'd the *most High,*
> If he op*pos'd;* and with am*b*itious *aim*
> A*gainst* the *Throne* and *M*onarchy of *God*
> Rais'd *im*pious *War* in *Heav'n* and *Battle proud*

> With *vain* at*tempt. Him* the A*lmighty Pow*er
> H*urld head*long *flam*ing from th' Ethereal *Skie*
> With *hideous ruine* and com*bustion down*
> To *bottomless perdition, there* to *dwell*
> In A*damantine Chains* and *pe*nal *Fire*
> Who *durst de*fie th' Om*ni*potent to *Arms*.

If sense is necessarily the guide to the major accents, a single word cannot here be settled on as definitely more prominent in stress than the others. Even allowing latitude of interpretation for more usual poems, primacy is still assigned to a single accent at the expense of others: if one argues that the first "cause" receives most stress in the line from *Othello*, then the second receives less; if one argues that they both receive the same, a persuasive interpretation, the line is given a strikingly abnormal reading, and "soul" is still put into the background—unless one assigns it primacy; but all three cannot have equal value here—and this is precisely the way we must read the lines of *Paradise Lost*.

As we inspect the sense of the first line, "who" calls for stress because of the magnitude of the question; "first" because of the tremendous action initiated here, the subject of the poem, "Of Man's *first* disobedience"; "seduc'd" because of the fantastic treachery involved; "fowl" because of the enormity of the act; "revolt" because of the all-embracing nature of what the sin was directed against. The sense of the line seems simultaneously to concentrate in almost each accented word, and so on through this quotation as I have marked it, and on through the poem. This passage, in fact, illustrates rather more normal latitude of accent than is to be found in the prayers and invocations of the poem, which present nearly unbroken series of five major accents to the line. The voice to read this poetry must almost never flag in soaring, however it modulates: a strong-ribbed structure of accents constantly buoys up line by line the mighty periods.

The rhythmic effect which Milton gains by assigning all his accents nearly equal value is unusually special, as compared, for example, with French verse. In that convention the accents have an equality not of prominence, as in Milton, but of uninsistence. While Milton achieves a strenuous personal rhythm which heightens each of the individual accented syllables over the unaccented, the French convention tends to level the difference between accented and unaccented syllables, giving the whole poem line by line a rhythm that subdues

the sense to wear its convention like a uniform. A similar effect is to
be found in Italian poetry, even that which Milton imitated, as F. T.
Prince points out (*The Italian Element in Milton's Verse*), in seeking
a Virgilian grandiosity and *durezza*. Accents are levelled, not heightened, too, in the English verse of Chaucer, which echoes French
conventions:

> Your ÿen two wol slee me sodenly;
> I may the beautee of hem not sustene,
> So woundeth hit thourghout my herte kene.

Spenser, also, in his equality of accent, resembles an Italian and
French limpidity more than the Miltonic grandeur:

> A gentle knight was pricking on the plaine,
> Ycladd in mightie armes and silver shielde,
> Wherein old dints of deepe woundes did remaine,
> The cruell markes of many a bloody fielde;
> Yet armes till that time did he never wield
> His angry steede did chide his foming bitt,
> As much disdayning to the curbe to yielde:
> Full jolly knight he seemes, and faire did sitt,
> As one for knightly giusts and fierce encounters fitt.

No sooner have we stepped within the faerie forest, than all designa-
tions exist on the same allegorical level; and as the concrete stands
throughout in a one-to-one relation to the abstract, so Spenser's syllabic convention operates to keep each word of the sentence, and here
each line of the stanza too, patterned to an identical and formal
emphasis. Even the rhythm has the two-dimensionality of the sort
of mediaeval tapestry to which *The Faerie Queene* has often been
compared.

Milton began with Spenser, and began by going beyond Spenser;
we find an allegorical pattern in *L'Allegro* and *Il Penseroso* stated at
the beginning of each poem and violated by the main contrasts between light and dark almost as soon as the broken, tuning-up rhythms
of each poem's introduction have been toned off to the prevailing
tetrameter line. *Paradise Lost* sets a poetic problem more simple in its
generality than that of Spenser's epic and more directly spiritual—Man
instead of twelve virtues; angels and devils instead of maids, giants,
and castles. And the poem enunciates more thoroughly a literal but
unknowable truth; given Spenser's conception detail may be prolifer-

ated on a relatively simple principle, but Milton must at every point solve anew the problem of representing the unfallen Adam of Genesis through a fallen imagination.

The uniqueness of Milton's rhythm—what Eliot calls "the peculiar feeling, almost a physical sensation of a breathless leap, communicated by Milton's long periods, and by his alone"—derives from what it expresses, an imaginative conception which creates an equivalence among the verbal terms and their accents which the terms may not rest back on, as Spenser's are allowed to do by the syllabic norms and by his conception. In *Paradise Lost*, every accented word stands out when spoken as the major one in the line, pulling against the rise of the accents, equally strong, which precede and follow. This creates a kind of tension analogous to the conflict of physical forces found in the structure of a baroque dome, whose mathematics, Siegfried Giedion tells us, introduces a new complexity of interrelated forces into architecture. Or, as Milton says in another connection:

> As in an Organ from one blast of wind
> To many a row of Pipes the sound-board breathes.

(We remember that the baroque period is also the high point for that instrument in church music.)

Thus Adam may be general Man (which his name, Milton was aware, means in Hebrew) by virtue of inhabiting a world where everything concrete, in the Garden and elsewhere, can be at once abstract and irrevocably concrete; where every aspect of speech and idea gains importance without suppressing the importance of another, just as angels gain rather than lose (as Satan wrongly thought) by the preeminence of the Son in Heaven. A rhythmic provisionality—the accent is major only while spoken—governs this mortal representation of "things invisible to mortal sight." And just so a rhythmic assertion —the accent is major while it occurs—governs the poetic union which attempts "things unattempted yet in prose or rhyme." We may note, in fact, that the "things" are unattempted even by the inspired, and superior (Milton would surely say), prose of Genesis, because Scripture, in being inspired by the Holy Ghost, does not have to work within the limit of a fallen imagination. Milton expresses this limit, I believe, by his doubling of Urania, the classical muse, with the Holy Spirit, and by calling Moses a shepherd in the Theocritan as well as the New Testament sense. Moses is seen partly as such a shepherd, within the poem; and Milton, in not being a writer of Scripture but a poet following classical conventions, cannot help *as a poet* seeing the Holy Spirit partly through Urania.

The rhythms of *Paradise Lost* are simultaneously rapt with feeling and, as Arnold Stein says, "an integral part of the high, unwavering illusion of mystical motionlessness." We may inspect another passage to see how this rhythmic intussusception arrives at its "breathless leap" (Eliot) of "no middle flight" (Milton):

> Him th' Almighty Power
> Hurl'd headlong flaming from th' Ethereal Skie
> With hideous ruine and combustion down
> To bottomless perdition, there to dwell
> In Adamantine Chains and penal Fire
> Who durst defie th' Omnipotent to Arms.
> Nine times the Space that measures Day and Night
> To mortal men, he with his horrid crew
> Lay vanquisht, rowling in the fiery Gulfe
> Confounded though immortal.

"Now the first thing to notice," Rajan says of this passage, "is its preponderance of stock epithets. 'Hideous' does not limit the suggestions of 'ruine' and 'penal' does little to control our reaction to 'Fire.' Perdition has always been 'bottomless' and chains in poetry are usually 'Adamantine.' The associations of these words moreover are not developed but accumulated. 'Fire,' 'Combustion,' 'flaming' and in this context 'perdition' all suggest much the same thing and a similar grouping can be made of 'ethereal,' 'down,' 'bottomless,' and 'headlong.'" And Rajan goes on to notice that there is a repetition of *m* and *n* sounds, often in conjunction with *i* and *o*, which "convey irresistibly the terror of Satan's downfall." We might add that this "terror" which Rajan hears in the phonemes, the terror of the distance, the (plastic and infinite) measure of the fall, also gets into the tone of the poetry's sound through the strength of each primary accent, because these accents are not levelled off as in French, but are each successively primary. The headlong rush is the more precipitate for the dominance of the accent on "headlong" while the word is being spoken and the equally dominant accent on "ethereal," which, so to speak, keeps the sky aloft, tonally and geographically, and produces a kind of leaped gap of sound in which the word "flaming," equally accented, can blaze the more by being set, in wrenched sound as in visual image, against the "ethereal sky."

So Rajan's point about Milton's diction, that its terms tend to inter-fuse, "hideous" tending to complement "ruine" rather than limiting it (the way *modifiers* usually work), is reinforced by the similar action of the major accents in the sound, which give "hideous" and "ruine" the successive major emphasis. A particular poetic force, then, may be seen to reside in the famous Miltonic vagueness, noted perhaps first by Macaulay and berated by modern critics who value precision highly. Milton gives us not precision, but inter-echoing overtones, in sound and in sense. He does so because his poetic purposes are those not of precision—categorizing the attitudes of sin, repentance, and virtue like Dante, organizing the gestures of virtue and vice like Spen-ser—but of generality:

> Man's First Disobedience and the Fruit
> Of that Forbidden Tree whose mortal taste
> Brought Death into the World and all our woe.

Here the terms "Man," "Fruit," "Tree," etc., are given more generality even than allegory (though Milton allows himself to capitalize them for quasi-allegorical emphasis): allegory implies system, and system a specification of function which Milton's whole poetic effort in *Paradise Lost* is to avoid.

If we introduce Valéry's idea, that a poet in some sense invents the meanings of the words he uses, then we may see that Milton's inven-tions are strengthened by the privacy of his diction. The word in a poem gets its particular newness, or at least its freshness, by appearing in vivid conjunction with other words. Milton's practice operates, we may say, only to free the words from a prose limitation, to allow them to assert their conjunction the more forcibly as a way of representing the plastic qualities of Man's theological experience.

In a world where God is known by analogies, "things invisible to mortal sight" must appear in a form mortal sight (physical and spirit-ual) can compass. God is Light, the invocation to Book III elaborates, and God (the Son) is a Word to such a degree that it is the Son, in the part of Book VII which puzzles some commentators, who goes forth as the agent of the Creation, presumably because the Creation is performed through Words ("Let there be light . . ."), and for God, Word is Act. There are for Milton the Word—Scripture—and words—those of his "private" language. To comment on Scripture in a poem is a perilous act, and a difficult one. One is following the Revealed with the fallen Imagination; therefore what one sees dazzles. The general-

ity of light carries one over, but its generality is factitious; Adam
imagined in a poem written by a post-lapsarian poet can be Man by
the same sort of supposition that Moses can be spoken of as like
Theocritus.

Milton's universe is as plastic as the sounds that describe it: a Dan-
tesque diagram cannot be made of it. "First"—of disobedience or of
parents—is used in the double sense of "original" and of "primal," and
the elaborate voice is at once building the general (but lost) original
situation, and regretting the lost (but always present) primal condition. The world itself is seen as a transmuted Eden; poetic analogies
from the fallen world are used to portray the unfallen. It is in a description of the Garden that the famous simile is introduced about
Proserpina, with its implied comparison to Eve:

> The Birds thir quire apply; aires, vernal aires,
> Breathing the smell of field and grove, attune
> The trembling leaves, while Universal *Pan*
> Knit with the *Graces* and the *Hours* in dance
> Led on th'Eternal Spring. Not that faire field
> Of *Enna,* where *Proserpin* gathring flowrs
> Her self a fairer Floure by gloomie Dis
> Was gatherd, which cost Ceres all that pain
> To seek her through the world; nor that sweet Grove
> Of *Daphne* by the *Orontes,* and th'inspir'd
> *Castalian* Spring might with this Paradise
> Of *Eden* strive; . . .

The simile is prepared for rhythmically by a pair of clauses just two
lines long apiece, each introduced, as often in English and Latin
verse, by a cadence somewhat shorter than those that follow. The
effect of a cadenced rise between the short phrase and the longer ones
is emphasized by the rhythmic connotation of the semicolon in the
first line, which tends to hold the voice rather than stop it as a period
would do; and also by the shorter rise from "aires" to "vernal aires"
(itself a kind of delayed near-rhyme to "faire" in the first clause of the
simile sentence) at the beginning of the first longer clause. In addition, there is an abrupt shift in tense from the present of the first
clause, "attune," to the past of the second, "led," which trails the
sense, with the voice, off, in letting the garden not hold its immediate
present tense. (This is prepared for, also, by the participial phrases,

the present of "breathing" and the past of "knit.")[1] Pan, then, in Adam's time and in the present of the poem, is at once factitious like the poem (Milton does not "believe in" the classical gods), and "universal," this word being but an expansion of the Greek meaning of Pan.

The voice quickens powerfully to pick up the beginning of the simile in the middle of the line, the more that it must leap the distance of the denial in "Not" (in which we also have perhaps the trope of preterition: to say the field is not so beautiful would be a way of hinting that in some sense it is). In this plastic world that Milton depicts, a part of the simile, Proserpina, moves to the centre and assumes some of the purport's freedom (the original comparison was of quality between a field and a grove). Proserpina's connection with Enna is rhythmically insisted on, by the strong enjambent from the line before, and by the major accent on each. She herself enforces the meaning, being compared to a flower with the same word—"fair"—which had governed the initial comparison of one garden to another. The world of the simile is allowed to expand and include Ceres' search, because the rhythm and the sense of the poem add a feeling of constant flight, in their breathless sound. This search is a constant simile for the conception of the poem and will always suggest the poetic comparison at the end of this passage, here that of the Castalian spring where the poet drank to be "inspir'd." We should note that "inspir'd" is the first end-word not a monosyllable since "Dis" (or, if "flowrs" may seem monosyllabic by being printed so, since "Pan"). Thus rhythmically we are made aware that it is by such a poem that we can imaginatively transcend "all that pain," our own being like Ceres'. It is but another line to the ending assonance of Paradise, expanding into its Hebrew equivalent (Eden, pleasant garden) in the next half-line, again through preterition ("nor . . . might . . . strive"). The loss implied, rhythmically, and also in sense, as Empson notes, by the word "all," is counterbalanced by this half line and is not as regretful as it would be if Milton had ended on "Paradise," with some such line as: "Castalian Spring might match this Paradise." The whole passage—and the poem—is such a trope as we find in the word "inspired," applied by metonymy to the spring, when actually referring to the poet who drinks the spring: so, Milton implies, Eden is actualized in the poem, a poem as lofty in its "no middle flight" as the Castalian spring is at "high" Delphi against the crags of Parnassus. Moses is "inspired" by the Holy Ghost and writes truth about Eden;

Milton is "inspired" to a poetic fiction that offers what of Eden can be approached by a fallen imagination.

The whole poem, in its sound, fuses the imaginative perception of Paradise with sorrow for its loss. The central idea and the language—which it took Milton so much of his lifetime to arrive at—create the forceful succession of major accents, the idiosyncratic tendency to generality and repetition in the diction, and the rhetorically "incoherent" expansiveness of the similes. These derive from the central insight of sound which Empson has attributed to the word "all" as a tonal equivalent for both the poem's cosmological scope and its *lacrimae rerum* (*Structure of Complex Words,* chap. IV):

> In a stylist, the word presumes economy of means; it raises the thing in hand absolutely without needing to list all the others. The sound rolls the tongue from back low (the inner man) to front high (throwing him out and upward), and the vowel is the "organ" note for which Milton is praised or the Virgilian moan at the sorrow inherent in the whole story.

Paradise Lost is "emotive" in Empson's terms; it is like music. And since its poetic idea of fallen humanity is a central abstraction, its music tends to be abstract in a way to be found only in Milton's work, and then only in *Paradise Lost* and the later sonnets.

II

Milton, at the beginning of his career, found uncongenial the logico-rhetorical, or metaphysical, style of the day, and some of his early efforts are notably clumsy or uncertain, in sound as in sense:

> This rich marble doth enterr
> The honour'd wife of *Winchester,*
> A Vicounts daughter, an Earls heir,
> Besides what her vertues fair
> Added to her noble birth,
> More than she could own from Earth.

The inept prosiness and the platitudes of this early attempt to write in the vein of "obsequie," at which Donne was such a master, find here a rhythm uncertain to the point of brokenness, without even the spontaneity of doggerel. Soon Milton was to achieve a kind of abstract musical balance in the tetrameters of *L'Allegro* and *Il Penseroso,* whose indeterminate mingling of light and dark as a sort of abstract antinomic image (in both poems, Cleanth Brooks points out) is matched by a syllabic indeterminacy between iamb and trochee, and by the nearly Spenserian tuning up rhythms of each poem's opening lines. Milton's father had been a musician, and it was to the accompaniment of music by Henry Lawes, his father's friend, that Milton early achieved a poetic consort for music in the masque *Comus*.

> Hence had the huntress Dian her dred bow
> Fair silver-shafted Queen for ever chaste,
> Wherwith she tam'd the brinded lioness
> And spotted mountain pard, but set at naught
> The frivolous bolt of Cupid, gods and men
> Fear'd her stern frown, and she was queen oth' Woods.

The "chaste" effect of such lines, the "sober certainty of waking bliss," likened by Randall Jarrell (in a discussion that takes place in *Pictures from an Institution*) to the poetry of Hoelderlin, arises from the rhythm's confinement within an almost normal syllabic pattern (preserved by such contractions as the violent "oth' Woods"). This lies midway between the levelled accents of Spenser and the rising accents of *Paradise Lost*. A broidery of near rhyme and assonance (lioness/men; chaste/nought/woods; gods/dred/woods; huntress/lioness; feared/stern/frown) keeps a heightened charm of echo smoothly associating the sounds, almost asleep at their own beauty to such a degree that the argument can allow us the grace notes of "spotted" and "brindled," which are no part of the Elder Brother's reasoning here, if not indeed contradictory to it. But the sounds never quite go to sleep, and we can enjoy them through the protection of Chastity, to which heaven would stoop, the last lines tell us, "if Virtue feeble were"; we can thrill at the sound of "frivolous," which allows delight in the act of reproof, just as the argument of Comus expounds the beauties of the world in such a way as to allow them some measure of good (though brutish, I feel, in the rhythms of his speech). To this pure, abstract music, all things can be pure, and it need not decide between syllable and accent any more than it need reconcile classical gods with Christian.

The kind of reconcilement between the two which Milton will woo on such a magnificent scale in *Paradise Lost* (where accent buoys up syllable as fallen classical fleshes out an imagined Eden) is first addressed in *Lycidas*. As music this poem is tuned perhaps too high for its theme; its achievement is carrying this off successfully—just as classical and Christian are allowed to conflict but are not reconciled, any more than grief and fame, Poetry and Church, are reconciled. Milton speaks of berries harsh and crude, of forced fingers rude, and there is no reason not to take him seriously. It may be a kind of sign of the proto-poetry he is writing here that he uses the nine unrhymed lines Ransom has strikingly noted. But, once written, *Lycidas* will not be repeated. There will be, he tells us at the end of this ambiguously autobiographical poem, "pastures new."

Milton had learned to create an artificial and high style, an abstract music as we have been calling it, partly through observing and writing classical hexameters on a quantitative pattern foreign, scholars tell us, even to Latin, and certainly to English; trying quantity in English was a mistake Milton, so far as we know, never made. He was to learn to rib his poems strongly with a simultaneity of sense from Hebrew poetry, which he read and translated during his long near-silence. Hebrew metres are based on parallelism of sense, a kind of logic foreign to Donne, and to anything else in English, Italian, and classical poetry. This logic, concentrated and simultaneous like that of the Prophets rather than successive, led Milton to the quite new achievements of the later sonnets. They ride over even the division of octave and sestet, these "Miltonic" sonnets as they are called, a form invented by Milton to express something quite new: a contribution of sense to the poem which the musical beauties of all his earlier work had lacked. The sonnets, are, however, spare as well as short. They go beyond, but have not incorporated the lushness of, *Lycidas* and *Comus*. We find the two—the strong ribs of simultaneous logic in the periods and accents of the sonnets and the nearly abstract musical lushness of the early poems—fused and transcended in *Paradise Lost*.

This was Milton's highest rhythmic achievement, but not his last. *Paradise Regained*, whose poetic and rhythmic excellence lies in an austerity barer even than that of the sonnets, proposes both a subject and a treatment more difficult than *Paradise Lost*: instead of Unfallen Man, the Man-God; and instead of a lofty treatment with an encyclopaedic range of imagery, a nearly bare presentation, in which the most mysterious side of the poem, the fact that the Man is God, is not allowed to be seen from the heavenly viewpoint, but is deduced from His human actions alone, as the Christ of the poem is said to have deduced His Divinity from His natural human intelligence. No longer the magnificent Father of Lies, but a shady old man with a bundle of sticks on his back, the Devil is not even allowed the gamut of false reasons, mendacities, contradictions, and perversions with which his speeches in *Paradise Lost* always abound. The "darkness Visible" in this poem, and the light of heaven, are covered fires, fires which the rhythm, like the moderate language, keeps covered:

> He added not; and Satan bowing low
> His gray dissimulation, disappear'd
> Into thin Air diffus'd: for now began
> Night with her sullen wing to double-shade
> The Desert, Fowls in thir clay nests were couch't;
> And now wild Beasts came forth the woods to roam.

One cannot say of the rhythm that there are special major accents in the line (as in Shakespeare and most poetry), or that the major accents are levelled off in a syllabic pattern (as in Spenser, and in French poetry, for example), or that each accent becomes successively major as pronounced (as in *Paradise Lost*). The directness, or near prosiness, of the style, which acts as a severe limit on paragraph-long flights (and on elaborate metaphors), is brought to bear on the rhythm in such a way that the syllabic pattern keeps the accents from being pronounced, and the accents keep the syllabic pattern from being incantatory: very much as Christ is confined to His humanity, and is presented not in his positive glories (as is God in *Paraside Lost*), but in his opposition to Satan. Just as Christ withstands temptation, the accents of the poetry that assert his steadfastness have a stark strength in their rugged, prosy resistance to absorption into the uniform syllabic norm of the poem. One could call it Biblical rather than classical, as Christ in the poem rejects Pindar and all classical poetry for the Prophets. The effect—of accents, and yet no one accent being major—is, we have been saying, almost peculiar to Milton; but here the rhythm is carried into a more extreme form than in *Paradise Lost*, where an equivalence of major accents kept the flight aloft. Here the syllabic pattern is brought to bear as a strenuous check, or mute, to keep any accent from being heard as major, but not to subdue the accents, as a syllabic norm works in all other syllabic poetry.

In *Samson Agonistes* we meet metrical practices so radical that they have puzzled generations of commentators; Hopkins recognized in the poem the kind of tension between underlying pattern and individual accent which he called "sprung rhythm," but actually the sound pattern of the choruses in *Samson* does not allow quite so many accented (or unaccented) syllables to the foot, nor is its underlying norm so unambiguously regular as that in Hopkins' work. The blank verse of the speeches in *Samson* rather resembles that of *Paradise Lost*, a heightened abstractness of successively major accents, except where the rhythms of the chorus invade the blank verse, which they do mostly in easy transitions from blank verse into some choral rhythm and occasionally in individual lines.

Samson is a kind of dramatic *tour de force* because the action of the drama—and action is central to a drama—turns on Samson's gradual attunement to the Divine Will. His decision to go with the Philistines, rather than to resist them, is both the peripety and the recognition in the play, and yet it is unprepared for, unmotivated, in the scenes with Manoah, Dalila, Harapha, and the officers. In fact, the effect of these dialogues is the opposite—to induce him to resist being taken to the festival of Dagon. The gradual stirring in Samson of the Divine Will is as inchoate, as indeterminate, as secret, as Christ's realization of His own Divinity, and His resistance to supreme temptation, in *Paradise Regained*. Milton's representation of this dramatic peripety not in the action but in the poetry of the play, and particularly in the rhythm, is a tremendous poetic feat. The rhythmic violence of Samson's despair is the beginning of this recognition;

> O dark, dark, dark, amid the blaze of noon,
> Irrecoverably dark, total Eclipse
> Without all hope of day!

Here the strength of the equivalent major accents on each "dark" is matched by that of "blaze" and "noon"; but that strength is swallowed up in the long, liquid, hovering adverb "irrecoverably," in a line that has only four accents. It rounds out in the slow, measured, nearly spondaic third line. We always recognize metre by position, and thus must always read both backwards and forwards. So this third line may be read, in conjunction with the second line, as a sprung-rhythm four-beat line (like the second); or, in the blank verse, as a trochaic half-line, with the sadness of the half-lines in Virgil (which echoed in Milton's mind); finally, one may read it a third way, as the very first line in the poem looking ahead to the varying line lengths of the choruses.

Each of these three ways—the very fact that there are three—points to Samson's stirring. If it is read the first way, as a sprung, four-beat line, Samson is gathering his forces; the line is stronger than the dissolution of "irrecoverably" in the line before. If it is read the second way, as a Virgilian half-line, the silence at the end of it points to the stillness of Samson's own mind, to that which he cannot voice because he is as yet unaware of it (the Divine Will which he will later recognize). Read the third way, as anticipating the choral measures, it echoes and sets the tone for both the humility which throughout characterizes the Chorus and the final triumph and joy of the choric passages which recount and formulate the sacrifice of Samson.

Milton has introduced a rhythmic indeterminacy—a sort of multiple possibility of reading which is not only functional, as it was in the iambic-trochaic indeterminacy of *L'Allegro* and *Il Penseroso* (and as are certain effects which Donne achieves if we accept the sensitive reading of Arnold Stein), but also dramatic. Further, it carries the burden of the drama, a burden which is almost always carried by stage action. Milton tells us, however, that this poem, seemingly more dramatic than the performed *Comus*, "never was intended" for the stage.

This indeterminacy appears in the very first line spoken by the Chorus:

> SAMSON Thir daily practice to afflict me more.
> CHORUS This, this is he; softly a while,
> Let us not break in upon him;
> O change beyond report, thought, or belief!

The Chorus's first line read as echoing Samson's last would be a catalectic blank-verse line read in sprung rhythm (with accents on "this," "this," "he," "soft," and "while"). So read, each accent—each one successively major—is like a plea to be quiet, the voice raised in a whisper, out of consideration for Samson as the second line tells us. It is a still small voice which asks not to be heard against the strong, resigned complaint of Samson's final line here. But one may also—and simultaneously—read the line by referring it to the line ahead, in which case it follows not a blank-verse pattern (only), but the pattern of the Chorus's second line, a trochaic tetrameter line with reversal in the second foot. This reading, it might be said, emphasizes the dance, and thus the ritual function of the Chorus, because trochee is a singsongish dance measure. In this reading, the second "this" would go unaccented, as if, underlying the stark presence of Samson, requiring the astonishment of two *this*'s (accented with syncopation according to our first, blank-verse reading), there were an image of Samson doubling his presence—an accented "this"—with something internal and hidden, all but silent—and a "this" slurred and unaccented. The next line, too, can be taken as iambic pentameter or trochaic tetrameter—but this time the rhythmic reference is altered, almost carried forward, by the fact that we must read ahead, rather than backward, to get the iambic norm and backward, rather than ahead, to pick up the trochaic.

The rhythm always opens out for an indeterminacy of purpose—which is a hope for Samson of internal and inspired change—by presenting rhythms not only chorally fluid—*Apolelymenon* or loosed is the Greek term Milton cites in his preface—but themselves so indeterminate as to allow of two or more simultaneous readings. This very indeterminacy permits Samson, as we have said, to voice, in his last appearance, the sudden and unmotivated decision, quiet as none of his previous statements have been, to accompany the Philistine officer—a decision he appropriately communicates to the Chorus rather than directly to the officer himself:

> Be of good courage, I begin to feel
> Some rouzing motions in me which dispose
> To something extraordinary my thoughts.

Here the rhythm is kept ordinary, in the convention of *Paradise Lost,* to allow the word "extraordinary" to carry accentually, and rhythmically, the whole burden of a decision which even at this point remains an indeterminacy, for "extraordinary" is still only an adjective modifying "something."

Rhythmic indeterminacy, having gloriously expressed so secret and divine a calling, appropriately accompanies the joy of the Chorus at the end:

> CHORUS   Of dire necessity, whose law in death conjoin'd
>   Thee with thy slaughter'd foes in number more
>   Then all thy life had slain before.
> SEMICHORUS While thir hearts were jocund and sublime,
>   Drunk with Idolatry, drunk with Wine,
>   And fat regorged of Bulls and Goats.

The first line of the Semichorus can be read as a blank-verse line, and therefore an echo most immediately of the Messenger's narrative, detached and reflective. One can also read it as the more dance-like trochaic measure which is begun in the preceding line of the Chorus— "Then all thy life had slain before"—and carried forth, almost to a joyous tramp, in the unambiguous tetrameter—iambic but with tro-chaic effect due to its position—of "And fat regorged of Bulls and Goats." Taking this first line as trochaic, however, one is left with not only reversal, but an extra "sprung" syllable in "jocund and sublime."

This extra syllable permits a third reading, an anapestic one. (The position, I believe, will not allow for reading this line as dactylic tetrameter catalectic. The strong accent at the beginning is not the first beat of a dactyl but the syncopation of an anapest.) Anapests are more strongly present in the next line, "Drunk with Idolatry, drunk with Wine." The anapest is a dance measure like the trochee, but here, perhaps, more rollicking, a mockery of the jocundity of the Phi-listines which the anapestic rhythm mimes in order to transcend, as the religious joy of the true God transcends the merely earthly, gross joy of the drunken festival of Dagon. But the Chorus catches itself up into trochee again after only two feet—in "drunk with Wine." The whole line can also be read as a blank-verse line. The rhythms look back to reflectiveness (iamb), ahead to controlled joy (trochee), and can momentarily, without forgetting the other feelings present, re-joice in the very wildness of the enemy—but only with reference to the enemies' false devotion ("idolatry" is an anapest), not to the stim-ulant against which the Nazarite Samson has taken a lifelong vow ("Wine" is in trochee).

In some of these cases of indeterminacy, the accent varies with the reading ("this" in the previous quotation is unaccented by one read-ing, accented by another); but in other cases, the accentual pattern is the same ("jócŭnd ănd sŭblíme") and the pattern is different accord-ingly as to whether it is read back as trochee or ahead as anapest. But this does affect the movement: if "and" here would be an extra sprung syllable, it shows a strength and assertiveness of its own; if it is read as the last of an anapestic series, it slurs onward the way the wildness of the anapests is here felt to slur.

For several accentual patterns to be present at once, and to be felt as coiling ahead and backwards, is Milton's achievement in *Samson,* an achievement new for him as it is for us. Milton, like Shakespeare, followed heroically, in his employment of rhythms, not only the artis-tic requirement that he should find his own imaginative means—to such an extent that he went almost unread by even his better con-temporaries—but also the more difficult principle of advancement with each work which Jean Cocteau states (but does not embody): "Learn what you can do as an artist, and then don't do it." In Milton's rhythms we find the work of a poet of greater range than even his present admirers, and his past imitators, have sometimes allowed.

NOTES

1. Lowry Nelson finds this shift in tense characteristic of what he and others call Baroque verse. "Góngora and Milton: Toward a Definition of the Baroque," *Comparative Literature* (1954), 53-63.

[EDITOR'S NOTE. For Mr. Cook's unlocated references, see A. Stein, *KR*, XV (1953), 166-71, and *Answerable Style*, 1953; T. S. Eliot, *On Poetry and Poets*, 1957; B. Rajan, *"Paradise Lost" and the Seventeenth Century Reader*; T. B. Macaulay, excerpted in *Milton Criticism*, ed. J. Thorpe, 1950; C. Brooks, *The Well Wrought Urn*, 1947; and see also W. B. Hunter, Jr., *PQ*, XXVIII (1949), 125-44; S. E. Sprott, *Milton's Art of Prosody*, 1953; D. Davie, in *The Living Milton*, ed. F. Kermode, 1961; L. Nelson, Jr., *Baroque Lyric Poetry*, 1961.]

WARNER G. RICE

Paradise Regained

Paradise Regained is generally read, and criticized, in the light of
Paradise Lost, to which it is supposed to be a pendant.[1] To be sure,
there have been objections to this view.[2] And indeed no very great
emphasis should be placed upon Thomas Ellwood's account of how
he asked the poet, "What hast thou to say of Paradise Found?" and
of how Milton subsequently showed him his shorter epic with the
remark, "This is owing to you, for you put it into my head by the
question which you put to me at Chalfont. . . ." But the evidence of
the invocation seems convincing:

> I who e're while the happy Garden sung,
> By one mans disobedience lost, now sing
> Recover'd Paradise to all mankind,

and the two poems obviously deal with some of the same themes—
temptation, for example, the conflict of truth with falseness, the attempt of Satan to pervert the good.

Many of those who are willing enough to agree that the later poem
is a kind of sequel to the earlier one urge, however, that like most
sequels it shows a decline of its author's powers. The style is criticized

From *Papers of the Michigan Academy of Science, Arts, and Letters,* XXII
(1936), 493-503. Reprinted by permission of the author and The University
of Michigan Press.

as being too bare in some places, in others overornate; it is asserted that there is too little action; that the long arguments are tiresome; that the character of Satan is faded; that Jesus is unsatisfactory; and that the whole conception is weak since, "given Christ's nature, the temptations are not tempting."[3]

It will be impossible, within the limits of a short paper, to consider all the points at issue; but at the outset, to clear our vision, we may well bear in mind that we are likely to be prejudiced in approaching the subject of *Paradise Regained* as we are not prejudiced when we approach that of *Paradise Lost.* For the story of the Fall of Man, with the eating of the apple and the rest, belongs to Christian mythology, so that we are not disturbed when Milton manipulates these materials freely and with originality in order to make them yield a new meaning. The case is different when we have to do with Jesus. Here we find ourselves in the realm of Christian truth and of Christian doctrine, not of mythology; we approach the Savior with reverence, and, regarding him as very God, instinctively resist any unfamiliar interpretation of his actions. Perhaps our difficulties arise partly from the fact that we have been more deeply impressed by the mysteries which theologians insist upon than by the simple story narrated in the Gospels.[4] At all events, we are somewhat repelled and puzzled by the unorthodox manner in which Milton handles his theme.

Remembering the first books of *Paradise Lost,* we are surprised to meet a Satan who is vastly different, certainly, from the indomitable commander of the rebellious legions who were cast out from Heaven. Yet this Satan is logically developed from that great Adversary. For the poet, as he himself declares in the invocation to the Ninth Book of the earlier poem, has gradually worked away from the established conventions of the epic style,

> Not sedulous by Nature to indite
> Warrs, hitherto the onely Argument
> Heroic deem'd, chief maistrie to dissect
> With long and tedious havoc fabl'd Knights
> In Battels feign'd; the better fortitude
> Of Patience and Heroic Martyrdom
> Unsung,

and has focused his subject by the presentation of an intense inner conflict, with Satan participating as the wily seducer, the plausible contriver, who, having found out Adam's weakness, and Eve's, de-

stroys them by craft, not by open assault. At the crisis there are no
battles on the glittering plains of Heaven—only contests of minds and
wills in the Garden. The great spiraling movements which lead up to
the fourth and ninth books culminate by fixing attention on Man in
Eden.

   Paradise Regained, likewise, is designed to tell

> of deeds
> Above Heroic, though in secret done;

its conflicts are carried on within; its tensions are psychological and
moral; it presents no physical encounters, but the shock of will against
will. And, accordingly, the Satan of *Paradise Regained* is no more a
panoplied warrior than is the Satan of the last books of *Paradise Lost.*
But he is not the less formidable or impressive on this account. From
the beginning he realizes, and forces upon us the realization, that he
stands in extremest jeopardy, in a danger far greater than that which
he proudly faced from his throne in Pandemonium at the first council.

> And now too soon for us the circling hours
> This dreaded time have compast, wherein we
> Must bide the stroak of that long threatn'd wound,
> At least if so we can, and by the head
> Broken be not intended all our power
> To be infring'd, our freedom and our being
> In this fair Empire won of Earth and Air;
> For this ill news I bring, the Womans seed
> Destin'd to this, is late of woman born,
>
>   (I, 57-65)

so that there is desperate need for his trial of all possible means

> to subvert whom he suspected rais'd
> To end his Raign on Earth so long enjoy'd.
>   (I, 124-125)

This enterprise involves first a discovery and a testing. Jesus has become known in the world; he has been baptized:

> I saw
> The Prophet do him reverence, on him rising
> Out of the water, Heav'n above the Clouds
> Unfold her Crystal Dores, thence on his head

> A perfect Dove descend, what e're it meant,
> And out of Heav'n the Sov'raign voice I heard,
> This is my Son belov'd, in him am pleas'd.
> His Mother then is mortal, but his Sire,
> He who obtains the Monarchy of Heav'n,
> And what will he not do to advance his Son?
> His first-begot we know, and sore have felt,
> When his fierce thunder drove us to the deep;
> Who this is we must learn, for man he seems
> In all his lineaments, though in his face
> The glimpses of his Fathers glory shine.
>
> (I, 79-93)

And, accordingly, the whole action of the poem turns upon the Devil's attempt to corrupt, and at the same time to find out the real Nature of, Christ.

Now much of our feeling concerning the events narrated is determined, necessarily, by our grasp of the conception which Milton presents of the character and being of the Savior of Man. Speculations concerning the Son of God are set forth at length in the fifth chapter of *De Doctrina Christiana*; but into that thicket of theology it is not necessary to penetrate now. It is enough to point out that from the first lines of *Paradise Regained* it is Jesus' manhood, Jesus' humanity, that the poet emphasizes. The Almighty, foreseeing what the Tempter will endeavor, declares,

> He now shall know I can produce a man
> Of female Seed, far abler to resist
> All his sollicitations, and at length
> All his vast force, and drive him back to Hell,
> Winning by Conquest what the first man lost
> By fallacy surpriz'd.[5]
>
> (I, 150-155)

All commentators note the Arianism here; but simply to say that Milton subscribes, or nearly subscribes, to a heresy is to confuse the issue. The point is that he is getting behind the accretions of theological speculation and dogma, and figuring forth the Christ of the New Testament, the greater Man who preached and walked with his humble disciples in Galilee, who asserted his kinship, and all men's kinship, to God, but not his Godhead; who, at last, cried out in agony on the Cross. Milton admirably imagines him as the inheritor of the Jewish tradition, a man brought up in the knowledge and love of the Law and of the Prophets—a Prophet himself, conscious of Messianic promptings. And this chosen One has at first shared the prevailing belief in the function of the Messiah

> To rescue *Israel* from the *Roman* yoke,
> Then to subdue and quell o're all the earth
> Brute violence and proud Tyrannick pow'r,
> Till truth were freed, and equity restor'd.
>   (I, 217-220)

If he has come at last to another view of his mission, finding it

> more humane, more heavenly first
> By winning words to conquer willing hearts,
> And make perswasion do the work of fear,

it is not, Milton makes plain, without being fired by thoughts of domination and glory. In him there has been an impulse toward self-assertion. Jesus' notable victory, then, has first of all been won over a tendency to go boldly against the mighty in the world, to trust in his "calling." He has schooled himself to humility, to a reliance upon Divine Providence and its guidance:

> And now by some strong motion I am led
> Into this wilderness, to what intent
> I learn not yet, perhaps I need not know;
> For what concerns my knowledge God reveals.
>   (I, 290-293)

Upon this pivot everything really turns. Satan, shrewdly guessing that if Jesus is to be attacked successfully on any side, it must be through an appeal to human impulses not less strong in him than in Adam, seeks first to entrap Christ by appearing in the guise of a hermit to suggest that he transform stones into bread.

> But if thou be the Son of God, Command
> That out of these hard stones be made thee bread;
> So shalt thou save thy self and us relieve
> With Food, whereof we wretched seldom taste.
>   (I, 342-345)

The request is devilishly designed. It is casual, as though the matter were no great one, and it is abrupt; it seems charitable; it glances at the Savior's human need, for he really is hungry; but it involves great things. If Jesus undertakes to perform the miracle, he will at once have arrogated to himself extraordinary power; he will also have tacitly called in question Heaven's intentions toward himself—in both particulars satisfying his tempter. But Jesus is not to be surprised into doubt:

> Think'st thou such force in Bread? is it not written
> (For I discern thee other than thou seem'st)
> Man lives not by Bread only, but each Word
> Proceeding from the mouth of God; who fed
> Our Fathers here with Manna; in the Mount
> *Moses* was forty days, nor eat nor drank,
> And forty days *Eliah* without food
> Wandred this barren waste, the same I now:
> Why dost thou then suggest to me distrust,
> Knowing who I am, as I know who thou art?
>
> (I, 347-356)

Thus unmasked and rebuffed, Satan is still persistent. He at once returns to the assault. His long speeches, beginning with

> 'Tis true, I am that Spirit unfortunate . . . ,

are not designed merely for self-revelation, nor are they intended chiefly to arouse Jesus' sympathies. Their real aim, half apparent throughout, emerges clearly at the end:

> Thy Father, who is holy, wise and pure,
> Suffers the Hypocrite or Atheous Priest
> To tread his Sacred Courts, and minister
> About his Altar, handling holy things,
> Praying or vowing, and vouchsaf'd his voice
> To *Balaam* Reprobate, a Prophet yet
> Inspir'd; disdain not such access to me.
>
> (I, 486-492)

And once more Jesus answers with perfect humility,

> Thy coming hither, though I know thy scope,
> I bid not or forbid; do as thou find'st
> Permission from above; thou canst not more.
>
> (I, 494-496)

The pattern thus established is worked out fully in the later books of the poem. The Messiah, still hungering, wondering what his long fast portends, but still trusting in God, dreams

> as appetite is wont to dream,
> Of meats and drinks, Natures refreshment sweet;
>
> (II, 264-265)

and waking, is again approached by the Tempter, who reminds him that

> Others of some note
> As story tells, have trod this Wilderness;
> The Fugitive Bond-woman with her Son
> Out cast *Nebaioth,* yet found he relief
> By a providing Angel; all the race
> Of *Israel* here had famish'd, had not God
> Rain'd from Heaven Manna, and that Prophet bold
> Native of *Thebez* wandring here was fed
> Twice by a voice inviting him to eat.
> Of thee these forty days none hath regard,
> Forty and more deserted here indeed.
>
> (II, 306-316)

It is proper enough to see in this invitation, as many critics have done, an appeal to Jesus' sense of brilliance and luxury, as well as to his strong desire for food; and Lamb was partly right in regarding his refusal as a triumph of temperance. But there is more here—a modesty and a reverent caution which will not admit the assumption implied in Satan's flattering questions,

> What doubts the Son of God to sit and eat? . . .
> What doubt'st thou Son of God? sit down and eat.

The indirectness of Christ's answers must not be taken, then, as indicating a wish to torment and exasperate Satan, though his words certainly have this effect: the point is that under the circumstances assertion would be unfitting; irony must suffice:

> Said'st thou not that to all things I had right?
> And who withholds my pow'r that right to use?
> Shall I receive by gift what of my own,
> When and where likes me best, I can command?
> I can at will, doubt not, assoon as thou,
> Command a Table in this Wilderness,
> And call swift flights of Angels ministrant
> Array'd in Glory on my cup to attend:
> Why shouldst thou then obtrude this diligence . . . ?
>
> (II, 379-387)

Still the Adversary continues—offers riches, fame, and finally glory, reminding the Son that glory is not disdained by the Father himself. It is a subtle shift, and the more dramatic because Satan, not the least of the angels, has fallen into irretrievable ruin precisely because he could not resist his desire to rival the Almighty in glory.[6] But Jesus is steadfast, not to be betrayed, though he is greatly moved as he "fervently" replies to Satan's insistence upon God's delight in glory,

> And reason; since his word all things produc'd,
> Though chiefly not for glory as prime end,
> But to shew forth his goodness, and impart
> His good communicable to every soul
> Freely; of whom what could he less expect,
> Then glory and benediction, that is thanks . . . ?
> But why should man seek glory? who of his own
> Hath nothing, and to whom nothing belongs
> But condemnation, ignominy, and shame? . . .
> Yet, sacrilegious, to himself would take
> That which to God alone of right belongs.
>
> (III, 122-141)

Though it is grandly elaborated, the promise of a kingdom seems something of an anticlimax after this. But we must not forget the power of the Messianic dream, of which the poet seeks to remind us by the opening passage in Book II, or of Jesus' youthful acceptance of the idea of conquest and domination over the princes of the earth. His lengthy replies to Satan are, then, more than displays of rhetoric; and they show more than the power of reason to discover falseness. They are outpourings of thoughts long revolved and treasured up, Christ's assurances to himself that his rejection of violent measures his decision to "make perswasion do the work of fear" are just. In a sense they serve the purpose of soliloquies. And again the conclusion is that God's will must be done. Not even to rescue the Chosen People can Jesus be tempted to think of accepting the proffered aid:

> no, let them serve
> Thir enemies, who serve Idols with God.
> Yet he at length, time to himself best known,
> Remembring *Abraham* by some wond'rous call
> May bring them back repentant and sincere,
> And at their passing cleave the *Assyrian* flood,
> While to their native land with joy they hast,
> As the Red Sea and *Jordan* once he cleft,
> When to the promis'd land thir Fathers pass'd;
> To his due time and providence I leave them.[7]

(III, 431-440)

The prospect of the glories of Greece, reserved until the end, closes up this series of trials, and it is the greatest of them all. That Milton should review the intellectual achievements of the mighty ancients only to reject them has seemed shocking to many; the violence of his renunciation has been thought to declare the strength of the claim of those secular studies which so long delighted and supported him. But it is equally proper to apply this interpretation to the protagonist of Milton's poem, to Jesus. It is accordant with the character here given him that the powerful appeal of human wisdom, of human philosophy, should call out a determined denial:

> Alas what can they teach, and not mislead;
> Ignorant of themselves, of God much more,
> And how the world began, and how man fell
> Degraded by himself, on grace depending?
> Much of the Soul they talk, but all awrie,
> And in themselves seek vertue, and to themselves
> All glory arrogate, to God give none.[8]

(IV, 309-315)

So we are brought to the final climax. Satan has gained no satisfaction, has won no victory, has found no answer to his question. Frustrated, "swoln with rage," he cries out that he has discovered in Jesus no more than human constancy,

> And opportunity I here have had
> To try thee, sift thee, and confess have found thee
> Proof against all temptation as a rock
> Of Adamant, and as a Center, firm
> To the utmost of meer man both wise and good,
> Not more; for Honours, Riches, Kingdoms, Glory
> Have been before contemn'd, and may agen:
> Therefore to know what more thou art then man,
> Worth naming Son of God by voice from Heav'n,
> Another method I must now begin.
>
> (IV, 530-540)

And this "method," indeed, seems certain to yield decisive results. He sets Christ upon the pinnacle of the Temple, challenging in scorn:

> There stand, if thou wilt stand; to stand upright
> Will ask thee skill; I to thy Fathers house
> Have brought thee, and highest plac't, highest is best,
> Now shew thy Progeny; if not to stand,
> Cast thy self down; safely if Son of God:
> For it is written, He will give command
> Concerning thee to his Angels, in their hands
> They shall up lift thee, lest at any time
> Thou chance to dash thy foot against a stone.
>
> (IV, 551-559)

Jesus' dilemma seems now desperate indeed; but once more the answer comes, confident, calm, crushing in its reproof. It is the answer of Samson: "All the contest is now 'twixt God and *Dagon*." In his moment of apparent peril he does not yield one whit. His trust is in the Almighty, in the Divine Providence which may dispose of him as it will for the accomplishment of its hidden purposes. He replies,

> Also it is written,
> Tempt not the Lord thy God, he said and stood.
> But Satan smitten with amazement fell.
>
> (IV, 560-562)

Thus by humility, by constant faith, the contest is decided.[9] Now can Christ be borne to Heaven, now declared "True Image of the Father," and assured that

> A fairer Paradise is founded now
> For *Adam* and his chosen Sons, whom thou
> A Saviour art come down to re-install.
>
>   (IV, 613-615)

And thus is sung

> Recover'd Paradise to all mankind,
> By one mans firm obedience fully tri'd. . . .

When we reflect upon it, we can scarcely think it surprising that the "second Adam" should thus illustrate the lesson which the first Adam learned as a result of the fall, namely,

> that to obey is best,
> And love with feare the onely God, to walk
> As in his presence, ever to observe
> His providence, and on him sole depend.
>
>   (P.L., XII, 561-564)

And it is surely fitting that a Christian poem should stress this idea; for man, after his ruin, can no longer trust to unobscured reason, but must depend upon God's grace to set him on even ground against his mortal foe, and so is bound to acknowledge a double debt. Milton learned to subdue his own assertiveness; its power in his nature marks the extent of his victory. His pride at last comes to be the pride of God's servant, the pride of one who, recognizing his true place, can say

> They also serve who only stand and waite.

It is this aspect of the poet's achievement which Landor has expressed in his fine lines on "Shakespeare and Milton":

> The tongue of England, that which myriads
> Have spoken and will speak, were paralyzed
> Hereafter, but two mighty men stand forth
> Above the flight of ages, two alone;
> One crying out,
>
>   All nations spoke thro' me.
> The other:
>
>   True; and thro' this trumpet burst
> God's word; the fall of Angels, and the doom
> First of immortal, then of mortal, Man.
> Glory! be glory! not to me, to God.

NOTES

1. All the important books which deal with Milton and his poetry include some discussion of *Paradise Regained;* the titles of the principal essays devoted to it are listed by David H. Stevens, *Reference Guide to Milton* (University of Chicago Press, Chicago, 1930), Nos. 1123-29.

2. See, for example, E. M. W. Tillyard's chapter, *"Paradise Regained:* Its Relation to *Paradise Lost,"* in his *Milton* (New York, 1930), pp. 297-301.

3. This phrase of William Vaughn Moody's in his Introduction to *Paradise Regained* (Student's Cambridge Edition of *The Complete Poetical Works of John Milton,* p. 250) has been frequently repeated by other critics, and in general Moody's unfavorable judgments upon the poem have found a wide acceptance.

4. It is salutary to turn, not only to the Scriptures, but also to such a book as T. R. Glover's *The Conflict of Religions in the Early Roman Empire* (London, 1909) to remind ourselves of what the historical Jesus of Nazareth actually said, did, and claimed for himself.

5. The mention of Job in the verses preceding this passage and elsewhere, and the fact that Jesus is often in the poem brought into comparison with the Prophets, add to the reader's sense of his human quality.

6. Charles Williams, in his stimulating essay on Milton in *The English Poetic Mind* (Oxford, 1932), pp. 122-123, puts the point well:

"Omnipotence is engaged upon something to which Satan is with his whole nature antagonistic. Reason bids him submit—God and Raphael both point this out: even after his fall from Heaven he considers the possibility. To do that, however, would be precisely to lose *himself;* he would be something other than he is. He must act from what he is, and he expresses this in a minor contradiction. When he is addressing his followers he points out that none of them will envy him his throne; no one will want 'the greatest share of endless pain.' Reasonable enough, true enough; only it is precisely this which he himself must demand. 'Better to reign in Hell than serve in Heaven.' This contradiction is not deliberate deceit; it is the irrational strength of his nature. . . . Milton stresses the moral choice in the contradiction, the choice which so many men have made, the preference for the existence of their own will as the final and absolute thing as against the knowledge (whatever that may be) of some 'great commanded Good.' "

Williams's excellent comments on *Paradise Regained* appear on pages 135-143 of his book.

7. Cf. III, 182-197.

8. Milton would have man's reason guide him in accordance with God's law in obedience. Metaphysical speculation, the pride of the mind, he distrusts. The fallen angels "found no end, in wandring mazes lost" (*P.L.*, II, 557-569), and the Angel warns Adam to be "lowlie wise."

9. This interpretation of the significance of Christ's answer does not agree with the usual view; see Dowden's essay on *Paradise Regained*, in *Milton Memorial Lectures, 1908* (London, 1909), pp. 209-210. Yet this interpretation seems to me to be fully in accord with the central meaning of the poem.

[EDITOR'S NOTE. For further references, see the essay following.]

NORTHROP FRYE

The Typology of *Paradise Regained*

The second of three main episodes in the agon of Christ and Satan is presented in *Paradise Regained*. First is the original war in heaven recounted in *Paradist Lost*, and third is the final binding of Satan in the second coming of Christ, prophesied in the Book of Revelation. The defeat of Satan as tempter fulfils the prophecy in Genesis that the seed of Adam shall "bruise the serpent's head"; the imagery suggests the romance theme of a knight-errant killing a dragon and is one of several such images in the Bible. Besides the serpent in Eden, the Old Testament speaks of a dragon or sea monster, called "leviathan" or "Rahab," who was defeated once at the Creation and is to be destroyed or, in the metaphor of the sea serpent, hooked and landed on the day of judgment. Isaiah refers both to the previous and to the future victories over this leviathan, and Ezekiel and Isaiah appear to identify him with Egypt as the symbolic land of bondage. In the Book of Revelation this figure becomes a dragon with seven heads and ten horns, whose tail draws a third of the stars from heaven, the basis of Milton's account of Satan's fall; and in the symbolism of the same book the Satan of Job and the Gospels, the serpent of the Eden story, and the leviathan of the prophecies are all identified.

From this is derived the conventional iconology of Christ as a

From *Modern Philology*, LIII (1956), 227-38. Reprinted by permission of the author and the publisher.

dragon-killer, such as we have in medieval sculptures portraying him with a dragon or basilisk under his feet. In the first book of *The Faerie Queene,* the story of St. George and the dragon is used as an allegory of the imitation of Christ. St. George's dragon in Spenser is clearly identified with the whole Satan-serpent-leviathan complex in the Bible, and as a result of St. George's victory the parents of his lady Una, who are Adam and Eve, are restored to their inheritance, the Garden of Eden, which is also the unfallen world. Milton's reference in *The Reason of Church Government* to the allegory of St. George and "the king's daughter, the Church" indicates his early absorption of this theme. Michael explains to Adam in *Paradise Lost,* however, that the agon of Christ and Satan will be not a physical but a spiritual and intellectual fight, the cutting weapons used being those of dialectic and the true dragon being a spiritual enemy.

Paradise Regained is clearly Milton's essay in the "brief epic," mentioned in a famous passage of *The Reason of Church Government,* for which the model is there said to be the Book of Job. We should therefore expect *Paradise Regained* to have a particularly close relation to that book. In the Book of Job the contest of God and Satan takes the form of a wager on Job's virtue, and the scheme of *Paradise Regained* is not greatly different, with Christ occupying the place of Job. Satan soon disappears from the action of Job, however, and when Job's mind is finally enlightened by God, God's speech consists very largely of discourses on two monsters, behemoth and leviathan, the latter of whom, the more important, is finally said to be "king over all the children of pride." These monsters seem to represent an order of nature over which Satan is permitted some control, but, in a larger perspective, they are seen to be creatures of God. By pointing these beasts out to Job, God has, so to speak, put them under Job's feet and taken Job into his own protection; thus the Book of Job presents, in terms of this symbolism, a dialectical victory over both Satan and leviathan.

In the Incarnation the precise point of the agon of Christ and Satan is more usually located between Christ's death and his resurrection. It is then that he descends to hell, harrows hell, and achieves his final victory over hell and death. In medieval paintings of the harrowing of hell, hell is usually represented as leviathan, a huge, open-mouthed monster into which, or whom, Christ descends, like the Jonah whom Christ accepted as a prototype of his own Passion. For Milton, however, the scriptural evidence for the descent into hell was weak, and, besides, Milton believed that the whole of Christ's human nature died on the cross, with no surviving soul or spirit able to visit hell. The temptation in the Synoptic Gospels immediately follows the baptism, and Milton's view of baptism represents one of the rare exceptions to his general antisacramental attitude toward biblical symbolism: he is willing to see in it a symbol of the three-day crisis of Christian redemption, death, burial, and resurrection. Hence the temptation becomes for Milton the scripturally authorized version of the descent into hell, the passing into the domain of Satan, and the reconquest of everything in it that is redeemable. Certain features, such as the bewilderment of the forsaken disciples and the elegiac complaint of the Virgin Mary at the beginning of the second book, might belong more naturally to the period immediately following Christ's death. Christ's withdrawal from the world at this point is the opposite of a "fugitive and cloistered virtue," as he is being led directly into the jaws of hell itself, and not yet as a conqueror.

In the typology of the Bible there are two parallel versions of the fall and redemption of man. Adam falls from a garden into a wilderness, losing the tree of life and the water of life; Christ, the second Adam, wins back the garden ("Eden raised in the waste wilderness") and restores to man the tree and river of life. Similarly, the fight between St. George and the dragon in Spenser takes place at the boundary of Eden, St. George being refreshed by the paradisal well of life and tree of life, which continue in the church as the sacraments of Baptism and Communion. And as the natural home of Christ on earth is a fertile garden, the Eden in which he walked in the cool of the day, so the natural home of devils is the wilderness, "A pathless desert dusk with horrid shades," a blasted land like the country traversed in the *City of Dreadful Night* or by Browning's Childe Roland, the sort of scene one instinctively calls "Godforsaken," where the panic inspired by hunger, lost direction, and loneliness would have unsettled the reason of most people in much less than forty days.

Inside the story of Adam is the story of Israel, who falls from the Promised Land into the bondage of Egypt and Babylon. Besides being a second Adam, Christ is also a second Israel, who wins back, in a spiritual form, the Promised Land and its capital city of Jerusalem. In this capacity the story of the Exodus, or deliverance of Israel from Egypt, prefigures his life in the Gospels. Israel is led to Egypt through a Joseph; Christ is taken to Egypt by a Joseph. Christ is saved from a wicked king who orders a massacre of infants; Israel is saved from the slaughter of Egyptian first-born. Moses organizes Israel into twelve tribes and separates it from Egypt at the crossing of the Red Sea; Christ gathers twelve followers and is marked out as the Redeemer at his baptism in the Jordan (which the Israelites also later cross). Israel wanders forty years in the wilderness; Christ forty days. The Israelites receive the law from Mount Sinai; the gospel is preached in the Sermon on the Mount, which in its structure is largely a commentary on the Decalogue. The Israelites are plagued by serpents and redeemed by a brazen serpent on a pole, also accepted as a prototype of the Crucifixion by Christ. The Israelites conquer the Promised Land under "Joshua, whom the Gentiles Jesus call" (i.e. Joshua and Jesus are the same word), corresponding to Christ's victory over death and hell, as in the church's calendar Easter immediately follows the commemorating of the temptation in Lent.

Thus when the Angel Gabriel tells the Virgin Mary to call her child's name Jesus (Joshua), the typological meaning is that the reign of the law is now over and the assault on the Promised Law has begun. Similarly, the death of Moses just outside the Promised Land typifies the inability of the law alone to redeem mankind.[1] The difficulty of the temptation for Christ is complicated by the fact that he is still, at this stage of his career, within the law; his temptation is only a part of a much subtler process of separating, in his own mind, the law which is to be annihilated from the law which is to be fulfilled. Milton explicitly says that Christ in the wilderness "into himself descended" and employed his time in clarifying his own mind about the nature of his messianic mission. We see little of what is actually passing in Christ's mind; but as his refusal of one after another of Satan's temptations drives Satan to display his resources in a steadily rising scale of subtlety, the poetic effect is that of a negative clarification of Christ's own thoughts. The climax of the temptation corresponds to the death of Moses in the Exodus; it is the point at which Jesus passes from obedience to the law to works of faith, from the last Hebrew prophet to the founder of Christianity.

The typical Old Testament figures who represent the law and the prophets, respectively, are Moses and Elijah, who accompany Jesus in his transfiguration and are the two "witnesses" to his teaching in the Book of Revelation. Both of them prefigured the forty-day retirement and fast of Jesus in their own lives. The Old Testament says that Elijah will come again before the Messiah, a prophecy fulfilled by John the Baptist, but in a sense Moses has to be reborn too, as the law is fulfilled in the gospel. The Bible suggests the possibility that Moses did not die but was, like Elijah, transported directly to Paradise —an early version of *Paradise Lost* was to have begun with some speculations on this point. In any case Eden, the Promised Land, and the inward Kingdom of Heaven proclaimed by Jesus are all the same place, and Jesus' victory as second Adam and Israel is identical with the central act of his ministry, the casting of devils out of the human mind.

Christ has fasted for forty days, and, as Luke remarks with some restraint, "he afterward hungered." He has a Freudian wish-fulfilment dream, in which memories of Old Testament stories of prophets are mingled with food. In Milton, however, Christ is not hungry until after the first temptation to turn stones to bread, which consequently has nothing to do with hunger but is superficially an appeal to his charity, corresponding to the miraculous provision of manna in the Exodus. Jesus' answer that man shall not live by bread alone is a quotation from a passage in Deuteronomy that refers to the giving of manna. A contrast is thus involved between the material bread of the law and the bread of life of the gospel, distinguishing the gospel from what for Milton was the sacramental fallacy, the tendency to translate the Jewish ceremonial code into Christian terms, which produces the doctrine of transubstantiation. But Milton's interest is less in the temptation than in the tactical maneuver which Satan makes after his disguise is penetrated.

In Giles Fletcher's *Christ's Victory and Triumph*, Milton's most obvious source, the first temptation is primarily a temptation of despair and closely follows the episode of Despair in the first book of *The Faerie Queene*. Milton's Christ uses only the term "distrust," but still Milton is here the poetic grandson of Spenser.[2] Despair's argument in Spenser is based on the logic of law without gospel: i.e. sin is inevitable, and the longer one lives, the more one sins. Satan's argument in Milton is a refinement of this: good and evil are inseparable in the fallen world, and, in a world where all instruments are corrupted, one must either use corrupt instruments or not act at all. The use of evil or Satanic means being inevitable, Satan himself must be a reluctant agent of the will of God—that is, as long as we can believe in the will of God. In terms of the law alone, which can discover but not remove sin, this argument is more difficult to refute than it looks— in fact, it could be a clever parody of the central argument of *Areopagitica*. Christ's answer, leading up as it does to a prophecy of the cessation of oracles and the coming of the Word of God to the human heart, is based on what is familiar to the reader as the gospel or spiritual view of Scripture. Satan has never met such a view before, however, and feels sufficiently baffled to retire and consult with his colleagues before going further.

The conflict in *Paradise Regained* is ultimately a spiritual one, but the basis of the human spirit is the physical body, and the body is the battlefield of the spirit. Phineas Fletcher's *The Purple Island* begins with a detailed allegory of the physical body and then expands into a psychomachia, in which the principals are Christ and the Dragon. This allegory is based on the defense of the House of Alma in the second book of *The Faerie Queene,* which presents the quest of Guyon, the knight of temperance or continence, the physical integrity which is not so much virtue as the prerequisite of virtue. The crucial ordeal of Guyon is the Bower of Bliss, where the tempting agent is female and the temptation itself primarily erotic. In Giles Fletcher's version of the temptation of Christ the final[3] temptation is modeled on the Bower of Bliss. Satan's rejection of Belial's proposal to tempt Christ with women indicates Milton's deliberate departure from his predecessors. Milton had already dealt with such themes in *Comus,* and *Comus* presents, so to speak, the temptation of innocence, in contrast to the temptation of experience, which is the theme of *Paradise Regained*.[4]

Nevertheless, the sequence of temptations, which now proceeds unbroken to the end of the poem, begins with an attack on Jesus' temperance or continence, the physical basis of his humanity. There are two of these temptations—a banquet and an offer of money; neither is biblical, and it is generally recognized that the temptations of "Beautie and money" in the second book of *The Faerie Queene* are mainly responsible for them. They take place in a pleasant grove, one line, "Nature's own work it seemed (Nature taught Art)," being a vestigial survival of the Bower of Bliss, with its triumph of artifice over nature. Attacks on temperance could be resisted by any genuine prophet or saint or even by a virtuous heathen. Satan is an imaginative oriental bargainer, and one has the feeling that, although, of course, he wishes to gain Christ as cheaply as possible, he is reconciled to seeing these temptations fail—his strategy, as we shall see, is cumulative, and individual temptations are expendable. The temptations of food and money continue the argument of the first temptation, in that they urge the necessary use of doubtful means for good ends. Their rejection establishes the principle, which is also in Spenser, that the moral status of the instrumental depends on the mental attitude toward it: if the initial attitude is one of passive dependence, the instrument will become an illusory end in itself. It is not immediately apparent, however, why Satan has so much higher an opinion of food than of women as a temptation, even granting that there is really only one temptation of food.

We should be careful not to take anything in Satan's reply to Belial, such as his remark that beauty stands "In the admiration only of weak minds," at its face value. Nothing that Satan says in the poem is as trustworthy as that. He is, of course, right in thinking that Christ cannot be tempted to sins which are foreign to his nature; he can be tempted only to be some form of Antichrist, some physical or material counterpart of himself. But he is right for the wrong reasons.

The epic is traditionally a poem of heroic action, and a Christian poet must decide, before writing an epic, what in Christian terms a hero is and what an act is. For Milton all real acts are good, and there are no real evil acts.[5] Christ in *Paradise Lost* illustrates the pattern of this positive or real act: all his acts are creative or re-creative (i.e. redemptive). Adam's fall was thus not an act but a failure to act, the sham act of disobedience. Satan's fall was the parody act of rebellion, which, unlike disobedience, involves an attempt at rivalry with God. In the fallen world (since Nimrod, who introduced political authority and with it the possibility of imitating the demonic), man naturally turns to the demonic pseudo-hero as the pattern of heroic action. The genuinely heroic act is found only in the imitation of Christ, in endurance and obedience, and its pattern is illustrated in Abdiel, the faithful angel. For Satan, of course, heroic action means his own type of aggressive and destructive parody-heroism. His assumption that the Messiah's heroism will be in some way of this type is genuine, and he is consequently willing to give Jesus credit for a heroic contempt of "effeminate slackness." His own contempt for the kind of heroism that Christ seems to prefer is also genuine, and for anyone else this would be itself a major temptation: Faithful in Bunyan, for example, remarks that "Shame," the sense of worldly contempt, was his worst enemy. Satan, the accuser of Israel, is what, since Milton's day, we have learned to call a Philistine. Both Satan and Christ divide the world into the material and the spiritual, but for Satan the material is real and the spiritual is imaginary or, as he says, "allegoric." It is only from Christ's point of view that he is an Archimago or master of illusion.

Hence, just as Comus puns on the word "nature," so all the elements of the dialectical conflict are attached to a material context by Satan and to a spiritual one by Christ. By rejecting everything that Satan offers in Satan's sense, Christ gets it again in its true or spiritual form, just as Adam, if he had successfully resisted his temptation, would still have become as the gods (i.e. the true gods or angels), knowing good, and evil as the possible negation of good. In the *Christian Doctrine* Milton speaks of the virtue of urbanity and its opposing vice of obscenity, which, he says, consists of taking words in a double sense. He means, of course, what we mean by the "double entendre"; still, Christ is the source of urbanity and Satan of obscenity, and something of the double entendre, the great words "the kingdom, the power, and the glory" "profaned" to their worldly opposites, runs all through Satan's speeches. As in the previous conflict, Satan is "scoffing in ambiguous words," and the opening colloquy between Satan and Christ in the first book is already a clash of oracular powers. Satan's dialectical instrument is the evasive or quibbling oracle; Christ's is the simplicity and plainness that Milton prizes so in Scripture, especially the Gospels. The climax of *Paradise Regained*, when Satan falls from the pinnacle and Christ stands on it, is marked by two very carefully placed classical allusions, almost the only mythological ones in the poem. One is to Hercules and Antaeus, of which more later; the other is to Oedipus and the Sphinx. Christ has not only overcome temptation, but, as the Word of God, he has solved the verbal riddle of human life, putting all the words which are properly attributes of God into their rightful context.

The temptations which follow are temptations to false heroic action and fall into three parts: the temptation of Parthia, or false power; the temptation of Rome, or false justice; and the temptation of Athens, or false wisdom. One problem of interpretation is raised by Milton's curious proportioning of emphasis. The temptation of Parthia seems much the crudest of the three; yet it takes up the entire third book, while the other two are huddled with the third temptation into the fourth.

In Jesus' day, with the memory of the Maccabees still vivid, the question of armed rebellion against Roman power was very insistent; it was the course that most Jews expected the Messiah to take and had already been in the mind of the youthful Christ:

> victorious deeds
> Flamed in my heart, heroic acts, one while
> To rescue Israel from the Roman yoke.

And, though even then Christ thought of putting down violence rather than of using violence, still Satan's arguments on this point are unanswerable: to defeat Roman power by arms requires princely virtues, and princely virtues, as Machiavelli demonstrated, are not moral virtues, far less spiritual ones; they are martial courage and cunning, both demonic gifts. What Satan unwittingly does for Christ in the temptations of Parthia and Rome is to dramatize the nature of that aspect of law that is to be annihilated by the gospel—law as a compelling external force in which spiritual authority is subject to and administered by temporal authority.

Satan is shrewd enough to throw in the suggestion that, by gaining the power of Parthia, Christ will be able to realize the patriotic dream of reuniting the lost ten tribes with the Jewish remnant. In rejecting this, Christ rejects also the legal conception of Israel as a chosen people and is ready to usher in the new Christian conception of Israel as the body of believers. There seems also to be some personal reference, however indirect, to the great blighted hope of Milton's political life. Some Milton scholars think that *Samson Agonistes* is earlier than *Paradise Regained:* if so, the latter is Milton's final poetic testament, and his treatment of this theme takes on an additional intensity and pathos.

The final binding of Satan, the third phase of the agon, is prophesied in the Book of Revelation, where, in the twelfth chapter, we have again a wilderness, a symbolic female figure representing the church, and a threatening dragon beaten off by Michael, the angelic champion of Israel, in a repetition of the first encounter. Milton, like everyone else, took the Book of Revelation to be in part a prophecy of the troubles the church was to suffer after the apostolic period. In *The Reason of Church Government* he attacks the supporters of tradition on the ground that they do not understand that the Book of Revelation foretells an apostasy of the church and "the Church's flight into the wilderness.'" Several times in the prose pamphlets Milton refers to the rebellion against Charles I in terms of the Exodus from Egypt and expresses a hope that England will be a new chosen people, chosen this time for the gospel instead of the law, the rescued apocalyptic church coming out of the wilderness with Michael into a new Promised Land. In this role the English nation would represent the returning lost tribes, a new Israel taking up the cross that the Jews had rejected. By the time he wrote *Paradise Regained,* the English had chosen, in the terrible phrase of *The Ready and Easy Way,* "a captain back for Egypt." Yet even Milton cannot allow Christ to dismiss the unfaithful tribes, who have lost their birthright rather than their home, without adding a few wistful cadences in another key, too gentle in tone to be a direct reply to Satan and at most only overheard by him:

> Yet he at length, time to himself best known,
> Rememb'ring Abraham, by some wondrous call
> May bring them back, repentant and sincere,
> And at their passing cleave the Assyrian flood,
> As the Red Sea and Jordan once he cleft,
> When to the Promised Land their fathers passed;
> To his due time and providence I leave them.

The temptation of Parthia, to ally the Messiah with an anti-Roman power in order to overthrow Rome, had, in short, been a temptation of Milton as well as of Christ. It is a commonplace that if Milton had written his epic around the time he wrote *The Reason of Church Government,* it would have been more closely affiliated to the epic-romance convention established by Boiardo, Ariosto, and Spenser, in which Arthur would probably have represented a crusader or Christian warrior and some heroine an aspect of "the king's daughter, the Church," like Spenser's Una. But the female figure over whom physical wars are fought is likely to be closer to the erotic conventions, "Inductive mainly to the sin of Eve," to Courtly Love, uxoriousness, and lust. The rejected Romantic tradition appears in Milton's reference to "The fairest of her sex, Angelica," where we might expect the more familiar Helen of Troy or Guinevere; one reason for his choice may be that Boiardo's landscape is more shadowy and insubstantial than Troy or Britain.

In *Paradise Regained* Satan displays all his kingdom; consequently, Christ must refuse all of it, including much that in other contexts he might handle fearlessly. Later in his career he shows no hesitation in providing miraculous food, sitting at table with sinners, or accepting money and other gifts. But he has not yet entered on his ministry: the teaching and healing Christ that we know, with his compassion and courtesy, his love of children, and his sense of humor, has no place in Satan's kingdom. The haughtiness and aloofness of Christ mean that, before Christ can work in the world, he must recognize and repudiate all worldliness. In *Paradise Regained* Christ is looking at the world as it is under the wrath, as the domain of Satan. Wrath is the reaction of goodness contemplating badness; it is disinterested and impersonal and is the opposite of anger or irritation. If God is capable of wrath, he is incapable of irritation. Milton goes to grotesque lengths in *Paradise Lost* in emphasizing this point: he transforms the Father into a monster of indifference, who merely smiles when he observes that a third of his angelic creation has revolted. The word "unmoved," so often applied to Christ in *Paradise Regained*, refers to his emotions as well as his intellect: Satan is condemned but not railed at. Christ cannot exercise mercy until he has separated it from sentimentality, and his comments on the misery of man under wrath are part of this separation. Hence *dramatically* Christ becomes an increasingly unsympathetic figure, a pusillanimous quietist in the temptation of Parthia, an inhuman snob in the temptation of Rome, a peevish obscurantist in the temptation of Athens.

When Adam in *Paradise Lost* decides to die with Eve rather than live without her, the reader is expected to feel some sympathy for Adam, to feel that he might well have done the same thing in Adam's place, as, of course, he would. Conversely, one might almost say that the point at which the reader loses sympathy with Jesus in *Paradise Regained* is the point at which he himself would have collapsed under the temptation. All of us are, like Christ, in the world and, unlike him, partly of it, and whatever in us is of the world is bound to condemn Christ's rejection of the world at some point or other. This aspect of the temptation story is the theme of the other great literary treatment of it, the Grand Inquisitor episode in *The Brothers Karamazov*, but it is present in Milton too.[6]

In *Paradise Regained*, as to some extent in *Comus*, the dramatic and the dialectical aspects of the conflict are opposed and in a paradoxical relation to one another. Comus and Satan get our dramatic attention because they show such energy and resourcefulness; the tempted figures are either motionless or unmoved and have only the ungracious dramatic function of saying No. Yet, of course, the real relation is the opposite of the apparent one: the real source of life and freedom and energy is in the frigid figure at the center. One would think that Milton had selected the temptation episode because it is, with the possible exception of the agony in the garden (on which Milton also meditated a "Christus patiens"), the only episode in which suspense and the feeling of the possible awful consequences of failure are consistently present. But Christ's ability to reply "Why art *thou* solicitous?" to every temptation destroys all opportunity for narrative suspense. Yet it is essential to Milton's plan that Christ should be able to see every card in Satan's hand, for if he is once puzzled, he is lost. Narrative suspense and dramatic sympathy go together; we can have them in *Samson Agonistes,* but they must be renounced here.

The reader may feel that the effect is to make both Christ and Satan seem bored with their roles and that such boredom is infectious. Of course, in long poems there are two areas of criticism—the structure or design and the poetic realization of details—and value-judgments established in one area are not transferable to the other. It is quite possible for a poem to be, as *Paradise Regained* may be, a magnificent success in its structure and yet often tired and perfunctory in its execution. In structure, however, *Paradise Regained* is not only a success but a technical experiment that is practically *sui generis.* None of the ordinary literary categories apply to it; its poetic predecessors are nothing like it, and it has left no descendants. If it is a "brief epic," it has little resemblance to the epyllion; its closest affinities are with the debate and with the dialectical colloquy of Plato and Boethius, to which most of the Book of Job also belongs. But these forms usually either incorporate one argument into another dialectically or build up two different cases rhetorically; Milton's feat of constructing a double argument on the same words, each highly plausible and yet as different as light from darkness, is, so far as I know, unique in English literature.

The rejecting of the temptation of Rome forces Satan to relinquish one of his trump cards, which is the appeal to opportunity, the panic inspired by the ticking clock. The aspect of temptation which suggests the temporal is an aspect with a particular significance for Milton himself, who for a great part of his life was torn between two contradictory, but equally powerful and valid, impulses—one to complete his epic, the other to postpone it until it was ready. This problem, in itself peculiar to Milton as a poet, was for him also a special case of the general principle that the Christian must learn to will to relax the will, to perform real acts in God's time and not pseudo-acts in his own. In the temptations of Adam and Samson, too, the same theme recurs of an action not so much wrong in itself as wrong at that time, a hasty snatching of a chance before the real time has fulfilled itself. Christ is older than Milton was at twenty-three when he wrote his famous sonnet, and Satan constantly urges him, from the first temptation on, to be his own providence, to release some of his own latent energies. The discipline of waiting is not only more difficult and inglorious but constantly subject to the danger of passing insensibly into procrastination.

The subtlest thing that Satan says in the poem is his remark that

each act is rightliest done,
Not when it must, but when it may be best.

The demonic hero judges the present by an intuitive sense of the immediate future. He is distinguished from other men by his capacity to take thought for the morrow, to be, in short, a diviner. In the classical epic, knowledge of the future is usually gained from a dark underworld, in contrast to the revelations of gods, which as a rule illuminate the present moment. Similarly in Dante the damned know the future but not the present, and in *Paradise Lost* Michael prophesies the future to Adam after he has gained his forbidden knowledge. Hence we are not surprised to find that Satan's oracular powers in *Paradise Regained* include a knowledge of Christ's future "fate" gained by astrology. In contrast, all times are present to the Father, and the Father is manifested as a real present, or presence, by the Son. Christ's main scriptural ally on this point is Ecclesiastes, with its doctrine that there is time for all things, but the sense of strain in waiting for God's time comes out in several places, not least in the reference to the lost tribes, already quoted.

The temptation of Athens has, as its Antichrist core, the Stoic ideal, the "apathy" of the invulnerable individual who feels that the wise man in a bad world can only do the best he can for himself. In rejecting it, Christ also rejects the contemplative life as an end: Christ's aim is to redeem the world, not to live a morally sinless life, which he might conceivably have done as a philosopher. In the temptation of Athens the clash of the two oracular traditions, the prophetic and the demonic, reaches its climax. Here again it is Greek philosophy in its context as part of Satan's kingdom that is being rejected. A Christian working outward from his faith might find the study of Plato and

Aristotle profitable enough; but if he were to *exchange* the direct tradition of revelation for their doctrines, which is what Christ is tempted to do, he would find in them only the fine flower of a great speculative tree, with its roots in the demonic metaphysics and theology described in the second book of *Paradise Lost*.

The third temptation begins with a night of storm, not in itself a temptation but an indispensable preliminary to one. Its object is to impress Christ with Satan's power as prince of an indifferent and mindless order of nature, to suggest that his Father has either forsaken him or is unable to reach him in a fallen world. It is, in short, another suggestion of despair or distrust, but with the specific aim of making Christ feel lonely and deserted, hence isolated, hence the self-contained ego which is the form of pride. It demonstrates the fact that in a world of death and mutability the light of nature is surrounded by the darkness of nature; but as Christ has already rejected all arguments based on the analogy of natural and revealed wisdom, this fact comes as no great surprise. The placing of Christ on the pinnacle of the temple follows and is, as Satan makes clear, a temptation of Jesus purely in his capacity as Son of God, an ordeal that no simple human nature would be able to survive. Here, for once, we can cautiously accept what Satan says, although, of course, his motive in saying it is to drop a suggestion of arrogance into Christ's mind.

The temptation of the pinnacle is equally a bodily and a mental assault. Christ has been weakened by forty days of fasting and by the night of storm. Satan won over Eve by instilling thoughts into her mind while her consciousness was preoccupied with the wonder of a talking snake; and Eve, when she came to search her own mind, found Satan's thoughts there and took them for her own. Christ is far more astute, but still the sequence of blinding visions of earthly glory may have left in his mind some faint trace of attachment, some unconscious sense of exaltation. If so, he will feel dizzy on the pinnacle. Mentally, then, Christ is being tested for *hybris,* or pride of mind. He is in the position of a tragic hero, on top of the wheel of fortune, subject to the fatal instant of distraction that will bring him down.

Physically, Christ is being tested for exhaustion, for a slight yielding to pressure that will make him stagger out of sheer weariness. Satan quotes the Psalms to show that the Messiah could fall, trusting in the support of angels; but Christ, though led by the Spirit into the wilderness, is not being led by the Spirit to fall off the pinnacle. That would be his own act, and the Antichrist core of it would be a trust not in angels but in his own fortune, and trusting to one's fortune is the same thing as trusting to Satan. It would perhaps be a reasonable definition of cowardice to say that a coward is a man whose instinct it is, in a crisis, to do what his enemy wants him to do. Christ's ordeal is one of fortitude as well as wisdom, and he has proved himself no coward; but even brave men have had traitors lurking within them, something that co-operated with an outward attack. If there is the smallest trace either of pride in Christ's mind or what we should now call the death-impulse in his body—the impulse that would make any other man accept the vinegar sponge on the cross—this final test will reveal it. If not, Christ is ready to be God's sacrificial victim, a martyr who, so far from being, like some martyrs, half in love with easeful death, dies as the implacable enemy of death.

Christ has been tempted *quasi homo,* purely as man. For Milton what man can do for himself is negative and iconoclastic: man does not save himself, but, by clearing his world of idols, he can indicate his willingness to be saved. Christ has resisted the whole of Satan's world; he has done what man can do, and the only possible next step is for God to indicate acceptance of what he has done. Thus the fact that Christ successfully stands on the pinnacle is miraculous, but not a miracle drawn from his own divine nature, not an ace hidden up his sleeve, which is what Satan is looking for. It means that his human will has been taken over by the omnipotent divine will at the necessary point and prefigures the commending of his spirit to the Father at the instant of his death on the cross.

Christ's answer, "Tempt not the Lord thy God," is the only remark Christ makes in the poem which employs ambiguity.[7] Primarily, it means "Do not put the Father to unnecessary tests," the meaning of the passage in Deuteronomy which Jesus is quoting. But here the Son carries the name and nature of the Father, and the statement bears the secondary meaning "Do not continue the temptation of the Son of God." At this point, probably, Satan for the first time recognizes in Jesus his old antagonist of the war in heaven. Earlier in the poem he had spoken of Christ as an opaque cloud which might be a cooling or shading screen between himself and the wrath of the Father. This is, of course, the direct opposite of Christ's true nature,

> In whose conspicuous countenance, without cloud,
> Made visible, the Almighty Father shines.

So far from screening the fire of the Father, the Son is focusing it like a burning glass, the two natures of the Godhead united as closely as Milton's Christology will permit. And just as this last temptation was of Christ in his specific role as Son of God, so with his victory Satan is defeated in his own headquarters, the lower heaven or element of air which is the spatial limit of his conquest at the Fall. That is why Christ's victory is immediately followed by a reference to the struggle of Hercules and Antaeus, in which Hercules (a prototype of Christ also in the "Nativity Ode" and elsewhere) overcame the monstrous son of earth in the air.

There is a hidden irony in Satan's quotation from the Ninety-first Psalm. He quotes the eleventh and twelfth verses; the thirteenth reads, "The lion and the adder, the young lion and the dragon shalt thou trample under foot." In his fall Satan assumes the position of the dragon under Christ's feet, the only place for him after his failure to gain entrance to Christ's body or mind. At this point a new center of gravity is established in the world, as the gospel is finally separated from the law. Judaism joins classical wisdom as part of the demonic illusion, as the center of religion passes from the temple Christ is standing on into the true Christian temple, the body of Christ above it. The destruction of the Garden of Eden at the Flood showed that God "attributes to place no sanctity," and the later destruction of the temple, prefigured at this point, illustrates the same principle. Christ's casting the devils out of heaven prefigured the cleansing of the temple, with which, according to John, his ministry began. Here, with the end of the temptation, Christ has chased the devils out of the temple of his own body and mind and is ready to repeat the process for each human soul.

The temptation of the pinnacle corresponds to the point in *Samson Agonistes* at which Samson, after beating off Manoah, Delilah, and Harapha, refuses to go to the Philistine festival. He is right in refusing but has come to the end of his own will. At that point he appears to change his mind, but what has happened is that God has accepted his efforts, taken over his will, and changed his mind for him. In *Samson Agonistes,* which is a tragedy, this point is the "peripety": Samson is now certain to die, though also certain of redemption. Jesus has also made it impossible for himself to avoid death, as his prototypes Elijah and perhaps Moses did; but *Paradise Regained* is less a tragedy than an episode in a divine comedy, and we need another term for the crucial point of the action.

In the *Christian Doctrine* Milton distinguishes between the literal and what he calls the "metaphorical" generation of the Son by the Father. By the latter he means what might more accurately be called "epiphany," the manifesting of Christ in a divine capacity to others. The showing of Christ to the angels in *Paradise Lost* is a metaphorical or epiphanic generation of him: the Father's phrase "This day have I begot" can hardly refer to literal generation. The same distinction recurs in the Incarnation. Two of the Gospels, Matthew and Luke, are nativity Gospels, beginning with Christ's infancy or physical generation in the world. The other two, Mark and John, are epiphanic Gospels and begin with his baptism, where he is pointed out to man as the Son of God. (In the Western churches epiphany means particularly the showing of the infant Christ to the Magi, but in the Eastern churches it means particularly the baptism, though the date of observance is the same.) Epiphany is the theological equivalent of what in literature is called "anagnorisis" or "recognition." The Father recognizes Jesus as the Son at the baptism: Satan recognizes him on the pinnacle in a different, yet closely related, sense. That is, the action of *Paradise Regained* begins with the baptism, an epiphany which Satan sees but does not understand, and ends with an epiphany to Satan alone, the nature of which he can hardly fail to understand. Behind this is the still larger scheme in which *Paradise Regained* is the sequel of *Paradise Lost*. The epiphany of Christ to the angels, which caused the original revolt of Satan, was chronologically the first event in *Paradise Lost*, and, with the climax of *Paradise Regained*, the great wheel of the quest of Christ comes full circle, as far as Milton's treatment of it is concerned.

NOTES

1. *De doct. Chr.*, I, xxvi (*Works* [Columbia ed.], XVI, 110-11).
2. For the homiletic tradition behind Milton's and Fletcher's treatment see E. M. Pope, *"Paradise Regained"; The Tradition and the Poem* (Baltimore, 1947). For Spenser's Despair see also E. Sirluck, "A Note on the Rhetoric of Spenser's Despair," *MP*, XLVII (1949), 8 ff.
3. Giles Fletcher follows the Matthew order of temptations; Milton, of course, follows Luke.
4. This contrast is symbolized by the fact that the action of *Comus* moves up to the sprinkling of the Lady by Sabrina, an act with some analogies to baptism, whereas the action of *Paradise Regained* follows

baptism (cf. A. S. P. Woodhouse, "Comus Once More," *University of Toronto Quarterly*, XIX [1950], 218 ff.).

5. *De doct. Chr.*, I, xi (*Works*, XV, 198-99).

6. For an explicit assertion that Satan was right and Christ wrong see the passage from the nineteenth-century anarchist Proudhon quoted in Karl Löwith, *Meaning in History* (Chicago, 1949), p. 64.

7. A. S. P. Woodhouse, "Paradise Regained," *University of Toronto Quarterly*, XXV (1956), 181.

[EDITOR'S NOTE. See also M. Y. Hughes, *SP*, XXXV (1938), 254-71; E. M. W. Tillyard, *SP*, XXXVI (1939), 247-52; I. Samuel, *PMLA*, LXIV (1949), 708-23; H. Schultz, *PMLA*, LXVII (1952), 790-808, and *Milton and Forbidden Knowledge*, 1955; D. C. Allen, *Harmonious Vision*, 1954; M. Fixler, *MLN*, LXX (1955), 573-7; A. S. P. Woodhouse, *UTQ*, XXV (1955-56), 167-82; A. Stein, *Heroic Knowledge*, 1957; B. K. Lewalski, *SP*, LVII (1960), 186-220; L. L. Martz, *ELH*, XXVII (1960), 223-47; H. R. MacCallum, *UTQ*, XXXI (1961-62), 397-415; J. M. Steadman, *HTR*, LIV (1961), 29-34 and *UTQ*, XXXI (1961-62), 416-30; J. Sims, *The Bible in Milton's Epics*, 1962; A. E. Barker, in *Essays in English Literature . . . Presented to A. S. P. Woodhouse*, ed. M. MacLure and F. W. Watt, 1964.]

A. S. P. WOODHOUSE

Tragic Effect in *Samson Agonistes*

The point of view from which I propose to look afresh at *Samson Agonistes*[1] seems perfectly simple and even obvious, and yet, so far as I know, it has never been tried.

Misled by Milton's prefatory emphasis on his Greek models, an emphasis entirely justified if properly understood, critics have assumed that the poet intended not only to follow them in structure and convention but to reproduce their spirit and effect, and that hence the only possible criterion for judging *Samson Agonistes* is Greek tragedy. Opinions on his success have differed. Jebb (to take a famous example) vigorously defends Milton against Johnson's charge that *Samson Agonistes* has a beginning and end but no middle, that nothing occurs to precipitate the catastrophe. But he goes on to condemn the drama as not truly tragic, as not Hellenic at all in spirit and effect, but thoroughly Hebraic. It does not, like Greek tragedy, pit the hero against superior powers before which he goes down to inevitable defeat, yet demonstrates his heroism even in his defeat. On the contrary, Samson is an instrument of the Supreme Power, and the only possible conclusion is that "All is best." Nor, in the most vigorous and effective defence against Jebb, does W. R. Parker ques-

From the *University of Toronto Quarterly*, XXVIII (1958-59), 205-22. Reprinted by permission of the Executors of the Estate of A. S. P. Woodhouse and the University of Toronto Press.

tion the assumption that Greek tragedy furnishes the sole and sufficient criterion. But it is precisely this assumption that I would question.

In *Paradise Lost* Milton follows his classical models every whit as
closely as in *Samson Agonistes;* yet no one supposes that he is trying
to reproduce the spirit and effect of Homer, or even of Virgil. His
purpose is to adapt the classical epic form to a Christian content and
outlook, and to achieve thereby a new but still genuinely epic effect.
And I would ask whether *mutatis mutandis* the same thing may not
be true of *Samson Agonistes.* The only way to find out is to re-examine the drama from this point of view, that is, with two questions in
mind: What is the effect actually achieved? And is it one that can be
legitimately described as tragic?

II

To attempt an answer, however tentative, to these questions we
must establish a proper understanding of the theme and action, and
on the way thereto may comment on the insufficiency of Jebb's. He
recognizes that "Samson's will is the agent of the catastrophe" and
that everything which "helps to determine his will and define his purpose" leads on to it. But he proceeds: "The force which is to produce
the catastrophe is the inward force of Samson's own despair, not an
external necessity pressing upon him." On the contrary (as I have
heretofore argued, and D. C. Allen has further demonstrated) it is
not Samson's despair that produces the catastrophe, but his gradual
rising out of his initial state of feeling, in which indeed the last heroic
act would have been quite impossible. Again, it is true that Samson
voluntarily precipitates the catastrophe (for Milton never surrenders
his robust belief in man's free will within God's providential scheme,
and could not possibly achieve the effect at which he aims if he did
so here). But if there is "no external necessity," there is still an overruling power: there is God who controls the outcome: and this fact,
paradoxically, Jebb later insists upon in order to explain Milton's
failure to achieve the Greek tragic effect. In his reading of the poem
Jebb altogether misses the interplay of these two forces, Samson's will
and God's, because while he oversimplifies the conception of God as
Providence, he ignores the intense religious experience undergone by
Samson as he comes to a realization that God's "ear is ever open; and
his eye / Gracious to readmit the suppliant" (1172-3). When Jebb
insists on the Hebraism of *Samson Agonistes,* he does not ask himself

how much of this adheres inevitably to the legend with which Milton is working, or whether the religion which permeates the poem is not in fact Christian, and whether it is not the Christianity, far more than the Hebraism, that differentiates it in effect from Greek tragedy. The problem of *Samson Agonistes* is part of the problem of Christian tragedy—of the problem and Milton's solution of it.

Act I (as we may call it: 1-331: Samson, Chorus) gives us Samson's situation and initial state of mind. He has sinned and been most dreadfully punished. But the punishment, be it noted (for this is characteristic of Milton's whole presentation), is the natural and inevitable outcome of Samson's actions, just as the sufferings of Oedipus are the natural and inevitable outcome of his. Blinded, now, enslaved, the mockery of his enemies, Samson knows that all these evils have come upon him through his own weakness. He experiences bitterest remorse; but this is not repentance: it is too entirely self-centred for that, and it has issued in a degree of despair (itself a sin in the Christian view) which can entertain no thought of forgiveness, no ray of hope. Yet Samson's foot is on the path that leads to repentance, though it will first lead him yet deeper into the Slough of Despond: he has acknowledged that the fault is wholly his. I can find, he says,

> Ease to the body some, none to the mind
> From restless thoughts, that like a deadly swarm
> Of hornets arm'd, no sooner found alone,
> But rush upon me thronging, and present
> Times past, what once I was, and what am now. . . .
> Why was my breeding order'd and prescrib'd
> As of a person separate to God,
> Design'd for great exploits, if I must die
> Betray'd, captiv'd, and both my eyes put out,
> Made of my enemies the scorn and gaze? . . .
>
>   Promise was that I
> Should Israel from Philistian yoke deliver;
> Ask for this great Deliverer now, and find him
> Eyeless in Gaza at the mill with slaves. . . .
> Yet stay, let me not rashly call in doubt
> Divine prediction; what if all foretold
> Had been fulfill'd but through mine own default;
> Whom have I to complain of but myself?
>
>   (18-46)

Doubts momentarily assail him, and complaints of Providence mingle with his self-reproach, so that the Chorus is fain to counsel, "Tax not Divine disposal" (210), though this is only the submission which Samson himself acknowledges as God's due, and indeed echoes his own words:

> But peace, I must not quarrel with the will
> Of highest dispensation, which herein
> Haply had ends beyond my reach to know.
>
> (60-2)

Taken in conjunction with Samson's full admission of his personal responsibility, these lines give us our first clue to the inner tension between man's freedom and God's Providence which only the final words of the poem will resolve.

From the conviction of his own responsibility Samson never wavers. Even of Dalila, "That specious monster, my accomplish'd snare," he can aver, "She was not the prime cause, but I myself" (230, 234). Still Samson is far from true repentance. His remorse (as we have said) is in large measure self-centred:

> [I] like a foolish pilot have shipwreckt
> My vessel trusted to me from above,
> Gloriously rigg'd; and for a word, a tear,
> Fool, have divulg'd the secret gift of God
> To a deceitful woman. Tell me, friends,
> Am I not sung and proverb'd for a fool
> In every street; do they not say, how well
> Are come upon him his deserts?
>
> (198-205)

These are the words of wounded pride, and pride, as Allen recognizes, has its issue in religious despair. Conformable to the truths of moral theology, this is also the fruit of Milton's imaginative insight. To the Chorus, Samson appears

> As one past hope, abandon'd
> And by himself given over.
>
> (120-1)

The principal purpose of this mainly expository first Act is, then, to underline Samson's remorse (not yet repentance) and his religious despair: to give us the starting point of the movement back to God—

and on to the catastrophe. But, incidentally, the Act brings home to us three other facts; and first, the remoteness of Milton's Samson from the sanctified barbarian of the Book of Judges, the tribal folk hero, incapable of religious experience. Secondly, we begin to be aware that in Milton's treatment (unlike Vondel's) the primary focus is religious and personal, not national (even from the depth of his self-reproach Samson can rouse himself to disclaim responsibility for Israel's plight—235 ff.), though the national aspect of the action will be present throughout in a secondary rôle and will have its place in the final resolution. And, thirdly, we already recognize the character and function of the Chorus: it is Hebrew in its outlook and offers as it were a Hebraic commentary on the story which the poet will present, consistently though unobtrusively, from a Christian standpoint, and thus it serves the purposes of historical realism; it is not the mouthpiece of the poet: it does not run ahead of events, but like the audience follows them step by step and learns from them what it can.

Less simple is the rôle of Manoa, whose entrance marks the beginning of Act II (332-709: Samson, Manoa, Chorus). True to his classical models Milton subordinates his people to the action and to the central figure of the hero, but Manoa's functions are varied and more than the others he gives the impression of a self-motivating character. Here, as again in the final Act, he supplements the Chorus, now joining in Samson's lament, now criticizing his "marriage choices," even, like Samson, and like the Chorus, seeming to question the ways of Providence, rebuked this time by Samson himself:

> Appoint not heavenly disposition, Father.
> Nothing of all these evils hath befallen me
> But justly; I myself have brought them on,
> Sole author I, sole cause. . . .
>
> (373-5)

In his main endeavor Manoa is deluded: his effort to ransom his son is a counter-action wholly ironic. Yet his words have an effect on Samson beyond, and sometimes contrary to, their intention. They bring home to Samson the offence against God and against Israel:

> Father I do acknowledge and confess
> That I this honour, I this pomp have brought to Dagon . . . ;
> to God have brought
> Dishonour . . . ;

> have brought scandal
> To Israel, diffidence of God and doubt
> To feeble hearts . . . ;
> Which is my chief affliction, shame, and sorrow,
> The anguish of my soul, that suffers not
> Mine eye to harbour sleep or thoughts to rest.
>
> (448-59)

This is a step forward, though for the time being it only deepens Samson's despair. More subtly still, in the course of his mistaken argument Manoa puts his finger on the insufficiency of Samson's remorse: it turns too much on the offence against himself: God, says Manoa,

> ever more approves and more accepts
> (Best pleas'd with humble and filial submission)
> Him who imploring mercy sues for life
> Than who self-rigorous chooses death as due;
> Which argues over-just and self-displeas'd
> For self-offence, more than for God offended.
>
> (510-15)

Rejecting his father's proposal and his optimistic inferences, Samson fastens on these words:

> His pardon I implore; but as for life
> To what end should I seek it?
>
> (521-2)

To conceive the possibility of pardon is of course to take another step forward; but to conceive it in this context is not immediately to lighten the burden. Indeed, in this Act, Samson reaches his lowest depth of despair;

> Oh, that torments should not be confin'd
> To the body's wounds and sores . . .
> But must secret passage find
> To th' inmost mind. . . .
>
> Sleep hath forsook me and giv'n me o'er
> To death's benumbing opium as my only cure.
> Thence faintings, swoonings of despair
> And sense of Heav'n's desertion.
>
> (606-32)

And from the Chorus, orthodox though it be, Samson's misery wrings the impassioned cry of bafflement:

> God of our Fathers, what is man!
> That thou towards him with a hand so various,
> Or might I say contrarious,
> Temper'st thy providence through his short course,
> Not evenly, as thou rul'st
> The Angelic orders and inferior creatures mute,
> Irrational and brute.
> Nor do I name of men the common rout . . .
> But such as thou hast solemnly elected,
> With gifts and graces eminently adorn'd,
> To some great work, thy glory
> And people's safety. . . .
>
> Nor only dost degrade them, or remit
> To life obscur'd, which were a fair dismission,
> But throw'st them lower than thou didst exalt them high,
> Unseemly falls in human eye,
> Too grievous for the trespass or omission. . . .
>
> (667-91)

The Chorus itself will correct this judgment in its final comment, but not so as to dispel the whole of the mystery. Meanwhile it makes its powerful contribution to the darkness, through which a gleam of light is presently to break. But first must come the two crucial encounters, with Dalila and with Harapha. For the first, if it is to have its due effect, the essential preparation is Samson's repentance; for the second, the conviction already voiced by Samson *de profundis,* that if with him the strife is over, God is still God and in his own good time and way will triumph over Dagon (460-71).

In Act III (710-1074: Samson, Dalila, Chorus) the coming of Dalila is described with incomparable vividness by the Chorus; but her motives are left by Milton obscure. They do not matter: she is there for the sake of Samson and the action, not in her own right. The primary function of the scene is to demonstrate by Dalila's powerlessness to reassert her sway the completeness of Samson's repentance. Only obedience, Milton believes, can remit the sin of disobedience—Christ's obedience for Adam's disobedience, Samson's for his own—and what is remitted is the sin, not all its consequences. But this is no mere demonstration or for the audience alone. It has its effect upon Samson himself and hence upon the action. He has won his first victory, over himself; and, though he does not realize it, he approaches his next decisive encounter with new possibilities of emotional response.

Act IV, if the divisions were marked, would fall into two scenes. The first (1075-1307): Samson, Harapha, Chorus) presents this encounter, with the champion of the Philistines. It will precipitate the summons to appear before the lords, the occasion of the final catastrophe; but, more important, it is just what is needed to rouse Samson, and draw him on to form and utter, almost unawares, a hope—the first in the whole action. Harapha jeers:

> Presume not on thy God, whate'er he be,
> Thee he regards not, owns not, hath cut off
> Quite from his people, and delivered up
> Into thine Enemies' hand—

to be bound, blinded, imprisoned and set to labour, companion of the slave and ass. It is only what Samson himself has said before. Nor does he seek now to mitigate his fault or deny the justice of his punishment; but in his mounting anger at Harapha he gives back for insult defiance:

> All these indignities, for such they are
> From thine, these evils I deserve and, more,
> Acknowledge them from God inflicted on me
> Justly, yet despair not of his final pardon
> Whose ear is ever open; and his eye
> Gracious to readmit the suppliant;
> In confidence whereof I once again
> Defy thee to the trial of mortal fight,
> By combat to decide whose god is God,
> Thine or whom I with Israel's sons adore.
>   (1156-77)

Nothing surely could be psychologically more true, or dramatically more effective. Samson, we remember, has reasserted his confidence in God; his remorse has become repentance, and he has sued for God's forgiveness; and but now, in the encounter with Dalila, he has stood firm: a deed has sealed his repentance and given a basis for returning confidence in himself. All this was necessary before the hope could be born that Samson might be indeed forgiven and, for one final exploit, be restored to God's service and the communion of his own people; but it was all latent, as it were, unrecognized by Samson himself. Till the hope was uttered, he did not dream that it existed: and utterance was born of the perfectly natural union of repentance and indignation.

Here, at length, is dawning the resolution necessary for Samson's last heroic act. The change is not too sudden or complete; but now to the passive desire for death is joined an active and more powerful motive. Harapha will seek vengeance for the scorn heaped upon him. Let him, says Samson, for

> come what may, my deadliest foe
> Will prove my speediest friend, by death to rid me hence,
> The worst that he can give, to me the best.
> Yet so it may fall out, because their end
> Is hate, not help to me, it may with mine
> Draw their own ruin who attempt the deed.
>
> (1262-7)

And this new resolution the Chorus instantly recognizes:

> Oh how comely it is and how reviving
> To the spirits of just men long oppress'd
> When God into the hands of their deliverer
> Puts invincible might. . . .
>
> (1268-71)

Samson, they feel, is once more doubly armed (and this is of crucial significance, as we shall see)—doubly armed with "celestial vigour" and with "plain heroic magnitude of mind" (1279-80).

In the second scene (1308-1444: Samson, Officer, Chorus), the summons arrives, and Samson, knowing his presence at a heathen festival unlawful, refuses: "I cannot come"; and then with mounting anger at the indignity designed him (for all thoughts of self have not been quenched): "I will not come," and again, "I will not come" (1321, 1332, 1342). But before the Officer returns, better thoughts have prevailed: the inner voice, so long silent, has spoken once more —the seal of Samson's restoration:

> I begin to feel
> Some rousing motions in me which dispose

> To something extraordinary my thoughts.
> I with this messenger will go along. . . .

> Happen what may, of me expect to hear
> Nothing dishonourable, impure, unworthy,
> Our God, our Law, my nation, or myself. . . .
>
>   (1381-4, 1423-5)

And the Chorus replies:

> Go, and the Holy One
> Of Israel be thy guide. . . .
>
>   (1427-8)

In Act V (1445-1758: Manoa, Messenger, Chorus), the futile counteraction, Manoa's effort to ransom his son, provides an overtone of pathos and a sustained note of irony, his narrative punctuated, from the main action, by shouts and the noise of ruin. The Messenger enters to recount the catastrophe; and Manoa and the Chorus comment antiphonally on Samson and his end.

It is of the first importance to observe that Samson's tragedy is considered, and the effect summed up, on the purely human level (1660-1744) before the Chorus is permitted to raise its eyes to the larger issue of the place of his sacrifice in God's providential plan, before it can determine that "All is best, though we oft doubt . . ." (1745-58). For this dual reference is not confined to the comments on the catastrophe. It extends to the whole situation and action. In an earlier reference to Samson's exploits, in the *Defence of the English People*, Milton had presented the alternative, "whether he acted in pursuance of a command from heaven or was prompted by his own valour." In the poem, the Chorus (as we have seen) recognizes Samson as doubly armed, with "celestial vigour" and "plain heroic magnitude of mind." The poet has found a way not to choose between the two views, but to combine and harmonize them. And of this we are reminded by Samson's attitude just before the last heroic effort: he stood "as one who pray'd / Or some great matter in his mind revolv'd" (1637-8): he was in fact doing both. Granted that the outcome is controlled by God's overruling power, and that his grace is operative from the first, though overtly so only as the catastrophe approaches, yet Samson's responses are at every point natural and humanly intelligible. If he is an instrument of Providence, he does not cease to be an individual, fallible, though corrigible, heroic—and by his own action doomed.

The effect of the final comments is at once to magnify Samson and to reconcile us to his fate: and this raises a problem. A common feature in all tragedies is a sense of disaster. A feature of very many is, at the end, some mitigation of this sense of disaster, some reconciling of the audience to the experience which they have witnessed and shared. This is true of many tragedies, but certainly not of all. We remember, for example, the grim closing words of the *Oedipus Tyrannus* ("Let no man be accounted happy till he has carried his happiness with him down to the grave"), nor could anyone, perhaps not Sophocles himself, foresee the consummation that awaited Oedipus at Colonus. Again, we remember how little of mitigation may attend the intervention of the god *ex machina*, as for example in the *Medea* of Euripides. In a word—despite some exceptions, such as Aeschylus' conclusion of the *Oresteia*—Greek tragedy generally leaves us with small ground for consolation or reassurance. But Greek tragedy, as we observed at the outset, is not necessarily the norm to which alone we should refer; and in Shakespeare the mitigation of our sense of disaster plays a larger part in the final effect, though it differs in kind and degree from play to play. There is the sense of a moral order vindicated and restored (*Macbeth*), of the task accomplished at whatever cost (*Hamlet*), of the transforming effect of suffering, as well as of death the deliverer (*Lear*), of a human heroism somehow greater than the entangling fate to which the hero succumbs (*Othello,* and indeed *Hamlet*); and finally there is a sense of life as something that goes on chastened by these experiences (the four tragedies). And of all these means, explicitly or by implication, Milton avails himself on the human level before invoking the providential:

> O dearly-bought revenge, yet glorious!
> Living or dying thou hast fulfill'd
> The work for which thou wast foretold
> To Israel, and now liest victorious
> Among thy slain, self-kill'd
> Not willingly, but tangl'd in the fold
> Of dire necessity, whose law in death conjoin'd
> Thee with thy slaughtered foes. . . .
>
> (1660-7)

But he, though blind of sight,
Despis'd and thought extinguish't quite,
With inward eyes illuminated
His fiery virtue rous'd
From under ashes into sudden flame. . . .

So virtue giv'n for lost,
Deprest and overthrown, as seem'd,
Like that self-begotten bird
In the Arabian woods embost,
That no second knows nor third,
But lay erewhile a Holocaust,
From out her ashy womb now teem'd,
Revives, reflourishes, then active most
When most unactive deem'd,
And though her body die, her fame survives,
A secular bird, ages of lives.

                                   (1687-1707)

Come, come, no time for lamentation now,
Nor much more cause, Samson hath quit himself
Like Samson, and heroically hath finish'd
A life heroic. . . .
                    To Israel
Honour hath left, and freedom, let but them
Fnd courage to lay hold on this occasion,
To himself and Father's house eternal fame;
And which is best and happiest yet, all this
With God not parted from him, as was fear'd.
But favouring and assisting to the end.
Nothing is here for tears, nothing to wail
Or knock the breast, no weakness, no contempt,
Dispraise or blame, nothing but well and fair
And what may quiet us in a death so noble.

                                   (1708-24)

This reconciliation, this mitigating of the sense of disaster, is restricted
to the human level, the level on which tragedy commonly moves (for
the reference to God is in relation less to the outcome than to Samson's personal experience and feelings, and the image of the phoenix,

which so often in Christian symbolism represents immortality, is carefully confined to the immortality of Samson's fame); and these considerations lead on to a first formulation of the tragic *katharsis* as Milton conceives it.

Only when this is accomplished is the Chorus allowed to raise its eyes to God's providential purpose and the place of Samson's sacrifice therein, and to correct, though not to deny, the doubts which have assailed it and Manoa and Samson himself. And since God's ways are just but also mysterious, acceptable by faith but often baffling to reason, the effect of the larger view is less to cancel than to confirm and complete the narrower, or so at least Milton's treatment would seem to say:

> All is best, though we oft doubt
> What th' unsearchable dispose
> Of highest wisdom brings about,
> And ever best found in the close.
> Oft he seems to hide his face,
> But unexpectedly returns
> And to his faithful champion hath in place
> Bore witness gloriously; whence Gaza mourns
> And all that band them to resist
> His uncontrollable intent.
> His servants he with new acquist
> Of true experience from this great event
> With peace and consolation hath dismist
> And calm of mind, all passion spent.
>
>   (1745-58)

And as if to confirm this reading of the lines, they again culminate in a formulation—perhaps the most famous in all literature—of the Aristotelian *katharsis*. Clearly Milton supposed that, with his basic Christian assumptions, he had still produced a genuinely tragic effect. Nor will the reader who clears his mind of prepossessions, and allows the poem to have its full effect, be likely to demur.

III

To say that *Samson Agonistes* is Milton's attempt to write a Christian tragedy is not to deny all relevance to his Greek models. It simply means that we must not expect divergent assumptions to issue in identical effects and must be willing to extend our terms of reference.

Though many critics have followed Macaulay in asserting that Euripides is Milton's principal model, there seems to be singularly little ground for this opinion. In spirit his closest affinity is with Aeschylus, whose ethical and theological emphasis Milton can hardly have failed to appreciate, and who, in the *Oresteia*, re-reads an ancient and barbaric legend with all the insight of a profound moral and religious sensibility. In form, on the other hand, as Jebb recognizes (though his choice of the *Trachiniae* is not the happiest example) Sophocles is the chief model; and this is confirmed by Parker, who rightly chooses the *Oedipus at Colonus* as the closest of all Greek analogues. But the similarity in form, and up to a point in content, serves to underline the difference in spirit and effect.

Though standing somewhat apart from Sophocles' other works, and modifying the inferences to be drawn from them, the *Oedipus at Colonus* is his deliberately chosen conclusion, which supplies the mitigation wholly lacking in the *Oedipus Tyrannus;* and it must be read in the light of the whole story and of the Sophoclean outlook. That outlook, if we follow H. D. F. Kitto, posits a cosmic order encompassing and governing the life of man. It is not a moral order such as Aeschylus presented as progressively realized; at most it subsumes such an order. Whoever runs athwart this cosmic order, whether wilfully or, like Oedipus, without intent, is (in Kitto's vivid image) like one who interrupts the flow of a powerful electric current, which destroys him and flows on. The gods have predicted, they have not decreed, the fate of Oedipus. Now he reaches Colonus, conscious that there he is to be released from suffering and the final prediction fulfilled. The prelude to this event is a series of encounters, much as in *Samson Agonistes*. The effect of these encounters is to magnify the figure of Oedipus from the blind and helpless wanderer of the opening scene to one of heroic proportions once more, with power to confer benefit and doom. In so far there is a parallel effect in Samson. But Oedipus' determination is not formed by these encounters: it is merely exhibited. Though (to steal a phrase from Dryden) it seems like treason in the court of Apollo to say it, the *Oedipus at Colonus* lies much more open to Johnson's charge than does *Samson Agonistes*: the action does not precipitate the catastrophe, as in Milton's tragedy it plainly does. Oedipus' reliance on divine prediction, and his determination to await its fulfilment at all hazards, had been already reached in the long interval since the ghastly revelations of the *Oedipus Tyrannus,* and especially in the year of wandering that had led at last to Colonus. Milton has chosen the much more difficult task of displaying in four acts a gradual change of mind in his hero comparable in extent to the whole development of Oedipus from the time when he stood before the palace blinded and desperate. The catastrophes, when at last they come, present some similarities: each hero goes to meet his end willingly and with a sense of fulfilment. But the effect in the two cases is very different. It must be so for dramatic reasons as well as philosophical—in the light, that is, not merely of the outlook of the two poets, but of the prior experiences of the two heroes. Oedipus has erred unwittingly: contemplating his deeds he has known an abyss of horror, but no remorse of conscience: his *hubris* perhaps supplied the trigger of the weapon that destroyed him, but certainly not the charge: and now he awaits release, as Samson has also done. But Samson's experience has been of a different order: he has sinned, been punished, and repented, and he has been miraculously restored to God's service. The *Oedipus at Colonus* ends in mystery, and, partly because the known reality is so intolerable, mystery is relief. *Samson Agonistes* ends in the transcending of mystery, and in something that is more like triumph than mere relief: death is indeed relief—but death is swallowed up in victory. Both plays announce an end to weeping and lamentation; but to realize to the full the difference, one has only to place beside Milton's final chorus the final chorus of Sophocles (as it is movingly rendered by a recent translator):

> This is the end of tears:
> No more lament.
> Through all the years
> Immutable stands this event.

It would be hard to imagine any comment more noncommittal.

IV

Since ours is a purely inductive study, let us try a comparison with Shakespeare. At first glance no two tragedies could be more unlike than *Samson Agonistes* and *Hamlet*. In form (at least in the narrower sense of the term) they have nothing in common, and in content little enough. Each has as its basis a barbaric legend and a folk hero (as indeed have many of the great tragic themes including the *Oresteia* and the Oedipus plays), and in both *Hamlet* and *Samson Agonistes* (as also in the *Oresteia*) a dominant motive in the legend is revenge, which, as Bacon reminds us, is "a kind of wild justice." These legends and heroes the poets by their superior insight transform, so as to bring into relief a profounder and subtler human significance without wholly eliminating the basic primitive elements. It is when we come to the pattern of the action in *Hamlet* and *Samson Agonistes* that we strike what may turn out to be a clue. For without confusing poet with philosopher, or art with life, one may, and I think must, concede that the imagined action in such serious works of literature as these does in some way represent the poet's intuition of what life is, or on occasion may be, like. Now the common factor in the action of *Hamlet* and *Samson Agonistes* is that each hero is moving, however hesitantly or unwittingly, towards the fulfilment of his task and (for they are conjoined) towards his own doom. Not that the task (Hamlet's execution of justice or Samson's service of God) necessarily of itself entails the destruction of the hero. It does so because of the hero's own conduct, because, that is, of the interplay of free will and circumstances which together weave a web of necessity no less inexorable than that in which Oedipus is entangled. The heroes do not, like Oedipus in the *Tyrannus,* unconsciously run athwart the order of things; they do not, like Macbeth, defy the moral order or, like Edmund, call its mandate in question. On the contrary, they perish at last in giving effect to it. They are on the side of the power—the overruling power—which destroys them. Irony is of the very substance of tragedy; and this is the element of irony common to the two plays. In *Samson Agonistes* the power is frankly identified as Providence. In *Hamlet* we detect at least in the hero a growing sense of a providential order: "There's a divinity that shapes our ends . . ."; "There's a special providence in the fall of a sparrow." Even if we interpret this as a purely subjective response on his part, it is apt to have some influence upon us; and even if it has not, there remains the pattern of action and the tragic irony which is inseparable from it.

These common features, which condition the kind of tragic effect achieved, spring from a common source, namely, the assumption, for the most part implicit in *Hamlet,* but much more explicit in *Samson Agonistes,* of a Christian view of man and the world. In *Hamlet* it is a Christian view of man in the order of nature, with no specific reference to grace: one could not, with any show of propriety or probability, speak of Hamlet's undergoing a religious experience. In *Samson Agonistes,* on the other hand, to miss the presence and purport of Samson's religious experience, and the silent operation of grace therein, is to but half read the play, and thus to throw it out of focus.

The greater precision, the more specific religious reference, in *Samson Agonistes* has a twofold result. First, it heightens the tragic irony of the catastrophe and, in retrospect, of the steady movement on towards it, for that movement is the very same as Samson's movement back towards God. Secondly, it supplies the ground of a more complete resolution, a stronger mitigation of the sense of disaster than is common in tragedy. In *Hamlet* the sense of disaster, though mitigated, is still predominant at the end; and Shakespeare does here what he does nowhere else: he looks, if only fleetingly, beyond the earthly scene, where the tragic action has worked itself out, to some resolution beyond it ("Good night, sweet Prince, / And flights of angels sing thee to thy rest"). From any such reference Milton has abstained, and critics have guessed at various explanations, including his mortalism; but the all-sufficient explanation is that tragic precedent was against it, and anyway it would have been superfluous.

V

The question has often been asked whether a Christian tragedy is really possible. No doubt on a total view Christianity presents the drama of existence as a divine comedy—or at most a divine tragicomedy—in which the overruling power is the Supreme Goodness and whatever or whoever opposes it is finally eliminated. Whether their fate is in any negotiable sense tragic is a question that need not detain us: it no more arises than does the question whether in *Samson Agonistes* the fate of the Philistines is tragic. If such a subject were ever given tragic treatment, it would have to be in a pagan, not a Christian context. If a Christian tragedy is possible, then its subject will be the saved, or those on the way to being saved, not the utterly lost. And clearly in the ample confines of the divine comedy there is plenty of room for tragic episodes. "I now must change / Those notes to tragic," writes Milton, as he introduces the subject of the first sin, and the first repentance, and their consequences. Christianity never denies the power of sin and suffering, though it envisages a final escape from them. In suffering, indeed, it discovers a new dimension. "Prosperity," said Bacon, "is the blessing of the Old Testament; adversity is the blessing of the New." This idea has entered deeply into the Christian consciousness, and not with the theologically minded alone: it receives its recognition not only in *Samson Agonistes*, but also, for example, in *Lear*, and even Cleopatra can say, "My desolation does begin to make / A better life." This is not theology: it is a profoundly true apprehension of one of the possibilities of human experience, on which Christianity has seized, and it is pregnant with drama, as Shakespeare knows and so does Milton.

Suffering may be the lot of either sinner or martyr, and Samson is both. He has sinned, and through suffering he has progressed to self-knowledge and repentance, the necessary prelude to readmission to God's service. But now God's service is martyrdom, if not precisely the usual kind. Patience, as the Chorus observes,

> is most oft the exercise
> Of saints, the trial of their fortitude,
> Making them each his own deliverer,
> And victor over all
> That tyranny or fortune can inflict.
>
> (1287-91)

This, however, is not the way of tragedy, and Samson is called upon to play a more active rôle: to be his own deliverer in a more literal sense and to achieve therewith a victory that dwarfs all his former triumphs. But suffering, though it may be a means of grace, is suffering still, and death, though it be the price of such a victory, and though it even come as a release from suffering, is still death. Thus some of the ingredients of tragedy are certainly available; and it only remains to be asked what the poet has been able to do with them. What Milton has done in respect of the action we have seen: he has made the way of repentance and restoration, the way back to God, also the way that leads inevitably to the catastrophe, and has thus achieved at a stroke the only kind of irony that is at once compatible with a Christian outlook and as potent as any to be found in tragedy anywhere. Moreover, he has shown the necessity which thus conjoins Samson's salvation and victory with his death to be no arbitrary imposition of the overruling Power, but the outcome of Samson's conduct—of his sin and of his subsequent repentance. That his repentance is achieved under the impulsion of divine grace does not alter the fact that it is Samson's own. If God is present and operative in the tragedy (as he must be in a Christian view) at least he does not operate arbitrarily—or from a machine!

So much for the poem, if it stopped short with the catastrophe. It does not. The conclusion, as we have also seen, is directed wholly to reconciliation, to mitigating the sense of disaster: first on the human level, and, when that is completed, by invoking the overruling Power, by showing the place of Samson's sacrifice, of his whole experience, in the providential order of God, who does not force men's wills but nevertheless controls the event. The emphasis of this comment is justified not only on doctrinal but on artistic grounds. The very strength of the element of tragic irony in the action both permits and demands it. And the irony and the resolution of irony alike depend on the fact that this is a Christian tragedy: that is to say, a tragedy which, however scrupulously it adheres to classical conventions, is written unfalteringly from a Christian point of view.

Christian exegesis of the Samson story had developed different and sometimes mutually incompatible interpretations. Samson had been regarded as a repentant sinner who, by God's mercy, had been restored to his service. He had also, like Moses, Joshua, David, and others, been regarded as a prophetic type of Christ, and his sacrifice as a type of Christ's on the Cross. There can be no doubt that Milton builds his drama wholly on the former conception; and we need not complicate the question of the possibility of a Christian tragedy by introducing the latter view.

In that possibility Milton, clearly, believed; but his artist's intuition taught him that it could be realized only under certain conditions. The first was the provision of a strong element of tragic irony in the pattern of the action. The second was a resolution of that irony by a final appeal to God's providential order, to the rhythm as it were of the divine comedy. Nor was this all. If one was to achieve an effect truly tragic, one must focus attention on the hero, and must so present his response to the outward pressures of circumstance, and the inward impulsions of grace, as to render that response intelligible in purely human terms. And here Milton's former sense of a dichotomy in Samson's motivation came to his aid; only now it presented itself not as a pair of alternatives but as two forces working to a common end: "celestial vigour" *and* "plain heroic magnitude of mind." The sense of Samson as heroic individual does not stop short with the catastrophe: it extends to the comment. The reconciliation, the mitigating of the sense of disaster, is worked out in purely human terms before the larger rhythm of the divine comedy is invoked, lest that rhythm should not only resolve the tragic irony of the action, but dissolve the whole tragic effect.

Since I have been considering *Samson Agonistes* as a Christian tragedy, I have inevitably dwelt upon the view of life implied as conditioning the kind of tragic effect achieved. This does not mean that I am overlooking, or relegating to second place, the distinguishable, though inseparable, contribution of the poem's form. I have in fact been silently taking it into account in every statement made and every line of the poem quoted. But it is proper that, at the end, this element of poetic form should receive overt recognition. Kitto remarks that the form which Sophocles imposes upon the Oedipus legend is a reflection and reinforcement of the whole Sophoclean view of life. And what is true of Sophocles is no less true of Milton. Every great poet adapts form to content in his own way. But the basic classical structure common to Milton and Sophocles is peculiarly effective because the framework which it supplies for every subtlety of insight and modification still retains its beautiful clarity and its insistent suggestion of inevitability. Here the true importance of Milton's adoption of his Greek models finally lies. It is not that he is seeking to reproduce their spirit and effect—far from it—but that he is adapting their means, to present and produce his own. To say that *Samson Agonistes* is a classical tragedy with a Christian theme and outlook does not completely define the effect or the means used to attain it; but it puts us, I think, on the right track. It gives us a point of view from which to read and judge the poem.

NOTES

1. To avoid a multiplicity of notes, the line references to *Samson Agonistes* are supplied in parentheses. The critical works alluded to are in order of occurrence, Sir Richard Jebb, "*Samson Agonistes* and Hellenic Drama," *Proceedings of the British Academy* (1907-08); W. R. Parker, "The Greek Spirit in Milton's *Samson Agonistes*," *Essays and Studies of the English Association*, XX (1935), 21-44; my own "*Samson Agonistes* and Milton's Experience," *Transactions of the Royal Society of Canada*, ser. 3, vol. XLIII (1949), Section II, pp. 157-75; D. C. Allen, *The Harmonious Vision* (1953), chap. iv; H. D. F. Kitto, *Greek Tragedy* (1954). The translator of Sophocles referred to is E. F. Walling, in his *Sophocles' Theban Plays* (1947).

[EDITOR'S NOTE. For further references, see the essay following.]

JOHN M. STEADMAN

"Faithful Champion": The Theological Basis of Milton's Hero of Faith

In the ordeal of Milton's "Heroic *Nazarite*" scholars have usually recognized one or more of several "themes"—repentance, regeneration, the trial of faith and patience.[1] Actually, in Milton's drama, as in his theology, these concepts are closely related, and a recognition of their interrelationship is essential for an adequate understanding of the fable of *Samson Agonistes*. According to Milton's *De Doctrina Christiana*, both repentance and faith are "effects of regeneration," and faith itself serves as "an instrumental and assisting cause" in the "gradual progress" of sanctification.[2] In the course of the drama Samson "becomes as it were a new creature"—a man "sanctified both in body and soul, for the service of God and the performance of good works."[3] Nevertheless, since regeneration is by definition a purely internal development, we are able to trace it only in its effects. We follow its gradual progress in the utterances which express Samson's repentance and faith. On the one hand, the pattern of his struggle follows the "progressive steps in repentance" outlined in the *De Doctrina*—"conviction of sin, contrition, confession, departure from evil, conversion to good."[4] On the other hand, his trial serves to manifest the strength of his faith and patience, the progressive recovery of his virtue.

From *Anglia,* LXXVII (1959), 12-28. Copyright © by Max Niemeyer Verlag, Tübingen. Reprinted by permission of the author and the publisher.

Thus, in the final analysis, neither repentance nor the trial of faith can be regarded as an exclusive "key" to the drama. Both are essentially aspects of a larger whole, the supernatural renovation of the elect. The dominant motif of the tragedy is the hero's spiritual rebirth, his sanctification.[5]

In the following pages I shall re-examine Milton's characterization of his protagonist as a "faithful Champion"—a hero of faith—against the background of his theological beliefs. In orienting the drama around Samson's internal development rather than around a concatenation of external events, Milton gave poetic expression to several commonplaces of Reformation theology—the relationship of faith and works; the trial of faith and patience; and the logical opposites of faith, hope, and trust. If his primary emphasis falls on what happens in the hero's soul, this psychic drama follows a moral pattern already set forth in the *De Doctrina*.

I

Milton's emphasis on Samson's faith derives (as Parker observed[6]) less from Judges than from Hebrews, where he is enrolled among the "heroes" of faith. Calvin's commentary on this passage is illuminating. Since the "chief thing" in the elders "and the root of all other virtues"[7] was faith, Hebrews 11:32 ascribed to faith "all that was praiseworthy" in Samson:

> Samson homo rusticanus, et qui non aliis quam agriculturae armis se exercuerat, quid poterat contra tam superbos victores, quorum potentia subactus fuerat totus populus? . . . Sed quoniam Deus omnes sequuntur ducem, et eius promissione animati iniunctum sibi munus suscipiunt, spiritus sancti testimonio ornantur. Ergo quidquid laudabile gesserunt, fidei apostolus tribuit, quamquam nullus est eorum cuius fides non claudicaverit.

Samson's surrender to Dalila manifested how "halting and imperfect" was his faith:

> Samson concubinae blanditiis victus suam et totius populi salutem inconsiderate prodit . . . Ita in omnibus sanctis semper invenietur aliquid reprehensibile. Fides tamen etiamsi mutila sit ac imperfecta, Deo probari non desinit. Quare non est quod

> nos frangant vel exaniment vitia quibus laboramus, modo fide
> pergamus in vocationis nostrae stadio.[8]

Did Milton, like Calvin, believe that Samson's disastrous revelation to Dalila was an evidence of "halting" faith? If so, it explains, to some extent, why Samson should first prove the constancy of his faith in his debate with himself, with the Chorus, and with Manoa, before re-encountering his wife. It also suggests that his rejection of Dalila's entreaties in the drama should, perhaps, be regarded as an additional confirmation and seal of his faith.

Beyond the central conception of the Nazarite as a hero of faith, *Samson Agonistes* reveals other analogies with Hebrews 11. The Chorus compares Samson with Gideon and Jephthah (lines 277-291) and recites how he had "stopped the mouths of lions, . . . waxed valiant in fight, turned to flight the armies of aliens." The catastrophe clearly ranks him among those who "through faith subdued kingdoms, wrought righteousness, obtained promises, . . . out of weakness were made strong." Finally, like other Old Testament heroes of faith, Milton's champion "had trial of cruel mockings" and "of bonds and imprisonment," but, in the end, "obtained a good report through faith."

Paradoxically, Milton's hero of faith belonged to the old dispensation, when knowledge of the objects of faith was still incomplete and obscure. Nevertheless, the seventeenth-century Protestant could regard him as all the more admirable in as much as he had "received not the promise." Had not Calvin interpreted Hebrews 11:13 as an exhortation for perseverance?

> Quum Deus gratiam, quae in nos large effusa est, patribus
> duntaxat gustandam praebuerit, quum eminus illis ostenderit
> obscuram Christi imaginem, qui nunc se conspiciendum quasi
> sub oculos nostros offert: tamen acquieverunt, nec unquam
> exciderunt a sua fide: quanto nobis hodie amplior datur perse-
> verandi materia? Si deficimus, bis sumus inexcusabiles.[9]

Saving faith, as Milton defined it, entails believing that "whatsoever things" God "has promised in Christ are ours, and especially the grace of eternal life."[10] The fact that Samson lived and died before the advent of Christ does not, however, lessen his value as a hero of faith. According to the *De Doctrina*, "the ultimate object of faith is not Christ the Mediator, but God the Father." Many "both Jews and

others, who lived before Christ," were "saved by faith in God alone:
still however through the sole merits of Christ":

> Hinc illi sub lege illustres viri, Heb. xi, verae fidei testimonio
> ornati, cum in Deum duntaxat credidisse dicantur; Abel,
> Enoch, Noe, &c.[11]

A contributing factor in Milton's conception of his protagonist's
ordeal was the Protestant doctrine of justification by faith rather than
by works. In stressing Samson's faith, he was emphasizing the "essential form of good works." Since "none . . . of our works can be good,
but by faith,"[12] it is actually faith which makes Samson's final exploit
an heroic act—a deed acceptable to God. Before describing the act
itself, Milton very logically demonstrates that his hero manifests the
form or essence of heroic action. Before the "trial of mortal fight" to
which Samson challenges Harapha and the "trial of strength" he exhibits to the Philistines, the poet subjects him to a trial of faith.

For a similar reason Milton delineates the gradual revival of Samson's virtue as an essential preliminary to his final act. While the
"primary efficient cause of good works" is God, the *proximate* causes
are virtues.[13] At the beginning of the drama the once "Heroic" and
"Irresistible *Samson*" is described as "one past hope, abandon'd And
by himself given over," one "whose strength, *while vertue was her
mate,* Might have subdu'd the Earth." Yet at the end the Semichorus
relates how the same man "His fierie vertue rouz'd From under ashes
into sudden flame," and concludes:

> So vertue giv'n for lost,
> Deprest, and overthrown, as seem'd . . .
> Revives, reflourishes, then vigorous most
> When most unactive deem'd . . .

In the interim Milton had shown the progressive renewal of Samson's
virtue; after his moral victories over Dalila and Harapha, the Chorus
is able to conceive him once again in the role of potential hero or saint
—as one who may yet deliver his people through "plain Heroic magnitude of mind" or else may prove "his own Deliverer," one "Whom
Patience finally must crown." Before his final victory over his country's foes, Samson exhibits in two personal encounters with his enemies the moral virtue which is the proximate cause of good works.

The "works of believers are the works of the Spirit itself," and "con-
formity not with the written, but with the unwritten law, that is, with

the law of the Spirit, . . . is to be accounted the true essential form of good works."[14] Though Samson lives under the old dispensation (and as he leaves for Dagon's festival he reiterates his determination to do nothing "that may dishonour Our Law"), he demonstrates, nevertheless, a preference for "the unwritten law" of the Spirit. In the first place, his marriages with *"Philistian* women" had been prompted by "intimate impulse" and "Divine impulsion." In the second place, it is only upon the instigation of the Spirit—after feeling "Some rouzing motions in me"—that he agrees to attend the "Idolatrous Rites." To emphasize the fact that Samson is actually conforming to the law of the Spirit in contradistinction with the written law, Milton first describes him as refusing to accompany the Public Officer on the grounds that "Our Law forbids at thir Religious Rites My presence; for that cause I cannot come." Moreover, the Chorus' final words to Samson are a prayer that the Spirit of the Lord may assist him:

> Go and the Holy One
> Of *Israel* be thy guide
> To what may serve his glory best, and spread his name
> Great among the Heathen round:
> . . . that Spirit that first rusht on thee
> In the camp of *Dan*
> Be efficacious in thee now at need.

In this context, the word *efficacious* is especially apt, inasmuch as the "primary efficient cause of good works . . . is God."

Significantly, this passage alludes directly or indirectly to several of the essential attributes of good works, as defined in the *De Doctrina*:

> Bona opera sunt quae *agente* in nobis *Dei spiritu* per *veram fidem* facimus, ad *Dei gloriam,* salutis nostrae spem certam, et proximi aedificationem.[15]

For the "edification of our neighbor" Milton substitutes the suggestion that Samson's act may spread God's name "Great among the Heathen round." The hero's "true faith" had already been established earlier in the drama.

II

As "triall is by what is contrary,"[16] Milton demonstrates Samson's faith primarily through contrast with its logical opposite, doubt. This is a vice "to which even the pious are sometimes liable, at least for a time," and its importance[17] in *Samson Agonistes* is emphasized by the explicit references to doubt in the first and final speeches of the drama and its prominence in the first *stasimon*. Since "the object of faith is the promise, that of hope, the thing promised,"[18] Samson's initial doubt centers around the prophecy that he should deliver Israel. His present condition seems a direct contradiction of the terms of the promise:

> Promise was that I
> Should *Israel* from *Philistian* yoke deliver;
> Ask for this great Deliverer now, and find him
> Eyeless in *Gaza* at the Mill with slaves,
> Himself in bonds under *Philistian* yoke . . .

It is the diametric opposition between prophecy and fact that tempts him to "call in doubt Divine Prediction." From the very beginning of the drama God's apparent failure to fulfill his promise serves as a test of faith and a stumblingblock, a suggestion that he is "to his own edicts, found contradicting." The tension created by the unfulfilled promise—the paradox that the proposed liberator is himself a slave—endures throughout the play and is not resolved until the catastrophe. In the miraculous execution of the prophecy the faithful find confirmation of their faith, indubitable evidence that God is true to his word.

Since hope and trust are closely linked with faith in Milton's theology, their opposites also serve to exercise Samson's faith or to bring it into clearer definition by contrast. To manifest hope, he must struggle not merely against doubt, but also against despair, a vice which "takes place only in the reprobate."[19]

In spite of "faintings, swoonings of despair, And sense of Heav'n's desertion," Samson does not abandon his belief in God's mercy or "despair . . . of his final pardon." He displays a "most assured expectation through faith"[20] that Jehovah will vindicate the glory of his name against Dagon's competition:

> This only hope relieves me, that the strife
> With me hath end; all the contest is now
> 'Twixt God and *Dagon* . . . He, be sure,
> Will not connive, or linger, thus provok'd,
> But will arise and his great name assert . . .

As hope is an effect of faith,[21] Samson's affirmation of hope is an additional confirmation of his faith.

His hope in God stands, however, in striking contrast to the absence of personal hope:

> Nor am I in the list of them that hope;
> Hopeless are all my evils, all remediless . . .

Like Abraham, Samson is one "who against hope believed in hope" (Romans 4:18, 19).[22]

In the strongest expression of his griefs (lines 606-651) the core of Samson's complaint is Heaven's desertion—that God "hath cast me off as never known." His terminology makes it perfectly obvious that he is struggling against "the tentation of dereliction"—a temptation he ultimately overcomes "by a strong confidence in his God."[23] In Wolleb's discussion of Christ's internal sufferings Milton had found the temptation to despair expressed in very similar terms:

> Internae sunt, Tristitia, Angores & Cruciatus, ex atrocitate irae divinae & conflictu cum tentatione abjectionis ac desertionis orti, qui & sanguineum ei sudorem, & miserabilem illam vocem, *Eli, Eli, lamma sabachthani, Deus mi, Deus mi, cur me deseruisti?* expresserunt.
>
> Etsi autem cum abjectionis tentatione luctatus sit, nec tamen desperavit, nec tentationi succubuit, sed eam fiducia firma in Deum superavit.[24]

This stage of Samson's ordeal involves a trial of faith and hope already familiar to Protestants from theological discussion of Christ's Passion, and Milton's contemporaries should have recognized it fairly readily as a temptation to despair. The analogy is intensified by such verbal similarities as 1. "desertion," "desertionis," *"deseruisti"* and 2. "cast me off," "abjectionis." Though *Samson Agonistes* is not a celebration of Christ's spiritual agony (as recent scholarship has argued),[25] Milton has expressed Samson's temptation to despair in terms reminiscent of Christ's.

If the earlier acts of the drama are darkened by temptations to doubt and despair, the final scenes are charged with renewed hope. Samson is confident that God will pardon his transgression and finally predicts that

> This day will be remarkable in my life
> By some great act, or of my days the last.

Manoa hopes that he may procure his son's liberty and that God will
restore his sight. The Chorus conceives Samson once again in the
role of potential Deliverer, triumphing over his enemies or himself:

> Either of these is in thy lot,
> Samson, with might endu'd
> Above the Sons of men . . .

And expectation comes close to the actual fiulfillment of "Divine Prediction" when the Danites, hearing the "rueful cry" from Dagon's
temple, suggest that Samson—"his eyesight by miracle restor'd"—is
again "dealing dole among his foes."

In these final scenes, there is a gradual orientation of hope towards
its proper object—"the thing promised." For the greater part of the
drama there has been a marked disparity between Samson's "assured
expectation" of God's imminent victory over Dagon and his lack of
hope for himself and his prophesied role as deliverer. Although he has
refused to distrust the promise itself, he does not look for its fulfillment. Nevertheless, the disparity narrows significantly during the
encounters with Harapha and the Philistine Officer, and in the final
utterances of Samson and the Chorus it has virtually disappeared. In
the event, the same act fulfills both predictions.

III

It is in the encounter with Harapha that, for the first time in the
drama, Samson appears once more in his ordained role as "Defensor
Fidei"—God's "faithful Champion," who thrice challenges Dagon's
"Champion bold" to combat. The giant's taunts call forth an explicit
avowal of the Hebrew's "trust . . . in the living God" and "confidence" in final pardon. The very jeers of his enemy are a testimony
of his faith:

> Fair honour that thou dost thy God, in trusting
> He will accept thee to defend his cause . . .

Trust and confidence are key words in this passage, as important in
Milton's delineation of his hero of faith as was hope in the earlier
scene (lines 460, 472). According to the De Doctrina, trust is an inseparable companion of saving faith and may therefore be used as a
synonym for faith itself. On the other hand, the term may also be

used, in a slightly different sense, to indicate "a particular effect or degree of faith, or a firm hope."[26] In this second sense, trust is one of the virtues belonging to the worship of God—"an effect of love, and . . . a part of internal worship, whereby we wholly repose on him."[27]

To Milton's readers, Samson's affirmation of his confidence in God, in the midst of his calamities, may have recalled Job's similar assertion of faith under trial: "though he slay me, yet will I trust in him."[28]

In the *De Doctrina* Milton distinguishes four opposites to trust in God (*fiducia*): 1: distrust of God (*diffidentia in Deum*), 2. an overweening presumption (*praefidentia sive praesumptio*), 3. carnal reliance (*fiducia carnalis*), and 4. a trust in idols (*fiducia idololatrica*).[29] All four of these serve, in varying degrees, as foils for Samson's faith; they cast into bolder relief his confidence in God.

Hanford has observed that, in the final work of Milton's imagination, "the temptation to distrust . . . becomes a dominant and controlling motive." In "the midst of failure and personal affliction," Samson "is definitely tempted to surrender his trust in Providence because of his inability to understand its dealing with himself."[30] Though we should avoid confusing *doubt* with *distrust* (inasmuch as Milton distinguishes them as the opposites of different, though related, virtues), we must, I think, regard the temptation to "call in doubt Divine Prediction" as a temptation to distrust. Though Samson checks himself before expressing actual disbelief in the promise, he comes very close to distrust, as Polanus had defined it:

> *Diffidentia erga Deum*, est peccatum, quum quis aut omnino non fidit soli, promissioni divinae, de re aliqua vel ad salutem aeternam vel ad praesentem vitam pertinente, quamvis certae: aut de promissionis illius impletione dubitat: proficiscens à nativa infidelitate hominum propter defectum mediorum ordinarium & apparentem impossibilitatem consequendi id quod Deus promisit.[31]

Samson is obviously tempted to "doubt the fulfillment of the promise" because of "the lack of ordinary means and the apparent impossibility of accomplishing what God has promised."

Strictly speaking, in questioning the workings of Providence (lines 32-42, 350-372), both Samson and Manoa show doubt, but not distrust. It is significant that, in Wolleb's opinion, doubt is compatible with trust:

> Yet we teach not such a firm confidence, as if no wayes tossed with doubtings; but such a one as doth not finally yield to doubtings.[32]

Again, according to Wilcox's translation of Polanus,

> Doubting is neither firmly to consent to the word of God, and in that word, to the promise of Grace especially, neither altogether to resist the same, but to flow, now into one part, and anon faintly to incline to the other part.[33]

In contrast to numerous references to doubt, the drama contains only one explicit allusion to distrust—Samson's regret that he has inspired "diffidence of God, and doubt In feeble hearts."

When Samson affirms his "trust . . . in the living God" and challenges "*Dagon* to the test," Harapha maintains that this confidence is really presumption:

> Presume not on thy God, whate'er he be,
> Thee he regards not, owns not . . .

Samson's challenge to a "test," to "the trial of mortal fight," might indeed seem presumptuous—a case of tempting God—were it not for his extraordinary commission from Heaven. Both Ames and Polanus define presumption essentially as the expectation of some benefit from God without promise:

> Temeraria ista praesumptio . . . aliquando . . . nititur Deo, sed perverse sine promissione ac fide, ut cum quis sperat veniam ac salutem, quamvis maneat impoenitens, aut retineat propositum in peccatis suis vivendi, aut aliquid aliud exspectat à Deo, quod non convenit ejus naturae vel voluntati revelatae.[34]
>
> *Confidentia temeraria,* est peccatum, quum quis aliquid ad praesentem vel futuram vitam pertinens, se posse à Deo impetrare confidit, aut potius confidere se inaniter gloriatur, aut neglectis mediis à Deo ordinatis aut adhibitis mediis voluntati Dei adversantibus quasi volens Deum ipsum antevertere: quum novam aut peculiarem non habeat à Deo extraordinariorum mediorum promissionem.[35]

But Samson refuses to mistake *fiducia* for *praefidentia* and reiterates his confidence in God.

Primarily, however, this encounter stresses the antithesis between trust in God and "carnal reliance"—between confidence in the unarmed might of God and trust in purely human force and arms. For Samson, this is a familiar dichotomy. Formerly, "weaponless himself," he had "Made Arms ridiculous" with "what trivial weapon came to hand." Now once again, in spite of his blindness, he is confident that, relying only on his "Heav'n-gifted strength"—"the power of *Israel's* God"—he can overcome a fully-armed giant with merely "an Oak'n staff." Knowing that his might is not his own, but a divine miracle, he opposes to "gorgeous arms" his "trust . . . in the living God."[36] Harapha, on the other hand, acclaims "glorious arms" as the "ornament and safety" of "greatest Heroes." Whereas Samson trusts in Jehovah alone, his adversary is one "that trusteth in man, and maketh flesh his arm."[37]

Nevertheless, it is not in Harapha alone that we must look for the antithesis of Samson's trust in God. When, "swoll'n with pride,"[38] he had walked "Fearless of danger, like a petty God," he was guilty both of presumption and carnal reliance. He has learned by experience, however, not to glory in his strength:

> God, when he gave me strength, to show withal
> How slight the gift was, hung it in my Hair.

Like Manoa, he knows how unreliable is our "ever failing trust In mortal strength."

A further instance of misplaced confidence in creatures instead of the Creator is to be found in Samson's experience with Dalila. Her "wedlock-treachery endangering life" contrasts not only with Samson's trust, but also with God's fidelity to his promise. Reliance on Jehovah is counterpointed by allusions to Samson's disastrous "trust" in his wife (lines 783, 1001) and her breach of "faith" (lines 388, 750, 986, 1115). The failure of this trust in the creature emphasizes, by contrast, the reliability of God.

Finally, the contrast between confidence in God and trust in idols is fundamental both to the drama as a whole and to Samson's role as Jehovah's champion in particular. Implicit in the interview with Dalila, it receives explicit statement in the encounter with Harapha, when Samson challenges Dagon "to the test." The focal point of this antithesis, however, is the "popular Feast" to honor the Philistine idol. In this celebration both Samson and Manoa recognize a direct affront to God ("So *Dagon* shall be magnifi'd, and God . . . compar'd with

Idol"), and both expect Jehovah's early and decisive answer to this challenge. Appropriately, it is when the provocation is at its height—when, drunk with idolatry and wine, the Philistines are "Chaunting thir Idol, and preferring Before our living Dread"—that the conflict between *fiducia in Deo* and *fiducia idololatrica* achieves its fullest dramatic expression. It is at this moment that God intervenes to "vindicate the glory of his name," to destroy the idolators, and to bear witness to his faithful Champion.

IV

Samson's ordeal shows most of the characteristics of the "good temptation," as Milton had defined it in the *De Doctrina*—the trial "whereby God tempts even the righteous for the purpose of proving them." First, it serves the "purpose of exercising or manifesting [his] faith or patience, as in the case of Abraham and Job." Secondly, it also achieves the end "of lessening [his] self-confidence, and reproving [his] weakness," so that he himself becomes "wiser by experience, and others . . . profit by [his] example." In his "sense of Heav'n's desertion" he resembles Hezekiah, "whom 'God left'—partially, or for a time—'to try him, that he might know all that was in his heart.' "[39] Thirdly, Samson's temptation has "a happy issue,"[40] for the trial of his faith is "found unto praise and honor and glory."[41]

His sufferings not only try his faith and patience, but also lead him to repentance and renewed trust in God. "Chastisement is often the instrumental cause of repentance," according to the *De Doctrina;* since God "supplies strength for our support even under those inflictions which . . . appear to us too heavy to be borne," misfortune instructs us [2 Corinthians 1:8-10] "that we should not trust in ourselves, but in God."[42] Similarly, Polanus maintains that temptations and afflictions are impulsive causes of trust in God:

> *Causae impellentes* nos ad eam [fiduciam in Deo] sunt tentationes & afflictiones in quibus versamur . . .[43]

On the whole, Samson's trial follows the causal and temporal pattern suggested by James 1:3 ("the trying of your faith worketh patience") and Romans 5:3-4 ("tribulation worketh patience; And patience, experience"). If the crisis of faith is strongest at the beginning of the drama, the test of patience is most pronounced during the interval between Manoa's departure to seek the Philistine lords and Samson's own departure with the Philistine Officer. Samson's lament (lines 606-651) and the immediate observations of the Chorus (lines 652-666) both emphasize his need for patience. His petition for "speedy death" is patently an instance of "impatience under the divine decrees; a temptation to which the saints themselves are at times liable."[44] There is little difference in substance between this outburst and similar outcries of impatience from Elijah, Jonah, and Job:

> 1 Reg. xix. 4. *expetebat apud se mori.*
> Iob. iii. 2, &c. *utinam periisset dies* . . .
> Ion. iv. 3. *praestat mori me quam vivere.*[45]

At this point the Chorus comments on the inutility of "sayings of the wise" extolling "Patience as the truest fortitude," to comfort the afflicted. Yet, immediately after the scenes with Dalila and Harapha, the same Chorus hails Samson as one whom patience may crown. After the sense of Heaven's desertion, he experiences "Favour renew'd" and "internal peace." His trial teaches him patience—to "acquiesce in the promises of God, through a confident reliance on his divine providence, power, and goodness, and bear inevitable evils with equanimity, as the dispensation of the supreme Father, and sent for our good."[46] Finally, the outcome of his temptation, the "great event," leaves his companions with "new acquist Of true experience."

In reply to Samuel Johnson's objection that *Samson Agonistes* lacks a middle, modern scholarship has stressed "Milton's inward interpretation of his theme."[47] This orientation is hardly surprising. Regeneration is, by definition, a "change operated" in the *inward* man,[48] and Milton's doctrine of the relationship of faith and works made it virtually imperative to place his primary emphasis on Samson's spiritual changes rather than on the movement of external events. Although a complex and tightly-knit structure of cause and effect underlies the drama, this pattern is essentially moral and theological. It is not until Samson is regenerated in understanding and will, until his repentance and faith demonstrate his sanctification in body and soul, that he is ready "for the service of God, and the performance of good works."[49] Nevertheless, Dr. Johnson's observation is not altogether unjust, for Milton has patently substituted the development of character for that of the plot or fable.

If "nothing passes between the first Act and the last, that either hastens or delays the Death of *Samson*," the primary reason is to be found in Milton's theology. According to the Protestant conception of the relation of faith to works, the spiritual regeneration of the inward man, rather than a concatenation of external events, was the really significant factor in heroic activity. The true causes of good works were to be found in a pattern of internal events—a spiritual "plot"—rather than in a sequence of causes entirely outside the mind and will of the agent. External events could provide an *occasion* for moral action—good or bad—but the primary causes were to be found within the soul itself.

A similar emphasis on the internal event was fostered by the Protestant attitude towards suffering. The chief significance of external misfortunes resided in their moral effects on the sufferer. Possessing little intrinsic interest in themselves, they were primarily important as instrumental causes of repentance and the trial of faith and patience.

Although the crowning event of *Samson Agonistes* is an external act, Milton invests it with probability and verisimilitude by presenting it as the logical culmination of a spiritual process rather than as the effect of purely external causes. To have led up to the final catastrophe in any other way would have blunted the whole point of the test of faith. The trial of Samson's faith and patience depends essentially on the apparent impossibility of fulfilling the promise that he should deliver Israel. If Milton had constructed his plot differently, around a chain of events pointing inevitably towards this catastrophe, he would have sacrificed the very foundation of the temptation motif.

NOTES

1. For these and related interpretations, see Walter C. Curry, "*Samson Agonistes* Yet Again," *Sewanee Review*, XXXII (1924), 336-352; James Holly Hanford, "The Temptation Motive in Milton," *SP*, XV (1918), 176-194; *idem, A Milton Handbook*, Fourth Edition (New York, 1947); William Riley Parker, *Milton's Debt to Greek Tragedy in Samson Agonistes* (Baltimore, 1937); Frank Kermode, "Milton's Hero," *RES*, n. s., IV (1953), 317-330; F. Michael Krouse, *Milton's Samson and the Christian Tradition* (Princeton, 1949); T. S. K. Scott-Craig, "Concerning Milton's Samson," *Renaissance News*, V (1952), 45-53; Arnold S. Stein, *Heroic Knowledge, An Interpretation of Paradise Regained and Samson Agonistes* (Minneapolis, 1957); E. L. Marilla, "*Samson Agonistes;* An Interpretation," *Studia Neophilologica*, XXIX (1957), 67-76; Merritt Y. Hughes (ed.), *Paradise Regained, The Minor Poems, and Samson Agonistes* (New

York, 1937). Marilla (p. 67n) gives a brief bibliography of studies which emphasize "the problem of determining the philosophic import of the poem."

2. *The Works of John Milton* (Columbia Edition), XV, 376-379. All references to the *De Doctrina* in this paper are based on the Latin text and the English translation by Charles R. Sumner, in the Columbia Edition.

3. *Ibid.*, 366-367.

4. *Ibid.*, 384-385.

5. *Ibid.*, 374, "Hinc regeneratio alio nomine sanctificatio dicitur, et quidem proprio; nam regeneratio metaphorica potius est." "Sanctificatio autem nonnunquam late sumitur pro quavis electione aut separatione vel gentis universæ ad cultum externum, vel hominis cuiusquam ad aliquod munus." As a Nazarite, consecrated to the particular office of delivering Israel, Samson had been sanctified from birth, in the latter, more general sense. Through his regeneration he is also "sanctified" in the former, more specialized sense.

6. Parker, 236; Krouse (pp. 130-131) observes that Samson was "an exemplar of faith" from "the time of the writing of the Epistle to the Hebrews" and that Milton's drama "deals with Samson's struggle to preserve his faith against all the temptations by which Man may be tried . . . In connection with each of these temptations, it is on Samson's faith that emphasis is placed."

7. John Calvin, *Commentaries on the Epistles of Paul the Apostle to the Hebrews*, tr. John Owen (Edinburgh, 1853), xxx.

8. Calvin, *Commentarius in Epistolam ad Hebraeos, Corpus Reformatorum*, LXXXIII (Brunsvigae, 1896), col. 166; Owen, 302-303. Cf. Krouse, 74.

9. Calvin, *Commentarius*, col. 155; Owen, 283.

10. Milton, XV, 392-393.

11. *Ibid.*, 402-405.

12. Milton, XVII, 6-9.

13. *Ibid.*, 26-27.

14. *Ibid.*, 8-9.

15. *Ibid.*, 4. Italics mine.

16. Milton, IV, 311; cf. VI, 178, "In *Logic* they teach, that contraries laid together more evidently appear . . ."

17. Milton, XVII, 58-59.

18. Milton, XV, 408-409. An essential feature of saving faith (XV, 392-393) is that "we believe, on the sole authority of the promise itself" ("propter ipsam promittentis Dei auctoritatem, credimus").

19. Milton, XVII, 58-59. Doubt is opposite to both faith and hope.

20. See Milton's definition of hope (XV, 406), "certissima . . . rerum earum expectatio futurarum quae in Christo iam nostrae per fidem sunt."

21. *Ibid.*, 408, "Differt spes a fide ut effectum a causa. . . ."

22. *Ibid.*, 406-407.

23. John Wollebius, *The Abridgement of Christian Divinitie,* tr. Alexander Ross, The Third Edition (London), 1660, 139-140.

24. *Christianae Theologiae Compendium . . . Authore Iohanne Wollebio* (Amstelodami, 1633), 124. See Maurice Kelley, "Milton's Debt to Wolleb's *Compendium,*" *PMLA,* L (1935), 156-165; T. S. K. Scott-Craig, "Milton's Use of Wolleb and Ames," *MLN* LV (1940), 403-407.

25. Scott-Craig, *Renaissance News,* 46.

26. Milton, XV, 396-397. The distinction between *fiducia* as 1. the *form* or essence of saving faith and 2. its *effect* was not uncommon among Reformation theologians. Cf. James Nichols (tr.), *The Works of James Arminius,* I (London, 1828), 318-319; Wollebius, *Abridgment,* 253-254, 324; *Theodori Bezae Annotationes Maiores in Novum Testamentum (s. l.,* 1594), Part II, 365.

27. Milton, XVII, 52-53.

28. *Ibid.*, 56-57.

29. *Ibid.*, 54-57.

30. Hanford, *SP,* 190.

31. *Syntagma Theologiae Christianae ab Amando Polano a Polansdorf* (Genevae, 1612), II, cols. 710-711.

32. Wollebius, *Abridgment,* 255.

33. Amandus Polanus, *The Substance of Christian Religion,* tr. Thomas Wilcocks (London, 1608), 470.

34. *Guliel. Amesii Medulla Theologica* (Amstelodami, 1648), 237.

35. Polanus, *Syntagma,* II, col. 711.

36. The antithesis between trust in God and confidence in arms also appears in Psalm 18:2, 3, which Milton quotes as an example of *fiducia* (XVII, 52-53): "Jehovah is my rock and my fortress . . . in whom I will trust, my buckler and the horn of my salvation, and my high tower."

37. Jeremiah 17:5. The opposition between Harapha and Samson can be epitomized by the antithesis between this text and Jeremiah 17:7, "blessed is the man that trusteth in Jehovah, and whose hope Jehovah is" ("benedictus vir ille qui fiduciam habet in Iehova, et cuius confidentia est Iehova"). Milton quotes these texts (XVII, 54-57) as examples of *fiducia carnalis and fiducia in Deo,* respectively.

38. For Milton's projected drama on *Samson Hybristes,* see Hughes, 428.

39. Milton, XV, 88-89.

40. *Ibid.*, 88-89, "Et felicem exitum promittit Deus."
41. 1 Peter 1:7. Cf. Milton,, XV, 88-89.
42. *Ibid.*, 388-389.
43. Polanus, *Syntagma*, II, col. 709.
44. Milton, XVII, 68-69.
45. *Ibid.*, 68.
46. *Ibid.*, 66-67.
47. Hanford, *Handbook*, 286; Parker, 23; M. E. Grenander, *"Samson's* Middle: Aristotle and Dr. Johnson," *University of Toronto Quarterly*, XXIV (1955), 377-389.
48. Milton, XV, 366-367.
49. *Ibid.*, 366-367.

[EDITOR'S NOTE. See also, on the preface, P. R. Sellin, *JEGP*, LX (1961), 712-30, and, on the title, *SEL*, IV (1964), 137-62; on the choruses, G. L. Finney, *PMLA*, LVIII (1943), 649-64, and *Musical Backgrounds for English Literature,* [1962]; F. T. Prince, *The Italian Element in Milton's Verse*, 1954; on ransom, A. G. Gossman, *RN*, XIII (1960), 11-15; on Harapha, D. C. Boughner, *ELH*, XI (1944), 297-306; G. R. Waggoner, *PQ*, XXXIX (1960), 82-92; J. M. Steadman, *JEGP*, LX (1961), 786-95; for further interpretation of the poem, J. B. Broadbent, *Milton: "Comus" and Samson Agonistes*, 1961; A Gossman, *JEGP*, LXI (1962), 528-41, and *ES*, XLV (1964), 212-24; A. B. Chambers, *PMLA*, LXXVIII (1963), 315-20; W. O. Harris, *ELH*, XXX (1963), 107-20; G. A. Wilkes, *H.L.Q.*, XXVI (1963), 363-79; A. E. Barker, in *Essays in English Literature . . . Presented to A. S. P. Woodhouse*, ed. M. MacLure and F. W. Watt, 1964.]